RANDOM RECORDS OF THE ROYAL MARINES

A COLLECTION OF EXTRACTS FROM THE DIARIES AND LETTERS OF SOME OF THEIR PAST AND PRESENT OFFICERS, NON-COMMISSIONED OFFICERS, AND MEN; FROM OFFICIAL DOCUMENTS, AND FROM NOTES AND ACCOUNTS FROM VARIOUS SOURCES, OF THEIR CHARACTER, HISTORY, UNIFORM AND COLOURS, THEIR BARRACKS AND OTHER MATTERS OF INTEREST.

COMPILED BY
GENERAL SIR H. E. BLUMBERG, K.C.B.,
AND COLONEL C FIELD

FIRST PUBLISHED IN CONNECTION WITH THE
"GLOBE & LAUREL"
THE JOURNAL OF THE CORPS. 1935

THIS EDITION PREPARED FOR PUBLICATION
BY COLONEL BRIAN CARTER, OBE

SERIES EDITOR JOHN RAWLINSON

RANDOM RECORDS OF THE ROYAL MARINES
REPRINTED 2024 BY THE ROYAL MARINES HISTORICAL SOCIETY
SPECIAL PUBLICATION NO XX
Copyright © Royal Marines Historical Society 2024

All Rights Reserved

No part of this book may be reproduced in any form
by photocopying or by any electronic or mechanical means,
including information storage or retrieval systems,
without permission in writing from the copyright owner.

ISBN
978-1-908123-29-9

First published 2024 by the
ROYAL MARINES HISTORICAL SOCIETY
The National Museum of the Royal Navy
Portsmouth PO1 3NH
United Kingdom

Cover, design and typesetting
Tim Mitchell | Piernine
www.piernine.co

Printed and bound in Great Britain by
CPI Antony Rowe Ltd, Chippenham and Eastbourne

Contents

Editor's Introduction	xiii
Foreword by Colonel C Field	xv

1.	Blumberg's Random Records	1
2.	The History of the Royal Marines Divisions 1755-1923	377

The Marines of Antiquity	4
Clothing and Equipment of The Marine Regiments in 1702	5
Some Personal Recollections of Royal Marine Uniform	13
The "Good" Old Times 1706	17
A Question Regarding Cabins	18
The Heart of The Prince of Hesse	19
Miscellaneous Documents by Col Field	19
Gibraltar	23
The Interegnum, 1713-1740	26
A Very Poor Detachment	27
A Marine's Experiences in the '45	28
Marine Recruiting Instructions, 1745	35
Anson and the Marines	36
"A Mixed Grill"	37
Some Documents in Connection with the Beginning Of The Present Corps of Royal Marines in 1755	38
The Fathers of the Corps of Royal Marines	43
Officers Appointed on Formation of the Present Corps of Marines in 1755	44
Artillerymen Serving Afloat Prior to 1804	49
The Marines in 1758	51
Belleisle	53
A Cool Request	55
Affray between Marines and Shipwrights	55
Major Pitcairn and the Marines in the Expedition to Lexington and Concord, 18th & 19th April, 1775	55
Defence of Boston	64
The Royal Marine Battalions in North America 1775-1778	65
Coxswain of the Marine Boat 1781	76
The Chatham Marine Band 1781	76
An Unpopular Order 1782	77
Repentance and Forgiveness	77
John Murray	78
The Evening Walk 1792	79

Evacuation of Nootka Sound by the Spaniards 1795	80
The First British Settlement in Australia 1787	81
Competence of a Naval Court-Martial Questioned.	89
Presentation of Colours to Marines at Constantinople in 1799	90
Memorandum of the Services of Colonel William Robinson	90
Mutiny on board HMS Temeraire in December 1801	94
The Service of Major-General Sir John Douglas, Kt. b1762 d1814	97
Portrait of The Earl of St. Vincent 1804	109
Precedence of the Corps of Royal Marines	111
Extracts from the Diary of Lieut. Wm. Clark, R.M.	113
"Johnson the Smuggler"	114
Marines in Action Afloat	124
The Night Attack 1810	125
Rations and Victualling Arrangements in the Royal Marines from 1755 to Present Day	128
Loyalty and Disloyalty a Century and a Quarter ago	135
Lord Howe and his Marine Pay	138
Orders for Marine Detachments	139
Foreigners in the Marines 1804	142
Extracts from the Diary of Major Christopher Noble of the Royal Marines 1792 to 1822	143
Extracts from My Uncle's Diary 1796-1820	149
Extracts from the Diary Of Major W. Pridham, R.M. 1799-1816	151
Marines on Impressment Duty in Plymouth 1803	158
The Buenos Ayres Fiasco of 1806	159
Pay of the Royal Marines in 1808	164
The Defence of Anholt, 1811	165
The Regent's Allowance	168
Cutting-Out Expedition at Corigeou 1815	170
The Waterloo Campaign and the Royal Marines	174
Presentiments of Death	175
Occupation of Van Dieman's Land and Melville Island 1824	176
Royal Marine Corps a Hundred Years Ago 1826	177
H.M.S. "Albion" at Navarino, 1827	179
The "Good" Old Days	187
Cessation of King as a General of Marines and First RM AdC to the King	189
An Admiralty Letter authorising a Naval School of Gunnery on HMS Excellent	189
Reminiscences. of the Late General Simon Fraser, R.M.	190
Lt.-Col. Molesworth Phillips, R.M. 1832	194
Official Return of the Naval Force of Great Britain on July 1st, 1833	196
The Battle of Hernani 1837	197

Contents

The Syrian Campaign 1840	199
"Palmerston's Own"	205
The Four Marines of HMS Wager	207
Life on the Island of Ascension 1843	207
Operations on the Parana River 1845	217
Ireland and the Baltic 1846-57	219
Marine Extravagance 1847	220
Royal Marine Battalions in Ireland 1848	220
Crimea – The Fleet	221
Bombardment of Odessa	223
Balaclava Heights	225
Charge of the Light Brigade – Balaclava	227
The Heights of Kamara	231
Bomarsund 1854	234
The Bombardment of Sveaborg 1855	239
Experiences of an Old Royal Marine in New Zealand	244
Ashantee 1873	247
The Occupation of Port Hamilton 1885-87	249
Sepoy Marine Battalion	259
Tamaai - 13th March, 1884	262
The Vitu Expedition 1890	269
The Work of an Officer of The Marines in the Opening Up of Japan 1892	274
The War on the Gambia 1894	275
Origin of the Divisional Fund	284
Annual Inspections	286
The Divisional Colours of the Royal Marines	286
The Sword in the Royal Marines	279
Honorary Colonel Commandant	283
The Commanding Officers, Royal Marines	285
Regiments Afloat	289
Blumberg's Notes from Corps History	291
The Royal Marines and HM Dockyards	333
Origin of Colour Sergeants	339
Recruiting in the Royal Marines	340
Antwerp 1914	350
V.C. Won by Major (Temporary Brigadier-General) F. W. Lumsden, D.S.O., R.M.A.	353
Royal Marines Drummers' Looping Lace	354
History of the Globe and Laurel	357
Field Gun Competitions	364
A Record of RM Successes at the Tournament 1824-1929	364
National Rifle Associations from 1860	371

History of the Royal Marines Divisions 1755-1923	377
History of The Portsmouth Division RM 1755-1923	379
History of The Depot Royal Marines, Deal	388
Record of the Bands of The Portsmouth Division, R.M.L.I. and of The Depot, Royal Marines, Deal.	404
History of The RMA Division	414
History of The Woolwich Division	430
History of The Plymouth Division	445
History of The Chatham Division	457
Index	492

LIST OF ILLUSTRATIONS

Gunboat in Action at the time of Henry VIII	2
Marine Officer's Uniform 1702	12
Rough Map of British Troop Movements around Lexington and Concord 1775	57
View of the Town of Concord	58
Major John Pitcairn	64
John Murray	78
Evening Walk 1792	79
Colours Captured at Buenos Ayres 1806	163
Colour Sergeant J Mullins RMA, the first man to live on Whale Island	189
Battle of Tamaai 13 March 1884	267
Badge of Royal Dockyard Battalion	335
Royal Marines Drummers' Looping Lace Patterns	356
History of the Royal Marine Divisions	
Old Clarence Barracks	379
Entrance Gate, R.M. Barracks. Forton, 1896	382
Plan of Forton Barracks	383
Officers Mess, Forton Barracks	384
Forton Barracks by W L Wylie	387
Dockyard Gates Deal 1860	388
Jubilee Gate	390
Cavalry Barracks	391
North Barracks	392
Deal Castle and the Old Naval Hospital, 1792	395
Kingsdown Rifle Range	398
12in Cartridge Case from the Kaiser William II Battery, Knocke, Belgium	403
The Duke of York in North Barracks	403
Depot Band 1922	405
Master of the Band 1829	407

Major George Miller MVO Mus Bac LRAM	410
Band of Portsmouth Division 1921	413
Plan of Fort Cumberland	418
Fort Cumberland and Eastney Village	420
Proe's Farm	422
Eastney Barracks 'Parade Looking East', circa 1870	422
Plan Showing Garden Battery and Mortar Batteries	424
Making the Football Field Eastney Barracks 1901-2	426
The Crinoline Church	429
Married Officers' Quarters and Tower	429
RM Barracks Woolwich nearing completion 1848	430
RM Barracks Woolwich completed	432
The Red Barracks (originally the Infirmary)	433
Officers and Colours 1869	434
The Drum and Fife Band	438
Royal Marines Barracks Stonehouse	446
Plan of Royal Marines Barracks Plymouth Prior to Alterations in 1900	450-451
Marine Barracks at Stonehouse Devonshire	452
Plans of HM Dockyard Chatham in the years 1688, 1698 and 1774 (Plan 'A')	460
A Prospect of Chatham Dock	461
Plan of Chatham Barracks 1856 (Plan 'B')	465
Royal Marines Barracks Chatham 1880 (Plan 'C')	468-469
18th Century Church at Chatham Dockyard	483
Upnor Castle	484
The Burning of the Kent	487
Extract from the East Surrey Regiment	488

Editor's Introduction.

By Colonel Brian Carter OBE.

This is the final assembly of papers put together by Colonel Field from the additional papers he and General Blumberg found and/or were sent after the publication of Britain's Sea Soldiers. He took some of the articles from copies of the Globe & Laurel of the time to complete the full picture.

I have corrected typographical mistakes, but kept all the spelling, grammar, punctuation and layout of the originals in order to give a feel for the times they are written in. This may irritate the reader as some of it is extremely strange and changes for every article depending on who wrote it and when. However it is after all a part of history in itself. Clearly there were no rules for military writing in those days and it is interesting to see how little attention was paid to such matters right up to WW1! I have inserted Blumberg's 'errata' into the text and consequently removed his list of errata.

I have also re-organised the contents into a more or less chronological order as far as possible in order to help the reader associate the various articles with others of the same period from around the world. The photographs/diagrams are as in the original and I have not added any. I am most grateful to John Gilbert for digitalising the original text, a thankless task, and Mark Bentinck for preliminary editing. I am also very grateful to Tim Mitchell who had the painstaking task of typesetting all these original texts and letters as written by the original authors, no easy task when every article/letter was written by a different author in a different style and on many occasions with no respect for grammar, spelling or punctuation.

As a result of the generosity and financial support once again of RMHS member Mark Phillips we are not only able to publish this volume, but to do so in hard back, a most fitting conclusion to the completion of the publication of General Blumberg's and Colonel Field's works.

A Foreward

By Colonel C Field.

AFTER the completion and publication of my book " Britain's Sea Soldiers," I came into possession of a large collection of manuscripts, etc., which had been amassed by the late Lieutenant-Colonel Lourenco Edye, R.M., as material for the continuation of his " History of the Royal Marine Forces," of which only Volume I, covering the period 1664-1701, has been published.

Among these, it may be remarked in passing, was a practically complete rough copy of his Second Volume, carrying the Corps History up to 1706 (the fair copy had been lost in a ship which was sunk by a German submarine), which is now to be seen in the Admiralty Library.

But there was also a mass of copies and extracts from documents in the Public Record Office relating to the Corps and its predecessors, as well as a number of excerpts from newsletters and journals of the early Eighteenth Century having reference to the Marines, besides a few private diaries and letters from their Officers.

It seemed to me that it would be a great pity that some of the more interesting items of this collection should be lost to the Corps generally, and this consideration induced me to suggest to the Editor of the Globe and Laurel that these should be issued with that Journal, separately paged, so that those subscribers who did not wish to keep the whole numbers, would be able to retain such historical items in a separate and convenient form. I had also many similar items among my notes for which space could not have been provided in Britain's Sea Soldiers, as well as others discovered after its publication. I hoped, too, that many more might have been obtained from existing members of the Corps, both on the Active and Retired lists, but until the late Sir H. Blumberg began contributing his interesting articles, very few were forthcoming, and I would suggest that this little Volume should be dedicated to his memory.

C. FIELD, Colonel

Blumberg's and Field's Random Records

THE MARINES OF ANTIQUITY
From "Sea Power in Ancient History."
By A. McCartney Shepard (London, 1925).

The ROWERS varied in number from 170 on the Athenian trireme to over five hundred in the largest rates . . .

The SAILORS, numbering about 17 on the trireme, and proportionally on the higher rates, were under the immediate supervision of two Non-commissioned Quartermasters. Their work, which was probably far less toilsome than that of the Rowers, consisted in looking after the rigging and sails, and in steering and navigating the vessel.

The MARINES were simply heavy-armed land troops (HOPLITES), detailed for duty on shipboard. They were used for boarding the enemy's ships, for repelling boarders, or for forming a mobile landing force to operate in the enemy's territory. Their numbers varied in accordance with the character and object of the expedition on which they were embarked. Generally speaking, in proportion as the expedition was strictly naval in character, the smaller was the number of Marines taken on board.

Thus, at Salamis, when the system of land warfare at sea largely prevailed, the number of Marines attached to each warship was 18, of whom four were archers and the rest heavy armed; while in the days of Phormio, half a century later, when naval tactics had reached a high stage of development, the total number had been reduced to ten, which was barely sufficient to repel boarders during the few seconds in which the warship was in contact with its rammed foe. When the object of the expedition was Military as well as Naval, a much larger number of Marines - often as high as fifty to a vessel - was embarked on a Greek warship.

The Romans, with their much larger vessels and their incurable instinct for land warfare at sea, went a great deal further. Their quinquiremes carried as high as 120 Marines to each ship, and to them, we are told, by the most competent of witnesses Rome's good fortune at sea was due. "For though nautical science," says Polybius, "contributes largely to success in sea-fights, still it is the courage of the Marines that turns the tide most decisively in favour of victory."
*Polybius VI 52.

NOTE - The Roman legions served as Marines in the naval actions in the Punic Wars. In the reigns of Nero and Vespasian two legions were formed from the Marines, and were quartered the 1st Adjutrix in Spain, and the 2nd Adjutrix on the Rhine in Batavia. There was also a Marine Cohort quartered on the wall of Adrian in Cumberland.

BADGES OF ROMAN MARINES.

According to some classical authorities the 1st Legio Adjutrix and the 2nd Legio Adjutrix were Marine Legions. Whether they were actually Marines in the modern sense of the word seems somewhat doubtful, for from various accounts of their constitution and doings they might well have been emergency Legions, formed from Naval ratings not required afloat. Assuming, however, that they were Marines, it is interesting to note that while both bore the Naval emblem Pegasus,"the 1st had the Badge of a "Goat" and the 2nd of a "Boar".

THE MARINES OF ANTIQUITY.

"The employment of Infantry as part of the regular complement of vessels of war was common to the Phoenicians and to all the maritime States of Greece, at least for centuries before the commencement of the Christian Era. In the earlier History it was not so… but as Naval Science progressed, and the size of vessels increased, there gradually sprang up distinct classes: the Rowers and Seamen proper, who had the general management of the vessel and sails, and Marines or fighting men. Marines are especially mentioned in the account of the Battle of Lade, the time of Darius, King of Persia, about 497 B.C… These men-at-arms, or soldiers, which formed part of the complement of the Greek Trireme, were called Epibatae, a word all authorities agree in rendering into English, by the word "Marines." The largest number of Marines found aboard such of the "Swift Ships," is, the regular men-of-war, as distinguished from transports, at this period was fifty… The learned Historian of Greece, Mr. Grote, speaks of "Epibatae" as "Marines" and observes that 'though not forming a Corps permanently distinct, they correspond in function to the English Marines.' In the statement that they did not form a distinct Corps, Mr. Grote seems to differ from other authorities. Boeckh, probably one of the best authorities on the antiquities of Athens, states, 'These Epibatae were entirely distinct from the land Soldiers and belonged to the vessel. They had, moreover, their own Officers, called Trierarchoi.'

From *"History of the U.S. Marine Corps,"*
By Capt. R. S. Collum, 1896.

GUNBOAT IN ACTION IN THE TIME OF HENRY VIII.
From a Cottonian MS.

This quaint picture is from a MS. on the subject of Artillery which is said to have belonged to King Henry VIII. It was re-produced in the Archaeological Journal about 50 years ago. The heaviest gun is apparently an ordinary light field-piece on a shore-going carriage. The two light pivot guns are without doubt breech-loaders, though the details of the breech closing apparatus do not appear. The archer and the halberdier - who may possibly be in command of the boat-complete a somewhat meagre crew.

This interesting picture is reproduced in the Record Section of the Globe and Laurel as it may be the earliest picture of Marine Artillery handling guns afloat.

CLOTHING AND EQUIPMENT OF THE MARINE REGIMENTS IN 1702.
By Colonel Lourenco Edye, R.M.L.I.

N.B. - This article, with slight abridgements and alterations in the wording is taken from the rough copy of the second volume of the late Colonel Edye's "History of the Royal Marine Forces."

"To the supreme command of the six Regiments of Marines Colonel William Seymour was appointed as Brigadier-General, whose duties were "to observe that the men were comfortably quartered, that their officers were attentive to their respective departments, and that the Marine soldiers when embarked on board ship were supplied with proper sea-clothes and other suitable necessaries.[1]

By a study of the personnel of the Officers of these Regiments it will be seen that the earlier Marine Regiments (including the Admiral's) are represented in the ranks of the new, whilst every foot regiment, many cavalry regiments, and the Navy itself also contributed officers. The force at its first raising may therefore be said to have been thoroughly representative of the then existing English fighting services.

The clothing of the new Marine Regiments, under the system prevailing during the 17th century, still remained in the hands of their Colonels.

The decision as to the colour of the "linings"[2] and general points of distinction in the uniform was their prerogative, as was also, subject to the Sovereign's approval, that of the Colours.

The manner in which the clothing of the soldier was supplied was no doubt objectionable, but the government of the day had not as yet considered it desirable to trench on the privileges of the commanding officer in this matter, and doubtless advisably so, seeing that they probably recognised the fact that the welfare of the soldier would be better safeguarded by this mode of supply, than by entrusting the same to contractors, whose sole object in those early days was robbery and jobbery wherever Government contracts were concerned.[3]

In contradistinction to the present mode of supply, the Marine soldier of the 18th century paid for all his own clothing, the "free kit" being unknown. From his pay the sum of sixpence per diem was deducted for "subsistence," the balance being termed his "off-reckonings."

From the total annual amount a shilling in the pound was also stopped, and paid to the Colonel in part payment of the sum advanced by him to clothe his regiment; or to the contractor if so arranged.[4]

That such arrangements were at times carried out may be seen by "An Agreement (made) between the Honble. Colonell Alexander Luttrell, William Churchill, and Richard Harnage, for Cloathing a Regiment of Marines," in which Colonel Luttrell owns "to have bargained with the said William Churchill and Richard Harnage for the goods, accoutrements, &c., &c., amounting to Seven thousand two hundred and thirty-two pounds, twopence, for payment of which some the said Richard Harnage and William Churchill are to take an assignment upon the off-reckonings of the Regiment, and that neither I the said Colonell Alexander Luttrell, my Executors, or Administrators shall be answerable for the payment thereof."[5]

Thanks to several very interesting MS documents concerning Colonel Luttrell's - (previously Villiers') - Regiment of Marines, drafted by Lieutenant Thomas Yard, Quartermaster of the Corps, we are able to determine the complete land and sea kit of the Marine soldier of that time, together with other details of much interest.

The first of these documents we may consider sets forth that the land kit of the rank and file is to consist of "One Coat, one Waistcoat, one pair of Breeches, one Sword, one Belt, one Cartridge-box, one pair of Stockings, one pair of Shoes, two Shirts, two Cravatts, and one Capp for each man for the first yeare," whilst in the second year he received "one pair of Breeches, one pair of Shoes, one Shirt, one Cravatt, and one pair of Stockings."

By this arrangement it will be seen that the Coat, Waistcoat and Cap were each intended to last for two years, and that the soldier received a second shirt and cravatt every other year in addition to his annual supply of clothing. These articles were known as a man's "Mountings,"[6] but they did not entirely complete that kit, for the payment of which he was in the end responsible; for we find that, in addition he was compelled to possess a "Surtout," as well as a "Bed, Rug and Pillow."

The cost of the equipment for each Non-commissioned Officer, Drummer and Private for the two years is set forth as follows:-

	£	s.	d
Sergeant	14	7	0
Corporal or Drummer	11	4	0
Centinel	4	17	0

As to the charge made for the various articles themselves, several of them are quoted by Lieutenant and Quartermaster Yard as below:-

	£	s.	d	£	s.	d
Surtout		11	0		10	2
Coat	1	10	0	1	5	0
Breeches	0	7	0		5	10
Waistcoat		8	0		6	8
Caps		6	4		5	4
Shirts		3	0		2	7
Shoes		4	7		3	10
Stockings		1	10		1	7
Cravats			9			71/2

The right hand column no doubt represents the cost of the various articles as purchased, whilst the left hand column represents the price demanded of the men themselves.[7]

The saving thus effected, together with that arising from casualties, such as "dead pays" and "non-effectives", enabled the Colonel of the Regiment, or the contractors concerned, to safeguard themselves against losses due to desertion and other unforeseen causes. The prices of the several articles above detailed was for the Corporals and "Centinels" only, as distinct from the Sergeants and Drummers, whose clothing differed in some respects, for by other documents we find that whereas the price of a "Centinel's" coat was £1 10s. 0d., that for a Sergeant was £3 12s. 0d., and for a Drummer £3. Similarly, whilst Sergeants' shirts and cravats cost 4/6 and 2/- respectively, those issued to the remainder, including drummers, cost only 2/7 and -/8 each. Sergeants and Drummers also wore superior caps, and probably waistcoats, but of the latter no mention is made by Mr. Yard. As regards Shoes, all were served alike, but while Sergeants paid 5/- a pair for their stockings, the remainder only paid 1/7 for theirs.

Besides the kit issued to N.C.Os. and men whilst serving on shore, it is proved by another document that a sea-kit was also issued to them when serving afloat, but whether all the items of this kit were, or were not, in excess of the land clothing is, unfortunately, not stated.

As this document is interesting in detailing not only the various items, but as shewing the difference in prices paid in London and in Plymouth for some of the articles, as well as the variation in cost between those issued to Sergeants and "Centinels" (including Corporals), it is here given in full: -

A Particular Acct. of the Sea things bought by Captain Piggott at Plymouth.

	s.	d.		s.	d.
For a Sergt.'s Frock	16	3	For a Sentinell's Frock	9	9¼
For a Shirt	4	6	For a Shirt	2	7
For a Cap		10	For a Mil'd Cap[8]		10½
For a Neck Cloth	2	0	For a Neck Cloth		8
For a Pair of Shoes	3	1	For a pair of shoes	3	1
For a Pair of Shoes	3	6	For a pair of Stockins	1	4
For a Bed		9 6	For a Bed	9	0
£1	19	9[9]	£1	7	9¾

An Acct. of the particulars bought in London.

	s.	d.		s.	d.
For a Sergt.'s Frock	10	4	For a Sentinell's Frock	5	8
For two Shirts	8	4	For two Shirts	5	0
For two Neckcloths	2	0	For two Neckcloths	1	4
For a red cloth Cap	2	6	For a red Cap		6

For a Bed	11	6	For a Bed	8	0
For a Pair of Stockins	3	6	For a Pair of Stockins	1	4
For a Pair of Shoes	3	1	For a Pair of Shoes	3	1
	£2 1	3		£1 4	11

From the above documents it is quite clear that for working purposes when serving afloat there were issued to the N.C.Os. and men an additional frock and cap of a less ornate description than those worn by them on shore, or possibly when on guard, or detailed for any special function whilst serving afloat.

It has been quite impossible to trace any description of this sea-service frock, but the cap was probably the same as that worn by the pioneers of this date[10] and similar to that now worn by yachtsmen and brewers of the present day.

In addition to the kits as detailed above, the several ranks were served out with the following articles of equipment:-

		Cost s.	d.
For Sergts.	Swords	10	0
	Belts	3	6
For Drummers	Drum Carriages	10	0
	Swords	4	6
	Waistbelts	4	6
For Centinels	Waistbelts	3	1
	Bayonett Swords[11]	4	6
	Collars of Bandaleers	5	6
	Cartridge Box and Sling	3	4
	Match Boxes	1	0
	Snapsacks[12]	3	6

From a further document it is found that the contract price of the cloth for the sea-frocks, which were made of white kersey, was 2/3 a yard for those furnished to the Sergeants, while that for the men's sea-frocks was 1/5 a yard. For the making of these garments, including buttons and thread 4/6 was charged for the Sergeants and 2/4 for the men's.

This contract seems to have been made at Plymouth on behalf of the Companies of Captains Courtenay, Docton, Pigott and Warre, then under orders to embark. The shoes provided were evidently made at Launceston, from the fact that the account shews an item of eleven shillings for "a Sergt. for horse hire and charges to goe to Launceston to bespeake the Shoes."

The Shirts contracted for on this occasion were "blew" and the Neckcloths "speckled,"[13] whilst all ranks wore "Mill'd Capps."

The men of the Grenadier Companies carried "Granadeer hangers" as distinct from the "Bayonett Swords" worn by the battalion companies. They were also equipped with Fuzees with Slings to each, Granade-puches, Hatchets with girdles to them, and "Granadeer Bags."

With regard to the make and description of the different articles of a man's clothing, all were ordered to be of a uniform pattern[14], except that Regiments were allowed to differ in those several minor details which served to identify them one from another.

The Surtout, or "Capitation Coat," issued at this date to all infantry Regiments, corresponded to our modern Great-coat and was scarlet for all but the Marine Regiments. Their Surtouts were made of Brown Cloth and lined with the same colour as the Regimental facings.[15]

The land service coat of scarlet cloth was also lined with a material which faced it with the livery of the regiment, which was also represented in the colour of the waistcoats, breeches, cap, and stockings.

The "cravatts" worn by the officers were as in the preceding century, generally very handsomely embroidered, whilst the "Neckcloths" of the men were worn in a manner more approaching the "stock" of later days, than had hitherto been the practice.

There is little doubt Grenadier Caps were worn by all the Regiments of Marines, for Mr. Yard never refers in the several documents of which he is the author to the word "Hats" as distinguished from "Caps," nor does he discriminate at any time between Granadiers and others, as regards their head-dress.

Among the articles of equipment carried by the Marines - possibly for the first time - was the Snapsack or Knapsack. In this bag Colonel Walton tells us[16] "the soldier carried all his kit, spare boots, clothing and food," it "was carried slung on the musket, or the rest, or on a stick, but more commonly, and more correctly, it used to he slung to the back by a strap passing across the chest, over one arm and under the other, just as pedlars or gipsies may be seen carrying their "packs" at the present day."

Mr. Yard has left sufficient evidence to prove that the Colours were furnished as well as determined on by the Colonel of the Regiment; for in one of his accounts, we find that £700 is assigned "by Coll: Villiers upon the off reckonings besides of cloathing out of wch: Mrs. Villiers is to have for Snap Sacks, Drum Cases, and Colours £74, wch: ye Coll: furnished for the Regt:"

On the raising of a new Regiment officers were to agree upon a pattern approved by the Colonel for their coats and to buy them where they liked.

The Silk Sash was like that now worn by all officers, but round the waist[17], the price of those for Colonel Villiers' Regiment of Marines being £3 16s. 0d. The Gorget was also worn by officers, possibly of the same make as obtained during the previous century, gilt for Captains, "Sanguined (Blued) Steel" studded with gold for Lieutenants, and Silver for Ensigns.

Lieutenant Yard's Quartermaster's Gorget cost him £1 4s. 0d., but whether it was a Lieutenant's or Ensign's is not clear.

Colonels also wore a Gorget when on duty[18]. The colour and description of the uniforms of the new Regiments of Marines can be in a measure gleaned from the descriptive returns given of deserters, and also from other sources, for whilst they varied in colour, facings, buttons and loopings, they were, without exception, similar in cut to those of the infantry of the line. The colour of the coat worn by the Marines on shore was red in all cases, and, as far as can be traced, the lining or facing varied for each regiment.

Of that worn by Mordaunt's and Lord Shannon's Marines, no record can be traced. In Colonel Holts Regiment the facings were Grey, as were also the breeches, stockings and waistcoats, the last beornamented with loops of a mixture of Red, Black and White. The "Grenadier Caps" were of the "same mounting"[19] whilst the Capitation Coat was Brown lined with Red. The Buttons were pewter, except those of the Grenadier Company, which were Brass.

In Colonel Fox's s Regiment the facings throughout were Light Green, as were also the waistcoats which had loopings of Silver Lace for the Sergeants and white worsted lace for the rank and file.

In Colonel Saunderson's Regiment the facings like those of "Holt's" were Grey, whilst in Colonel Villier's Regiment they were Yellow. In neither of these two Regiments does there appear to have been any "loopings" on the waistcoats.

NOTES.

N.B. - *These notes are in Colonel Edye's Manuscript, with the exception of those initialled "C.F.", which are added by the Editor of the Article.*

1. Nicholas. - "Historical Record of the R.M. Forces.- Vol. 1. Page 8.
2. Facings of the modern day.
3. As a matter of fact the Commanding Officers of that day were very frequently as ready to rob the soldier as were the Contractors, with whom they were often in league. Says Colonel Walton in his "History of the British Standing Army," (p. 391): The off-reckonings were barely sufficient to cover the expense of the clothing; nevertheless the Colonels contrived to screw a very considerable income out of them, varying from £200 to £600 a year. This money they, in plain language, embezzled, inasmuch as, although it was handed to them for a particular purpose, they diverted it to their private benefit. That it was the fashion "of their class to steal does not render the theft less disgraceful." - C.F.
4. According to the system then in vogue the soldier practically got no pay and was lucky if he got his clothing and subsistence. The following taken from Colonel Walton, shews his highly unsatisfactory balance sheet for the year: -

	£	s.	d.
Total pay at 8d. per diem	12	3	4
Deduct Subsistence at 6d.	9	2	6
Gross off-reckonings	3	0	10
Deduct 1s. per £ on annual pay		12	2
One day's pay for Chelsea Hospital			8
Net off-reckonings	2	8	0

And out of the net off-reckonings was to come his kit! - C.F.

5. From MS. In possession of G.F. Luttrell, Esq., of Dunster castle.

6. The old term for the soldier's outfit or kit; half-mounting is a limited or partial issue of clothing, etc. The term is still used in the Indian Army in regard to Native Soldiers. (Vide Army Regulations. India. Clothing, 1914). C.F.

7. A similar Document, but clearer in detail, exists among Harleian MSS. No. 6844.

8. "Mill'd," i.e., Cleansed and thickened cloth." - C.F.

9. The addition is in both cases incorrect,

10. An illustration in "The burning of the Pope at Temple in London 1679 shews this cap. The above is a pamphlet, which states "First marched six Whifflers to clear the way in pioneer caps and red waistcoats. - C.F.

11. Issued new every third year. - Dublin State Papers.

12. From the German "Schnappsack."

13. "Speckled."

14. Proclamation 26th July, 1697. - Dublin State Papers.

15. As will he seen later the Surtouts of Holt's Marines were lined with red. - C.F.

16. "History of the British Standing Army," page 377.

17. When Colonel Edye wrote the Sash was worn over the left shoulder. - C.F.

18. McKinrion's History of the Coldstream Guards, Vol. I., page 187.

19. Mounting here evidently means of the same colour as the facings area decorated with the regimental lace. - C.F.

The above caps are of interest, as it is probable that the Marine "Cap," so frequently referred to in Colonel Edye's article entitled "Clothing and Equipment of the Marine Regiments in 1702", which appeared on pages 85 to 88 of the Record Section in the October issue, approximated in shape to one of them.

* * * *

The illustration of the coat was copied by Colonel Field from a tracing taken from the original drawing in a tailor's pattern book by the Rev. P. Sumner, a great authority on old Military Uniforms. The coat is interesting, as dating from the time immediately after the Corps was made Royal, also because from the tailor's accompanying description it is evident that each Division wore different buttons.

N.B. - Only three buttons are shown on cuff, but it distinctly states there were four, and this was apparently always the number up to the appearance of the tunic in 1856. The epaulette is merely indicated, and no detail is given.

1. GRENADIER CAP. 1ST FOOT GUARDS. 1686 - 2. GRENADIERS CAP. 2ND. QUEEN'S. 1715.

TAILOR'S DESCRIPTION.

Superfine Scarlet Coat, cut as regulation - 10 holes in lapel by twos - 4 blue long holes on top of lapel, and the rest of the holes on forepart scarlet - Lapel full 4 inches at top - Blue lapels, cuff and standup collar with 1 hole and breast button on each side, - two on each side behind - soldier's side - four holes on flaps and cuffs, by pairs White cassimere - Embroidered skirt ornaments, a Heart - Gold Epaulette - Gilt buttons of whatever Division they are of, whether Plymouth or Chatham. ROYAL MARINES. - For Lieut. Sampson, Feb. 1803.

Fr. Messrs. Welch & Stalker's Pattern Bk.

SOME PERSONAL RECOLLECTIONS OF ROYAL MARINE UNIFORM
By The Late Major-General Simon Fraser and Colonel C. Field.

Among a number of the late Major-General Simon Fraser's notes and papers which have come into my possession I have come across the following personal recollections of the uniform which he wore on joining the Service, and also later on in his career. My own recollections as to the Corps uniform, which commence in 1879, would appear to follow on pretty closely the last portion of the General's reminiscences, so that I have added them in order to continue the "sartorial story" more or less to date.

"When I first received my commission (writes General Fraser) I was appointed to the old Woolwich division. Being at home, and in the country at the time (Scotland), I was, after some deliberation, taken to the old family tailor in Edinburgh. At that time there were not so many regular outfitters as there are now, and the tailor was consequently much perplexed as to how to get me correctly "rigged out", but he did his best (though no one there knew much about the uniform of our Corps), and only understood the undress of the Corps. This was a long dark blue coat, with a gold cord on the shoulder, gilt buttons, and a crimson sash round the waist; the trousers black and plain; a dark blue cloth cap with a badge, and a deep red band (sign of Royal).

Having reached London, I waited on my father's two old friends, Lord Melville (the first Lord of that time), and Sir George Clark. Being approved of by them, and carrying with me their hearty good wishes, I started the same evening for Woolwich, reported myself to the Commandant and was invited to breakfast the next morning. Accordingly I went at the hour appointed, was ushered in, and there for the first time met our good kind-hearted Commandant, Colonel MacClaverty, a most popular officer, and one, the thought of whom, has always been a sincere pleasure to me from the first day I entered the Service until now. I have found many a warm, true friend, many a brave comrade during my long service ashore and afloat, but none more true or single-hearted than he was, a gentleman in every sense of the word.

On the occasion of our first meeting, after Colonel MacClaverty and his daughter had shaken hands with me, and glanced curiously at my uniform, they both laughed heartily, and at last the Colonel, hoping I would excuse them asked where I had procured it and told me that the buttons - two and two - were as old as the hills, and not of our Corps at all.

Though hot all over, and my youthful dignity being somewhat upset, I made a satisfactory breakfast, seeing that the Colonel and his charming daughter were very kind to me, after their laugh was over and mutual explanations had been given. The Colonel then told me to go to my quarters and put on my plain clothes, and come to him on parade. This I did quickly enough, having been introduced to the Adjutant, who was told I might go to my drills in plain clothes.

I was then handed over to the drill sergeant. On the second day he reported me as "the most apt hand at drill and sword exercise that he had ever had." Upon being questioned by the Adjutant, I told him that I had received the silver medal at the Royal Scottish Military Academy for special skill in military exercises. I next went through the drills before the Colonel, and was reported qualified to join the Battalion at once.

Not a word more was ever said about the unfortunate buttons; they were soon cut off and consigned to the flames.

The full dress uniform at that time was scarlet as it has always been since I entered the Service and it was so in the time of my Grand Uncle, Sir John Douglas.

When I joined the Service the full dress uniform was very handsome: A red tail-coat with blue facings, and richly embroidered with gold lace. Epaulettes of gold bullion. The trousers were white in summer and black in winter, with a red piping down the side. The full dress hat was of a very peculiar shape, very tall, large and exceedingly heavy, broad at the crown, and small and narrow on the forehead, a very tall, stiff white aigrette, and a handsome gold badge in front; also a gold cord and tassels attached by one end to the hat, the other being fastened on the breast. These hats were most difficult to manage, being so awkward in shape, and so top-heavy, that if any officer chanced to stoop or bend forward, the hat was certain to fall over his face.

After this followed various styles of uniform which at this date I cannot remember minutely. We had an endless variety of hats and caps: there was the shako, high and low crowned, with white balls, green balls, stiff aigrettes, and drooping green plumes. Afterwards we had another style of shako, and finally the helmets now worn. We also wore swallow-tail coats, with white lining, and many different styles, until the tunics of the present day were chosen.

For a long time epaulettes were worn, and sashes round the waist, with white belts across the shoulder; then the epaulettes were abolished, white belts worn round the waist, and crimson sashes across the shoulder. White trousers in summer, black, with at one time a narrow red piping, at a later date a wider stripe down the sides.

Just before I joined the 2nd and 1st Lieutenants wore only one epaulette, the Captains two, Majors and Colonels wore two, but their epaulettes were made of handsomer bullion than the Captains. At the time I entered the Service the Corps had just appeared in the handsome new uniform, with the gold embroidery, as I have already described; the 2nd Lieutenants then wearing two epaulettes of gold bullion.

At that time we attended mess in our full dress uniform, the mess jackets being a later innovation. When at Lisbon, the Admiral used to take my Captain of Marines and myself ashore with him in his own boat, to the Queen's Levees (to be presented). At that time we were wearing the handsome uniform described above, and Her Majesty (the Queen of Portugal) was pleased to examine it minutely, and expressed great admiration, so did also her own officers.

* * * *

My own recollections of the uniform with which I joined the Portsmouth Division in the autumn of 1879 are perfectly clear, although so many years have since elapsed. The spiked helmet, supposed to have been a poor imitation of the German "Pikel-haube," which became so famous in the Franco-German War of nine years before, had only very lately superseded the shako, which, indeed, was still being worn by some regiments in the garrison about that time. The helmet, I was informed by those of my brother officers who had just discarded the shako, was a vast improvement upon that head-dress, which they say caused a headache, from all its weight being in front and bearing on the forehead, while, unlike the helmet, it gave no protection to the nape of the neck either from sun or rain.

The tunic of the time and battle-honoured scarlet, the traditional British soldier's colour, was similar in shape and lacing to that shewn in the coloured plate facing page 190, Vol. II. of "Britain's Sea Soldiers." But the collar was cut much lower and bore no Corps badge. Instead was the badge of rank embroidered in silver, a Crown for Subalterns, Captains a Crown and Star, Majors a Star, and Lieut.-Colonels a Crown and Star. It had simple plain gold loops as shoulder straps.

The undress was a jacket of blue faced cloth, decorated with black mohair braid, after the fashion of a Hussar jacket. There were no shoulder straps or marks or badges of rank for Captains or Subalterns, but Field Officers wore theirs in gold upon the collar. This Patrol Jacket, as it was called, was a very useful garment, both for drill, manoeuvre and social functions, but rather too elaborate and expensive a garment for field training, gunnery, etc., for which a rank and file blue serge or kersey frock was often "taken up" and worn, though there was no provision for it in the regulations. The French Army between the Crimean War and its "debacle" in 1870 was considered the military model, and the patrol jacket was doubtless suggested by that worn by the officers of the Imperial French Army. In the "sixties" the tendency was to imitate our present allies more or less closely in matters of uniform. Hence the small shakoes, trousers cut as loose as the regulations would admit, and full skirts to the tunic. The very low collar, which was only beginning to disappear about the time I joined, was another Gallic fashion, and I have seen some officers wearing tunics and patrol jackets which shewed but the merest line of cloth below the lace or braid. The forage cap had a straight peak and a more or less soft top. Although it should have been made of green cloth-as the Corps was at that time Light Infantry - it was blue, and surrounded by a wide band of silk oak-leaf braid. It had a black button on the crown, with loops of narrow black braid embroidered around it. Some regiments at this time had strained the regulations in order to wear these caps altered to something the shape of the French Kepi; I think the 24th was one of these.

The silver Globe, with gold embroidered laurels, was worn on the front of the cap, with a gold embroidered bugle above it. A year or so after I joined, however, these caps were superseded by a stiff round cap, copied, apparently, from that worn by the Guards at that time, though it differed in that the button and braid of the old cap was retained. The peak came close to the forehead and was gold embroidered for all ranks. Field Officers had a very narrow gold cord or "halo" round the top edge of their caps. Although this cap still wrongly remained blue instead of green, it was an improvement, in that the black band was replaced by a red cloth one, which had long been the mark of a "Royal" Regiment or Corps.

At the same time a Glengarry cap, a head-dress which had for some time been worn by the rank and file, was introduced for the officers, but it was spoilt for the work for which it was intended by being decorated with an elaborately embroidered Globe and Laurel, instead of one of silver and gilt metal.

At full-dress balls, levees, etc., a crimson and gold sash, waistbelt and trousers with a crimson and gold stripe were worn. These were abolished in 1902 under the pretext of economy. But except in first cost these articles were really no expense at all, as they would last the whole of an officer's service without difficulty. The lace on the trousers was even an economy, since it always looked well and kept the trousers in shape, while for the occasions on which they were worn no trousers with the ordinary red welt looked anything but shabby unless practically brand new. At the same time the very serviceable patrol jacket was replaced by the more expensive frock coat, which, being quite unsuitable for many of the occasions on which the patrol jacket could be worn, had to be augmented by a blue serge jacket, which the tailors took good care should cost nearly as much as the "patrol" of much more expensive material, with its embroidery of mohair braid. Very little economy in this change. It was at this period that the slashed cuff, common to the Royal Marines and the rest of the Army in the sixties was reverted to. It is a pity that while they were about it the distinctive 4-button slash was not re-instituted. I say "distinctive," because in a letter which I received from the late Captain W. Portlock-Dadson, R.M.L.I., in 1911, he says:-

"Before 1849 the coatee had four pieces of gold lace round as many buttons on the tail skirt, that of the N.C.O.s and rank and file being of white braid, just as now worn by the Guard Regiments on the skirt of their tunics. This was discontinued shortly before I joined the Service in August 1849. There is a picture in the series of uniforms of the British Army published by Ackermann about that date, of which I have a copy, - bequeathed hereafter to the Plymouth Division - but it is wrong in one item; the cuff of the coatee has 3 buttons with lace, we had four, like the Guards, while Infantry had three only. A doubt having been thrown on this, I went to my old brother subaltern, Capt. Rowland Brookes, R.M.A., and he showed me his portrait as a 2nd Lieutenant, painted for his mother, which distinctly shews 4 buttons."

If, as I hope may someday sooner or later be the case, the present blue abortion is consigned to the limbo of inappropriate monstrosities, and the old red tunic comes to its own again, perhaps the opportunity may be taken to revert to our distinctive 4 buttons. Long before the "slash" came into vogue, by the way, the 4 buttons were worn on the cuffs of the Marines, generally set on in pairs.

It may be in the interest of some persons to obliterate the many small military differences and distinctions which connect the Royal Marines with their ancestors, but it is certainly to the interest of the Corps itself to hold on to those they have, and to resuscitate as many as possible, for these things, small and puerile as they may seem to the civilian mind, are among those which go to foster that esprit de corps, which is of priceless value to any militant organisation.

During the greater part of my own service the blue cloth helmet remained the full-dress head-dress, the white helmet, as in the Army, only being worn on foreign service in hot climates. To my mind it is a great pity that it was abolished, for independently of the fact that the white helmet is quite unsuitable for cold and wet climates, it leaves the Royal Marines in the position of being the only military body in H.M. Service without a full-dress head-dress. I don't know that anybody is particularly in love with the blue helmet, but some full-dress head-covering ought to be supplied to place the Royal Marines on a par with other corps.

Something like this seems to have taken place at the end of the 18th century. As being more adapted for active service the wide flaps of the uniform cocked hats were "cropped," much like the one worn by the Marines through the Napoleonic Wars was the result. But it was a makeshift, and the Army adopted the cap which later developed into the shako, about 1800. But the Marines were left with their "makeshift" till a proper shako was adopted in 1823.

––––––––

THE "GOOD" OLD TIMES.

Well - perhaps. Not very good in the way of Pay however, which small as it was, was sometimes very difficult to get hold of at all.

Witness the following Petition:-

"To the Right Honble: Sidney Lord Godolphin, Lord High Treasurer of England.

The humble petition of the Subaltern Officers of the Two late Marine Regiments commanded by the Marquis of Carmarthen and Sr Cloudsley Shovel'.[1]

Humbly Sheweth: That the said Subaltern Officers have been kept out of their Pay for their Service in the said Regiments near Eight Yeares, in which time they have had many assurances they shou'd be clear'd[2], but all of them (except three) are still unpaid, by which most of them and their poor Famillyes are in a miserable condition and are nott able to appear abroad 'till it shall please yr Lordsp to Order the payment.

therefore most humbly pray yr Lordsp wou'd Comisserat the Condition of yr poor petitrs. by payment of their just Right.

And they shall (as in duty, bound) pray, etc., etc.

7. Nov., 1706.

1. Raised 1690. Disbanded 1698.
2. "Cleared" i.e., Regimental accounts settled and pay due issued.

Ed note:- The above is exactly as written!

––––––––

A QUESTION REGARDING CABINS.

From Captain Robert Bockenham, R.N.

H.M.S. "Auguste".
Hamoaze, 8th Jany: 1706.

"The Marine Officer on board Her Majesty's Ship under my command having applyed himself to me either to have the steerage divided or a cabin built there for him, I informed the Comsr here of the same, who hath answered me that there are Cabins built for the Commission and Warrant Officers according to the establishment, and that he will order no more to be built without and order from His Royal Highns, alledging that I have applyed one Cabbin for the use of my clarke, wherein I humbly conceive I have not offended, there being no other convenience for him, for the keeping and securing my papers and accounts, and in every ship some place is allotted for that end, Therefore desire His Royal Highness's Order either to have the steerage divided, or a Cabbin to be built there for the convenience of the Marine Officer, and am, &c., &c.

Endorsed –
  "An Order to have the steerage divided or a Cabbin built as may be most convenient.

From Captain Robert Bockenham,

22nd January 1706.

I recd. yours of the 13th inst: in relation to ye building of a Cabbin for ye convenience of ye Officer of Marines, but when ye Joyners came off, found there was not roome there being but four foote from ye gun to ye bulkhead of my Cabbin, and but three foote to the bulkhead of ye steerage, wch ye Joyners themselves acquainted me was not length, and my Chaplain complaining of the frequent noise occasioned by the Officers servants who wait on them in the coach, who prevent him studying, chose to change with the Lieutenant of Marines, and desired his cabbin might be built in the gunroom where he should he more quiet. After the joyners had been down and brought me word a good cabbin might be built there, clear of my guns and might always stand. My Lieutenant (whom I sent) confirming the same, made me ready to consent to it since the Marine Officer and Chaplain were pleased.

The Cabbin was just finished when yesterday two men belonging to the Yard came off and without acquainting me or any of my officers with the reasons, went and beat down the Cabbin, for which together with his ill language I corrected him with 3 or 4 blows, one whereof happened breake his head, who by the Commsrs letter in answer to one I wrote him, desiring to know if he had recd: any directions for breaking down, the aforesaid Cabbin, he alledging it was not in the proper place the Prince had appointed, and that the man I beat was the Joyner of the Yard which at that time I was a stranger too, all which misunderstanding proceeds from the builder who has been so free with his language tongue as to give me unmannerly language even to my face (which to avoid complaints of this nature) I have turned my head and seemed not to hear, but humbly hope he will not be encouraged in it, and the Commissioner is angry because I wrote to His Royal Highness, and did not make any application to the Navy Board for ye building of ye Cabbin, which I begg may be ordered in the Gunroom, where 'tis clear of my guns at all times, and am &c &c.

THE HEART OF THE PRINCE OF HESSE.

From Captain Charles Gibson,
A Prisoner at St. Malo.   Jany. 13/14. 1706.

"In my voiadge from Lisbon in ye Latitude of 40 & 30, I had ye misfortune to meet with French Privateer of St. Malo, of 20 guns and 130 men.

She chased me into ye latitude of 47 and then come up with me, it was on ye 3rd instant at 7 in ye morning; we fought him five hours, with our small arms and stern chase, not being able to use any other gunns, for ye enemy attacked us in ye lee quarter, and ye wind blowing fresh, my gunns were under water, and the major part of my men like cowardly rascalls run down into ye hold, otherwise I did not doubt of saving the Queen's ship. I had several land officers on board with whom I consulted, and having 4 foot water in ye hold and not above 10 men to stand by me, it was their oppinion to strike, otherwise we must have sunk.

I therefore ordered ye colours to be struck, having thrown overboard 3 males, with the Ambassador's Packetts and all other letters: one of my officers has lost an arm and his son one leg, five more wounded but not dangerous; we were landed here ye 8th instant and ye commissary has promised ye land officers with myself and company shall depart with ye first Transport which will sayle in 10 days time.

The officers taken with me are: -
Capt. Benson of my Lord Raby's Dragoons.
Capt. Hamilton of my Lord Portmore's
Lieut. Lloyd of Col: Elliotts. and
the late Prince of Hesse's Secretary who has got ye Prince's Heart to carry into Germany.
(Admiralty. Captains' Letter Books).

MISCELLANEOUS DOCUMENTS
From Notes kindly lent by Col. C. Field, R.M. (ret.)

DEDUCTION OF 6d. IN THE £.

Rawl. M.S.C. 914, fol. 35.
His Royal Highness Prince George of Denmark, etc., Ld. high Admiral of England, etc.,

Ireland, etc., and of all her Majts.' Plantations, etc., and Generalissimo of all her Majts.' Forces, etc.

Whereas by the late Instructions given by her Majty for the better Government of the Marine Regiments, it was ordered that Sixpence in ye pound should be deducted from all money which should from time to time be Issued for the use of the Said Regiments, you are hereby required and directed to make the same deduction of Sixpence out of every Twenty Shillings wch you shall Issue, pursuant to the foregoing Establishment, to be by you paid by Such proportions and in such manner as I shall from time to time direct you, by warrant: under my hand, of all wch you are to keep a distinct Account in Wrighting, to be laid before me at such times as I shall require the Same. Given under my hand this 12th day of May, 1704, in the Third Year of her Majty's Reign.

GEORGE

To Walter Whitfield, Esqr., Pay Ma'r
   of the Marine Regiments.
By Command of his Royall highness
   George Clarke.

MEMORIAL OF CAPT. HY. DAVYS.

S.P. Domestic Petitions, Vol. VI., 1712.
To the Rt. Hon'ble the Earl of Dartmouth.
   The Humble Memoriall of Capt. Henry Davys sheweth -
   That he has served these Seventeen years in Flanders and Spain, and is at present Captain of a Company in Col. Nassau's Regt. of foot. His father having lately died and left him a sum of money, he is desirous to advance himself in her Majesty's Army by purchasing a better post.
   Humbly prays your Lord'p will be pleased to move her Majesty that he may have leave to dispose of his company in order to purchase another post, for which he has partly agreed, as also to part with his post to Lieut. William Boseville, who is at present Lieut. in Lord Shannon's Regt. of Marines.
   His Grace the Duke of Argyle has been pleased to consent to his disposal and to make use of his name for obtaining leave.
   We do Certify that the particulars in the above are true, and that Capt. Davys has served with great Reputation both in Flanders and Spain.

J. WEBB
GEO. CARPENTER
CHARLES WILLS

Undated.   (Original Signatures)

DESERTERS.

The Post Man (No. 1006)

From Saturday, August 22nd, to Tuesday, August 25th, 1702.

July 27th, Deserted from Portsmouth, out of Capt. Jo. Harrison's Company of Grenadeers, in the Honourable Coll. Holts' Regiment of Marines, with their Mountings, viz., Red lin'd with Grey, Grey Wastcoats, with loops of mixture of Red, Black and White, Grey Stockings and Caps of the same, John Carlisle, aged 21, well set man, about 5 foot 5 inches high, of a Swarthy Complexion, with short black Hair; has been a sailor; generally carried his wife with him on an Ass, selling Powder and Wash Balls about the Streets of London - she is a likely brown woman. Wm. Lensadell, a brisk young fellow of a swarthy complexion, with Black Hair, about 20 years old, 5 foot 8 inches high, born at Colerton Moore in Leicestershire.

Deserted also August 14th from the above said Capt. Harrison, one Henry Parkeson, aged about 23, a tall thin man, near 5 foot 11 inches high, fair Complexion, thin visage, long nose, with Wastcoat, Britches and stockings of the said Mountings, and an old brown Capitation Coat; born near Preston in Lancashire, or in Blackburn Hundred in the said County. Alexander Huit, a tall well set man, about 40 years of age, some grey Hairs in his Head, deserted out of Capt. Edward Morrison's Company, the beginning of August 1702. Whoever secures them, or gives notice of 'em, so that they may be secured to the said Capt. at Portsmouth, or to the Agent of the said Regiment, at Young Man's Coffee-house, Charing Cross, shall have 5 Guineas reward for each of them, with reasonable charges, but if they will return to their said Companies before the 15th of September next, they shall he kindly received.

BRIGDR. SEYMOUR EMPOWERED TO TRY BY COURT-MARTIAL.

H.O. Military Entry Book, Vol. 5,
    Anne R

Whereas we have Order'd Our Marine Regimts. to go on board Our Fleet, and it being necessary, if those Regimts, or any part of them, should be employ'd on Shore during their being abroad upon this intended expedition, that they should be kept in good order and discipline. Our Will and pleasure is, and we do hereby Authorize and Empower you, or the Commanding Officer for the time being not under the Degree of a Field Officer, to call and Assemble Courts Martialls from time to time as there shall be occasion, and to be president of ye same; which Courts Martiall are to be Constituted according to an Act past in the last Session of this Present Parliament. Entituled an Act for Punishing Officrs and Soldiers who shall Mutiny or Desert Her Ma'ty's Service in England or Ireland, and for Punishing False Musters, and to meet at such time or times as you the said President shall appoint for the Punishing such Mutiny, Desertion or False Musters as shall be committed by any Officer or Soldier of Our said Marine Regimts under your Command, while they shall be on shore, and we do hereby further Authorize and Empower the said Courts Martial' to hear and Examine all such matters and Informations as shall be brought before them touching the Misbehaviour of any Officer or Soldier by Mutiny, Desertion or False Musters as aforesaid, and to proceed in the Tryalls of such Offenders, and in giving of Sentence, and inflicting of Punishment, according to ye Powers and Directions mentioned in the said Act of Parliament (a copy whereof is hereunto annexed) and according to such other Rules and Orders as are or shall be given for the better discipline and Govermt of Our Forces, and for so doing this shall be a sufficient Warrt. Given at our Court at Windsor this 22nd day of May 1703, In the Second year of our Reign.

By Her Ma'ty s Command,
NOTTINGHAM.

To our Trusty and Welbeloved
Wm. Seymour, Esqr., of the
Brigadrs. of Our Forces and
Coll. of one of our Regimts. of
Marines.

SUPPLY OF ARMS.

S.P. Dom. Anne, Vol. 17-1710, Aug.- Nov., Fol. 116.
May it please Your Majesty,

In obedience to Your Majesty's Commands signified by a letter of the 24th instant from the Rt. Hon'ble the Lord Dartmouth, Your Maj'ties' Principal Secretary of State - we have considered of the enclosed Memorial from the Lord Commissioners of the Admiralty relating to the furnishing Arms for the Additional men of Collonel Churchill's Regiment. And beg leave to inform Your Majesty that the general pratice of this office is to Arm Regiments when first raised, but after that the respective Colonels are to take care to keep their Regiments Armed. It is true, some Regiments that have been sent upon a sudden Service and wanted Arms, we have supplied them, by a particular Warrant from Your Majesty, for which payment was to be made out of the Arrears of the Regiment, but when we have apply'd for the same to the Paymaster of the Army we have met with so many difficultys and very little of what has been due has been paid to this office that we are humbly of the opinion it is for Your Majesty's Service that the Regiments here buy such Arms as they want, having a Fund already settled for that service.

Your Majesty's most obedient Servant,
C. MUSCRAVE.

Office of Ordnance,
    26th Oct., 1710.

ORDERS FOR LANDING, 1708.

REPORT ON KETTON MSS., VOL. 26.
1708, July 24th. - "Orders to be observed before and after landing the forces:
1. That all officers on board take care to look over their men's arms every day and see that they be well fixed and have good flints.
2. That before they land they take care to have six cartridges fixed in their hats and to tie their cartridge boxes and pouches about their necks so as to keep them dry.
3. That when they land no officer or soldier shall stir out of the ranks on any pretence whatsoever on pain of death, which shall be immediately executed on them.

4. That the adjutant-general be attended by an orderly adjutant of each brigade, each of the majors of brigade by a sergeant of each regiment, who are to repair to the adjutant-general and the majors of brigade as soon as ever they land.
5. That the men be all ordered on the decks, and that the officers on board each ship do read the articles of war to them, with notice that if any of them transgress they shall be proceeded against according to the said articles without mercy.

THOS. ERLE."

———————

MINORCA.

REPORT ON KETTON MSS., VOL. 26.

1712, Feb. 9th - Toulon. Unsigned letter beginning "Dear brother," containing a description of the Island of Minorca, the fortifications of which the writer thinks are "three times" as strong as Gibraltar. - A good many of these are English fortifications by Brigadier Durrant, of whose engineering people have so good an opinion that nobody thinks a stone is placed wrong.

———————

GIBRALTAR.

REPORT ON WELBECK MSS., No. 28A

1704, Dec. 23rd – ROBT. HARLEY to the DUKE (OF NEWCASTLE).

The Portugal letters came this morning, which gave an account that our recruits for Gibraltar sailed away the 9th new style, so that I hope there was no danger of the place, the garrison having a thousand healthy men. They are assured from Madrid that the Marquis de Villadarias has remonstrated at the hazard of continuing the seige, that it ruins their best troops, but that notwithstanding this repeated remonstrance that Court are obstinate in pressing the recovery of the place. I hope our recruits have prevented that expectation, and that there will be an opportunity for our ships to bring home to Lisbon the Six millions at least of patacoons, which the Portuguese seized sometime since at Brazil coming to Spain.

———————

GIBRALTAR.
SESSION TO GREAT BRITAIN.
SEC. X OF THE TREATY OF UTRECHT.

"The Catholick King does hereby, for himself, his Heirs and Successors, yield to the Crown of Great Britain the full and entire Propriety of the Town and Castle of Gibraltar, together with the Port, Fortifications and Forts thereunto belonging; and he gives up the said Propriety to he held and enjoyed absolutely with all manner of Right for ever, without any Exception or Impediment whatsoever.

"But that Abuses and Frauds may he avoided by Importing any kind of Goods, the Catholick King wills, and takes it to be understood, that the abovenamed Propriety be yielded to Great

Britain without any Territorial Jurisdiction, and without any open Communication by Land with the Country round about.

"Yet whereas Communication by Sea with the Coast of Spain may not at all Times be safe or open, and thereby it may happen that the Garrison and other Inhabitants of Gibraltar may be brought to great Streights; And as it is the Intention of the Catholick King, only that fraudulent Importations of Goods, should, as is abovesaid, be hindered by an Inland Communication, it is therefore provided, That in such Cases it may be Lawful to purchase, for ready Money, of the neighbouring Territories of Spain, provisions and other Things necessary for the Use of the Garrison, the Inhabitants and the Ships that lie in Harbour.

"But if any Goods be found Imported by Gibraltar, either by way of Barter for purchasing Provisions, or under any other Pretence, the same shall be confiscated, and on complaint made thereof, those Persons who have acted contrary to the Faith of this Treaty, shall be severely punished.

And her Britannick Majesty, at the Request of the Catholick King, does consent and agree, That no Leave shall be given under any Pretence whatsoever, either to Jews or Moors to reside or have their Dwellings in the said Town of Gibraltar And that no Refuge or Shelter shall be allowed to any Moorish Ships of War in the Harbour of the said Town, whereby the Communication between Spain and Ceuta may he obstructed, or the Coasts of Spain be infested by the Excursions of the Moors.

"But whereas Treaties of Friendship, and a Liberty and Intercourse of Commerce are between the British and certain Territories situate on the Coast of Africa, it is always to be understood, That the British subjects cannot refuse the Moors and their Ships entry into the Port of Gibraltar purely upon the Account of Merchandizing.

"Her Majesty the Queen of Great Britain does further promise, That the free Exercise of their Religion shall be indulged to the Roman Catholick Inhabitants of the aforesaid Town. And in case it shall hereafter seem meet to the Crown of Great Britain to grant, sell, or by any means to allieniate therefrom the Propriety of the said Town of Gibraltar, it is hereby agreed and concluded, that the Preference of having the same shall always be given to the Crown of Spain before any others.

From "A Compleat History of Europe for the year 1713," pp. 145-146.

NOTE.-Although the Royal Marines are not mentioned, the above is of interest, as the Cession was due to the Capture and Defence of Gibraltar by the Royal Marines.

GIBRALTAR.

An account of the number of Marines on board the Ships sayled with Sr. Geo. Rooke.
(Compiled by Colonel C. Field, R.M.L.I.)

SHIPS	REGIMENT	COMPANY	No.
*Royal Katherine**	Br. Seymour's	Major Purcells	59
*Monmouth**	do.	Capt. Kempenfeldt's	52
*Montague**	do.	Capt. Bisset's	59
Antelope	do.	Brigadier's	48
*Kent**	do.	Lt. Col. Rook's	60
Expedition	Col. Lutterell's	Capt. Hedges	15
do.	do.	Capt. Adam's	11
do.	do.	Capt. Dodton's	4
do.	do.	Capt. Piggott's	1
do.	do.	Capt. Warr's	1
do.	do.	Capt. Devereux's	4
*Bedford**	Col. Holt's	Capt. Morrison's	40
do.	do.	Capt. Rodney's	30
Suffolk	do,	Capt. Dahlem's	40
do.	do.	Capt. Wilson's	40
*Newport**	do,	Major Lawrence's	5
do.	do.	Capt. Kemp's	5
Expedition	Col. Fox's	Capt. Wildbore's	34
*Hampton Court**	do,	Major Cobham's	87
do.	do.	Capt. Mullin's	
Advice	do,	Lt.-Col Borr's	16
Leopard	do,	do.	19
*Eagle**	Col. Saunderson's	Capt. Brerton's	66
		Total	696

An account of the numbers of Marines on board the ships which are to follow Sr. Geo. Rooke to *Lisbon*.

*Nassau**	Col. Holt's	Capt. Harrison's	41
*Shrewsbury**	do,	Capt. Henley's	39
Berwick	do,	Major Lawrence's	30
*Somersett**	do,	Col. Holt's	34
do.	do.	Capt. Manley's	45
do.	do.	Capt. Leslie's	52
*Boyne**	Col. Saunderson's	Capt. Palliser's	57
do.	do.	Capt. Burston's	50
*Royal Oak**	do,	Capt. Ord's	43

*Cambridge**	do,	Lt.-Col. Pownall's	55
do.	do.	Capt. Bedford's	56
*Firm Prize**	do,	Sr. Wm. Mansell's	47
do.	do.	Capt. Ward's	48
*Swiftsure**	Col. Lutterell's	Capt. Dodton's	59
*Somersett**	do,	Capt. Tynte's	55
*Prince George**	do,	Col. Lutterell's	53
do.	do.	Capt. Blynman's	57
*Burford**	do,	Major Blakeney's	47
*Royal Oak**	Lord Shannon's	Capt. Webb's	46
*Tor Bay**	do,	Capt. Bradshaw's	49
do.	do.	Capt. Thompson's	34
*Grafton**	do,	Lt.-Col. Markham's	43
do.	do.	Capt. William's	46
*Dorsetshire**	do,	Capt. Masham's	53
do.	do.	Capt. Lennard's	38
Essex	do,	Capt. Carter's	52
do.	do.	Capt. Hutton's	60
*Yarmouth**	Col. Fox's	Capt. Van Alphen's	58
do.	do.	Capt. Stewart's	47
*Shrewsbury**	do.	Capt. Kemp's	30
*Burford**	do.	Capt. Foulk's	30
*Warspright**	Br. Seymour's	Capt. Savill's	55
		Total	1493

Home Office and Admiralty Correspondence No. 16, 141-142.

The two totals of these lists are added together in the MS. I have copied and made a grand total of 2189, but as it is evident that some of the ships returned home between the first and second lists, it is impossible, even if there had been no casualties, to reckon that the above Grand Total represents the number of Marines concerned in the Taking of Gibraltar.

N.B.–The ships marked* were all at the capture of the Rock.

THE INTEREGNUM, 1713-1740.
(THE PERIOD WHEN THERE WERE NO MARINES)
By Colonel C. Field, R.M.

Between the Peace of Utrecht in 1713, when the existing regiments of Marines were either disbanded or transferred to the Line, and the institution of a fresh Marine establishment at the very end of 1739, the Royal Navy attempted to carry on without Marine soldiers. During the few peaceful years that succeeded 1713 it seems to have managed pretty well in their absence, but as soon as hostilities broke out again, Naval Officers began to feel the want of them. In the usual close quarter fighting that was then usual in a sea engagement, their musketry had been a very valuable auxiliary to the fire of the great guns, and in 1720 an attempt was made to provide our men-of-war with a specially trained force of seamen, who were to be known as "small shot men." The number of these carried was to be ten less than the ship's established number of guns. An additional Lieutenant, "or the youngest lieutenant appointed to the ship," was to be put in especial charge of these men and their arms, and two years later (4th May, 1722) the Admiralty had collected a stock of special "slop-clothes, designed for small-shot men," which were to be sent on board and sold to them-if they could be induced to buy them at £1 12s. 0d. a set. How these clothes differed from the grey jackets and red breeches which were established as the seamen uniform by Prince George of Denmark in 1705, does not appear, but from the above wording it would seem that there was something distinctive about them, possibly-at a guess-it was in the buttons. For in a contract for seamen's clothing dated 9th September, 1717, the Grey jackets and Red waistcoats were to have brass buttons and buttonholes stitched with gold-coloured thread, while in a similar contract dated 3rd February, 1724-5, these garments were to have "thread" buttons and stitching of the colour of the cloth. It seems just possible that the earlier contract was especially for the "small-shot men," the brass buttons being intended to give them a more "military" appearance.

Although we are accustomed to associate red breeches or trousers with the French Army, they were as a matter of fact, considered essentially military garments in this country as far back as the Civil War, and worn with the buff coat, to give the wearer a specially smart and soldier-like appearance. They were, moreover, the usual wear of the British Infantryman up to about 1770. In instituting them in the Navy, Prince George may have had in mind the original uniform of his old Regiment - The Admiral's - though it is only fair to say that when he assumed command of it, he changed its red breeches to grey ones.
Authority: Hist. M.S. Comm. Lady Du Cane, p.p. 2-10-22-28.

_____

A VERY POOR DETACHMENT.

The following letter from Capt. Philip Cavendish, of H.M.S. *Antelope*, shews the bad results of a personnel not numerous enough to allow of a proper training before embarkation. The letter is dated 4th November, 1707, the ship lying in the Hamoaze. "I beg the favour of you to acquaint His Royal Highness[1] yt of the forty marins yt were put aboard me at the Nore, what by death, putt ashore sick, and unfitt for service, I have but 22 left. They were pickt, as I am told by the Lieut, out of 11 of the 12 Compys of the Regt. of Wills[2], and not three of ym yt* had ever clapt a musquett on his shoulder before he came on board my ship, but all raw recruits, and the very scum of the party yt were in those quarters at Canterbury. There are so many wanting now and I believe this cruize will end the days of half the remainder. I desire that I may have a Sergeant and 20 men from some other regiment to make good what I have lost, against I come in again, for I have no manner of dependence on these that I have."

Notes:-

1. Prince George of Denmark, brother of Queen Ann, Lord High Admiral and in special charge of the Marine Regiments.
2. Now 30th, 1st Battallion East Lancashire Regiment.
* Editor's note. These 'yt's and 'ym' in this text are as originally written!

A MARINE'S EXPERIENCES IN THE '45.
From the Historical MS. Commission's Report on the Laing MS. in the University of Edinburgh. Vol. II.

James Grant in his "British Battles by Land and Sea," in describing the Battle of Culloden, refers to the 48th Regiment as having been present at the action and further describes it as the 5th Marines. The "48th (or 5th Marines)" he says. Now at this time – 1746 - the 5th Marines was commanded by Colonel James Cochrane (or Cokran), whereas the 48th Regiment at Culloden was commanded by Colonel Ligonier, and is actually referred to by Grant in another paragraph as "Ligonier's."

The 44th, 46th and 52nd Regiments were also engaged in the Scottish campaign against the Pretender, but as a matter of fact these numbers really refer to the numbers they became entitled to after the abolition of the Marine Regiments in 1748. Before that the 44th was actually the 55th, 45th - 56th and so forth. But in 1748 they inherited the places on the Army List left vacant by the removal of the ten Marine Regiments.

But although there was no complete Regiment of Marines engaged in the Scottish Campaign, they were, as usual when anything in the way of active service is forward, well represented by individuals and small detachments.

There was a rumour in 1745 that Admiral Byng was to land 3,000 Marines in the North of Scotland, but in all probability this operation was never carried out. But it is certain that one detachment, at any rate, was landed - witness the following extract from a letter from H.R.H. the Duke of Cumberland to the Duke of Newcastle, dated 23rd April, 1746:-

"His Majesty having been pleased to prefer Major Lawrie to be Major in his own Regt. of Horse, I take the liberty to recommend to His Majesty to succeed him Capt. Gardner, the 2nd Capt. in Lord Mark Kerr's Regt. who is a very active and diligent officer and behaved very well in the last affair, the eldest Captain being quite worn out, and left as unfit for service at Berwick. And if His Maty. shall think fit to give the troop to Capt. Gore of Pawlet's Marines, who was landed by Admiral Byng with 100 Marines at Montrose, and acted with so much prudence and judgement there, that when I reembarked the Marines, I took him with me, and he was with me at the last affair, where he behaved so well that I have taken this first occasion to recommend him to His Majesty's favour."[1]

Arthur Tooker Collins of Lowther's Marines seems also to have been employed with a detachment - whether of Marines or other troops cannot be said - in searching for rebels and arms in the Highlands, while Captain Richmond Webb of Cotterell's (6th) Marines[2] served through the campaign in Scotland as A.D.C. to General Huske.

I have recently come across a portion of a diary kept by this officer, parts of which, at any rate, may be of some interest to present day Marines. Perhaps the word "diary is a misnomer, as Captain Webb's writings consist of a series of letters addressed to "William Allan, Pall Mall, London." Still they are pretty consecutive and so practically form a diary. He writes first from Newcastle on 18th October, 1745:-

"We are still very quiet here and not at all apprehensive of the attempts of the rebels in town, they have given us sufficient time to put it in a posture of defence. The latest advices from Berwick say that the rebels have quitted their camp and got it to Edinburgh. I am sorry to tell you that it's reported they have had a French ship put into Montrose,that has landed 150 officers, £100,000 in money and 4,000 stand of arms, which will give them spirits. Our Army is assembling at Doncaster. I wish for a fair wind to bring the troops from Flanders. General Huske is extreamly well, and has gone through an immense deal of business. I have bought a horse, etc., for our campaign, which obliges me to draw a bill on you payable to Cuthbert Ogle, for £40.

"He writes again on 1st November: "At length the Army so wished for has come up, except Sinclair's battalion, which is to come in to-day, and the horse and dragoons, who, I beleive, are to follow on or go another route. I beleive we shall march on Sunday next. I have no news of the rebels, except their marching and counter-marching about Edinburgh. It is said they are near 10,000 effective men. We have 20 battalions of foot besides 2 regiments of horse, and with Hamilton's and Gardner's 3 regiments of dragoons. I will not pretend to give my small judgement of affairs. I know hitherto we are all extreamly healthy, but just now it begins to rain, which is very bad for our marches and encampments. The General is extreamly well, and I need not tell you that know him, is vastly civil. I believe I shall sett out for Morpeth to-morrow. When we have crossed the Tweed do myself the pleasure to write to you. I have directed a letter for Colonel Cottrell to be left at your house, not knowing whether he is at Bath or Portsmouth, therefore I beg you'll forward it. I hope you order all the ship accounts to be sent to Maxwell[3] to enter, and likewise DoIlas's accounts, otherwise the money will be lost, if the men are cleared and those articles not known how to be charged. I wish with all my heart Lieutenant Cramer[4] was at sea. He is very much in the regiment debt, and by staying on shore he'll never pay it. I hear there have been several people who have got majoritys, etc., in some new levies. I wish I had staid to have sollicited one of them. However, I hope the service I go upon now and the time I have been a Captain, if there are any more new levies, will give me at least as good pretensions to ask for a majority as those who were originally Arabians."[5]

Webb again writes from Newcastle on 5th November: "You'll see by the enclosed letter from Graham that his money may be had of Captain Wilkinson. Therefore I beg the favour you will be so good as to call for it, which I suppose will be paid you on shewing the enclosed letter. I should be glad it might be done as soon as possible to secure the money for poor Graham's use, lest my Lord Crawford should alter his mind. I set out with General Huske for Morpeth last Sunday. The army was to follow on Monday, but an express arrived with certain advice that the rebels are marching in order to slip by us by way of Carlisle, the Marshall has ordered the army to halt awhile. This day I saw an order from one Lord Kilmarnock, who calls himself Colonel of the Prince's Horse Grenadiers, to the magistrates of Kelso to provide billets, etc., for 4,000 foot and 1,000 horse, to be there on Monday the 4th, and then to send the same order to Wooler, in Northumberland, where is Colonel Legonier with those damned runaway dragoons. However, he is a good officer, and we have great hopes he'll make them do their duty. Shall I tell you the numbers of our army? I fancy it's needless. You have the list of the regiments, so can guess; but don't reckon the 8 battalions of Dutch compleat, nor don't imagine we are without a sick man, lying up to their knees in mudd; and, by the way, part of our army, viz., Price's, Legonier's, 5 companies of Barrell's and 6 companys and 2 of Flemming s, with 150 Dutch, are at Berwick, and can't come at us if the rebels are marched by Wooller. However, I beleive they are only feigning to come into England to prevent our going to Scotland. The General sends his compliments."

Nov. 22. - Newcastle: "The last letter I wrote to you was from Hexham, where we received advice of Carlisle's being surrendred, so that our army is this day come back to Newcastle, and beleive on Sunday we shall march from thence southward. Our men are all quartered under cover in this town, either in publick, private or empty houses, which will be a great refreshment after their miserable encampment. If Colonel Cottrell is in London, pray make my compliments to him and apologys for not writing. Tell him Major Jeffreys is well, and sends his service, but his fingers are so cold he can't hold a pen. The campaign is like to hold much longer than I expected or desired. However, I hope it will have a fortunate end."

Nov. 24. - Newcastle: "Yesterday we were order'd to march from hence in three divisions southward, but now it is determined the whole army is to march on Tuesday next to Chester le Street, and from thence to Durham, etc., in order to follow the rebels who have marched on southward."

Nov. 26 - Chester le Street: "This night the army came to the camp marked out in this place in fine order, fine weather and health; pray God it may continue. General Huske is very well and greets you. I was obliged to draw a bill on you payable to Alderman Matthew Ridley for £20, which I hope you'll honour. I had an ugly fall with my horse this day, almost broke my legg. It's in pain. However, this is only *inter nos*. The General orders me to conclude with informing you we are now drinking your health."

Nov. 29 - Camp at Peise Bridge: "As paper is scarce I have only just room to set down the following route of our army as is settled for the present, viz.:-

FOR THE HORSE.
North Allerton ...   Saturday

Thursk and Villages	Sunday
York	Monday
Tadcaster ...	Tuesday (there halt)

DRAGOONS.

Bedell and Masham	Fryday
Rypley and Knaresborough	Saturday
Halt till further orders	

ENCAMPMENTS OF THE FOOT.

Catterick ...	Saturday
Bedel ...	Sunday
Borough Bridge ...	Monday
Weatherby ...	Tuesday, Dec 3

As to news, I have none, but we have tolerable good weather."

Dec. 3 - Camp at Burrow Bridge: "I received this day yours of the 28. We marched in here yesterday, and upon account of the long marches and great fatigues the troops had undergone were obliged to halt here this day. To-morrow we march to Wetherby, and when or where we march after I can't tell, but I fear it will be northward. Sure the rebels are not fools enough to get between two armys, or hardy enough to fight one. Our fatigues are great. I can't tell how our credit stands in the coffee houses, etc. I communicated that paragraph of your letter to the General relating to the cover directed by General Huske which you received from Newcastle. He desires you'll for the future take no notice of any request that may come in a letter directed by him unless the request is made by him."

Dec. 7 (Saturday) - Ferrybridge: "The army was to have marched this day to Doncaster, but was countermanded by expresses which came from the south. I hope it's true that the rebels have been stop'd by his Royal Highness, and I hope likewise we shall come up with them before they get to the vile holes from whence they came; a dreadful situation for any other people but they, to have nothing but death or the Highlands before their eyes. I should be glad to hear from you when your business will permit. I had forgot to tell you that commissarys are sent to Wetherby for forage, etc., so I suppose we shall dance to the northward again. I thought we were improving every day's march to the southward, but we must return to misery, frost and snow."

Dec. 9 - Ferrybridge : "General Huske presents his service to you. He desires you'll send him down an almanack for the next year, also that Mr. Adair[6] will buy him three lottery tickets, and when he has bought them send him down the numbers of them. We march tomorrow towards Halifax. I hope things goes on pretty well at Maidstone, tho' I have never had one line from Maxwell since I left London. If there's anything extraordinary, pray be so kind as to let me know. I desired Maxwell to confine his payments to subsisting the men on shore, to paying the sea pay to such as went on board, and not to meddle too much with the officers or recruiting parties, but referr them to you. I don't know how he goes on, as he never writes. The general's almanack must be Ryders, bound up in a marble cover, of the same size with the enclosed."

Dec. 10 (Tuesday) - Camp at Wakefeild: The army came here this day and was to march tomorrow to Hallifax, but upon advice that the rebels were yesterday at Manchester and bending their march towards Preston in their way to Scotland, it's thought proper to alter our route, as they have a 2nd time slipt us, and go tomorrow towards Leeds, and from thence northwards to cover Newcastle, and where then I can't tell; however, you shall hear of our proceedings. For my part I have given over any thoughts of seeing the rebels, but I'll still continue to dance o're the ice, and march thro' the dirt, because other prople do. I hear nothing at all of Maxwell or how he goes on. As I'm answerable for his actions in some measure, I should be glad to hear from him. However, I've wrote Maidstone about the campaign a letter a little longer that I expected or desired. I wish it was ended, meerly because of my accounts at the regiment, which will be long and intricate, and I don't find accounts here likely to turn out to advantage, where everybody is put to their trumps. The General is very well."

Dec. 15 (6 o'clock in the morning) - Burrow Bridge: "Yesterday it was at last determined to canton the army, and march it in three divisions to Newcastle. General Huske marches away this morning with 1,000 men to Northaltern, and so on in 4 days to Newcastle, if the men can perform it. The weather is deplorably bad, the army much reduced, so that it was high time to put it under cover. General Huske is very well."

Dec. 20 (Friday) - Newcastle: "Without doubt the Gazette informs you of our several motions, by which you'll see the army has marched a great tract of ground since they departed from Newcastle, till at last we were obliged to leave off encampments to save the men from perishing. The camp broke up at Borrow Bridge and marches in divisions by cantonments to Newcastle and thereabouts. Major-General Huske was detached from the army with 1,000 foot to Newcastle, which he marched in four days from Burrough Bridge with those men after all their fatigues, thro' very bad roads to Hexham, which is at least 90 miles. The General does not go with them, but they are to be commanded by Brigadier Mordaunt. The General stays here in expectation of going to Scotland. We have an express come in from Penrith which says there has been a skirmish between some of his Royal Highnesses' dragoons and the rebels, in which there were some killed on both sides; that the rebels have plunder'd Penrith, and are flying before the Duke's troops. Colonel Honeywood is wounded, as it is reported. General Huske desires you will enquire as well as you can into McClauchan's merits, what sort of principles he has as to publick affairs, and also as to his private behaviour, and to inform him by the very first opportunity you can, because if he is such a person as you think the General can confide in, he believes he shall have occasion to send for him when he goes to Scotland, where if he is honest he may be of great use from his thorough knowledge of the country.

There is a gap here in the continuity of Richmond Webb's letters, the next being dated from Nairn on 15th April, 1746:-

"I can now be able to acquaint you of our having passed the river Spey, from whence in 2 days we reached this camp. We have continually chaced the rebels before us, who, to the number of about 3,000, shewd themselves, but never suffered us to come near them. They have all gone to Inverness, where we shall march to-morrow, and I beleive they'l certainly fight us if they have anything like the numbers which are reported to us, which is about 11,000. We have a good army and expect the transports with the four regiments from England.

I have the only opportunity of buying the commission of a leiutenant colonel that will ever happen perhaps in my life, and that if I can find a possibility of raising £500. I can't pretend to say that I am in possession of so much or till my accounts are settled I can have any credit on you. Yet if you would be so good as to advance me £200 on this important occasion, I shall make it a point of conscience and honour to repay you by the most speedy and safest way, and don't doubt that if I can get a few weeks' leave of absence to finish my accounts, I shall do it to every one's satisfaction and have more than that sume comeing to me. The case is this: Leiutenant Colonel Catherwood of our regiment is old and infirm, and on the point of disposeing, and if he does not hasten it the Duke will oblige him. General Huske, who is my very good friend, by the good offices you have been so kind as to do to me, will forward the thing. Therefore, Sir, I beg this addition of your freindly offices, and that you would mention it to Colonel Cottrell, who I don't doubt will still be so much my friend as to advance me the other sum on such security as I can give. This is sturdy begging, but I flatter myself you'l not only forgive but comply with this. I shall soon have it in my power to repay both the Colonel and you, otherwise I would not ask it without a prospect of making good my engagements."

There seems to be no letter actually describing the Battle of Culloden, but the following, written from Inverness on 17th April, makes a slight reference to it :- "I had not time to finish the letter before we were order'd to march, and now I congratulate you on the glorious work of yesterday. Lord Bury without doubt you have seen, who has given more particulars than I can relate. I am very well, thank God, and you may swear we are in good spirits without puffing. Pray favour me with a line in answer to this. P.S. - Pray excuse the dirtiness of this letter, and send me downe the Gazette that publishes the relation of the battle."

NOTES.
1. CAVALRY COMMISSIONS FOR MARINE OFFICERS.

    Besides the promotion of Captain Gore of Pawlet's Marines to a Troop of Horse, Lieut. W. Graham (probably of the 2nd Marines) was promoted to a Troop in the 4th Dragoons about this time (vide "Britain's Sea Soldiers" Vol. I., p.128), and there may have been others, since the Marine Regiments then formed a more or less integral part of the Army, and their officers could and often did, rise to the highest ranks in it. On the other hand, to quote a note from Col. R. S. Liddell's "Memoirs of the 10th Royal Hussars"- "several instances occur at this period of Cavalry Officers being transferred to the Marines." Richmond Webb is a case in point, Colonel John Jordan (or Jordain) who was promoted from a Lieutenant-Colonelcy in Churchill's Dragoons (now 10th Hussars) to command the 8th Marines is another; Lieut. Matthew Sewell, of Sir Robert Rich's Dragoons (now 4th Hussars), who was promoted to Captain in Jeffery's (10th Marines), is yet another; and there were doubtless several other similar promotions.

2. CAPTAIN RICHMOND WEBB.

   This officer was born in 1714, and was a cousin of the General Webb who so distinguished himself in the battle of Wynendael in September 1708. He received a commission as Cornet in the Queen's Own Dragoons (now 3rd Hussars) in 1735, and joined the 6th Marines, commanded by the Honble, Ducie Moreton, on 1st December, 1739. He was promoted to Captain in the same Regiment in 1741. In that year Lt.-Col. Cotterell, of Wolfe's (1st) Marines, succeeded to the command, vice Moreton, who died at Cartegena. Several references to Col. Cotterell are made in Webb's letters. Besides being aide-de-camp to General Huske, Webb - according to the Dictionary of National Biography" - commanded a company for King George at Culloden." It was probably not a company of Marines, but of some regiment which was short of a captain at the time of the action. If he succeeded in purchasing the Lieutenant-Colonelcy in his own regiment to which he refers in one of his letters, he cannot have held it for long, as all the Marine Regiments were disbanded in 1748. After Culloden, however, he was recommended for a majority in Battereau's Regiment (now 52nd). He seems to have eventually arrived at the rank of Colonel, although I cannot find in what regiment. He retired from the service in 1758, and died on 27 May 1785, at the age of 70. He is buried in the East Cloister of Westminster Abbey.

3. MAXWELL.

   This may have been Lieutenant James Maxwell of Webb's regiment. He might have been his subaltern, and left in charge of his company.

4. CRAMER.

   This would be Lieutenant Samuel Cramer of the same Regiment. This officer, with two others, are the only officers serving in 1740 whose names appear in the Army List of 1755.

5. "ARABIANS."

   I have not been able to discover the meaning of this expression. I imagine it to have been some cant term of the day used in disparagement of those officers who were continually dodging from one regiment to another in search of promotion-military "nomads."

6. MR. ADAIR.

   There was a Captain James Adair in Webb's Regiment in 1740, and it may be he to whom reference is made. Or guessing from the context, he may have been the Regimental Agent-unless Mr. William Allan occupied that position.

There is, however, among the same collection of papers a draft letter, with no name or address, which may very well supplement those written by Richmond Webb. It is dated Edinburgh, April 22, and runs as follows:-

I can now assure you that the Rebellion has at last most effectually got its death's wound by a most glorious and complete victory obtained over the rebells by the Duke of Cumberland at Culloden Moor near Inverness, the story of which runs thus:- Tuesday the 15th the Duke lay all night at Nairn. It was his birthday. The rebells took it for granted that his army would be drunk, etc., and accordingly marched all night to attack him at break of day. But when they came near his camp they found the Duke in a posture of defence. This occasioned a council of war, in which it was resolved to march back to their camp at Culloden Moor, where they had entrenched themselves and placed cannon upon their entrenchments. The Duke began his march after them at 5 in the morning, and got up with them about half an hour after 12, when they were just entered their camp. They began immediately to play their cannon upon him, which did but little execution except on the *corps de reserve*, most of it flying over their heads. The Duke's cannon soon returned the compliments by which theirs were presently dismounted and then he continued to play incessantly upon them for the space of 20 minutes. This did terrible execution. The rebels, finding no safety for them in their trenches, came out and their right wing, consisting of the Macdonalds and Frazers, made a furious attack on our left, which consisted of Ligonier's, Price's and Munro's foot, commanded by Generall Husk. The Highlanders, after one fire threw aside their guns and attempted once and again to break in sword in hand, but our foot first gave them one fire, the fore rank kept them off with their bayonets till the 2 hind ranks charged again and gave them so close a fire that our fore rank was bespattered with their blood and brains. At this instant the Duke of Kingstone's Light Horse brake in and then followed an universall root, which ended in a dreadful slaughter for half an hour without giving any quarter. The whole way from the field to Inverness was strewed with dead bodys. The rebells fled to all quarters. Some went to Fort Augustus, others towards the West Highlands, and a great many into Rosshyre. Our accounts bear that there are vast numbers of their leaders fallen besides at least 1,000 men, 400 prisoners with 300 French and their ambassador, which was all that remained of them. Other accounts make the number of the killed, wounded and prisoners 3,500, which is not impossible. . . . The Duke behaved as usuall, led on his men on foot in a plain soldier's coat, with a common gun and bayonet. Not a man in the whole army behaved ill. On the contrary an uncommon spirit appeared through the whole of the men. The Argyleshire Campbells and Kingstone's Light Horses behaved in an extraordinary way. This is the substance of what we have had yet, which may be depended on as true, seeing we had it from no less authority than Lord Burry, one of the Duke's aids-de-camp, in his way to London to give an account of it to the King.

C. FIELD.

MARINE RECRUITING INSTRUCTIONS, 1745.

"1745, - Pursuant to the Right Hon'ble. Field Marshall Earl of Stair's order, dated the 26 of March, 1745, which I herewith send you, for the receiving of impress'd men for the service of the regiment of marines under my command, you are to go with Lieutenant William Gordon and Lieutenant Ravenscroft of my regiment, with two serjeants, two corporals, two drums and twelve private men, with side arms, to the town where the generall quarter sessions are held in Somersetshire, and to be there by the 20 of this month, without fail, there to receive such impress'd men as shall be delivered to you, or the subaltern officers under your command, by the commissioners appointed for that purpose, strictly conforming in everything to the act of parliament in that case made and provided. You are to transmit constant retirns to the Secretary at War of all the men who shall be inlisted, and brought to the county, town or place of security. And you are to send me, once a week, a list of such men's names as you shall receive from the commissioners, together with their age, size, where born, where listed, trade or occupation, with the respective days of their being listed, and entering into the regiment's pay. You are to subsist such recruits as you shall receive from the commissioners at six pence per day, and when you return from this service you are to make up an account with the agent or paymaster for what subsistence you have paid while on this duty, and account for all the moneys you shall have received from the agent, on account of the regiment. You are to continue on this service till you receive orders to the contrary. You, and the officers under your command on this duty are to inlist what volontiers you can, but you are to inlist no man that is under the age of seventeen and above thirty; they must be full five feet four inches high, without shoes, well shoulder'd, well limb'd, properly turn'd for musquetiers, free from ruptures, and every other distemper, bodily weakness or infirmities. You are in your returns to me to distinguish such men as shall be inlisted, from the press'd men, specifying the officers' names by whom rais'd who shall be allowed four pounds for each man they shall inlist conformable to the above instructions, they subsisting them till they are approv'd of at the regiment's quarters."

From Colonel John Cottrell (6th Marines)
To Captain Shafto (6th Marines).

Hist. M.S. Corn. Laing, M.S. in University of Edinburgh. Vol. II. P.359

ANSON AND THE MARINES.

"To Anson is due the credit of, for the first time, enabling a fleet to be started forth on an emergency with a body of permanently organised sea-soldiers, the Marines. Heretofore the Country had been obliged to depend on regiments, specially raised indeed for the purpose, but disbanded when not immediately wanted, and combined in one Corps. He had long pressed for this great reform, which had been an old scheme of Lord Sandwich's, but now took the organic form with which we have been familiar ever since that day, *and to which no little of the success of the British Navy has been due.*

Like so many other simple improvements, it seems strange that the country should ever have hesitated to adopt it; but less strange when one reflects upon the difficulties which have been so often placed in the way of a hearty and generous recognition of the value of the services of the Royal Marines.

No less than fifty companies were raised at this period, but not with sufficient promptitude to satisfy Hawke's eager wish to substitute them altogether for the regiments of the Line with which some part of his fleet was supplied. He probably had some hand in the establishment of the force, for he writes as if it was a scheme long familiar to himself as well as to the Admiralty. By the year 1759 the numbers of the Corps had mounted up to 18,000."

"Life of Edward Lord Hawke," by Capt. Montagu Burrows, R.N., p.224 and Barrow's "Anson," p. 235.

"A MIXED GRILL."
SOME MARINE DETACHMENTS BEFORE THE INSTITUTION OF THE PRESENT CORPS.

In the old days when the Marines were divided into different Regiments, it was naturally very difficult to keep to the original intention of having complete detachments from the same regiments in the various men-of-war put in commission.

Sooner or later, owing to various casualties, the numbers of an embarked detachment had to be made up from other regiments than that which originally supplied the detachment. Here is an example in 1711, taken from the weekly return from H.M.S. *Portland*, then lying off Yarmouth[1].

No. of Marines on board	*Regiment*	*Company Officer*	
30	Lord Shannon's	Lt.-Col. Markham	
1	"	Capt. Byng	
3	General Wills'	Col. Buston	Lt. Williams
4	"	Major Williams	
3	"	Capt. Palliser	
2	"	Capt. (?)	
9	"	Capt. Merson (?)	
52			

That the same thing was liable to occur between 1739 and 1748 in the Marine Establishment which immediately preceded the present one, is evident from the returns of H.M.S. *Buckingham* for December 1741. It will be seen that the numbers of the detachment varied considerably during the month[2].

No. of Marnes on board	*Date*	*Regiments*
32	2nd December	*Jefferies & Paulett's*
26	9th December	*Jefferies & Paulett's*
22	16th December	*Jefferies & Paulett's*
69	23rd December	*Jefferies & Paulett's and Hanmer's & Cotterell's*
79	30th December	*Jefferies & Paulett's and Hanmer's & Cotterell's*

The *Buckingham's* detachment, with their buff, green, light and dark yellow facings and caps, and their canvas or striped ticking leggings must have presented very much the appearance of Falstaff's "men in motley." It is little wonder that the Admiralty in 1747 decided that all Marine Regiments were to wear deep yellow facings and caps. Or that when the new Marine Corps was formed in 1755 that its subdivision into separate regiments was not repeated.

NOTES.
1. Admiralty: Captains Letters B., Vol. 9.
2. " Lists of Marines or soldiers on board ships in Commission.

SOME DOCUMENTS IN CONNECTION WITH THE BEGINNING OF THE PRESENT CORPS OF ROYAL MARINES IN 1755.
By Colonel C. Field, R.M.L.I.
Colonel Field's remarks are in italics.

The ten Regiments of Marines dating from 1739-41 were abolished in 1748. But by the beginning of the year 1755 there were evidently rumours of the intention of the Admiralty to establish a new organisation of Marines. Witness the following letter: -

(Brit. Mus. Additional MS. 32,852)
Folio 410.

Maidstone,
Feb. 8, 1755.

May it please your Grace

To pardon my presumption in begging your Grace's Interest for one of the Companys, in the Regt. of Marines, which we are inform'd is speedily to be Revised.
I am at present eldest Lieutnt. but one in Wolfe's Regt. and have served near eleven years.
I am,
May it please your Grace,
Your Grace's most dutiful!
and most obt. Godson,
Thos. SPENR. WILSON.

(Brit. Mus., Ibid)
Folio 432.

Who his Grace was does not appear. Most probably it was the Duke of Newcastle, who was appointed head of the Government in March 1754. Here are other applications addressed to him: -

Plymouth Dock in Duke Street.
11 Febry. 1755.

My Lord Duke,

May it please yr Grace, I humbly beg leave to acquaint your Grace, That upon hearing a Regiment or Two of Marines are to be immediately Rais'd, and having been an Ensign in the Dockyard Regiment at Plymouth in the late War. I do with Great and Humble Submission offer myself as a Lieut. of Marines to Serve His Majesty. As this offers, and flows from a Heart full of Zeal, and Well Attach'd to His Majy. and Good Family, I am in hopes your Honour will Grant my Request and Pardon my Giving Your Grace this Trouble.

I enclose a Copy of my Ensign's Commission, and humbly beg leave to acquaint your Grace that I served my time to the Sea in His Majesty's Service. And being in the Country and Ready to Inlist Men, having a Serjeant of Marines in last War here Ready to assist me in Rising Men. If this meets Your Grace's Approbation, my Age is 36 years, Active and Heartilly Willing to Serve His Majesty

King George the 2d. against all his Enemys with my Life, etc., etc.
Being with Great Submission,
Your Grace's Most Dutiful and Obedt.
Humble Servt.,
WILLIAM SHEPHARD.

To
His Grace the Duke of
Newcastle, etc., etc., etc.

The final decision to establish the present Corps seems to have been settled at the meeting referred to below:
-

March 17, 1755.   MARINES.
At Lord Anson's

                             That all Commissions be signed
Lord Anson   by the King, to be carried by
Mr. Fox   the first Commissioner of the
Mr. Philipson   Admiralty and countersigned by
Mr. West   three Commissioners of the
Mr. Cleveland.   Admiralty.
                             The Officers to have rank in
                             the Army, but not to expect to
                             rise among His Majesties Land
                             Forces.
                             All orders to flow from the
                             Admiralty. The Captains to be
                             made out of the Half Pay,

(Brit. Mus. Ad. M.S. 33046)
Folio 333.

The following letter from Mr. West, apparently to the Duke of Newcastle, gives further opinions as to the proposals regarding the Marines: -

(Brit. Mus. Ibid)   Treasury Chambers,
Folio 330.   March 17, 1755.

    Mr. West saw Mr. Fox yesterday as soon as he came to Town, and before he saw the Duke. He seemed to think it right, That the Marines should be under the Admiralty, as to Discipline, Clothing, etc., but that they should have their Commissions from the King, countersigned by the Secretary of War that in case of merit and recommendation from the Admiralty or others, they might have some Rank and View of promotion. That the late Regulations were so bad in many respects that they must be greatly altered and that he hoped something might be planned at the meeting this morning at Lord

Anson's, that might answer the end of raising them. Mr. Fox said nothing was determined in relation to the appointment of Majors, so that Mr. West did not mention Capt. Fletcher, only gave him Mr. Waller's recommendation, which he said might be easily done.

Mr. West humbly begs Your Grace would please to send the proposal for Marines, which he delivered to Your Grace, on Saturday morning, to him at Lord Anson's.

The following is a letter from the Captain Fletcher referred to by Mr. West addressed to Lord Lincoln:-

(Brit. Mus. Ad. MS. 32,861, Folio 518)

My Lord,

Since I wrote from Coll. Mostyn's I've seen Mr. Fisher the Agent, who told me yt 5000 Marines were to be raised in Company (? Companies). and a Major to every 1000 to reside at the Head Quarters with an Adjutant and Surgeon to Discipline the Men and send Detachmts. backwards and forwds as the Service shall require, all which Service I've gone thro' when I was in the Marines last Warr.

I'm pretty sure of my Intelligence, for Mr. Fisher have already been asked his scheem of raising 'em, etc., which I believe he have given in already, and yt Mr. Phillipson and some body is to meet tomorrow or next day in order to settle scheem for to lay before his Majesty for his approbation. There is but one Major (viz., Brown) on the Half Pay as I can recollect, so if four will be appointed, and if your Lordship can get me one of those 'twill be in my next step of Rank, and in a Service yt. I think I have a right to ask it in, as your Lordship well knows how long I served last Warr on the Watery World - and if Lord Anson would enquire my character of the Gentlemen of the Navy I am sure 'twill stand ye test. I beg your Lordship's Pardon for giving you so much Trouble and am with Complimts to ye Gentlemen, of my acquaintance yt surround yr Lordship's Oatlands Mutton.

    Your Lordships,
     most obliged obedtt.,
      JACK FLETCHER.

Past 4 0'clock

"Jack Fletcher" does not seem to have been successful in his application, if we may judge from the following letter from Lord Newcastle to Mr. Fox: -

(Brit. Mus. Ibid)   Newcastle House
(Folio 364)   March 18, 1755.

Dear Sir,

I this moment have received the enclos'd Letter from my cousin, Colonel Vane. I really believe, He would do very well, If you would have the Goodness to recommend him. I have always heard that he was a good Officer; and I should be very much oblig'd if this could be done for him.

Poor Jack Fletcher, I suppose, must be out the Question, as there are to be no Majors.

Mr. Morrice, who is an old Lieut., and recommended to me by My Lord Granby and Mr. Waller, who is an Ensign, would be very happy If the one could be made a Captain and the other First Lieut. of Marines upon this occasion.

I am, etc.,

HOLLES NEWCASTLE.

Rt. Honble. Mr, Fox.

Other applications for Commissions in the Marines continued to come in. Here is one of somewhat curious character: -

(Brit. Mus. Ad. MS. 32,855, Folio 98)
My Lord Duke,

Lord Albermarle have to get rid of my son Edwd. Cobden, Draughted him into the Marines and as now Serjeant, and Captain Prossers' Company, att Plymouth, so I have I expect no moar from his Lordship nor Mr. Fox - all that can be done for him now is to Recomend him to Lord Anson for a Lieutcy in the Marines, as he is well skilled enough in his Exercise To Serve in ye poast, having served in ye Army 8 years, and with a good Carackter. If your Grace will be so good as to Oblydg me on This Request you c(an) make me and my wife Happy, as this boy is my Eldest son and entituled to Some thing after us that will Enable him to be Gratfull to your Grace And Family as his good benefactors. As I hope he will be endued with Gratitude to all his friends.

I am with Gratest Duty to
your Grace and humble
Servant two Command,

EDWD. COBDEN.

Draught in Singleton,
near Midhurst in Sussex,
May ye 21st 1755.

Below is yet another request for a Commission, some months later:-

(Brit. Mus. Ad. MS. 32,858, Folio 316)

TO HIS GRACE THE DUKE OF NEWCASTLE.

My Lord,

Pray pardon this Fredom as Necessity is the Obligation thereof. Your Grace was so Good in the Late War, through the Intrest of Mr. Peck of Spittle Fields to make me Lieut. of Marines. Upon Breaking the said Corps I was put on the half pay for four years, since which time I have been Adjutant to the Regimt. of Invalids at Portsmouth, and yesterday Received a Lieut.'s Commission in Col. Walsh's Regimt, serving in Jamacai.

At the time your Grace gave me the Commission in the late Marines, Your Grace was then

Pleased to Promise Mr. Peck and myself to give me Company the first Opportunity. As there now is Several Vacancies in America I hope your Grace will be so good as to Provide for me there or otherwise as your Grace may think Proper - and am Your Grace's

Most Obedient Servant,

JNO. WYNN.

London, Augt. 27, 1755.

It does not seem quite certain that this applicant was desirous of a Marine Commission, but he is probably hinting at it. The first batch of Officers, all from Half-pay, was dated 2nd April, 1755, and it may be that by the end of August there were Companies or Detachments of the newly raised Corps already ashore or afloat on the further side of the Atlantic. The most insistent demand for a Marine Commission seems to have been made by a Mr. Thornhagh, who in his second letter to the Duke of Newcastle assumes almost a threatening attitude. He writes:-

(Brit. Mus. Ad. MS. 32,854, Folio 532)

My Lord Duke,

After I asked the favour of your Grace to procure an Ensign Commission for the younger son of my friend Mr. Watson in the Marines wch. I apprehend are soon to be raised, I ought sooner have wrote to your Grace, according to your commands, but I was uncertain whether the young Gentleman's name was Gilbert or John till I this day heard from the country that it was Gilbert. If you are so kind as to assist me on this occasion I am sure it will greatly oblige a worthy family of very considerable interest in our Country.

I am

Your Grace's

Oblig'd Humble Scrvt.

THORNHACH.

March ye 31st, 1755.

He writes again on May 11th:-

(Brit. Mus. Ad. MS. Ibid, Folio 495)

May the 11th, 1755.

My Lord Duke, Upon your Graces. assurances that you would procure a Commission in the Marine Service for Mr. Watson, I sent for him to this town that he might be ready to obey the Commands of his Superiors, and by your Command troubled you with a letter that you might know his Christian Name, and now I find all the Commissions are disposed of and that my friend has none.

If nothing is to be done for him I must most earnestly press your Grace's most serious consideration in what light I shall appear in Nottingham upon the Occasion and whether your Grace may not meet with some remarks from those who don't wish you well, as I can only justify myself under those assurances you gave.

I have severall times call'd at Newcastle house with intention to mention this affair, but having been disappointed of the honour of seeing your Grace and going into Nottinghamshire tomorrow morning obliges me to give you this trouble, and as it is so important an affair, and as you have alwaies done me the honour to express great friendship for me, I flatter myself an answer will be given to

Your Grace's
most Obedient Servant,
J. THORNHAGH.

This epistle perhaps procured further promises, for the next letter is in rather a different key: -

(Brit. Mus. Ad. MSS. 32,858, Folio 189)

Augst ye 16th, 1755.

My Lord Duke,

As you are pleas'd to interest yourself on Mr. Watsin's behalf, I flatter myself that I shall be excus'd if I now acquaint your Grace. there are two vacancies of Second Lieutenants in the Marine Service, Sullivan's of the 12th Company, Smith's of the 22nd Company, one of which I should hope might be procured for him.

I am with the greatest respect
Your Grace's
Most Obedient Servt.
THORNAGH

None of these applicants appear in the list of first appointments to the Corps (vide p. 117, Records G. & L.) except Watson, personally recommended by the Duke of Newcastle, though as 100 more Commissions were given soon after, they may be among them. C. FIELD.

Colonel Field's remarks are in italics.

THE FATHERS OF THE CORPS OF ROYAL MARINES.

Although there were various establishments of Marine Troops at earlier dates, it is well known that the present Corps of Marines - created in 1802 - dates from the year 1755.

The following list of the 106 Officers originally appointed upon its creation should, therefore, be of interest, as from them the present Officers of the Royal Marines can trace an unbroken descent and they may thus be fairly called "The Fathers of the Corps."

The list was found among the papers of the late Colonel L. Edye, and is noted as having been copied from "Stray Letters, Navy, 1686-1787" - probably preserved in the Record Office.

The more modern and numerical designations of the various Regiments that are referred to under their Colonel's names, have been added by another hand probably - from the handwriting - by Col. Edye himself.

An interesting point in this List is the fact that more than half the Officers appointed to the new Marine Corps had previously borne commissions in the ten Regiments of Marines raised in 1739 and 1740 and disbanded in 1748, so that a strong connection of the present Corps with the previous Marine Regiments is established.

It will be observed that Nicholas in his History of the Royal Marine Corps, states that in addition to the 106 Field Officers, Captains and 1st Lieutenants who are mentioned in this list, 100 2nd Lieutenants were appointed at the same time. Probably this is correct, but their names do not appear here. As very likely none of them had served before, and so had a previous military history, it may be that Colonel Edye did not think it worthwhile to have their names copied out.

The Notes I have added at the end are not in the original, but are my own.

The spelling of the note as to the cancellation of the commission given to John Harris is somewhat erratic, and some of the names of the Colonels of the former Marine Regiments are spelt in a different way to that to be found in some other accounts and documents in which they are mentioned. For instance, here "Cochrane" is spelt "Cochran" or "Cockran"; "Fraser" appears as "Frazier," while "Powlett" really should be "Paulet," i.e., The Hon. Charles Armand Paulet, who became Duke of Bolton in 1758.

Ed note:- In the original there are handwritten (in ink) notations against some of the names.

OFFICERS APPOINTED ON FORMATION OF THE PRESENT CORPS OF MARINES IN 1755.
Marine Commissions dated 2nd April, 1755.

Names	From what Regiment	Date of previous Commissions
To Be LT-COLONELS OF MARINES[3]		
Lt-Col Paterson	½ Pay Cornwall's (7th Marines)	24 Jan. 1740/1
Lt-Col Dury (? Drury)	½ Pay Loudon's (30th Regt.)	30 Mar. 1742
Lt-Col Gordon	½ Pay Laforey's (6th Marines)	1 May 1745
To be MAJORS[3]		
Major Bendish	½ Pay Cornewall's (7th Marines)	1 May 1745
Major Leighton	½ Pay Laforey's (6th Marines)	1 May 1745
Major Burleigh	Late Falmouth's (Disbanded)	4 Oct. 1745
To be CAPTAINS (50) - (From Half-Pay)		
Hector Boisrond	Torrington's (4th Marines)	8 Jan. 1740/1
Gabriel Sediere	Cochran's (5th Marines)	24 Mar. 1740/41

John McKenzie[1]	Torrington's (4th Marines)	15 April 1741
Charles Repington	Churchill's (1st Marines)	22 April 1741
Alexr. Cumming[2]	Holmes's (3rd Marines)	7 May 1741
Sr Robt. Abercrombie	Cochran's (5th Marines)	12th Oct. 1741
Alexr. Douglas	Cochran's (5th Marines)	1 June 1742
Edward Rycaut	Churchill's (1st Marines)	12 June 1742
John Wright	Jordan's (8th Marines)	22 Sept. 1742
Thomas Dawes	Cornwall's (7th Marines)	14 May 1744
John Tufton Mason	Pepperell's[3]	6 Sept. 1745,
Thomas Sheldon	Agnew's (10th Marines)	27 Sept. 1745
Thomas Moore	Cornwall's (7th Marines)	29 Nov. 1745
John Gordon	Powlet's (9th Marines)	26 Feb. 1745
Richard Barker *	Holmes's (3rd Marines)	12 May 1746
James Dundas	Panmure's (25th K.O.Bs)	18 April 1747
George Maxwell	Battereau's (Disbanded 1748)	18 May 1747
James Robertson	St. Clair's (Royal Scots)	7 Jan. 1747/8
John Campbell	Ld. John Murray's (Black Watch)	17 May 1748

(From Half-Pay Capt. - Lieutenants)

Claud Hamilton	Torrington's (4th Marines)	25 June 1741
John Bell	Laforey's (6th Marines)	29 Nov. 1745
John Dennis	Holmes's (3rd Marines)	12 May 1746
Thomas Dalton	Albemarle's (Coldstreams)	1 June 1750

(From Lieutenants)

Thomas Whitwick	Holmes's (3rd Marines)	20 Aug. 1741
James Hamilton	The Royals	7 May 1742
Roger Basket	Torrington's (4th Marines)	3 June 1742
Henry Grame[2]	Stuart's (37th N. Hampshire)	2 July 1742
John Beaghan	Holmes's (3rd Marines)	13 Aug. 1743
Samuel Prosser	Powlet's (9th Marines)	24 Feb. 1743/4
Patrick McDowal	Holmes's (5th Marines)	29 May 1745
Alexander Irons	Laforey's (6th Marines)	26 July 1745
Charles Webb	Warburton's (45th Sherwood Foresters)	13 Sept. 1745
William Stacey	Ld. Effingham's (34th Cumberland Regiment)	2 Dec. 1745
Richard Brough	Pole's (10th N. Lincolns)	9 April 1746
Henry Smith	Bocland's (11th N. Devon)	11 April 1746
Leathes Johnston	Braddock's (14th Buckingham)	14 Dec. 1746
John Johnston[2]	Ld. Geo. Beauclerk's (19th, 1st York N. Riding)	17 June 1746

*Next on the list to Richard Barker came Campbell Edmonston, from "Campbell's" Regiment, in which his commission was dated 25 Aug., 1746, but it is noted "Hath desired to be excused accepting the Commission."

Christopher Gauntlet	Skelton's (12th E. Suffolk)	11 April 1747
Tooker Collins	Kennedy's (43rd Monmouth)	27 May 1747
Walter Caruthers	Torrington's (4th Marines)	21 July 1747
John Vere	Bocland's (11th N. Devon)	24 Oct. 1747
William Picton[2]	Skelton's (12 E. Suffolk)	16 Jan. 1747/8
Richard Shuckburgh*	Agnew's (10th Marines)	23 July 1748
Richard Hawkins	Handasyde's (16th Bedfords)	24 Jan. 1752
George Maddison	Pole's (10th N. Lincolns)	27 Nov. 1752
Charles Grey[2]	Guise's (6th Royal Warwicks)	23 Dec. 1752

SUB-BRIGADIER

Robert Burdet	Earl of Hertford's (Horse Gds)	13 Oct. 1741

CORNET

John Yeo	Bland's (3rd King's Own Hussars)	18 May 1744
Robt. Parkhurst	Bland's (3rd King's Own Hussars)	13 Jan. 1753

ENSIGN

Alexr. Leslie[2]	Earl of Dunmore's (3rd F. Gds.)	22 Dec. 1753

To be FIRST LIEUTENANTS (50)

Daniel Campbell	Americans[4]	31 May 1746
Dudley Crofts	Americans	1 June 1746

Captains received by the intended Canada Expedition, Recommended by Mr. Stone.

CAPT.-LIEUT.

George Langley	Powis's[5]	Oct. 1745

Was Ensign in Otway's[6] from May 1742. Recommended by Earl Powis.

From LIEUTENANTS

James Hill	Holmes's (3rd Marines)	21 Aug. 1741
	Recommended by Sir Wm. Priddleton	
Alexr. Cathcart	Holmes's (3rd Marines)	2 June 1742
	Recommended by Major Brown	
Francis Hay	Bruce's[7]	28 Dec. 1744
	Recommended by the Earl of Rothes	
Donald McDonald	Loudon's (Disbanded 1747/8)	8 June 1745
	Recommended by Lt.-Col. Watson	
John Suttie	Pepperell's	1 Sept. 1745
	Recommended by Lord Cathcart	
Edward Howarth	Jordan's (8th Marines)	29 Nov. 1745
	Recommended by Lord Bateman	
Robert Douglas	Frasier's (2nd Marines)	29 Nov. 1745
	Recommended by the Earl of Morton	

*Next on the list to Richard Shuckburgh came John Harris from Waldegrave's Regt., in which his commission was dated 14 May, 1749, but his name is erased, with the note "Superseded at the request of the Secretary of War, by Captain John Johnston."

John Phillips	Holmes's (3rd Marines)	21 May 1746
	Recommended by Admiral Boscawen	
John Brown	Rich's (4th King's Own)	10 Mar. 1746/7
	Recommended by the Earl of Finlaker	
Colin Campbel	Independent Companies[8]	4 June 1747
	"A Good Character"	
Robert Enver	Frazier's (2nd Marines)	24 Oct 1747
	"A Good Character"	
Archd. Campbell	North British Fusileers	23 Mar. 1748
	Recommended by Lt.-Genl. Campbell	
George Ord	Bruce's	26 Aug. 1748
	Recommended by Lord Barrington	
Lancelot Willan	Richbell's (39th Dorset Regt.)	22 Oct. 1748
	Recommended by Mr. Reynolds of Lancaster	

2ND LIEUTENANTS

William Fraser	Cornwall's (2nd Marines)	8 Jan, 1740/1
	Recommended by Lord Anson	
James Short	Holmes's (3rd Marines)	21 Aug. 1741
	Recommended by Major Brown	
Geo. Bossigne	Laforey's (6th Marines)	26 June 1742
	"Good Character"	
James Mercer	Churchill's (1st Marines)	28 Sept. 1743
	Recommended by Lord John Murray	
John Fraser	Richbell's (39th Dorsets)	27 Mar. 1744
	"Good Character"	
Wm. Aytoun Douglas	Fraser's (2nd Marines)	27 Mar 1744
	"Good Character"	
Dennis Bond	Holmes's (3rd Marines)	27 Mar. 1744
	"Good Character"	
Thos. Backhouse	Battereau's (Disbanded 1748)	1 May 1744
	"Good Character"	
Gerrard Dennet	Agnew's (10th Marines)	25 June 1744
	Recommended by Sir Edward Winnington	
Thomas Troy	Cockran's (5th Marines)	18 Aug, 1744
	"Good Character"	
Edward Kyffin	Churchill's (1st Marines)	31 Aug. 1744
	Recommended by Lord Granby	
Geo. Gulston	Agnew's (10th Marines)	26 July 1745
	Recommended by the Duke of Marlborough	
Richd. Dennison	Holmes's (3rd Marines)	27 Sept. 1745
	Recommended by the Duke of Bedford	

Wm. Thompson	Cockran's (5th Marines) "Fit to Serve"	1 Dec. 1745
John Elliot	Frazier's (2nd Marines) Recommended by Mr. Chaigneau	9 April 1746
John Pitcairn	Cornwall's (7th Marines) Recommended by Mr. Hamilton of Pekinfield	30 April 1746
James Perkins	Powlet's (9th Marines) "Good Character"	21 May 1746
Wm. Dennis	Cornwall's (7th Marines) Recommended by Mr, Walpole, Senior	17 June 1746
Ralph Teesdale	Torrington's (4th Marines) Recommended by Mr. Lambton of Durham	23 June 1746
Pierce Dent	Powlet's (9th Marines) "Good Character"	23 June 1746
Robert Shirley	Cockran's (5th Marines) Recommended by Mr. Guerin	13 Oct. 1746
Danl. Campbell	Independent Companies[8] Recommended by Lt,-Genl. Campbell	9 June 1747
John Blinkhorn	Hohnes's (3rd Marines) Recommended by Dr. Guernier	14 Oct. 1747
William Lutman	Holmes's (3rd Marines) Recommended by Mr. Page of Chichester	8 Mar. 1747/8
Thomas Wight	Cornwall's (7th Marines) Recommended by Lord Coventry	15 Mar. 1747/8
William Rowley	Huske's (23rd R. Welsh Fus.) Recommended by Admiral Rowley	10 Feb. 1753

From ENSIGNS

Thomas Stamper	Pepperell's Recommended by Mr. Fox, Chichester	3 Sept. 1745
Thomas Airy	Howard's (3rd Buffs) Recommended by Mr. Ridley of Newcastle	25 July 1747
Thomas Smith	Hopson's (40th Somersets) Recommended by Lord Anson	7 Nov. 1747
Thomas Waller	Handasyd's (16th Bedfordshire) Recommended by the Duke of Newcastle	16 April 1748
Charles Fletcher	Pulteney's (13th Somersets) Recommended by Lt.-Col. Stanwix	27 Nov. 1752
Benj. Edwards	Leighton's (32nd Cornwall L.I.) Recommended by Lord Maipas	29 Oct. 1753
Enoch Markham	Cornwallis's (24th S. Wales Bds.) Recommended by Mr. Ellis	22 Dec. 1753

NOTES.

1. Charles Repington first served as an Ensign in Harrison's (15th Foot).
2. These Officers and six others on this Captain's list transferred or exchanged to the Line in the course of the next few years, and in 1766 eight of these were Lieutenant-Colonels and four Majors (Vide Nicholas, Vol. I., p. xi.).
3. "Pepperell's." This was a Regiment raised in 1754 by Colonel Pepperell, who had seen considerable service in America. It was numbered 51st in the Line, served in America, and seems to have disbanded in 1756.
4. "Americans." Probably "Gooch's," raised as auxilliaries to the Marine Regiments employed at Cartagena. It had four Battalions. It was disbanded in 1742, but probably many of its Officers and men remained in the Independent Companies of Foot, which at that time garrisoned our Western possessions.
5. "Powis's." I can find nothing further as to this Regiment.
6. Otway's," Later the 35th Foot.
7. "Bruce's." Later the 100th Foot.
8. "Independent Companies." These seem to have been formed from time to time as required. Two Battalions of the Boscawen's Expedition to the East Indies. The 23 Officers of Marines who sailed round the world with Anson seem to have come from Independent Companies. Eight such Companies serving in the West Indies were formed into a Regiment in 1743 (the 49th Foot), now 1st Battalion Princess Charlotte of Wales' Royal Berkshire Regiment.

It appears that in the case of a Lieutenant's Commission a recommendation of some kind was required, but not, apparently, for a Captains Commission.

———

ARTILLERYMEN SERVING AFLOAT PRIOR TO 1804.
From Col. L. Edye's "History of the Royal Marine Forces," Vol. II.

The presence of Colonel George Browne as "Chief Bombardeer and Engineer" in the fleet[1] deserves more than a passing notice, for not only did he represent the Train[2] for land service but also that portion if it embarked for service afloat, and as such may be regarded as one of the first representatives of the present Corps of Royal Marine Artillery.

As early as 1693[3], it had been determined to embark on board certain ships, in addition to the Seamen and Marines, a certain number officers and men of the Artillery Train[4], the object being for the working of the mortars, and as an experiment the bomb-vessels *Serpent*, *Mortar*, *Firedrake* and *Grenade* were so manned[5]. These vessels formed part of Commodore Benbow's squadron which bombarded St Malo in the same year, and Dieppe in the year following. In 1695, following presumably on the success of the previous trials, it was considered "requisite and necessary for . . . . service that several bomb-vessels with mortars, and fitting proportion of ammunition and other stores should be provided for . . . (the) fleet in the Streights."[6]

In consequence of this decision, Colonel Sir Martin Beckman[7], Major John Henry Hopkey[8], Adjutant John Hanway[9], Chaplain John Galloway, with two Commissaries, a Medical Officer and his "Mate," three Firemasters[10] fourteen Fire-workers, twenty-six Bombardiers, eight Conductors, a Master-Carpenter and his mate," twelve Carpenters, a Master Smith and three Smiths, were ordered to embark for service in the Fleet, as part complement to the bomb-vessels[11].

Later in the year a second detachment of the Train of Artillery was ordered to embark in the bomb-vessels for service with the fleet about to operate in the Channel, and which subsequently bombarded St. Malo, Granville, Dunkerque and Calais, Colonel Jacob Richards in command[12], an Adjutant, one Pay and Commissary, five Clerks, three Firemasters, fourteen Fire-workers, forty four Bombardiers; whilst the Machine vessels[13] were also to receive a smaller detachment under the command of an officer named Alexander Eustace[14].

In 1698 we again find a detachment of Artillery with Vice-Admiral Aylmer's fleet, embarked under the command of Colonel George Brown[15] with Major Albert Borgard[16] as second in command[17].

No further embarkation of the Train took place until the present year, when a large force formed part of both the Duke of Ormonde's and Sir George Rooke's respective commands.

In connection with those serving in the capacity of Marine Artillerymen on this occasion, we find two Petitions of Major Borgard's, stating "they were in action at the taking and burning of the French men-of-war and Spanish galleons . . . . and Desire their share of the Prize-Money," as also a report[18] from Major Borgard "that hee nor any of the Bombardeers[19] ordered on board have any places or Cabbins to sleep in, nor can have any victualls as ye Captain informs him"[20], although it would appear "the Captains had orders to receive them and furnish them with ye usual allowance of provisions"[21].

From this date until 1804 detachments of the Royal Artillery always formed part of the complement of certain of H.M. Ships of War.

NOTES.

1. i.e., the fleet destined to attack Vigo, etc.
2. Now the Royal Regiment of Artillery.
3. They had been embarked in 1692, but were on this occasion for transport only.
4. "Cleaveland Papers," page 132.
5. Idem, page 133.
6. Idem, page 136.
7. A Swedish Captain of Artillery in 1667, appointed by Royal Warrant Engineer to the Ordnance 19 Oct,, 1670 ; Capt. in Prince Rupert's Regiment of Dragoons, 27 August, 1673; Capt. in Royal Regiment of Fusiliers (now Royal Fusiliers) 14 June, 1685. Succeeded Sir Bernand de Gonune as Chief Engineer 30 Nov. 1685 Ktd. 20 March 1686. (Dalton's English Army List and Commission Register. Vols. 1. 11., pp. 157. 205, 28, 137. See also Col Duncan s History of the Royal Artillery.)
8. or Hopeke.
9. Served in Flanders. An Engineer in 1698, afterwards Chief Engineer at Gibraltar. Present at Barcelona, and in 1703 went to Jamaica with Admiral Graydon. (Loftus' History R.E., Vol. 1., pp, 70, 119. 137.)
10. The Firemaster was charged "with the direction of the laboratory, the manufacture of powder, rockets, fire-balls. petards, and all similar instruments of war, as well as air and water balloons."

11. Cleaveland Papers, p. 137.
12. In 1685 Mr. Jacob Richards was appointed "to travel and inform himself." (See his report Stowe Coll., Richards Papers I., iii.) as Lieut.-Col of Train. He served at the Battles of Steenkirke (1693) and Landen (1693); died 1701. (Porter's Hist. R.E., Vol. L. pp. 51, 52, 53, 54, 55, 56.)
13. ie., Explosion vessels, one of which created great havoc at St. Malo.
14. Cleaveland Papers, p. 153.
15. This Officer in 1701 submitted a proposal to the Navy Board "for instructing the gunners of His Matie's Ships in the Art of Gunnery . . . . thinking it may very much contribute to the good of the Sea Service." (Lords' Letters to the Secretary of State. Vol. II., Folio 49.)
16. Originally in the Danish, subsequently in the Prussian service. Present at the Sieges of Buda, Bonn and Maintz, and afterwards at the Battle of StzIankerman. Joined the English service in Flanders and present at the Steenkirke and Landen and Siege of Namdr (Parnell's "Wars of the Spanish Succession" II. p. 68t)
17. Cleaveland Papers, p. 153.
18. Admiralty Office. Ordnance Account. Vol. 1.
19. Bombardiers and Fire-workers were always, apparently, allowed a cabin; consequently so must also have been Firemasters. (Admiralty Office of Ordnance, Vol. V. 26 June 1708.)
20. Admiralty Office of Ordnance, Vol, 1., 3 April, 1703
21. Idem Vol 1., 23 June, 1703

————

THE MARINES IN 1758.

LETTER FROM A YOUNG OFFICER.
AN AFFAIR OF HONOUR.

To the Editor of The Times.

Sir,- In connexion with the anniversary of Trafalgar, the following letter, written at Gibraltar in 1758, by a young Marine, and addressed to the house of his sister, Mrs. Browne, of Derby, my great-great-grandmother, may be of interest:

To Miss E. Buckston
At Mrs. Brownes
  in Derby Derbyshire
    England.

Gibraltar 23rd Decemr 1758.

Dear Sister,- I am sorry to inform you yt I have never had ye pleshur of receiving a letter either from you or Brother Geare since I left England and what is most wonder of surprise to me is yt Mr. Beard who is my agent in Westminster frequently sends letters to this place but there is never any for me. We are laitely arived from Leghorn after a very inactive or merchantman voyage for ye french have very few or no ships of war at sea so yt we are returned without anything extraordinary hapening except yt we have taken never a prize for this ten months past but we expect to go out on a separate cruise in a few days to ye westward and then we shall stand sum chance to catch a frenchman. I have been at Florence Leuca and Peasa last summer ye first of them in perticular is very gay. I went by Land from Leghorn.

Yesterday I had a dispute with one Ensign Gouldfinch of Col: Geffers Regim: who is a very hot headed young man: in ye dispute he yoused some words yt no man of Honor could possably put up without his beging pardon in as bublick a maner as he gave the affrunt and I have been with him this morning to talke ye affaire cooley over but he still persists in his errar and absolutely refuses to make acknerlidgement at all, so yt must absolutely end in a duell wh. is a very disagreeable thing and wh. no prudent man would undertake if he could avoide it with Honor, but this I cannot tho' he might as he was ye aggresser. I have left every thing I have in this part of ye world to ye care of my very good friend Lieut. Bob. Wright of Eame, who will send every thing belonging to me to you and also pay ye all ye money yt is due to me of prize money. I will write to B. G. at the same time and have desired that he would assist you in every thing that he can. When you receive this letter you may be shure I am dead for I shall not send it myself but leave it with Mr. Wright to send it after my death. My arreares as Capt. of Marines are due to me from ye first of Jany 1757 to this time wh. is about 72 pounds for two years; my subsistence is all due to me from ye first of October 1757 to this time wh. at 7s. 6d. pr day is about 170 pounds, and which you will get from Mr. Beard in downing street, Westminster. I wish all ye hapiness yt you can hope for may attend you, and am,

Dear Sister
Your sincere friend and loving Brother till Death
THOS. BUCKSTON.

P.s. You will find a piece of flowered silk in my large trunk to make you a gound.

We do not know that the duel was fought, but we do know that Captain Thomas Buckston lived to old age, and was buried in Bradhourne Church, Derbyshire, under the following inscription :-

In memory of Thomas Buckston, Esq., who died in the year 1811 aged 87. Many years Captain in the Royal Marines, during which period he served in many engagements, and lived to be one of the oldest officers in his Majesty's service. He was formerly a lieutenant in the 30th Regiment of foot, and was at the battle of Culloden. A man warmly attached to his family and friends, charitable and religious in his principles and conduct. Elizabeth his wife died 27th of August 1810, aged 75.

A portrait of "Bob Wright" continues to hang in the ancient and beautiful Hall at Eyam, still inhabited by the old Wright family.

Yours, &c.,
GEORGE BUCKSTON BROWNE.

Wimpole-street.
From The Times of 21-10-26.

BELLEISLE.

Some Account of Captain David Hepburn.
Vide "Britain's Sea Soldiers,"
Portrait facing p. 101 and p. 107.

Captain David Hepburn was originally in the Dutch Service. He then served in the Marines and distinguished himself at the Siege of Palais in the Belleisle Expedition. He did not, however, remain in the Corps, probably because he, like many other officers who left it round about the same time, awoke to the fact that there was no "top of the tree" for them, Naval officers being already perched on the highest branches of the Marine Service. We next hear of him as Major, and later on, Lieut.-Colonel of Graeme's Regiment (probably a Highland Corps), and finally as Deputy Adjutant-General in Ireland.

He was the son of James Hepburn, of Keith Marischal, a well-known Jacobite, frequently mentioned by Home in his "History of the Rebellion of 1745."

He was father of Major-General Francis Hepburn, a distinguished Peninsula and Waterloo officer, who commanded a battalion of the Scots Guards at the Defence of Hougomont."

THE MARINES AT BELLEISLE, 1761.

"The following instance of the bravery of our Marines must not be omitted. The French were in possession of a village that annoyed us much; the General had it reconnoitred, and gave it as his opinion that the place might be stormed with two or three hundred men; others said it could not be taken without cannon. While they were thus undetermined, one night a corporal with four men, relieving the advanced sentinels, was fired upon by the French from the village, on which he stood his ground and returned the fire, and sent one of his men to acquaint the commanding officer, that if he would send him a few more men he would take the village. The officer gave little faith to his message, but sent a party to bring them off. Before they came the corporal with the three men had drove the French, to the number of fifty men, out of the village and was in possession of it. Such is the undaunted courage of that Corps on this expedition."

"On the 21st, in the evening arrived the *Fly* sloop, Captain Gayton, with an account that the garrison had made another sally, but were repulsed by our Marines, who pursued them so closely as to enter the town with them, and gallantly sustained their superior force till a reinforcement came up. We are now in possession of the town, and it is thought the citadel will soon surrender. Captain Carruthers of the Marines was wounded, but we hear not dangerously."

"May 13th. This morning there happened the most extraordinary thing in the Marine camp ever heard of, viz., Lieutenant White of the Marines, lying in his tent in a cot, a shell fell under him and burst, which overturned him, and wrapt him all up in the tent; but he was not hurt, though his cot was blown to pieces. A little after another shell fell into a serjeant's tent, where were three men, three women, and a child or two, which blew all the tent and bedding to shatters, but not a person was hurt. One woman, who was big with child slept over the shell while the fuze was burning-this is affirmed by many of good credit."

"May 26th. The Marines have gained immortal glory, and as a reward have been appointed to every post of honour."
From Letters and Reports from Belleisle in the news Columns of "The Royal Magazine," 1761.

SEAMEN AT BELLEISLE.

"Our sailors are denied going into the town, some of them having been a little too rude with the French ladies who, by the way, are not at all displeased with their amorous disposition, and John will run the hazard of flogging to stay till dark."

BELLEISLE.
Gallant Conduct of a Party of Marines.
Youghall,
October 18th, 1761.

"This evening arrived the *St Ann*, schooner, of Lisbon, Captain William Bamfield, last from St. Sebastian's, who spoke with H.M.S. *Lively*, 20 leagues off Cape Clear, from whom we had the following particulars of a truly heroic action, viz., That on the 11th last three French men-of-war appeared about four miles off Belleisle, and within them lay the above-mentioned frigate at anchor, not a mile from the shore. The French manned six large boats, in order to board and take the *Lively*, in sight, though not in the power of the garrison, who concluded she must be in some danger from the place she lay at; but part of Colonel Morgan's Light Infantry (the then 90th Regiment) and some Marines that were on shore (and also for the most part Irish), applied to General Hodgson for leave to assist the frigate, which he immediately complied with.

On this eighty-five men set off in four boats, and as they were lighter and had the heels of the French, soon came up with, resolutely attacked, and took four of their boats; the other two immediately ran, and so soon as their people could secure their prisoners, they pursued, but could come up with only one of them, which they also took, and carried their five prizes safe to shore, in which there had been 102 seamen and marines, 15 of whom were killed and 16 wounded.

Among the French prisoners are seven marine and sea officers, the chief of whom is mortally wounded. On this occasion we had four men killed and eleven wounded. This attempt of the French may prove to be no less fatal to their ships, as they were immediately pursued to sea by five men-of-war, and it is hoped will be met with.

The Royal Magazine for Nov., 1761.

A COOL REQUEST.

Second-Lieutenant William Carroll, Marines, asked to be made a First-Lieutenant with the rank of Captain for his conduct of His Majesty's affairs at the Court of Dresden having merited His Majesty's entire approbation."

His application was rejected as "totally unreasonable, and if allowed would be a discouragement to officers who had served long and satisfactorilly, and be very prejudicial to His Majesty's Service." (Admiralty - 14th March, 1769).

This officer joined in February, 1761, and was put on Half-Pay, 1st May, 1763.

From Home Office Papers, 1679, p 458, Sec. 1143.

AFFRAY BETWEEN MARINES AND SHIPWRIGHTS.

A quarrel happened between the Shipwrights in Portsmouth Dockyard and the Marines then on duty there, in consequence of the Marines having taken the bundles of chips, which the Shipwrights had made up and claimed as their perquisite, and carried them to the guard-house. Both sides drew up in a line of battle, the Shipwrights armed with adzes and axes, and the Marines with their muskets and bayonets fixed, but happily, the superior officer, having notice of this fray, arrived time enough, and prevented the consequences by ordering the Marines to restore the chips.

From an old Magazine (probably "The Gentleman's"), April, 1768.

MAJOR PITCAIRN AND THE MARINES IN THE EXPEDITION TO LEXINGTON AND CONCORD, 18th & 19th April, 1775.
By Colonel C. Field.

PART I

The expedition from Boston to Concord, in which Major Pitcairn of the Marines — who afterwards fell gloriously in the moment of victory at Bunker's Hill - has been briefly mentioned in Chapter XI of my "Britain's Sea Soldiers." I have lately come across a great number of very interesting details of the doings of this little expedition in the course of which the shot was fired that signalised the birth of the United States.[1] I propose in this article to combine those passages which deal especially with Major Pitcairn and the Marines who were present.

It is common knowledge that General Gage, who commanded in Boston, sent out this flying column as it may be called, for the purpose of capturing and destroying various military stores which had been hidden away in the township of Concord by the disaffected colonists, generally referred to as Whigs or Provincials.

The troops detailed were the Grenadier and Light Infantry companies of the following Corps: 4th, 5th, 10th, 18th, 23rd, 38th, 43rd, 47th, 59th Regiments and of the 1st and 2nd Battalions of Marines.

Lt.-Colonel Smith of the 10th went in command, Major Pitcairn as second in command. Smith seems to have been a stout heavy individual, but, from the point of view of military efficiency - to quote Euclid - "of no parts or magnitude." In every account of the affair he seems to slide into the background, Pitcairn being always the prominent figure.

It must be noted in passing that the 22 companies above enumerated by no means represented anything like 2,200 men. It is generally agreed that the force amounted to not more than between seven hundred and eight hundred men altogether, so that the average strength of these Flank Companies must have been under 50 men apiece.

According to one story, Pitcairn was chosen to go as "he had previously examined the road to Concord, and had studied the town in disguise." This can be traced to no contemporary source. But as we read in an old work that he had been "Military Commandant at Boston" before the war, it is extremely likely that he was well acquainted both with Concord and the routes to that place. It seems quite possible, not to say probable, that a detachment of Marines was the first British force to be landed in the city, very likely some little time before the arrival of a considerable military contingent. It would have been only one instance out of many in the history of the Corps in which a similar event has taken place.

In the case of Pitcairn's choice for the Concord expedition, however, we are told that he was a seasoned veteran and general favourite, popular with Whigs as well as Tories. For these reasons alone he may have been selected for a post which was likely to demand discretion and good temper.[2]

Pitcairn was a "veteran" since he had obtained his commission as a Lieutenant in Cornwall's (7th Marines) on 30th April, 1746, and it is quite on the cards that he may have been transferred to that Regiment from some other corps. He was given a Lieutenant's commission in the present Marine Corps on its first establishment in April, 1755, on the recommendation of "Mr. Hamilton of Pekinfield." That he was a general favourite is borne out by the statement in the old work previously quoted, that when in command at Boston "he had endeared himself to the people," and that at Bunker's Hill, "no officer fell more regretted, for he was beloved, even by his enemy."[3]

As a matter of fact it appears that both Smith and Pitcairn were detailed as "the two Field Officers first for duty, and the senior of each rank."[4]

Gage determined that the expedition should be sudden and secret, but in a city and neighbourhood swarming with Whig sympathisers, the cloak of mystery with which he enveloped his orders and proceedings, actually drew more attention to something "being in the wind" than if he had moved in a more open fashion.

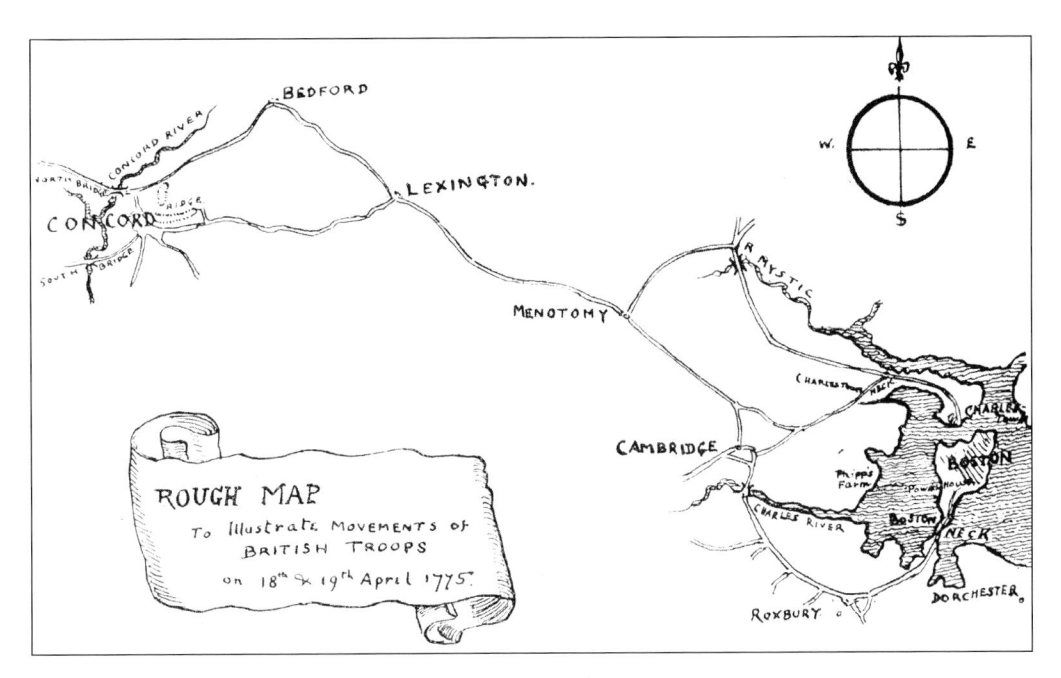

ROUGH MAP
To Illustrate Movements of British Troops on 18th & 19th April 1775.

The rank and file of the Flank Companies detailed "were not apprised of the design, till just as it was time to march, they were waked up by the sergeants putting their hands on them and whispering gently to them; and were even conducted by a back way out of the barracks, without the knowledge of their comrades, and without the observation of the sentries. They walked through the street with the utmost silence. It being about ten o'clock, no sound was heard but that of their feet; a dog, happening to bark, was instantly killed by a bayonet. They proceeded to the beach under the new powder house[5] - the most unfrequented part of the town, and there embarked on board the boats, which had their oars muffled to prevent a noise."[6]

The town of Boston is situated on a more or less pear-shaped peninsula attached to the south side of a large eastern-facing bay, by a narrow isthmus or stalk, known as "Boston Neck." Bunker's Hill and Charlestown occupy a peninsula of somewhat similar shape attached by its "stalk" - Charlestown Neck - to the north-west corner of the bay. A strait runs between the outer ends of the two peninsulas, which may possibly have been connected with each other at some very remote period.

The spot selected for the embarkation of the expedition was on the western side of the Boston peninsula, where it was separated from the mainland about the mouth of the Charles or Cambridge river, where was the selected landing-place, at a spot known as Phipps Farm, by over a mile of water.

The secrecy with which the operation orders were issued was all very well, so far as it went, but as it was known early on the 18th from seamen coming ashore "that provisions were being dressed on board the transports for a body of troops, that the boats were ordered to be on the beach near the Common at night, and that several officers had gone out towards Concord in the afternoon,"[7] there was quite enough rumour afloat to arouse suspicion among the Whigs of some move of importance.

The Officers in question were all mounted, Gage's idea being that they would be able to intercept messengers sent from Boston to warn the Provincials. But it seems rather that they served as a warning themselves. It was they who, after Paul Revere in his celebrated ride had escaped them once, caught him again between Lexington and Concord, and foolishly released him. But another rider, William Dawes, also got away by a different route, and independently of these two messengers, we all know how fast news flies in country districts in an almost unaccountable manner, and in short the expedition failed altogether as a surprise.

VIEW OF THE TOWN OF CONCORD.

1. Companies of the Regulars marching into Concord.
2. Companies of the Regulars drawn up in order.
3. Regulars destroying the Provincials' Stores.
4. & 5. Colonel Smith and Major Pitcairn viewing the Provincials mustering on East Hill.
6. The Town House.
7. The Meeting House.

N.B.—Major Pitcairn and Colonel Smith are seen in the foreground, standing in the Cemetery, which was at the western end of the ridge which flanked the Lexington Road. The large house in the centre of the picture is the Wright Tavern, which is still standing. Beyond it to the left is seen the Mill Pond on the further side of which the stores are being destroyed and dumped into the Pond by the British working parties.

Moreover, there was delay and miscalculation from the very beginning. Although the troops should have been at the place of embarkation at 10 p.m., it was nearer 11 before all were present. The number of boats provided by the men-of-war and transports proved to be too few, and two trips had to be made, so that the whole force was not ashore till nearly one o'clock in the morning. Another hour was lost in serving out the cooked provisions which had been prepared, so that the expedition did not begin its march till 2 a.m. Nor had its route been arranged with sufficient care and forethought, since the tide had not been taken into consideration, the result being that having got wet to the knees in a marshy landing place, waiting for their provisions to be issued, "which most of the men threw away, having carried some with 'em,"[8] the troops had to wade through two inlets, one of them at any rate up to their middles, before reaching the high road. Colonel Smith then advanced at a great rate, to make up for lost time, and probably also to warm the men after their prolonged wetting. Whether Smith perceived any indication of alarm in the countryside or not after his first halt, he gave orders to Pitcairn to push on full speed ahead of him to Lexington with six of the Light Infantry companies. Almost immediately afterwards the ringing of bells and firing of guns echoed on every hand through the early morning stillness. The Provincials were awake. Pitcairn, nearing Lexington met some of the mounted officers who had gone out the previous afternoon, who informed him that there were 500 militiamen drawn up on Lexington Green to oppose him. Pitcairn halted, ordered his men to prime and load, but "on no account to fire, nor even to attempt it without orders."[9]

In the meantime, there now being no doubt that the whole countryside was alarmed, Colonel Smith sent back to General Gage asking for reinforcements.

Lexington Green was triangular in shape, and Pitcairn entered by the apex and rounding the Meeting House, which stood, with its belfry, to one side of it near that corner, found, not 500, but something over 100 Militia and Minute men[10] drawn up with arms near the base.

What happened next? There seems no doubt that Pitcairn ordered the Provincials to lay down their arms and disperse. Their leader, a Captain Parker, asserted that he also ordered his men to disperse, but he did not, apparently, tell them to lay down their arms. Pitcairn, it seems, who had with him one or two mounted officers, galloped on to the Green round the left of the Meeting House, and probably gave his order immediately he saw the Militiamen. It is said that his men rushed forward somewhat tumultuously, and with loud "huzzas." What probably happened was that the leading companies doubled round the other side of the Meeting House, in order to overtake their Commanding Officer, but did not rush upon the rebels, as the latter evidently thought they were about to do, but formed up in two companies or half-companies facing them. It is in this order that they are shewn in an engraving made on the spot by an American, Amos Doolittle, only a few weeks later.[11]

About this time it seems that the Minute men began to disperse; but now came the fatal shot which had such momentous consequences. Who fired it will never be known, "each party imputing it to the other." Pitcairn denied positively that he gave any order to fire, but in any case the first shot was followed by fire from his men, which killed eight and wounded several others of the Minute men, though it is admitted by various American accounts that he did all he possibly could to stop the firing. The question as to which side fired the first shot is not worth arguing about. In the state of extreme tension which then existed between the armed Provincials and the British troops, it was a dead certainty that it was only a matter of hours, or at most days, before it was fired, if not at Lexington, at some other place in the district.

About this time Colonel Smith seems to have joined up with the Grenadiers and the rest of the Light Infantry.

After what had occurred, and considering the general alarm in the country, several of his officers suggested that it would be advisable to retire to Boston. Smith, however, was determined to push on to Concord, his original objective. It was a five miles march. On nearing the town the Grenadiers kept to the road and the Light Infantry moved up to a ridge which ran parallel to it on the right. Provincials had been seen drawn up on the end of this ridge, but they retired to the far end just above the town on the advance of the British, and when the latter entered Concord, again retreated to an elevated piece of ground on the farther side of the Concord River which ran roughly at right angles to the British line of advance, at some little distance beyond the town. Here, during the time the troops were destroying the warlike stores they found, their numbers were continually augmented by arrivals from the surrounding townships and villages.

There was a bridge at this point, known as the North Bridge, and another a good deal further to the left, known as the South Bridge. Smith sent one company, under Captain Parsons, to hold the last mentioned bridge, and pushed on six to the North Bridge, three to hold it, while the other three went over and on some distance to search the farm of a Colonel Barrett. The search there and in the town itself seems to have been carried out with a great deal of consideration, for though a considerable quantity of arms and ammunition were discovered and destroyed including two 24-pound guns, whose trunnions were knocked off and their carriages burnt, other stores escaped, on account of the good nature of the searchers, who allowed themselves to be put off by plausible excuses. According to General Gage's report, one sulky inhabitant even struck Major Pitcairn without being punished for it.

While the search proceeded and parties were employed in dumping powder, flour, etc., into the large mill-pond which occupied the centre of the village, according to the deposition of one Martha Moulton, an old lady of seventy-one[12], who lived in a little house in the centre of the town, she waited on Major Pitcairn and four or five other officers "who sat at the door viewing their men," with chairs, water, "or what we had." She went on to say that when the gun-carriages were burnt she saw smoke coming out of the Town House. She begged of the officers to have the fire put out, "When they only said, 'O, mother we won't do you any harm!' 'Don't be concerned, mother,' and such like talk." However, according to her own account, she presently prevailed with them to have the fire extinguished, on the strength of which she petitioned the Provincial authorities for a gratuity.

But the smoke of this fire led to trouble. The Provincials massed on the further side of the river, saw it, and determined to fight rather than allow as they thought, their town to be burned down. They advanced towards the North Bridge. The British Companies there fired a few single shots into the river as a warning, and this being disregarded, another shot, which wounded a Provincial. Both sides now began to fire in earnest, but for some unaccountable reason the British abandoned the bridge and fell back towards the town in some disorder. Possibly they feared to be cut off from the main body, or again they might have received orders not to become too closely engaged.

The Provincials now crossed the bridge and took up a position on the end of a ridge that ran at right angles to the one they had occupied on the first appearance of the British, and at some little distance from it. All the outlying companies were now called in, and Captain Parsons, with his three companies, recrossed the North Bridge without any opposition.

It was now about noon and Smith started on his homeward journey. But he was at once attacked by the Provincials, who re-occupied their original position on the ridge, parallel to the road to Lexington. Thence onward the British were fired on from every side, the rebels running from tree to tree and from wall to wall, every man on his own. Some even were mounted, and having fired from one position, galloped ahead to select a fresh position from which to fire on the retreating British, who were practically confined to the road, where their column of route offered a most favourable target to the enemy.

"All the hills on each side of us were covered with rebels," wrote an officer who was present[13]. "…they kept the road always lined and a very hot fire on us without intermission. We at first kept our order and returned their fire as hot as we received it, but when we arrived within a mile of Lexington, our ammunition began to fail, and the light companies were so fatigued with flanking they were scarce able to act, and a great number of wounded scarce able to get forward, made a great confusion." Colonel Smith was hit in the leg and several other officers wounded. Smith and Pitcairn made desperate efforts to straighten things out and form a rear-guard. "An officer, mounted on an elegant horse," wrote an American eye-witness "and with a drawn sword in hand, was riding backwards and forwards, commanding and urging on the British troops. A number of Americans behind a pile of rails, raised their guns and fired with deadly effect. The officer fell, and the horse took fright, leaped the wall, and ran directly towards those who had killed his rider."

The rider was Pitcairn, but he was not killed, or even wounded, but he had to march the rest of the way on foot. He also lost his Highland pistols, which were carried during the rest of the war by the American General, Isaac Putnam, and are now preserved at Lexington.

In the meanwhile Smith's request for reinforcements had reached Boston. Gage seems to have foreseen the probability of their being required, for he had already on the evening of the 18th ordered the 1st Brigade, consisting of the 1st Marine Battalion, the 4th, 23rd and 47th Regiments, under Lord Percy, to parade at 4 o'clock on the following morning. When he got Smith's letter, he thought he had merely to give the order to march. This was about 5, but there was no one on parade. It then appeared that his order of the evening before had been left at the Brigade Major's house. He was out, and the letter was left on his table, and no one told him of its arrival when he got home. When Smith's letter arrived every effort was made to assemble the brigade. By 6 it was on parade, except the Marines. It then turned out that their orders had been addressed to Major Pitcairn and left at his house, although the Brigade Major must have known perfectly well that he was away. This caused further delay, so that it was getting on for 9 o'clock before Lord Percy was able to start, and by this time rumours of the fighting had filtered into the town. Lord Percy's Brigade, accompanied by a couple of field guns, marched off by way of Boston Neck, Roxbury, Cambridge and Menotomy. "Few people were to be seen, and the houses were in general shut up." [14]

There was no one about from whom to get news, and it was not till Percy had passed Menotomy that he heard that the Flank Companies were retreating under fire and that their ammunition was giving out. He now pushed on with all speed and met Smith's almost exhausted troops in the neighbourhood of Lexington. The reinforcing brigade drew up in line on the near side of that place, and the flank companies formed up behind it. The rebels were close on their heels, and the whole force began to retire on Boston, followed and flanked by the enemy the whole way. "We also advanced a few of our best marksmen," wrote a British officer, who fired on those who shewed themselves."

The 23rd Royal Welch Fusiliers formed the rear-guard for the first seven miles, and after they had expended most of their ammunition, their place was taken by the Marines.

As the brigade neared Cambridge the firing grew hotter and hotter, and Lord Percy, thinking that the bridge over the Charles River which he had crossed on his way out, "might either be broken down (which indeed was the case) or require to be forced," took the resolution of returning by way of Charlestown, which was the shortest road, and which could be defended against any number of rebels."

The two guns probably prevented the retreat from being more disastrous than it was, for whenever a cannon-shot was fired at any considerable number, they instantly dispersed.[15]

They were of great use, too, in demolishing houses and walls behind which the rebels took cover. Before reaching Charlestown Neck the Marines had been relieved as rear-guard by the 47th, and that regiment in its turn by the 4th.

As soon as the Brigade passed Charlestown Neck the rebels ceased firing. After remaining for some time drawn up on the heights above Charlestown, soon to be the scene of the bloody engagement of Bunker's Hill, the sorely tried Flank Companies were sent across to Boston, followed as boats became available by Lord Percy's Brigade. The first detachment of boats returned with the picquets of the 2nd and 3rd Brigades, the 10th Regiment, and 200 men of the 64th. The Marines of the Squadron were also landed, so that Charlestown Neck was occupied in considerable force, H.M.S. *Somerset* covered the crossing of the troops, and her guns were ready to flank any attack on the Neck.

The British casualties were heavy on this unfortunate day - 68 killed, 167 wounded and 22 missing, not including the officers, who had 17 wounded (2 mortally). The Marines suffered by far the most heavily of all. Their "butcher's bill" amounted to 3 officers wounded, and of other ranks 31 killed, 38 wounded and 2 missing.

The 4th Regiment came next with 2 officers wounded (1 mortally) and of other ranks 7 killed, 25 wounded and 8 missing. There is nothing in the various reports and narratives of the fighting which throws any light upon this, but at a guess it may be surmised that the reason for the heavy losses of the Marines was the fact that they took on as rear-guard in the neighbourhood of Cambridge, where the fighting seems to have been the fiercest, and where probably they had to cover the change of direction of the main body to Charlestown Neck, almost at right angles to the previous line of retreat.

Notes:-
1. "The Day of Concord and Lexington." By Allen French (Boston, 1925). "A British Fusilier in Revolutionary Boston." Diary of Lieut. Frederick Mackenzie, Adjt. Royal Welch Fusiliers, Jan. 5th to April 30th, 1775. Edited by Allen French (Cambridge, Harvard University Press, 1926).
2. "The Day of Lexington and Concord."
3. "The Stranger in America" (C. W. Janson, 1807).
4. "A British Fusilier."
5. Vide Map of Boston and Environs in "Britain's Sea Soldiers," Vol 1, facing page 152.
6. Jeremy Belknap. Journal Massachussetts Hist. Society, IV.
7. "A British Fusilier."
8. "Diary of Lieut. John Barker, King's Own Regiment."
9. General Gage's Report.
10. "The Day of Concord and Lexington "; Minute Men - Men to be ready at a moment's warning.
11. "When the Governor's Guard of the Connecticut Militia came in late April to the siege of Boston, there were in it two young men, Ralph Earl and Amos Doolittle. In some interval of their three weeks' stay on duty they went to Lexington and Concord, with the purpose of producing a set of engravings presenting the more important events of the 19th. On that trip, Earl, being a budding portrait painter, made sketches of his backgrounds; and Doolittle, the engraver, since his friend was not particularly skilful in drawing the human figure, posed as lay figure . . . From the four finished drawings Doolittle made his engravings, which were sold in New Haven in the following December for six shillings the set plain, eight shillings coloured. The originals are now among the rarest of American engravings, and fetch a high price because of their historic interest . . . There is nothing romantic in their composition. No artistic licence is taken . . . and not a little because of the technical crudity . . . they speak for themselves ... Both the artists were only 21."-The Day of Concord and Lexington.
12. Martha Moulton's petition is found in Frothingham's "Siege of Boston."
13. Ensign Henry De Berniere: "General Gage's Instructions, etc., 1779."
14. "A British Fusilier."
15. Ibid.

Note.- The print on page 55 "A View of the Town of Concord" - is a copy by Colonel C. Field of the rare original by Amos Doolittle, vide Note 11.

FROM A CONTEMPORARY PORTRAIT LENT BY COLONEL C. FIELD.

MAJOR JOHN PITCAIRN.

This Officer's career is noted in Chapter XI. of "Britain's Sea Soldiers," by Colonel C. Field, and on pp. 53 et seq. and 269 of the "Records of the Royal Marines."

DEFENCE OF BOSTON, 1775-6.

Handbill circulated from the American lines to induce British soldiers to desert and endeavouring to seduce our men from their duty.

PROSPECT HILL.

I.	Seven Dollars a month.
II.	Fresh Provisions, and in plenty.
III.	Health.
IV.	Freedom, Ease, Affluence, and a good Farm.

BUNKER'S HILL.

I.	Three Pence a day.
II.	Rotten Salt Pork.
III.	The Scurvy.
IV.	Slavery, Beggary and Want.

Prospect Hill was the centre of the American lines opposed to Charlestown Neck, then defended by British works on Bunker's Hill.

On the back of the handbill was an "Address to the Soldiers," purporting to come from "An Old Soldier," and beginning:-

"Gentlemen,

You are about to embark for America to compel your fellow subjects there to submit to *Popery and Slavery*"

THE ROYAL MARINE BATTALIONS IN NORTH AMERICA.

AUTHORITIES: Gillespie's "History of the Royal Marine Forces;" Fortecues "History of the British Army;" Letter Books, Portsmouth and Chatham Divisions: Plymouth Divisional Orders; Order Books of the Marine Battalion in MSS. at Eastney; "Britain' Sea Soldiers," Vol. 1.

The preparation and adventures of these Battalions, which brought such renown to the Corps, may be of interest to the Corps of the present day. Comparison with the Battalions of more modern times shows how history generally repeats itself.

Owing to the incapacity and obstinacy of the English Ministry, together with their unwise imposition of Taxes on the American Colonies, matters were fast coming to a head in 1774 and the Colonies were on the verge of rebellion. The first record we have is an Admiralty letter dated 10th October, 1774 to the Divisions: "As it is possible that tents, kettles and camp equipage may be ordered to accompany the party of Marines intended to proceed to N. America, I shall be obliged if you will send me an account by return of post what articles of each sort there are in store and whether they are in a proper condition for use." (Signed) Geo. Jackson, D.S.

In N. America the Headquarters of the British Army, under Gen. Gage, was at Boston, where he had a considerable force; to this was attached a body of Marines under Major Pitcairn. The Naval Squadron was commanded by Vice-Admiral Graves.

This Marine detachment appears to have been drawn from the ships on the station as several of the officers shortly before are shown as afloat.

The strength is not known, but probably about 4 Companies of 60 each (see later).

Meanwhile drafts were being got ready in England. On 21st January, 1775, the Admiralty notified that a reinforcement of 2 Majors, 10 Capts., 27 Subalterns, 28 Sgts., 25 Cpls., 29 Drs., and 600 Privates were to be sent to Vice-Admiral Graves in N. America as soon as transports could be got ready to receive them.

Portsmouth were to send Major Tupper and Adjutant Fielding with 3 Coys. consisting of 3 Capts., 6 Subalterns, 6 Sgts., 6 C pls., 6 Drs., and 180 Ptes. Plymouth sent Major Short and Adjutant Waller with 6 Coys., consisting of 6 Capts., 12 Subalterns, 2 Sgts., 12 Cpls. 12 Drs., and 360 Ptes. Chatham sent I Coy. of 1 Capt., 2 Subalterns, 2 Sgts., 2 Cpls., and 2 Drs and 60 Ptes. Also 7 Subalterns, 8 Sgts., and 5 Cpls., were sent by Portsmouth and Plymouth for the companies already in America.

If there were insufficient men at H.Q. the S.N.O.s at the Ports were ordered, on the 25th Jan., to disembark the numbers necessary from the harbour ships; Portsmouth drew as many as 130 Ptes from this source and Plymouth Division probably the same. (c.f. 11th Bn. in 1921). Chatham was evidently cleared out of men as it drew from the Harbour ships after the Draft had sailed.

At the end of January the Majors and Adjutants were sent to the Admiralty to receive instructions, and on 2nd Feb., 1775, important orders were issued. Portsmouth and Plymouth were ordered to "send the Colours of your Division to Boston with the Marines and to acquaint you that they will be replaced with new ones." Chatham, Portsmouth and probably Plymouth were ordered to send 60 Grenadier Caps with this detachment so that the formation of Grenadier Companies was evidently contemplated. (Samples of these caps and of the L.I. caps can be seen in the Officers Mess at Eastney).

Provision was made in the Transports for women to accompany the draft: Chatham provided 6 and 4 for detachments already there, Portsmouth provided 18 and 6 for detachments already there, and Plymouth provided 36 and 10 for detachments already there.

From this it seems that companies were allowed six each. It must be remembered that these women performed the duties of medical orderlies as well as doing the laundry and some of the cooking.

The Captain of one of the light Companies (the Hon., J. Maitland) seems to have been amember of Parliament as he could not sail at the same time as the draft. He signally distinguished himself later at Savannah in 1779 in command of a Light Infantry Battalion of the Army.

From the Plymouth orders of 8 Feb., 1775, we learn that the kit taken was as follows:- Officers to have long leather gaiters with Hessian tops (as pattern) except to have buttons Instead of springs, and also with proper accoutrements.
Men to have following Kit:-
4 good white shirts
4 good pr. of Stockings white (2 pr. worsted)
1 Cheque Shirt
3 pr. good shoes
1 pr. Long Gaiters with Hussar Tops
1 Pr. Short
2 pr. good Prussian Drab Drawers
1 Brush, Wire, Picker, Turnkey, etc.
1 set Uniform Shoe and Knee Buckles
1 Knapsack each (which are arriving in Transport)
2 Black Manchester Velvet Stocks, Buckles for Grenadiers, Clasps for Bn companies.
Sea Kit:-
1 Old Hat
1 Jacket, etc.

On the 24th March, 1775, Plymouth orders state, "They will muster at 5.30 for muster master parade and will march off parade (the old parade in the Barbican) at 5.30 a.m. tomorrow."

They arrived at Boston on 20th May, 1775.

In the meantime events had been hurrying on in America.

On the 5th Sept. 1774., the Americans held a Congress, but the proposals they put forward were rejected by the English Ministry, Gage therefore took steps to protect Boston; he fortified the Neck, leading to the Dorchester Heights on which it stood, and seized the Provincial Arsenal at Cambridge, and at Charlestown on the other side of the harbour.

Early in the New Year, Gage obtained information that the Americans were collecting a quantity of Military stores at Concord, and he determined to seize them.

On the 26th Feb., a small force under Major Pitcairn came into collision with the Militia, but without serious result.

On the 18th April, General Gage despatched a force composed of the Grenadier and Light infantry companies, under Lt. - Col. Smith and Major, Pitcairn, to destroy the stores at Concord. The force proceeded up the Charles River, disembarked at Phipps Farm, and advanced on Concord. The Militia had been roused by Paul Revere and had assembled at Lexington at 5 a.m. Six Companies of Light Infantry under Pitcairn had been detached to hold the bridges beyond Lexington, whilst the remainder went on and destroyed the stores at Concord; the Militia attacked the Light Infantry and the detachment fell back and retreated to Lexington.

On the 19th, Brigadier Lord Percy was sent with 10 Companies and a body of Marines to help Smith's force and arrived at Lexington; they had two field pieces which materially helped in keeping the Americans off. Pitcairn's horse was wounded. The Americans in large numbers had assembled on the route of advance to harass the retreat, but Lord Percy retired by a different road, via Charlestown, and reached the heights of Bunker's Hill about 8 p.m. Nicholas says that the Marines of the Fleet, under Lt.-Col. Johnston, were landed to cover the passage of the troops from Charlestown, which was also covered by the guns of H.M.S. *Somerset*. Casualties were 65 killed and 270 wounded. Major Pitcairn's Detachment was attached to Lord Percy's Brigade and, on the arrival of the reinforcements, "The C.O. finds it necessary for the good of the service to form the whole under his command into two Battalions." H.Q. Companies at this time were 1 Capt., 2 Subs., 3 Sgts., 3 Cpls., 2 Drs., and 50 Privates and so presumably this was followed.

The Battalion staffs were: -

	1st Bn.	2nd Bn.
C.O.,	Major Short	Major Tupper
Adjt.,	Lt. J. Waller	Lt. J. Fielding

Q.M.   Lt. J. Pitcairn   Lt. Thos. Smith
Superintending Adjt. and Deputy Paymaster-Capt. D. Johnston, 2nd Bn.

The Grenadier Coys. were commanded by: -
1st Bn. Capt. T. Averne, afterwards C.O. of the Grenadiers of the Army (see later) and later Commandant at Portsmouth.
2nd Bn. Capt. Geo. Logan, killed at Bunkers Hill.
Light Companies.
1st Bn., Capt. W. Souter, afterwards Commandant at Plymouth and later D.A.G.
2nd Bn., Capt. A. Campbell, killed at Bunker's Hill.

The Americans after the affair at Concord, invested Boston and gradually closed on the town; General Gage determined to attack the Dorchester Heights to the South of the town but, on the morning of the 17th June, the Americans were seen building a redoubt and breastwork on the hill known. as Bunker's Hill, or rather Breed's Hill, at the end of the ridge above the town of Charlestown on the opposite side of the harbour. At dawn, H.M.S. *Lively* bombarded Charlestown. General Gage at once issued the following Morning Order: -

General Morning Order 17th June, 1775.
The 10 Eldest Companies of Grenadiers and 10 eldest companies of Light Infantry (exclusive of regiments lately landed), the 5th and 38th Regiments to parade at 11.30 a.m., with arms, Ammunition, Blankets and Provisions cooked, and march by files to the Long Wharf; - The 52nd and 43rd, with remaining Companies of Grenadiers and Light Infantry to parade at the same time with same directions and march to the North Battery: - The 47th and 1 Bn. Marines will also march as above directed to the same Battery, after the rest are embarked, and be ready to embark when ordered. Rest of troops to be kept in readiness to march at a moment's warning. 1 Subaltern, 1 Sergt., 1 Corp!. 1 Dr., and 20 Ptes. to be left by each Corps for the security of respective encampments.

The Order of Battle was: -

C.-in-C. Gen. Howe
Maj.-Gen . Burgoyne

1st Brigade	2nd Brigade
Brig.-Gen. Lord Percy	Brig.-Gen. Pigot
23rd	38th
59th	1/Marines
44th	47th
4th	10th

4th Brigade
Brig.-Gen. Jones
18th & 65th
49th

2/Marines
40th

Maj.-Gen. Clinton

3rd Brigade	5th Brigade
Brig.-Gen. Grant	Brig.-Gen. Robertson
43rd	5th
52nd	45th
22nd	63rd
	35th

Note. - Fortescue says that the Grenadiers and Light Inf. Companies were drawn from 4th, 10th, 18th, 22nd, 23rd, 35th, 59th, 63rd and 65th. According to the above order the Grenadiers and L.I. Coys. of 2./Marines must have completed the ten companies, because we know that these companies of the 1st Bn., were with their own Battalion.

For the interesting personal narratives of officers who were present, see B.S.S. Vol. 1; the following is a purely tactical account from the History of the British Army (Fortescue) and Gillespie's History of the Marines.

The Americans had actually placed their redoubt on Breed's Hill, which was just above Charlestown, on the end of the Bunker's Hill Ridge. It consisted of a strong redoubt on the summit with a line of trenches from the redoubt to the water on the North Side. The British could have landed anywhere to take the trenches in rear, or even on the Charlestown Neck itself, but instead a more or less frontal attack was made.

The Grenadier and Light Companies under Gen. Howe, with the 5th and 38th Regts., under Gen. Pigot, landed on the extreme east point of the Charlestown peninsula, under the fire of the ships which had opened on the entrenchments at daylight. The Generals, after a reconnaissance, asked for two more Battalions. The 52nd and 43rd Regts. with 6 more companies of Grenadiers and L.I. were disembarked. The attackers were drawn up in 3 lines; the left wing, under Howe, in column of Battalions formed of the Grenadiers, 5th and 52nd ; the Right Wing, under Pigot, formed of the L.I. Companies, the 38th and 43rd.

They were covered by the fire of 8 guns and Howitzers, which was ineffectual as the wrong ammunition had been sent over. The day was very hot, the grass was up to the men's Knees and the ground was broken by a succession of fences. The men were carrying their Knapsacks and 3 days' provisions.

The infantry advanced, and during this advance of 600 yards the columns deployed. The L.I. companies were directed against the left of the Americans with a view to outflanking them; during the advance the left wing was galled by fire from the village of Charlestown, but that place was quickly set on Fire by a Battery at Boston, which had been built by the Seamen and Marines of the Fleet and was called the Admiral's Battery and which mounted Six 24 prs., and was manned by the R. Artillery. The smoke of the burning town was driven into the eyes of the attackers. Not a shot was fired by the enemy until the troops nearly reached the entrenchments, when a tremendous and effective fire was opened which staggered the attackers; the American Riflemen picked off the British Officers. Howe rallied the troops and led them to a similar attack - from left to right – Grenadiers, 52nd, 43rd, 5th and L.I. They were again swept down and fell back with heavy loss. Howe ordered the packs to be thrown off and the bayonet to be used; he abandoned the attack on the left flank and directed all his force on to the redoubt and breastwork.

The 1/Marines and 47th had now arrived with Gen. Clinton; as Gillespie says "Having been formed in two lines they advanced with slow but steady steps to the conflict, Majors Pitcairn, Short, and Tupper led the Corps." The advance was covered by fire from the ships and batteries. The British advanced without firing a shot, and the Americans reserved their fire; the last volley mortally wounded Major Pitcairn who died shortly after in the arms of his son. Major Short, commanding the Battalion was also killed, but the Americans shrunk from meeting the bayonets and were driven down and across the neck of Charlestown, where they were harrassed by the fire of H.M.S. *Glasgow* and suffered heavily.

Lt. and Adjt. Waller, 1/Marines, says that 2 companies of 1/Marines and part of the 47th were the first to cross the breastworks. The troops on the hill were reinforced the next morning by the 2/Marines and 4 Line Regts., with a company of Artillery, entrenchments were thrown up on the neck, the troops being encamped on the hill.

The British Casualties were heavy:- 1 Lt.-Col. 2 Majors, 7 Capts., and 9 Subalterns were killed, including 2 Majors, 2 Capts., and 3 Subalterns of Marines. 70 Officers were wounded of whom 6 were Marines. The Grenadier and L.I. Companies of 2 Marines lost 2 killed and 3 wounded out of 6 officers. Other Ranks casualties were 207 killed (22 Marines) 758 wounded (87 Marines). Major Tupper was mentioned in dispatches.

On 19th June the C.-in.-C. published the following order, "The C.-in-C. returns his most grateful thanks to Maj.-Gen. Howe for the extraordinary exertion of his military abilities on 17th inst. He returns thanks to Maj.-Gen. Clinton and Brigadier Pigot for the share they took in the success of the day as well as . . . . Major Tupper . . . . and the rest of the officers and soldiers who by remarkable efforts of courage and gallantry overcame every disadvantage and drove the rebels from the redoubt and strong-holds on the heights of Charlestown and gained a complete victory."

From Orders at H.Q. ordering subalterns to embark, the casualties were evidently soon made good; and on 16th July orders were issued for Lt.-Col. Gauntlett to proceed to Boston to take over command, but he had already left for Ireland, where he had been detailed for recruiting duty and could not be got hold of. This officer died when 2nd Commandant at Portsmouth.

During the following months they must have drawn on the ships for reinforcements, as, on 15th

November, a list was sent to the Divisions of N.C.O.s and Men who were serving ashore from 17th June to 9th October 1775.

After Bunker's Hill, the Americans set to work to fortify themselves on the Dorchester Heights to the South of the town and mounted guns there, so that Boston was isolated from the Mainland. The garrison remained passively on the defensive, the 1/Marines were certainly left in Charlestown, and Gillespie says that during the winter of 1775-76, the Marines were in tents on Bunker's Hill. The position was most difficult; they were cut off from communication with the Continent and could get no supplies. Storeships arrived slowly and several were intercepted by the enemy, and in 1776, we find orders from the Admiralty that armed guards of Marines, generally of 1 officer and 20 men, were put on board Transports with stores to protect them from the Rebel cruisers. (c.f. the same work of the Corps in 1914-18).

A Detachment of Marines was sent to Savannah under escort of an armed ship to collect supplies, but there was a fight; 7 laden ships were burnt and the party returned to Boston.

At the beginning of March, American Batteries on Dorchester Heights and at Phipps Farm, commenced a severe bombardment and an attack on Dorchester Heights ordered for the 5th March was cancelled owing to the weather.

General Howe had succeeded General Gage in command, and, in the middle of March, the combined effects of hunger and the bombardment determined them to evacuate the town; the embarkation was carried out on 17th.

The Marines were embarked in the Grand Duchess of Russia, 200 in the Centurion and 200 in the Chatham and Renown and the Army sailed for Halifax, Nova Scotia, where they landed early in April the strength of the Force being 9000 effectives. The Marines were told off to garrison the place. The Battalions were re-organised, the 1st under Col. Collins and the 2nd under Major Tupper.

The Grenadier Companies under Capt. Averne accompanied General Howe in his expedition as follows: -

General Howe had a plan of campaign to seize New York and by an advance up the Hudson River, to join hands with the forces from Canada, and so cut off the New England States; he was however diverted to Philadelphia. He embarked in the first days of July and got away from Halifax on 23rd. On 31st he was off Delaware Bay, but on the advice of the Naval Authorities, he went on to Chesapeake Bay and disembarked his troops on 25th August at the head of the Elk River (only 13 miles from Delaware Bay) and then advanced on Philadelphia.

The Armies came into collision on the 3rd September near Wilmington; the Americans were assembled at Brandy Wine Creek, barring the road to Philadelphia. Washington was strongly posted with his left on a Cliff, the centre at Chad's Ford and the right up stream in thick wooded country. Although Howe was inferior in numbers, he decided to turn their right flank; Gen Knyphausen attacked the centre, Gen. Cornwallis, whose force included the 2 Bns. of Grenadiers, of which the two Marine Companies formed part, attacked the American right after a march of 18 miles; they were formed in 2 lines, 8 Bns. in the first line, 7 in the second and 4 in reserve. Washington was driven off, retreated to Chester and Philadelphia was occupied.

In order to secure the communications of the Army it was necessary to clear the Delaware River. The Americans had sent the Delaware, 32 guns. with gallies etc., to harass the batteries guarding the town; she anchored within 500 yards, and as the tide fell the British Field guns caused her to strike her Colours and she was taken possession of by Capt. Averne and the Marine Grenadiers.

Admiral Lord Howe then tried to enter the river with the Fleet, but owing to the enemy batteries, we had to anchor between Reedy Island and Newcastle on 8th October. The Americans were holding Batteries at Mud Fort, near the junction of the River Schuykill, and at Red Bank opposite on the New Jersey shore and had sunk chevaux de frise in the river.

Till the river was cleared, the Army supplies had to come overland from the Chesapeake River. The enemy were first driven from a post, called Billinghurst and then, in conjunction with fire on the Mud Fort from guns on the Pennsylvania bank, the Auguste, 64, and Merlin sloop attacked Red Bank; both ran aground and were destroyed by fire Capt. Barclay (afterwards D.A.G.) was the Marine Officer of the Augusta.

The Hessians, under Von Donop, also attacked Red Bank on 22nd October and were repulsed with heavy losses. Guns were then established at Providence Island and, under cover of their fire on the 18th November, the ships attacked various points of the Mud Fort and, after a long and destructive cannonade, the enemy deserted it in the night. The Army then occupied Red Bank and the enemy withdrew after partly destroying the works, but left their Artillery and set fire to some of their vessels; the navigation was thus opened for the supply of the Army. We need not follow the Army any further.

Reverting to the Battalions in garrison at Halifax. The Admiralty forwarded a return to the Divisions, on the 12th June, 1776, showing the Marines who had been transferred from H.M.S. *Somerset* and *Glasgow*, with a report from Col. Collins, the Commanding Officer, saving that he was keeping some of his invalids for garrison duty and sending the rest to England in the Glasgow. We learn incidentally of a great hardship; apparently N.C.O.s so invalided had to revert to the ranks when sent on board, as others were appointed in lieu; Col. Collins asked that they might be reinstated on reaching H.Q.s. The Adjutants also had a moan because, when at H.Q. they received a certain amount of the Levy Money for recruits, which of course, they could not get while abroad; and both of them were really H.Q. Adjutants.

On the 12th July, Major Tupper was given leave to England and did not rejoin. He was succeeded by Major Souter.

In September, 1775, Captains of companies were given 1/- a day Contingent Allowance for paying their companies. Whilst at Halifax this was increased to 1/6 for providing necessaries, repairing arms, and burying the dead! (Contingent Allowance was not abolished until 1919).

Apparently on the 19th December, 1776, the Light infantry Companies had a skirmish for which they were commended by the G.O.C.

A letter from Major Souter is interesting as it shows that promotion of N.C.O.s was made on the same principles as now. He writes on the 21st December, 1770. "that he understands many of the Corporals serving in the Battalions have been appointed Sergeants in their respective Divisions at home, and asks that when such promotions take place he may be informed."

A Board Order was issued on the 1st January, 1777, ordering the two Battalions to be consolidated into one on the 2nd of April.
"Companies to consist of I Capt., 4 Subalterns, 5 Sergts'. 5 Cpls., 4 Drs., and 100 Private men each, 11 conformable to the present establishment of the Corps, together with the following Field Officers and Staff, 2 Majors, 1 Adjutant, 1 Quartermaster, 1 Chaplain, 1 Surgeon and 1 Surgeon's Mate. The balance to be embarked in H.M. Ships short of complement; the officers to be sent to England.
      By order of their Lordships,
       (Sgd.) Philip Stephens."

Gillespie gives the full list of officers (p. 232). Detachments were trained at the guns in the Batteries which defended the harbour and the command was given to Lieut. Tantum, thus again we find a Marine Battalion defending a Naval Base.

On the 25th August the Marine Battalion was struck off the strength of the Garrison and embarked on the 1st September for England.

On the 11th November the Commandant at Portsmouth reported that the first part of the Battalion had arrived (the remainder landed on the 21st November). The accounts were to be settled before they rejoined their Divisions or were embarked, and this was to be completed by the 24th November.

Plymouth, however, started panicking to get their Corporals and men recommended for promotion sent round, and eventually these and the officers were sent to Plymouth, the remainder being retained at Portsmouth for embarkation;- no furloughs in those days. The officers found themselves first for sea; Chatham officers and men were sent to Chatham.

On the 17th January, 1779 the Commandant at Portsmouth was ordered to report the number of men of the Battalion still remaining at Portsmouth, and they were ordered to be embarked in the Royal George, flagship of Admiral Rodney in his great battles on the West Indies in 1781 and 1782.

73

THE ROYAL MARINE BATTALIONS IN NORTH AMERICA, 1775 - 1778.
By General Sir H. E. Blumberg, K.C.B.

PART II.

Since writing the first part of this story, Colonel Field has most kindly lent me some of his papers, which enable the account to be amplified in some particulars.

From the Diary of an officer (Lieut. Barker) of the 4th King's Own Regiment we learn that Major Pitcairne's detachment consisted of 460 men, and that they arrived at Boston in the Asia, Boyne and Somerset men-of-war, the first ship, the Asia, arriving on 4th December, 1774, with Major Pitcairne on board, but there is no word of whether they came from England, or had been collected from ships on the station. From some American papers Pitcairne seems to have been in Boston before, and to have been well known. One of the Captains was Capt. Souter, who eventually brought the Battalion home in 1778. As late as 26th December Lieut. Barker says that the Admiral would not land them, but the reason he gives is strange, viz.; ". . . .as he wants to have the advantage of victualling them." Any rate, they were landed during the next few days, because on the 30th December, 1774, they were detailed with the 43rd Regiment to defend the passage between Barton Point and Charlestown Ferry.

On 20th January Major Pitcairne's Battalion was ordered to do duty with the 1st Brigade, under Lord Percy; up till then they had not done duty, because they had "no watchcoats or leggings."

In addition to the account of the fighting at Lexington and Concord, of which Colonel Field has given such an excellent account on pp. 68-70 of the Globe and Laurel Records (in one point Colonel Field is in error, as he speaks of the presence of the 2nd Battalion of Marines, but as we have seen, they were not formed till after the arrival of the draft in May, an article has recently appeared (March 1931) in the New York *Herald Tribune*, by Mr. R. G. Adams, from which we learn that General Gage's papers have been purchased by an American, and are now in the Clements Library of the University of Michigan. Among these papers are General Gage's instructions to Colonel Smith as to the guns, ammunition and stores to be destroyed at Concord, and their location, which show that his intelligence service must have been very good. Whilst for us Marines still more interesting is Major Pitcairne's own report of the affair, which is as follows: -

"Sir,

As you are anxious to know the particulars that happened near and at Lexington on the 19th inst., agreeable to your desire, I will in as concise a manner as possible state the facts, for my time at present is so much employ'd as to prevent a more particular narrative of the occurrences of that day.

"Six companies of Light Infantry were detached by Lt.-Col: Smith to take possession of the Two Bridges on the other side of Concord. Near three in the morning, when we were advanced within about Two Miles of Lexington, Intelligence was received that about 500 men in arms were assembled, determined to oppose the King's Troops and retard them in their march. On this intelligence I mounted my horse and galloped up to the Six Light Companies. When I arrived at the head of the advanced company, two officers came and informed me that a man of the Rebels advanced from those that were there assembled, had presented a musquet and attempted to shoot them, but the piece flashed in the pan. On this I gave direction to the troops to move forward, but on no account to fire, or even attempt it without orders; when I arrived at the end of the village I observed drawn up on a Green near 200 of the Rebels; when I came within about one hundred yards of them they began to file off towards some stone walls on our right flank. The Light Infantry observing this ran after them. I instantly called out to the soldiers not to fire, but to surround and disarm them, and after several repetitions of those positive orders, not to fire, etc., some of the Rebels who had jumped over the wall fired four or five shot at the soldiers, which wounded a man in the Tenth and my horse was wounded in two places. From some quarter or other, and at the same time, several shott were fired from a Meeting House on our left. Upon this, without any order or regularity the Light Infantry began a scattered fire and continued in that situation for some little time, contrary to the repeated orders of me and the officers that were present. It will be needless to mention what happened after, as I suppose Colo: Smith hath given a particular account of it.

I am, Sir,
Your most obedient humble servant,
JOHN PITCAIRN.

Boston Camp, 26th April, 1775."

Coming to a later date, Lieut. Barker says the first portion of the reinforcing draft arrived on 15th May and the remainder on 23rd, when the two Battalions as we know were formed, with their Grenadier and Light companies, by an order dated 20th May, 1775.

In addition to the details already given as to Battle of Bunker's Hill I am enabled to add the following:-

In Hist. MS. Commission XIV Report Vol. Appendix, Part I, page 2, there is an interesting account of the nature of the ground on Bunker's Hill, over which our troops had to attack: "The ground on the peninsula is the strongest I can conceive for the kind of defence the rebels made, which is exactly like that of the Indians, viz., small enclosures, with narrow lanes bounded by stone fences, small heights which command the passes, proper trees to fire from, and very rough and marshy ground for troops to get over. The rebels defended well and inch by inch."

This writer says that floating batteries had been ordered to go close in and prevent rebels moving reinforcements over the Neck, but that they did not go close enough and withdrew too early, and that the rebels consequently had been reinforced to a strength of 7,000 men.

The papers do not add much to our knowledge of the actual battle of Bunkers Hill, except that the 17th June was a Saturday, and that after the Americans withdrew from the redoubt they retired over Charlestown Neck to a position on a hill on the road to Cambridge (see Col. Field's map), about two miles off, called Prospect Hill, which they commenced to fortify, and that the 2nd Bn. of Marines and the 63rd Regiment were sent over to Charlestown on the night of the 17th, and not the 18th, as I stated.

Col. Field tells me that contrary to legend, he has recently learnt from Major Tupper's official report to the Admiralty that Major Pitcairne "was wounded a few minutes before the attack was made on the Redoubt, and he died about two or three hours after." Major Pitcairne belonged to the Plymouth Division.

On Sunday the 18th there were apparently skirmishes, but the rebels on each occasion were driven off by the Artillery, and the British troops finished the entrenchment guarding the neck, "extending from the left of the hill quite to the waterside on the right." The tents were sent over and the troops encamped, except the Light companies, who had to guard the works. On 23rd June the 2nd Bn. returned to Boston. No further details have come to light.

So ends the story of these Battalions, so typical of the Marine Corps.

COXSWAIN OF THE MARINE BOAT, 1781.

22nd May, 1781. David Pring, Pte., in the 123rd Company, having been Quarter Master in the Navy several years, and thereby understanding the Steering and Management of a Vessel, is appointed Coxswain of the Marine Boat, which being lately repaired, painted and put in good order, he is hereby directed to take charge of, with her sails, oars, awning and other furniture belonging, under the Inspection of the Quarter-Master, an Inventory of which he is to sign, a chain and lock being provided; he is to keep the boat constantly moored, and in such clean proper order, as to be fit for Service on the shortest notice, and no person is to employ or make use of the Marine Boat, but by Permission first obtain'd thro' the Quarter-Master, and in order to exert a proper Command over the Boat's Crew, and encouragement to behave well, he to act as Lance Corporal with an allowance of one shilling a week out of the Musical Fund till further orders.

Order Book, Chatham Division

THE CHATHAM MARINE BAND, 1781

"8th October, 1781. In order that the Marine Musical Band may not hereafter be looked upon in the light of common Fidlers, and permitted at the desire of indifferent persons to play in that capacity at ordinary and common Balls and Concerts, it is directed that in future, the Band or any part of them, shall not have liberty to play anywhere out of Barracks, but where the Divisional Business calls upon them, or where Government may take any Concern."

Order Book, Chatham Division

AN UNPOPULAR ORDER, 1782.

"17 August, 1782.

As it will greatly conduce to the good order and happiness of the Inhabitants of the Barracks that Military good example of attention in the Officers who lodge there be adhered to by keeping proper and reasonable Hours, in repairing thither regularly in the Evenings. It is therefore earnestly wished and expected, if any Officer who lodges in the Barracks is engaged abroad for the Evening, that he will be pleased to repair to his Appartment at Ten o'clock, or at furthest half an hour thereafter. For as the Commanding Officer will endeavour to carry on the several Duties at the Marine Barracks, so as in a little time to give the Young Officers, in as pleasing a method as can be devised, a small idea of Garrison Modes. He is therefore resolved that at half an hour after Ten, or at furthest a Quarter before Eleven o'clock every Night, the Keys of all the Gates and Doors shall be brought to him by the Serjeant of the Guard, and not returned to the Guard till full Daylight next Morning, unless some very particular or extraordinary business may require any of the Gates or Doors to be opened in the intermediate time."

General MacKenzie, who issued the above order, could not have had much experience of Barrack routine, as in his earlier days there were practically no Barracks in existence, the custom being to billet soldiers or Marines about the districts where they were quartered. The Marine Barracks at Chatham were only opened and occupied on 3rd Sept., 1779.

On the 28th a respectfully worded Representation was prepared for submission to General McKenzie, who however, flatly refused to receive it. The matter was eventually submitted to the Lords of the Admiralty, who apparently considered that the order was unreasonable, and seem to have indicated their opinion to General McKenzie, since he shortly afterwards issued various modifications of his original order.

Order Book, Chatham Division.

REPENTANCE AND FORGIVENESS.
By Colonel C. Field.

The following two extracts from the Order Book of the Chatham Division in 1782 strike one nowadays as being somewhat remarkable :-

"*8th November*, 1782. 28th Company, Edw: Jones, Private, who lately was reduced from being Serjeant, for his Profligate and Unmilitary Conduct, and having shewn a Compunctive Remorse for his bad behaviour, and the Corps of Serjeants, whom the C:O: greatly respects, having by letter to him petitioned the Forgiveness and Restoration of the said Jones to his former Station; In Compliance with their request he is reinstated in his former Rank and appointed Serjeant to the 28th Company, Commencing Pay as such tomorrow ; at the same time the C:O: wishes this may create in him, and all others, who may have deviated from Military Propriety; such a Return, as may truly mark their Gratitude and prevent their being insidiously and ignorantly led astray by those who can have only Selfish, Poor, Low, Dirty business in View."

21st November, 1782. 147 Co., Robt: Haycroft, Pte. having shewn a Compunctive Remorse for his Unmilitary Conduct, is forgiven the remainder of the Punishment sentenced by his Court-Martial, and restored to the Rank and Pay of Serjeant in the 147th Co:

"Compunctive Remorse," seems to have been what would now be called "a good egg." But it would be interesting to know in what way these old soldiers contrived to "shew" it!

JOHN MURRAY.

JOHN McMURRAY, the founder of the great firm of publishers, was a Scotchman, and like Sir Walter Scott, the son of an Edinburgh writer to The Signet. He was born in Edinburgh on 27th November, 1745. Seventeen years later he obtained a commission in the Royal Marines, but at the age of 23, owing to slowness of promotion, he resigned his commission and bought the bookselling business of Paul Sandby, at 32 Fleet Street, London. He was apparently without any previous training, yet he founded what is now and has long been one of the most famous and fruitful of English publishing houses. Not only so, he narrowly missed having as his partner another young Scotchman, at that time in the Naval Service of his country, who is doubly remembered as the author of almost our solitary nautical epic, and by the melancholy circumstance of his death. There has long been in print the letter in which Lieut. McMurray, of the Marines, invited his friend William Falconer, author of "The Shipwreck," and at that time a purser in the Navy to join him in purchasing and working a bookselling and publishing business in London, for the acquisition of which he himself was then negotiating. The letter dated 16th October, 1768, from Brompton, in Kent, which is a continuation of Chatham, still a chief station of the Royal Marines, is addressed to Falconer, at Dover. It gives, lucidly and tersely, particulars of a contemplated purchase, and describes the character and the promise of the business of William Sandby, of Fleet Street, opposite St. Dunstan's Church, and close to Falcon Court, so called from the sign of the falcon, which had been that of the venerable old printer

PHOTO SUPPLIED BY GENERAL PHOTOGRAPHIC AGENCY, 173-5 FLEET ST., LONDON.

Wynkyn de Worde, the successor of the still more venerable William Caxton. The sum required for the purchase, bound stock included, would not probably be more than £400," and Lieut McMurray added alluringly, "the shop has been long established in the trade, it retains a good many old customers, and I am to be ushered immediately into public notice by the sale of a new edition of 'Lord Lyttelton's Dialogues,' and afterwards by a like edition his history. These works I shall sell by commission, upon a certain profit, without risque; and Mr. Sandby has promised to me always his good offices and recommendation." The young Lieutenant of Marines had confidence in himself, and seems to have known something of the new arena which he was about to enter, since he proceeds to say - "Many blockheads in the trade are making fortunes, and did we not succeed as well as they, I think it must be imputed only to ourselves." Unfortunately for himself, Falconer did not accept his friend's offer, which was of partnership on equal terms. On starting as a bookseller and publisher in Fleet Street, Ex-Lieutenant McMurray dropped the Mc, and called himself simply "Murray." This was a curtailment of surname significant of and due to the keenly anti-scottish feeling then prevalent in London and in England. The popularity of John Wilkes, of the North Briton, the reviler of Scotsmen in general and of Lord Bute in particular, was at its height, and in the year of Lieut. McMurray's offer to Falconer, Boswell is found recording "Dr. Johnson's prejudice against Scotland appeared remarkably strong at that time." One old association, however, of his pre-bibliopolic days the new John Murray, of Fleet Street, cherished so fondly that as memorial of his Lieutenancy of Marines and service afloat, "a ship in full sail" figured in the billheads of his accounts. This founder of the publishing house of Murray was an able energetic, and enterprising man, though perhaps more of a bookseller than a publisher; in old records of the trade there is frequent mention "Mr. Murray," the medical bookseller of Fleet Street. After selling and publishing books in Fleet Street, for a quarter of a century, the first John Murray died in November, 1793, leaving a son, then only fifteen years of age, who was destined to become one of the foremost of British publishers, and to make the name of Murray known wherever English books found and find readers.

"THE EVENING WALK."
PORTRAIT OF CAPTAIN JAMES JUSTICE OF MARINES IN 1792.

The accompanying sketch is traced from one of a large series of portraits etched by John Kay an Edinburgh miniature painter, between 1784 and about 1817. They nearly all represent Scottish notabilities seen in Edinburgh. They are of all sorts and conditions, from dukes to dustmen, and many of them are caricatures. Among them are a considerable number of striking representations of military officers and n.c.o.'s of various regiments, including Fencibles and Volunteers. The details of their uniforms are clear, and have every appearance of being correct, and one would naturally expect this from an artist who as a miniature painter was accustomed to closely study his subject.

These etchings were collected and published in two quarto volumes in 1837, with biographical notes and anecdotes of the persons represented, compiled from material left by Kay, who died in 1826 at the age of 84. Where necessary this was supplemented by the compiler of the work. No details are given as to the military or naval services of Captain James

PORTRAIT OF CAPTAIN JAMES JUSTICE - ETCHED BY JOHN KAY

Justice, except that "He entered the army as an officer in the marine service; served abroad during the American War, and attained the rank of Captain." Neither can I find any mention of him in Nicholas.

He was born in 1755, and was the son of James Justice, who was one of the principal Clerks of the Court of Session, and lived at Justice Hall, near Ugston, in the county of Berwick. "He was above six feet in height and well proportioned. His address was perticularly agreeable and fascinating; and both in appearance and manner he bore no slight resemblance to George IV."

He married a Miss Campbell, but they did not get on well together, and eventually separated. "Shortly after this unfortunate separation, a friend of his, accompanied by an acquaintance went to visit him at Justice Hall. They found the Captain just returned from a solitary stroll in the fields, and a little in dishabile. He apologised for his appearance, and on the stranger being introduced to him, 'O,' said he, in his usual voluble manner, know your father well; not at all like him; no doubt of your mother - but, pshaw! never mind, welcome to Bachelor's Hall -tis Bachelor's Hall now, you know - Mrs. Justice has left me. No matter, she was a good sort of person for all that - a little hot-tempered - only three days after marriage a leg of mutton made to fly at my head; never mind, plenty of wine, eggs, at Bachelor's Hall, we can make ourselves merry!"

Captain Justice was a good amateur actor, a great patron of the drama, and even wrote one or two plays himself.

The picture is interesting, as giving an excellent idea of the uniform of the Corps in 1792. The white facings and anchor buttons are well in evidence. The latter are interesting, as though a "uniform button" is frequently mentioned in Orders, the design upon it is not. The top boots, to judge from other military portraits in the series, were a usual wear of officers at this time, and always as in this case, with the tabs hanging outside.

The lady with Captain Justice is stated to be a "fair one," at one time well known in the beau monde of Prince's Street.

EVACUATION OF NOOTKA SOUND BY THE SPANIARDS.
Extract of a letter from Lieut. Pearce, of the Marines, to His Grace the Duke of Portland* dated Tepic, New Galicia, 200 Leagues to the N.W. of the City of Mexico, April 25th 1795.
* The Home Secretary.

"I have the honour of acquainting your grace that in obedience to your instructions, I proceeded from Monterley to Nootka, in company with Brigadier-General Alava, the officer appointed on the part of the Court of Spain for finally terminating the negotiations relative to that port; where, having satisfied myself respecting the state of the country at the time of the arrival of the Spaniards, preparations were immediately made for dismantling the fort which the Spaniards had erected on an island that guarded the mouth of the harbour, and embarking the ordnance. By the morning of the 28th (? March) all the artillery were embarked, part on board his Catholic majesty's sloop of war Active, and part on board of the San Carlos guardship. Brigadier-General Alava and myself then met, agreeably to our respective instructions, on the place where formerly the British buildings stood, where we signed and exchanged the declaration and counter declaration for restoring those lands to his majesty as agreed upon by the two Courts. After which ceremony I ordered the British flag to be hoisted in token of possession, and the General gave directions for the troops to embark."

From "The Britannic Magazine," 1795.

N.B. - A small British settlement at Nootka Sound on the West Coast of America had been seized by the Spaniards, on the ground that Spaniards, not British, had discovered the country. Pitt replied that the claim to possession rested not on discovery, but on occupation, and prepared to back his argument with a fleet. Failing to get support from France, Spain surrendered completely.

THE FIRST BRITISH SETTLEMENT IN AUSTRALIA.
(By Captain H. S. N. White, R.M.L.I.)
(Reprinted from the "Globe & Laurel" of 1st Dec., 1892).

On the 13th May, 1787, an expedition started from Portsmouth which was destined to have an enormous influence on the future development of our Colonial Empire. Its departure occasioned no excitement; it was not even recognized as a national event in the historical records of the time, and the Annual Register makes no mention of it.

The destination of this important expedition was Botany Bay in New South Wales, or New Holland, as the whole continent of Australia was then termed. Captain Cook had discovered New South Wales in 1770, but it was not till 1783 that any proposal was made to utilise and turn to account the territory on which he had hoisted the English flag, and it is possible that, but for the loss of our American Colonies, the colonisation of the vast continent of Australia might have been deferred to a still later date. The manner in which it was eventually decided to establish a settlement in Australia seems curious to us at the present day, but at that time, and for a long time previous, the work of colonisation was so associated with the employment of convict labour that, when a new colony was projected, the despatch of convicts to its shores formed an indispensable part of the programme. Hitherto most of the convicts had been sent to the American plantations. That place of exile being no longer available, another had to be found and, to empty the crowded gaols, it was decided to transport them to form a settlement in New South Wales. Though this was the ostensible object of the Government, it cannot be doubted that they had other motives beyond the mere removal of convicts, who might well have been sent to some nearer place of banishment, and that they hoped in some measure to redress in Australia the losses of England on the American Continent.

The expeditionary force which left the shores of England, as above stated, in May, 1787, consisted of H.M.S. *Sirius* (commanded by Captain Arthur Phillip, who was to be Governor of

New South Wales), the armed tender Supply, six transports and three store-ships with provisions for two years, farming implements, clothing, etc. The transports carried 775 convicts (of whom about 190 were women)* and each had a detachment of Marines on board, the total strength being 19 officers and 192 men.

The names of the officers were as follows: -

Major-Commandant:
R. Ross (Lieut.-Governor and Judge of the Vice-Admiralty Court).

Captains:	First-Lieutenants (contd.)
J. Campbell,	J. Furzer (Quartermaster),
J. Shea,	J. Poulden,
D. Collins (Judge-Advocate and Secretary to Governor).	J. Johnstone,
	J. M. Shairp,
Captain-Lieutenants:	T. Davey:
J. Meredith,	T. Timmins.
W. Tench.	Second-Lieutenants:
First-Lieutenants	R. Clarke,
G. Johnston (Aide-de-Camp the Governor),	W. Dawes (Officer of Engineers and Artillery),
J. Cresswell,	J. Long (Adjutant),
R. Kellow,	W. Feddy (or Faddy).

That the selection of Marines for this duty was not unpleasing to the Corps generally may be gathered from the following extract from a letter from Major Ross to Mr. Evan Nepean, Under Secretary of the Home Department†: -

"I have now only to add that this is the first instance in which the Corps of Marines has been employed in any way out of the usual line of duty, and as I firmly believe that any part of it being so employed is entirely owing to your friendly wish of drawing the Corps forth from that subordinate obscurity in which it has hitherto moved, - impressed with this belief, permit me to offer you my own as well as the sincerest thanks of the officers of the detachment under my command for the generous opinion you have shown in favour of the Corps, and to assure you that every nerve shall be strained in the faithful and diligent discharge of our duty; and I entertain not a doubt but that the conduct of the whole will be such as will not only do credit to your recommendation, but give satisfaction to the Administration. These much wished for objects obtained, shall then ardently hope that what you once hinted to me might be the consequence will, with your assistance, take place, and that we shall no more return to our original obscurity, 'but become an active Corps of your creation."

With these protestations and promises before us it is difficult to understand the line of conduct adopted by Major Ross and the Marine Officers at Sydney, and the want of success which attended the Marine Garrison generally.

The first point touched at by the expedition was Teneriffe, where, it is recorded, the Marines were allowed a daily ration of one pint of wine apiece. It is interesting to note that they were sent to sea without any supply of "musquet balls," or even paper for making musquet cartridges," and they had no armourers tools to keep small arms in repair. The want of cartridges was to some extent remedied at the next port of touch, Rio Janeiro, where 10,000 were purchased for the arsenal. No soap was provided for the convicts, and they had to borrow it from the Marines, who were repaid out of a supply bought at Rio. The only other port touched at was the Cape and, after a voyage of just over eight months all the ships were at anchor in Botany Bay on the 20th January, 1788, one or two having arrived on the 18th. Only one Marine died on the way out. Forty women, wives of the Marines, were allowed to go out with the garrison.

The stay at Botany Bay was not long, Captain Phillip finding the shores marshy and in other ways unsuitable for a settlement, and on the 26th all the vessels moved to Port Jackson, where Phillip had selected a small bay on the south shore, some five miles from the entrance, at which to commence operations.

The disembarkation at Sydney Cove occupied two days, the Marine encampment being fixed at the head of the cove. Two guards were established, each consisting of two lieutenants and 48 men, under a captain of the day, to preserve public security, while the Provost-Marshal was responsible for the prevention of straggling. Captain Phillip's house was constructed near what are now the grounds of Government House, while at the head of Sydney Cove stretches, at the present day, what is known as the Circular Quay.

On the 7th February, 1788, the various public commissions were read by the Judge-Advocate, the Marines marching with music playing (presumably supplied by the band of the *Sirius*) and colours flying, to an adjoining stretch of ground and, at the conclusion, firing three volleys.

On the 15th February a detachment was sent to Norfolk Island, which had been discovered by Cook, two Marines being amongst the number. In October of the same year eight more marines and an officer were sent there.

Meanwhile barracks were built, consisting of four large buildings for the men and separate huts for the officers. This accommodation was, however, only considered temporary, and the plan of a town was drawn out on a large scale, the principal street being 200 feet wide, and the rest of corresponding proportion. An observatory was established on the point at the west of the bay (subsequently known as Dawes Point) whence Lieutenant Dawes was to observe an expected comet, and various expeditions were made into the interior by Philip accompanied by several officers and men of the Marines.

Finding Sydney Cove unsuited for agriculture, Philip despatched a detachment of one captain,

83

two lieutenants, 25 men and 50 convicts to the upper end of Port Jackson, to cultivate a stretch of land at a place called Rose Hill, the native name being Paramatta, by which name the town there is now known.

In the autumn of 1788 the marines were asked whether, at the end of their three years – for which period they had volunteered - they would remain in the Colony as Settlers. The list sent in contained only nine names, most of these being conditional on the Government affording them some encouragement to remain.

Among the many difficulties with which Phillip had to contend, the most serious was that arising from the want of co-operation on the part of the marines. No instructions had been conveyed to the officers of the Marines for the purpose of ensuring their obedience to the Governor's orders; the consequence being that they were no sooner encamped than they refused to obey any orders outside their ordinary duty, insisting that they would not interfere with the convicts under any circumstances, except as a garrison force. The Judge - Advocate appointed to preside over the courts of civil and criminal jurisdiction was a Captain of Marines without any legal training or experience, while the presiding Judge was in no way qualified to administer justice "according to the laws of England." Thus Phillip's attempts to distribute impartial justice were hampered at the outset, and the law, as administered, was strictly military.

The prime mover in this antagonism of the military to the Governor appears to have been Major Ross. The life evidently did not suit him, for his letters home in the first year are full of complaints of all kinds. "Never," he said, "was a set of people so much upon the parish as this garrison is"; "This country will never answer to settle in"; "If ever able to maintain the people sent here it cannot be less than, probably, a hundred years hence"; "In the whole world there is not a worse country than what we have yet seen of this." In fact, according to Major Ross, there was general discontent in the settlement.

In May, Phillip wrote home that the officers disliked controlling the convicts "except when employed for their own particular service"; not having anticipated it, they thought it a hardship to sit as members of a criminal court. Another grievance was the absence of power in the Governor to "immediately grant lands" to the officers.

There had been a court-martial on one soldier for striking another, and Major Ross put the five officers on the court under arrest "for passing what they call a sentence . . . .of such a nature as . . .tends greatly to subversion of all Military discipline." With five officers under arrest, if a general court-martial were held, only one would be left for duty, and this Phillip considered unpracticable.

Affairs reached a climax in October, 1788, when, at the request of Major Ross, Phillip issued a warrant for a court-martial on an officer for neglect of duty, and contempt and disrespect to Ross. The thirteen senior officers when assembled declared they could not sit as members under Phillip's warrant, being amenable only to the Commissioners of the Admiralty. Phillip ordered a court of enquiry into the particulars of the charge, but was again foiled, the officers refusing to sit after a warrant for a court-martial had already been issued. Shortly afterwards Ross informed the Governor that the offending officer had satisfied him, and Phillip ordered him to return to his duty. The Judge-Advocate appears to have thought that the Marines, being amenable to the Articles of War and the Act for the regulation of the Marine Forces, were not subservient to the Act of Parliament under which Philip governed, though he wrote home that, considering the circumstances, distance from home, etc., he thought they might waive their privilege, and "act under the authority" of the Governor, "throwing themselves with the strong plea of necessity" on the Lords of the Admiralty to procure them "an indemnification for having so acted."

It was not until June, 1789, that the Secretary of State at home dealt seriously with the obstructions which were constantly mentioned in Phillip's despatches, and in the same month fresh troubles were reported.

Phillip had, by the exercise of great tact, secured the services of no less than fifteen criminal courts, but now Captain Campbell refused to sit, and whilst it was unknown whether others would join him, Ross suggested that they might do so, saying "he knew of no Articles of War to compel them" to sit. Accordingly, Phillip ordered a court of enquiry, but the members did not think themselves competent to give an opinion on a private dispute, which appeared to them to involve a point of law." The court was therefore dissolved, and Phillip sent for several of the officers and pointed out the consequences which would follow their refusal to sit on a Criminal Court, and they all assured him they had never doubted its being a part of their duty to so sit after they had heard the Act of Parliament and the Commission read which established the court. Major Ross, however, informed the Governor that some officers still objected to sit so he called for a report of the opinion of each individual officer, when nearly all declared they had thought it their duty ever since they had read the Act of Parliament, which, however, most of them had never seen until after their arrival in the Colony. Captain-Lieutenant G. Johnstone's expressed opinion was as follows: "I do not recollect that the Major asked the officers to join in refusing with Captain Campbell to sit as members of the Criminal Court, but recollect his saying that officers were not to be driven, and believe he wished them to concur with Captain Campbell's refusal; he also called it an oppressive duty."

It was not till February, 1791, that this point was finally settled in a despatch from Mr. Grenville, stating "Military Officers are bound to perform the duties of members of a Criminal Court when they shall be duly summoned for the purpose.

Meanwhile the supplies were exhausted, no fresh store-ships arrived and the gardens were not, as yet, very productive. A watch of twelve convicts was set to prevent robbery of the gardens and orchards with orders, amongst others, to detain any seaman or soldier found straggling "after the taptoo has beat," or who might be found in the convicts huts, and to give information to the nearest guard-house. Ross, while not denying that robberies had been thereby checked, considered that this order put the soldiers under the command of the convicts, and informed the Judge-Advocate that he considered a soldier's being stopped, when not committing any unlawful act, as an insult offered to the Corps, and that they would not suffer themselves to be treated in that manner, or to be controlled by the convicts while they had bayonets in their hands. This instruction was subsequently modified into one ordering that no soldiers were in future to be stopped unless found in a riot or committing an unlawful act, though Phillip pointedly writes in his despatch that "the last sentence respecting the bayonets was never mentioned to me till this business was settled. I should not have been induced to withdraw the order by so pointed a menace, for I should not have thought it could tend to the good of His Majesty's Service."

Ross found fault with others besides the Governor, as may be seen by his arrest of the five officers. Phillip also reports that both the Adjutant and Quartermaster had been under his displeasure, while the Judge-Advocate had applied to resign owing to his treatment by the Lieut. Governor.

Amongst the records is a letter from Phillip in reply to some petulant complaints of Ross, containing the following sentence: - "The time cannot be far distant when a legal inquiry can take place, and all complaints will then be attended to; till then His Majesty's Service requires some little forbearance on your part as well as my own."

That Phillip was forbearing there can be no doubt. A man of indomitable courage, he was also possessed of great self-control, which stood him in good stead throughout the whole of his Governship of New South Wales. He had many difficulties to face which were inevitable owing to the faulty preparations made by the Government for the expedition. In the first place many of the convicts were so old as to be past work. In addition, there were no farmers in the Colony, no mechanics, no skilled workmen, no geologists, no botanists or other scientific men, and no overseers for the convicts, while the health of the settlement was in jeopardy owing to want of proper clothing and anti-scorbutics. These deficiencies, arising from want of proper preparation, were aggravated by the subsequent despatch of convict ships, one after the other, at a time when the settlement was suffering from want of the actual necessaries of life, ships, too, sent out with such a total disregard for human life, that the fevers on board left the few survivors in such a crippled state that, on landing, they had to be kept in hospital among a starving population. With difficulties such as these to struggle with, it was not too much to expect a more cordial co-operation on the part of the garrison.

In June, 1789, a despatch from home announced that the detachment of marines was shortly to be withdrawn, their discontent and desire to return having led to the making arrangements for reliefing them. A corps would be raised for that particular service, and 300 men would be ready to leave home in October, 1790. Any marines wishing to be discharged abroad and settle there were to be encouraged to do so, but the preferable plan, if possible, was that they should be induced to enlist and add strength to the new Corps, receiving a bounty of £3 and their discharge, as well as a grant of land after five years further service - each non-commissioned officer was to receive a grant of 100 acres of land, each private 50 acres.

A later despatch announced that the marines were to return under Major Ross, any volunteers to remain being formed into a company under three Marine officers and incorporated in the New South Wales Corps, the officers to have the ranks of Captain, Lieutenant and Ensign, respectively. Phillip's attempts to form this Company were not successful at first, owing, he says, to the "doubts the men had as to receiving any allowance of spirits and the fear of being obliged to pay for their rations. This difficulty was removed by an injunction from England that the usual ration, except spirits, would be allowed, and no deduction would be made from their pay, the result being that on the arrival of Major Grose with a company of the new Corps in February, 1792, sixty-three marines under Captain-Lieutenant G. Johnston remained behind. This officer did good work in the Colony at a later date.

Amongst the punishments of marines recorded at Sydney is that of Joseph Hunt, who, being found absent from his post "when stationed as a sentinel," was tried by court-martial and sentenced to receive 700 lashes. Six other marines also were executed tor breaking into the spirit stores.

One other act of Major Ross may be mentioned. On the death of Captain Shea, he promoted Lieut. G. Johnston to fill the vacancy, at the same time asking the Governor whether he approved of his giving his own son a commission as Second Lieutenant. The Governor declined to express approbation of the proposal, which, however, Ross carried out, officially presenting his son to Phillip at the same time as the other promoted officers.

The Governor managed at last to get rid of Major Ross by appointing him Commandant of Norfolk Island in March, 1790, in place of Lieutenant King, whom he had sent to England. Ross remained there till October, 1791, and eventually returned to England in December of that year, his place being taken by Major Grose.

Of the other officers, Captain-Lieutenant G. Johnston subsequently became Major in the New South Wales Corps, and became a well-known character in the history of the Colony. In January, 1808, he arrested Governor Bligh of New South Wales, and in May, 1811, he was tried by court-martial for mutiny in so doing and was cashiered. This mild and lenient sentence for such an offence was passed in consideration of the "novel and extraordinary circumstances" which appear to have existed at the time at Sydney, and indeed the whole history of this remarkable case is well worth reading. Johnston returned to the Colony where he lived and died universally respected.

Captain Collins remained at Sydney till 1796, and then returned to England. After waiting many years for a well-deserved promotion he was, in 1803, appointed Lieutenant-Governor of Port Phillip, which however he abandoned, going across to the banks of the Derwent in Tasmania. Besides being Judge-Advocate he was Secretary to the Governor, and the Annalist of the Colony, in which capacity he rendered great service. His book, entitled An account of the English Colony in New South Wales, was published in 1798;

Captain Tench's book, entitled A narrative of the Expedition to Botany Bay, and published in 1789, was one of the first books to attract attention in England to the new Colony. It was translated into many languages and ran through several editions. He published a larger volume in 1793.

* These figures are taken from the nominal list given in Phillip's Voyage (1889). No two accounts agree as to the number of Convicts, and three different totals are given even in Phillip's Book.

†This Department of State administered the Colonies in 1757.

AUSTRALIA.

In amplification of the Article on Australia, it may be of interest to quote the original Admiralty letter: -

8 Oct., 1786: -

"Lord Sydney having signified to the Lords Commissioners of the Admiralty that a Corps of Marines consisting of 160 Privates with a competent number of Commissioned and Non-Commissioned officers should be embarked in H.M. Ships that are to escort the vessels destined for transporting a considerable number of convicts to Botany Bay in South Wales and to be landed for the protection of the settlement intended to be made there, as well as for preserving good order and regularity among the convicts.

My Lords intend that they should be formed into 4 Companies. Volunteers to be specially preferred upon this occasion. N.C.O.s and men making a voluntary tender, will, if they desire it, be allowed their discharge on their return to England, after they have been relieved (which is intended to be done at the expiration of 3 years) provided their good behaviour in the meantime shall entitle them to such favour (enlistment in those days was for life - ED.) or they will be discharged abroad upon the Relief and be permitted to settle in the Country if they prefer it. The Marines are to be victualled by a commissary immediately upon their landing and provision will be made for supplying them with such tools, implements and utensils as they may have occasion for, while they are employed for the protection of the new settlement. In the Appointment of Commissioned Officers, those at full pay at the different Divisions will have the first option Commandants will please, therefore, send a list of names who may tender their services, that the requisite appointments may be made; the same offer will be made to officers on half-pay if number of officers on full pay is insufficient. (This led to an indignant protest from officers of Plymouth Division, especially as many on half-pay volunteered. - ED.)

By 8 Nov., 1786 the Admiralty notified they had received so many offers from officers that they did not want any more.

On 24 Nov. 1786 the Order in Council was issued increasing the Corps by 4 Companies, each consisting of 1 Captain, 2 First Lieuts., 1 Second Lieut., 3 Sergts., 3 Cpls., 2 Drummers and 48 Privates. Nos. 61 and 63 were allotted to Portsmouth, Nos. 62 and 64 to Plymouth.

On 14 Oct., 1786 the Commandant at Plymouth reported that 200 men had volunteered and that he had chosen a fine detachment amongst which were men of all trades.

On 3 Jan., 1787 permission was given for 10 wives per company to accompany the draft, for which the King's authority had to be obtained.

On 23 Nov., 1786 the Companies were ordered to be rearmed with 200 short land musquets with steel rammers (instead of firelocks); the Sergeants to have 12 Sergeant's Carbines with steel rammers.

Quite a big supply of spare parts were sent, but no ammunition; Major Ross borrowed what he could at Portsmouth.

The men were also supplied with 2 cotton Cheque shirts and 2 years "Light Clothing," at their own expense be it noted; and on 2 Jan., 1787 the Commandant at Plymouth was authorised to supply one of the setts of Colours now at Plymouth Headquarters, if they can be spared."

In addition to these companies, H.M.S. *Sirius* had a detachment - 2/Lt. Davies (the Engineer Officer) 1 Sergt., 1 Cpl., 1 Dr. and 18 Privates and the Supply, storeship, 1 Sergt., 1 Cpl. and 10 Privates.

But the Plymouth Order, dated ? March, 1787, is too typical of the Corps not to be quoted:

"8 March. Detachments for Botany Bay to embark at 10 a.m., tomorrow."

When we think they were going out into the Blue - the place had once been seen by Capt. Cook - no one knew its possibilities or what lay before them; but the same routine that has gone on for the last 300 years was observed.

When I first joined, a very favourite song at all sing-songs was "Botany Bay," with a roaring refrain; this must have been a survival of these old days. I unfortunately have lost the words and the music, I wonder if any one knows them now; I never saw them in writing, so they must have been traditional.

––––––––

COMPETENCE OF A NAVAL COURT-MARTIAL QUESTIONED.

A circumstance, to which is attached a question of infinite magnitude to naval and military men, lately occurred in the Mediterranean. An officer of the 11th Regiment, detached with a party of duty men to do duty as Marines on board one of the ships in Admiral Hotham's fleet having been guilty of disobedience of orders and contemptuous conduct towards the captain of the ship, was by him, as his superior officer, brought to a court martial, at which Admiral Goodall presided. The

charges being fully proved he was sentenced to be dismissed the Service, and rendered incapable of ever serving His Majesty again. He however denied the legality of their proceedings, alleging a naval court to be incompetent to decide what he deemed a military cause; and in consequence wrote to General Briggs, Commander in Chief at Gibraltar, who, disregarding the judgement of the court-martial, ordered him to do his duty till he had His Majesty's directions to the contrary. The affair is now before the War Office, and we trust will be terminated without creating any differences between the two professions.
From "The Britannic Magazine," 1795.

PRESENTATION OF COLOURS TO MARINES AT CONSTANTINOPLE,
7th January, 1799.

It would seem that the Marines of the Fleet destined for the defence of Acre were presented with Colours by Mrs. Smith, wife of the British Plenipotentiary at Constantinople, for in the Journal of Midshipman (afterwards Commander) N. H. Budd, R.N., of H.M.S. *Tigre*, appears the following entry under date of 7th January 1799.

"Moored in Harbour of Constantinople. Fired a salute of 21 guns, and man'd Ship on occasion of Marine Corps being presented with a stand of Colours from H.B. Majesty's Ambassador's Lady."

I wonder if any other non-Royal lady ever had the honour of presenting Colours to the Corps?

MEMORANDUM OF THE SERVICES OF COLONEL WILLIAM ROBINSON
Companion of the Most Noble Military Order of the Bath; Colonel in the Navy of the King of the Two Sicilies; Commander of the Honourable Military Order of St. Ferdinand and of Merit, and a Major of the Royal Marine Artillery.
Compiled by Mr. D. B. Smith, Admiralty Library.
(Reproduced by permission of the Librarians - War Office and Admiralty).

Entered the Marine Service as Lieutenant in the month of February, 1797, and was embarked on board the Iris frigate at the Nore, in command of a detachment of Marines during the mutiny in June following.

Was slightly wounded in the head in boarding and cutting out the French privateer Hero from a small port near Gottenburgh in August of the same year.

In 1798 was employed in boarding and cutting out the Dutch national schooner Pegasus of 12 guns from a port on the coast of Norway. In 1799 assisted in the boarding and capture of the French national privateer Legere from a port in the coast of Jutland, being also employed during part of these two years in the blockade of Holland under Admirals Duncan, Onslow and Dickson.

Embarked in 1801 on board Lord Nelson's flagship the *Amazon*, in command of the Marines of the squadron employed on a particular service off Boulogne. Here termined the war.

In 1803, at the commencement of the new war, embarked on board the Antelope, bearing Commodore Sir Sidney Smith's broad pendant, in command of the detachment of Royal Marines.

In the month of October was wounded in the neck by a rifle ball at Bergen-op-Zee, on the coast of Holland, in boarding and destroying a considerable number of the enemy's vessels on their way to join the Boulogne flotilla, and also in burning and destroying several others on the same day at Scheveling under a heavy fire of cannon and musketry.

Accompanied Sir Sidney Smith on board the King George cutter into the Harbour of Flushing, where she was sunk in shoal water by the fire of the enemy's batteries and the Dutch flotilla. Her shot holes being stopped during low water, she floated at the return of the tide, beat off a very superior force, and was saved.

In May the same year shared in the action with the Dutch flotilla of 59 sail near Ostend, on their way to Boulogne (vide Sir Sidney Smith's despatch).

In 1804 was appointed by the Rt. Hon. William Pitt to superintend the equipment of a secret service expedition against the French flotilla at Boulogne, consisting of fire vessels, explosion vessels and submarine bombs. In order to prove the practicability of the new system of destroying vessels by means of the torpedo, the Dorothea, a vessel of 300 tons, was purchased and anchored in Walmer Roads. She was blown up and totally destroyed by me in the presence of the Naval officers of the station, who were assembled to witness the effect of the explosion of gunpowder under water, as detailed in my reports to the Secretary of State on that occasion.

In 1805 commanded the boats with submarine bombs at the bombardment of Boulogne, destined to blow up the enemy's vessels in the outer roads by the squadron under Commodore Sir Sidney Smith. Was sent in 1806 to the Mediterranean, having the direction of a large equipment of Congreve's rockets destined for the destruction of Constantinople, but arriving too late for this service was ordered to Sicily to assist in the defence of that Island, and to instruct officers and men in the use of this newly-invented instrument of war.

In 1807-8, it being found necessary to arm for the defence of the Faro of Messina, a number of gunboats and rocket boats which were attached to the Quartermaster General's Department, I was also attached to that department and appointed Director of the Rocket System, having the entire arrangement of the Arsenal at Messina for the equipment of the numerous flotilla.

In 1809 accompanied the expedition under Sir J. Stuart to the Gulf of Naples, was at the capture of Ischia and Procida, also at the capture and destruction of the French flotilla, consisting of about 40 sail.

Commanded a division of boats at the bombardment of Gallipoli, in the destruction of several Martelle towers, and in the burning and capture of 13 of the enemy's vessels in the port of Castello on the coast of Calabria.

In 1810 appointed second in command of the British Army flotilla and sent to the Ionian Islands, there to equip a division of armed vessels, which I commanded at the siege and surrender of the fortress of the Island of Santa Maura. An expedition consisting of one thousand gun-boats and transports having been fitted out at Naples to attack Sicily, I was immediately recalled to Messina, and on the 10th June the telegraph signal was made for 50 of the enemy's vessels being in sight, which were immediately attacked under a very heavy fire from the shore, 17 of which vessels were captured and almost all the remainder sunk and destroyed; for which service I was thanked in the General Orders of the Army. On the arrival of the remainder's of the enemy's expedition from Naples in the Faro of Messina, frequent attacks were made upon them, as well as on the French batteries along the line of coast from Seilla to Reggio. On the day the enemy landed at Mili in Sicily, five of his vessels were captured (with troops on board) by the division of the flotilla under my immediate command. On the day Murat retired from Calabria with his army and flotilla, nine of his transports were captured by the division of the flotilla under my command.

I was second in command of the Army flotilla at the bombardment of the city of Reggio, and in the destruction of a French privateer at anchor in the roads.

In 1811, on the arrival of Lord William Bentinck to command the army in Sicily, it was deemed necessary to turn the Sicilian flotilla to some account, which by reason of the heavy construction of the vessels had been for some time inactive and in consequence of the high rank of many of its Sicilian officers, Captain Robert Hall, of the, Royal Navy, was appointed, with the rank of Brigadier in the Sicilian service, to command the two flotillas, which were then called the combined British and Sicilian flotillas, the former of which I commanded at the attack made on the enemy's armed vessels at Pietra Nera, on the coast of Calabria, when 24 of them were totally burnt and destroyed. Commanded the British flotilla under Brigadier Hall at the bombardment of the city of Reggio and the destruction of an English merchant vessel captured by the enemy in the month of February.

At this period it was thought expedient from motives of economy to consolidate the flotillas and to wear the flag of His Sicilian Majesty. It was then called the SICILIAN FLOTILLA, in which service My Lords Commissioners of the Admiralty permitted me to accept the rank of Captain of a frigate.

In 1814 commanded a division of the Sicilian flotilla under Commodore Sir Robert Hall at an attack made on the enemy's vessels and batteries at Pietra Nera, on the coast of Calabria, when we succeeded in capturing and burning 54 of the enemy's vessels, destroyed the batteries and made the French General, La Roche, a prisoner, together with the whole field artillery, cavalry, and a portion of the infantry; for which service His Majesty the King of Sicily was graciously pleased to decorate me with the Insignia of a Companion of the Honourable Military Order of St. Ferdinand and of

Merit, and I was promoted by my own Sovereign to the rank of Major in the Army.

Commodore Hall being appointed to command on the Lakes of Canada, the command of the flotilla again devolved on me, in which I continued, till the Short Peace, when the boats and vessels belonging to the British Government were sold and the crews discharged with the exception of a few which were kept for communication with the Ionian Islands.

On the escape of Buonaparte from Elba, it was thought necessary to re-equip the British flotilla for the defence of Sicily and other service on the coast of Italy, which I was appointed to command by Lord William Bentinck, this being afterwards approved by Lord Bathurst, His Majesty's Secretary of State for the Colonial Department. About this period His Majesty the King of Sicily was pleased to take my services into his gracious consideration and confer on me the rank of Colonel in his Royal Navy, with the command of his flotilla in Messina.

1815. In this year Murat's flotilla again made its appearance on the Calabrian coast, ultimately arriving at Scilla, where he was closely blockaded by the flotilla under my command, and various attacks were made upon it. Several of their merchant vessels and transports were captured, carrying provisions and grain which the army in Calabria then very much wanted. On account of the success of the armies of the north, the march of the Austrians into Italy, and an expedition having sailed from Sicily to the coast of Naples, preparations were made to attack the enemy in Calabria, previous to which I was sent by His Majesty with a flag of truce to summon General Duvanoir (commanding Murat's force) to surrender, who occupied an entrenched camp above St. Giovanni, with 4,000 men and 20 pieces of field artillery. He enterd into capitulation with me, of which the primary articles being agreed to, subject to the approval of His Sicilian Majesty, on the following morning he surrendered at discretion when I took possession of the Castle of Scilla, the batteries on the coast, and the flotilla. On making my report of these services, His Majesty was pleased in person to confer on me the Insignia of a Commander of the Honourable Military Order of St. Ferdinand and of Merit.

The fortress of Gaeta still holding out, I proceeded thither in command of the flotilla, pursuant to my instructions, remaining at Naples a few days at the request of Admiral Sir C. Penrose, in order to equip some Neapolitan gun boats, which I succeeded in doing, and these being placed under my command, the flotilla then became the combined BRITISH, SICILIAN AND NEAPOLITAN flotilla. On my arrival at Gaeta, a close blockade was immediately formed by the combined flotilla and the boats of His Britannic Majesty's ships of war at that place, while every facility was afforded by me to the Austrian General Lawre to complete the batteries then erecting to carry on the siege of the fortress, for which purpose I dismantled the Island of Ponzo, supplying the Austrians with all the entrenching tools, platforms, etc. The results are best shewn in the dispatches of Admirals Lord Exmouth and Sir Charles Penrose.

I had the honour here to fire the last shot in the war; to sign the capitulation on the part of the British and to deliver the keys of the fortress of Gaeta into the hands of His Majesty.

Returned to Naples with the combined flotilla for the purpose of giving up the command of the Sicilian and Neapolitan parts of it, when His Majesty was pleased to confirm me in the rank of permanent Colonel in his Navy, and by a special decree was further pleased to give me seniority over all his officers who had not been employed in actual service, as well as over those who had served with Murat. Arrived at Messina with the British flotilla for the purpose of again disposing of it in obedience to instructions to that effect, and to discharge the crews. Here I received a dispatch from the Neapolitan Ministry of War and Marine putting the whole of the Sicilian flotilla under my command, with secret instructions how to dispose of a part of it, leaving me at liberty to act with the remainder as circumstances might occur. This dispatch also contained information of Murat being about to sail from Corsica, where he had assembled a number of boats and men for the purpose of making a descent on some part of Naples or Calabria. After being at sea for several days, they arrived on the coast of Calabria, where they were captured - some escaped, and the boat in which Murat was embarked succeeded in making the shore at Pizo in the Gulf of St. Euphemia, where he was seized. I arrived shortly after him and remained in joint charge of his person during his confinement. Being the senior officer present, it fell to my lot to sit as President of a Commission ordered to try him, which office I thought proper to decline, but I remained with Murat to the moment of his execution.

(Signed) W. ROBINSON.

MUTINY ON BOARD H.M.S. *TEMERAIRE* IN DECEMBER 1801.

The following extracts from the "Life and Letters of Admiral Collingwood," by G. Cornwallis-West, recently published. (London: R. Holden & Co., 1927) demonstrate how effectively when properly handled the Marine Detachment of one of H.M. ships was able to deal with the outbreak of a mutiny. Yet, curiously enough, it seems to have been the misbehaviour of a Marine which was the match which ignited the accumulated fuel of discontent in the ship's company.

An armistice had just been made with our French opponents. At this time half the Channel Fleet was lying in Bantry Bay, and the crews seem to have thought that now that hostilities were at an end, at least for a time, they ought to at once sail for England. It was a natural expectation, and it must be remembered that a great number of the bluejackets were pressed men, taken by force from their families and employment.[1]

But some means the rumour spread that the ships were to "go foreign" again, and discontent with this prospect rose to such a pitch that the ship's company of the Temeraire - the flagship of Rear-Admiral Campbell - mustered on the upper deck and announced to their Captain that they "would not start an anchor but to go to England." He, Captain Eyles, said he was unaware of their destination, and that they must obey orders, upon which, it appears, they went below. This was on the morning of the 3rd December, 1801. Somewhat similar scenes seem to have taken place on board the Formidable, Majestic and Vengeance.

What followed is best told by an extract from Captain Eyles' official narrative:-

"On Sunday the 6th of December, 1801, after the sails were bent, agreable to the Rear-Admiral's orders, the major part of the ship's company of this ship were heard cheering on the lower deck, between one and two o'clock; they lowered the ports and were in the act of barring them in, and attempted to unship the ladders, when Lieutenants Douglas, Brown and the rest of the officers immediately went amongst them, when they exclaimed, 'We will fight for our King and Country, but not start an anchor except for England.' They further stated that they had no grievances, and appear to have been pacified for the time being. On Wednesday evening, however, the crew having put their views and demands into the form of a letter to the Rear-Admiral, pushed it through the lattice of the Admiral's pantry. The day following the Admiral addressed the crew on the impropriety of their conduct, and telling the Marines that they were mentioned in the letter as being in agreement with the rest of the ship s company, asked them if they knew anything of it. No answer was given; the ship's company then went below quietly.

"In the evening about five o'clock," continues Captain Eyles, "Lieutenant Pogson reported to me in the Admiral's cabin that Jas. McAvoy, one of the Marines, was drunk, and very insolent to Lieutenant Williams and a Corporal. I then went on deck and ordered him in irons. About a quarter after five Mr. King (Master's Mate), when going the rounds, observed John Filcher, John Fitzgerald and James Lockyer running from the larboard bay up the fore ladder, calling out 'Jack,' and returned again instantly in the same hurry. Mr. King, knowing them to be suspicious characters, and that a man had Just been put in irons, supposed there was something going on, and reported the same to Lieut. Pogson, who immediately went with him on the middle deck and up the fore ladder, when they found a mob collected under the forecastle. Mr. King again came up, and reported the same to Lieutenant Welsh, who sent him to Captain Vallack[2] to order the Marines under Arms, at the same time desired him to acquaint me of it, as Lieut. Welsh did not think it proper to leave the deck at that crisis. Mr. King then came into the Admiral's cabin, and said the men were beginning a disturbance again. The Admiral, as well as myself and the officers, went immediately on deck. By this time a Guard was collecting under arms. Lieutenant Pogson, Officer of the Watch, informed me the people were going to cobb a man under the forecastle, and that he had been to say he would not suffer anything of the sort to take place in his watch. They persisted in doing it, and when he had seized two men to bring them aft, he was hustled, and the men rescued by the mob, they saying there should be no prisoners, no punishment. The people then called all hands on deck and cheered on the forecastle. I instantly went forward and asked them what they wanted (it was about dusk); a general cry was heard, 'There is a man in irons.' I said, yes, there is, and there he shall remain. Their answer was, 'We will have him out, no prisoners, and cheered again, saying we will have him out, we will punish him ourselves.' I then seized a man, believing him to be one of those who cheered, to bring him aft, desiring the people to make a lane. They open'd a little, which gave me an opportunity of seeing the Admiral coming forward with the officers, but they, again cheering, immediately surrounded and began to hustle me. John Collins, the butcher, closed and pushed me about, holding up his arm and preventing me going aft with the man I had seized; when Mr. Douglass, the boatswain, threw his hand across Collin's breast, saying, 'You damned rascal, do you know who you are touching of' (or words to that effect), the man was passed aft and I remained with the Admiral and some of the officers on the forecastle.

By this time all the Marines were under arms on the quarter-deck and poop. The Admiral then seized James Lockyer on the forecastle and brought him aft under the poop. He again came forward and began successively to call out the men pointed out by me and the other officers as most suspected, when every officer conducted them aft, as they were called out. The Admiral, Captain Vallack, and Lieut. Welsh, as well as myself, went aft and spoke to the Marines, saying we trusted they would do their duty; when they answered they would. Lieut. Garrick, Mr. Charlton and the Carpenter were ordered to lay the grating on fore and aft, which was done.

Leaving the quarter-deck in charge of Lieutenant Douglas (first Lieutenant), the Marines were brought forward on each gangway with the officer in front, forced the people over the bows. some of them getting in at the head doors, main, and middle deck ports, and the starboard gangway ladder, and some of them overboard.

Supposing they were gone below to assemble in the bay, leaving a guard on the quarter-deck, the Admiral, myself and Captain Vallack, with the Marines, proceeded to the bay on the lower deck. Finding nobody there, we went round the middle deck, where there were a few men, which we sent up; after coming on deck again, placing guards on the main deck, quarter deck and ladders. The Admiral then called aft several more men, who were pointed out to him by myself and the officers as most suspected, and sent them under guard to the Windsor Castle. All hands were then called and ordered to assemble on the booms, when James McAvoy (the prisoner) was punished with three dozen lashes at the quarter deck netting, abreast of the main rigging, and then put in charge of a sentry.

After the Admiral taking every means of explaining to the men the impropriety of their conduct on the quarter deck, I at the same time endeavouring to explain to those on the fore part of the booms that they had been premature, how very wrong they had acted after what they had heard to-day as they had not been called on to unmoor. Alter waiting some time everybody was sent aft, when the Admiral addressed them, saying: Temeraires, if you will promise me to be quiet, orderly and attentive, I will allow you to go to your hammocks; if not, you shall remain up till daylight, and to daylight again. When in a general voice they answered 'We will-we will,' they were allowed to go below, and the Watch was called.

The officers were then put to watch, the watch armed, and the Marines also armed, and the watch below were ordered not to undress.

There was a certain amount of trouble on board other ships of the squadron, but the officers were able to deal with it, owing to the steadfastness of the Marines on board the ships of the Fleet."

* * * *

Some reference to this mutiny is made on pp. 205-206, Vol. 1. "Britain's Sea Soldiers," and it is somewhat curious that there is a good deal of difference in the wording of the letter from the Resolution's Detachment, signed "Wm. HEANS on page 206 (taken from Nicholas) and the same letter as reproduced in the work from which the above extracts are taken. In this it runs as follows:-

Sir, -

We hope you'll excuse the liberty we take in addressing you but as we understand that certain Ships Companies have refused obeying the just Commands of their Superior Officers in different respects, and knowing as we do the dreadful consequences that formerly attended such like proceedings, which was so prejudicial to that regularity which is so highly necessary to promote good order. For our part we abhor the idea, and are determined to support and maintain the Officers in any Point which they may think proper.

We hope you'll inform Capt. Gardner and the Admiral of our determination, as we think it highly incumbent on us to act in such a manner as may best promote the welfare of our King and Country.

I have the honour of subscribing Myself and on behalf of the detachment of Marines, Your most obedient, humble servant,

Wm. HEARNS, Sergt."

NOTES.
1. Many had not seen their families for nine years.
2. Commanding Marines.

_____

BRIEF STATEMENT OF SERVICE OF
Major-General SIR JOHN DOUGLAS, Kt.,
Colonel of the Royal Marines in Syria and Egypt,
During The Years 1799 and 1800.

Sir John Douglas went out with Sir Sidney Smith in the Tigre to Constantinople, after the Treaty of tripple alliance between England and Russia and the Porte, concluded by Sir Sidney Smith and Mr. Spencer Smith, Sir Sidney sailed from Constantinople for the coast of Egypt.

On his arrival off Alexandria he found a general movement in the Turkish Army, which he concluded from various circumstances and other information, was intended for Syria. His conjectures were so well founded, and his penetration so correct, that he immediately ordered a course to be shapen for Mount Carmell, and on his arrival off that mountain, he was fortunate enough to fall in with, and to capture, the flotilla of Bonaparte, containing his battering cannon, powder, and all his implements for the Siege of Acre.

At that time Sir John Douglas was invested with a special commission from Sir Sidney Smith, giving him additional rank from that of Lieut.-Colonel to Colonel, in order that he might take the command of the Turkish forces, as well as the seamen and marines that were landed from the Fleet.

Sir John Douglas led, and commanded in person the memorable sortie there, when a handful of British Marines and seamen took possession of the first and second lines of the enemy's trenches, parallel to the Mine, although defended by the very flower of Bonaparte's army; and kept possession of them until the Mine was totally destroyed and brought back into garrison under a most tremendous fire the remains of his gallant detachment. In this most hazardous service Sir John was ably aided by the gallantry of Lieut. Wright and Major Oldfield, of the Marines, the latter of whom unfortunately fell in that memorable sortie.

Colonel Philipeaux (an able Engineer officer) died early in the siege, and this unfortunate circumstance caused the whole duty of erecting batteries, etc., to devolve upon Sir John Douglas, aided by the councils of Sir Sidney Smith. It is needless to mention the minute details of this arduous Siege of sixty-two days, during which the enemy made no less than fourteen general assaults, and was each time vigorously and successfully repulsed; or is it needful to dwell upon the bodily fatigue and the terrible anxiety of mind that the almost momentarily expectation of the place being carried, must have occasioned to Sir Sidney Smith and Sir John Douglas. Bonaparte, finding all his most assaults ineffectual, and finding himself defeated, he retreated from the walls of Acre, and the world knows how effectually Sir Sidney Smith harassed him in his march along the sea coast on his forced return to Egypt.

Sir Sidney afterwards returned to Cyprus and collected there, through his great zeal and popularity, a considerable army, with which when, united with the Turkish Fleet, he proceeded to Aboukir, where that army was landed. Sir John Douglas then volunteered his services to lead these troops against General Bonaparte in Persia, but from their total want of subordination and order, the whole of the Ottoman Army was put to flight, notwithstanding the utmost exertions of Sir John Douglas, and the whole of them, consisting of about 13,000 men, were driven into the sea, killed, or taken prisoners.

Sir John Douglas, with Colonel Bromley (a French emigrant officer), narrowly escaped being cut to pieces, by boldly riding into the sea, which was rough and stormy at the time. They were picked up by Sir Sidney Smith, who, with a field piece in the bow of his boat, gallantly rowed in shore and kept the French cavalry at bay.

After this unfortunate defeat, Sir Sidney again collected a considerable force from Rhodes and other islands, and made an attack on the French forces at Damietta, where Sir John Douglas accompanied Sir Sidney Smith. They took possession of an old Monastery, close to the enemy's redoubt where they erected cannon and destroyed their magazine; but, unfortunately, the Turkish forces, as at Aboukir, did not take advantage of this misfortune of the enemy, but allowed the French cavalry to get upon their flank, and was, by the Corps of Reserve, quitting the position in which Sir Sidney and Sir John had placed it. The consequences which followed were precisely the same as at Aboukir.

Sometime after this, at the particular request of His Highness the Vizier, then at Jaffa, by application to Sir Sidney Smith for Sir John Douglas to direct and assist his army, Sir John again went out of his own proper line of duty and took upon himself that very arduous charge. He continued with the Vizier four months, suffering every degree of hardship in the desert, being obliged to drink brackish water, sleep in the open air and subsist upon about two ounces of rice per day sent dressed from the Grand Vizier's table, at which no chieftain can sit, and which was all His Highness could spare for the daily subsistence of each man in the British detachment.

Under all these difficulties and hardships, Sir John Douglas completed the capture of the garrison of El Arish, and prevented the dispersion of the Ottoman Army, by getting possession of the Wells of El Arish, and a supply of provisions, of which they were in the greatest want. This Post, which Sir John had most difficulty in persuading the Vizier to attack, is the only post taken from the French which the Turks now possess, and is the key to the desert on the Syrian side. It is of such immense importance, that no army can march across the desert, or obtain water, without first possessing themselves of it.

Sir John Douglas never felt himself more proud than by being embraced by Sir Sidney Smith on his arrival there with the French Commissaries, and warmly thanked for his having captured that important place, which he feared the Turks would never have accomplished, and which they would not have effected had it not been for that gallant detachment of the British seamen and marines, as acknowledged by Monsieur Cazel (the French Commandant), who delivered up his sword to Sir John Douglas, and put the garrison under his protection from the fury of the Turks.

The capture of this valuable fortress greatly facilitated the ever memorable Convention concluded there, and which probably would not have taken place but for that event, as General Kleber was on his march to its relief, which he would undoubtedly have effected in two days after the surrender to Sir John Douglas.

Sir John hopes he will not be deemed vain by thinking himself much honoured in being selected by Sir Sidney Smith to carry home the account of this convention, which Sir Sidney Smith and Sir John Douglas then presumed to think was a most brilliant termination of the French expedition to Egypt, by which, according to Denan, the enemy promised themselves the conquest of that country, the subjection of the Ottoman Empire and a direct intercourse with India.

An exact translation of the Grand Vizier's letter to Sir Sidney Smith, omitting the numerous titles customary in the Oriental languages, begins as follows:-

"To the Commander of His Brittanic Majesty's Fleet, to our most esteemed and beloved friend, Sir Sidney Smith, our best greeting. May your destiny be ever prosperous and your health flourishing.

"We send you by the present our friendly advice and information concerning His Brittanic Majesty's Officer, Colonel John Douglas, to make known unto you, that during his stay at, and cooperation with the Army under our command, he has evinced, not only great skill, but also the most undaunted courage and bravery, as his glorious and faithful services have afforded us the highest satisfaction, so do we wish the same may prove to him most honourable and advantageous, and as we think it just and expedient for all powers and Sovereigns nobly to reward eminent merit, so have we written this letter for the express purpose to beg you to transmit to our dear, most respected, and great Friend and Ally, the King of Great Britain a faithful narrative of Colonel Douglass' gallant behaviour, that accordingly he may be raised to the rank he so well deserves.

"We hope and trust, that at the receipt of our letter you will act in conformity with this our sincere desire.

Given at our Camp before El Arish, in the Desert, 2nd Febry. 1800."

N.B. - *The original of the above letter is vested in the Foreign Office, written in the Turkish language, and emblazoned on vellum.*

Besides this he has the pride and felicity to say, that when Sir Sidney Smith was enrobed for his very eminent services with a Royal Pelice and an Aigrette taken from the turban of the Grand Signior, and put into his hat by the Pasha of Cyprus, Sir Sidney, after that ceremony, presented Sir John Douglas with a valuable and elegant sword, as a lasting mark of the esteem in which he held his faithful coadjutor.

By the kind order of Lord Keith, Sir John Douglas, having put all his valuables on board the *Queen Charlotte* at Syracuse, to a great amount and some of which had been presented to Sir John in Syria and in Egypt for his services, by the Grand Vizier, and various chiefs, and which presents he considered more for his honour than for their intrinsic value, they were all together with his own private property destroyed, by the calamitous accident which befel that ship. For this very considerable loss, to the amount of many thousands Sir John has not been able to obtain the smallest remuneration, although he hopes he is not presuming when he adds, that he feels himself in some degree entitled to some solid mark of his country's approbation for his very arduous and perilous services, and in zealously endeavouring upon every occasion, at Syria, and at Egypt, to be an active instrument in promoting the interest and the glory of the British Empire.

The Turks were very much devoted to Sir John Douglas they had great faith in his valour, and a high appreciation of his leadership. On one occasion, during the siege of Acre, he exposed himself too much to danger, and the Turks became anxious about him, knowing the need they had of his help, they determined to prevent him from thus recklessly risking his life. Two or three of these Turks seized hold of him and used their utmost strength to pull him off the rocks, trying at the same time to hide him from the enemy with their own persons. They were soon put aside, however, by Sir John, who coolly and bravely maintained his perilous position, urging and cheering his men in his bright, hopeful manner, and leading them onward with the greatest gallantry.

He was followed by two courageous boys (young favorites of his), a midshipman and a marine drummer, who kept as close to him as possible, evidently inspired by the undaunted spirit of their leader.

In addition to the numerous other presentations made to Sir John Douglas at the conclusion of the Syrian Campaign, he also received from the Sultan a jewelled sword of great value, as a token of acknowledgment of his brilliant services, besides a solid mark of his own country's approbation in a grant of a yearly pension of £400.

It was at this time that the Royal Marines, for their great valour, and the important victory they had gained, were given the right to wear a wreath of laurels as a portion of the badge of their Corps.

* * * *

Some of the Services of Major General Sir John Douglas, Knt., of the Royal Marines.

This Officer particularly distinguished himself during the great mutinies at Spithead and the Nore, when important mention was made of the gallantry of Captain John Douglas, who, with his small party of loyal true Marines (and a brave little drummer, who would not leave for a moment the side of the Captain he loved so well and so faithfully) was literally surrounded by hundreds of desperate and threatening men, who had gained entire possession of the ship.

They told Captain Douglas that he and his Marines must immediately leave the ship, or they would shoot every man of them.

Captain Douglas, knowing that previous to the mutiny he had been a great favourite with the seamen, as well as with his own men, turned to the Naval Captain and said earnestly to him, "Give me the command of this ship but for half an hour, and I will quell the mutiny "This request being determinedly refused, the seamen again told Captain Douglas that he, with his Marines must leave the ship, and once more repeated their fierce threats. Then it was that, turning indignantly to the mutineers, he made his memorable speech: "Oh! that the heads of all you mutineers were on the shoulders of one man, that I could cut them off with one stroke of my sword, and so should perish all who would be disloyal to my King and Country!"

Yet notwithstanding this daring speech, so much did the seamen respect and admire Captain Douglas for his great courage that they said to him: "Well, we will allow you, sir, and your party of Marines to leave this ship with the honours of war, in full marching order."

Captain Douglas, finding that the Naval Captain was still unwilling that he should attempt to pacify the seamen in any way, or be the means of quelling the mutiny on board, and not wishing that the lives of his few brave marines should be sacrificed to no purpose, he accordingly gathered his men together and left the ship, the little drummer in the bow of the boat (after boldly "speaking his mind" to the mutineers), triumphantly playing The British Grenadiers - all the way to shore, the boats having been made bright and clean for the occasion.

* * * *

During the Irish Rebellion of 1798, especial mention was made of the bravery of Captain John Douglas, who had by this time gained the sobriquet of "Brave Douglas of the Marines." His never failing courage, and great skill in the use of arms, caused many the most famous duellists of the time, both at home and abroad, to be very wary of quarrelling with him or with any of his friends.

* * * *

His death called forth the following General Order to his Corps:-
"Whilst the impressions of the awfully inspiring rites and solemnities attendant upon the remains of our late Brother Officer, Sir John Douglas, are at present in our minds, I would fain draw the serious attention of the Junior members of his Corps to the animating prospects which his career holds out, in him will be perceived an Officer of a Corps almost constitutionally serving in subordinate detachments possessing the confidence of all in command with the love of those who obey. He is seen equally esteemed, admired, and entrusted on every service, whether in the West Indies or Cape of Good Hope; whether animating his Corps in defending one fortress, or leading them to the reduction of another, whether in executing the most arduous duties, or in bearing the most confidential and important despatches.

I need not repeat to you the distinguished part he acted in the long, glorious and successful struggle in the Defence of Acre; or the reduction of El Arish, the siege of which he conducted in person, commanding the Allied British and Ottoman Forces.

The historian will associate Douglas and Marines with the first discomfiture of the Greatest Conqueror on record. In his life will be found not only every honourable incentive to the Soldier, but in his example the Marine Officer will see that Royal approbation, confidence and the bounty of a grateful country have been opened to award his exertion.

Death is equally the fate of all; may we be held in readiness for the unknown summons, and may the successes of this Brave Soldier and worthy man be indelibly engraven upon the memory of the young Marine, as on the walls of Acre and El Arish.
       (Signed) ANDREW BURN,
           Major-General."

INCIDENTS IN THE LIFE OF SIR JOHN DOUGLAS.

Sir John Douglas was well known among his brother officers for his brave, undaunted spirit, and had frequently been called upon to prove it.

On one occasion, when embarked as Captain of Marines, in a ship anchored off Dublin, he went ashore with several other officers. When they landed the question arose as to what hotel they should go to, so that they might hear the latest news.

Sir John mentioned one, but the other officers, knowing his indomitable spirit, anxiously cautioned him not to go there explaining to him that the hotel was frequented by a notorious bully and his friends, the said bully having already met several officers in duels, and being always ready to promote a quarrel and "call out" his antagonist.

"That is the best of all reasons why I should go there," said Sir John; and accordingly there he went, accompanied by several of his brother officers.

He was also told that the bully was in the habit of occupying two or three of the best chairs in the public rooms, with his hat, sword, gloves, etc., and daring any fresh arrivals to touch them. On Sir John Douglas and his companions entering the room, the bully's friends looked knowingly at each other, Sir John being a stranger to them. He noticed at once that two chairs were occupied, the one with a pair of gloves, the other with a cocked hat. So he immediately walked up to one of them, and receiving no reply, save an insolent stare, to his courteous request that the owner of the hat would remove his property, he, with the point of his sword, sent the said hat rolling into a distant corner of the room, and then quietly sat down in the chair himself, at the same time taking up a paper which was lying on a table near him and commencing to read.

The bully, finding himself thus boldly defied, came forward and shouted loudly "Who has dared to do that dishonour to my hat?"

"I did, Captain John Douglas, of the Marines," was the quiet reply.

Then looking hard at Sir John, the bully said threateningly, "You, sir, shall pay dearly for this outrage!"

Sir John, however, just glanced at him for a moment, gave him a cool nod, and continued reading the newspaper, while the bully, shaking the dust off his hat, put it on, and walked out of the room, to which he never returned until Captain Douglas had left the neighbourhood. There was great delight at the bully's prolonged absence among the constant frequenters of the hotel, and considerable satisfaction expressed that he had at last met his match in the person of the young Marine officer. No doubt, learning afterwards with whom he would have to deal, the duellist thought it wiser not to meet so formidable a foe, for Sir Douglas had been in his earlier days a great deal in France, with some of his noble relatives, and was quite master of the cut and thrust rapier then in use. Although easily roused, and of a most fearless, daring spirit, he was naturally of a kind and gentle disposition, courteous and generous, much beloved by his brother officers and the men of his Corps.

On another occasion we hear of Sir John Douglas having played a very different part.

A large ball was taking place at the house of a wealthy Welsh gentleman, the head of an old county family, when a young kinsman of Sir John Douglas, then only eighteen years of age, and an Ensign in a line regiment, ran away with the host's daughter, a charming maiden of sweet seventeen. It was a real genuine love affair, a romance of the good old times. The respective families of the youthful couple were in no way averse to their marriage at some future date, but insisted that they should wait a reasonable time, until both were certain that they knew their own minds. The boy lover's regiment, however, was ordered abroad on foreign service, and the pair were determined they would not be separated. So, while the mirth of the ball was at its merriest, and the gaiety at its height, the young hero (a determined youth of good old Scottish family) and his fair partner, instead of being soberly "treading a measure" in the ballroom, were fast speeding on their way to the far-famed Gretna Green.

Sir John Douglas, as well as his kinsman, Sir Sydney Smith (the celebrated naval hero) were both present at the ball, and were in the greatest consternation when it was discovered what had occurred. Sir John was distressed on his host's account, as well as that of his own family, for in a moment the idea flashed upon him that his young kinsman's regiment would start the following day, and that he might be detained on the road (travelling not being so easy in those days as it is now), and so be too late to join his comrades, and thus disgraced for ever in the Service.

To think, with Sir John, was to act, and ere a very short time had elapsed he had started, accompanied by Sir Sydney Smith (the latter being always ready for any exploits of this kind, where love or war were concerned) in hot pursuit of the fugitives.

They arrived, however, just too late to be present at the interesting Gretna Green ceremony; but after seeing that the couple were also married both according to the forms of the Presbyterian and English Church (to save disputes that might thereafter arise), and the hero fairly en route to join his regiment, the two gallant officers returned to play the part of peacemakers to the respective families of the youthful bride and bridegroom.

* * * *

Sir John Douglas was born at Jeanfield, Dalkeith, in the County of Midlothian, on the 12th of October, 1762.

He was the second son of Lewis Douglas, of Garvauld, and Jeanfield, Scotland, grandson of Sir Robert Douglas of Glenhervie, Bart., and lineal descendant of the Earls of Angus, through

Sir Robert Douglas of Glenbervie, second son of William, ninth Earl of Angus, who married his cousin, the Lady Catherine Douglas, daughter of William, eleventh Earl of Angus, and first Marquis of Douglas, and the Lady Mary Gordon, his wife, daughter of George, first Marquis of Huntly.

Sir John Douglas was also related to William Douglas, Earl of Selkirk, afterwards Duke of Hamilton, and to George, Earl of Dunbarton.

He died on the 4th March, 1814, at Douglas House, Greenwich, and was buried at old Charlton Church. His residence, which used to be called Douglas House, is still standing; it is situated on Maze Hill, near the entrance gates into Greenwich Park, and it was said that the last of the funeral procession had not left Blackheath when the gun carriage arrived at Charlton Church.

Sir John died in the arms of his favourite comrade and great friend, Captain Coryton,* of the Marines, whose brilliant services and great gallantry will no doubt find a prominent place in the history of the Corps.

*Vide.-"Britain's Sea Soldiers". Vol. 1. p. 243.

The foregoing account of the services and incidents in the life of Sir John Douglas is from the pen of MISS JULIA A. FRASER, daughter of the late General Simon Fraser. R.M., and great-niece of Sir John Douglas. Her statement that the Laurel Wreath was granted as a Badge of Honour to the Corps at the time of the Defence of Acre is, of course, entirely incorrect.

SIR JOHN DOUGLAS.
(Miscellaneous Documents)

(Copy)   27 Novembre.

Monsieur,
J'ai l'honneur de vous informer que je suis destiné à diriger les opérations de l'armée Ottomane, contre votre garnison. La force est si considérable que je suis convaincu que vous trouverez juste pour l'amour de l'humanité et vous sauver reclusion du sang, que je vous requiesse d'accepter les conditions offertes, qui certainment ne peuvent pas être contraire à votre honneur et je n'ai pas besoin de vous dire combien il ne sera difficile de préserver les vies des braves soldats que vous commandez, en cas que vous refusiez et que nous soyons obligés de vous attaquer.
J'ai l'honneur d'être avec la plus grande considération.
(Signed) John DOUGLAS,
Colonel au service de S.M. Brittanique.

————

(*Copy of Original*)
El-Arish le Frimaire au
8 de la Rep. Fce.

Cazal, Chef de Battalion du Genie,
    Commandant, à El-Arishe.

Monsieur,

Je viens de recevoir la lettre que vous m'avez fait l'honneur de m'écrire pour apprendre que vous etiez destiné à diriger les oppérations de l'Armée Ottomane, contre la garnison que je commande, et pour m'engager à accepter les conditions que vous m'offrez.

J'ai l'honneur de vous répondre, Monsieur le Général, qu'ayant l'ordre du Général en Chef de l'Armée Francaise de défendre la place qu'il m'a confiée jusqu' à Ia dernière extrémité, les lois de l'honneur, et du devoir m'empêchent d'accepter vos propositions. Je ne puis vous dissimuler, Monsieur le Général, que j'ai été surpris de recevoir votre sommation, dans un moment où le Général en Chef Kléber, traite de la paix avec le Grand Vizier et avec Monsieur le Commodore Schmit, Plénipotentiare de la Cour de Londres. J'ajouterrai, Monsieur le Général, que d'apres les loix de la Guerre, je ne puis recevoir de sommation, l'Armée Ottomane ne l'étant pas presentée devant El-Ariche. Du reste, Monsieur le Général, puisqu'il-ya des conférences établies en Egypte pour un accommodement, c'est au Général en Chef lui même à qui il faut s'adresser: lui seul ayant l'autorité nécéssaire, et le pouvoir de satisfaire a vos demandes.

J'ai l'honneur d'être, Monsieur le Général, avec la considération Ia plus distinguée,
    Votre trés humble, et trés obéissant serviteur,
            (Signed) CAZAL.

––––––––

CAMP AT GAZA, 9th December, 1799.
    Copy of a letter from Colonel Douglas to Mr. Smith H.B.M. Minister Plenipotentiary
                (at Constantinople).

Sir,

By a courier, who departs from hence this day for Constantinople I have the honour to send you this letter, feeling it my duty to afford you every information concerning the movements of this Army.

At the request of His Highness the Vizier, to Sir Sidney for an English officer to direct the operations of the Turkish Army, he has honoured me with that very important appointment, in company with Lieutenant-Colonel Bromley, Captain Troth Winter, and Mr Smith as my aide-de-camp. We landed at Jaffa the 30th November. The Tigre sailed from that place the 3rd inst. for Damietta, in order to receive on board two French Generals for the purpose of proposing a truce.

The Ottoman camp began to move from Jaffa on the 5th inst. and arrived here on the 7th. I had the honour on the 8th of an interview with His Highness the Vizier; he demanded my opinion respecting an attack upon El-Arish. I answered that I thought his dignity was involved in the question, as well as that of the Turkish Empire, and that it was absolutely necessary he should be in possession of that garrison, being the key on this side of the desert, and a barrier from whence he might treat in a more honourable manner than by allowing as small a fortress to remain in the hands of the enemy and in the near neighbourhood of his numerous army. He approved the idea, and proposed sending the enclosed letter No. 1 from a French Lieutenant taken near El-Arish, accompanied only by a Tartar. I, however, recommended an Officer of information for that purpose, and yesterday sent Lieutenant-Colonel Bromley with the Orders marked No. 2, and Letters No, 3 and 4. I hope the arguments he will use may prevail on the garrison to surrender. I have directed him to say that I am preparing everything for the attack the moment he returns, in case of a refusal, and that I shall bring such a force as to render it impossible for them to defend themselves, and as no succour can possibly arrive to their assistance, they will do well to consider the matter seriously, as the Turks are most determined that they will give no quarter, and I shall do everything in my power to fulfil my promise, and to ensure success. Indeed, sir, I am most sensible of my inability to act in this new and very extraordinary scene, where the eyes of all Europe are directed towards our operations, and I long most anxiously for the return of your most worthy brother whose counsel I much want - he is the oracle of everything here, and I am certain no one is so capable of directing these extraordinary people, or to move them towards anything for their own preservation. In the meantime be assured I shall do everything in my power to deserve his good opinion and that of the Allied Powers.

I beg now, sir, to offer my most respectful compliments to Mrs. Smith, and do me the favour to say I must do much to deserve the honour she has conferred upon me in being her champion.

I beg also to present my good wishes to Count and Madame Tamara. I have been much obliged to the good offices of Mr. Frankini, who begs to be remembered to you.

I have the honour to be, with much respect,
Your most obedient and very humble servant,
(Signed) JOHN DOUGLAS.

To His Excellency J. S. Smith,
    H.B.M. Minister Plenipotentiary.

———

Copy of a letter from Sir Sidney Smith to
Sir John Douglas.
(Copy of Original)

Tigre, 25 Decr. 1799.

My dear Colonel,

I lose not a moment in informing you that a truce was the first object of our arrangement on the Commissioners meeting me on board the Tigre, off Damietta, where the weather permitted our communication. I send the necessary official papers to the Vizier, the Ras Effendi and Mr Frankini. The truce is to commence on the new moon of the 27th December, as you will see by my answer to the note of the French Commissioners, which latter note I send you in original, to operate, as an order to the Commandant of El-Arish, in case he should doubt of the communication a certified copy may be sent.

When the truce is concluded you may perhaps wish to quit a situation which cannot have charms for you any longer than there is active service going on. I have therefore ordered Mr.

Hervey to receive you on board, or such part of the detachment as you may judge proper to send back. I have likewise directed Captain Cane to offer you passage with him, as you will see by the order which Mr Hervey will show you. You are, however at liberty to stay if you judge your presence in the camp of any utility to the Service.

I am, dear sir,
>Your sincere friend and faithful humble servant,
>>(Signed) W. SIDNEY SMITH.

(The above letter was received by Sir John (then Colonel) Douglas, of the Royal Marines, on the 11th January, 1800. It was addressed to - Colonel Douglas, Commander of the British Detachment at the Ottoman Camp, conducting the Siege of El-Arish, Gaza.) - W.S.S.

———

Copy of a letter from Sir John Douglas, but to whom it is addressed is not stated in the copy.

Sir,

In compliance with the desire you were pleased to express to be acquainted with the circumstances under which the Grand Vizier acted immediately preceding, and at the time of the Convention with the French, I have the honour to inform you that the multitude under the supposed command of His Sublime Highness, and denominated "The Turkish Army," were destitute of almost everything which constitutes strength, except numbers, and in a state of general insubordination. The Body which I am to call the Turkish Army is recruited by an advance of six months pay to each individual. During the long period the French had been in Egypt, 200,000 men were assembled by the Port, 80,000 of whom deserted on the march from Constantinople to El Arish. But this was the least evil; the vast residue was infected by a similar spirit. Plunder and desolation had marked alike the progress of those who continued, and those that had dispersed, and the country being unable to afford proper sustenance to the troops of the Vizier, they were kept together only by the account that the French General had proposed to capitulate, and the expectation that by such an event they would be restored sooner to their homes than they could by any other. Under these circumstances the Vizier perceived that it would be impossible to continue inactive, or to proceed against the enemy. He never had more than five days provisions at a time, and was once reduced to two. He could not procure a third part of the leather bags that were requisite to contain water for the six days' march across the desert, and in consequence of a mortality amongst the camels, he had not even enough of them to convey the few bags and the quantum of provisions that were left, added to which, Gezzar Pacha, Governor of Acre, was in actual hostility against him, and he was convinced from the popularity of that Chief, that the Turkish Army, in its then state of disorganisation, would join his standard, or disperse on his apprehended speedy approach.

But supposing the reverse of all these facts; that the conduct of the Governor of Acre should not have tended to augment the disorganisation of the Turkish Army; that they were able to surmount so desperate a march without water, or provisions, and that they were inclined to do so; the Vizier would not yet lose sight of the more than possible, the almost certain, calamitous issue. HQ did not forget that 18,000 Albanians and other chosen Turkish troops, collected through the zeal and popularity, and attempted to be inspired by the valour of Sir Sidney Smith, were defeated, and 14,000 of them cut to pieces, or drowned, by a detachment of French, only 800 of whom got into action at Aboukir, and that the residue murdered their General, Patrona Bey, at Cyprus. He did not forget that another numerous body assembled by Sir Sidney Smith at Rhodes, Candia, etc. were nearly destroyed at Damietta, and their General, Seid Ally Bey, notwithstanding his individual exertions, beheaded on arriving at Constantinople. He did not forget the recent Siege of El-Arish, where, though he had 100,000 men, that place defended by 700 French, for nine days resisted his utmost efforts, and would have continued to resist them, but that a battery of two guns worked by the English, enfiladed to extreme injury the ditch facing the entrance, and made a breach in the north-east angle of the great square. He could not forget the alarm created by the success and tactics of the enemy, and that if it were ever possible to cross the desert under the circumstances in which he stood, that he would then have but a few bad eight pounders, and shot considerably too small for their calibre, to attack the French Army, with a perfect park of artillery, and entrenched in such a manner upon the walls of Sesostris is to render them almost invulnerable to even troops not exhausted by famine and fatigue, or paralyzed by terror, or disaffection. With a conviction that a total defeat would be the consequence of action, he knew that even a check would be attended with the immediate desertion, and that the exhausted state of the treasury precluded the chance of levying other forces, if even the Government were permitted to exist for the two or three years which would be requisite for the purpose; but he knew that the heterogeneous and frequently hostile particles of which the Turkish people are composed, and which by force alone are rendered amenable to authority, would instantly and finally separate, and that the power of the French would be permanently established by the subversion of the Turkish Empire. Thus left without an alternative, he felt that his first duty was an expeditious compliance with the instructions transmitted from Constantinople, through the Commissioners deputed by the Porte, to offer to the French the terms uniformly held out to them, as well by printed and other papers thrown from the walls of Acre, with the signature of Gezzar Pacha and Sir Sidney Smith, as upon every other occasion during the way, namely - To convey any part of the entire Army to France at the charge of the Turkish Government.

The Vizier therefore sent repeated messages and letters, and even despatched Lieutenant-Colonel Bromley to Sir Sidney Smith to Damietta, urging him to instantly repair with the French Commissioners, deputed by General Kléber to His Excellency at El-Arish, declaring that his and their presence, and the immediate conclusion of the Convention are the only terms upon which the enemy would treat, and were indispensable to the existence of the Turkish Army, and of the Turkish Empire.

I have the honour to be, sir,
Your most humble and obedient servant
(Signed) JOHN DOUGLAS.

PORTRAIT OF THE EARL OF ST. VINCENT.
Compiled by General Sir H. E. Blumberg, K.C.B.

The following letters with reference to the portrait of Earl St. Vincent in the Portsmouth Mess are abstracted from the Portsmouth Letter Books to the Admiralty 1802 to 1806.

> Royal Marine Barracks, Portsmouth,
> May 17th, 1804

My Lord,

The Officers of the Division, which I have the honor to command, impressed with lasting gratitude for the many benefits conferred by your Lordship on their Corps; beg leave, as a small testimony of their sense of obligation, to solicit through me that you will be pleased to allow some Artist of eminence (whoever your Lordship may approve of) to take your portrait that it may be placed in the Mess Room at this Headquarters. Permit me to express particular pleasure in communicating this wish to your Lordship and also to assure you, that I am with the most profound respect, My Lord,

> Your Lordships Most obedient servant
> Geo. Elliot, Major General R. Marines.

To Lieut. Gen. Campbell, Commandant in Town.

> Royal Marine Barracks Portsmouth
> 20th May, 1804

Sir,

By particular desire of the officers of the Division a Letter of which the enclosed is a copy, was forwarded to Earl St. Vincent, a copy of whose letter in return is likewise transmitted for your information. You will perceive that Sir William Beechy is the Artist alluded to, & I am to request you will wait on that gentleman & give him directions to take a painting of His Lordship, near the size of that of Earl Spencer at Plymouth; our Mess Room not being capable of containing a picture of larger dimensions; & also to wait on his Lordship & express the high sense of the satisfaction we feel at his indulgence & request he will be pleased to inform you of the time it will be most convenient for Sir W. Beechy to wait on him.

> I am Sir
> Your most humble servant,
> Geo. Elliot, Major General.

The following letters are taken from the Letters of Earl St. Vincent (Navy Record Society Publications) –

"Earl St. Vincent agrees to sit to Sir W. Beechy for his portrait for the officers of the Portsmouth Division Royal Marines.

Maj. Gen. Elliot

> May 1804

29th May, 1804.

Col. Burn,

"I am much gratified by the sentiments which the officers of the Chatham Division of Royal Marines have been pleased to express of the attention I have paid to honour and interest of the Corps, & although I feel the sitting for my portrait very irksome shall comply with their request & hope they will approve of Sir William Beechy."

It is probable that there is a similar letter to account for the portrait of Lord St. Vincent in the Plymouth Mess.

_____

PRECEDENCE OF THE CORPS OF ROYAL MARINES.
Summary of Appendix to the Historical Record of the Royal Marines, by R. Cannonby, Adjutant General's Department of War Office, published 1845.

"Following memoranda…….to show relative positions in which the Marine Regiments were placed in respect to rank and precedence with Regiments of Infantry during the period the Marine Regiments were borne on the establishment of the Regular Army, and the ground upon which the present *Corps of Royal Marines* has been authorised, when acting with the Infantry of the Line, to take their station next to the Forty-ninth Regiment according to the date of their formation in the year 1755."

The rank of the several regiments of the British Army was first regulated by a Board of General Officers assembled in the Netherlands, by command of William III., on 10th June, 1694.

Another Board of General Officers was assembled by order of Queen Anne in 1713, to decide on rank and precedence of regiments raised subsequently to 1694.

A third Board was assembled by command of King George I. in 1715 for the same purpose.

* * * *

The numerical titles of Regiments, as fixed on the principles laid down in the Reports, were confirmed by Royal Warrant of King George II. on 1st July, 1751, and again by King George III. on 19th December, 1768; previously regiments were generally designated by names of their Colonels.
1. The regiments which had been formed by King Charles II. in 1660, and those raisedby Kings James II. and William III. were numbered according to dates of being placed on the English establishment, from the First or Royal Regiment to the Twenty-seventh.
2. Regiments added during reign of Queen Anne from 1702-1713 and retained on establishment after Treaty of Utrecht 1713 were numbered from Twenty-eighth to Thirty-ninth regiments.

3. 40th Regiment formed from independent companies in N. America and West Indies in 1717.
4. 41st Regiment formed from invalids in 1719.
5. Regiments raised by King George I. on augmentation in 1715 were disbanded in 1718, after the Monarchy in the line of Brunswick had been established.
6. 42nd Highland Regiment formed in reign of George II. from independent companies in Scotland in 1739.
7. 43rd Regiment raised for service in America in 1740, disbanded in 1743. (Also known as Goochie's Marines.-Ed.).
8. The 10 Regiments of Marines raised in 1739 and 1740 were numbered from 44th to 53rd Regiments. These were disbanded in November 1748.
9. The following seven regiments were raised and added to the Army in January 1741, in consequence of disbandment of Gooche's American Provincials and also the 10 regiments of Marines - the numerical titles of six of these regiments were changed after the peace of 1748. The 54th to 59th Regiments became the 43rd to 48th Regiments; the 60th Regiment was disbanded.
10. The 49th Regiment was formed in 1743 of two companies of a regiment raised in reign of Queen Anne, which had remained in Jamaica, and of six other companies formed in that colony. Retained on the establishment in 1748 and numbered 49th Regiment.
11. On recommencement of hostilities with France in 1755, 50 companies of Marines were raised, under the control of the L.C. of the Admiralty, and formed into three divisions, at Chatham, Portsmouth and Plymouth.

The Corps of Marines having been raised in 1755, and since that period retained on the establishment as a branch of the permanent National Force of Navy, Army and Marines, H.M. King George IV. directed the following General Order to be issued:-

"Horse Guards,
30 March, 1820.

" In reference to the Regulations regarding the Precedence of Regiments (as contained in page 10 of the General Regulations and Orders for the Army), His Majesty has been graciously pleased to command that the Royal Marines when acting with Troops of the Line shall take their station next to the Forty-ninth Regiment.

By Command of H.R.H. the Comdr.-in-Chief,
(Signed) HENRY TORRENS,
Adjutant General."

EXTRACTS FROM THE DIARY OF LIEUT. WM. CLARK, R.M.

EPPERSTONE,
NOTTS,
November, 1839.

Commodore Sir Samuel Hood, whose zeal, skill and enterprise were never surpassed, even in the British Navy, could not long remain quietly looking at the enemy, and both they and ourselves were soon in something like perpetual motion, and boats and small craft were in constant activity. Amongst other means of annoyance, the Government at that period employed, I believe, various persons, and means devised by them to endeavour to destroy in various ways the enemy's vessels at that time collected in different ports on the French coast, and amongst others they employed a most notorious smuggler, of the name of Johnson, whose escape from either the fleet prison or Newgate by escalade, and some other most extraordinary feats of desperate enterprise (worthy of buccaneers of former days), rendered him at the time a sort of "public character." This man, in command of a small cutter, was sent out to Sir Samuel Hood, to attempt the destruction of some of the enemy's ships in Basque Roads (Rocheford). He was provided with gigs, or swift pulling boats, and machines of peculiar construction, partly, I believe of his own invention, one of which, called a Catamaran, was filled with combustible materials, and could be so far sunk in the water as to render the person conducting it scarcely visible above it. This machine was to be attached to the cable of a ship lying at anchor and allowed to drop under her bows, where by the aid of clockwork it was to explode after a given time, and it was expected it would drive in her bows, and cause her immediate destruction.

Well, this fellow was with us, I don't remember how long, but some weeks, anchoring his vessel near the French squadron most nights, and waiting for a favourable opportunity of carrying his scheme into execution; but something or other, according to his own account, always presented some obstacle: either the moon was too bright, and would cause his premature discovery or it was too dark to enable him to secure his "infernal machine" in its proper position. And at last Sir Samuel's patience began to tire; indeed, I have no doubt he considered him a humbug from the first, as he professed to row round the enemy's ships night after night, making the necessary observations to secure the success of his plans, when matured. The Commodore resolved to send an officer with him, who could form some judgment respecting what might be expected from him. So Sibley, our First Lieutenant, accompanied him one night, and on that occasion he did row close to the *Majestueux*, the French Admiral's flagship - if I remember right, round her. Yet, however, time passed on, and nothing more was done, and he and his vessel were ordered home, and the Frenchmen remained in whole ships and with whole skins. The cutter; I believe, was his own, and the Government paid so much per month for her; if so, his dilatory proceedings are sufficiently accounted for - delay, not promptitude, was his interest - the only object likely to be pursued by such a character. During his stay he very nearly caused us a serious loss by a false report, and his desertion of us at the time of trial. He reported to the Commodore that a very large French man-of-war brig had anchored off Rochelle; that he had been sufficiently near her to see the men on her deck, and could not be mistaken. Sibley instantly requested, and Sir Samuel granted permission, to attempt her capture with the boats, and we thought ourselves secure of being laid gallantly alongside by engaging Johnson himself to pilot us. It was arranged accordingly that he was to anchor his cutter between the French squadron and our intended object of attack, which being about one of his usual anchorages, was not likely to create any suspicion of our intentions, and when sufficiently dark, we were to quit the squadron and rendezvous alongside his vessel, when he was to join and lead us to glory. Accordingly, with eight boats, under the command of Sibley (with whom I was), we reached the cutter about ten o'clock, when to our utter dismay, the gallant smuggler was gone. His mate, or first officer, informed us, that finding the night favourable for operations, he was gone to see what could be done. He (the mate) said there was a brig, and that appeared to be all he knew. However, we insisted on his accompanying us, and away we went, and pulled and pulled, without meeting with anything, until near daybreak, and were about to return, when we saw a brig sure enough. And now we were inclined to forgive the traitor, and away we dashed, the crew of the first boat jumping on board, when all was still as death - she was an American merchantman. A pistol went off by accident, which woke her captain, who, poor fellow, wondered what in the name of God all the row meant. And now we had to pass at no great distance from the enemy's squadron, some of which having espied us, got under sail to cut us off, and it became doubtful whether they would not do so before we could join our ships, which were nearly becalmed. Fortunately a breeze sprang up, and brought them in so fast that the French ships were obliged to allow us to pass or risk an action with our squadron, which with their usual courtesy they declined, and we returned unharmed, but cursedly cross, and venting invectives both loud and deep against Johnson, who, doubtless, would as soon have betrayed one party as the other, provided the balance of interest was in his favour.

* * * *

Some Notes on "Johnson, the Smuggler."
COLONEL C. FIELD.

This more or less adventurous person was born in 1772, and is said to have been at one time an Officer in the British Navy. This, however, is probably somewhat doubtful. In 1798 he was imprisoned for smuggling, but escaped, and was considered of sufficient importance to have a reward of £500 offered for his capture. He probably succeeded in evading the authorities, for we next hear of him as acting as pilot to the British expedition to Holland in 1799, for which service he received a pardon for his smuggling offences.

He again reverted to smuggling, and was again imprisoned in 1802 not this time for his old offence, but for debt. He again escaped and got across to Calais and Flushing. Napoleon is said to have asked him to pilot his proposed invasion of England, but Johnson answered, "I am a smuggler, but a true lover of my country and no traitor." For this spirited reply he spent nine months in a French prison. Whether he escaped, more suo, or whether he was released, does not appear, but in October 1805 he was evidently at liberty and in correspondence with Lord Castlereagh, who wrote to Sir Sidney Smith:

"Mr. Johnson was employed in the late war in various services of a confidential nature by

Government, wherein he proved himself of much utility by his dexterity and boldness, and by his knowledge of the coasts of the enemy."

Sir Sidney Smith seems to have been persuaded by Johnson that if given a suitable vessel - a small craft, cutter or lugger - he would be a valuable assistant in the projected attack on the Boulogne Flotilla, assembled ready for the descent on the English coast. In what way does not seem clear, but probably in reconnoitring the enemy. After some correspondence as to the status of the vessel, it was decided by Lord Barham, "If the cutter is purchased by the Government, she must, of course, be commanded by a King's officer, and cannot be placed under any other authority. If hired by the month, Johnson may command her and his crew navigate her."

Eventually Sir Sidney Smith was informed (25 Oct. 1805) that Lord Castlereagh approved of the Nile cutter being purchased for Johnson for £2,600. "There will," continued the memo "be great difficulty in having her fitted and coppered in a King's yard. His Lordship therefore, wishes you would direct the equipment in a merchant's yard."

In 1806 Johnson seems to have been with Lord St. Vincent, and evidently had some scheme for the destruction of the French shipping for on 8th August the Admiral wrote to Lord Howick - "The vigilance of the enemy alone prevented Tom Johnson (sic) from doing what he proposed."

In 1809 he was attached to the ill-fated Walcheren expedition, and was probably borne on the books of H.M.S. *Caesar*, for the Gunner of that ship wrote in his memoirs* that they received a number of "copper submarine carcasses," holding from 405 to 540 pounds of powder apiece, intended for use as mines. "Johnstone (sic) the smuggler, "he adds, "laid one down near the gate of the new harbour before Flushing surrendered, but we never heard of any damage being done by it. As for our part, we never tried them - indeed our Admiral said it was not a fair proceeding."

Although the expedition - and Johnson himself apparently - was a failure, he received another pardon for his smuggling propensities, and probably with the idea of "setting a thief to catch a thief was given command of the Fox, Revenue Cutter, and a pension of £100 a year. However he soon tired of this, or the Admiralty tired of him, and paid him off on the conclusion of peace with France, and it seems probable that then it was that he turned his attention to the construction of submarine vessels. The story goes that he actually did carry out some experiments in some kind of a submarine, either his own or somebody else's invention, and during one of these, he was on board when she got foul of a ship's cable and remained immovable. Johnson calmly pulled out his watch and said to his assistant, "We have but two minutes and a half to live unless we get clear of that cable." They did get clear in time, and Johnson lived to build a couple of submarines, of which he wrote in 1821, "I constructed two submarine ships, which I intended should be engaged in the meritorious and humane service of rescuing the immortal Emperor Napoleon." Why "meritorious and humane" it is difficult to imagine. They were named the "Eagle" and the "Etna," and are said to have been propelled by steam and to have carried "twenty torpedoes."†

*"A Mariner of England." (1780-1819). Edited by Col Spencer Childers, 1908.

† Letter in the "Sunday Times" of 7th January, 1917, from J. P. Bacon Phillips, Crowhurst Rectory.

Johnson says he built two for Napoleon's escape, but only one is generally spoken of. It is said to have been 100 feet long, and provided with two folding masts. This is more likely than the steam propulsion referred to above. It was probably intended that she should make the greater part of the passage above water, and when near St. Helena dive to avoid the British cruisers, and get close enough inshore to send a message to the Emperor that she was waiting to receive him on board.

Johnson was promised £40,000 by Napoleon's friends the day his boat was finished, and "wealth beyond the dreams of avarice" should the project prove successful. But as the great Emperor died just before the boat was completed, the whole thing was a bad "wash out" as far as Johnson was concerned. Moreover, the Government got wind of his intentions about this time, and ordered Sir Robert Seppings, the Surveyor of the Navy, to inspect the boat and report whether he thought Johnson's plan would have been feasible. Sir Robert reported in the affirmative, upon which the vessel was ordered to be destroyed.

It seems possible that Johnson may have had the second boat he mentions under construction somewhere out of the Government's ken, for it seems that later on he exhibited a submarine in London, which he was hoping to sell to the Spanish Committee, which meditated its use against the French Fleet then blockading Cadiz. The project fell through, and Johnson and his inventions seems to have faded into obscurity. All that can be further told of him is that he died in the Vauxhall Bridge Road at the age of 67. C.F.

Our next enterprise proved of a more serious and formidable nature. In July we were informed by an American ship from Bordeaux that a convoy of merchant vessels, under the protection of two men-of-war brigs, were lying in the Verdun Roads (some distance up the river Garronne), whence Lord Cockrane had succeeded some months before in cutting out a ship of war (the Tapageuse.). Our First Lieutenant, E. R. Sibley, immediately solicited the Commodore for permission to attempt their capture with the boats of the squadron. Sir Samuel detached Captain Rodd in the *Indefatigable* frigate to reconnoitre, and to confirm the correctness of the American's information. The signal was made to the squadron for each ship to send a barge, manned and armed, for immediate service alongside the Centaur, our own being preparing at the time. The Commodore, with his usual kindness, granted me permission to accompany Sibley, with such Marines as I chose to select, and we all proceeded on board the *Indefatigable*, boats, officers and boats' crews, and made sail from the squadron for the mouth of the Garronne, where we joined the Iris frigate who reported all to be the same state as when the *Indefatigable* left and on the night of the 14th July we were all in the boats and preparing to quit the ship, when it came on to blow so hard, that it was not deemed prudent to proceed that night. (I mention this, because we learnt afterwards our preparations had been observed from the shore, and the enemy being put on their guard, took their measures accordingly). However, the next evening saw us all thirteen boats, including those of the two frigates, quit the ships and steal along with muffled oars (like poor old King Lear's troop of horse shod with felt). We left the frigates about nine o'clock, the boats in two lines, six in ours (Sibley's) and seven in the other, commanded by Lieut. Ivy, first of the Iris, the two commanding officers abreast of each other, the rest following in succession. After pulling some time we made sail, the wind blowing strong and the boats keeping excellent order. We passed the Corduan lighthouse, and reached the river's entrance, when we struck sail and again took to our oars, pulling in the direction in which we expected to find the objects of our search. It was now exceedingly dark, blowing strong, with thunder and lightning. We pulled a considerable time, and began to fear we should miss our objects, if we had not already passed them, when Sibley cautiously gave the word "oars" (that is, cease rowing). He had observed the masts of a vessel through the gloom. The two lines of boats were still in excellent order, and the two commanding officers now closed each other, and we distinctly made out two men-of-war by their masts, and other tokens familiar to the practised eye of an old man-of-war man. They were riding to the tide, which ran strongly, and Sibley determined to attack the headmost, which appeared the largest, with his division of the boats, leaving the sternmost one to be dealt with by the other. This was clearly understood before we parted, when wishing each other success, each gave way with the utmost impetuosity towards his destined bark. The high wind, the thunder and the extreme darkness were in favour of our approaching our enemy unheard and unseen, and I believe a vivid flash of lightning betray'd us at the last; but we were alongside at the instant, or at least nearly alongside as protruding beams would allow us to get, when she opened her broadside upon us, and followed it up by a rapid discharge of musketry, and when we at length reached her side and grappled the boat to her, muskets with bayonets fixed were darted into the boat and we found that we had not yet cleared the principal obstacle to our entrance; she had boarding nettings triced up to her mast heads, and secured down to her hull, barring all entrance, until Sibley, whilst clinging to the rigging, with a most fortunate stroke with his sword, severed the tracing line, and down came the netting whip with a simultaneous rush. Those who were not entangled in the netting, sprang forward, and a most determined struggle hand to hand ensued. But it was too terrible to last long, and the Frenchmen who were able, ran below and left us masters of the deck, when we gave three hearty cheers, to give notice to the party which we hoped were in possession of the other brig.

Our Winter Quarters at Madeira we could not but enjoy in so delightful climate, nothing of a hostile nature occurred with one exception on the part of the Comus, her boats cutting out a small Merchant Vessel from one of the Canary Islands and having, if I remember right, a Lieutenant and two or three men wounded. I forget what time we left Madeira, though I know I very lately ungallantly destroyed a Copy of complimentary verses addressed to us in the name of the ladies of the Island, on our sailing from Funchal Bay with the date attached to it.

I am now at a loss, I know we had to refit at Plymouth, I know that we had a cruise without the Commodore in the North Sea. I well remember fishing on the dogger Bank, the Broad Fourteens, and various other fishing grounds off the coast of Holland, but I can bring nothing to book until I find ourselves with the Broad Pendant again flying at Yarmouth in the fleet, under Admiral

Gambier, with an army of some Six or Eight and Twenty Thousand Men, under Lord Cathcart, destined as we supposed, to make a descent on the shores of the Baltic, in aid of the Swedes then beseiged in the fortress of Stralsund, in Swedish Pomerania. We sailed the latter end of July, 1807, and passed Cronborg Castle and anchored in the sound early in August. Our (*Centaur's*) station was near the Town of Elsinore, where I went on shore several times and visited amongst other places, what is known as Hamlets Gardens, and you who know my veneration for our immortal Shakespeare, will believe with what sensations of enthusiasm and delight I traversed the spot, rendered for ever classic ground, by his unrivalled pen. We were received with every rite of friendship and hospitality, and were supplied with whatever refreshments we required, and a pretty return we shortly made. A Plenipotentiary (Mr. Jackson) had reached Copenhagen a few days before us, to endeavour to prevail upon the Court of Denmark to deliver up to us in trust, the Danish Navy, to prevent its falling into the hands of the French, guaranteeing of course its return when such danger should cease to exist, this proposition with a becoming spirit was refused to Mr. Jackson, but he dealt only in words, but a far more potent negotiator was at hand to back him, Lord Cathcart with seven or eight and twenty thousand men were disembarked a few miles from Copenhagen on the sixteenth of August, and by the eighteenth the City was invested and preparations were commenced for bombarding it, both by land and sea. The Danes were not idle, but did all that could be done against a force so overpowering, several skirmishes took place whilst advancing on the Town, and some lives were lost. The Gun boats were very active and found some warm employment for boats and small craft. Detachments of seamen were landed from the ships to assist in transporting the heavy guns, Mortars, Ammunition and stores from the landing places to the batteries preparing for them, and all was activity and bustle. The fleet was so distributed as to afford aid whenever and wherever it was in their power to give it. Commodore Sir Richard Keats, and a Squadron occupied the great Belt on the opposite side of the island of Zealand, Sir Samuel with another detachment moved on towards the further end of the Sound, near the town of Drago, on the Isle of Amack, so that if you glance your eye on the Map of Denmark, you will see that the Fleets completely surrounded the Island as the Army did the City. Between the time of landing the Army, and the completion of the preparations for bombarding the ill fated City, many gallant exploits were performed, both ashore and afloat, though on no grand scale. The principle affair was the defeat of a body of Danish Troops near Kioge, by a British Brigade under Sir Arthur Wellesley (The Duke of Wellington). At length all being ready, and every effort to induce the Danes to comply with the demands having failed, the fearful scene commenced, and I cannot do better than use the brief but terrible description given by Admiral Gambier: "The Mortar Batteries which had been erected by the Army, in the several positions they had taken round Copenhagen, together with the Bombing Vessels, which were placed in convenient situations, began the Bombardment on the Morning of the second September, with such power and effect that in a short time the Town was set on fire and by the repeated discharges of our artillery was kept in flames in different places, till the evening of the fifteenth, when a considerable part of it being consumed, and the conflagration arrived at a great hight, threatening the speedy destruction of the whole City, the General Commanding the Garrison, sent out a flag of truce." From this time hostilities ceased, and the Danes were enabled without molestation to take the best means in their powere to arrest the fearful conflagration of their almost ruined Capital. For dreadful indeed had been the wide spread destruction perpetrated during the last four days and three nights, the whole of which time the devoted city had been a prey to the devouring flames, for though they had I believe one of the best organised Corps of Firemen of any City in Europe, the furious element soon reached a height which set all their best directed efforts at defiance, it had been ascertained where the greatest stores of combustible material were accumulated, and there were directed the shells, carcasses, red hot shot and Congreve's rockets (the last were a new invention of Sir William Congreve's, then first used on active service with a most destructive effect), and whenever the conflagration was observed to rage with the greatest fury, there again did a portion of the Batteries ply their missives with increased rapidity, for the purpose of defeating the exertions of the Firemen and inhabitants to check its progress and I was told that very few of the former escaped death or mutilation. Our attention was directed late one night to the Cathedral Church , the body of which appeared to be in flames, beautiful spire towering majestically above them towards it we could distinctly see flying through the dark gloom of night, the burning fuses of numerous shells, whilst the rockets rushed through the air to the same destination with a roar of a distant hurricane; from time to time, portions of ruins appeared to fall and dense columns of smoke arise, soon again to be succeeded by fresh torrents of increasing flames, at length, between three and four o'clock in the morning, the body of the sacred edifice being a complete ruin, its magnificent Spire which as yet had appeared erect and uninjured, dropped perpendicularly to the ground. Hundreds of families which but a few days previous had been living in peace and comfort, without the least anticipation of approaching danger were thus ruined and rendered houseless, and hundreds of their members, including females and children, killed or crippled and rendered a burden to themselves, their kindred and their country for the remainder of their existence - and this is Civilised and Christian Warfare. From our detachment of ships, we had observed a number of small vessels assemble at the Town of Drago, and suspecting they were collecting for some hostile purpose, Sir Samuel determined to send in the Boats to ascertain, and if so to attempt their destruction. Wobrige our First Lieutenant was ordered to proceed with the boats of the Squadron, and I was appointed to command the Marines, though several superior and doubtless much abler Officers than myself were in the in the Squadron and volunteered their services (of this proof Sir Samuel's good opinion and confidence in me I feel I may be justly proud). Lt. H. C. Thompson was ordered to support us with the launches armed with Cannonades in case we should be attacked from the Town whilst occupied in firing the Vessels. On reaching the outside pier we found a boom across which with some difficulty we displaced, and pulled in and boarded several of the vessels there assembled, they proved to be craft little calculated for warlike work of any kind, small heavy coasters and lighters. We then mounted the wooden pier and advanced towards the Town, but soon found ourselves unable to proceed as we could not find any communication with the shore, but were involved in a labyrinth of pier within pier, and now the Danes being alarmed were beating to arms in the Town and we thought it best to fire some of the largest vessels, which we did, and by the time we had done so, the enemy had apparently mustered a considerable force and commenced to fire some field pieces, the launches under Thompson had opened fire from their Cannonades upon the Town, and as all we at first contemplated, was executed we re-embarked in the boats, and when doing so a party of Danish Troops came down the pier which we were leaving, and a smartish brush took place between them and the last of our party embarking, and I being the last, got a slight tap on the head, we immediately pushed off leaving several of the vessels burning. When we had cleared the harbour, we hoisted a light, or rather the Cox-swain of the barge held out a lantern as a signal for the other boats to form and follow, we had not proceeded far, when a shot from a field piece dashed the lantern to atoms out of his hand, the fellow exclaiming " a d---d good shot by G-d, and a marine immediately mounted another on his bayonet and shouldered his musket, when the whole of the boats soon joined us and we returned to our ships. The Bombardment was always severest at night, as it could be best seen where the flames raged with the greatest fury, and the spectacle was undoubtedly one of awful grandeur, the burning carcasses the ignited fuzes of the shells crossing each other in their courses looked like so many meteors, whilst the Congreve Rockets streamed blazing through the air like comets hastening furiously onwards to accelerate the destruction of the flaming City. When the conflagration was at its height, you may form some idea of its magnitude when I tell you I could at midnight read without difficulty, by its light alone, any ordinary print (a newspaper for instance) when distance from it at least four miles. I have before said hostilities ceased on the fifth, and on the seventh (I think) the army marched into the City and the Navy took possession of the Naval Arsenal. Officers, Seamen and Marines were landed, and immediately commenced fitting out the Danish Fleet. The Norge, a fine Seventy Four, fell to the *Centaur's* lot, and Lieut. Wobrige and I were put in charge, the greatest activity prevailed in the Arsenal as you may imagine, for though the Danish Ships were quite dismantled when we took possession, we brought away early in October (I don't remember the day) Sixteen ships of the line, Thirteen Frigates and Six Brigs of war. The excellent arrangments in the Naval Arsenal gave great faculity in expediating the equipment, each ship having a separate store house assigned for her rigging store, all of which was in the most complete and efficient order, the ships themselves lying alongside the various jetties ready to receive them. Besides those brought away, we towed out of the harbour an old line of battle ship and a frigate, and burnt them and destroyed another ship of the line which was building and nearly complete.

We now proceeded up the Baltic with all the expedition we could, hoping to find a reinforcment on our way, and we happily were joined by H.M.S. *Implacable* (74) Capt. Byam Martin (now Admiral Sir B. Martin) an officer for skill and enterprise unsurpassed in his profession. At the entrance to the Gulf of Finland, we were reconnoitred by two Russian Frigates and had we known the coast and the relative situation of our friends and foes, I fancy we could have cut them off from their Fleet, but we were ignorant of both, and it was our policy to act with great precaution and particularly to avoid being decoyed from our primary object, the succour of our friends and Allies the Swedes, and we assuredly found them in considerable jeopardy, the two Fleets were anchored in sight of each other, the Swedes in the Ora Sound, the Russians near Hange Head, but the Swedish Fleet was devided and of eleven sail of the Line, only seven were anchored together, four being at an anchorage considerably detached, amongst the multitudinous mass of rocky islands with which the whole of the coast of Finland is thickly studded. Why the Russians had not attacked the seven Swedes, the Russian Admiral could have explained, to us it did appear unaccountable, for they were unprotected by a single gun on the land, and the Russian Fleet consisted of eleven Sail of the Line, two of them three deckers and a number of large Frigates, I think eight or ten (the Swedes were all two deckers, some only Sixty Fours). After communicating by signals, we joined the Swedish Ships, and on the following day the whole of the Russian Fleet appeared standing off and on, reminding us of the old times of Blockade, only with the tables turned, we were now blockaded. As they had not attacked the Swedes before our arrival, we did not expect they would now they were reinforced by us, but they daily cruised off and appeared either to dare us than otherwise, but it was not our time yet. They one morning sent in a Frigate under cover of a flag of Truce, with a proposal to liberate some Swedish prisoners, but in fact to reconnoitre and ascertain whether we were really what we outwardly appeared, British Ships, the Frigate kept out of Gun Shot, but the Officer sent on board the Centaur, had been trained (as many Russian Officers were), and on stepping on our deck, immediately recognised an old Messmate in one of our Midshipmen: The Admiral sent him off with a flea in his ear, desiring him to report to his Captain that he had a great mind to detain the boat, and that had the Frigate come within range, he would have fired upon her under the circumstances, as she was evidently sent as a spy; the proffered release of a few prisoners being merely a pretence.

All hands were now set to work to assist the Swedes, their four sail of the line were brought round and all was active preparation for an anticipated Battle, for the Russians still cruising off generally standing close in in the forenoon and evening, and appeared braving us to conflict. Sir Samuel visited some of the Swedish ships almost daily in company with the Swedish Admiral (Nickoff) and Captains Martin and Webley, and was quite satisfied with their state of preparation, their discipline and enthusiasm. How long we were employed I do not exactly recollect, I think about a fortnight, at length, the morning of the Twenty-fifth of August saw us quit Ora Roads, the whole of the sick of the Swedish Fleet were put on board an old Four, which on leaving the roads steered for Carlscona. The Fleet now consisted of Thirteen Sail of the Line, Eleven Swedes several of them Sixty Fours and two British Seventy Fours with two Swedish Frigates, the Enemy we expected to meet consisted of eleven Sail of the Line, two of them Three Deckers, and a host of large Frigates, I think ten if not more. The Swedes formed their line of Battle the two British Ships serving themselves independant, in order to enable them to act wherever the judgement of the Admiral they could do it with the greatest effect, but I believe it was his intention if practicable, to have laid them both upon the Russian Commander-in-Chief, whose Flag was in a magnificent Three Decker of 120 Guns. But we soon found that notwithstanding the bold face they had assumed whilst we were quietly at anchor, they were by no means eager for the conflict on our assuming the offensive. We came in sight of them before noon, when they tacked and stood from us, we supposed the better to collect their ships and from their Fleet for the attack, we made all sail expecting they would either bring to or having formed their line would put about and meet us, but no such thing, they stood on, and our expected fight became a chase, the two British ships sailed better than the Russians, but they could much outsail the Swedes, few of which were coppered, we thus shortly became unsupported, except by each other, we were determined however to stick close to their skirts, and be ready if any opportunity should occur to cut off or disable any straggler. We remained at Quarters and thus continued the chase all night, about five in the morning of the twenty-sixth, the Implacable having headed the Centaur considerably, was enabled to bring the stern-most ship of the enemy to action, and steering upon her lee quarter, poured in a broadside, and heaving stays, gave her the other as she came round, receiving a few shots in return, she stood on until she hoped to fetch to windward of her, tacked again, but could not weather her, if she could only have done so it was Captain Martin's intention to have hooked on her bows, and have run right before the wind down upon the Swedish Fleet, now almost hull down to leeward, when they must have abandoned her, or have risked a general action, she, however, fetched within pistol shot of her lee quarter and opened a tremendous fire, when her colours came down (shot away the Russians said), but her pandant was halfway down when the Russian admiral (Hennikoff) with the whole Fleet bore up to the rescue, the Centaur was now well up, but we were both obliged to sheer off from such overwhelming odds, but only so far as to be ready to seize the first favourable opportunity of renewing the attack, the Implacable lost in the affair I think, eight killed and fifteen wounded, the Russians acknowledged to about eighty killed and wounded, a large shot passed through the Implacable's copper and spilled the ships companies' breakfast. A very fine large frigate took the lame duck in tow in a very seaman like manner, when our First Lieut. (Paul Lawless) observed by G--. if my bold friend Niminsky is in the Fleet, he commands that Frigate" and sure enough, so it turned out, Lawless had been shipmate with several young Russians in our service, where opportunity of learning their profession was afforded to such as voluntarily chose to have applied himself successfully, as soon as they had secured their beaten ship, they again made sail, the two British Ships hanging on their quarters, but the Swedes were some five or six leagues dead to leaward and increasing their distance hourly, in the afternoon we came in sight of the Russian Coast, and saw to our mortification, the Russian Fleet stand into Rogerwick (or Port Baltic), they could but just fetch in, and the damaged ship could not do so, but anchored about three of four miles to leeward, close to the shore, we had no Pilot for the coast, nor any Officer who was acquainted with it, and we thought at one time she had grounded, and dare not risk ourselves too near, so stood off, and the crew having been fagging hard, and not having been in bed the night before, the hammocks were piped down at six o'clock that they might have a good snooze, the Boats of the enemy's Fleet about this time, appeared actively engaged about their damaged ship. The Admiral was anxiously and perserveringly observing their proceedings through his telescope, when suddenly he turned around exclaiming "why she's afloat, if theres water for her there is water for us; turn the hands to make sail," which was instantly done, the hammocks were piped up and restowed, and we again beat to quarters and bore away with a free wind and a nice breeze, but which felt light as we approached the shore, thirteen boats which were assisting in towing the enemy cast off on seeing our determination to attack, and the ship cast round her head off shore. The Admiral ordered the guns to be treble shotted with round shot, and he himself took to con the ship into action, not a grain of powder was burnt on either side until the enemy's jib boom was through our foretopsail, and the bow of the two ships were in contact (somewhere about eight o'clock, the Admiral gave the order to fire as the guns came to bear, I was quartered with a small party on the forecastle, and we had the honour to open the Ball, we had sufficient way upon the ship to drag across her bows slowly, and I believe scarcely a shot was thrown away, and as she occasionally hang fast for a bit, some of the guns got a second shot in before she passed them, when her bowsprit came as far as the foremost mizen shroud, the Admiral ordered the master to lash her there "Lash her Ned lash her " cried the Admiral "thats it now she's safe." A party of the enemy now rushed out and attempted to board us along the bowsprit, but were I believe, nearly all killed or knocked overboard in the attempt, a second and a third attack with the same desperate intent followed, and one Officer, the Commander of the Soldiers on board, succeeded in reaching our poop sword in hand, and wonderfull to say unwounded, and the brave fellow was disarmed and conducted down into the cockpit, when the last forlorn hope was repulsed they were followed by a party of our boarders, and a desperate conflict took place on her quarter deck; when she surrendered, she proved to be the Sewoled, a Seventy Four, Commanded by Capt. Roodnof, her loss had been enormous, as near as we could make out about 350 killed and wounded, principally the former, and that in addition to the eighty lost by the Implacable's attack in the morning, to account in some measure both for the severity of her loss and the desperate defence she had put up, she had been crowned with a reinforcement of men from the Fleet to assist her defence. The Implacable had been detached towards the Swedish Fleet before we discovered the enemy to be afloat, she now joined us, but the Centaur and the Sewoled were both aground side by side, and the rocks so close ahead that some of the Russians attempted to reach them by dropping from her bows, but were picked up by the boats, we got an anchor out astern, but could not succeed in getting the ship off, Captain Martin came on board, and after consulting with Sir Samuel, returned to the Implacable and anchored her astern of us, we got hawsers from the stern posts of each ship and manning both capstans, strained very hard, but in vain to get the old ship afloat. At this time we could perceive with night glasses that several of the enemy's Ships had their sails set and we expected they would come down upon us. Captain Martin's observation was, "Well, if we can't get you off, we are afloat - we can bring our stern to yours, and with a spring on our cable we can form such a battery as will give a warm reception to any of them that dare attempt to approach us". We now proceeded to lighten the ship forward, by getting the foremost guns aft, and then with a mutual good heave away heartily on board both ships, and at length to our sincere delight, the old Lady glided off, and all was soon again right and ready. As soon as we could, we commenced removing the prisoners from the prize, which we found so desperately battered, that the Admiral determined to destroy her, her bows were literally beaten to a mass of splinters, and she could scarcely have been made sufficiently seaworthy to have ensured her safely down the Baltic, nor under our circumstances could we either spare the men to man her or a ship to convoy her, so after taking out the living and nothing more, she was set on fire about seven a.m., and a glorious bonfire she made to consummate our victory. Gun after Gun kept discharging as the fire reached them, and when her grand magazine at length exploded the spectacle was awfully magnificent. Her mainmast topmast shot up in a stream of fire to a considerable height, straight as an arrow, surmounting a dense mass of curling clouds, and fragments of her were flung in all directions: the hull continued burning the whole of the following day. The *Centaur's* loss was four killed and twenty-seven wounded. One of our sailors had a somewhat singular escape, he was a very fine young fellow, and had been a boatswain's mate, he was in the Boat with us when we left the ship on our expedition up the Garonne, but got drunk whilst on board the *Indefatigable*, and when we left that ship was unfit for duty, and one of her crew took his place, for this disgraceful conduct he was disrated and punished and a canvas label bearing the words "A disgrace to the Ship" was sewn on the back of his jacket, which he bore for many months, the fellow made a vow that he would redeem his character the first opportunity, and he now did so, he was one of the first that boarded, every true sailor in those days was especially proud of an enormous pigtail, it was the pride of his heart, and his was the very beau ideal of a tail, so thick, so long and so firmly tied, and a good service it rendered him when rushing along the Enemy's gangway towards her quarterdeck, he received a most tremendous blow, supposed from a tomahawk which falling just on the back of his neck, severed his tail from his head as clean as it could have been done with a pair of shears, inflicting a very severe wound, had it not been for the interposition of his tail, it would no doubt have killed him on the spot.

We sent the boats with the most severely wounded prisoners towards the Russian Fleet under white flags without subjecting them to the torture of successive removals. One Russian sailor had lost both legs above the knees by a cannon ball, and though he had been fourteen hours without the least surgical assistance, or having the stumps touched, when he came alongside he asked for a drink of water, and when he had drank, washed his hands and face, whether the shot had acted as an actual cautery or what, had prevented hemorrhage, I am not qualified to say. They were gladly received and I believe the courtesy as well as the humanity of the act properly appreciated, and eventually all the Russian prisoners were given up, on the understanding that they were not to serve again during the war, unless regularly exchanged. Amongst our own wounded was the First Lieutenant (Lawless), who after assisting in lashing the ships together was in the act of heading the boarders, when he received a musket shot near the hip joint, which came out near the spine making a wound fourteen inches long, but without causing any fracture of bone, and he eventually recovered, but poor fellow to meet at last a melancholy fate, he commanded the Vantour Brig and sailed for the West Indies, and it is supposed, foundered with all hands, as she was never afterwards heard of.

MARINES IN ACTION AFLOAT.

From "The Sailor Boy," A Poem in Four Cantos Illustrative of The Navy of Great Britain."
By H. C. Esq. London. 1809.

"Now within gun-shot, with three cheers the tars
The foe salute, and welcome bloody Mars;
While Duncan, from the quarter-deck, employs
His trumpet, bawling out Stand by, my boys.
'All ready,' cry the men who court the fray:
`Then at 'em, says the captain, 'fire away.'
A broadside roars, while French return the sound
Din salutes din, and echoes wide around.
Duncan intrepid, issues orders cool,
The first-lieutenant bold maintains his rule
While at the wheel the steady master reigns,
Who, spite of battle, steers thro' liquid plains.
As each Marine and his piece o'er quarter fires,
With officer, who thus his troop inspires;
Now hotter still, and hotter grows the fight,
Yard-arm and yard-arm, each essays his might.
`Coolly, my lads - keep cool.' the captain cries;
'Mind the sea's heaving - mark ye how she lies –

> 'Now pour away, my boys - strike, strike it in,
> 'Hearty, my lads' - Anon resounds the din,
> Which to increase, a whizzing shot comes by,
> Rending the deck, on all sides splinters fly,
> That level five Marines, with three ship's men,
> Brave souls thus destin'd ne'er to rise again; &c.

Marines have nothing to do in working the ship; their duty is merely to defend it in war, and attack the enemy when fighting. There is generally a company on board each ship, about forty in number under a captain and two lieutenants; and there are seventy companies of the Marines in the whole. In a sea-fight their small arms are of very great advantage in scouring the decks of the enemy; and when they have been long enough at sea to stand firm, as the ship rocks, they must be infinitely preferable to seamen if the enemy attempts to board, by raising a battalion of fixed bayonets to oppose them."

––––––––

THE NIGHT ATTACK.
(From "Nelsonian Reminiscences," by G. S. Parsons, Lieut., R.N., 1843.)

(27 Sept., 1810)

The boatswain's shrill pipe, re-echoed by his mates, called attention, and "Boarders away" resounded through the decks of H.M.S.--------.

It wanted an hour of midnight, and was intensely dark, when I ordered the boats to follow my motions without noise, and proceeded in search of a cutter, anchored between Rochelle and Rochfort, round which the boats of that division of the Channel Fleet, commanded by Sir Harry Wurrard Neale, were ordered to rendezvous, for the purpose of cutting out a convoy that had left Rochelle and chased into a bay near that place some days previously. Its strongly guarded state forbade any prospect of success in daylight, as a (very high promontory, called Point Du Che, furnished with long thirty-two pounders, afforded effectual resistance, even to the approach of an adverse squadron. A regiment of infantry were moved from Rochelle, and encamped round the very pretty bay, their white tents glittering on the plain, and giving more effect to its beautiful scenery. The Admiral and officers, that had volunteered on this desperate undertaking, had closely recconnoitred the place this day, and each officer had the plan of attack fully explained to him by Sir Harry, with the particular duty expected from him.

The Marine Artillery were selected, and volunteers from that admirable corps, headed by Lieutenant Liddle, composed the forlorn hope. It was on recconnoitring we found that a regiment of infantry had arrived from Rochelle in the bay, and had taken an excellent position both for defending the shipping and the promontory of Point Dy Che. The plan of attack was skilfully arranged by Sir Harry. Darkness was the first requisite, and it was most essential that a landing should be effected, or the boats got so much under the promontory that the heavy metal with which it bristled could not be depressed to bear on the approaching force. One hundred Marines, commanded by their Captain from the "Caledonian" were to secure the retreat of the storming party, headed by Lieutenant Liddle; and for that purpose were to take up a position between the boats and French regiment, whose encampment so much enlivened the plain.

The boats were to move in six divisions from the cutter, their oars muffled, and each division having a different duty assigned it. Some were to board and cut out the shipping; others conveyed the storming, and covering party; mine, in a seventy-four's launch, was to flank the Marines, and, with an eighteen-pounder mounted in her bow, to check the advance of the French infantry.

Now, imagine the cutter - and she was found with great difficulty, not daring to shew a light - imagine the cutter's deck thronged with the officers commanding the different boats, receiving the final orders of the youthful flag-lieutenant representative of the Rear-Admiral, each as he made his parting bow to the gallant youngster - for so he was compared to the senior officers under him - each drew tighter the belt of his sword, and placed his hand on the butt of his pistols. The quick ear might have detected the half-drawn sigh and the rapid glance, had there been light, the slight suffusion of the eye, as some replaced the locket they had most affectionately pressed to their lips, arguing, from the dangerous nature of their service, a possibility of no other opportunity of bidding farewell to the much-prized tokens of love or friendship.

At this moment some awkward fellow accidentally discharged his pistol, and the stifled exclamation of displeasure burst from numerous lips. All eyes turned eagerly to the dangerous battery of Point Du Che, and then swept the bay where the regiment had encamped, but nothing denoted alarm. The sentinel still paced his lonely round, and a few minutes' observation convinced us they had not observed our unguarded conduct.

"Gentlemen, to your boats" said our youthful commander, and they formed in the divisions previously planned. As we slowly approached the intended scene of disembarkation, for the strictest orders were given for silence, and the muffled oars just touched the unruffled water, we plainly perceived the sentinel, as he stood on the topmost pinnacle of the high bluff cliff. His figure, as viewed by us so far beneath, appeared unnaturally large, and swelled out into gigantic proportions between earth and sky. Sometimes he would slowly pace the edge, then would he rest on his musket, casting a wary eye on the dark waters below.

Every man held his breath, for, this was the trying time. Death or victory hung on the vigilance of that man, and each eye strained to watch his motions.

"Hush!" was faintly heard among the divisions and I thought I could distinguish the beating of the heart, as the sentinel was observed to stop and apparently stretch himself forward from the cliff.

A discharge of grape and canister at this moment, from their heavy guns, would have swept us like a flash of lightening, from the face of the ocean.

Thank God! He drew back, and, seemingly satisfied with his gaze, resumed his slow pace. Each person drew his breath more freely; at least I can answer for myself, who felt as if a ton weight had suddenly been lifted from my breast.

Every yard had now life or death depending on it. Yet we could not exert more speed without drawing on us the attention of our wary and vigilant foe. With us all was profound stillness and inactivity, far different from the bustle and noise of action; and I am confident many a good resolution was formed, and many a silent aspiration ascended to the throne of Heaven for mercy. During the forty-two years I have been in the Service, never did I feel my mind called upon for more fortitude than on this eventful ten minutes. Again the sentinel stood still, and stretched himself over the cliff, gazing on the deep, deep sea, like a man alarmed, for the dip of our oars had reached his quick ears.

"Qui vive?" from his hoarse, manly voice, rang in our ears like thunder. Again we heard the challenge, quickly followed by the report of his musket.

Now hissed the rockets as they ascended the sky, and the blue lights innumerable threw a ghastly glare on the frowning promontory and bay below. The grape and canister splashed and tore the waters into foam just outside of us, and the British cheer rang high and merrily, as our youthful commander shouted "Give way for your lives men, and remember your orders!"

The divisions of boats flew through the placid waters, as the rowers bent both back and oar to their work; and as they neared the shore, diverged to their different duties. The forlorn hope, under the gallant Liddle, jumped from their boats, and rushed up the steep to the attack of the battery with incredible speed. I drew off to the right of the Marines, and directly in front of the French regiment, whose bugles at intervals could be heard above the roar of the heavy artillery and field-pieces, that thickly lined the beach, and now opened in earnest on the boats.

A sudden nervous start, and - "I was afraid my right arm was off," said the midshipman, seated near me; but it is only confoundedly bruised by a shot striking the gunnel."

"It is well you preserved it, for I want its assistance in training the carronade. So - oars, lay in the six foremost ones, bowse the forward gun, and load it with double canister. Now, cockswain, keep the bow of the boat directed towards the centre of that scattered fire you see advancing;" for the regiment has thrown out its sharpshooters to feel their way, and give some knowledge of the attacking force. Of these gentlemen I took no notice, confident that the main body was advancing in close column, and reserving my welcome for them alone.

By this time Lieutenant Liddle's storming party had gained the crown of the promontory, and were halted to reform and gain breath, but finding the enemy endeavouring to turn one of their heavy guns upon them, the gallant Liddle gave the word to charge bayonets, and advance in double-quick time; sparks flew as they crossed each other, and many a gallant breast was transfixed by that truly British weapon.

At this moment their gallant leader received a ball in his sword arm, which shattered the bone, so as to require amputation, and the wounded hero was supported to the boats with the wreath of victory on his brow. The tramp of masses of infantry was plainly heard in the launch and the sharpshooters retired on their main body.

"Depress the gun, and stand clear of its recoil!" Nearer, and still nearer came the heavy tread. I heard the command to our Marines, to make ready and close their files. "Fire?" and thirty-six pounds of small balls imperatively commanded a halt, which the Frenchman acknowledged by prompt obedience.

The flames from the grounded shipping, that had been set on fire, now gave a glimpse of the retreating infantry, and our gun, by its playing, accelerated their march.

The commanding officer now ordered the bugle to sound a retreat, and the Marines rushed into the boats in double-quick movement. Never was a night attack better planned, or more ably executed. Our youthful commanding officer, now Captain Hamilton, then received his promotion, and we the thanks of Sir Harry Burrard Neale.

I feel myself called on in gratitude, here to notice the extreme kindness of our reception by our excellent Captain, now a full Admiral, as he welcomed each officer by a warm shake of the hand, and "Thank God I see you all safe!" with the capital breakfast laid out in his cabin, to which I, for one, did ample justice. There is a warmth of feeling and susceptibility about a true Irish gentleman, that is most pleasant to experience, and is excelled by no other nation on the surface on this fair globe.

NOTE – This cutting-out expedition was carried out by the crews of the "Caledonian" and "Valiant." Three brigs were attacked, two of which were brought off and the third destroyed. The Marines stormed the battery and spiked the guns. Lieutenant Little (Liddell is a misspelling) received a reward from the Patriotic Fund, a pension of £70 a year for his wound, and an appointment at the Woolwich Division of Marines.

RATIONS AND VICTUALLING ARRANGEMENTS IN THE ROYAL MARINES FROM 1755 TO PRESENT DAY.
By General Sir H. E. Blumberg, K.C.B.

In view of the care now taken in the Corps as to food and its arrangements, it may be of interest to glance back at the manner in which our forefathers fared in this respect.

When the Corps was forming in 1755 no barracks were available, and it was therefore necessary to put officers and men into Quarters, or as we should say, into Billets.

Billetting in England had always been unpopular, and was forbidden by law, except when authorised by the several Mutiny Acts for the government of the Standing Army; as these did not cover the Marines, the Marine Mutiny Act of that year contained the necessary provisions for billeting Marines in Inns, Alehouses, Victualling houses, etc.; billeting in private houses was absolutely illegal. The Marine Mutiny Act was passed yearly by Parliament, and after signature by the Lords of the Admiralty was promulgated to the Divisions; this continued until the Army Regulation and Discipline Act of 1878, which included provisions for the Marines on shore, and is now embodied in the Army Act of 1881, which is brought into force yearly by the Army Annual Act.

The Innkeeper besides providing accommodation was obliged to provide n.c.o.'s and men with meals if required, for which deductions were made from their pay; the ration apparently included an allowance of beer. Officers made their own arrangements for providing their meals, for which they paid themselves. There was therefore no need for Quartermasters and their stores.

As the pay of a Private was only 8d, a day, from which he was put under stoppages for rations, necessaries, Greenwich Hospital, and the Chaplain, he cannot have received much actual cash - they seem to have generally only had money when they drew their sea pay, which, luckily for them, was generally increased by prize-money; they usually, however, embarked heavily in debt.

There is an order extant, dated 4th February, 1756, showing that Drummers were deducted 3/- a week for subsistence until trained.

As war broke out in 1756 and the bulk of the Corps, which rose to about 25,000 strong, were at sea or in battalions all over the world, no doubt billeting met the needs, but after the demobilisation in 1763 we find bitter complaints from the Commanding Officers about the prevalence of desertion, which they attributed largely to the miserable conditions of the billets. Arrangements were consequently made to build barracks for the Marines, though it was nearly twenty years before Plymouth Division, which was the last, took over the Barracks at Stonehouse; even then - particularly at Portsmouth - there were still a considerable number of officers and men in billets.

When the Dockyard Guards were instituted in 1764, Plymouth Division, or some portion of them, appear to have been in barracks at Devonport, because on 11th December there is an order that 1s. 6d. per week is to be laid out by each Marine on butcher's meat, vegetables and bread - provisions must have been very cheap in those days.

The principle of stoppages for rations established in 1755 remained in force for Marines for 150 years, as it was not until 1904 that free rations were finally granted to Marines on shore.

In 1779, in the middle of the War of American Independence, the Government, probably due to shortage of supplies, had to make some sort of issue or arrangements, because from a Plymouth order of the 5th July, 1779, we learn that "a well-baked loaf weighing 6 lbs. of good English wheat, out of which the first or coarse bran had been taken by means of an 8-cloth, is allowed for each soldier for four days; men to be stopped 4½ d for the loaf."

When barracks were taken into occupation, arrangements for victualling were placed in the hands of the companies, as the supply of necessaries always had been. The quartermasters (who were ordinary duty officers told off for the duty), who only dealt with arms and clothing did not come into the picture. Definite orders were issued about messing: "Plymouth, 8th Dec., 1783 - men in each barrack-room to form a mess for the short half week to lay out 6d. and the other half week 8d. (presumably per man) for butcher's meat and vegetables. One sergeant or corporal of each barrack to go with the men to market and see that the above proportion of money is laid out for that purpose." The company pay captain (or, as he was called then, the Squad Officer) made the necessary stoppages out of their pay.

This method cannot have been very satisfactory, because there is an order of 23 Oct. 1784 - "Because the men are living so much on vegetables, the Commandant directs that each man is to contribute 1s. on pay day. The sergeant who collects the money is to go to market with some of the mess and lay out the money to the best advantage, and we are given the first example of a mess account: -

For 14 Men	14.0	42 lbs. of Beef @ 3d. a lb.	10.6
		Vegetables	8
		Salt, Pepper, & Baking	4
			11.6
		Remains	2/6

This gives some idea of the number of men in a room, and also the price of provisions.

There is no mention of tea or coffee, and presumably the liquid refreshment was Small Beer, as we shall see presently. Afloat there seems to have been an issue of wine, spirits, or beer; the ration of beer per man a day was one gallon. This lasted until 1797, when grog was substituted.

In the French Wars, from 1792 till 1815, we see the increasing difficulty of rationing, and the steps that had to be taken by the Government to ensure that the men had bread and meat.

According to the Portsmouth letters, 20th June, 1792, an allowance of 10 ½ d. per week was made to purchase bread, whilst in quarters or barracks in Great Britain; and Corporals, Drummers and Private Marines were to have this allowance of bread, and to be supplied whilst serving on shore out of their pay and allowances with food to the value of 3s. a week.

"A Committee was appointed, consisting, of one Field Officer, two Captains and two Subalterns, to examine the books of each Parade Company once every month, and also whenever the Captain or Commanding Officer of a company shall be embarked or removed, causing amount of each Marine to be stated, and the balance paid into his hands; reporting in writing to the Commandant of the state they find the Company. Sergeants to have "an allowance of 9s. a year out of Poundage (?) to every sergeant whether in barracks or quarters, commencing from 1st Jan. 1792"; but this did not last long, because on 13th October of the same year the Sergeants were to have the same ration of bread as the men.

On 12th June, 1794 the Admiralty issued an order "That an Allowance of Small Beer (as for the Army) not exceeding the quantity which those in quarters (i.e., Billets) were entitled to receive gratis from their landlord, viz., five pints of Small Beer per day for each N.C.O. and Man was to be made to the Marines; but they were to have the option of three pints of 12' - Table Beer per diem instead of the five pints of small beer." Commandants were directed to obtain contracts for the supply. The small beer must have been mighty poor stuff.

Meat and bread must have been getting scarce in 1795, and the price going up, because there was an Order in Council and an Admiralty Order 21st April, 1795, directing that N.C.Os. and Men were to be supplied with bread at the same rate as when in camp, i.e., the difference between the usual camp stoppage of 5d. a loaf and the actual price will be charged to Marine Contingencies. From this we also learn that when in camp issues in kind were made.

And again, on 12th May, 1795, "Owing to high price of butcher's meat, all beyond 4 ½d. a lb. is to be allowed extraordinary to N.C.Os. and Men, the extra expense to be charged to the Contingent account."

As we know, one of the great causes of the Mutinies in 1797 were the complaints of the bad victualling.

Speaking of 1797, Gillespie, in his History of the Royal Marines, says "Liberal allowances of provisions were also granted to the Sailors and Marines of the Fleet; as upon a general aggregate they are more than they can possibly consume the overplus being converted into money is nearly adequate to the purchase of those cordials of which they stand in need, a prudent man is under little necessity to encroach upon his pecuniary gain." We wonder!

Prices went on rising, until finally the Government had to decide in 1800 to supply all the forces throughout England on a regular and uniform plan; and Messrs. Dacres, Adams & Giles Welsford were appointed Contractors to make the supply, and the following order was sent to the Marine Divisions: 25th March, 1800, "Marines to be put on the same footing as Marching regiments, and an extract of the War Office letter is forwarded to Commandants to make the same arrangements with the Contractors: 'Bread is to be made of good marketable English or Foreign wheat, out of which the bran has been taken by means of a twelve shilling seamed cloth; each soldier's allowance of this bread for four days being a well baked loaf of 4 lbs., for which a stoppage of 6d. will be made from his pay and paid to the Contractors; excess beyond that price is to be paid by the public; contract is not fixed, but the payment to be made on current market prices. This was followed by difficulties in supplying the Recruiting parties, who were scattered all over the country, and on 24th April orders were given that when they could not be supplied by the contractors they were to have a money allowance in lieu.

This year the question of the beer ration came up, and on 1st May "an allowance of 1d. a day was made to each N.C.O. Trumpeter, Drummer and Private stationed in barracks in lieu of the present allowance of small beer," the charge being made against the Contingent Account. This allowance was continued until 29th November, 1881, in the case of N.C.Os., and until 8th August, 1899, in the case of Privates, as we shall see. There is some amusing correspondence about closing the contracts with the local brewers, and at Portsmouth it was continued till the end of June, the brewers being Messrs. Deacon.

We wonder if this innovation was due to the introduction of tea and coffee, but orders are silent on this.

The food must have been very poor and scanty, and it was many years before any improvement took place. Cooking was apparently done in the barrack rooms and each mess catered for itself.

The first mention of an evening meal is in Plymouth Orders of 8th August, 1845, when the G.O.C. Western District directed that an evening meal of tea and coffee, with a proportion of bread, shall be furnished to soldiers depots throughout the Western District, in addition to breakfast and dinner," and suggests the hour of 6 p.m., after the evening roll call.

Whether it was due to the Government undertaking the issue of rations I am not certain, but by Order in Council of 19th May, 1846, a 2nd Quartermaster was authorised for each Division, to be promoted from the Staff Sergeants and the Sergeants of the Corps. Hitherto the Lieutenant and Quartermaster had been an ordinary duty officer, who held the appointment for a period like the Adjutant; his extra pay must have been good, because there are complaints that the Adjutants, "who ought to be the best officers," were always applying to exchange to Quartermaster. He seems to have only been concerned with arms and clothing. Lieutenants and Q.M. were abolished on 3rd August, 1867, when a second Quartermaster was added; special rates of pay, etc., for quartermasters having been laid down.

As late as 1890 breakfast and tea consisted of tea and "slingers," i.e., dry bread; one may conclude therefore that it was even worse in those days.

Somewhere in the 1840's stoppages for rations of Naval ratings afloat must have ceased, because an Order in Council of 6th October, 1849. represents that no class of Naval Officer is liable to such deduction, nor are soldiers of the Army, and directs that the deduction of 1/1 a day from the shore pay of captains R.M., when afloat, to meet the cost of provisions was to cease from 1st July, 1849; but the deduction from N.C.Os. and Men of the Marines continued until the publication of the following most illuminating Order in Council of 1854, which deserves to be quoted in full for the light it throws on Marine conditions and their work afloat: 11th August. 1854 - "Army when afloat are not subject to any deduction for rations. etc. N.C.Os. and Men. Royal Marines are still liable to deductions from pay, originally intended to meet cost of sea provisions when afloat; this position has become anomalous, compared with Soldiers of the line and their own officers, and in consequence of the increased pay to Continuous Service Seamen of the Navy; no corresponding advantage having been granted to the Royal Marines." The grounds upon which additional pay to Seamen entered for continuous service was granted had reference to the value which unquestionably attaches to the services of skilful and trained Seamen, and to the great demand for such men in the Mercantile Marine; but the bearing of this increase as affecting the relative conditions of the Marines when embarked was not taken into account, and it cannot be denied that the reasons which have led unavoidably to an increase in the wages of seamen in R.N. when entered for long periods, apply in many respects with equal force to the services of the R.M. when afloat. Of late years, and more especially since the Order in Council of 1st.july, 1849, great care and pains have been bestowed in training the Royal Marines when ashore, not merely in the exercise of the ship's gun batteries, but also to some of the duties of seamen, and the proficiency which these men have acquired before embarkation renders them so fully equal to those duties, that in the recent equipment of the Fleet (i.e., for the Crimean War) they have been found capable, of rendering very efficient and valuable services."

"Another consideration which should not be overlooked in weighing the claims of the R.M, is the fact that at all times, and under all circumstances, but more especially during the repair and equipment of ships in port, they are liable to the performance of many harassing and laborious duties, which have been known to deter seamen, when not entered for continuous service, from volunteering during the period of equipment. Royal Marines are exposed to much wear and tear of clothing, without any additional remuneration, and that as regards the general discipline of H.M. Fleet, too much importance cannot be attached to the contentment and efficiency of the Marine Corps; therefore their Lordships consider that N.C.Os. and Men should be placed on a more equitable footing as regards ration deductions." This order therefore approved removal entirely of differences of pay between R.M. ashore and afloat, and deductions for rations afloat ceased from 1st October, 1854 - but it was 50 years before deductions ceased when ashore!

By the Instructions for Marine Divisions 1888, and probably for many years before, the stoppages ashore was 7d. a day, viz., 4 ½ d. for 1 lb. of bread and ¾ lb. of meat provided by the Government, and 2 ½ d. for tea, coffee, vegetables, etc., expended by the messes under the supervision of the Captain of the Company.

Improvements were made in the cooking; the establishment of Dry Canteens enabled a better use to be made of the Mess Money, but there is no doubt the men, and particularly the recruits, were much underfed. This led in 1898 to an Order in Council (3rd February, 1898) by which recruits were granted an increased ration up to 1lb. of meat and 1 ½ lbs. of bread a day, without any increase in the stoppage. This was due "to the increased importance of physical training."

At last in 1899 (8th August) Sergeant Cooks, who had been trained in the Army Schools of Cookery, were granted extra pay, and an effort was made to improve the methods of serving the food. Perhaps some will remember how the tea, milk and sugar used to be boiled up together in the coppers that were used for cooking vegetables.

In 1898 the Army deductions for rations had ceased, but it took the Admiralty 18 months to make up their minds to do anything, and the R.M. Order in Council was dated 8th August, 1899. But even then the method could only have occurred to the Civilian mind of the Admiralty!

They announced that from the 1st July, 1899, the emoluments of N.C.Os. and Men, Royal Marines, would be increased by 2d. a day, and we wonder what great mind evolved the following scheme: -
    (a) The 1d. a day Beer Money for Privates was abolished. It had been abolished for N.C. officers on 29th November, 1881, when alterations were made in pay, etc.
    (b) The deductions for bread and meat were to be in future:
        for N.C.Os. 2 ½d. instead of 4 ½d. per diem
        for Men 1 ½d.   "   4 ½d.   "
    (c) When rations were not issued in kind N.C.Os. to receive 2d. and Men 3d., except on furlough, when both received 2d.

In August 1903 great improvements were made in rations afloat, in which naturally the Marines shared, but it was not till the following year that Free rations were at last given to men ashore. By Order in Council 7th March, 1904, the stoppage of 4 ½d. for bread and meat was discontinued, and an allowance of 2 1/2 d. a day was made to each N.C.O and man to cover the cost of groceries, etc., for each day on which he drew pay ashore - provided he had been under training for six months and completed recruit training, or attained the age of 19 years, whichever occurred first. Those who could not draw rations in kind received 6d. a day. Married men were therefore now able to draw their rations in kind, a very welcome addition to the family budget, as hitherto they were not liable for the 7d. deduction, but had to purchase food in the town.

In 1907 further great improvements were made afloat by the introduction of the Standard Ration and the 4d. a day Mess allowance, but no alteration was made for the Marines ashore.

When war broke out in 1914 a scale of standard ration suited for active service conditions, which had been drawn up by the Director of Victualling and the Adjutant General Royal Marines to meet the case of manoeuvres and active service was brought into force, and continued with slight variations as regards savings until 1919, when the Royal Marines on shore were put on to the Naval scales of victualling.

Various attempts to make full use of these, such as formation of company messes and dining rooms were made, and then the great plunge was made with the building of dining halls and the introduction of the General Mess as it exists to-day. This with trained cooks and all the accumulated experience makes the present day feeding of the Corps a great advance on the haphazard methods of the past, and compare favourably with the civilian standard of living, whilst in the latter part of the last century it was definitely below it.

LOYALTY AND DISLOYALTY A CENTURY AND A QUARTER AGO.

"Bolshevism," that fell disease of the body politic, engendered and disseminated by gangs of international cranks and criminals, is no new thing. The name alone is new and is attributable to the fact that the latest and bloodiest manifestation of its virulence has been in Russia. Like most diseases, it fastens on its victims when in an enfeebled state. Russia, when the Bolsheviks seized her in their greedy clutches, was staggering under the strain of a prolonged war, and similarly when a like collection of evil-disposed miscreants, then known as Communists, took possession of Paris in 1871, France had just suffered a heavy defeat at the hands of the Germans. In this case however, the French Republican Government stamped out the infection with a heavy and effective foot.

"Communism, by the way would seem to be the best and most nearly descriptive name for those evil or misguided persons who profess tenets which are to the effect that "What's yours is mine, and mine's my own." However they may endeavour to conceal their true nature by, more or less plausible political "shiboleths," their open and insolent use and adoration of "The Red Flag" gives them away every time.

For the "Red Flag" means, and always has meant, nothing more or less than "Blood and Bloodshed." In the ancient Greecian Navy it was the signal to engage the enemy; in mediaeval times it signified certain death and mortal strife to all sailors everywhere"; in the 16th, 17th and 18th centuries, when it was generally known as the "Bloody Flag," it was hoisted afloat when the opposing ships came to close quarters, and it has been stated that though pirates sometimes gave quarter when fighting under the black flag and cross-bones, they never did so after hoisting a red flag.

Just about a century and a quarter ago there was a serious manifestation of Communism in this country and in Ireland. In those days it was referred to as "Jacobinism" from its promoters, the members of the Jacobin Club formed in Paris in 1789 responsible for the bloodshed and atrocities of the French Revolution. In this country it produced what were known as the Corresponding Societies; in Ireland it incited the "United Irishmen" to rebellion, murder and arson. The two together were mainly responsible for the notorious mutinies of the seamen of the Navy at Spithead and the Nore.

The same dissemination of handbills and pamphlets, urging the armed forces of the Crown to sedition and mutiny, for which certain Communists of our own day have recently been imprisoned, were scattered broadcast throughout Ships and Barracks. The wording was not far from being identical. That their effect was more marked in the Navy than in the Army may be accounted for by the fact that the seamen were many of them pressed men, others committed by the magistrates to serve in the Navy in lieu of imprisonment, and to the presence in the ships' companies of members of the treasonable societies above referred to, who had enlisted for the express purpose of exploiting the undoubted grievances of the seamen and organising revolt. The Army turned a deaf ear to the sedition-mongers, as did the Marines, who, had the authorities utilised their loyalty in the same prompt and effective way that Lord St. Vincent did in the Mediterranean Fleet, would have nipped the mutiny in the bud. Their attitude is well set out in the following answer made by the Chatham Division to an attempt to seduce it from its allegiance:-

"AN ANSWER TO A HANDBILL
FOUND ON THE 21st DAY OF MAY, 1797, IN THE MARINE BARRACKS, CHATHAM.

"As we know not who you are that have taken the liberty to address us as Bretheren, but from the tenor of whose address we have every reason to disown as such, - Yet, lest ye might be led to imagine from our silence, that we in the smallest degree acquiesce in your sentiments, we consider it necessary for the establishment of our own honour, to reply to your Several observations:-

"You say, are we not men?

"We are men; we know it; and should the Enemies of our King, our Country, or Constitution (either Foreign or Domestic) ever oppose us, we will prove ourselves such; we should only lose our natural claim to the name of man did we ever in the smallest degree swerve from that fidelity and attachment which we owe to our beloved Sovereign and to our Country"

"You ask us are we respected as men?

"Yes - we are not only respected as men, but by every good man regarded as the Protectors of our Country. If there are any class of men who hold us not in proper respect, we are well assured it is only those, who, lost to every sense of virtue, and blind to the real interests of their Country, endeavour to disseminate principles of Jacobinism and Sedition, with a view to destroy that Constitution and Government which has so long been the admiration of surrounding nations; and to introduce a system of anarchy and confusion, by which alone their diabolical schemes of murder, rapine and plunder can be brought to bear; but we are united and resolved to shed the last drop of our blood in the opposition of such detestable doctrines, and such we trust is the resolution of all our virtuous Bretheren.

"You say wrong notions of Discipline have led us to be despised.

"We as good soldiers glory in proper Discipline, and in paying that necessary and proper obedience to the commands of our Officers, who treat us with all that respect and humane attention that every good Soldier deserves.

We believe, and our Officers acknowledge, that Serjeants are a principal spring in the Military Machine; but that is no argument that the Army could act as well, or indeed could exist at all, without superior and commissioned Officers; they only form one of the gradations of rank necessary to the well-being of the whole.

"We place every dependence in the wisdom of his Majesty and Parliament for the amelioration of our situation, and we have every reason to be satisfied with their declared intentions in our favour.

"We know by experience that Barracks are far better for us than quarters, where a want of necessary conveniences for Soldiers used to cause us, much trouble. In Barracks we have everything convenient.

"We acknowledge that a great number of our Brother Soldiers are harassed by long marches through the country, to prevent the base designs of the disaffected and disloyal, who endeavour to disorganise the Army, unhinge the Constitution and strike at the very vitals of all good Government. And you ask us, that labouring under so many grievances, what are we to do? We briefly answer; Our Duty as Soldiers and not as slaves, in protecting our King and Country to which we have bound Ourselves, by a just and Voluntary Obligation.

"You desire us in conclusion to be Sober, be ready. We will be sober and ready, but it will be in the Opposition of all such invidious Endeavours to poison our Minds, and to make us throw off that necessary Obedience and respect to the just and legal commands of our Officers, whom we love and respect, and to the Chief of whom, in this Division we have every reason to pay the highest degree of Veneration.

"Cease, therefore, your vile endeavours to poison our minds, for we are too steadily attached to our Country, to our King, and to our Constitution, ever to be led astray by such absurd and wicked attempts.

Signed by the Serjeant-Major, Serjeants and Corporals."

The Light Company issued a shorter but similar declaration of loyalty of its own, signed by each member of it.

The "Red Flag" was at this time being flown by the Naval Mutineers, but with a better eye to artistic effect than the present day Communists with their staring red ties they wore in their hats "large bunches of blue and pink ribbons" - "which are called the signal of defiance." The "delegates" or ringleaders wore in addition "a broad band of blue paper, with the following words marked upon it in gold letters, 'Success to the Delegates of the Fleet.' "The Great Mutiny before long "petered out" and came to an end, but the troubles fostered by our enemies in Ireland continued to grow. A letter from County Down gives the following picture of the state of affairs there at the time of the Naval Mutinies, which were doubtless paralleled in other counties :-

"All business is at a stand - John Gordon, the Glennys, Walker, and many others in custody, and their houses full of Military. Ab: Walker, S Turner, etc., etc., have made their escape; 3 Pieces of cannon, 1,000 rounds of Ball Cartridge, 3 barrels of Powder were got in Walker place; 36 Pikes in Lawson's, - a great number of Arms are brought in every day from the Country - the Houses deserted and the Inhabitants flying."

It is noteworthy that no distinctly Irish name appears among those of the rebels mentioned.

But in those days there was a strong and determined loyalist population in Ireland besides the perennial malcontents. The manifesto published by the Marines, a Corps always renowned for its loyalty, would excite no surprise if it had been issued in reply to our modern sowers of evil seeds but we should rub our eyes if we opened our paper and saw the following manifesto from the "LIMERICK MILITIA."

Yet here it is, just as it appeared in the Limerick Chronicle for 31st May, 1797:-

"COUNTY OF LIMERICK REGIMENT OF MILITIA.

WE, the Serjeants, Corporals, Drummers and Privates of His Majesty's 21st, or County Limerick Royal Regiment of Militia, having heard with concern that several Seditious Means are using to Mislead and Decoy the Army of this Kingdom from their Allegiance to their King and Country, Unanimously Resolve, That we hold in the greatest Abhorrence such diabolical Schemes, and that we will use our utmost Endeavours to detect and bring to Punishment any Person presuming to tamper with our Loyalty in any Shape whatever, and for the better carrying into effect these our determined Resolutions, we do hereby offer a Reward of TWENTY GUINEAS to any Person who shall make known, and prosecute to Conviction, any Traitor so offending.
Signed by desire of the Serjeants, Corporals and Drummers of the Regiment,
ROBERT GORDON, Serjeant-Major.

Waterford, May 19, 1797."

It may be added that when the Irish Rebellion of the year following broke out, it was defeated and subdued almost entirely by the Irish Loyalists. Of the army of 80,000 men that defeated the rebels and re-established order and authority, not more than 10,000 were British Regular troops.

What has become of the strong stratum of loyalists who then preserved the unity of the Kingdom? Is its disappearance due to the propaganda of Sinn Fein and earlier anti-British societies, or may it not rather be laid to the charge of successive British Governments - of all parties with their wobbly Irish Policies, which while alternately punishing and placating or bribing the malcontents, have been only consistent in discouraging and handicapping the loyal and law-abiding inhabitants in the South of Ireland?

History seems to have no attractions for our politicians, probably because its lessons mostly run counter to what they would like to believe, to most things they say, and to many things that they do, but in times like the present, when licensed agitators abound in the land, it might be a very good thing for the country if they would study the history of Ireland, and our dealings with it and the story of the Communist efforts in this Kingdom between 1795 and the year of Trafalgar. Nor would it do any harm to the thousands of apathetic optimists among us to study these things as well.

LORD HOWE AND HIS MARINE PAY.

"In the beginning of 1798 was passed an Act, empowering the Bank to receive voluntary contributions for defraying the expenses of the war. At this time Earl Howe's only pecuniary emolument, for all his past services, was the stipend arising from his post as General of the Marines.

(N.B. - This was in accordance with the old abuse of giving the best appointments in the Corps to Naval Officers.-C.F.)

Being himself confined to his bed, he commissioned the Countess to receive his annual salary at the Marine Pay Office, with instructions to carry the whole of it (upwards of £1,800) immediately to the Bank as his contribution."

Naval Chronicle, Vol. IX., p. 399.

ORDERS FOR MARINE DETACHMENTS.
ADMIRAL LORD ST VINCENT.

Ville de Paris
6th July, 1798

Gen. Memo.

Having found it necessary to appoint Lieut.-Col. Highs Inspector of the Marines serving in the fleet under my command, he is to be received as such and be permitted to have the Marines of the respective ships under arms, to inspect their necessaries, visit the storerooms, and every other department attached to the Marines, and he has my orders to report any departure from the regulations of the Service and the instructions I have thought fit to give.

Issued to Capt. of Ships.

(Signed) ST. VINCENT.

* * * *

Ville de Paris,
18th August, 1798.

Memo.

Whereas there is great propriety and (in case of disembarkation) necessity that the cloathing of the Marine Forces serving on board H.M. Fleet under my command should be uniform - and as the new cloathing may be expected by the next convoy, the Commanding Officers of Marines of the ships of the Squadron before Cadiz are required to come on board the Ville de Paris in the course of next week, accompanied by an intelligent Sergeant and their Master Tailor, to look at the pattern winter and summer regimental working jacket, hat, etc., to which they are enjoined strictly to conform in future.

To Capts.

ST. VINCENT.

* * * *

Aug. 18, 1798.

Memo.

Having taken into consideration the state of the cloathing of the Marine Forces serving in the Fleet under my command, and the approach of the rains, I judge it expedient that the long regimental cloathes shall be made into working jackets with as much dispatch as the work to be done and the number of tailors on board each ship will admit.

And in future the following regulation touching the Working Jackets, Summer Regimentals and Hats are to be strictly complied with - Working Jackets to have no white facing, Summer regimentals to have no mixture of Red whatever in it; Hats to be cocked on one side only, according to patterns to be seen on board the "Ville de Paris."

To Captains.

ST. VINCENT.

* * * *

Ville de Paris,
Off Ushant, 1 July, 1800.

Every order or regulation issued by me touching the duties of Marines in his Majesty's Ships under my command, is to be communicated immediately to the Commanding Officer of Marines in each ship, and a copy given to him if desired.

ST. VINCENT.

* * * **

Ville de Paris,
Off Ushant, 23 June, 1800.

Gen. Orders.

For the maintenance of order and the preservation of his Majesty's Ships of the Line from fire and the dreadful calamities incident thereto, the following regulations are henceforth to be strictly observed when all or any of them are moored or at single anchor in Torbay, Spithead, Cawsand Bay, Portland Roads, or in any other bay or roadstead in Great Britain or Ireland, at Gibraltar, in Port Mahon, and the Tagus, and on the coasts of France, Spain, Portugal, Italy, and Bombay.

1.

Guard to be paraded on the poop every morning at half past 8 o'clock, with the form and order practised on the best regulated parades, and after going through a short exercise, to descend to the quarter-deck at nine o'clock precisely, where all the accustomed formalities are to be gone through, with the respect or decorem due to the occasion (although no colours are allowed), and where there is a band of musick - after the Troop, "God save the King" is to be played, while the Guard is under presented Arms, and all persons present are required to stand with their hats off, until the Guard shoulders, and after the Commanding Officer of the Detachment has received his orders from the Captain or Commanding Sea Officer on the quarter-deck, the arms are to be lodged, and the Guard held in constant readiness for occasional service.

2.

No Non-commissioned Officer, Marine or Soldier told off for the Guard shall be called upon to perform any of the duties of the ship for which the seamen are fully competent.

3.

The annexed detail of Guards for Ships of the Fleet, second and third rates, is to be established, with permission of an increase of the number, according to the discretion of the respective Captains of Ships of the Line.

	Guards					Centenels where Posted											
	Subalterns	Sergeants	Corporals	Drummers	Privates	Qr. Deck	Poop	Gangways	Forcastle	Ladder between Entering Port	Ward Room	Gun Room	Fore Cockpit	After Cockpit	Galley	Bits	Prisoners	Cabin Door	Total
First and Second Rates	1	2	2	1	54	2	2	2	2	1	1	1	1	1	1	1	1	2	18
Third Rates	1	2	2	1	45	2	2	2	2	-	1	1	1	1	1	1	1	-	15

4.

A Sergeant or Corporal of the Guard to patrole the ship every half-hour during the night, with two privates.

5.

The Guard to continue three days, and the relief to be exempt from Duty the day before they mount, to clean their cloaths and accoutrements.

The signal for Commanding Officers of Marines - a Red pendant over a Union Jack at the mizen topmast head.

ST VINCENT

* * * *

23 Aug., 1798.

Memo.

Altho' my order of 22nd June literally taken expresses that the Marines are only to perform Garrison Duty while at this anchorage, I judge it necessary to extend its influence to all anchorages, both abroad and at home - mooring, unmooring, coming to sail and swaying up topmasts and lower yards being the only exceptions thereto, and upon these occasions the Subaltern's Guard of the Day is upon no account to be broke in upon or disturbed.

To Captains.

ST. VINCENT.

Another example of Orders for a Marine Officer in the 18th Century.
ORDERS FOR MARINE OFFICER OF THALIA,
BY CAPT. POWLETT.

13th Sept., 1796

The Marine Officer will have charge of his own people, taking care to see they comply with the regulations of the Ship, and report to the Captain any neglect; he is to exercise his people as often as he may see fit when the duty will admit and on coming to anchor he is to take care to have centinels placed on each gangway, properly dressed, and that the reliefs are regularly made.

FOREIGNERS IN THE MARINES.
ATTESTATION OF AN ITALIAN, 1804.

I, Gaetan Loyagalo, do make oath that I am by trade a Bricklayer, and to the best of my information and belief was born at MILAN, and am entirely free from all engagements, and that I have no rupture nor ever was troubled with fits and that I am no wise disabled by lameness or otherwise but have the perfect use of my limbs and that I have voluntarilly enlisted myself to serve his Britannic Majesty King George the third in his Royal Marine forces during the present war under an agreement that I shall be discharged at the end of it and a passage free of expense to the Mediterranean.

| Witness | C: W: Adair Capt. |
| present | Inspectg Officer of Recruits for the R.M. |

As witness my hand this 22 day of March 1804

His

Gaetan X Loyagalo.

mark

I, Gaetan Loyagalo do swear to be true to his Sovereign Lord King George the third of Great Britain and serve him honestly and faithfully in defence of his person, Crown, and dignity against all his enemies and oppressors whatsoever and to observe and obey his Majestys orders and the orders of the Generals and Officers set over me by His Majesty

So help me God.

These are to certify that Gaetan Loyagalo aforesaid aged 27 years 5 feet 10 inches high Sandy Hair Grey Eyes Freckeled Complexion came before me and declared that he had voluntarilly enlisted himself to serve his B. Majesty King George the third in his Royal Marine forces, he therefore is duly enlisted and the second and third articles of war Against Mutiny and desertion were likewise read to him and he has taken the oath of fidelity mentioned in the said articles of war.

I have examined the said
Gaetan Loyagalo and find
him in every respect sound
and fit for his Majesty's
Service.

Surgeon. "*Victory.*"

Sworn before me on board
H.M.S. "*Victory*" this 22 day of March 1804.
Nelson & Bronte.

I do acknowledge to have Received from Capt. C: W: Adair Five Pounds Five Shillings Bounty.

Witness	C: W: Adair	His
present	Capt. & Inspg.	Gaetan X Loyagalo.
	Officer of Recruits	Mark
	for the R: M:	

Embarked on board H.M.S. *Niger* before orders reached the Inspecting Officer of Recruits in the Mediterranean to class Recruits to Companies or Divisions.

103 Co:

––––––––

EXTRACTS FROM THE DIARY OF MAJOR CHRISTOPHER NOBLE OF THE ROYAL MARINES, 1792 To 1822.
By Colonel C. Field.

There has lately come into my hands a thin little MS. book in small quarto, which is a species of Diary kept by Christopher Noble, of Henley in Arden (Warwickshire) who served as an Officer in the Marines from about 1792 to 1822.

"Diary" is perhaps hardly the right word to describe this little manuscript. It does not give any of the many details we should like to find of his life and experiences "Per Mare, per Terram," but merely notes of his movements. Still, reading between the lines, we may obtain a general idea of the Service life of an Officer of Marines a hundred years ago.

On what date Noble obtained his first Commission is not clear. His first entry is that he "Sailed from Hull March 22nd, 1792," but there is a note: Hull, March 11th, Yorkshire to March 21st, from which we may gather that he went to that place from which together with "Hell and Halifax" the seaman prays to be delivered, for the purpose of joining one of His Majesty's ships. How long before this he got his Commission we do not know - not long probably, as in those days embarkation followed closely upon joining the Corps.

His ship "lay Yarmouth side 11 days," and Noble relates that on March 26th "it thundered very much." From Yarmouth a course was set for Oporto, where the ship arrived on 28th April and remained till 29th May, when she paid a short visit to St. John's before returning home. We have a few notes as to the way our subaltern employed his time during his visit to Portugal. The entry "Was on board all day" is frequent, but we hear that he dined with a Mr. Nassaw on May the 10th and "took a walk after dinner" and "drank tea at his country house with a Mrs. Johnson." After dining on another occasion with a Mr. Croft, he "borrowed the Adventures of Telemachus." We will hope he enjoyed reading them.

We are left in the dark as to the happenings of the rest of 1792, of 1793, and of most of 1794, but by 16th December of that year Noble seems to have been on board H.M. Frigate "*Hind*." The *Hind* spent the first half of 1795 "batterfanging about" between Sheerness, Portsmouth, Cork and Dublin, sometimes with a convoy, more often not. The only incident out of everyday routine seems to have been on May 27, when after leaving Dunmore with a convoy she "saw a Lugger out at Sea, gave chase and came up with her; she proved to be a smuggler, and took her as a prize to the *Hind*.

Three days previously Noble had been promoted to 1st Lieutenant and appointed to the 34th Company at Chatham but he probably did not hear of this until the *Hind* arrived at Dublin on June 11th after leaving her prize at Carrickfergus.

The remainder of the year passed like the first half in endless cruises backwards and forwards in home waters, and 1796 seemed likely to follow suit. Another smuggler, the *Guernsey* of Guernsey was captured to the westward of the Scillies on May 25th, after which things went on as usual till the 12th August, when the *Hind* sailed "from Portsmouth to Quebec with convoy." She "made the Land supposed to be Chapeau Rouge on Newfoundland on September 25th, and on the next day but one was "chased by two French line-of-battleships, one near gun shot, when she carried away her fore topmast and main topgallant mast."

The *Hind* therefore was able to escape from her formidable pursuers, made Gaspe Bay on October the 4th, and arrived at Quebec on the 18th. Sailing again on the 7th November she arrived at Cork on the 28th December, but on 4th January, 1797, left that place "on a cruise in company with the *Powerful* and several frigates, and on the 8th "joined Lord Bridport with the Grand Fleet." After taking "possession of the *Favorite*, a French Brig Privateer, as a prize to the fleet," she returned to her old duty of dodging about from one Channel port to another; but we find that on the 17th March Mr. Christopher Noble "Left the *Hind* and came to Sick Quarters at Gosport."

How long he remained "sick" does not appear, as there are no more entries for that year, but on New Year's Day 1798 he embarked on board H.M.S. *Vanguard* at Chatham. After calling at Portsmouth, Noble's new ship sailed for Lisbon, where she arrived on 23rd April. Leaving that place on the 27th she joined Lord St. Vincent's Fleet off Cadiz, but in a couple of days was detached to Gibraltar, where she joined a squadron of three line-of-battleships and three frigates with whom she went "up the straits" in to the Mediterranean.

A 6-gunned privateer named the *Peter* chased and captured off Toulon, and also a French merchantman bound from Smyrna to Marseilles, after which the *Vanguard* seems to have encountered heavy weather, since three days later, on the 23rd May, Noble records that she "Put into St. Pierre (Island of Sardinia) with the loss of our foremast, main topmast and mizen topmast." However no time was lost in repairing damages, and putting to sea again on the 27th, two Spanish brigs and a ship from Genoa were made prizes of in the next ten days, On June 7th, the day the last two ships were captured, the *Vanguard* joined "a fleet of 10 sail of the line." Noble adds "these ships were not in sight when the above prizes were taken."

After calling at Syracuse this fleet proceeded further eastwards, and on 28th July "Took a French brig out of Coron (in Greece) Harbour from Cyprus bound to Venice.

On the 1st August Noble took part in the famous Battle of the Nile, but if we hope to get any interesting particulars of the action, we are doomed to disappointment. All he has to say about it is;

"August 1st. Fought the French fleet at anchor off Alexandrie, consisting of 13 sail of the line and several frigates took 10 sail of the line and burnt one three-decker and one frigate and sunk one frigate. Capt. Faddy of the Marines and six privates killed and seven wounded." He adds a nominal list of "French ships taken and destroyed." On the 11th we have the bald entry "took the *Le Fortune*, a French corvett of 18 guns." Leaving Alexandrie on the 19th in company with two sail of the line and one frigate, the *Vanguard* arrived at Messina on the 11th September, and seems to have spent the rest of the year cruising between that place, Naples, Marcella (? Marsala), Palermo, Malta and Leghorn. Here are a few of the more interesting entries:-

"Oct. 26th.-Took a French and a Spanish Polacca bound to Valett (Island of Malta) in possession of the French.
Oct. 29th.- Island of Crozo surrendered to the Squadron.
Oct. 30th.- Sail'd from Malta for Naples with prisoners.
Nov. 22nd- Sail'd from Naples to Leghorn with troops.
Nov. 28th.- Arriv'd at Leghorn with 7,000 troops.
Dec. 23rd.- Sail'd from Naples for Palermo with the King on board.
Dec. 25th.- Arriv'd at Palermo with the King and family."

The first six months of 1799 were spent in apparently uneventful cruises in that part of the Mediterranean, but after arriving at Naples on 24th June we find the following entries:-

"June 29th.- Landed the Marines.
"June 30th.- Had an action with some Jackobins (John Hickson kill'd, Daniel Elliott and Christr. Caroline wounded; Lieut. Millbank of the Artillery kill'd."

The detachment would appear to have remained on shore for some weeks, but we have no further entries regarding encounters with the Jackobins, or of anything else, till under the date August 20th we find: "Return'd on board the *Vanguard* at Minorca.

Noble does not say how they got there, but it is evident that they must have been sent to that island in transports or been borne in other men-of-war for passage only.

Nothing of particular interest seems to have occurred during the remainder of the year, beyond that on the 28th September it is noted that "four Spanish Settees were taken prizes to the *Vanguard* and *Zealous*, laden with wine, paper and corn.

At the end of 1799 the *Vanguard* sailed for England, arriving at Spithead on 5th January, 1800, and on the 25th "went into the harbour to be paid off." Noble disembarked on the 17th February and the following day "March'd from Portsmouth for Chatham."

There are no further entries for that year till 9th October, when it is recorded that he "went to Huntington on the Recruiting Service." Here the day following he took lodgings at Hartford, at Mr. Luke Richards'."

The next entry is rather cabalistic: "Nov. 13th M.M.O. at Harford." Does this mean "Married M.O., or Miss O"? It might, for having got back to Chatham on the 5th March 1801, we find the entry: "March 24th- Mrs. Noble left Chatham for Henley." This is the first mention of the lady.

Noble again went on recruiting service on 6th June, this time to Northampton, but as Peace "broke out" in 1802 he was recalled to Chatham. However, he got another recruiting billet in March 1803 at Ware, in Hertfordshire, but did not hold it very long as he was recalled to Chatham early in August, most probably on promotion, as he was promoted to Captain on the 10th July and appointed to the 47th Company at Portsmouth. He joined that Division on the 10th August, and on the 27th of the same month embarked on board H.M.S. *Princess Royal*, with 5 months and 21 days sea credit."

Up to 4th February 1804 Noble's new ship seems to have spent her time between Cowes, Spithead and St. Helens, but upon that date she sailed to join the fleet off Brest, war with France having again broken out. But after a few months, during which the *Princess Royal* made several trips backwards and forwards from the fleet to Plymouth, Noble disembarked to Plymouth Headquarters on 31st July.

He then apparently, went on leave to Henley in Arden, but gives us no information as to when he returned, unless his leave was extended to March 19th. 1805, when we find that he "Left Ludlow for Plymouth." He arrived there on the 22nd, and on the 15th April "Embark'd on board H.M.S. *Terrible*, with 7 months and 3 days sea credit." The *Terrible* cruised during the rest of the Year between the Brest Fleet, Ferrol and our Channel ports, but early in 1806 she joined Sir Richard Strachan's fleet of 5 sail of the line and 2 frigates, with which, after a preliminary cruise to Madeira, she sailed from Cawsand Bay on the 19th May to the West Indies, arriving at Carlisle Bay, Barbadoes, on August 8th. Sailing again on the 19th, "A hurricane came on at half past twelve in the morning and continued till ten o'clock, totally dismasted the *Terrible*." Damages, however, seem to have been pretty quickly made good, since the *Terrible* got back to Cawsand Bay on 27th September.

Noble makes no further entries in his record till 1st January, 1807, when, still apparently in the *Terrible*, he sailed for Cadiz, joining the fleet off that place on the 12th, and cruising between there and Gibraltar till the end of August 1808, when his ship went up the Mediterranean, joining the fleet off Toulon, and after two or three days, cruised to Genoa and Leghorn. The rest of the year and the year following was occupied with cruising between the Toulon fleet and Minorca, Malta, Palermo and Port Mahone.

This brings us to the year 1810, in which the first entry Noble makes is on 16th February, apparently at Malta, when he notes: "At a quarter before eleven at night felt the shock of an earthquake at eleven, very violent one." Another slight shock was experienced at 2 p.m. the day following. On the 3rd March the *Terrible* left Malta with a convoy for England, finally arriving at Chatham on the 29th May. Noble disembarked on the 7th June, and the next day march'd from Chatham to Portsmouth."

Thence he made his way to his own headquarters at Plymouth - how he does not say-and went on leave to Henley.

There are no entries for the year 1811, but on the 3rd March, 1812, we find that he "Left Frome for Plymouth," arriving on the 5th, and embarking on board H.M.S. *Magnificent*," with 8 months and 27 days (sea credit, presumably) on 21st April.

This seems to have been Noble's last embarkation. His ship after cruising about in the Channel proceeded to the north coast of Spain and anchored off La Queita, then held by the French, and apparently besieged by the British. The place surrendered on the 21st June, and Noble records that 295 prisoners were taken. Guttarez, Portugalette, Bermes and Castro were all visited, the latter place surrendering with 141 prisoners on July 8th. On the 23rd the *Magnificent* anchored off Santander and the 27th Noble was landed there, "wounded and taken prisoner." On the 30th he was "Exchanged and sent on board the *Insolent* Gun Brig, which must have sailed at once for England, probably with wounded and prisoners, for Noble was landed at Paignton Hospital on the 4th August. His wound must have been serious, for his next entry is on 26th April, 1813, when he "Took lodgings at Mrs. Parkhouse (Paignton)." He does not seem to have been able to travel till 21st September, when he "Left Paignton for Henley," where he arrived in three days.

Here ends our diarist's active service, so far as we can tell by the notes which he has left us. He may have served a few months at Headquarters - since it appears from official records that he received the rank of Brevet Major on 4th June 1814. But on the 3rd October in the same year he writes "Accepted Half-pay." This seems to have been really going on the retired list, since on 9th December, 1815, we find the entry: Received a letter from the Admiralty saying the Prince Regent had increased my pension to £250 a year from the 1st July last.

Noble appears to have died at Henley about 1823, and to have spent a considerable part of the time between his retirement and death in visiting various places in England and Wales - Tenby, Portsmouth, Southsea, Shanklin, Teignmouth, Barmouth and Scarborough are all mentioned in his diary as having been visited, some more than once.

There are a few odd and end notes on the fly leaves and elsewhere, which have some little interest. He mentions for instance; that he purchased a "Silver watch, maker's name Arnold, £13. 13s. 0d." on 6th April, 1812. Also that he "took a paper at 7s. a quarter-"Mirror of the Times," editor's name John Stokes, No. 5 Hind Court, Fleet Street." Another note is;-

"Last Paper 'Lloyd's Evening Post,' April 28th, 1815.

First ditto 'English Chronicle,' April 29th, 1815."

Whether this means that the first mentioned paper became defunct and the other made its first appearance, or whether it merely means that Noble changed his subscription does not appear.

In May 1792 he "Bought a Monkey," and at the end of 1807 "A Parrot." In 1812 he seems to have purchased "A Terrier Dog." and there are several notes of sums paid "for the keep of a dog." Noble was evidently fond of animals. As regards amusements he seems to have taken up "netting" at one time, when at Frome, probably on his way to or from his home at Henley in Arden. This was in April 1811, and immediately below we find "Nov. 7th. 1812 - finished half the Cloak, fifty-eight inches." A netted cloak seems rather a curious garment - possibly it was in the nature of a lace cloak or shawl for his wife. Perhaps, too, he was thinking at a much earlier date of the same lady, when he wrote-

"Read	That I	But	Your
Up	Love	If I	Love
and	You	find	to
Down	if	you	me
And	you	Love	is
you			
shall	Love	me	soon
See	me	not	forgot"

On another page we find a note, probably of small sums won and lost at cards, thus:-

	Lost	s.	d.		Won	s.	d.
Oct. 5th		5	0	Oct. 13th		2	6
Oct. 12th		1	8½	Oct. 19th		1	6
Oct. 14th		2	6	Oct. 21st		3	0
Oct. 15th		1	0				
Oct. 20th		4	0				

If this is a fair specimen of Noble's usual gambling account, he would not seem to have been a very successful player. Let us hope that in his case the adage "Unlucky at cards, lucky in love" fulfilled itself.

Perhaps the quaintest thing in his MS. to our modern eyes is the following list of his plain clothes kit about the time he joined the Service, as it is dated "Ch.: Augst. 21st, 1793."
"27 Shirts
18 pare of Wite Stockings, Six pare Silk
2 pare of Worsted do.
12 Neckcloth
10 pocket hankerchief
3 Wite Wascoat
3 Under Do.
1 Yallow Do.
2 Black Do.

2 Nankeen Britches
1 Black Silk Do.
2 Black Cloth Do.
1 Light Cloth Do.
1 Knite Do.
4 Draws
2 Black Coats
1 Blew Do.
2 Night Caps
6 Hand Towles
2 Pare of Sheets
2 Pillow Case
2 Blankets
1 Bed Quilt
1 Boulster
1 Pillow"

For the credit of Lieutenant Noble's spelling we may fairly assume that this list, the writing of which is somewhat different to that of our diarist, was the work of his soldier servant.

EXTRACTS FROM MY UNCLE'S DIARY.
1796-1820
(Communicated By An Officer Of The Corps.)
Born-November 8, 1780, at Portsmouth.
At Westminster School from 1788 to 1792.
Commission dated - 2nd Lieut., R.M., 17th June, 1796.

April 16, 1799.- Sailed from Plymouth Sound.

May 11.- Crossed the Tropic of Cancer, receiving the usual visit from Neptune.

May 25.- In the afternoon anchored in Carlisle Bay (Barbadoes).

May 27.- In consequence of a drunken quarrel at Nancy Clarke's tavern, a duel was fought next morning between T. Tapper, surgeon of the *Arab*, and Lieut. Dundas, of the Army; the latter had his thigh shattered. In the evening the Captain came on board drunk and confined all the officers in a most extraordinary manner, leaving me in charge of the ship. Next morning he released all but the Master.

May 31.-…..Master released,

June 23.- Hove too of the Grand Caymans, purchased turtle, parrots, etc. Died - Dennis Day and John Wilson, being the first victims to the yellow fever in this ship (*which on her return to England brought home, from different losses, only 11 out of 155 men.*)

July 10 (Gulf of Florida).- In chase all day, and at night came up with and engaged three Spanish frigates - the *Amphitrite*, 36 guns, 44, and *Sn. Lorenzo*, 44 ; beat them off. Lost three seamen killed, and two Marines wounded; one gun dismantled. Killed - Martin Newland, John Fullarton, J.

Armstrong. Wounded - Mills, corporal; Edmund Garvey, private. About half-an-hour before the action commenced, Mr. George Shanks, midshipman, departed this life, and we had 60 men sick and convalescent, the fever making severe ravages.

August 3.-Took a beautiful brig, *The Maria*, of New York, bound to Vera Cruz with a cargo of jewellery and silks worth a million dollars; found the Spanish owner and papers on board, and conveyed her to New Providence. In the night, while waiting for daybreak for the pilot to take her over the bar, the commander made our men a present of rum medicated with opium, and at the same time coaxed the officer down to a card table. The plan succeeded, and a cloud coming over the moon, they seized the vessel and got safe off to Charlestown, South Carolina.

August 17.- This day officers and ship's company signed the agreement to share prize money with the *Quebec*.

August 19.- At night saw a brig, supposed a slave vessel from Africa, on the Maranilla Reef, firing signals of distress; impossible to assist her.

September 2.- Spoke the *Quebec*, found she had taken the *Porcupine*, American brig. (*For which I never received the money till 1807*.)

September 30.- A schooner we had detained to search carrying sail to keep company with us in chase, was capsized, but the people got into our large cutter, which we had fortunately cast adrift to them on passing them in the morning, and got on board about daylight next day.

October 3.- Fell in (at 8 o'clock this morning) with the wreck of the schooner floating on her broadside, unrigged her and got as much as we could out of her, principally silks, and had we persevered might have saved her. Self and party on her all day naked, the ship having gone in chase, without refreshment of any kind ; the skin so scalded as to confine me to my bed for several days and at length the cuticle came off in large strips.

Oct. 9.- Took the *Nostra Senora del Carmen Natranesa*, value 24,000 dollars.

Oct. 21.- All went in chace different ways; the *Aramanthe* lost off St. Augustine two days afterwards.

Nov. 17.- Arrived in Port Royal.

Nov. 27.- Boatswain broke by a court-martial for drunkenness.

Nov. 30.- Lieut. Parsons dismissed the ship and placed at the bottom of the list, an instance of injustice seldom equalled. The Captain, on going on shore, ordered the studding sail booms to be scraped; Parsons, leaving the ship, repeated the order to the Master, who got drunk and forgot it. For this neglect the Lieutenant was tried. The Carlisle Bay business scraped up, but my evidence squashed that; in fact, poor Parsons was disliked by the Captain and consequently sacrificed. (*He was afterwards drowned in command of the "Hecate," gun brig.*)

Dec. 28.- Died - Mr. W. Edwin, gunner; according to a mutual, agreement, saw him buryed the next day.

Dec. 30.- Sailed from Port Royal, and while looking up at a new mainsail just bent, and having been called to breakfast, I was suddenly seized with the fever, in an instant, as it were. To cure this the Master insisted on my drinking half-a-pint or more of half rum and water hot, and being covered up with blankets. My own case and that of a seaman were the only two known to recover after the black vomit had made its appearance.

January 12, 1800.- Attempted to cut some vessels out of Port au Plata, in St. Domingo, but failed. Went up in the evening and lay in the hammock netting to see the firing, being my first leaving the gun room.

January 17.- Mr. John Dawes, the purser, died. Self just able to walk about.

January 24.- Retook an American sloop from a French privateer.

January 29.- Went in the boat at night and attacked a schooner becalmed, but found her a heavy privateer and too strong for us.

February 7.- Went on shore in Porto Rico, seized a schooner and loaded her with mahogany.

February 11.- Appointed to the command of the Liberty, schooner.

February 19.- Arrived at Port Royal.

February 26.- Sailed on a cruize in the *Retribution* (prize re-named by the Admiralty.- Ed.). While my vessel was lying at Kingston, the Captain (Thomson) of the *Potomack*, an American we had detained, complained to me that one Leatherborough, the prize master, and who was quartermaster of the *Arab*, had illtreated him by drinking his wine from the cabin. On my remonstrance Leatherboro' promised amendment, but a short time afterwards one of Thomson's crew came on shore and begged of him to go off, saying the cabin was full of sailors, and that they threatened to murder me if I came on board. I went off, and having ordered them to leave the vessel, they went upon deck, and Leatherborough armed himself to keep me below. Assisted by Thomson, I forced my way up the ladder, when he immediately seized me, and swearing he would throw me overboard, actually try'd to do it, when, finding he would probably succeed, I drew my dirk and warning him of his mutinous conduct, threatened him with death if he did not cease. He renewed his efforts, and called for assistance from his associates, when I plunged the dagger in his body; he immediately fell. I put him to bed and sent to the *Diana Guineaman* for a surgeon, who declared him in no immediate danger. He begged pardon, owned he deserved it, and entreated I would not send him to the flag ship, as I at first threatened. At the request of the surgeon I forgave him; yet this villain, on rejoining his ship reported I had stabbed him while endeavouring to prevent my plundering the vessel.

[*No reference to this in earlier portion of Diary.- Ed].

EXTRACTS FROM THE DIARY OF MAJOR W. PRIDHAM, R.M. 1799-1816.

Lieutenant Pridham appears to have joined the Marines in the same year in which he first went afloat, since on leaving the service in 1816, he states that he had served for seventeen years. This was no unusual occurrence, either for officers or men, in those days, or for that matter at a much earlier period. As far back as 1707 we find the Captain of H.M.S. *Antelope* writing to complain, that of the detachment of Marines selected from Wills' Regiment, "not three of them that had ever clapt a musquett on his shoulder before he came on board my ship, but all raw recruits."

Lieutenant Pridham's first entry in his diary is that he "Join'd His Majesty's Ship *Charon* in Sheerness Harbour the 23rd November 1799."

She was apparently fitting out, since she did not sail before the 15th of March, 1800, and then only got as far as Margate. Here she remained for nearly a fortnight, and then spent another week in the Downs. She was probably waiting to complete her complement - no easy matter in those days. Eventually she sailed for the Mediterranean, called at Port Mahon, and arrived off Genoa, then held by the French, on May 20th. The same night "the enemy were attack'd; one large galley was taken from the harbour mouth by our boats."

"5th June, anchored in Genoa Mole, the City having surrendered to the united forces of the British and Austrians. Same night sail'd with about 700 French prisoners for Antibes."

The rest of the summer passed in cruising to and fro in the Mediterranean without further incident, except that on the 30th August the *Charon* "fell in with and captured two latine sail boats, one laden with leather, soap and iron the other with oil and skins, from Marseilles, bound to Corsica." This was in sight of that island.

But, "on the night of the 14th between the hours of 9 and 10, we discovered ourselves to be in a most perilous position, about a cable's length from the shore, with the breakers close aboard surrounding us. At half past 9 let go the small bower anchor; a few minutes after let go the best bower, and then finding the ship drove nearer the shore, let go the sheet anchor, when we found her to ride without driving. At daybreak we discover'd ourselves within a cable's length of the shore (about Malaga), with the surf running tremendously high, expecting to go ashore every moment. We also discovered several ships of the convoy some distance from the shore under sail. We made the signal of distress, on which the *Incendiary*, fireship, sent her boat with the greatest hazard to our assistance, but by the Blessing of God, before she arrived to us a breeze sprang up off the land and the surf abated a little, at which time we got a spring on one bower and cut the other, and at the (same) time set our topsails and courses, with jibbs and spanker, which by the greatest Providence carried us off the land. (We had taken up the sheet anchor.) Arrived at Gibraltar with the loss of 3 cables and 2 anchors the 16th October, the gale continuing for several days after. God be praised for our Providential Escape."

The convoy which is referred to in the above entry consisted of about 120 sail of transports and troopships, carrying the army of 25,000* men destined for Egypt. The passage eastwards seems to have been a very slow one, but a considerable time was spent in Malta, where other troops were picked up, so that what with calling at Marmorice for a stay of nearly two months, Aboukir Bay was not reached till 2nd March 1801.

(To be continued.)

---

* "25,000 men" is Pridham's estimate. As a matter of fact there were not over 20,000, if as many, and the Army that eventually landed in Egypt was only about half this number.

EXTRACTS FROM THE DIARY OF MAJOR W. PRIDHAM, R.M. 1799-1816
(concluded)

We will now let Pridham take up his story:-

"The Army landed under a very severe fire from the enemy, on the 5th March 1801, in Aboukir. The 12th of March, early in the morning, the signal for the Marines to land was made, in consequence of which I immediately prepared to land. About 12 o'clock the greater part of the Battalion of Marines were on shore. About 6 in the evening Col. Abercrombie came express from the Army for the Marines to march immediately. We march'd about ten miles, over sand, which often came over our ankles, and at 12 the next morning we arriv'd at the Army, after the most fatiguing march I ever experienced; great numbers of our men were not able to march more than half way, being entirely exhausted.

At daylight next morning (13th March) the whole Army (the Marines included) were in motion. About 6 o'clock the firing commenc'd. Shortly after we were in close action with the enemy, and many experienced officers said they never saw so brisk a fire. The battle lasted until about twelve. The Marines lost upwards of seventy men, kill'd and wounded. Two officers kill'd and several (7 or 8) wounded. The Army altogether lost about one thousand men kill'd and wounded.

The enemy were driven into Alexandria, about four miles from where the action commenced.

The Marines received the thanks of Sir Ralph Abercrombie, with the 90th, 92nd and the Regiment of Dillon[2] after the action.

On the 14th of March, at the request of Lord Keith, the Marines were order'd to blockade the Castle of Aboukir, in consequence of which we had the same fatiguing march back again to Aboukir.

On the 18th of March the Castle of Aboukir surrendered to the British forces before it, which were the Queen's Regt., a half Regt. of Dismounted Cavalry, Marines and Artillery. The Grenadier Company of the Marines took possession of it. Marines lost 2 men here.

On the 21st of March, before daylight, the 92nd Regt. were order'd to relieve the Marines at Aboukir (who were to join the Army), but in consequence of the action the same day taking place shortly after they had left the camp, they were ordered back, and did not march to relieve the Marines until the Battle was over.

After the action a dispatch came to Aboukir for the Marines to march immediately to the Army. Arrived to the Army the same night (the 21st March). This march was as fatiguing as the former ones. We lay all night under arms in front of the line, expecting a second attack. We were all under Army (orders) for several nights afterwards.

The Marines remain'd from this day until the 6th August 1801, when they were order'd to embark."

The *Charon* sailed for Malta with invalids and prisoners, and in the interval between her arrival there and the signing of the Peace of Amiens in October 1801,[3] made two or three trips to Alexandria with provisions and troops.

Pridham makes no entries in his diary beyond dates of leaving and arrival at various Mediterranean ports, except that in 1802 he writes: "At sunset, 5th October, saw the Mountain of Zaguan in Africa, at about 140 miles distance, the highest, except Etna, in the Mediterranean.

Cruising continued without incident until war broke out again[4], when the *Charon* got busy among the enemy's shipping. In June she detained the *Constanxa*, sailing under Venetian colours, off the Faro of Messina, bound to Leghorn, laden with flax, coffee and sugar. The month following "took a French polacce ship, laden with corn, called Les Trois Freres, from the Black Sea, bound for Marseilles, and on 6th August 1803, the *Corona*, a Danish brig, bound to Genoa with cotton and various other merchandise from Smyrna.

The commission was, however, drawing to an end, and on the 30th October 1803 the *Charon* "sail'd from Malta for old England in company with H.M.S. *Cyclops* and 23 sail of merchant vessels." Other vessels joined the convoy at Gibraltar, and Pridham makes the following entry in his journal:

"Arrived at the Motherbank with the *Ambuscade* and convoy after a prosperous passage of 18 days from Gibraltar the 13th January 1804."

We should not consider 18 days from Gibraltar a very "prosperous passage" nowadays.

Pridham disembarked at Woolwich on 17th March, embarked on board H.M.S. *Eagle*, apparently for "passage only," and joined the Plymouth Division on April 2nd. He seems to have gone on leave to Dudley in Worcestershire in the following September, till March 1805, after which he joined the Portsmouth Division, but almost immediately was transferred back to Plymouth. In May he went off to Greenock on Recruiting duty, but at the end of the year was sent over to Newry in Ireland on the same service. He remained there till January 1807, on the 22nd of which month he got back to Head Quarters, Plymouth.

Three months later Pridham embarked on board H.M.S. *Alfred*, and after sundry coastal trips found himself at Elsinore, his ship forming part of the Expedition against Copenhagen, off which city she anchored 15th August 1807.[5]

"The Army." he writes, "under Lord Cathcart, landed without opposition about nine miles from Copenhagen 16th August. The Fleet weighed and anchor'd again nearer to Copenhagen August 17th 1807.

The Army opened their entrenchments on the evening of the second September, when a very heavy bombardment commenced, which set the city on fire. Copenhagen surrendered to the British forces on the 7th September 1807." The *Alfred* seems to have been then employed to carry Danish prisoners of war to Yarmouth, sailing in company with other ships, which brought back the 43rd Regiment.

On 6th December she "sail'd from St. Helen's, with the *Ganges*, (Capt. Halkett, Commodore) *Defence*, *Ruby* and *Agamemnon*" for Lisbon, where she joined three other men-of-war, in company with which she sailed exactly three months later" for the Bayonne Islands, off Vigo, to water."

This important operation effected the fleet returned to Lisbon, where it seems to have remained till July, when the *Alfred*, at any rate, proceeded to Figuera, where Pridham "disembarked with a detachment of Marines on service," and remained till the 2nd August, after which the ship returned to Lisbon.

The landing at Figueras was a much more important affair than would appear by the bare mention in Pridham's diary. From a note he made of his services many years later, we find that 300 Marines were landed under Captain Lewis, R.M., thus being the first British troops to set foot in the Peninsula, and held the place for three weeks, in spite of 4,000 French troops being in the vicinity and so secured a landing place for the British Army, which arrived there under General Anstruther on August 19th.

The *Alfred* returned to Lisbon on the 30th August; and the city capitulated to the British forces on the day following. A Russian fleet lying in the Tagus surrendered a few days later, and the Alfred sailed for England with the squadron under Rear-Admiral Tyler on September 11th, arriving at Spithead on 7th October.[6]

Pridham disembarked, made his way to Plymouth Division, but shortly afterwards went to Manchester on the Recruiting service. He remained in that city till the end of March 1809, when he was recalled to Head Quarters and embarked on board H.M.S. *Amazon* on 2nd May. Our diarist soon found himself again on the coast of Spain, and "on the 29th the boats of the *Amazon* and *Arethusa* brought out from the river Pravia, near Cape Pinas a large ship laden with cocoa, bark, etc. name unknown." A couple of days later "the *Amazon* captured a French schooner called the *Aimable Mariette*, from Guadeloupe, bound to Bayonne with cotton, coffee and sugar."

"On the 14th June," writes Pridham, "I landed with a party of Seamen and Marines on Cape Priorima, near Ferrol, when they destroyed a battery of eight 24-pounders by throwing them with their carriages over the rocks, razed a furnace for heating shot.

On the 27th "I had the honour of commanding 160 Marines from the *Defiance* and *Amazon*, which were landed, together with 40 armed seamen under the command of Captain Parker, near Ferrol, when they took possession of Castle of St. Philipe and Las Parma, the guns of which were spiked, after which they re-embarked for the Town of Ferrol, where they were received with the joyful acclamations of the people, whose enthusiasm in the cause of their country exceeded description. This, the almost extinguished flame of patriotism, has again burst forth in this part of Spain so long oppressed by the French. After taking prisoner the Governor of St. Philipe, a Spaniard in the French interest, the whole returned to the ships in the evening, amidst the shouts and caresses of thousands." July was passed in cruising off the coast, calling at Vigo, Corunna and other ports, during which time the *Amazon* detained two American schooners bound to St. Sebastian with fish, coffee and sugar; these were afterwards released.

"On 17th August, working out of Ferrol Harbour, the ship got ashore and remained about twelve hours, when she again floated, after receiving some damage to her bottom."

Off St. Andro a week or so later the *Amazon* chased a French lugger, which apparently escaped her by running under the protection of batteries on shore. These batteries the *Amazon* and *Arethusa* tackled a few days later, "about two hours being becalmed under them. Luckily no lives were lost. The *Amazon*'s main top and gallant mast and sail were shot through, the fore-topsail haulyards, back-stay, topsail jib, and fore-topmast staysail also received other damage from their shot."

Early in September the *Amazon* received orders to return to England, and Pridham disembarked to Plymouth Head Quarters on the 28th. He apparently remained there till the middle of July 1810, when he "took a most pleasant excursion into the County of Cornwall, visited most of the principal towns, a mine, etc." On the 3rd January 1811 he embarked with Major Dickenson and Lieut. Lidder on board the North Star, sloop, for passage to Lisbon, where he joined the Battalion of the Royal Marines under Major Robert Williams, R.M.A., which had been sent there at the end of the previous year.[7] After spending some time on detachment at Belem, Pridham re-joined the Battalion "for the duty of the City." Shortly afterwards "a general illumination and rejoicings took place in Lisbon - in consequence of the expulsion of the French from Portugal by Lord Wellington."

After the fall of Cuidad Rodrigo on the 19th January 1812, the R.M. Battalion received orders to return to England.

In a Lisbon Garrison Order of 11th February 1812 we find the following: "The Royal Marine Battalion will embark on Thursday next, according to the arrangement already announced. The Major-General cannot part with the Royal Marine Battalion without expressing the lively concern he feels in being deprived of their valuable services, and requesting their acceptance of his best thanks for their uniform good conduct whilst in this garrison, which, prepared as he was by the high reputation always maintained by the Corps of Royal Marines, has exceeded his most sanguine expectations. The Major-General begs to assure Major Williams and the Battalion that wherever their new career may take them, they will carry with them his sincere and ardent wishes for their welfare and prosperity."

Pridham, probably by this time a Captain, left for England rather earlier than the rest of the Battalion, as he was sent on board the transport *Latona* with a guard in charge of 170 French prisoners. He arrived "after a most tempestuous and perilous passage" on the 25th February.

On August 27th 1812 he left Plymouth for Portsmouth, whence he at once proceeded on Recruiting duty to Oxford, where he remained till 27th April 1814, when recruiting was suspended "in consequence of the Peace."[8] Three months later he records that he "embarked with a heavy heart on board H.M.S. *Galatea* in Portsmouth Harbour, August 6th, 1814."

Sailing for the North America and West Indies Station at the end of the month the *Galatea*, a few days out from Plymouth, "recaptured the ship *James* from Rio Plata to London, with hides, tallow and peruvian bark. She had been taken by the Chasseur, American privateer." The *Galatea*, with her prize in company, arrived at St. John's, Newfoundland, on 28th September. For the next twelve months Pridham cruised about the station in his ship without finding any incident worth special record, till on the 5th October 1815 she left St. John's for home, with part of the 93rd Regiment on board, arriving at Portsmouth "after a short passage of 12 days."

On November 8th he disembarked from H.M.S. *Galatea*, with hopes that she is the last man-of-war I am to belong to."

Pridham's hopes were justified in the event. Being re-appointed to Plymouth at the end of the year "at the Peace reduction of the Corps," he was sent to the Royal Naval Hospital at that port, in consequence of an injury and contraction of the muscles of the right leg, caused by a check of perspiration at Newfoundland in June 1815." That we should now call a chill, presumably.

How long he remained in hospital is not stated, but he seems to have applied for retirement on full pay, on account of the injury to his leg. Much to his disappointment and disgust he found himself retired on half-pay, a flagrant act of injustice," he says, "after upwards of seventeen years' service, and as disgraceful to an upright and liberal Government as ever was committed!"

However, Pridham appealed against the edict, and thanks to his energetic remonstrance and "the assistance of a good friend," he was re-surveyed and granted a retirement on full pay," and thus, he writes, "I am at once liberated from a Service I always disliked, after having been in it seventeen years and four months. This I esteem the happiest event of my life. God be praised!!!"

There is nothing more of interest in this diary of a somewhat disgruntled Marine, the remainder of it being concerned entirely with his private affairs, a chronicle of births, deaths and marriages.

He seems to have become a partner in a brewing business in 1817, or as he puts it, "Commenced the Business of Common Brewer."

We will hope that he, like some others, liked dealing with Ale better than with Salt Water, and that he prospered in his new life. Reading between the lines of the later entries in his diary, it seems probable that he did.

2 "The Regiment of "Dillon," originally an Irish Regiment, raised in 1653. It served in the French Army, where it had a most distinguished career in the Irish Brigade. In 1793 the 1st Battalion was quartered at Lille and became the 87e Regiment d'Infanterié. The 2nd Battalion was at St. Domingo, and capitulated on 22nd Sept the same year to Commamder Ford, R.N. It joined the British Army in 1794, but was disbanded in 1798. In the meantime, in 1795, Colonel Edward Dillon raised the Regiment which fought at Alexandria, at which time it was generally known as "Dillon's Emigres."

3. The preliminary Articles of Peace were signed in London on 1st October, 1801, and finally at Amiens, 25th March, 1802.

4. War was again declared 16th May, 1803.

5. In consequence of the Treaty of Tilsett, Denmark was required by England to hand over her Fleet, to be retained to a general peace. On her refusal the attack on Copenhagen took place.

6. In 1807, Russia, hitherto an ally, declared war on Great Britain, in accordance with the Treaty of Tilsett. Admiral Senyavin, who had 11 line-of-battle ships in the Mediterranean, bolted for the Baltic, but got no further than the Tagus, where he was blockaded by Sir Sidney Smith. He offered to surrender, on condition that his ships should be returned to Russia after the war, and that he and his crews should be allowed to return home. This was agreed to.

7. Vide "Britain's Sea Soldiers," Vol. I., p. 289-290 anti Vol. II. p. 329.

8. The Treaty of Paris, 20th November, 1815.

(Editor's Note. There is no Note 1 in the original. This is not a misprint.)

MARINES ON IMPRESSMENT DUTY IN PLYMOUTH.
MARCH 10TH, 1803.

Yesterday at 4 a.m., an Admiralty Messenger arrived express in 32 hours from London with important despatches for the Port Admiral Dacres. In a few minutes orders were sent to the Col. Commandant of the Marines at Stonehouse and Mill Barracks, on the receipt of which the Barrack Gates were immediately shut, and no person permitted to go in, or come out of barracks. About 7 p.m. the town was alarmed by the marching of several parties of Royal Marines, in parties of 12 or 14 each with their officers, and a naval officer, armed, towards the quays. So secret were the orders kept, that they did not know the nature of the service on which they were going until they boarded the tier of colliers at the New Quay, and other gangs the ships in Catwater, the Pool and the gin shops. A great number of prime seamen were taken out and sent on board the Admiral's ship. They also pressed landmen of all descriptions, and the town looked as if in a state of siege. At Stonehouse, Mutton Cove, North Corner, Morris Town, and in all the receiving and gin shops at Dock, several hundreds of seamen and landmen were picked up and sent directly on board the flagship. By the returns this morning it appears that upwards of 400 useful hands were pressed last night in the three towns.

Too much credit cannot be given to the different officers and their gangs for the spirit, secrecy and address and humanity with which they executed their orders. One press-gang entered the Dock Theatre and cleared the whole gallery, except the women.

Naval Chronicle IX, 243.

THE BUENOS AYRES FIASCO OF 1806.
By Col. C. Field.

In a little book published in Buenos Ayres in 1882 and entitled "Trofeos de la reconquista de la Ciudad de Buenos Ayres en el ano 1806," appears a coloured plate of the Royal Marine Colour which is here reproduced in black and white. There are also other pictures of a Union Jack, a Red Ensign, King's and Regimental Colours of the 71st Highland Light Infantry and of one of their Pipe Banners, together with a red colour bearing Black Crossbones and two Black Skulls which belonged to a St. Helena Corps. All these are trophies of which the Argentines are naturally very proud and which are preserved in the Convent of Santo Domingo in Buenos Ayres. All were taken when in 1806 the diminutive British Force which was attempting to hold the city against overwhelming numbers was compelled to surrender. In similar cases the surrendering troops have sometimes burnt or buried their colours to prevent them falling into the hands of their enemies, but, personally, I am inclined to think that it is more honourable on such occasions to surrender them to a victorious enemy than to endeavour to cheat him of the legitimate spoils of his victory.

I propose to give a short account of the operations whose unfortunate ending is commemorated by these trophies, but before doing so, the somewhat curious circumstance which led to the publication of the coloured representations of the captured British Flags and Colours, is worth mention.

It seems that in 1882, a certain Chilian gentleman, Don Santiago de Lorca by name, offered the Duke of Cambridge a British Flag which he said had been captured by his grandfather, Don Santiago Fernandez de Lorca in the Buenos Ayres and Montevidean Campaign of 1806. What warrant he had for saying so does not appear, but the Municipality of Buenos Ayres disputed his claim, and at once published the above little brochure "to prove that all the flags lost by the British troops in these operations are kept in the Convent of Santo Domingo del Rosario,"

No sooner had the army sent out to the Cape of Good Hope effected the complete reduction of that settlement, than the Senior Naval Officer, Sir Home Popham, conceived the idea of attacking the Spanish Colonies in South America. According to an officer of the H.L.I[1] who participated in this ill-fated expedition, his principal object was loot, for just before Buenos Ayres had to be surrendered he wrote in his diary:- I cannot too often repeat, let the consequences be what they will, that Sir Home Popham ought to be brought to an account when he arrives in England for having advised the attack on this place. His ideas are turned on the money altogether instead of advising an honourable mode of defence. Anyway, as the event proved, the British Forces were ridiculously inadequate to hold a city of the size of Buenos Ayres in the face of a hostile population. But his proposal was approved by Sir David Baird the General in Command at the Cape who had just received some re-enforcements from England, and on April 14th,1806, the troops under the command of Colonel Beresford sailed for St. Helena on board the *Diadem, Raisonable, Diomede, Leda* and *Narcissus*, with the Encounter gunboat and five transports. At St. Helena a detachment of the St. Helena Regiment and some Artillery were taken on board, and on the 25th June, the ships all anchored off Punta Quilmes about a dozen miles from Buenos Ayres. The same evening the troops were landed near the village of Reduction, six miles nearer to the city, without the least opposition. According to the already quoted booklet their total strength did not exceed 1,641 men, 16 horses and 8 small cannon. The 71st H.L.I. battalion was the strongest unit and "Second in importance for its numerical strength was the Battalion of Marines, 340 men, which number included the following officers:- Major A. McKenzie (in Command), Major Gillespie, Capt. Ballinghall and Lieuts. Swale, Pilcher, Pollard, Sandell, Forbes and Fernyhough. Together with 90 seamen, who had been given what training in infantry work was possible on the voyage over from the Cape, and 10 Naval Officers, the Marines formed what we should now call a Naval Brigade under the command of Captain King of H.M.S. *Diadem*.

It may be noted in passing that in former times, forces of Seamen or Seamen and Marines landed from ships, were sometimes referred to as " Marine Battalions"[2] and it may be that instead of particularly referring to the Royal Marines, the flag with R.M.B. in the centre may have been considered as the "Regimental Colour" of the Naval Brigade, its King's Colour being represented by the plain red ensign which was also carried.

The Artillery consisted of four 6 prs. manned by a small detachment of the R.A., two 5 ½ -inch howitzers brought by the St. Helena Artillery - about 100 strong - and a couple of light 3 prs. manned by the seamen. The St. Helena Infantry mustered 175 men with 7 officers. Although the landing had not been opposed, the enemy had watched it from the rising ground round about the village of Reduction, and it was necessary that this force should be dislodged before it would be safe for the British to move along the coast on Buenos Ayres itself.

The high ground which ran parallel to the coast for many miles towards the mouth of the river turned inland at Reduction and formed a valley between it and the City through which the River Chuelo meandered down to the sea. All the ground between this high ridge and the sea-shore was flat and very swampy.

The British bivouacked for the night, and on the morning of the 26th prepared to attack the enemy who consisted of about 2,000 men, mostly mounted, with eight field guns.

Colonel Beresford found that only a frontal attack was possible on account of the marshy nature of the ground. He formed the Royal Marines and the H.L.I. in a single line with his two howitzers in the centre and two 6 prs. on either flank. The St. Helena Infantry was formed 150 paces in rear of the line with the two Naval guns with orders to face right or left if a flank attack should be threatened by the enemy s cavalry.

Just as the enemy's guns opened fire, the advance was held up by a tongus of swamp, impassable for our guns, so that the line was halted while they tried to find a way round. This they failed to do, so that the line pushed on again as fast as the boggy ground would allow, and on seeing it arrive at the foot of the hill the enemy retired and eventually fled in disorder, leaving four guns behind them. After resting for a couple of hours, while the guns were being extricated from the morass, Beresford moved off towards Buenos Ayres hoping to gain the bridge over the River Chuelo before the enemy should have destroyed it. A column of fire and smoke some way ahead betokened its destruction and the main British body halted a mile short of the bridge, while three companies of the H.L.I. with two Howitzers pushed on in the forlorn hope of saving at least some of it. But it was too late, and as the enemy during the night was heard bringing guns down to the further side of the river, Col Pack, who commanded the advanced detachment considered it best to fall back on the main body. At daybreak the enemy was found to be strongly posted under cover of houses, hedges and shipping, and on the British advancing opened a heavy fire of cannon and musketry. This was ill-directed and pretty ineffective, and our field pieces pushed down to the water's edge escorted by the Grenadier and Light Infantry companies of the H.L.I., soon silenced the enemy's guns. Their musketry was too futile to stay our further advance and the Naval Brigade under the direction of Captain King having prepared and collected rafts and boats, the troops crossed the river with little or no opposition from the enemy who not only deserted their position but the city itself, which surrendered before the British had actually reached it.

So far so good, but for a force of less than 2,000 men to attempt to hold a city of 70,000 inhabitants, mostly hostile, with enemy forces collecting in the neighbouring country was a preposterous proposition which could only have one ending.

A considerable amount of specie fell into the hands of the British, said to have exceeded 1,290,000 dollars of which 1,086,000 dollars were sent to England in the *Narcissus*, the remainder being retained for the exigencies of the expeditionary forces.

In a very few weeks it was apparant that not only was there imminent danger of a rising in the city itself, but that two separate armies were being formed for its recapture. One of these was assembling in Monte Video on the other side of the Rio de la Plata under Captain Liniers, a Frenchman in the Spanish service, the other under a Buenos Ayrean official named Puereydon at Pedriel about 20 miles to the westward of the city.

To attack the latter force 450 men of the H.L.I., 50 Royal Marines and 2 guns left at 2 o'clock in the morning of 1st August and at 8 discovered the enemy, 2,000 strong with 10 guns drawn up in a well chosen position.

The instant and determined advance of the British detachment dispersed their opponents in about twenty minutes. They lost about 100 men, killed, wounded or taken, and all their guns.

Although well beaten the Spaniards appear to have fought with a good deal of determination for the short time the affair lasted, their cavalry charging our guns and very nearly succeeding in killing Colonel Beresford, who was commanding in person. His life was saved by his orderly, a Sergeant of the Marines, and two or three of the Grenadiers of the H.L.I.

Satisfactory as was this victory it did little or nothing to stay the impending disaster. Two days later Liniers evading the British squadron, brought his men over the river in 28 vessels and landed them at Las Conchas, about 20 miles above the City. Buenos Ayres at this time extended about two miles along the sea front and about one mile inland. It was all laid out in square blocks of lofty well built houses with flat parapeted roofs. In the centre of the sea front was the fort, which formed the British headquarters. Parallel to the land face of the fort at some yards distance was a long colonaded building, beyond which was the Plaza Mayor, or Great Square. Two streets at right angles to each other issued from each angle of the square. At the north end of the city, not far from the sea, was the Bull Ring, and here on the night of the 10th August, the enemy attacked and slaughtered in circumstances of great barbarity the picket of a sergeant, a corporal and 20 men.

This was the beginning of the attack from outside, but prior to this there had been several unpleasant happenings within the city. A number of German soldiers belonging to the H.L.I. had deserted late in July, one, Echart by name, was captured in the skirmish of the 1st August, tried by Court Martial and shot on the 9th. On the night of the fifth in a storm of rain and wind, four Spaniards fell upon a young Marine of sixteen who was sentry on a tobacco store near the Square and took his firelock from him, but did not seem to have injured him. But on the 9th another sentry was attacked in the same way, and an officer of the H.L.I. who went to his assistance was stabbed in the shoulder.

As soon as the enemy had established himself in the north quarter of the city, Liniers sent in a summons to surrender, which was refused. Thereupon a general attack began, the enemy continually reinforced by the inhabitants worked from house to house and gradually pervaded the whole city till the British had to fall back on their position immediately in front of the Fort. The H.L.I., with the exception of two companies occupied the building forming the east side of the Plaza Mayor in front of the Fort, the Royal Marines and Seamen were in the square itself while The St. Helena Infantry were placed in rear to cover the passages on either end of the building.

On the 12th, the British were completely surrounded with evergrowing swarms of assailants, every roof and window vomited musketry and men were falling fast. At length Colonel Beresford decided that surrender was inevitable and hoisted the white flag. Colonel Liniers did everything he could to maintain a proper order, but great difficulties were experienced in dealing with the exultant rabble which formed the bulk of his forces. Major McKenzie, R.M. was wounded while the white flag was flying, while conveying orders to the men in one of the bastions of the fort to cease firing. "The British troops were marched from the fort to the Cairldo," wrote an officer of the H.L.I.[3] through a line, I am almost ashamed to say of what sort of soldiery, and then delivered up their arms and honours, in exchange for a prison and perhaps starvation." Liniers had promised to exchange them for the Spanish troops who had been captured, and without doubt would have carried out his promise, but was prevented from doing so by the infuriated population, and Beresford and his men were sent hundreds of miles up country. So ended this unfortunate and ill-advised expedition which resulted among other things in the collection of surrendered British Colours and Flags now in the Convent of San Domingo. The following description of the Flag illustrated is published in the brochure already mentioned.

Ordinary wool, 1.64 metres by 1.7 metres. It bears in the centre three large letters in light coloured cloth R.M.B. (Royal Marine Battalion), but it lacks the Globe with the official motto "Ubique, per Mare per Terram." This flag was brought to the garrison by the Marines (Royal Blues), who disembarked at Los Quilmes to augment the invading forces, and which were commanded by Captain William King of the flagship *Diadem*. The flag is all red because the British Fleet, a century earlier in order to faciliate the service, had been divided into three great sections according to the British tri-colour, i.e., red, blue and white, the white being the highest rank; the expeditionary ships belonged to the red section and Sir Home Riggs Popham was flying the Red Ensign. There is another small Red Ensign about the same size but with a plain fly, probably both were boats' ensigns.

What the Spanish writer calls "ordinary wool" is probably bunting. The "Ubique" in the Corps motto is curious. Did it ever appear in it? I have seen the motto similarly written in the preface of a little book by Davenport Adams entitled "Famous Regiments of the British Army" published sometime in the 'sixties. We know that our motto has not always had quite its present wording; for instance on the pouch ornament illustrated on page 275, Vol. I., "Britain's Sea Soldiers," it reads Per Mare et per Terram," while on the title page of Gillespie's History of the corps (1803) it appears as "Per Mare Terramque Vincimus." It would be interesting to ascertain whether either this or the "Ubique" one was ever official or actually used and when the present wording was officially adopted.

The words "Royal Blues" are rather puzzling. Do they refer to the Marines or to the blue-jackets? In an account of the operations published in 1838, it refers to "the marine battalion, under the orders of Captain King of the *Diadem* which was composed of the marines of the squadron, augmented by the incorporation of some seamen, and three companies of royal blues." Here they seem to be in addition to both seamen and marines.

The other Naval Flag is described as being "4 metres by 1.45 metres" and to be "crossed on all its surface with the English national colours." It flew on the flagstaff of El Retiro, which was converted into an ammunition depot as it was within range of the ships' guns. It has been mended in many places.

The arrangement of the "Union" in all these flags is very curious. In the two smaller ones there is no white fiumbration to the upright arm of the St. George's Cross, and in all three the arms of the diagonal crosses of St. Andrew and the Fitzgeralds cannot meet in the centre. The "Union" in the Colours of the H.L.I. hanging with them is correct.

These flags when deposited with great ceremony in the Convent of St. Domingo on 24th August, 1806, had inscribed below them:- " In memory of the retribution upon the English and of the glory of Liniers in Buenos Ayres."

Notes:
1. Captain Pococke. Journal published in "H.L.I. Chronicle" the opinion of Popham is corroborated by Fortescue (History British Army Vol. V.p. 315) who says "with a knowledge of Pophams antecedents and character, it may also be suspected that the Commodore doubted the success of an attack on Mont Video and that he therefore declared an immediate movement on Buenos Ayres, where he would be sure of finding the object which he was really in search, namely prize money."
2. Vide "Britains Sea Soldiers" I. p. 24 – II. p. 311.
3. Captain Pococke in his Journal.

PAY OF THE ROYAL MARINES IN 1808.

"There are however some things, - in which the Army enjoy advantages which are not extended to the Navy. Wherever the soldiers go, each regiment takes with it its paymaster; but sailors and Marines are never paid anywhere except in England, however long they may be absent. Upon the Marines this is particularly hard, as there is a practice of drafting them out of vessels which are going home into those which are to remain upon the foreign station. This is done to keep up the complement, because no men are forced into this, as they are into the Navy Service, and no addition is made to it abroad, unless any prisoners should enter, which the Dutch soldiers frequently do. 'I knew' said this officer, (a Naval fellow-traveller) 'a private Marine who had been nine years on a foreign station, and never received one farthing of pay; and he would have been drafted again into another ship still to remain there, if the captain had not stated to the commander-in-chief that he was quite blind at night, a common disease within the tropics.' This is one reason why so many men in those seas desert from the English ships to the American."

Fr "Letters from England"
By Don Manuel Alvarez Espriella 1808.

THE DEFENCE OF ANHOLT IN MARCH, 1811.
(Reprinted from the "Globe & Laurel" of 1st Sept. 1892).

There are now on view (and for sale) at Messrs Spink and Son's, the well-known Medallists, 17 and 18, Piccadilly, some relics which commemorate one of the most gallant defences on record, and should appeal specially to the Corps of Royal Marines. There can have been but few engagements on such a scale, in which the honour of the British flag has been upheld solely by Marines, and yet it is probable that the majority of the members of the Corps have never heard of the defence of Anholt.*

The principal relic, which the writer has seen through the courtesy of Messrs. Spink & Son, is a presentation sword with a magnificently chased gilt scabbard, and a blade inlaid with gold, on which is the following inscription: - "Presented by the Officers, Non-commissioned Officers, Gunners and Privates of the Royal Marines and Royal Marine Artillery in garrison at Anholt, to their esteemed Governor, Captain James Wilkes Maurice, of the Royal Navy, in token of their admiration of his personal bravery in the battle of the 27th March, 1811, and as a grateful memorial for his liberal, forbearing and kind consideration of their feelings during his government.

Besides the sword are to be seen Captain Maurice's Medal (the Naval General Service), with the clasp, for "Anholt, 27 March, 1811," two seals used by him (one bearing an impression of the Diamond Rock) and two letters, one from himself (signed) announcing the loss of the Diamond Rock and the other from Lord Nelson (signed), complimenting him on his splendid defence.

The defence of the Diamond Rock where six years before Captain Maurice had already gained such distinction, concerns the Corps less intimately than the repulse of the Danes at Anholt in March, 1811.

The garrison of the island, which we had captured from the Danes in 1809, consisted, according to James's Naval History, of 350 Royal Marines and 31 Royal Marine Artillery. The Marines were under the command of Captain (with local rank of Major) Robert Torrens, and the whole were under Captain Maurice, R.N., the Governor of the island, whose second in command was Lieut. H. L. Baker, R.N. The following Marine Officers are mentioned in Captain Maurice's despatch, but it is not known whether any others were present at the time: -

Royal Marine Artillery - Lieut. and Adjt. R. C. Steele (Commanding the Howitzer Brigade) and Lieut. Bezant. Royal Marines - Capt. Torrens (Commandant of Garrison), Lieut. and Quartermaster Fisher, Lieuts. Stewart, Gray, Ford, Jellico, Atkinson, Curtayne and Turnbull (Commanding the Light Company).

The island was attacked just before daybreak on the 27th March, 1811, by a Danish flotilla of 18 gun boats,* accompanied by transports, the whole force, according to Capt. Maurice, consisting of nearly 4,000 men,† owing to darkness and thick fog the landing was effected on the south shore without opposition, and Capt. Maurice on arriving at the hill above the beach found his force of 200 men and 4 howitzers so outnumbered and outflanked on both sides by the invaders that he deemed it prudent to retreat, to avoid being cut off from the forts. A body of 200 Danish seamen followed, but were compelled to retire to the beach by the heavy fire from the Massareene and Yorke batteries.

Meanwhile the main body of the enemy had crossed the island and taken up a position on the northern shore, and a body of 150 men was sent forward by the Danish Commander to commence the attack on the forts. This force, though advancing bravely and rallying frequently, was at length beaten back, and the Danish seamen having by this time succeeded in bringing up a field piece, which enfiladed the Massareene battery, a general assault on the works was ordered.

In spite of the support from the Danish gun boats the attack was unsuccessful. The discharges of grape and musketry from the British batteries were irresistible, and strewed the ground with dead and wounded, amongst the former being the three senior Danish officers. The discomfiture of the enemy was completed by the appearance on their flank of the Anholt schooner, a small armed vessel attached to the island, manned by volunteers, and commanded by Lieut. Baker, R.N. (with whom was Lieut. Turnbull). Finding the sandhills no protection against the fire of the schooner, and both advance and retreat impossible, the Danes offered to surrender on terms; but the Governor would accept of nothing less than an unconditional surrender, to which the Danes, after some deliberation, acceded.

By this time the Danish gunboats, being much galled by the fire of the batteries, and observing the approach of British 32-gun frigate Tartar, got underweigh and stood to the westward, and the column of the enemy on the south shore, finding their retreat no longer covered by the flotilla, surrendered. The remainder of the assailants fled to the west shore, where their re-embarkation was assured by the presence of 14 gunboats, and Capt. Maurice, having only 40 men (with 4 howitzers) at his disposal, the remainder being in charge of the prisoners, did not feel justified in offering any opposition.

Thus after a close combat of 4 ½ hours, the enemy received a most complete and decisive defeat, with a loss of 4 officers and 30 to 40 men killed, 23 wounded, exclusive of a large number carried to the boats, and 16 officers and 504 men taken prisoners. In addition they lost 3 pieces of cannon, 484 muskets, 470 swords, and a large amount of ammunition and shell. The loss of the garrison was 2 killed and 30 wounded (including Capt. Torrens).

The retreating Danes were pursued by the *Tartar* and the *Sheldrake* (a 16-gun brig-sloop), which had reached the island the night before, but had been too far to leeward to assist the garrison. The latter captured two and sank a third gun vessel, while the *Tartar*, after capturing two transports, was compelled, owing to shoal water, to haul off and discontinue the chase.

Capt. Torrens was gazetted to a brevet majority on the 1st June, 1811.

It is hoped that the above short account of this brilliant action may be of sufficient interest to stimulate some generous reader to purchase these relics and present them to a Corps which, while it has surely the highest title to them, would also certainly most appreciate them.

*The Marine Artillery should be excepted, as there is in the Mess at Eastney a quaint picture, the work of Lieut. Turnbull, mentioned in this account, depicting the repulse of the Danes in this memorable engagement.

*Each of these gunboats mounted two long 24 or 18 pounders, and 4 brass howitzers, and had a crew of from 60 to 70 men.

†It should be stated that the Danish official account puts the strength of the troops at 1,000 men, including an organised body of 200 seamen, and Capt. Brenton gives the number of troops and seamen at 1,590, which number James accepts as a fair estimate.

DEFENCE OF ANHOLT.
By Gen. Sir H. E. Blumberg, K.C.B., R.M. (Ret.)

With reference to the article in last month's Records pages, it may be of interest to relate the disposal of this gallant garrison.

They must have remained in garrison until August, 1812, because in September, 1812, the Records give the Orders to the Commandant at Portsmouth; that as the garrison of Anholt arrive the R.M.A. are to be sent back to Chthm, but the Infantry to be formed into 6 companies; to be equipped the same as the 1st and 2nd Battalions but with no battalion organisation, colours, pioneer equipment, etc., and to be embarked in the *Nemesis* (order dated 13 Oct., 1812) and sent to join 1st and 2nd battalions on the North Coast of Spain, where no doubt, they took part in the investment of Santona. Captain Sterling was in command as orders re Regiment's Allowance are addressed to him; and we learn later that Major Gorrens was serving in H.M.S. *Blenheim* with the Marines in South Holland in 1813.

These companies returned to England with the 1st and 2nd Battalions and were incorporated with them for service in America (Admiralty letter 2 Jan., 1813).

———

THE REGENT'S ALLOWANCE
Compiled By
General Sir H. E. Blumberg, K.C.B. R.M. (Ret.)

This old allowance, which was taken away from the Royal Marines in 1921, was once of great interest to young officers, and as the knowledge of its provisions is becoming lost in the shades of antiquity, it may be of interest to recall them to the young officers of the present generation.

Legend states that the Prince Regent (afterwards King George IV.) when dining with the officers of a certain regiment, noticed that several officers did not drink the King's health after dinner, and he was informed that the reason was that they could not afford it. He therefore determined that an allowance should be made to enable them to do so. This seems to have occurred somewhere about 1809; but as far as the Royal Marines are concerned the first notice is in an Admiralty letter dated 25th September, 1811, addressed to the Commandants as follows:

"H.R.H. was pleased to order an allowance in aid of the expences of the Regimental Mess should be granted to every regiment, battalion or corps when stationed in Great Britain, and that the said allowance should be apportioned according to the establishment of the corps and under the direction of the Commanding Officer on the following scale: -

For every Regiment or Battalion consisting of 10 Troops or Companies and upwards at rate of £250 per annum

Ditto of 9 Troops or Companies	£225 per ann.	
Ditto of 8 " "	£200 "
Ditto of 7 " "	£175 "
Ditto of 6 " "	£150 "
Ditto of 5 " "	£125 "
Ditto of 4 " "	£100 "
For a Corps of 300	£75 "
" " 200	£50 "
" " 100	£25 "

H.R.H. the Prince Regent has approved of a similar indulgence being extended to the Royal Marine Corps and to the Royal Marine Artillery, to be in a like manner apportioned to the strength of the Corps at Headquarters, in aid of the expences of their respective messes, according to aforementioned scale. Directions to be given to the Paymaster to issue an allowance accordingly in aid of the mess of your Division, the same to commence this day.

(Signed) JOHN BARROW.

The Commandants
R.M. Divisions."

This soon led to correspondence on the subject of the commencing date, and on the 4th October the Commandant at Portsmouth was informed that the commencing date was "25th Sept., 1811, and is not to go further back"; but in response to further appeals the Admiralty relented and on 10th December, 1811, approved that "Allowance was to commence from 25th December, 1809."

That the allowance was in aid of the wine drunk at mess is shewn by several letters in the Divisional letter books; e.g. when the 1st Battalion returned from Spain prior to going to America: "25th March, 1812, Major Williams having applied for Regent's Allowance, the Commandant is called on to state whether the Battalion messes with the Division."

22nd April, 1812: "Major Williams having requested about charge made to officers of the Battalion for wine drunk by them at Mess, the Paymaster is to make them an allowance for the same."

On 30th Oct., 1812: "There is approval for an allowance for wine for the Anholt Battalion while serving on shore. The Admiralty addressed a letter to Captain Sterling, R.M., on board the *Nemesis* (the companies were then on their way to North Spain) and said application is to be made to Lieut.-General Elliott (i.e., the Commandant at Portsmouth), who will cause it to be paid according to strength of Battalion and the time it was on shore at Portsmouth. This letter is endorsed 'Approved' in old General Elliott's handwriting and marked by him to the Deputy Paymaster.

Regent's Allowance was payable under this order for many years, but from entries in various Mess Minute books it undoubtedly became merged in an Admiralty allowance paid towards upkeep of messes.

An entry in Plymouth Minutes, 3rd March, 1832, states "Resolved also that the Plate Fund (subscription from new member of the mess) and Regent's Allowance be kept separate; the Plate Fund to be carried to the surplus of the Regent's Allowance as a fund for the purchase of indispensable mess necessaries." The only official note beyond the first order in Council (quoted at the beginning) I have been able to find is the Order in Council of 31st December, 1883, where it says "Mess Allowance for Officers Mess, £450 per annum; ditto for Deal, £250 per annum." This allowance, which evidently included the Regent's Allowance, was paid up to September, 1921, when the Admiralty took over the upkeep of Officers Messes under Naval Conditions.

When I was a Subaltern the lump sum was paid to the Mess, and each dining member was credited with the princely sum of 3d. per day for each day on which he was in Mess, presumably to pay for the pint of wine which was charged to each member on public days.

Even when on Army Courses, such as Hythe, etc., an officer had to bring back a certificate that he had duly paid for so many days messing, which at that time was the regulated charge for mess dinner only; in those days at Plymouth the charge for dinner was 2/4, less the 3d. – net charge 2/1 per diem. As Regent's Allowance in the Army was paid at 4d. per diem, officers of the Corps lost

1d. per diem on this transaction. Alas! for us young subalterns, the small weekly sum of 1/9 went a very little way in paying for the wine.

On guest nights, which took place regularly every Friday night, all dining members, whether present or not, had to pay an equal share of all wine opened after dinner, whether they partook of it or not. As the least opened on these occasions was two bottles of claret (of the very best vintage), two bottles of port (none such obtainable in our cellar nowadays), two bottles of madeira (that had gone round the world) and two bottles of the very finest old sherry, it may be imagined that the cost was not light, and with the thoughts of the large pay of 5/3 a day in our minds, we contemplated a wine bill amounting to 10/- or 12/- for that day, and the fact that we might drink free what was let over on Saturday or Sunday as ullage was small compensation.

It was not till some years later, when strong Commandants like Colonels Way and Byam were in power, that they ordered that only the cost of the first two rounds of the after dinner wine should be divided equally, the rest being paid for by those who partook; and it was many years before the present sensible rules and customs were introduced, and His gracious Majesty King Edward VII. gave permission for his health to be drunk in pure water should we so desire.

CUTTING-OUT EXPEDITION AT CORIGEOU.

During the Napoleonic Wars the Marines nowhere proved their usefulness to the Navy to a greater extent than in the almost innumerable "cutting out" affairs which were carried out, almost always successfully against enemy ships anchored in bays and harbours under the protection of shore forts and batteries.

Their work it was, to quote a Plymouth Dock poet of 1811:-
"When 'gainst the hostile shore th' attack is plann'd,
To storm the batteries that guard the land;
Destroy the magazine, the tower, the fort,
And open and defenceless leave the port."

while their bluejacket shipmates boarded and carried out the enemy's vessels from the anchorage which they had hoped to find security.

Probably the very last of these operations was carried out in the Bay of Coriegou on the night of July 18th, 1815, and of this well executed enterprise we have not only first-hand accounts from two out of the three officers of the Corps who were present, but a rough sketch of the proceedings. This was made by Lieut Burton, and the following letter from him to his brother gives an interesting narrative of his experiences:

H.M.S. *MENELAUS*,
PLYMOUTH SOUND.
Friday, 4th August, 1815.

My dear William,

The above sketch will give you some idea of our affair. I believe it is tolerably correct as to most essential points, except that the French brig and cutter are placed a very little too far to the eastward, perhaps a furlong.

To begin the narrative methodically, you must know that on Saturday the 15th ultimo we saw the convoy under the tricolour coming from Abreverak, and chased them into the Bay of Plounejou or Correjou, and about seven miles to the eastward of the former place and about 18 miles from Brest. It was protected, as we afterwards found, by two batteries of two guns each. The coast is so very rocky that no large ship can act. The country near the beach is equally rugged, but more inland it is well cultivated and wooded. The fences are all low stone or sod banks. The peasantry live in stone cottages and speak the Breton tongue, not one in twenty understanding French.

On Tuesday the 18th the *Rhin* and *Havannah* frigates and *Fly* and *Ferret* brigs being in company and Captain Malcolm of the *Rhin* senior officer, an attack with the seamen and marines was determined on. The Marines of the other ships - about 120 in number, commanded by Lieut. Bunce, R.M. of the *Rhin*-and about 80 seamen, under Captain Hamilton of the *Havannah*, composed the main body. My party (45 rank and file) formed the advanced guard and skirmishing party; my orders were to cover the main body and act discretionally, Captain Malcolm commanding the whole.

The boats left the ships in the offing about 10 at night. The weather was calm and moonlight. At half-past 11 we came to a grapnel, under a range of rocks about a quarter of a mile from the shore. Here we lay waiting till the moon should set, intending to nick the time between her going down and the day dawning. All around us was quite still, and the time passed a little anxiously, as you may suppose; at half past 2 we moved on again, and after a quarter of an hour's pull reached the beach.

The landing was effected without discovery; the boat in which I was, happened to touch the rocks first, and just above high-water mark were three little stumps or piles standing in a row, and by that uncertain light they looked exactly like so many cannon pointed at us. Even after I had waded out of the boat and scrambled over the crags half way to them I became still more persuaded that we were close to a battery. I went back softly to the water's edge, and collecting the men who had got on shore, returned. To add to the effect a figure was now seen creeping towards the supposed battery - this I guessed was the French sentinel. I, first taking aim at him, demanded who he was. It proved to be an English officer from another boat, under the same mistake as myself. In a few minutes all the men were landed, and we moved off by the routes in the sketch at a very quick rate.

I had never seen any map of the place, and was quite unacquainted with the country (which had only been reconnoitred by Captain Malcolm), consequently knew not where to expect or look for an enemy. When we came to the spot marked in the sketch "High Ground and rocky," we saw a rock which we took for some sort of fortification, and I made a movement to my left in order to examine it. At this instant the main body came up abreast of us, and a minute afterwards, as we moved forward again, we saw the Convoy before us, moored to the rocks, with boarding nettings up and every precaution taken for defence.

It was now grey daylight. They immediately perceived us on the brow of the hill, and as immediately opened their broadsides. We ran down the hill and along the sandy isthmus under a shower of grape. The first battery was completely surprised; the enemy instantly abandoned it and retreated to the second, which was covered by rocks and a stone guard-house.

The main body halted in the first battery and (?) by the hill were waiting for the support of the *Ferret* and *Fly*, who were seen coming through the rocks to attack the Convoy.

My men now passed rapidly along their front and pushed over the hill and across the cornfields towards the second battery. This was the most bustling part of the business - the musquetry from the rocks and guard-house on our left, the grape and canister from the vessels in our front, made noise enough. I believe our escape is attributable to the rapidity of our advance down the declivity, since the enemy could not depress their guns quick enough.

(Not signed)
LT. ALFRED BURTON R M

For the Rev, Wm, C. Burton,
    Friars Place,
        Reading, Berks.

Additional particulars of the affair are to be found in letters from Lieut. Thomas Hurdle, who was also present:-

"The convoy was driven into the harbour of Corgiou immediately after the *Havannah* left, when the *Menelaus* was joined by the *Rhin*. The *Havannah* rejoined on the 18th July. In the interval the senior officer, with a view to an attack, had kept the frigates out of sight of land - the *Ferret* watching the port. In her an officer was sent to examine the neighbourhood for a favourable place to land. A very high house, built on the highest spot in the village, could be seen from a long distance, and as it stood near to the precipitous descent to the harbour, formed an excellent point of direction to the narrow sandy isthmus connecting the peninsula on which the Fort and Battery stood with the main land. From the masthead of the *Ferret* it was easily seen over the heath, and the bearing by compass taken from the place selected for landing. So although not yet light when we landed, there was no difficulty in deciding on the route.

On first landing the Marines formed in line in front of their boats, the *Havannahs* on the right, then the *Rhins*, and the *Menelaus* on their left. Before moving off the *Rhins* were moved to the *Havannahs*' right. The Captain of the *Rhin* being the senior naval officer and Lieut. Bunce of the *Rhin* the senior Marine officer, explains, why the *Rhin's* Marines took the right and led the movement followed by those of the *Havannah*. The *Menelaus* Marines were supposed to be following the *Havannahs*, and the seamen, who were to form a support, following the *Menelaus*.

The direction being known, we marched rapidly-never deviating until after we had passed the long sandy isthmus, when we turned sharply to the left, ascending a little hill to a small loop-holed stone building, which we found abandoned, and then proceeded on to the battery, also found to have been abandoned.

The three Naval Captains accompanied us, each with a seaman - one carrying a spy-glass, another a Union jack, and the 3rd (I believe) a compass. They remained on the little hill, supposed to be considering on which side the fort should he assaulted. They remained rather long, when I went back to learn the cause. A minute after the men-of-war opened a fire of grape upon the hill, one of which killed a man on board the *Ferret,* then passing about half a mile beyond the battery. We were then ordered to assault the fort on the east face. The Marines who were formed near the battery, moved rapidly round to the assault, and found little difficult in scaling the east wall; a wicket gate between the east wall and the stone barrack was easily forced. The fort was quickly carried, after some resistance, in which a fine young French officer was killed. The vessels now opened a fire of musketry upon us. The Marines replied, driving the enemy off their decks, but they did not strike their colours. The enemy seeing us training one of the guns to bear on them, hauled down their colours.

Up to this time I had not seen the seamen; on subsequent inquiry I was told they had mistaken the route.

All the Marines except the *Havannah's* were immediately ordered up to the village to avoid surprise, occupying favourable points of observation, until ordered to re-embark in the boats within the Bay. It was more than half an hour after our success before the boats came round, when, owing to the rapid fall of the tide, it was round impracticable to get the boats over the bar that tide, as had been the intention."

Here ends as much of Hurdle's account as I can make out. There is more of his writing in red ink, apparently written with a pin, and very confused, but he seems to be principally endeavouring to traverse everything Lieut. Burton had said in the letter to his brother. But his criticisms do not amount to anything worth "writing home about," and it is a common experience that the accounts of eye-witnesses of the same incident, even of such a small affair as the raid at Corigeou, generally differ in a remarkable way.

We should have liked to have heard that the landing parties got off to their ships without further difficulty. However, we may assume that they were able to do this, in spite of having to wait for the next tide, since from another account, though only a dozen lines are devoted to the operation we learn that "after a sharp conflict the whole convoy was in the possession of the British. The enemy had four men killed, and several, including officers, wounded, and the British party had one mortally and three slightly wounded."

Still one could wish that we had the end of the story, either from one or other of the two officers of Marines who have handed down to us their experiences on what was our last hostile landing on the shores of our present friends and allies.

THE WATERLOO CAMPAIGN AND THE ROYAL MARINES.
By Brigadier R. D. Ormsby, C.B.E., R.M.

In the Journals and Letters of Admiral of the Fleet Sir T. Byam Martin G.C.B., published by the Navy Records Society, an interesting note is given which is probably unknown to most members of the Corps.

In 1815 Rear Admiral Sir T. B. Martin was second-in-command at Plymouth. He was sent early in April 1815 with a small squadron to the Scheldt in order to afford naval co-operation with the allied forces in Belgium under the Duke of Wellington.

In a letter to the Secretary of the Admiralty dated 17th April 1815, Admiral Martin in giving details of his interview with the Duke states "his Grace intimated a hope that the Admiralty would be able to assist him by making a diversion in the mouth of the Seine with a force of ten thousand marines." The letter goes on to state how much importance the Duke attached to this proposal and the Admiral then states "but knowing that it would not be possible to collect such a body of marines, I thought it my duty to say so distinctly." His Grace then asked, "Can they do you think make up 5,000 men and pass them off for ten?" I made the same negative reply, observing that several of the largest class of ships had lately been commissioned and that I knew that the whole of the marine divisions could not produce anything like the number of men required for the completion of those ships, and that even with the marines now returning from America I was persuaded that there would be much difficulty in collecting an adequate number for the wants of the service, as many of them would be entitled to their discharge. On a renewal of the conversation the following morning the Duke inquired if two of three thousand marines might be reckoned upon, and I felt myself again under the mortifying necessity of discouraging (as far as my opinion went) all expectation of such assistance, and I concluded by saying that I would only venture to state that his Grace might rely on the cordial desire of the Admiralty to afford him the most un-limited co-operation in their power, but that I could not imagine the possibility of their exertions enabling them to meet his wishes on this occasion."

Admiral Martin goes on to say that "In speaking of the return of the marines from America I meant only those in ships, not knowing whether the marine battalions are in Canada, and likely to return home time enough for the service alluded to by the Duke of Wellington." (See Britain's Sea Soldiers, Vol. I, Ch XIX.)

In a note inserted by Admiral Martin he states "When I left Plymouth a fortnight previous to this conversation there were only 29 marines at headquarters, and the ships all short of their complements."

————

PRESENTIMENTS OF DEATH.*

"A still more remarkable instance was that of Lieut. Bissett, of the Royal Marine Artillery, who went out, in 1816, to Algiers, in His Majesty's bomb 'Infernal.' He over and again stated, even before the fleet got to Gibraltar, that he well knew he should 'be one of the first;' and after sailing from that place, passed his time principally in devotions, audible outside his cabin. Latterly he said but little to anyone, and on the morning of the battle, he several times repeated that he knew he should 'be one of the first.' With the exception of this, he hardly spoke on that day, unless to give the necessary directions at the mortars. The action began at about 2 o'clock in the afternoon, and he was in the act of aiming either the fourth or fifth shell when the fatal shot struck him.

Before this she had been a good deal cut up; she had had her springs shot away, boats swamped, and was severely raked for some time. During all this he seemed calmly waiting for death with the cool yet determined resolution of a gallant spirit who knows his last hour has come. I never could imagine what sort of a missile it was that ended his mortal career. He was cut in three pieces. One leg went forward on the gangway; and the other and part of his body, remained nearly where he had been standing; and his upper works went overboard - certainly on that day the Algerines threw about some queer articles, such as crow-bars, iron bolts, hand-spikes, glass bottles, bags of nails, &c. &c., 'ad libitum.'

A lance corporal, named Potter, fired all the other shells from the "Infernal" during that action. Where is he? What has been done for that man? They were well thrown, that, every body allowed.

I was told too, that poor Bisset was the only support of his sisters and an aged mother. What has been done for them? Where was our famed 'Patriotic Fund' &c. in 1816? Alas! how true it is, that not half the horrors of war are confined to the field of battle."

From "The United Service Journal and Naval and Military Magazine," 1832 Part 1 page 228.

*N.B. – Part of this was reproduced in Britains' Sea Soldiers, Vol 11, page 14

————.

OCCUPATION OF VAN DIEMAN'S LAND AND MELVILLE ISLAND.

The following account was taken from the "Demerara Gazette" of 29th June, 1825, and had been copied from a Portsmouth paper, probably the "Hampshire Telegraph and Post."

We have stated that his Majesty's ship Tamar, Capt. Gordon Bremer, was despatched from England, under the direction of Lord Bathurst, to take possession of the North part of New Holland, called Van Dieman's Land, and of Melville Island, in the Gulph of Carpentaria.

The following particulars, which we have received, written by an officer employed in the service will be read with much interest: -

"King's Cove, Port Cockburn, Melville Island, Australia, Nov. 12, 1824.- On our arrival at Sydney from England, we hired a merchant vessel (*the Countess of Harcourt*), which we loaded with various provisions and stores, and embarked in her a detachment of 25 men of the 3rd regiment of Buffs, commanded by Captain Barlow. We also loaded a Colonial brig, with various agricultural and mechanical instruments, necessary to form a settlement. After a pleasant passage of six weeks we arrived at the destined spot, at the N. extremity of New Holland (now called Australasia), named Port Essington, in long. 181, E. of Greenwich, where we landed all our marines (46 in number) and immediately hoisted the British flag, on a high tree, amidst a salute of 21 guns from the Tamar, a volley of small arms from the troops, and the repeated huzzas of all hands. Perhaps, never was a martial sound heard here before. The natives were so struck with terror, that they all fled away. After the other usual formalities, we divided ourselves into two small parties to go in search of fresh water, and discover the retreat of the natives. The next morning we found some fresh water, but could only trace the natives to a certain distance. In two days after, we proceeded towards Melville Island, which we reached in three days, at a point called Apsley Straits, which is about 30 miles in length formed by the said Island and another Island, named Bathurst Island, which lies to the westward. We also took possession of these places in the King's name, with all due formalities. The port has been named "Cockburn," and the spot of ground selected upon which to form the settlement, "King's Cove." The Islands are covered with the most luxuriant plants and trees, a great number of which we have cut down, to clear the ground, and in six weeks we have erected a fort, two large houses, about eighteen cottages, a large store-house, a good landing-place, and dug a deep well of spring water. Having completed our establishment, we had a grand dinner party, hoisted the flag in the fort, with a royal salute, drank bumpers to the King's health, and toasts out of number, not forgetting our dear absent friends, and the fair sex of England. The establishment consists of Capt. Barlow, Commandant, with a Lieutenant and 24 privates of the 2nd Buffs; Lieutenant Williamson and 27 Royal Marines; a Commissary, with 2 Clerks and a Surgeon, with some merchants - forming altogether 90 persons in the Colony. After we had been here nearly a month, the natives made in the appearance suddenly from the woods, with a great noise, which we hardly knew if it proceeded from the human or brute part of the creation. They were black men quite naked, holding their hands above their heads, as a sign of being friendly. They all at once made a stop and some of them came towards us, with whom we shook hands, but they appeared very suspicious of our attentions. Most of their words were Vara, Vara, this last expression we understood to be, give us some axes, which we did, and various other trinkets; after which they ran away making the same noise as before. They returned again, begging more axes, and what they could not obtain by gift they stole with all the dexterity of thorough-bred metropolitan thieves. We shall proceed hence shortly for the East India station.

Portsmouth Paper.

———————

ROYAL MARINE CORPS A HUNDRED YEARS AGO.
FROM "THE NAVAL SKETCH BOOK."
By "An Officer of Rank" (Capt. Glascock. R.N.) (Published 1826)

The Corps of Royal Marines have always constituted an important arm of our Naval force. Their value, however, was never fully appreciated until the last war, when it became necessary, in consequence of the shyness of the enemy's vessels, as well as for the frequency of combined operations by sea and land, to invade their harbours, and attack not only the shipping under the protection of the forts, but to storm the batteries themselves. In these services they deported themselves with so much zeal and steady valour, that a generous rivalry between them and the sailors employed on such expeditions awakened the latter to a just sense of their merits, and extinguished happily that feeling of discontent - almost approaching to contempt - with which they had previously, no doubt, from the comparative inactivity of that service, been regarded by men whose cheerful and undaunted intrepidity had rendered them the idol of their country, and the object of reluctant admiration to other nations.

The coast of Spain, during the Peninsula War; that of North. America, when they acted in battalion; and, above all, though precedently in point of time, the gallant defence of Anholt, have entitled this branch of the service to grateful recollection (? recognition - C.F.).

Their obvious utility in operations, either by land or sea, has at length overcome the scruples of those patriots in and out of Parliament, whose jealousy never fails to rouse itself into invective at the mention of a red-coat; and they are, despite of their cloth, now considered a portion of that which emphatically denominated the constitutional force of the country. The late improvements made in the Corps have extended even to their uniforms; and for soldier-like appearance they are not inferior to any troops in the service. Singular as it may appear taking their confined situation into consideration, they now rank among the best drilled corps. The practice of the broad-sword exercise has been introduced on board many ships, most of the serjeants being expert in the use of that weapon.[1]

Nor should it be unnoticed that a decided preference, as to general adaptability, may safely be given to a military body comprising exclusively with these advantages another, which must often be of the last importance - regular instruction and acquaintance with the management of great guns.

Though few instances of the kind, perhaps, have occurred on board large vessels since the peace, yet the Marines have, not unfrequently, volunteered on board our smaller ships of war to "furl the courses" and constantly go aloft, though contrary to regulation.[2]

Perhaps, to render a service so useful and eligible as nearly as possible perfect, it would only be necessary to admit them, when abroad, within the improved regulation, suggested under the head of "Discipline," relative to their pay.

During war, too, it might with little inconvenience, and certainly with great advantage to the service, be contrived that the Marines should not be suffered to continue on board, without relief, for two or three years together; a practice which, in a Corps calculated alike for land and sea service, deprives them often of opportunities of keeping pace with their comrades on shore in the daily improving system of drill and military tactics.

If there were yet a doubt remaining as to the policy of always keeping up the Marines on a liberal establishment, it might be sufficient to urge that, from its being necessary they should be inured to the sea, they are a force which cannot be suddenly created so as to be effective; that in harbour, when there are no other hands, they prepare every ship, on being commissioned, for the reception of a crew; and, what is still of greater importance, both as regards the discipline and safety of vessels of war, in every instance of insubordination or mutiny in our crews, the firmest reliance has been most properly placed on the well-known fidelity of this brave, though comparatively inconsiderable part of the ship's company. In such a crisis, every officer must be keenly sensible of the vital and inestimable value of a few loyal and courageous hearts. Though severely tried, their courage and loyalty has remained proof against temptation and peril; and like the high-minded chevalier, they may, without ostentation, assume the motto "Sans peur et sans reproche."

1. The writer mentions that several complaints were made by the Board of Ordnance about the jagged edges of the seamen's cutlasses and he suggests that the Captains reprimanded for this might well have replied that "the country was at war, and well knowing that nothing gave sailors so much confidence in boarding as the knowledge of the use of the broad sword, he had caused his crew to be regularly excercised by the Serjeant of Marines being in hourly expectation of an engagement with an enemy's cruizer".

2. "And yet we are told by a writer in the 81st number of the Edinburgh Review, page 174, that 'when on board ship, they, the Marines have no other exclusive duty to perform than to keep impressed men in obedience.' Doubtless the Marines, particularly the privates, would be too happy to find this a fact. 'Sailors,' continues the writer 'can easily be trained to all the duties of soldiers; but soldiers sent on board ship for the purpose of keeping the sailors in obedience, cannot mix with them, and therefore never learn the duty of sailors.' The ignorance of the writer betrays on this subject is really deplorable. In the first place, the very reverse of this reviewer's statement happens to be the fact; for instead of 'sailors being easily trained to do all the duty of soldiers,' they invariably so detest and despise the manual of a musket, that they actually consider excellence in a soldier's drill derogatory to the character of a sailor; whilst, on the contrary a Marine is prouder of excelling in the duties of a seaman than of a soldier. It is true, that the Brigades of seamen embodied to act with our troops in America, as well as in the North Coast of Spain, contrived to 'ship a bagnet' on a pinch, and to 'toe' (that was the phrase) 'a tolerable line'; but, had the reviewer reviewed our tars in the field instead of on paper, he would have discovered that various evolutions of 'forming four deep.' 'changing the front' or advancing in (as they termed it) 'shove along' (eschelon) were particularly perplexing to sailors, though quite au fait to mount guns in a battery, or serve them with effect, as at Walcheren, and under Sir Sidney Smith at Acre."

H.M.S. *"ALBION"* AT NAVARINO, 1827.
By Lieut. (afterwards General) Hurdle, R.M.

The official account of the battle states: "The *Asia* led in, followed by the *Genoa* and *Albion*, and anchored close alongside a ship of the line, bearing the flag of the Capitana Bey, another ship of the line, and a large double-banked frigate, each thus having their opponent in the front line of the Turkish fleet."

The *Albion's* opponent is therein stated to be "a large double-banked frigate." *The only mention made of the Albion's part in the action.*

The *Asia* was even nearer to the ship of the Egyptian Bey than to the ship of the Capitana Bey - and both are represented as "effectually destroyed by the *Asia's* fire – falling to leeward mere wrecks "- this early in the action — one account says before "the action became general"; another, "the action now became general."

It is stated "the smoke was so thick during the action that the guns of the *Asia* were pointed from the flag at the masthead of the Capitana Bey's ship "- it was the only object discernible.

The truth is, her cable nearest to the *Asia* was quickly shot away, when the strong current soon carried her past her other anchor, till it brought her up alongside of the *Albion*. Her masts, yards and rigging were then, apparently, in perfect order. She continued to ride by that anchor until two days after the action.

The *Albion* passed very close to the ship of the line (the *Genoa's* opponent) and immediately anchored, swinging to the current, which soon swept her port quarter to the starboard bow of a very large Turkish frigate, whose crew made a most gallant and determined attempt to board. It may be here mentioned that 40 Marines were stationed below at the *Albion's* guns, and two or three hours before she entered the harbour, of the 72 Privates called "small-arm men" stationed on her poop under the Captain of Marines, 40 were taken away and stationed below to carry powder from the magazine to the powder boys, and 20 more were taken to man four guns on the quarter-deck, leaving only twelve Privates on the poop - a small force to resist the impetuous and resolute attempt to board.

The collision was not at first observed on the quarter-deck; there were no bluejackets, nor any naval officer on the poop, but Mr. Addington, the boatswain, reached the poop at the moment of collision, and letting himself down by a rope, with an axe kept on the poop, quickly cut the frigate's cable.

The Captain of Marines having been one of the first persons killed, the command had devolved on the Senior Subaltern*, who had enough to do to repel the Turks' attempt to board. A Sergeant touching his left arm was shot through the head, and a Private on his right hand was shot through the shoulder; he himself was obliged to use a double-barrelled pistol twice.

The boarders having been called, the Subaltern was about to board with his men, when the Captain called to him through his speaking trumpet, "Don't board!" On looking along the port side he saw an immense ship (evidently a line-of-battle ship) approaching fast with the current; she seemed likely to scrape the *Albion's* side. She proved to be the Capitana Pasha's ship, which the *Asia* thought she was then engaging, by directing her guns at a flag at her supposed masthead.

An active seaman of the *Albion* ran his boarding-pike through the Turkish captain's back before he could get to the main deck. Immediately flames rose up to ten or twelve feet above her taffrail, from materials set on fire on the after part of the frigate's main deck.

The gallant boatswain, who had cut the cable, got on the frigate's bowsprit, and was in the act of hauling down her Jack, when he lost his arm by a musket ball. The Marine officer, though ordered not to board, seeing he was disabled, hastened over to him, took the flag from him and gave it to a sergeant on the poop; he then rushed back again to aid Mr. Addington, in which he was assisted by a late boarder, in getting him over the awkward ropes of the frigate, on board the *Albion* again - not any too soon, as the current was moving her astern.

As soon as the fire appeared the boarders hurried back to the ship, and some had to make fearful jumps to regain the vessel.

The 86-gun ship now opened fire on the *Albion* and was for a short time joined on the same (the port) side by the 76, she being very much nearer to the *Albion* than to her opponent, the *Genoa*.

The *Albion* was engaged on her starboard side with the double-banked frigate; a Turkish line-of-battle ship, about 300 or 400 yards astern, also opened a raking fire on her for some time.

The Marine officer was slightly wounded in the hand by a musket ball from the 86, which he concealed so far as to prevent being returned wounded.

The *Albion* was in excellent fighting order, and was closely engaged with her huge opponent more than three hours, when she ceased to fire. At this time the current moved the stern of the 86 nearer, so that her broadside looked across the *Albion's* bows towards the *Genoa*; she then suddenly fired six or eight of her lower deck guns at the *Genoa*; a broadside from the *Albion* now silenced her. She was then a "perfect wreck."

When the Marine officer the next morning boarded her, her immense fore and main masts each lay in three pieces on her deck, her bowsprit was shot away close to her head, her mizzen-top-mast, her mizzen top, and the yard on which the spanker is set, were shot away; there did not appear to be a square foot in her side that a round shot had not passed through, and her quarter-deck was encumbered with splinters. Her rigging on both sides was hanging down in the water, with about sixty dead bodies entangled in it on the port side, on which we boarded.

The Turkish Secretary (said to be of more importance than the Admiral), who was writing his despatches on board the *Albion*, stated the Capitana Pasha's ship lost 650 killed and wounded, and the 76, 400. The then condition of the former fully justified the statement, large as it was.

In about 15 or 20 minutes after the frigate was on fire she blew up, at which time one of the large plate glasses in the *Albion's* light room fell out; a man in the magazine promptly replaced it, holding it fast until secured. The accident, which might have been fatal, was attributed to the shock of the blowing up of the frigate.

Sir Edward Codrington, at an early hour the morning after the action, wrote to the Turkish Admiral, and to the Pasha commanding on shore, that if a single shot or musket ball should be fired at any one of the allied ships or boats, all the Turkish vessels remaining in the harbour would be destroyed. No answer having been returned to Sir Edward's letter, and as there were two small men-of-war in an angle of the fortress, thought to be fire-vessels, that might be used against the combined fleet at night, Sir Edward (who said he would not order anyone on the service) called for volunteers to capture or destroy them. The senior subaltern of the *Albion* volunteered and three times the number of Marines required volunteered to go with him. About 2 p.m. the barge with the Commander, Norman Campbell, who was also a volunteer. The different boats had rendezvoused alongside the *Asia*, when the Turkish Admiral went on board her. He solemnly pledged his word that no shot should be fired, upon which the expedition was abandoned and all returned to their ships. Of the three Captains of Marines seriously engaged, two were killed and the third mortally wounded, surviving about 48 hours.

The Lord High Admiral (then the Duke of Clarence) acquainted Sir Edward Codrington that in future he should promote surviving officers into the vacancies of Marine Officers killed in action, and that the Commissions would be sent to Sir Edward to fill in the names of the officers entitled to them. Sir Edward told the Captain of the *Albion* to acquaint his senior Marine Officer as soon as he (Sir Edward) received the Commissions he would insert his name in one and send it to him immediately. In the Battle of Trafalgar one Captain of Marines was killed and one mortally wounded. At Navarin, two were killed and one mortally wounded.

Compared with the number of Captains of Marines killed or mortally wounded in the Battle of Trafalgar, the similar casualties in Navarino were very much greater in proportion viz., in Trafalgar, of 23 Captains of Marines present, two were killed or mortally wounded; at Navarino, three were killed or mortally wounded. The Captain of Marines mortally wounded was promoted Brevet-Major. On his death being reported, Captain Seward, of the *Glasgow*, the only other Captain of Marines in the Squadron (whose ship only entered the harbour when the action had nearly ceased) received the Brevet of Major in his place.

Two of the Subalterns of Marines, whose Captains had been killed, were 15 ½ and 16 ½ years standing as *Second Lieutenants* one of them had seen some good active service. His Captain of Marines was killed very early, and the ship he belonged to (the *Albion*) bore a most distinguished part in the action, and captured the Capitana Pasha's ship, and yet no promotion was extended to either of them. The Lord High Admiral intended to do so, but he had not the power - it would have required an Order of the King in Council.

Denuding the poop of Marines increased the difficulty of effectually resisting the Turkish attempt to board; but it afterwards enabled the *Albion* to maintain such a rapid and destructive fire on her powerful adversary - the Capitana Bey's ship - as greatly facilitated her surrender.

The Russian line-of-battle ships came in last, and suffered severely from the batteries on the Island of Spacteria. One of their officers, who spoke English, when on board the *Albion* the next day, expressed his admiration and astonishment at the rapidity of the *Albion's* fire from both sides; his expression was, "*she appeared like a perfect fire devil.*"

NOTE. - The remark that the Capitan Pasha's ship *rode for two days after the action by the anchor she had down at the beginning*, needs some explanation. She brought up with her head touching the stern of the Turkish 76. The second day after the action, at 10 a.m., the Albion received an order to cut them both adrift, an order that surprised us, as they were incapable of doing us any harm. The senior Turkish officer wrote a letter of remonstrance to Sir Edward, stating they could not injure us and if sent into the more open part of the harbour, they would probably sink, from the numerous shot holes near the waterline; that they had no boat to save their lives, nor any anchor to prevent them drifting on a shoal. The answer insisted on their being cut adrift, but that a boat would be furnished from a Turkish vessel with a cable.

The cause, though not known at the time, was evidently to prevent the French or Russian Admiral knowing that the Capitana Psaha's ship was not driven to leeward by Sir Edward's ship, as appeared in the official account, but continued to ride by her second anchor after the first had been shot away.

The Russian Admiral's ship, the *Azoff*, suffered severely, the French *Breslau* rendered her assistance.

*Hurdle himself.

NAVARINO.
EXTRACTS FROM LIEUT. THOMAS BROWN-GRAY'S DIARY.
By kind permission of "The Morning Post."

Having kept close off the harbour during the night the combined squadrons were all in readiness to form in line, the men having got their dinner and also the officers. About 12 the signal was made to form line and make sail. The French squadron came next to us, the Russians astern of the French, leaving our squadron the van to lead into the harbour.

Each captain had a form where he was to anchor and their stations in going in. About half-past twelve the line was formed and we were leading in under topsails and top gallant sails, with a slight breeze from the southwards not going more than two or three knots.

About 11.30 we were gliding slowly past the battery, being the leaders of a long line, which looked quite beautiful following each other closely. When abreast of the battery a boat with two or three Turks came alongside: they came on board with a message from the Turkish commander to say that he had no orders to allow us in and that if we wanted anything we must send our boats. Our Admiral, through the interpreter, told this messenger that "we were not come here to ask permission to enter the harbour, nor receive orders, but we were come to give them or to see they were obeyed, and that if they attempted to fire a single shot at either of our flags we should destroy every one of them and be glad of the opportunity of punishing them for their breach of faith in sending their fleet to sea after promising that they would not leave the harbour for the space of twenty days."

We now found ourselves passing their fireships, which were anchored a little inside the battery and in front of their line. They were six of them. About this time the *Dartmouth*, who came in on our starboard beam, anchored between these fireships and the town.

We passed on, and in a few minutes anchored between the Turkish Admiral's ship, with flag at the main (86 guns) and the Egyptian Admiral's frigate of 64 guns. We let go both anchors and immediately furled sails and sprung the ship, bringing our starboard broadside to bear on the Turkish Admiral's ship, and had the Egyptian Admiral on our larboard quarter. Our guns and those of the squadron were double shotted; every man was at his quarters.

About this time the *Dartmouth* sent her boats to remove some of the fireships in her way; and also to make certain that they should not fire them and come down on us in the night, which we learnt they intended to do.

As soon as the *Dartmouth* boats attempted to go alongside the fireship, the Turks opened a fire, and the Lieutenant (Fitzroy) was killed, and several men, together with Browne-Smith, a cousin of mine, who attempted to board her. He was cut down by a Turk, fell inboard, where he was cut to pieces. The Dartmouth seeing this, opened a fire of musketry with her marines on the vessel. At this time a round shot was fired by one of the Turkish corvettes at the French Admiral and another at Dartmouth. Our vessels had now nearly all got in and the greater part of the French, but Russians were still outside.

The action now got tolerably general (2 p.m.) and the Turkish ship had opened her fire upon us. Our men were now all ready for the word, which was given in a loud voice by the Admiral, who stood cool and collected in front of the poop. In a moment we poured our broadside with tremendous destruction into our opponent. Almost every shot went through her, as we were within pistol shot and every gun was laid point blank.

The Admiral sent a boat to the Egyptian Admiral with the Flag Lieutenant and pilot Mitchell (a Greek) to say if he did not fire we should not fire at him. The grape came very thick about our rigging and cut it to pieces, but fortunately they fired a little high.

At about 3 p.m. my captain of Marines, who, an instant before, stood by my side, had crossed the poop and a double-headed shot came in through the poop, cut his body in two pieces, passed through the bulwark killing him dead on the spot. He was immediately carried down.

The next person I saw killed was our drummer, who received a shoal of grape, knocking him to pieces. We were now making a terrible example of our opponent, who kept up a very heavy fire for the first three-quarters of an hour. His masts and yards soon began to fall and his fire slackened much about 3.15. The Egyptian Admiral, who had promised not to fire now opened a heavy fire on us. We immediately manned the larboard broadside (fighting both sides), and turning the guns aft gave him a few broadsides, which cut him up severely, and cutting away his cables, he went adrift, leaving us to finish our old friend, who now only kept up a weak fire with grape and round. They managed to kill or wound the greater part of those on "the poop," the quarter deck at the same time suffering in proportion. Once or twice we ceased firing, to see if they had struck, but we were obliged to commence again; although he had, notwithstanding, but the stump of his foremast, and his sides were like a riddle.

4 p.m. Several vessels blew up with a tremendous crash, which we were happy to observe were not ours, but the enemy's. About 4.30 observed the *Hind* cutter, who had run in during the action with her boom in the port of a Turkish frigate who she had fired upon. The Turks were attempting to board her, but were beaten off by this gallant little crew, who bayoneted them with pikes, muskets, etc. as they tried to go on her deck. The Admiral at this time appeared more anxious than during the action. She fortunately got disengaged.

The Turks, finding they could not board her through their ports got into a boat to the number of 50 and attempted to board her, but Lieutenant Robb, with his gallant little crew, foiled their attempt by levelling one of his guns at the boat with round and grape. It fortunately struck her, knocking her to pieces and leaving the Turks floating in the water, as they had lost anchors and cables.

During this time a Turkish frigate on fire came drifting down on our beam and threatened us with destruction if we could not avoid her; but tarpaulin was spread on the deck, and everything made wet in case she should blow up and any of the burning ship come on board. Fortunately for us, when within fifty yards, she blew up - a dreadful but beautiful sight, which shook the ship very much and for a time stunned every other noise. The combustibles flew into the air, but all luckily fell without a piece coming on board us.

At this time the other ships, fearing we were on fire by this explosion, sent assistance to us.

The Turks were now blowing up and burning with great rapidity. The *Scipion*, French ship of the line, was observed to have been set on fire by a fireship which had run down across her bows, but it had been turned aside by the boats of the *Dartmouth* and *Rose*. The bowsprit was the only part on fire, and some of her crew ran out and with saws cut it away, which saved her.

We had now suffered very much about the stern, poop, and quarter deck, in consequence of not being protected by the *Cambrian*, who was to have anchored across our stern, to take off the fire of some corvettes or brigs. This she could not do, as she did not get into the harbour till the action was half over. She had then anchored abreast of the battery, being unable to see her place for smoke. She opened her fire on the battery with great precision.

Having tolerably well finished our other opponents we got our stern guns out and opened a heavy fire on a corvette which lay directly across our stern and cut us up severely. All our spanker boom had been cut to pieces, our mizzen mast cut away, which fell about 5 p.m. The Admiral ordered me down to tell the officers of the after quarters on each deck to fire at the corvettes and ordered everyone off the poop. I went to one of the after guns on the starboard side of the main deck, which was keeping up a fire on two frigates, which we soon disabled.

Here I found they had suffered severely, many of the men being killed and wounded, and among them I found my own servant. He had been killed by a round shot which had taken off part of his head. One or two of the guns had lost their muzzles and by the fall of the mizzen mast which threw the mizzen topsail over the larboard stern port, we could not use that gun against the corvette, who raked us with great precision and loss. They knocked the Admiral's cabin and stern walk to pieces, wounded the Admiral's son, and took an arm off a young mid. In a short time the corvette was silenced.

On going on the lower deck, I found the Master had been killed early in the action as he was returning up the main ladder after having sprung the ship. I also saw stretched by the gun-room Mitchell the pilot, who had gone with the Flag Lieutenant to Mocharem Bay's ship to interpret, was treacherously shot alongside. I suppose he was recognised as a Greek and as the person who had interpreted the Admiral's answer to the Turkish messenger on our coming into the harbour.

We sprung ship different ways to fire on some vessels still keeping up a fire on the *Genoa*. They had cut her up severely. She had lost her mizzen mast and also the French Admiral's ship *Sirene*.

We found all our rigging cut away, not a shroud standing, and our main mast so fearfully wounded that we feared every moment it would fall. We had the upper deck cleared, fearing it would kill some of our men. When the mizzen mast went overboard the two captains of the top were thrown overboard, but fortunately were not hurt, and they got in by the stern ports. We found all our boats stove and knocked to pieces with shot; so much so, that when the frigate blew up on our beam, we had not a boat to send for the unfortunate creatures who were holding on and dying on the wreck. On our lower deck we found several Greeks who had swum on board, with chains round their legs, having been prisoners to the Turks and chained to their guns.

The line of battleships which we had engaged had drifted on shore, nearly a perfect wreck. The little *Hind* cutter about 6 p.m. had got hold of our stern and held on by a hawser, having neither anchor nor cable.

6.30 p.m. - The action was now nearly over, except a parting fire kept up by some of the ships. The *Hind* we found had been much cut up, and half her crew killed or wounded. A little before this the *Albion* had boarded a frigate which she had engaged and fell aboard of. In all parts of the harbour the Turkish vessels were on fire and blowing up. We found that on the western and eastern line of the enemy, where the Russian and French squadrons with some English frigates were engaged, the enemy had suffered in proportion to the centre where the British ships of line were.

6.45. - The defeat was now quite complete, and as it was now past sunset and evening was closing in we retired from our quarters and established guard boats. This duty was taken by the Russians. We began to secure our fore and main masts, as they were in a trembling condition; the former had 18 round shot and the latter 28, independent of grape. Our bow-sprit was severely wounded, and there were about 123 round shot in our hull, while the poop bulwarks were torn to pieces with shot, and altogether we had suffered very much from having had at different times the fire of five or six vessels.

In the evening we had Tahir Pacha on hoard, who promised to the Admiral that no further hostilities should take place, or he would destroy the remaining vessels. This Pacha was second in command, a fine old fellow. He shed tears when in the cabin with the Admiral. We also had the Turkish Admiral's secretary on board, a fine looking old Turk. He told us he was in the line of battleship we engaged, and that out of 850 men they had on board we had killed or wounded 650. He said the decks and beams were all tumbling in and scarcely a gun standing.

In the evening the three Admirals had met on board, and congratulated each other on the victory we gained.

Oct. 25; - All the combined squadrons being perfectly ready for sea at 9 a.m., all the different ships weighed, it having been previously arranged how they were to lead out. Each ship had her boats towing. The wind was light but favourable and with the assistance of the boats, we drew out tolerably quickly. The dead bodies were now all rising to the surface, as they had been five days dead and this not only made it unpleasant to the smell, but also the sight of the mangled bodies which presented themselves on all sides black, swollen, and distorted into different shapes, was very horrible.

They floated alongside, and, indeed, one might say, we were sailing through mangled human bodies rather than through water.

As we passed the battery the Turks sat looking at us with the greatest composure, smoking their pipes, cross-legged, in the embrasures. All the squadron were now under weigh, each ship cleared and ready for quarters in case they should fire on us from the battery. The *Cambrian* and *Glasgow* frigates brought up the rear. They were but little damaged by the action.

The breeze freshened as the day advanced, and about 11.30 a.m. all the ships were clear of the harbour. When we got about a mile outside all the French and Russian ships came under stern and gave three cheers, and we returned it to them.

H.M.S. *ALBION* AT NAVARINO.

"The *'Albion'* Capt. Ommanney, anchored within pistol-shot of the third Turkish line-of-battle ship, and a double-banked frigate; on casting anchor, she swung aboard a large frigate of 56 guns, which she boarded and carried. The Turks ran below and fired up the hatchways, and wounded some of the men in the feet; they afterwards set fire to the ship, and her cables were scarcely disengaged, when she blew up, with great part of her crew on board. The *'Albion's'* fire was so destructive, that in half an hour she entirely disabled the Turkish liner, whose crew cut her cables and deserted her in boats; after drifting past the *'Azoff,'* this ship ran on shore with her fore-topmasts stay-sail set, and was burnt and blown up on Sunday. The two line of battle ships that had engaged the *'Asia'* and *'Genoa'* drifted past the *'Albion'* toward the close of the action, and fired occasional guns as they past. Capt. C. J. Stevens, Royal Marines, killed, with 10 men, 50 wounded."

————

The "Good" Old Days.
REMINISCENCES OF A VETERAN.

The following reminiscences were collected from Sergt.-Major Lowe, in 1867. Sergt.Major Lowe was then aged 80, and had been brought up in barracks from his boyhood.

UNIFORMS, ARMS AND BADGES. - Officers of Marines wore gorgets as late as 1810. (They lasted till about 1830.)

Sergeants carried halberds till 1827, when they were furnished with small firelocks, but not for use, no ammunition being supplied, and indeed none being manufactured for so small a bore.

The pricker and brush (for cleaning the musket) were carried by Marines, hung by two brass chains from the brass plate of the cartouch belt, hanging down to the stomach.

PUNISHMENTS. - He has seen 17 or 20 men in a morning receive 500 lashes, by drum-head court-martial, for slight offences.

"Kissing the wall" was abolished among Marines about 1815.

During the practise of Back-boards, he has seen a man (nicknamed "Long Joe"), determined not to hold himself up, lashed to a ladder for hours together. This man was later promoted and got on. He has seen the same punishment frequently applied in 1815 to "radicals."

Manual correction by Officers and N.C.O.'s began to disappear about 1815. On one occasion, in 1816, he saw a Sergt.-Major strike a man in the belly with a pace-stick. The man came to the charge, and would have chased the Sergt.-Major to stick him, had not the Adjutant come up and held him back. The Adjutant ordered the Sergt.-Major never to strike a man in the ranks again.

Partial reduction was used in the Marines within his recollection, and was termed "suspension" for a certain period.

PRECEDENCE. - In or about 1815 there was a dispute at Chatham as to the power of a General Officer of Marines to take command of a Colonel of land forces, then in command of the garrison at Chatham. The General was removed to obviate the difficulty.

Music. - Cymbals and tambourines were played by black men about 1823. "Jingle Johnny," being a "pole of bells," was used by the bands about the same time.

Brass instruments began to be used instead of the fifes about 1817, the key-bugle being one of the first.

Portugal, 1832. - " On Thursday morning at 6 o'clock, 3 officers and 200 rank and file of the R.M., and 5 officers and 90 gunners R.M.A., embarked on board H.M.Ss. *Talavera* and *Britannia*, left Portsmouth for Plymouth, where they were joined by 7 officers and 200 rank and file from that Division and the *Romney* troopship. They took with them four guns and a Brigade of Rockets. Never did a finer body of men quit the shores of England. They have orders to join Admiral Parker, and it is said Don Miguel will very soon be acquainted with the object of their mission." The officers were Lieut.-Col. T. Adair, C.B., Bvt.-Major T. L. Lawrence, Captains Clements, R. Kellow, Wm. Baker, Jas. Cottell, 1st Lieuts. E. Rea, Griffin, F. Spry, J. B. Castiau, Delacombe and Palliser, and 2nd Lieuts. J. Fraser, T. Holloway and Priest.

30th May, 1832.

ADMIRALTY OFFICE,
July 16th, 1830.

ROYAL MARINES. His Majesty having been pleased on his Accession to the Throne to discontinue in his own person the office of General of Marines, has commanded the Lords Commissioners of the Admiralty to signify to the several Divisions of Royal Marines, and to the Royal Marine Artillery, His Majesty's gracious approbation of their conduct, and his satisfaction at the high state of efficiency which they have attained. His Majesty relies on the continuance on their part of the same honourable course of loyalty, gallantry and discipline, to which they are indebted for the applause and confidence of their country, and which they may be assured will not fail to preserve to them His Majesty's favour and protection.

By command of their Lordships,
(Signed) JOHN BARROW,

FIRST ROYAL MARINE A.D.C.'s TO THE KING
ST. JAMES'S.
December, 1830.

"We are happy to observe by the Gazette of the 28th ult., which appeared too late for insertion in our present number, that His Majesty has conferred a similar distinction on the Corps of Royal Marines as that already granted to the other branches of the United Service, by appointing Lieut.-Colonels Walter Tremenheere and Harry Percival Lewis, of that distinguished Corps Aides-de-Camp." (From the "*United Service Magazine.*")

AN ADMIRALTY LETTER.
EXTRACTS FROM-dated February 1832

Authorising the Establishment of a School of Naval Gunnery on board H.M.S. *Excellent* at Portsmouth.

"As in the establishment of the officers and crew of the Excellent a lieutenant, three non-commissioned officers, and two privates of the Royal Marine Artillery are included in her complement of Marines, it is intended that the theoretical instruction required for the officers and seamen gunners should be furnished by them, and you will take care that every facility and assistance be given them to insure the performance of this duty, the most material points of which are the names of the different parts of a gun and carriage, the disport in terms of lineal magnitude and in degrees how taken, what constitutes point blank and what line of metal range, windage - the errors and loss of force attending it, the importance of preserving shot from rust the theory of the most material effects of different charges of powder applied to practice with a single shot, also with a plurality of balls, showing how these effect accuracy penetration and splinters, to qualify them to judge of the condition of gunpowder by inspection, to ascertain its quality by the ordinary tests and trials, as well as by actual proof, these being very indispensable qualifications; to instruct them also in the laboratory works required for the Naval service, such as making rockets for signals, filling

COLOUR SERGEANT J. MULLINS, R.M.A., THE FIRST MAN TO LIVE ON WHALE ISLAND. THE PHOTO SHOWS THE DRESS OF THE ROYAL MARINE ARTILLERY IN 1858.

tubes, new priming them, and filling cartridges, precautions in airing and drying powder, care and inspection of locks, choice of flints, correct mode of fitting them, etc., etc."

REMINISCENCES. OF THE LATE GENERAL SIMON FRASER, R.M.

I. - THE DUTCH BLOCKADE OF 1832.

Note. – After Belgium had revolted from Holland and obtained its independence, which was recognised by the Great Powers, the Dutch troops still held on to Antwerp and refused to evacuate it. This led to the intervention of Great Britain and France in 1832, the French sending an army of 70,000 men, which laid siege to Antwerp and eventually captured it for the Belgians, while we, on our part, established a blockade of the Dutch coast.

The *Vernon** having completed her equipment, was ordered to move to Deal to join some other ships at anchor there, some rumours having been brought on board that we were going to blockade the Dutch coast. This report proved true, so we were at once all alive, having visions of active service, with much glory, promotion, and rich prizes for the result.

Two days after arrival at Deal we were fated to have a taste of the North Sea climate. At daybreak there was a fresh northerly breeze, which soon increased to a heavy gale, accompanied with a fierce driving snow and hail. All hands were soon at work, yards were housed, and we were riding with bare poles and double anchors. Very fortunately, about the same time next morning the gale passed over us, and the sun shone forth bright and clear again, little damage having been done by the heavy gale, so that two days after we were all prepared for our orders which then arrived. The *Vernon* was to proceed at once to assist in the blockade of the Dutch coast off the Scheld.

Having a fair wind we soon reached our station, and we were scarcely there when the signalman reported "A large ship in sight, all sail set." The drum beat to quarters and a certain amount of readiness was held. The stranger did not alter her course, but came right down to us, and as we approached each other it was seen that she was a large merchantman, very much weather-beaten from a long voyage. On first meeting neither ship showed her colours, but at last the Vernon hoisted her Ensign and fired a gun, and then up went the Dutch flag,

The merchantman at the same time shortening sail, as she saw a heavy boat with armed men leave the frigate.

They knew very little English on board the Dutch ship, but enough to understand that England and Holland were at war with each other. Great was the astonishment and consternation of the poor Dutchman, captain of the merchantman, and he persisted in saying: "It is impossible that England can be at war with Holland, it must be a mistake, and that he was from Batavia, with a very rich cargo.

*Probably the late Torpedo School.

He was soon undeceived, however, when he was conveyed on board the *Vernon*, his officers and crew being first put under arrest; and when in return for a boat-load of them we sent a number of marines and seamen on board the Dutch ship, with several officers to conduct the prize to England. The Dutch Captain and his crew were treated by all on board the *Vernon* with the greatest kindness, the men being quite merry with our marines and seamen in the messes below, saying: " We do not mind; we quite sure we soon be all free again." The people of Holland seemed to be pleasant and kindly; they were very industrious and active, and at that time crime in any serious form was said to be exceedingly rare among them.

What became of our prize, with all her rich cargo, I know not, only the *Vernon* gained nothing by her capture.

After getting clear of the Dutchman we continued our cruise without any important change. The cold was intense, and the Captain allowed all the officers to don purser's jackets and trousers, to our great comfort and delight. We encountered a thick fog continually, more or less, and at night we thoroughly enjoyed a warm tumbler of rum punch. At first the question arose as to how to procure the hot water. At last, however, a thought struck me, and I speedily had the brass mess kettle rigged out so that when the wardroom lamp was lighted I was able to hang the kettle right over the flame (being half warmed at the galley), and it was soon quite hot and steaming.

The Purser and some of my messmates were frightened at the thought of what the Captain might say. To save himself the Purser informed the Captain of what was going on, but the latter only laughed and said: "A right good thought! I shall go down myself and tell Fraser as much." Accordingly that night our kindly, genial Captain did come down to have a game of whist, expressed great admiration of the brass kettle hanging over his head, and thoroughly enjoyed a good steaming tumbler of punch, nodding over to me at the same time. The few frightened ones took theirs cold, and out of sight, but on the following night they all came sneaking in for a glass of warm punch from "Fraser's kettle," and the Captain afterwards frequently joined us.

For a few days more we rumbled and tumbled about in a heavy fog, seeing nothing (at least, so our signalman reported to the Captain), and at last we got into such a thick dense black cloud of fog that our good old Master could take no observations whatever-neither sun, moon, nor stars were to be seen. We therefore came to an anchor at once, and so remained for eight days, truly miserable. On the ninth day the mist lifted all at once, and the Master then discovered that we were anchored between two large sandbanks, to have gone on either of which would have speedily made an end of the *Vernon* and all on board. As soon as the Master was satisfied, the Captain ordered a course to be shaped for the Downs, and right glad we were, for there was neither glory nor gain to be obtained in this blockade.

When we reached the Downs there was great excitement, for it had been reported that we were lost. One of the blockading ships on her way to the Downs, when all the fleet were assembled except the *Vernon*, came across a Dutch fishing boat, and those on board having been asked if any ships were lost, replied in their broken English, "Der—vere—none," which was mistaken for "*The Vernon.*"

This caused much visiting from other ships, as well as from shore, and I was glad to find that a letter I at once sent off to my home in Scotland and a newspaper reporting "the loss of the *Vernon* with all hands arrived on the same day, to the great joy of my parents. And so ended the *Vernon*'s" North Sea Blockade Cruise."

II. - H.M.S. VERNON - WEST INDIAN STATION.

The *Vernon*, having received a thorough refit after her cruise in the Dutch Blockade, was now commissioned to bear the flag of Sir George Cockburn on the West India and North American Station. With a few alterations her complement was the same, and my Captain of Marines, Captain Coryton, was the friend of my grand uncle, Sir John Douglas, in former days. I was also especially introduced to the notice of my good kind Admiral by my father's friends, Lord Melville and Sir George Clark, so I went under the best auspices.

When we started we had quite a friendly party on board, Lady Cockburn and her daughter, and a young lady companion, with two waiting maids. It was rather rough weather going down the Channel, and the *Vernon* soon began to "cut capers." She had an ugly way of rolling, and dipping her head deep in the sea, and then rising suddenly with a shiver that made everything which chanced to be loose fly about in all directions. It became so bad that at last we were forced to run into Torbay and shelter. There we found the flagship for the South American Station at anchor, having taken shelter before us, so there were two flagships in this snug bay. Next day, however, we both got away. I need scarcely say that our lady friends and their maids had a sore time of it, both day and night, during the rough weather, and had all our sympathy.

The remainder of our passage to Bermuda was uneventful. When we reached the Island, the black pilot who came out to take us in was utterly dismayed at the immense size of the ship, the like of which he had never before seen. The channel leading to the Admiral's anchorage ran between two ledges of rocks, very narrow in some parts, but he was somewhat assured by our Master telling him with great pride: "Why! The *Vernon* can do everything but speak, and if you don't take her in hand at once, I shall take her in myself!"

At last we got safely to our anchorage, right opposite Admiralty House. Here we had nothing to do but stroll about. The water was as clear as crystal to any depth, and when bathing in shore among the rocks, clear of the sharks, we were surrounded by thousands of fish of the most gorgeous and beautiful colours; it was difficult to drive them away and prevent them from nibbling at one's legs and feet. The numerous sharks abounding in those waters soon found out that there was a ship at anchor, and one morning two very large specimens were reported just off our ship. Hands were at once set about making a bait for them, and being hungry, one at once took a lump of beef and was made fast and hoisted well out of the water. There he hung until the Admiral ordered him to be towed on shore, so that he might be inspected by the ladies. Unfortunately before he was landed his wicked consort had torn away a large portion of his tail and eaten it, though the seamen tried hard to harpoon him. There was enough left, however, for inspection, great monster that he was. When near the shore he suddenly turned back to the ship, and next day he disappeared altogether.

With the exception of visiting the small guard kept at Government House I had little to do in the way of duty and my Captain and I were always heartily welcomed at Admiralty House. The time passed quickly, and at last we sailed for Halifax, visiting Jamaica and Barbados, and then returning once more to Bermuda.

When at Halifax the seamen brought on board a young brown bear, which proved an endless amusement to all on board. The young midshipmen used to entice him to follow them to the maintop, and when half way up they would tease him sadly, and the same coming down. On the main deck they lifted him to a cot hook, and there left him roaring lustily, when he would suddenly start down after them in full chase, to Jack's great amusement.

One day the Carpenter left his cabin door open, and Bruin entered stealthily, while the marine sentry's eye was off him and helped himself to a large jar of honey, of which he ate every bit, and then wrapped himself comfortably in a midshipman's night-coat which chanced to be at hand, and quite destroyed it. But poor Bruin's end was near. He was in the habit of strictly attending to the beef block, and the ship's butcher had to watch him closely, he was at all times ready to help himself. One day he did so more liberally than usual, and the butcher (an ill-natured man) struck at him so viciously that he wounded him severely. This proved unlucky for the man as well as for the poor creature which had been the pet of the ship. The wound grew to an abscess, and our poor Bruin died, to the great distress and grief of all on board. The night he died the enraged seamen, when it was dark and all was quiet, pulled the cruel butcher out of his hammock and gave him a severe thrashing before the guard could go to his assistance (not that the guard felt any desire to do so, for the love of animals among our marines and seamen is well known). On board, below deck, a quid of tobacco, or any other choice dainty that may be at hand, is always kept ready for the poor cow (if not well watched) or for any livestock that may be in the ship; and strange to say, the cow especially seemed to appreciate these offerings given with the best of intentions, if not over judicious. We all missed poor Bruin, and I think, unless obliged to do so in the course of duty, no one ever spoke to the man who had been the cause of his death for the rest of the voyage.

The *Vernon's* eccentric behaviour in rough weather having been reported to the Admiralty, we were ordered home, and a miserable small frigate was sent out to relieve us, instead of a two-decker as was expected. When the relief arrived a few changes were made among the naval officers, and a new Captain and Commander took charge of the *Vernon*. When ready we, with great regret, left our dear old Admiral, his charming family circle, and the Island of Bermuda, and once more set sail for England, where in due time we arrived safely.

1828.

The old Colours of the Royal Marines, which amount to eight in number, were, on the 29th August presented by Sir James Cockburn to Admiral Sir Richard Keats, the Governor of Greenwich Hospital, to be placed in the Painted Hall. Some of them were literally in tatters, and were used in the Battle of Bunker's Hill in 1775.

PROMOTION.

On 1st October, 1831, there were 120 Lieutenants on the list the senior of whom had served 26 years and the junior 20.

CAPT. WALTER TAIT.
(Said to be the original of Sir W. Scott's Captain Clutterbuck.)

25th October, 1836. "At his villa near Melrose, on the 21st inst., Captain Walter Tait, Royal Marines, aged 60. This distinguished officer was in the hard-fought engagement between the *Mars* (64) and the French *Hercule*, of 74 guns, when the latter was captured, both the captains being killed. In an attack on the French batteries in Cherburgh Roads, he lost a leg, and was invalided. So great was the respect of the ship's crew H.M. frigate *Trent*, that on (his) leaving the vessel they came aft and tendered a subscription of 100 guineas from their pay, to purchase him a sword, which was however feelingly and generously declined. He resided some years at his native village of Melrose, a*nd is understood to be the original Capt. Clutterbuck of Sir Walter Scott*."

From a Contemporary Journal.

LT.-COL. MOLESWORTH PHILLIPS, R.M.
From "The Gentleman's Magazine," 1832.

Lieut.-Colonel Phillips was born on the 15th August, 1755, of a good family in Ireland, where he once possessed considerable property. He at first entered the Royal Navy, but by the advice of his friend Sir Joseph Banks, shortly altered his course - without, however, abandoning that sea life to which his predilections originally led him, by accepting a Commission in the Marines. As Lieutenant in this service, he had the honour (for an honour in the best meaning of the word it was) to be selected to command the detachment which accompanied Captain Cook on his third or last voyage. Lieut. Phillips, whose bravery and presence of mind were well known to Captain Cook, was on shore at Owhyhee, and by his side in the fatal affray which robbed this country of one of its brightest ornaments, and mankind of a benefactor. Phillips certainly wounded the savage who struck the deadly blow, for the man was seen instantly to fall, but, whether actually killed or not, the confusion that ensued rendered it impossible, as it would have been fruitless to discover. Lieut. Phillips was himself severely wounded, which is particularly alluded to in the History of the Voyage, by Capt. King, L.L.D. and F.R.S.; and Phillips is represented in the interesting representation of that melancholy catastrophe by Weber, so well engraved by Bartolozzi, or Byrne. An accident which immediately followed this mournful event, displays the heroic courage and deeply seated humanity of the young officer, in a more clear and beautiful light than they could be placed by any effort of language. Wounded in two or three places and foreseeing the inevitable slaughter of all such parts of the ship's company as remained on shore after the Captain's death, he, with his men, swam off to the boats, which he reached, and was safe under the protection of their musquetry, when, looking around, he saw at a distance a marine, badly wounded, and making but slow progress through the waves, pursued by some of the natives, who were gaining on him so fast that without assistance it was evidently impossible he could escape. Lieut Phillips immediately turned back, lent his aid to the disabled marine, kept off his pursuers by his loud threats and menacing gestures, and finally after a struggle in which his strength was nearly exhausted, succeeded in getting his charge on board in safety. It may be asserted without risk of contradiction, that ancient and modern history would in vain search for a nobler instance of disinterested, unostentatious bravery, or a more undeniable proof of genuine goodness a of heart.

In consequence of a dispute with Mr. Williamson, one of the Lieutenants of the *Resolution* (afterwards Capt Williamson, broke for misconduct in the battle of Camperdown), he and Mr. Phillips took the earliest opportunity of settling their quarrel on shore. Williamson armed himself with one of the ship's long pistols; Phillips was provided only with a small one that he usually carried in his pocket. They fired, missed, and were preparing to reload, when an old officer, who acted as second to both required the parties to exchange pistols. Williamson refused, and the affair, consequently thus far ended. But meeting afterwards in an assembly room at the Cape of Good Hope, Williamson suddenly, and quite unexpectedly drew his sword and ran at Phillips, who was unarmed. The latter, however, avoided the thrust, instantly snatched a sword from the scabbard of a gentleman who was standing close to him, disarmed his assailant, and most likely would have punished him for his assassin-like attack, had not the company present interfered to prevent further mischief.

Colonel Phillips was well acquainted with the ex Bishop of Antun, M. de Talleyrand, when he was an exile in this country, showing him much kindness and hospitality; and when the latter was obliged by our Government to seek refuge in America, his English friend, thinking him rather harshly dealt by, assisted in fitting him out for his voyage, and accompanied him to Falmouth. Some years afterwards Colonel Phillips and his family were among the detenus under Napoleon's arbitrary decree. The Colonel made an appeal to the gratitude of M. Talleyrand, then in full power, who suffered two letters to remain unanswered. A third, couched in warm, if not rather strong terms, produced an order for the release of the whole of the English family; but in passing through Paris on their way to England, the head of it in vain solicited an audience of his former friend, the Minister, to thank him for his interference, though tardy, in their behalf.

Colonel Phillips married a daughter of Dr. Burney, the elegant historian of music, and thus allied himself to a family highly distinguished in the literary world - to Dr. Charles Burney, the great Greek scholar; to Madame D'Arblay, the celebrated novelist and to Admiral Burney, the laborious and faithful author of "A History of Voyages of Discovery," who was one of Cook's Lieutenants in both his last voyages, and hence originated a friendship between the latter and the subject of this notice which continued uninterrupted by any of those vexations that too often embitter the cup of life, till the death of the Admiral dissolved it. But Colonel Phillips cherished to the latest moment his love for the memory of his companion in danger, his last request having, been that his remains should be deposited in the grave of his earliest and most deservedly respected friend.

Mrs. Phillips died on the 6th January, 1800. Colonel Phillips married as his second wife in 1800 or 1801 Miss Ann Maturin. He was buried beside Admiral Burney in St. Margaret's churchyard, Westminster.

OFFICIAL RETURN OF THE NAVAL FORCE OF GREAT BRITAIN ON JULY 1ST, 1833

"The number of vessels composing the British Navy amounts to 557, carrying from 2 to 120 guns each, of various calibre.

This immense fleet, the largest in the world, employs in time of peace 20,000 sailors and 12,000 Royal Marines, stationed as follows: - 1st Division at Chatham, consisting of 26 companies; 2nd Division at Portsmouth, 29 companies; 3rd Division at Plymouth, 27 companies; 4th Division at Woolwich, 18 companies; and 2 companies of Royal Marine Artillery at Portsmouth - in the whole, 102 companies.

From a Contemporary Newspaper.

ABOLITION OF NAVAL INSPECTOR-GENERAL OF THE ROYAL MARINES.

"Major-General Sir James Cockburn (*an Admiral*) has taken leave of the Royal Marine Corps, on the abolition of the office of Inspector-General, in the following brigade order:-

ROYAL MARINE OFFICE,
May 21st, 1836

"The Lords Commissioners of the Admiralty having been pleased to abolish the office of Inspector-General of Royal Marines, all reports and communications heretofore made to Major General Sir James Cockburn, Bart., G.C.H in future to be addressed to Colonel Sir John B Savage, C.B. and K.C.H. Major-General Sir James Cockburn cannot quit the command which he has so long been honoured without expressing to the Corps of Royal Marines the gratification which he has upon all occasions derived from it and assuring them that he ever consider the period of his communication with the Corps as one of the proudest and most satisfactory in his life. He leaves them, impressed, from long experience, with the deepest sense of loyalty, discipline, and professional value; and confident of their upholding in all aftertimes the high and distinguished reputation which they have always so deservedly attained, he requests that they will accept the assurance of his everlasting best wishes and regards, and that he shall never cease to feel the liveliest interest in their welfare, prosperity, and renown."

J. WILSON, A.A. General.

THE BATTLE OF HERNANI,
16th March, 1837.

[This battle was fought between the Carlists and the Spanish Royalist troops, assisted by a Legion recruited in England, and a Battalion of the Royal Marines with guns of the Royal Marine Artillery. The Royalists were under the command of General Sir de Lacy Evans].

"Wednesday, 15th March. Left Loyola early for Passages and brought back the two days rations of pork which were cooked on Sunday last. On my way back heard that the Battalion had moved round to the Hernani Road from St. Sebastian by the bridge at St. Sebastian. Reached Loyola about one clock and found the mules detained at the pontoon bridge by the passing of Spanish troops. - Soon, afterwards heard the commencement of Evans' attack on the Carlists' positions.

As soon as I could get the ammunition &c on the mules, I moved on after the Battalion by a road ankle deep in fluid mud and joined the Battalion in a field close to the Harnani Road and within what had been the advanced Carlists' lines. - Here we remained till the business of the day was finished. A little before dusk Evans made a general advance I believe, and the Carlists ceased firing almost immediately and ran from all their positions, and thus the Venta Hill and all their breastworks were taken. Evans had with much skill outflanked their right wing, and he conducted the affair to-day with a good deal of talent and shewed great personal courage.

Two pieces of cannon were taken on the Venta. The loss of the Legion I have not been able to ascertain exactly in this day's work. Colonel Delancy was mortally wounded. We took up our quarters for the night in some houses on the Hernani Road, but I found it very cold from the wind that blew into the room.

Thursday, 16th March. Rose at three o'clock and about four started for Loyola to bring the provisions left there. Reached that place about six o'clock, distance, I should think, about seven miles. Got the mules loaded as fast as I could and returned across the country. Passed over the ground we advanced on on Tuesday. - The route was a very tiresome one from the ground being so wet and dirty, though the weather was very fine overhead. Before we got back to the house where we slept last night, we found that the Battalion had moved on in advance. Left the mules at the house to rest and to be fed, and moved on after the Battalion. Found it in position on a kind of tableland forming the right shoulder of the Venta. The position good and easy of defence so long as the rear could be protected. Before me lay a very pretty landscape. The town of Hernani in a valley on the left, and heights of Santa Barbara in front, while on the right the country seemed very beautifully broken into hill and dale with the village of Lasarte about three miles distant. - In a military view there was a redoubt to our right of Hernani from whence the Carlists were firing at the attacking parties from two guns. They afterwards also opened a small gun from the angle of the wall in front of Hernani.

The attack on the Carlists had then been going on nearly two hours. Soon after I joined we saw some lancers bringing in a Carlist prisoner up the road. He proved to be the Colonel of the Carlist Lancers, some of whom having come out of the town to cut off the Chapelgorries[1] were charged by the Lancers of the Legion and three of them killed and their Colonel taken prisoner, having been unhorsed as they were turning round to return to the town. Lieutenant Langford with a guard of our men was sent to escort him into St. Sebastian.

Up to twelve o'clock the affair seemed to be going very well. Evans was gaining ground, though slowly. Our men had just finished their dinners, and I was taking a luncheon, when I perseived the attention of some Spaniards earnestly directed towards the gorge in the range of Santa Barbara.

On looking in that direction I saw several Carlist columns coming through the gorge. One of these columns then advanced to attack a Spanish battalion in their front, throwing out skirmishers. When the Carlists arrived within (as it appeared to me) three or four hundred yards, the Christinos[2] fired a volley and turned round and ran off as fast as they could. It is true they did afterwards make a show of advancing, but they soon retreated on the other battalions in support of them. In the meantime other Carlists advanced from the town of Hernani and turned Evan's left flank and threw his left wing into confusion. Others of those columns which came through the gorge moved on until they became opposite to our centre when they advanced to the attack.

On the extreme right we saw at the same time a great number of Carlists who completely turned that flank. At the first appearance of these reinforcements there might have been perhaps three or four thousand troops in our front, including one or two regiments of the Legion. In less than half an hour afterwards the whole of these, with the exception of the Artillery and Lancers, was a broken mass in full flight.

This soon brought the Carlists to our position, and for nearly two hours our men were more or less engaged[3]. The 6th Regiment of the Legion was rallied in rear of us and recovered a hill on the reverse of our flank. Some Spanish troops also rallied in our rear. All praise be to God and most thankful ought we to be for his mercy and kindness to us this day. His Providence protected us, and our loss being one killed and twenty wounded. The check the Carlists had thus received on the right gave time to draw the Artillery off, and it is probable that we should have continued to hold our position had it not been for the disorganised state of the left wing. We withdrew to the position we occupied yesterday in as calm and orderly a manner as if the Battalion had been moving on a Parade at home. The Battalion at a later period in the evening marched into St. Sebastian where it was quartered for the night. If the Carlists had succeeded in throwing a strong force on the road from our right the consequence would probably have been most disastrous to General Evans Army."

From a private and unpublished Diary kept by Captain (afterwards Sir Richard) Steele of the Royal Marines Artillery.
NOTES.
1. "Red Caps" an irregular Royalist Corps. The Carlists wore White Caps.
2. The Royalist Spanish troops.
3. The Diarist gives no details of this but it is related in the Memoirs of Lord Malmesbury that "The heavy loss which Evans suffered would have been still greater if it had not been for the gallant conduct of our Marines, who not more than 400 or 500 in number, withstood the attack of the whole Carlist Army, and protected his retreat, or more properly speaking, his flight."

THE SYRIAN CAMPAIGN, 1840.
Extracts from the Diary of General Simon Fraser, Royal Marines.

ACRE.
THE FLEET,
UNDER COMMAND OF SIR ROBERT STOPFORD.

The Fleet, having returned to Malta from a cruise we found orders awaiting us to proceed forthwith to Syria. This seeming like active, service with a will, we were soon on our way to Acre, before which fortress we anchored.

The usual preliminaries having taken place, we were ordered to clear for action. This was soon done and the wardroom guns were allotted to the compliment of the *Marines alone*, under my command (Lieutenant Simon Fraser). Soundings having been taken by our Master. Mr. Elson, it was found that there was deep water, inside a reach of rock which ran along the front of the fortress. Great care was therefore required, and Sir Charles Napier, always ready for a dash, was allowed next morning, to lead in the Fleet, his ship, the *Powerful*, being, smaller than the flagship, *Princess Charlotte*. As soon as the Egyptian garrison saw the *Powerful* head inside the rocky way, they commenced firing, but not a shot was returned by the *Powerful* until safe at anchor; which was however, rather too soon, and ships were thus left outside the reef.

Firing then became general, and shot and shell began to play wild work with Acre's guns and walls; some of the garrison guns were regularly split open and every man killed. Our Captain of the ship (Fanshawe), amidst the fight, came down to the wardroom, calling out "Well done Marines! Well done! You are doing famous practise; the Admiral compliments you!

Towards sunset the firing ceased, but only to commence again next morning with renewed vigour. Storming parties were then arranged, of which I was to have one, and then we all lay down to sleep, or rest just where we were at the time, each one in readiness for immediate action, case of a sudden call "to arms." Just as another day began to dawn the Drummers beat "to quarters," but ere the sounds had well ceased, loud cheering on the quarter-deck told us in the wardroom that something good had come to pass, and the words "The White Flag is up" were quickly passed along with "Cease firing on all decks."

The remainder of the day was spent in diplomacy on board, and by the Egyptians in clearing the ramparts of their dead, by casting them into the sea.

On the third day officers were allowed to go on shore to inspect the stronghold though strongly recommended not to do so. However a party was formed and ashore we went, myself among the number, as I was anxious and curious to see the gun which I knew had been destroyed by my party in the wardroom. I accordingly wended my way at once to the ramparts; but to get there I had first to pass through the large square inside the fortress and I was quite unprepared for the awful sight which met my gaze. The whole square was strewn with the dead bodies of men and animals of all kinds, which were thickly covered all over with a fine dust from the ruins above, and around them, and swollen to an awful size by the heat, which was intense. There was scarcely room to place one's feet when passing over them. I was truly glad when I arrived at the now forsaken ramparts, but the memory of that terrible scene of carnage and ruin haunted me for long afterwards.

I soon found the gun I went to inspect; a shot had entered the muzzle, splitting it open, and knocking it over. I was told every man had been killed and their bodies thrown into the sea.

Having seen all I wanted on this spot I took a look over on the sea from the ramparts, when to my astonishment, I saw what for the moment I thought were some hundreds of the enemy dancing about in the water, with a peculiar silent gliding movement, all dressed in their white garments, and all quite upright. The sea was clear as crystal to the very bottom, which served to heighten the illusion. But I soon discovered that they were the bodies of the poor fellows who had been killed in action, and afterwards tossed into the sea by their comrades, and being now moved by the ripple of the water in a dancing motion.

While taking a last look around me. my heart warmed within me, when I thought that I might even then he standing on a spot where my gallant relative, Sir John Douglas, with his few brave Marines, had stood and fought, and with terrible odds against them, gallantly repulsed the flower of the old French Army in the former seige of Acre in 1798-99. Bravest of the brave our loyal Marines proved then, as now, and always; never turning their backs to the foe, ever true as steel to King or Queen and Country.

Having thus mused I slowly retraced my steps, as a strong body of prisoners had commenced to remove the dead from the square. I had just reached an opening to the sea a nice fresh breeze blowing, and was all by myself - my companions having gone across the square; but the smell was becoming so unpleasant, I could not stand it, and was hastening away from the spot, when a sudden flash and loud report startled me; then followed another, and yet another, and at last shot and shell were flying about fast in every direction. I at once took shelter, and two or three more of our party joined me outside the high wall, pieces of shell falling fast around us. We soon found out the cause of the firing and uproar. As the square was being cleared, the smouldering shells and rubbish, buried in thick dust, were lighted, and a great explosion took place, hundreds of the poor prisoners being killed and several naval officers badly hurt. After a while, however, the explosions ceased and all was quiet once more. We who were together then set about searching anxiously for those of our party who were missing. Soon they all turned up, with the exception of our Chaplain and one Marine officer; and at last, to our sorrow, we were obliged to go on board without them, someone having said that they had been last seen in a boat, just before the explosion, but no boat was visible now. Sad enough we all sat down to dinner, when behold, in the midst thereof our two missing comrades were brought into the wardroom, covered thickly with a white dust from the explosions, so that we could scarce recognise them. They had been considerably knocked about, though not actually wounded. The chaplain had only half of his coat skirt left, the marine officer's coat was also decidedly the worse for the expedition, and was slashed in a manner scarcely in accordance with the regulation cut. But we were all truly glad to welcome them hack to the shelter of the *Princess Charlotte*.

LEBANON.

After the seige and fall of Acre, the Marines were disembarked and were ordered to proceed to camp. During our Occupation of the camp I was despatched with a small party of Marines from the *Princess Charlotte*, with strict orders to keep a constant look-out, and prevent the Egyptians from approaching the camp through the Lebanon mountains, by the Dog River. We were also accompanied by a force of Turkish troops (at a respectful distance), under the command of the Turkish General Jackmos.

Having left the camp at daybreak, at mid-day we were all heartily glad to reach the Dog River, where we set to work and had a general wash, drying our shirts (or what remained of them) to our great relief on the rocks.

In the cool of the evening we once more started, after a frugal meal of rotten salt beef, too hard to cut, we could only scrape it with our knives and the mouldy shells of old biscuits, some of which were full of large maggots. At a late hour in the evening we again halted, on a spot sheltered from the sea breeze, and lay down where we best could find a resting place. During the night the cold was intense, and leap-frog was the occupation on the men waking up. At this time I took a sergeant and file of men to visit the posted sentries on the ridge overlooking the sea; there was a slight mist; but great was our surprise, when all at once the frigate which was anchored off the Dog River, opened fire upon us with shot and shell. We lay down quietly, however, and let them fire away. The men folded their overcoats as soon as the mist cleared, and those on board the frigate then saw their mistake; they had taken us for the enemy in our old grey overcoats.

Ere long a boat came ashore in hot haste, and an officer and two men appeared, laden with a heavy basket of provisions for us. It was full of good things, which the kind and thoughtful captain and officers of the frigate had sent, and which proved most welcome, as our little party were by this time well nigh famished with hunger, and still suffering from the bitter cold. Those on board had also been most anxious to express their sorrow for the mistake they had made in firing upon us, and to know if any of us were wounded; after which our welcome visitors departed, and once more we set out on our march.

We came at last upon a convent - a very large one - and we asked the Prior if he could sell us any provisions, my men being sadly in want of them after their long weary march, but he refused saying, "We are starving ourselves; we have nothing to give or to sell." When we had left, however, one of my men told me that he had heard both hens and sheep "making a row." We found out that this was the case, and that there were sheep, poultry, and excellent wine in the convent; the Prior himself afterwards confessed as much, but said, "I was obliged to refuse to supply provisions, because I was afraid that if I owned to having anything, the soldiers would make a forcible entrance into the convent and take all we had, without giving us anything in return." I indignantly explained that this was not the way our brave, trusty Marines acted in peace or war.

Shortly after this we halted and piled arms beneath a cluster of beautiful trees (the famous cedars of Lebanon), from which I cut a stick as a momento of our march. Our men here discovered a bees nest in an old wall, and began to dig them out, in the hope of obtaining some honey. A private, rejoicing in the celebrated name of Wellington, manfully taking the lead, when out came the bees all round his head (he happened to have a very large one, and had always been much joked about it by his comrades); these bees stung the poor fellow fearfully, and it took a number of the men to drive them off him, and our unfortunate Wellington was disfigured past all recognition; and of course we had no remedies there, only plenty of advice, which however was quite useless, seeing that as we were then situated he had no means of carrying it out. Wellington was a good-natured, lively lad, however, and bravely tried to laugh at the whole affair, though he must have suffered great pain.

It was a considerable time before any of us could go near the arms, as when driven off Wellington, the bees had clung around the piled arms, and were furious at their nest having been disturbed.

At daybreak on our second morning on the heights of Lebanon, at my order, the British reveille was sounded on drum and fife, this being the first time those ancient mountains had echoed to the sound of martial music. We had no covering at night, and slept where we best could in the open.

In two more days we returned to camp, wearied and hungry, our rotten beef and old biscuit being by this time quite finished.

SIDON.

Having been conveyed by steamer to Sidon, the flagship's Marines were landed under fire, along with the remainder of the 1st Battalion, the flagship's Marines forming the leading companies. Sir Charles Napier, commanding the expedition, here joined us. When ready, he ordered the first three companies under my command (Lieutenant Simon Fraser) to proceed to the citadel gate, under a desultory fire of *cut shot*.

We soon arrived there, and finding the citadel gate fastened, Sir Charles Napier ordered me to break it open with the *Marines' bayonets*. At this order I demurred, but seeing some old wood, which by some lucky chance had been left near the gate, I told him that we would use them instead of the Marines' bayonets. This I and my men did most effectually with a few heavy blows, and some of the men at the same time passing a strong plank under the gate, it was soon raised, until the huge iron bolt was clear of its hold, and with a hearty cheer, in we went, thus making our triumphal entry into Sidon. As we entered the enemy mysteriously disappeared down a long crooked lane, some of them pausing to fire at us at each turn.

Suspecting, however, that some of the buildings on each side (stores and cells, etc.) were occupied, and not wishing to be trapped, I ordered one of them to be broken open. We found that it was full of soldiers, but they at once laid down their arms, and were marched to the rear under guard. Several other buildings of the same description we also found occupied by considerable numbers of soldiers, who, like the first, laid down their arms upon our entry.

In one place there was a finely caparisoned horse fastened up to a nail in the wall; I turned to loose him, when one of the enemy caught up his musket and thrust his bayonet at my neck (which just grazed me) and firing at the same time. He was, however, instantly knocked down by one of my men; his companions stood quietly looking on, and were all afterwards marched off to the rear.

A little further on I discovered an officer, well dressed and well mounted, his horse beautifully caparisoned. He saw that he had got between two fires, the 2nd Battalion of Marines having just that morning arrived from England, and having disembarked with all haste, had now entered at the other end of the town, and were working their way upwards to meet us. Only just in time I saw that this officer was preparing to take aim at me, and I fired my pistol at him (a heavy ship's one); I think he was struck, but he made off somehow, and his charger came right up to us. I having caught the horse I sent him to the rear. That was the last I ever saw of my possession of two prize horses; they were taken by some of the *seniors*.

The attacking parties now met, and the 1st and 2nd representatives joined forces, and Sidon was ours. The garrison soldiers were made prisoners and marched down to the boats, to be drafted off on board our ships until the Sultan's ships came for them. I secured a large battle-axe, which I found in one of the buildings, and have kept it ever since as a momento of the Syrian campaign.

That night the 2nd Battalion occupied the upper and the 1st Battalion the lower part of the citadel. Our beef and biscuit were both done, so we went to sleep on cold water (and that none of the best). In the morning a great dispute arose, and the Major commanding the 1st Battalion came rushing in upon me, accusing my men (the *Princess Charlotte's* Marines) of having stolen a calf belonging to a man of the town, a Syrian. In vain I denied, and told him we had only had cold water the day before for dinner or supper; but he said, "Why, my dear Fraser, I feel the smell of roast meat now!" "Well, Major." I replied, "and so do I, and if you will just step upstairs you will no doubt see the *remains* of something good." Up he went accordingly, and there he found (to his great disgust) the Marines of his own ship busily engaged boiling and frying meat, and parts of the missing calf were scattered about (they had not the grace, however, to send us even a cutlet). As you may be sure, no more was said about the calf, and the indignant Major made no further enquiries about the matter.

Next day the 1st Battalion was once more embarked and we sailed for Beyrout.

BEYROUT.

Having been safely conveyed by a steamer to Beyrout, the 1st Battalion of Royal Marines, all ready for fight, found that the garrison had laid down their arms, and were to the number of 2,500, lying starving outside the walls. We were landed at once, and I, with a company of the 1st Battalion, was placed in charge of the main gate, where a company of Turkish troops joined us. These Turks had strict orders "to follow all the movements of the Marines," but the relieving of the two sentries and giving the orders was a great puzzle to them at first. However, I took my watch, and showed the young Turkish officer how we acted, and with much use of the cane and considerable noise and hubbub, they at last did all very fairly. It was most amusing to see the Turks watching intently and copying every movement of the Marines.

When the Colonel and the Grand Rounds visited us at midnight however, they were at first full of consternation, but drew up their guard and threw out their advance party just as we did, and fine men they were. When the Colonel had looked them over and said-"Good! Very Good!" to them, they were full of pride and joy, and their officer pointing to me said "Good, good Angliss!" their field officer at the same time saluting me.

When asked what accommodation I and my guard had, I pointed to the bare ground of a cell. Next morning a seat and some old tents to tie on were furnished to us (also a bottle of good wine was sent to me by some kind friend), and some good boiled beef for dinner. Seeing the Turkish officer looking into my cell as if he were very hungry, I gave him a wave of my hand, and in he came and squatted down beside me. Turkish fashion. Having procured the lid of one of my men's canteens, I put some of my mess into it and handed it to my strange guest; this he joyfully accepted and soon ate up, patting his chest in great satisfaction afterwards and saying, "Good! Good!" My man having cleared the old board (which did duty for a table) after our frugal repast, I drew out my bottle of wine (which proved to be very fine sherry), took out my leather drinking cup and a small corkscrew, drew the cork and filled the cup (my new friend all the time looking on wonderingly). I then offered it to him, but before taking it he rose slowly to his feet, and cautiously looked all round, then taking his Turkish sentry by the collar, he turned him round with his face from us, at the same time saying something sharp to him then returned to his old position,- not seeming to mind my sentry - took the cup and drained it to the bottom, and then leaning back in the usual Turkish manner, and looking at me for a few minutes with a soft innocent expression in his dark eyes, and once more patting his chest and murmuring "Good! Good!" he fell fast asleep.

My sentry, who had been a witness to the above scene, was evidently highly amused, and laughed quietly as he passed to and fro. The night passed as before, only the poor prisoners were clamouring for food. The Turks turned out like good soldiers, with my guard of steady Marines, to receive the Grand Rounds, and were again complimented, to their evident satisfaction.

Next morning we had some coffee and biscuits, and at noon a Turkish sub-officer and two file of men arrived, bringing with them the guard's dinner. To my astonishment they brought their officer's dinner into my retreat, and having uncovered it, displayed a whole boiled fowl, smothered in rice. To this my Turkish friend, with real grace, waved me to share with him, which of course I did. We had just finished, when my dinner of boiled beef arrived, and which was set aside for another occasion, and the Turkish sentry having been duly directed to look elsewhere we once more drew out the bottle and enjoyed a hearty *double sip*, to the great delight of my companion.

During the afternoon orders arrived for my party to be in marching order early next morning. A Sultan's ship had arrived with troops and an order to embark the prisoners. Having gathered them together at an early hour, with our young drummer and fifer, playing the "British Grenadiers," we escorted them to the boats, and then we ourselves embarked in a steamer to rejoin the flagship, and from thence to Malta, and old England.

When we left Beyrout the Turkish guard turned out and saluted us, the officer (my friend) taking a most affectionate farewell, and beating his breast, while he repeated with great enthusiasm, "Good, good Angliss!"

"PALMERSTON'S OWN."

Good Luck to you, noble Lord George,
You have stuck to the poor "Jollies" boldly,
Though the House - how it raised our gorge -
Has treated our advocate coldly.
The Home truths you told had told well,
And the House might have opened its eyes,
If the few had not been there to tell,
As usual, their Admiralty lies.
"The Corps" has received with a groan,
Lord George, it was mischievous wit

To call us "Lord Palmerston's Own."

To be sure if we battled in Spain
In the great cause of non-intervention,
Where 'twas hard any laurels to gain,
And our wounds had their "smart" for their pension.
If the Isle of Dogs' Legion was saved
When it fled for support to our ranks-
A fact which by Evans is waived,
But nobody asks for his thanks.
If through all this we acted with tact,
When we fought, or fell, fighting ashore,
Then, Lord George, you are right, for in fact
We must be "Lord Palmerston's Own."

If in Portugal we have campaigned,
Till the Portuguese think us no strangers,
And some of us haply have gained
The name of "The Old Tagus Rangers."
If we've fought little wars far and wide,
And our ships, like the famed horse of Troy,
Have carried an army inside
For the "non-intervention" employ.
If 'tis true we in Syria have played
First fiddle to Napier's trombone,
Then, my Lord, you're correct, I'm afraid,
In calling us "Lord Palmerston's Own"

Yet though we have run such a "Muck,"
Still such a nick name is the "Devil,"
When he can't get "the Devil's Own Luck,"
Although we're the children of evil.
While ambassadors often are told
When two foreign factions compete,
"Should you watch either faction controlled,
Just land the Marines of the Fleet."
Yet in sharing the loaves and the fishes,
We scarce get a crust or a bone,
Then, My Lord, prey attend to our wishes-
Don't call us "Lord Palmerston's Own."

From "United Service Gazette," 10 July 1841

THE FOUR MARINES OF H.M.S. *WAGER*.

Since writing the account of these four fellows, who, abandoned on the coast of Patagonia to an almost certain death in December 1741, gave "three cheers and called out 'God save the King,' because as Stevenson wrote, they liked to do things nobly for their own satisfaction" (vide "Britain's Sea Soldiers," Vol. I. pp. 313, 314), I have come across a note of their names, which assuredly ought to be preserved in the annals of the Corps. These Marines, of whom we may well be proud were:-
Corporal Crosslet
Private Smith
Private Hobbs
Private Hertford

LIFE ON THE ISLAND OF ASCENSION.
(Extracts from the diary of General Simon Fraser, Royal Marines, written about 1843.)

We had been eagerly watching for the first glimpse of our new home. In the moonlight it looked so beautiful that we thought all the stories we had heard of its many discomforts must have been untrue, or at all events much exaggerated; but we soon found that the first glance had been deceptive, and that in the morning, and on closer inspection it did not appear quite such an enchanted island as when etherealized by the moon's soft, tender light.

In 1501, it was a desert cinder, without a single inhabitant, either man or beast. It was called Ascension on account of its having been discovered on Ascension Day, the discoverer being Joao de Nova Galezo, a Portuguese navigator.

It lies between Africa and Brazil in South Atlantic Ocean; and is seven and a half miles long and six miles wide. The Island is of volcanic origin, and presents a surface of conical hills 200 feet high and upwards.

Of these, no fewer than twenty-four have craters, but they emit neither fire nor smoke. Desolation is stamped upon all these hills, with one exception. Between the hills are valleys strewed with various volcanic substances. In the eastern part rises a double-peaked mountain, and this, from its verdant appearance is rightly named the "Green Mountain."

Such then was to be, for some time, the home of our party of Royal Marines, now arrived from the Transport. We were landed early in the morning, by means of small boats. The entrance to the harbour is protected by a fort, in which are a few guns, and also a supply of small arms.

Georgetown was the next object to meet our view on shore, it is built in the form of a square, and here are the quarters of the married soldiers, the single men occupying the barracks, a large building encircled with a wide verandah. There are small cottages for the Officers' quarters, and two hospitals, one of the latter being exclusively for fever patients and these are all the buildings that constitute the small garrison. The commandant's cottage was on the slope of a hill, from whence orders could he signalled to the Green Mountain. The black men's quarters were all built near the shore, and were called Krootown.

Every house was surrounded by a wide verandah, which was an absolute necessity in that climate, being the only means of making any dwelling habitable. The houses themselves were built of stone from the shore; the sand consists of finely pulverized shells, or coral, which becomes firm by the action of the waves, and becomes in time susceptible of a clear polish like marble. Our cottage had neither fireplace nor window-glass in any of the rooms, but the latter was scarcely required - there was no change of season at Ascension, the heat was intense all the year round; so that the window places were always open during the day, and closed at night by venetian shutters, kept as open as possible to admit the air. Our walls were whitewashed, instead of being papered, or painted, so that such venomous insects as centipedes and scorpions might be easily seen on them and for the same reason carpets were also avoided, and very light matting used in their stead.

Our baggage having arrived we soon had the furniture and our other possessions arranged, and the rooms looked more home-like. The kitchen was built separately, and at some little distance from the house, and there our black cook reigned triumphantly.

The black men employed on the island as cooks and servants, were, for the most part, liberated Africans. Only the Marine Officers had a white man for personal attendance in addition to the cook. The black people on the island had been rescued from slavers, and landed at Sierra Leone. It was of their own free will they engaged to stay at Ascension for three years, and were then replaced by others for a like period. Their great ambition was to save money enough to buy wives on their return, but they were only allowed one wife on the island. Sometimes they would send for a wife to Sierra Leone, marrying women they had never seen before.

Our first cook had sent for a wife in this way, just after he came to us. On his wedding day he came up to the house dressed in gorgeous fashion, pure white trousers, bright blue coat with brass buttons, two very gay coloured waistcoats, both being displayed to the best advantage, a brilliant silk neck-tie, in which yellow predominated, and out of each coat pocket appeared the corner of a gorgeous coloured silk pocket handkerchief.

His bride was attired in a white dress, which contrasted strangely with her dusky skin, and was relieved only by the brilliant colouring of her head-gear. As there was neither church nor clergyman on the island, the marriage ceremony was performed by the Commandant of the Marines, who was legally empowered to marry and to christen.

At this time Ascension was the headquarters of the West African squadron, which was engaged in the prevention of the slave trade; and the hospitals contained a good many invalids from the various ships.

On Sundays we all assembled in the verandah of the barracks, that being the largest, and the Commandant or Adjutant read prayers and a sermon. Just before we left, however, the foundation of a church was laid.

There being no shops we were dependent upon passing ships for most of our household necessaries such as tea, sugar, butter and flour. Champagne could sometimes be procured from the French ships, and also brandy; but neither wine nor spirits could be landed, without especial permission from the commandant.

Water was very scarce, it was kept locked up in tanks, and a small quantity doled out to each family, according to its numbers. Officers and men shared alike the Commandant receiving no more than the private, and this same rule was strictly followed in the distribution of the fish and turtle. At a certain hour the water tanks were again locked up for twenty-four hours. These tanks were filled by the heavy rainfall which occurred two or three times a year, pipes being laid to receive it, and the verandahs around the different buildings being literally surrounded by every available tub, basin and jug, and these were filled from the roof with the precious fluid.

How often we used to wish for Scotland's bonnie burnies. One season the rain failed, and we had to procure water from St. Helena. Clothes had to be washed with sea water, and there were at that date nothing known of the condensing apparatus, or any such means of supplying us in our need, and great was our joy when, after two months, our kind commodore arrived, bringing with him a barrel of water for every family on the island, and it may he imagined how thankfully this gift was received by all.

The happiest time for us was when the Commodore's frigate was anchored in the Bay. During his stay he used to look after the comfort of all in our little garrison, and do all he could for us. He came about four times in the year, and as other ships from the squadron came at the same time to receive orders, we used to have a gay time. The commodore organized parties to the Green Mountain, and the ladies used to accompany us upon these pleasant excursions which we all enjoyed thoroughly. The Commodore was our best and kindest friend.

All the mason, wright, carpenter and smith work was done by the Marines, who had learned these trades previous to their enlistment; and very clever workmen they proved themselves.

Both men and officers wore suits of white duck, and broad Panama hats, as a protection against the sun. Ascension being so near the Equator the sun always rose at 6 a.m. and set at 6 p.m., there being no twilight.

It was intensely hot throughout the day, but nights were refreshingly cool, and the light was so clear and brilliant that we could sit in the verandah and read, as easily as by daylight. The insects in Ascension were both troublesome and dangerous scorpions and centipedes being numerous. My sister-in-law had a very narrow escape from one of the latter, whose bite is often fatal. The creature had crawled up her back, and got into the plait of her hair. On entering the room I fortunately chanced to see it in time, for, at that moment it was erecting itself preparatory to its venomous bite, but quickly snatching up a pair of scissors, I went behind her, grasped the centipede with them, and drew it out of the plait. Had the creature bitten my sister-in-law on the head she would have had but little chance of recovery.

There were large cockroaches which, though harmless, proved very disagreeable, for they imparted a strong odour to everything they touched. Streams of ants too, used to pay us regular and repeated visits, entering by the front door, marching through the dining room, and finally wending their way to one or other of the bedrooms, and at last making their exit through the window-place. These insect marches were conducted with a regularity that was surprising. At first we attempted to get rid of them, but found it quite impossible, so we were obliged to let them have their way. Mosquitos were furious, and unwearied in their attacks, and their peculiar hum was very irritating. Sleep was impossible unless when quite surrounded by mosquito curtains. But one of the greatest and most trying pests of all was the common house-fly; they were round us at all times in myriads. Neither breakfast nor dinner service could be set down until the very moment of use, and every glass or tumbler had a cover which was only removed for a moment and then replaced; reading or writing was a most difficult task, as the fly-switcher was in constant use. When the lamp was lighted was our only time of peace, our tormentors then beat a hasty retreat and clustering together like bees they retired to rest until morning.

One of our female servants was a young African woman, who had been brought up on the island; she had been rescued from a slaver when only three years old. Being too young to be set on shore alone at Sierra Leone, she had been brought to Ascension; and successive officer's ladies had taken kindly care of her, and had given her a good, plain education. She had the instinctive love of her race for gay colours, but otherwise her ideas were entirely European. We were sorry to lose our first black cook; he was a round faced, pleasant looking man, and we all liked him; but his time being out returned to his native land. His successor was frightful to see; from brow to chin his face was gathered in knots like the back-bone of a fish, and in addition to this he had fearful gashes across his cheeks. These, we were informed, were the marks of his tribe. His wife came to me with a formal complaint that: "Seurs beat her plenty too much," and she "want to go in big ship to Sierra Leone."

It was with great difficulty that I at last made her understand she could not be sent from the island without her husband's consent. But at last I summoned Seurs, by ringing the large bell in the verandah. He denied the charge of "beating plenty too much," and, enumerated all the articles of dress he had bought for her, she said indignantly that she "gib dem all back, no want dem." To which he replied most emphatically, "Him no want dem neider, dey no use, him want de money." On hearing this the wife hurried to Krootown, sold her belongings and brought back the money; her affectionate husband then gave her permission to depart whither she would, of which she speedily availed herself on the first opportunity. Seurs afterwards became very much attached to us, and was even anxious to accompany us home to England; but as that could not be, he took service with our successors, and whenever any letters arrived from our friends at Ascension they contained the message that Seurs sent "his best memory to us all." The society belonging to the Island was very limited, but we had pleasant visitors sometimes, independent of our Island garrison; convalescent officers from the hospitals, and friends from the ships in the Bay. Often in the evening they would come in, those who were musical bringing their instruments with them; and so enlivening us with music and singing.

Hours were very early. Those who belonged to the ships had to leave at 9 p.m., no boats being allowed to leave the pier-head later. Their departure was followed by that of our other guests belonging to the Island, and by ten o'clock everyone had retired to rest.

All were astir once more in the early morning, at five, to enjoy a cool hour before sunrise.

At one time we used to keep a number of birds, but we found they would not live in that climate for any length of time. We tried English and Cape canaries, love birds, whydah-birds and doves of various kinds, but the most tender care could not prolong their lives. Two parrots only survived and were brought, home to England.

We had some kind friends at St. Helena whom we never saw; they used to send quantities of fruit from time to time, and wrote pressing invitations for us to visit them, but being Adjutant I could not leave the island even for a short time, so we could not avail ourselves of their kindness. One day, however, we made an excursion to Comfort Cove, by sea it was rather more than three miles distant from Ascension; we lunched previously on board the Commodore's ship.

Comfort Cove is the place of quarantine for ships having had fever, or other infectious disease, on board. Near the sea is the graveyard, where those are buried who die on board the ships undergoing quarantine.

It is a peculiar spot round, and quite flat, surrounded by steep hillocks, and having only one entrance. A plant of the Madagascar rose was the only green thing visible; the flower is of a deep purple hue, and the plant grows low on the ground; it has no thorns; the want of verdure, and the bare hillocks, makes the spot look very desolate.

In spite of every precaution, fever will sometimes find its way into the garrison, and always proves very fatal. Some years before we were there nearly half the officers and men fell victims to it, the Commandant being one of the first.

The water on the island, in spite of careful filtering, was very unwholesome, the great heat caused incessant thirst, and brought on a feeling of lassitude and weariness.

The thunder storms on the coast were awful, but neither thunder nor lightning were ever known at Ascension.

There were two fairs on the island, which were held entirely by birds, eggs being the only commodity to be obtained. These strange fairs were called "Wideawake Fair" and "Gannet Fair." The former is so named from the peculiar cry of the birds as they fly through the air, constantly repeating what sounds to the hearers like "Wideawake," "Wideawake." The fair is a level piece of ground surrounded on all sides by hills, with a few sickly looking plants of the castor-oil and Madagascar rose. Thousands of birds congregate on this spot three times in two years. They always come here and to no other part of the island. When they depart no one knows where they go, as they have never been seen in any other place. On approaching the fair the noise is quite deafening from the screaming of its feathered occupants. All the residents on the island, and the sailors and marines of ships of any nation lying at anchor, are allowed to go out to the fair and bring back as many eggs as they please. Of this permission all on the island eagerly avail themselves; and, though vast numbers of eggs are carried away, up to the last there seems little diminution of the stock. No one is allowed to fire a gun in, or near the Fair, for fear, of frightening away the birds. "Gannet Fair" was occupied entirely by sea birds, about the size of a goose; but their eggs were not in so much request.

The *Erebus* and *Terror* discovery ships called at Ascension on their way home from the South Pole. Alas! as we stood on the shore and watched their departure, little did we forsee the sad fate awaiting them in the Artic regions.

We were also honoured by a visit of the *Belle Poule*, which was commanded by the Prince de Joinville, son of Louis Phillippe, on which occasion the French language was in great requisition. The Prince, with some of his officers, landed at my quarters, and proved charming guests.

The first vessel that steamed from England to India, the *Hindustan*, remained two days at the Island, on her way out, for the purpose of coaling; coals having been previously sent there for her use. The Captain was a Naval officer, an old friend of mine. We spent a most delightful day on board, the Captains wife, who was with him on the voyage, treating us with the greatest hospitality. One great trouble to us was the irregularity with which we received letters from home, months would often pass, and then a Transport would bring several at a time. We had more chances of sending letters home, as kept them ready, and Captains of ships calling on their homeward voyage were most kind in carrying our various despatches to England, and there posting them.

We were allowed during our stay on the island to spend a month on the Green Mountain, during which time we occupied the Mountain House, taking our whole establishment with us. The Island gig, a small carriage without springs (the only approach to a carriage at Ascension) was sent for the ladies, it was drawn by three mules. A small cart, also drawn by a mule, carried our baggage; and horses were sent for the rest of the party. The distance was seven miles, so we started very early in the morning to escape the heat.

The base of the Green Mountain is four miles from the garrison, it rises almost perpendicularly, the summit being reached by a rugged road along its side, very zig-zag and about three miles long, it is named "the ramps." It is a dangerous road in some parts, and one morning the mountain cart fell over the edge, and the two poor mules were killed.

The gate at the top is always guarded by a Marine sentry; and as we - poor dwellers in the perpetual heat, dust and desolation below - were rejoiced at the sight of what seemed to us like a paradise; the sweet cool air was so refreshing, and round the mountain cottage were clustered the only trees to be found on the whole Island.

The flower garden was a special delight: to us, it seemed so long since we had seen roses, fuschias, and other flowers, and they were growing in profusion in the garden at the Green Mountain, but, although in every other respect like those in our own far off home, here they were devoid of sweet perfume; want of dew was said to be the cause of the fair blossoms being scentless. Among the flowers there was one called the "Fly-catcher," from its custom of closing its petals tightly around any unfortunate fly that might chance to light upon it. There was also the "Sensitive-plant," which shrinks from the gentlest touch of the fingers, and cannot remain still for a moment if placed in the palm of the hand.

The scenery at the mountain is very beautiful, especially to those who admire the bold grandeur of rocks and rugged hills. In the distance is seen the crater, known as "The Devil's Punch Bowl," also the famous locality called "Bottle Point," which is most difficult to reach, many who attempted it being obliged to return disappointed and unsuccessful. The spot is so called from some adventurous person, in the year 1824, having placed a bottle there for the reception of visiting cards.

Our party daily enjoyed some delightful rambles. There was one beautiful glen which could only be reached by going through a long dark tunnel, high hills surrounding it on all sides. The glen was bright with flowers, golden gorse, daisies and flowers of the Indian cress climbing up the sides of the ravine; and how sweet the gorse and the simple daisies seemed to us, reminding us of home and the old Country.

Another favourite walk was round "Break-neck Pass," but it was only safe for those having good nerves and steady heads. On one side of the path rises a perpendicular rock of great height, on the other is a deep, dark chasm; to fall into this would be instant death. On one occasion a visitor having gone part of the way suddenly became giddy, and standing with his back against the rock called to the others of his party that he was unable to go on or to return. It was with the greatest difficulty that he was rescued from his perilous position.

Those however who could traverse the Pass were well repaid, for the pure, fresh south-east wind was most invigorating in its effect upon frames weakened with the great heat of the plain. It is 2,000 feet above sea-level. Quantities of the common brambleberry grow on the slopes leading to the peak, and also the Cape gooseberry plant. Banana trees grow in some of the ravines, and seem to flourish.

The shrubs and plants in the ravines and on the slopes give shelter to a herd of wild goats, and coveys of guinea-fowl, but neither could be shot or caught without an order from the Commandant. The eggs and young of the guinea fowl were often destroyed by the large wild cats, which were numerous in that part of the Island. A reward was given for each wild cat that was killed, but it was not easy to get near them.

There was a pet monkey at the Mountain, a marmozet, belonging to the Assistant-Surgeon. Jacko was a pretty little creature of his kind, very small, very intelligent and amusing. Jacko and I soon became great friends, he having taken a fancy for my society. Master Jacko had the most intense horror of tobacco smoke, and if anyone chanced, in fun, to give him a puff of it he would bury his face in his hands, carefully covering both eyes and ears.

There was a stove in the mess-room, but we never cared to have it lighted, the coolness being a perfect luxury to us. Some natural caves were said to have been the storing places where pirates had, in the days of old, before the Island was inhabited, hidden their plunder. If such was the case, the labour and danger of dragging it up the mountain-side must have been great.

The most pleasant times of life seem to end soonest. Our month of leave passed away all too quickly, and the day came round when we had to set out on our return to the garrison, and the heat and discomforts of the plain.

We left the Green Mountain with keen regret, but with gratitude for the renewed health and strength we had derived from our delightful sojourn there.

Our friends in the garrison were pleased to have us back again, and said that the Island had appeared quite deserted in our absence. At this time there arrived the medals for those who had distinguished themselves in the war of the Levant. They were sent to me as the only officer on the Island entitled to one. No ribbons were sent: but as some of the ladies had ribbons of the requisite colours my sister-in-law made as near an approach to the orthodox medal ribbon as possible; and when I - wearing my own - decorated the Marines who were entitled to have them (some of whom had been under my command during the war) and informed them who had made the ribbons, and that the lady herself was a soldier's daughter, they seemed very proud of wearing the handiwork of the only young unmarried lady on the Island.

I may here mention that the whole of the buildings were built solely by the small detachment of Royal Marines, composing the garrisons; two large hospitals, a large barracks and fort, Officers' Quarters and Married Men's Quarters, and they were the admiration of all strangers who visited the Island.

Frequently officers on board passing ships purchased a few turtle to take home: during the season the pond at Ascension often held as many as 300 turtle, mostly very large, and these constituted our fresh provisions, along with a small supply of bullocks occasionally from St. Helena. The pond was generally swarming with young turtle, about the size of large walnuts, and these were taken a mile out to sea and set free, to escape the small sharks and black fish. Where they went no one could tell, but a small one never turned up again. During the season the beach where they came to lay their eggs was strictly watched at night, and no one but the black man on watch, was allowed near it. A short time after each turtle landed it was turned over on its back, and lay there quietly until boat came to fetch it to the pond.

When I went my rounds in the mornings I was always attended by my faithful dog, and constant companion Pincher; he was a beautiful Scotch terrier, and was brave as well as handsome, caring nothing for the small sharks round him in the water, and the fierce War Birds flying just over his head; he was very fond of the water.

The day after we landed, Pincher took a walk to look at the barracks (by himself) when he was at once attacked by a whole pack of curs kept by the men for hunting the wild cats and rats of the Green Mountain, on their Saturday afternoons. He was very roughly treated, and came home bleeding all over so I kept him confined for a few days. The first day I again took him with me, to my surprise, he with ears erect and tailed curled, walked straight through the midst of them, looking at them right and left, but none of them ventured to interfere with him, and from that day Pincher ranged free and unmolested and was chief of the pack, and not a stray wild cat or any of the large black cinder rats were to be seen near my cooking-house or quarters; and when he saw a scorpion or centipede on the walls, he never rested until he had informed me of the fact.

The scarcity of water in the garrison was greatly felt at times; during one season no water came from the Green Mountain, and our tank was getting very empty, so that we had to kill off all our extra live stock. No rain had fallen for a great length of time, and whenever a dark cloud was seen, every piece of crockery about the house was brought out and ranged along in front of the verandah, so that we might catch any rain that fell, but none came. When we had reached our worst strait, however, our kind Commodore, Captain Foote, with a supply of water on board, and a large water tank followed, to our great relief and delight. All our water used to come streaming down the mountain; but on this occasion it was dried up on its way down, and not even a single cloud passed over the mountains to reward our anxious watching.

Generally the sea came in in moderate rolls, but at other times with very little notice it came in in huge rollers. On one occasion the Purser of one of our ships came to me to request leave to land a large quantity of coal and other stores on the wharf for a day or two. I told him it would be very dangerous to do so; as the rollers, came in often very rapidly and with quite without notice. At this remark he only laughed and said, "Oh! I will run that risk".

Accordingly, for two days, stores of all kinds were landed and piled up along the wharf; but on the third day, about midnight, the garrison was roused by the ringing of the great bell and roll of the drum. The waves came suddenly rolling in with even more than their usual force, without the least warning, and by ten o'clock the next day (Sunday) everything was swept entirely away, the rollers were rising mountain high and the wharf washed clean and clear. No one could land, and the poor Purser could only stand on the deck of his ship and from a distance view his loss.

Not a breath of air was blowing, and a short distance out to sea the water was quite smooth. The cause of this strange phenomenon, like the coming and going of the turtle, remains hidden from our knowledge: from no quarter comes the slightest breeze, all is calm and still outside the rollers.

On another occasion, a very fine Merchant ship with a valuable cargo, coming in for a supply of water and commanded by Captain Hamlin, of and bound for Greenock, Scotland, was totally lost close to the landing place. The Captain had been there before this occasion, therefore nothing but fool-hardiness or gross carelessness could have made him take his ship inside the danger buoy, and right upon the coral rocks, where she stuck fast.

The Sergeant-Major of Marines (who was the smartest non-commissioned officer I have ever known) with our men did all they could to save the ship, but she soon rolled her masts overboard and began to leak.

The Captain then seeing her lost state formally handed the ship and cargo over to the Commandant of the Island. To save the valuable cargo, every spare man on the island was at once set to work from daylight until darkness set in they worked hard, and fortunately the whole of the immense and valuable cargo was safely landed and housed in the Fort, only one bag of coffee getting a dip in the sea.

The Captain and his crew struck work, and were housed in a tent on the beach. Not long afterwards three ships arrived to take home the cargo, all of which our men re-shipped; they expected to have reaped a considerable sum as salvage money, and for their good and faithful service, but not a farthing did either officers or men receive, nor even thanks for their trouble.

In due time my term of service having expired, I was relieved, and we bade adieu for ever to the island of Ascension.

OPERATIONS ON THE PARANA RIVER
1845.
Colonel E. C. Domville, R.M.

In consequence of the disturbed state of affairs in the River Plate in 1845, it was decided to land the Marines from the squadron serving on the south-east coast of America, for the protection of British lives and property at Monte Video.

Accordingly the Marines, composing the detachments from the *Alfred* (50), Commodore Purvis' flagship, and *Gorgon, Satelite, Comus* and *Racer* were placed in charge of the Custom House, in conjunction with a large detachment of French from the frigates *Erigone* (?) and *Africaine*. These were specially augmented by the detachments from H.M. Ships *Eagle, Firebrand, Melampus* and *Vernon*, the *Alfred's* Marines returning to England. The town was then besieged by General Oribe with a combined force of the troops of General Rosas[1] and the revolutionary party in the Banda Oriental.

No aggressive operations were begun by the English and French, but the troopships *Apollo* and *Resistance*, with the 45th and 73rd[2] English Regiments, were sent on from Rio Janiero by the British Plenipotentiary at that place.

About this time the Buenos Ayrean leader Rosas proclaimed a blockade of the Rivers Parana and Uruguay, which so precipitated matters that the English and French Ministers at Monte Video decided on seizing the Buenos Ayrean Squadron which was done without loss of life, and soon after a combined force of English and French, accompanied by some Monte Videan troops under Garibaldi[3] was despatched to Colonia, which was attacked, and after a short but ineffective resistance, was abandoned and occupied by the allies.

About the end of October 1845 it was decided by the English and French Plenipotentiaries to force the passage of the Parana, which was closed by President Rosas. Some very strong batteries at Point Obligado were erected, and the passage of the river closed by a number of ships moored right across the stream, with strong cables over and under.

A force of English and French vessels was despatched to attack the position. A number of Marines were sent up from Monte Video, and a small battalion of four companies - in all about 200 men – was formed under the command of Captain Hurdle, R.M., with Lieutenants Lawrence Barnard, Morrison and Domville.

After the ships had taken up their position in front of the batteries which mounted in all 40 guns, some 32 and 24 pounders, and a large brigantine with 6 brass guns of some size at the opposite bank, a furious cannonade began, which lasted incessantly until the cutting of the chains by Captain Hope, R.N., attended by Midshipman Commerell, when the steamers proceeded up through the gap in the boom, and under a heavy fire, took up a fresh position above the batteries, until about six o'clock, when the seamen and marines landed and formed in two columns of sections; Marines' left in front, leading company 2nd Lieut. Domville, 2 companies with sergeants, the right company, 2nd Lieut. Barnard, R.M.A. the whole commanded by Captain Hurdle. He was most effectively assisted by 2nd Lieut. Morrison as acting Adjutant.

The two little columns vied with each other in breasting the hill, but reached the summit almost, if not quite, simultaneously, when they formed line, and were met with a volley of musketry, very badly directed, as only one seaman was killed, called Pollyblank, one of the gun-spiking party. However, on they went with a rush, and the enemy soon bolted, and the Union Jack was hoisted and the guns spiked.

There still remained a number of men who fired in a desultory manner from the wood in rear of the battery. A party was sent out under 2nd Lieut. Domville to clear the wood, and on passing over some wounded men who were lying about, with many killed, one man raised his carbine, and behind the carcase of his horse, aimed at Lieut. Domville, but fortunately missed him. He was soon quieted by the musket of Sergeant Phelps. After a short time the company was relieved by one under Lieut. Lawrence, R.M.A., who had been acting as aide-de-camp to Captain Hotham, R.N.

As it was getting dark the force returned to the ships and completed the work of dismounting the guns the next day. There were several smaller affairs subsequently in the Parana, but after the vessels, which had been trading since the opening of the passage of the river, had loaded and were returning, information was received that strong batteries were being erected at San Lorenzo.

It was determined to land a rocket party on the island opposite, which was done so quietly, that the enemy was quite unaware of it, and as soon as fire was opened on the leading merchantmen, a discharge of rockets was thrown into the enemy's battery and among the large force of cavalry in the rear. This was done under the able direction of Lieut. Barnard, Royal Marine Artillery.

After these operations the Marines, under Major Lennard, were frequently exposed to fire from Oribe's forces at Monte Video, and their presence undoubtedly saved that town from the plunder and atrocities so peculiar to the people of the River Plate.

NOTES.
1. Juan Manuel Rosas, Dictator of Buenos Ayres who may be regarded as the founder of the Argentine Republic. His attempt to assert his authority over Monte Video and the Plate River generally raised a host of enemies, to whom he finally succumbed in 1852.
2. These Regiments were on their way to the Cape, to take part in the war then proceeding with the Kaffirs. They had run short of water and put into Rio to refill their tanks, when Mr. Ouseley (afterwards Sir William Ouseley), in virtue of his authority as Queen Victoria's representative, diverted them to Monte Video.
3. The famous Italian patriot and guerilla leader, then in the Monte Videan service.

IRELAND AND THE BALTIC.
SERVICES OF LIEUT. A. O. LEWIS, R.M., 1846-1857.

A sword was recently discovered by a retired officer of the Corps in a pawnbroker's shop at Middleton, Lancs, bearing the following inscription: -

PRESENTED BY THE DIRECTORS OF THE CORK STEAMSHIP COMPANY TO LIEUT. LEWIS OF THE ROYAL MARINES, AS A SMALL TOKEN OF THEIR ACKNOWLEDGMENT FOR THE SERVICES RENDERED BY HIM ON THE 16TH JANUARY, 1847, AT BALLYCOTTON, IN PROTECTING THE WRECK OF THE "SIRIUS" STEAM PACKET.

An extract from *The Times* gives the following account: - "The *Sirius* is notable as having been the first steamer ever to cross the Atlantic. She was afterwards employed between London and St. Petersburg, and then purchased by the Cork Steam Packet Company.

She left Dublin on her last voyage for Cork on Friday, 15th January, 1847. Unfortunately, running into a thick fog about 3 o'clock on Saturday morning, she struck on some rocks, and though got off by backing the engines, she made water rapidly, and boats were got out. The first boat, lowered in a hurry, capsized and all on board her, mostly police and soldiers, perished.

The vessel was found to be on rocks about 50 yards from some cliffs, and Capt. Macameron, a passenger, swam with a hawser to a rock mid-way between the wreck and cliff, by which one or two sailors descended to help him, and so assisted the remainder of the passengers were got off. The hawser was then transferred by Capt. Macameron ashore, and made fast to a rock, and after two hours suspense in the darkness, the passengers were all safely ashore. By this time, nearly 6 o'clock, the Coastguard from Ballycotton came out and rescued those on deck.

The cliffs were now alive with wreckers, who swarmed down from all parts in hundreds, intent on plunder, and not giving aid to anyone. The handful of Coastguard men could do nothing against them, and an express was sent for police and military. The *Sirius* was literally smashed to pieces, not a vestige of her hull, framework or spars remaining. The only object discernible on the rock when she went to pieces was the boiler and part of the engine, which resisted the lashing of the waves.

The country people made away with everything they could lay their hands on, even threatening the C.G. men if they interfered with their rights until the arrival of a Magistrate from Middleton, with military and police.

Though not mentioned by name in the extract from The Times, it is probable that Lieut. Lewis was in charge of this party, as the date on the inscription shows, when the services were rendered. The cause of the presence of a battalion in Ireland at this date is noted in "Britains Sea Soldiers," Vol. II., p. 182.

Lieut. Arthur Onslow Lake Lewis joined the Corps in February 1846, and served with the R.M. Battalion in Ireland from October of that year until August 1847. He afterwards saw service in the Baltic in H.M.S. "*Odin*" in 1854 and 1855. The "*Odin*" first took part in a small expedition under Admiral Plumbridge, to examine the intricate channels of the Aaland Islands. The vessels were the "*Leopard*" (flag) "*Valorous,*" "*Vulture*" and "*Odin.*" He then commanded the Marines landed for destruction of the shipping and Russian stores at Brahasted on 30th May, 1854, and for a similar duty at Uleaborg on 1st and 2nd June. He was senior officer of Royal Marines at the attack on Gamla Carleby and at Bomarsund. He was also engaged in the "*Odin*" in the reconnaissance at Abo.

He was promoted to Captain in 1857, was invalided in August the same year, and died in London on 27th November, 1858.

MARINE EXTRAVAGANCE.

"Two privates of the Royal Marines, just paid off from Her Majesty's steam-vessel *Pluto*, Lieutenant-Commander Low, at Woolwich, for a trifling wager, commenced eating several £5 Bank of England notes 'with bread, cheese and onions.' but were stopped by some of their more sensible comrades, who came up at the time, and compelled them to desist. Fortunately the numbers of the notes remained unmutilated. The *Prometheus*, Commander Hay, and the *Phoenix*, Commander Dennis, have just been paid off, and the seamen have been playing similar absurd tricks. Most of the sailors have received nearly £100 each."

Illustrated London News, 11th Sept., 1847.

THE ROYAL MARINE BATTALION IN IRELAND,
1848
By Col. E. C. Domville, R.M.

In July 1848 an order was received at Plymouth Division for a battalion of 300 men to proceed to Ireland, under Colonel Miller. They embarked in the *Birkenhead*, and proceeded to Kingston, and were afterwards despatched with all speed to Waterford, and there joined the Marines of the Fleet, amounting to about 1,100 men in all (Artillery and Infantry), and were encamped at Gibbet Hill, Waterford. Shortly afterwards the Marines of the Fleet reembarked, and the Battalion under Colonel Miller remained, and was embarked on board the troopers *Rhadamanthus* and *Alban* moored off the city of Waterford. The rapidity with which Marines are landed was shewn in a very marked manner. It was agreed that on a certain sound of bugle on the quay, the men should land at once. One morning about 7 a.m. the bugle suddenly sounded, and in 20 minutes the men were fully accoutred, with 60 rounds of ball each, and ready to move off from the quay. They were stationed in three divisions at the entrances to the town, as an armed force was in motion at Curaghmore, and the 4th Light Dragoons and 85th Light Infantry were sent out to oppose them as soon as that force appeared on the scene. The rebels took to their heels and rushed to the woods, which were scoured, and 23 prisoners brought in and passed over to the Marines, who soon lodged them in the city gaol. The Marines had much arduous duty in the shape of night work, patrolling the county for some distance round Waterford.

_____

CRIMEA - THE FLEET.
H.M.S. BRITANNIA.

When at anchor some distance below the entrance to the Dardanelles, a severe epidemic of cholera broke out on board our ship and carried off a great number of our men. The seamen and officers were at once shipped on board a transport, and the good old Admiral, Sir James Dundas, gave leave to all who wished to do so to leave the ship also, whilst the ship was cleared out, but he remained on board himself with his staff, and not one officer or man of the Royal Marines would leave him. We all decided to remain with him on board.

When the ship had been cleared out and all right again, we waited for orders, and we had not to wait long. On a Sunday morning while at Divine service, the flag lieutenant came hastily down and whispered to the Admiral that a steamer was approaching in hot haste. We were just finishing church service, when all hands were called, and the dear old Admiral, hat in hand, declared that England was now at war with Russia, and that she expected every man would do his duty. Three loud cheers were given by every officer and man on board, the war flag was unfurled, captains of other ships came on board, and every ship in the fleet manned yards and cheered lustily, and "up anchor" was the word.

The Turkish Firman being all right, we entered the Dardanelles, and, sailing up slowly, we passed Constantinople early in the morning, making the frail houses shake to their foundations with our salutes, as each ship passed onward. At some distance from the city we came to an anchor in a snug bay, some seven miles from the entrance to the Black Sea. There the Turkish Fleet was anchored inside the bay. While at anchor outside the Black Sea several of the officers from our flag-ship made up a party to go ashore to see the celebrated big guns, placed by the Turks to defend the entrance to or from the Black Sea.

As it was my day off duty and guard, I intended to be one of the party; but in this I was disappointed, having been delayed in coming off guard, and so the party started without me. However as soon as I was free, I started in their wake, and as I got near the Battery I was surprised to meet the party returning so soon and evidently not in the best of spirits. Our Colonel of Marines (in full dress, brass scabbard, spurs, said to me "Ah Fraser! There you are, but you may just turn back with us again, as they will not let us in!"

"No," I replied, "since I am here I shall go and try my luck!"

So away went the Party, laughing heartily at me. Caring little, however, for their mirth, and calling over my shoulder that I was glad to have afforded them some little amusement. I proceeded on my way alone. When I reached the battery gate and knocked, the Turkish sentry who came to the wicket only shook his head, (after carefully inspecting me for some moments), but would not unbar the gate.

At last a thought struck me. I had served with the Turks during a previous campaign, and I uncovered the silver Turkish medal I was then wearing, given by the Sultan, and which bore his initials. I held it up to the sentry, who, having examined it eagerly, retired hastily to call out his officer. In a very short space of time the sentry returned, accompanied by a handsome young Turkish officer, who also examined the medal and myself minutely, then gave a loud call to his guard to "turn out," and began to lay about him vigorously with a cane which he carried, until his men had all "fallen in"- (it appeared that the Turkish officers could do little with their men without this cane practise). The gate then flew open, and I entered - the guard "carrying arms."

Having had the honour to inspect the guard (and very fine men they were, some twenty of them), I saluted, and put my hand on the medal caressingly. The guard then "turned in", leaving a file with the officer. After making him understand that I wished to inspect the Great Guns, he bowed elaborately and gracefully waved me on, accompanying me to the first gun, the file of the guard still following us. I then saw, and fully inspected, the three guns and the immense shot, taking a rough measurement of each (which I am sorry to say I afterwards lost). Having seen all I wanted, I saluted the officer, and was conducted as before to the gates the guard once more being "turned out." When I reached the landing place a boat came ashore and took me off to the ship. I went at once to my cabin, but when the dinner drum beat, I came out, and found a laughing party all ready to greet me, and learn disappointment at being kept out of the barracks as they had been. "Well, Fraser, my boy!" said my Colonel, "how do you like the Turkish courtesy on a warm day like this?"

"Colonel," I replied coolly, "I like it very much, and was truly pleased with the result of my expedition!"

"What?" he demanded, "pleased at having the gate shut in your face?"

"Certainly, after seeing all I wanted and more even than I expected to see" I returned.

Dinner here stopped the conversation for the time, but afterwards, to the astonishment of them all I told them of all I had seen, and pointing to the medal, I explained how it had assisted me to effect an entrance into the Turkish barracks (the Colonel's pride being considerably soothed thereby). Next day at the Admiral's table at dinner I had to go through the story all over again, to the great amusement of my good old friend Sir James Dundas and the others who were present.

The medal for some days after became quite a show. - Medals and decorations in those days were few. The Admiral was greatly delighted to have a copy of the measurements of the guns and stone shot.

About a week after this a boat pushed alongside our ship to inform the Admiral that heavy firing was heard in the Black Sea. A steamship was at once sent up, and we prepared to follow. When near the entrance we met the steamer, and then pushed on. When we entered, to our great horror we found the Turkish fleet completely smashed, particularly the flagship, the Admiral only just living, with both legs shot away, while the sea and shore were strewn with the dead and dying, but the Russian ships were no where to be seen, they having by this time entered Sebastopol Harbour, leaving the poor town of Sinope sadly smashed.

After a rest of two days, during which time we were all fully occupied in doing what we could for the poor unhappy Turks, the fleet sailed for Balaclava. On the way thither we sighted a Russian steamer, sent out to look at us. The *Terrible* was at once sent after her, but the Russian vessel steamed fast ahead, and the *Terrible* could only send a shot after her, which went from stern to bow, before she took shelter under the guns of Sebastopol.

Note -The Colonel mentioned above had been sent out in our ship to take command of the Battalion of Marines should they be required to land as such.

BOMBARDMENT OF ODESSA.
FROM THE DIARY OF MAJ.-GEN. S. FRASER.

Among others of Russia's outlying ports, Odessa had to feel the power of England's fleet. This city has a very large population, and is of considerable commercial importance; it is, moreover the chief landing stage for the corn exported from Southern Russia. Its total destruction therefore would prove most disastrous to the inhabitants.

On a lovely summer morning the English fleet was seen slowly and warily creeping in to an anchorage opposite the city of Odessa. Not a sound was to be heard, save the rasping of the great cables as they ran to ground. The flags of Russia fluttered aloft on shore, and every gun was manned on board the English fleet; the men sat round their guns getting a peep where they best could see what was going on on shore.

A boat carrying the ultimatum, with a white flag in its bow, now left the flagship, and was received on shore. After a short time it returned, and a signal from the flagship was made to one of our steamers, on receipt of which she at once drew out of line and took post opposite the Royal Dockyard at Odessa.

Profound silence reigned all around for some time, but just at one minute past the half-hour our ship unfurled a masthead flag, and the roar of a big gun broke the silence.

In a moment all was life and action on board, and whatever peep-holes could be obtained were at a decided premium.

Calmly and deliberately the steamer gave the City (from her starboard) gun after gun, continuing her course right along its front, while shot and shell whistled around her from the enemy. Having reached the limit of the front defences, she gracefully moved round, with her port towards the City and gave them each gun as she moved quietly along.

This practice she continued for some time, and great confusion was consequently now seen on shore; the Royal Dockyard and all the Russian buildings and shipping in dock and harbour were in flames, while many a flag was seen no more.

Our Admiral (Sir James Deans Dundas), who was liked by every officer and man on board, showed his mercy to the people of Odessa, by sparing as much as possible their private houses, and the flag on the hospital still fluttered aloft. Great good sense prevailed on shore and not a shot was fired by the enemy upon the fleet, nor was one fired from the fleet upon the town, the discharge of cannon at this time passing only between the steamer and the city.

Towards noon the firing slackened, and by sunset the white flag was seen hoisted on shore. Preliminaries were at once commenced, and next evening the whole fleet left the bay, with the shipping and buildings still burning on shore, and the avenging steamer not greatly the worse for her exchange of shot and shell with the town.

Had the ships of the fleet fired upon the city there would probably not have been one building left standing by nightfall, Odessa would have been completely destroyed, and the people killed, or left homeless and destitute, but my good old friend, Admiral Dundas, was kind-hearted, as well as brave, and true to the core, and so Odessa was spared.

LANDING OF THE ROYAL MARINES AT THE CRIMEA.
FROM THE DIARY OF MAJ.-GEN. S. FRASER.

The first Battalion of Royal Marines, landed from the fleet, were located on a small sheltered plain, and were under command of Colonel Hurdle. There we had a little drill, with Captains Meheuse and Simon Fraser acting Majors. Shortly after we were moved to the side of the hill facing the harbour, where we began to feel the rigours of a war footing. A quantity of old dilapidated tents were served out to our Battalion, which it sorely tried us to make fast at the outset. No lines were formed, each party choosing his own ground. There were plenty of holes in the tents through which to peep out at one another, and which let in a constant current of fresh air to keep us cool. Carrying shot in bags (hung over the shoulder) to the front was our chief employment at first, and hard work it was for our men along with forming daylight watering parties to places which were some distance off. There was water nearer at hand, but when not closely watched, the wretched Turks would strip for a wash in this water; when caught, however, they received no mercy from either their own chiefs or our men.

Miserable shelter and little food (and that little as bad as could be) soon brought dire sickness upon us, and typhus fever carried off a considerable number of our men, among the rest, I am sorry to say, my good and faithful servant, William Barrows, who was long remembered with sincere regret by officers and men for his kind attention to many a comrade, until he too was stricken with the terrible fever that raged among us. My groom also (John Finch), a fine, soldierly young lad, just escaped with his life, being very ill, so ill, indeed, that those around him feared there was but little hope of his recovery. In the mornings I had to mount my poor charger with the icicles hanging a foot long about him. There was only a very scanty supply of barley for our horses; they had no covering night or day, and were often standing nearly knee deep picketed in snow slush. My horse used to be nearly frantic with joy whenever I went near him, always faithful and affectionate - a true friend in that time of trial and peril, and seeming to be endowed with almost human instinct.

My poor servant had been very handy, and with my groom had scooped out a cell in the hillside for me; in the centre was my sleeping and resting place, the lower strata of small stones to let the water that dripped from the sides flow away by the entrance, and larger stones to step on, when inclined to sleep or rest on the couch, and which was only reached by the help of these stones; the water drip was carried out by a small drain running round the primitive couch, and on this a small quantity of the tips of bushes brought from a long distance, was laid. At night an old copy of The Times newspaper (which I had found invaluable at this time) served to cover my head and shoulders, and save me from the overhead drip, which ran free into the drain.

Sickness now fell still more heavily upon us and the Sardinian troops, located farther down the slope; and here I lost my kind, faithful servant, William Barrows, who was buried by his comrades on the hillside. Little food, and bad food, no proper shelter from the bitter cold and damp, and above all the green coffee sent out to us when we had no firing to roast it-helped many a fine fellow, and good soldier out of the world. We could do but little to help our poor sick comrades, we all fared alike; we had no luxuries to give them, scarcely even the bare necessaries to keep body and soul together (and this at the very outset of the campaign); we could only do our best, by kindly care and attention to cheer them, and to alleviate as much as possible their pain and sufferings.

At last I was ordered, with a company of the Royal Marines, to proceed and occupy No. 3 Battery, facing the centre of Balaclava Plain and Land Hills.

BALACLAVA HEIGHTS.
No3.BATTERY, ROYAL MARINES.
UNDER COMMAND OF MAJOR SIMON FRASER.
From the Diary of Maj.-Gen. S. Fraser.

Having occupied No. 3 Battery with a company of Royal Marines, 1st Battalion, with Lieutenant Taylor, we lost no time in trying to put it in thorough fighting order. There was a piece of wall, with six brass guns (short), and *one mortar looking over it*, but no covering whatever, and no defence from Horse or Foot. Hard work for a few days put matters so far to rights, when, one night, without much warning, a furious gale came and everything that could be moved was levelled with the ground. All the old tents were blown away, and I myself, covered with the heavy wet canvas of my tent, and the broken pole, was unable to move, until help came from my servant; there was no standing upright, the rain and wind being awful. The men were lying down, all around, wherever an old root or tuft of grass could be found to form some slight shelter.

That night the Transport "*Black Prince*" was blown all to pieces at her anchorage, and all lost; and Colonel Hurdle (commanding the Brigade of Royal Marines higher up the heights) was carried down the hill, rolled up inside his tent.

Fortunately, as the day advanced, the storm gradually passed away, and Colonel Sir Colin Campbell (who was then in command of the Balaclava Division) paid a visit to our Battery, and seeing the sad state we were in, he sent some men to repair the magazine, and a few more old tents. He asked me if I had seen any movement of the enemy. "Yes," I said, "I have seen the heads of men just behind the sand hills, moving actively about, but only two mounted troopers were to be seen on the hill top, looking out."

Sir Colin then gave me positive orders to defend to the last our Battery in case of attack; and in case of retreat, to spike the guns and roll them down the hill, and blow up the magazine, as he said anxiously to me: "The safety of Balaclava chiefly depends upon your Battery." My dear old friend and countryman! In memory I can see him clearly before me now, as if it were but yesterday. He was always so anxious and considerate for the comfort and well-being of every officer and man serving with him. Ever just and kind in his actions. "Duty and Honour" before all else was his motto. As a man he was loyal and true in his friendship, and most surely one of the finest, bravest soldiers the service has ever known.

Immediately on his leaving our Battery that day, I had the distance to and across the Plain taken, and fuses cut. In this I was greatly assisted by my excellent friend Lieutenant Bradley Roberts, of the Royal Marine Artillery, who went from one battery to the other, doing what he could to help us all, and leaving one of his men with me. Lieutenant Roberts was an able and a popular officer, and was of great assistance in the batteries.

Cases of deadly sickness still haunted us from time to time. Among others my favourite young Drummer was taken ill; I had a great liking for the lad, and we did all we could for him; but we had no medicine, and only a little very bad salt beef and biscuit. He was a Roman Catholic, and a short time before he died he said to me: "Oh, Major dear! Sure I think I could recover if only I had a spoonful of rice!" This we tried our utmost to procure for him, but failed. He used to speak often of his home and his mother, and begged one of his comrades to find her when he was gone, and tell her how he had thought of her, and died for his country. He had a beautiful face, this soldier laddie. I have often since thought of my poor little comrade dying before my eyes from sheer weakness, and want of the very simplest nourishment, that untold wealth could not have procured for him there - dying far from home and friends and country. One day, when the end drew nigh, after lying watching me wistfully for some time, he said: "Major, dear! It's home I'm goin' fast now, an' I've been wantin' to ax yer honour if ye'd read a prayer over me before I'm buried! I reminded him that our religious faith was not the same. "Oh, Major," he replied, "you have been so good and kind to meself and to all of us round you, sure I would so wish your prayer over me." I gave him my promise to do as he asked, and he seemed content, dying peacefully in my arms a short time after. Mindful of my promise, I read the church service over my little comrade, as he rested in one of the few green spots outside the Battery.

I had been much attached to him. He was a fine, bright young lad, a true soldier at heart, and Irish every inch of him. I think we all missed him in our battery, for he was a general favourite.

The case of my poor drummer was only one of many equally sad scenes which occurred in our midst. Brave young lads were stricken unto death before the fighting really had commenced, and we, their comrades, were powerless to help them.

Our hearts ached when we thought of the loved ones at home, who would so soon be mourning the loss of those who had probably been the joy and pride of their lives but whom they would never more see this side of the grave.

CHARGE OF THE LIGHT BRIGADE-BALACLAVA.
No. 3 BATTERY.
From the Diary of Maj.-Gen. S. Fraser.

A very few days sufficed to place the Battery somewhat in order; Sir Cohn Campbell coming each morning to the Battery, a little before the mist rose from the Plain, to see what the enemy was doing, and on one occasion he said to me: "I can assure you, Major, that I would not guarantee the safety of the ships in harbour for 48 hours were it not for my friends the Marines."

The Marines were always great favourites with Sir Colin Campbell; he used to put the utmost faith in their steadiness and gallantry.

At last, one morning, all the bagpipes of the Highland Brigade were heard to play "John Cope," and the cavalry trumpets to sound the "Alarm." The Marines higher up fell in, and the batteries were manned (when all was quiet once more "Highland Mary" was sounded, and then we did not man the trenches). Soon the cause of this was seen. As the mist rose slowly from the Plain, a cloud of Russian cavalry was observed coming round the sand hills and entering the plain, but warily keeping out of gun range of the batteries. As soon as the leading squadrons had rounded the sand hills, they formed up for charging, and at the same time we saw our gallant British Light Brigade at the other end of the plain, formed up to meet the foe.

Short was the word and quick the motion when both divisions advanced to meet each other, and then, like the flash of a great gun, our noble Britishers dashed into the ranks of the enemy, sabre to sabre, red and blue mixed together, and none to help our brave fellows, while we in No 3 Battery looked down upon this awful strife with beating hearts. Officers and men were frantic to be doing something, as they stood by their guns, ready and waiting, in the vain hope that some chance move on the part of the enemy might enable us to render some assistance to our comrades in arms. Every face bore a look of intense anxiety, and I know that to myself, and to each soldier present in our Battery that day, the trial of watching those brave fellows and their noble chargers cut down before our very eyes, while we stood powerless to help them, was terrible. I, for one, can never forget the fearful scene of that wild, mad, and glorious charge through – literally - "the valley of death."

I had to threaten in case of our men firing without orders, for the divisions engaged in the conflict were quite mixed up. At last, however each party began to gather themselves together and retire somewhat, and the Russians, being reinforced, evidently intended again to renew the fight, and now came our time (the distance had been marked off some days before). The Russians had quite overlooked the batteries, and in sweeping round after reforming, they just came neatly within reach of my guns.

"Now is our time, my lads! Do you cover?" I cried. "Yes, sir!" was the quick, hearty reply from my steady Marines. "Then fire from No. 1 gun, and so on" was my next order. Every shot went right into the midst of the enemy. As men and horses rolled over there was evidently great consternation among the Russian cavalry, and with a parting salute from our No. 1 gun, they went to the right about, and with men's breasts to horses' manes, they galloped out of sight round the sand hills. Black night closed this eventful day, and the plain was left to the dead, the dying and the wounded- men and horses - the cries of the latter being pitiful to hear, and thus ended the fatal charge, so renowned in the history of British battles.

The Turks were driven from the sand hills few days before, having little store of ammunition or food, they were shot down and their bodies left on the hillside.

BALACLAVA.
No. 3 BATTERY.
From the Diary of Maj.-Gen. S. Fraser.

The great event of the day, the glorious charge of the Light Brigade, together with the doings of our little Battery in giving our comrades in arms all the assistance we could in their great need, had passed. My senior Lieutenant in the Battery (and a fine bold young fellow he was, an Irishman, and full of "go" and pluck in every respect) had slipped down in the early morning at dawn, and captured a small horse, which had been slightly wounded, and brought him in safely. He gave a sad description of all that he had seen in the plain beneath our Battery, where there were nought around him save the dead or the dying. The wounded horses were still screaming for water, while their riders, a few short hours before, full of strength and courage, and in the vigour of health and manly spirits, now lay dead beside them.

The fatal order, the attack, the gallant charge, all came upon us so suddenly, and with such overwhelming force, followed by the awful and solemn lull in the storm of battle, the cessation of the firing, and the retreat of the enemy, all seemed like some wild, terrible dream, from which we were rudely awakened by the sights and sounds that followed, and the stern realities of the sad end and consequences of the fearful conflict and the events of the day before.

But there was duty to be done, and we all felt the necessity, as well as the benefit, of work at such a time.

Next day joint arrangements were made to bury the dead; and while my men were still flushed and eager for the fray, we set to work with a will to put things in order about the Battery.

The enemy were still in great force behind the sand hills in front of us, having driven the poor Turks right away, with the loss of everything but their lives. Two days afterwards Sir Colin Campbell visited the Battery and highly complimented us for our doings on the famous Balaclava day, and my great friend, the Honourable Major Bollo, his A.D.C., was quite jolly accordingly.

I then showed Sir Colin the defenceless state of the Battery, and that I had nothing but a few old wheelbarrows, which were scattered along the entrance, to help in case of attack. Sir Colin said: "My dear Fraser! I can do nothing for you: I am myself quite powerless!" "Could you not let me have a few Turks, Sir Colin?" I asked. "A few Turks?" he cried, laughing heartily. "Why, you might have the whole lot of them; but they would be useless, for they won't work a stroke!"

"I can but try them, sir," I replied, "and my compliment is small too," I said, "especially for bayonet exercise!"

"Well, Fraser," he answered, as he turned away, laughing, "You are determined, as usual, I see. I will do the best I can for you!"

The second day after the above conversation, 80 convalescent Guardsmen (who had been ill or wounded, and were not yet strong enough for hard work), with two officers, marched in to do duty in the Battery, to my great delight - and good duty men they were. The very first night they were with us, the youngest officer, seeing that I was very much fatigued, insisted on taking a half night watch for me. To this I consented, and at dark I gladly lay down to have a sleep, in which luxury I had not been able to indulge for some nights. My bed was between two rows of empty shell boxes, my sword and pistols lay ready at hand upon the top of one of these boxes; the moonlight was shining through the large rents in my old tent, openings for a plentiful supply of snow, rain and wind, when there was any (and it was only on rare occasions that we were free of one or the other). My new friend and comrade (the young Guardsman) was to call me at two o'clock in the morning.

I had slept until that hour, when I was aroused by a voice at the entrance to my tent, and on looking up I saw, to my astonishment, a tall soldier, appearing taller still in the dim uncertain light, and with his high fur cap and grey greatcoat, and seemingly talking in an unknown language. I had lifted my pistol, and was just about to fire, when I heard the name "Major Fraser," and springing up, I discovered at once that the intruder was my young friend the Guardsman. I was greatly shocked when I thought how nearly he had met his death at my hands. The cause of the mistake, which might have proved fatal for him, was that at times he stammered, or had some impediment in his speech, and had a great difficulty in expressing himself. My Lieutenant at the other end of the Battery could only lift up his hands in horror when the above incident was related to him. After having calmed down a little, and congratulated the Guardsman on his escape, he was just about to leave us, to obtain, if possible, a few hours' rest upon his own comfortless couch, when I saw far down on the plain a bright little flash, which I knew was outside the line of the outlying sentries. I at once ordered a blue light to be fired, and then a second, which fell close to where I had seen the flash, and from their light I distinctly saw men moving away among the brush-wood, but there was no move near the outposts, except that of the guards turning out. Our own men manned the guns, and the Guards lined the ground outside the Battery. We were still anxiously waiting the upshot of all this, when the sound of a horse galloping towards us was heard. The challenge was given and answered, and a mounted officer was seen rapidly approaching the entrance when suddenly a great commotion was observed: the horse had taken fright at seeing the Guards lying on the grass, and the old wheelbarrows piled up above them to help in the defence, and the officer was thrown violently to the ground, being quite unprepared for the sudden movement of his horse. The horse at once made for our lights, and fortunately the officer was only slightly bruised in body, though very much hurt in temper by the accident. He got up quickly and demanded to see the commanding officer. When I appeared he said, somewhat brusquely: "I have been sent by Colonel-------- to know who gave orders to fire the blue lights?"

"Tell your commanding officer," I replied, "that the safety of the Plain has been given over to me by Sir Colin Campbell, and I shall faithfully keep that trust as long as I am able to do so!"

"And pray, sir, may I ask," he next demanded, "what was the necessity for firing the blue lights?"

"For the information of your commanding officer," I answered, "I have to state that lights were seen by myself in the brushwood beyond the outposts, and men were moving about.

"Have you any further information to give me?" he asked.

"None," I replied, and I turned away and left him, wondering in my own mind if his aches and pains from the fall he had received had been the cause of his brusqueness and want of courtesy, or if his exceedingly unpleasant manner was natural to him. Such ways seemed strange at a time when we, comrades in arms, of whatever rank or position, felt more than an ordinary friendliness in our hearts towards each other; we knew not what a day or hour might bring forth; what dangers we might have to face together, or whether we might still be alive to greet our comrades at the dawn of another day.

Early next morning a large party of Turks joined us, bringing with them some old working implements, and after meeting with a kindly reception, both officers and men quietly lay down on the grass outside the battery. It was in vain that I urged the Turkish officers to order their men to commence digging the ditch round the Battery; they only shook their heads and grinned at me. At last the thought struck me of the good service my silver Turkish medal had been to me on more than one occasion, so now, taking it out I went up to the senior officer and held it up before his eyes. No sooner had he seen the Sultan's cipher, than he sprang up, calling loudly to his men, and with his cane began to lay about the heads and shoulders of them all, with the strictest impartiality. A few words from him made them understand, and to work they went.

It was somewhat later in the day, when as usual, Sir Cohn Campbell visited the Battery. When he arrived he held up his hands in astonishment on seeing the Turks working away like good ones. He was still more surprised when I explained the reason and told him of my former use of the Turkish medal.

Sir Colin Campbell then told me that Colonel....... had complained to him of my curt answers given to his messenger, but he had said nothing about the officer's fall, which Sir Colin said, laughing might possibly account for the brusqueness of his manner. Sir Colin also told me that he had explained to the Colonel that I had full power regarding the Plain and all movements thereon. During the next few days many officer visitors came up to see how the poor starved Turks could work, and very soon a good deep ditch was formed, to at least prevent the cavalry enemy from taking us in flank.

Not much was seen of the enemy until, one morning, a group of their officers appeared on a sand hill, just in front of my battery. I had only one shell ready for the distance, the fuse cut by our only Marine Artilleryman; but quietly taking our time, we laid the gun for the group, then fired, and off went the shell, falling in the very midst of them. They did not wait for another, but disappeared entirely. Next day we were informed that a great number of the enemy had crossed the Tchernaye, and our troops occupied the sand hills.

The Turks were very much delighted at the work the one shell had done. They came regularly to receive all the hard biscuit that we could spare at our meals, which was very little, for we were well-nigh starving ourselves.

But I soon had to leave them, being sent in command of a detachment to form an outpost ie outpost (the extreme outpost of the British Army), on the heights of Kamara, to prevent the enemy from creeping in upon our flank.

I think my poor friends the Turks were sorry for my departure, for they left off working, and began talking eagerly to each other; they then came forward and gave the grand salaam, the officers repeating "Bono Anglay! Bono Anglay!

I may here mention that on one occasion, before the above incident, and while I was at the Battery, having heard that a store ship had arrived laiden with good things, sent out from England by our good friends, and others, to be sold to us at a low rate, I left my Lieutenant in charge and slipped down to Balaclava to see what I could pick up.

On my way down I came across two jaunty looking chaps, one having a large turkey and the other a fowl dangling in his hand. "I hope you have left something for us on board," I said in passing. "Oh, you may see for yourself; she is cleared out fore and aft," was the laughing reply; "but go on, the walk will do you no harm," and the young man with the turkey here tossed it up like a football, as he and his companion with the fowl once more started on their way.

As I went along I met a Sergeant with the same badge as that worn by the two men to whom I had just been speaking, so I asked him if he knew them at all; he said that the one was Major and the other Lieutenant of the same regiment. Their uniform had all been worn out, and they were now wearing somewhat singular costumes of blanket pattern.

When I reached the ship, I found that there was nothing to be got in the way of clothing or provisions, so, tired, weary and disappointed I turned towards the town, in order to get, if possible, some warm socks. There I found that instead of a low rate, the sellers were asking double the London prices-they were Jews, Maltese, Greeks, and such like. However, there was nothing for it but to pay the exorbitant price they demanded.

Just then an orderly from Sir Colin Campbell found me out, and told me that the General was anxious to know if I would soon be able to return to the Battery, as he always liked to know that I was there. I could only say: "Tell the General that I shall return at once, as I have purchased my socks, etc." At this remark the orderly smiled and replied, "I will acquaint the General with your answer, sir!" When I returned to the Battery I opened my parcel, being anxious to enjoy the warmth and comfort of my new socks, when, to my consternation, I found that the rascals who had sold them had changed the men's socks I had seen and purchased for small boy's socks. I at once sent for the Provost Sergeant and gave him the parcel and its history. Down he went to the town, recovered my socks at a reduced price, and gave the guilty ones two dozen lashes each, well laid on, afterwards locking them up until the ship was to sail with them in it. There were some very good bargains to be had next day for those who were able to go for them; the Provost Sergeant's punishment to the delinquents of the day before proving a timely warning to the other traders.

THE HEIGHTS OF KAMARA.
From the Diary of Maj.-Gen. S. Fraser.

My duty in the Battery had now come to an end, and I received orders to proceed with my party to join my Battalion on the Heights, as an important move forward was expected the next day. Accordingly, early next morning, our whole Brigade of Royal Marines proceeded on the march to the Heights of Kamara. Our way lay through a perfect field of wild flowers, and fruit trees in full blossom, but not even a bird was to be seen for some time. At last, however, a solitary Russian trooper was seen making off before us, and then another. The advance guard gave them a right and left shot, and two of our mounted officers went off in pursuit; but the Russian soldiers were too clever, and they speedily made their escape, no one knew how.

As we proceeded on our march, we beheld through the opening in the trees the brilliant advance of the combined armies of all classes low down in the plain beneath us. It was a truly grand sight, with the bright morning sun shining upon them as they approached the river, and as our Brigade touched theirs, we formed the right wing of the whole great line.

The Russians, who had re-crossed the river, were drawn up facing our line, with the river between them. All at once the infantry on both sides commenced firing. Some of the Russian regiments, who were closer than was good for them, withstood for some time our heavy fire, but were at last compelled to retire, when their artillery then came to the front, and a fierce combat ensued between their own and ours. They also stood bravely under fire, but like the other Russian regiments, they too gave in, and retreated towards the Mackenzie Heights, leaving their smashed and dismounted guns to their fate. The whole Plain was now free of the enemy, and a wise decision was arrived at by the authorities, not to assault the Mackenzie Heights, which was a most formidable position; tons of rock were ready to be launched upon the heads of any advancing enemy, and hundreds of great guns were posted along, so that thousands of lives would have been lost in any attempt to assault the Heights; besides this fact, the route by which stores and provisions reached Sebastopol was now entirely cut off.

After a tiresome day the Royal Marines re-mounted the hill on their return to camp. On the way I was left with two companies in command of an outpost, at the very extreme point of the whole line of our armies, on the ridge of the hill above Kadikoa, and looking down upon the plain and river. This spot was quite a little amphitheatre, with smooth green turf and young trees growing all round it. We at once threw out sentries, and having found out a well as we came up, parties of our men were in turn sent down to fill their wooden canteens with the fresh cool water. We had no tents or coverings of any description; night was fast creeping on, so each one of us had to look for the best and most comfortable places, and then and there we laid ourselves down to enjoy what rest we could.

The next day was one of hard work. A path had to be cut to the well, and the tents, which had now arrived, to be set up; and we also cut our peep-hole of the Plain a great deal larger, so that we might see what was going on there and the Mackenzie Ridges. In all this my brother officers took a large and willing share, being always cheerful and active through all our time of peril and hardship.

About mid-day my friend and General Sir Colin Campbell (afterwards Lord Clyde) paid us a visit and highly complimented us on what we had done. Luckily there was a fine large stone close to my tent, on which our good old soldier used to sit and smoke his pipe; this stone we used to call the "General's seat," and it was always well cared for. How often I have thought of him since those long years ago, as he sat and smoked and chatted to us, with the grave, anxious, yet kindly expression on his fine face, and with always cheering, courteous words ready for us all. It was little wonder that he was so truly loved and respected both by officers and men who had the honour and privilege of serving under him.

I told him that the enemy were very busy on their own heights, but that not a single man ever came down. The control of the river was a great gain to us, as our cavalry were dreadfully ill of for want of water, the horses were dying in great numbers every day. At a stagnant pool near my old battery a number of troopers could be seen carrying away the bridles and cloths of their horses which had died while attempting to get a drink.

For some time matters remained very quiet, and I took a ride some distance round our outpost. One day I met a very large snow-white dog, which I supposed to be of a half-bred deer or greyhound. When he saw me advancing he stood looking at me, and my horse refused to move a step forward. However, when I spoke to the dog caressingly, his tail began to wag vigorously, and when I waved my hand to him he came right up to me and prostrated himself at my horse's feet. This was enough for me - I am a great lover of horses and dogs so I dismounted and caressed him, and he seemed only too delighted to go with me to our post, and when we arrived there he was admired by all. On the fourth day after I had found my new pet, I required to go into camp, and I left him carefully tied up and in charge of our Assistant Surgeon, who was sharing my tent. When I returned I did not see him, and so asked my companion in the tent where he was. He replied that he did not know. I never saw my beautiful dog again, but I knew that the Assistant Surgeon hated animals of all kinds, and from all I heard, I believe he had let the dog loose and ordered him off. After this I was much delighted when I once more had my tent to myself and the surgeon went to his own, for I grieved very much for the loss of my dog and blamed him as the cause.

I was seldom without visitors at this time, and a number of the French officers frequently came up to have a peep at the English outpost, and in this way the days passed; but it was a time of the greatest anxiety and suspense for us all.

The combined authorities being now in treaty with the Russians, I was ordered to withdraw my party and to rejoin the camp. My poor horse was then suffering from large boils on the back; we had no oats, and the barley we had instead was too heating. Our horses, too, were picketed out in the open, and they suffered greatly, so I never used mine when I could possibly avoid. He knew my tent, and where I was, and when the reveille sounded, and I looked out, he kept dancing on his hind legs and whinnying until I went to him, when he kissed my hand as I caressed him.

In the morning during the time we were in camp the cold was intense, and the poor, faithful creature was a mass of icicles, and little of him to be seen but his bright eyes, always so full of affection for me. He was always standing knee-deep among the snow and slush; but he used to have more than half of my ration of biscuits.

The miserable, only half-roasted coffee killed hundreds of our fine men, of all ranks, for we had no fuel to roast it.

And now, for the first time during many long years of service, I had an ailment, a severe attack of acute rheumatism in my right knee, from which I suffered a great deal, and on the very day Russia capitulated, the Surgeon took me down to the Brigade hospital. He was kind as man could possibly be to myself and to everyone under his care.

The Sardinians and Turks were dying in great numbers. After a few days, with warm covering and a roof over my head (of which I soon began to feel the comfort) I was sent on board a transport which was just about to sail for Constantinople; another officer, also an invalid, came on board at the same time.

Immediately on our arrival at Constantinople we were put into good quarters, but in different localities. My room, which was large and beautifully painted all over, had been occupied by some of the Turkish ladies, and vacated for the sick English officers. We enjoyed luxurious comfort and good food now, and the doctors were most kind and attentive. In a short time my invalid brother officer and I had greatly improved in health, but the doctor thought there was no use in sending us back to camp, so we were sent home by a company's ship and joyfully received by our relatives in old England and Scotland.

I could not, unfortunately, bring my beautiful horse with me, and so it was given to the doctor at the Marine Hospital when I left. Neither horse nor master have I ever seen since, but I grieved sincerely at parting with my faithful horse, and losing my loving dog, my companions through days of peril and hardship. I had many stories to tell of my four-footed friends to the dear ones around our fireside at home.

BOMARSUND, 1854

Extracts from the Diary of Colonel (then Lieut.) E. C. L. Durnford, R.M.A.

Lieutenant Durnford appears to have left Portsmouth on 3rd January, 1854, and joined the screw line-of-battleship *James Watt* on 2nd Feb. – where he does not say. The first entry in his diary seems to have been made on the 31st July, following when he records that "General Baraguay d'Hilliers arrived in the *Reine Hortense*. Had a visit in the afternoon from a Swedish family, 2 men, 2 women and a boy. They seemed pleased with the ship.

August 1. - General d'Hilliers and a large staff went up to Bomarsund in the *Reine Hortense*. Sent letters via Dantzig home. Russian deserters state that its force consists of 1,700 men - 500 riflemen.

August 2. - More troops arrived.

August 3. - No symptoms of a move yet.

August 4. - A battery of four guns to go. I am one of the officers.

August 5. - More troops, etc., arrived. Former arrangements knocked over. The battery not to go. Disgusting.

August 6. - I go up with Hamley, which is rather a consolation.

August 7. - Started for Bomarsund in the *Driver* at 3 p.m. Anchored to the N.N.E. of the Fort ready for landing in the morning. Lay down in the quietest corner I could find, in the endeavour of obtaining a few hours sleep, which was rather a failure.

August 8. - Got under arms at 2 a.m. and by 3 had landed. The Marines immediately advanced, I remaining with the Co. of Marine Artillery to which I was attached till 12 noon, waiting for rockets, which were in the *Julia* transport. When she came in found that the tubes were for sea service, so our wait was for nothing. Rejoined main body about 2, and shortly after the whole moved on to about 1,000 yards from Fort Tzee, where we encamped; in a measure protected from the fire of the fort by a ridge. Very busy all the evening constructing a wigwam.

August 9. - Reveille sounded at 2 ½ a.m. Remained under arms about an hour, then lay down again till 7. First shot fired at us to-day. Pitched in potato field which adjoins the camp, and some of the case fell in camp - the shot were about 1lb. The field at the time was full of men digging potatoes; fortunately no one was hurt. A round shot was also fired; passed over. Busy re-building our wigwam.

August 10. - Fort Tzee fired a couple of shot at us about noon. About one assisted in catching about a dozen horses close to fort, but under cover of a low ridge. Went on outlying picket at 8 p.m. When posting sentries at 9 ½, enemy opened upon us with rifles, shot whizzing by unpleasantly close. Then amused themselves for an hour or so firing grape and round shot; made a great deal of noise, but did no execution. On my legs the whole night visiting and posting sentries, as we of course might expect an attack at any moment. Got into camp at 5 a.m.

August 11. - Nothing particular occurred during the day except a few shot at us. Marched off on outlying picket at 9 p.m. Posted at Picket House under Capt. Clavell with 100 men. Everything quiet till about midnight when suddenly we heard an outcry, accompanied by a tremendous volley of musketry; the Fort immediately opened a tremendous fire of round, grape and case, firing in all directions. We, of course, thought the Russians had made a sortie, and got under arms. Almost the first shot was a case; we heard the balls pattering on the rocks and then they came about our ears, fortunately hurting no one. An uninterrupted shower of round, etc., was whirring about for an hour or so, rather too near to be pleasant. Most fortunately not a man on our side was touched, though we had 300 of the pills. The cause of the rumpus was, we afterwards heard, a Lieutenant of Chasseurs was shot, immediately the whole battalion rushed forward and let fly right into the Fort. Of course, the Fort thought we were going to storm, and acted accordingly. A dropping fire of rifles was kept up all night. Got into camp at 7 a.m.

August 12. - Pretty quiet today - filling sandbags, etc. A good deal of shot and shell over and near the camp.

August 13. (Sunday). - French batteries opened fire at 4 a.m., to which the Fort immediately replied, and the main work peppered at them with shot and shell like fun. Most of the shot went over them and came into disagreeable proximity to us. Tzee also peppered us pretty considerably. Whilst half a dozen of us were at breakfast a round shot pitched a dozen yards off, exactly in line with us, and hopped over our heads, not many inches to spare, and whilst I was walking with Ward, close to camp, a large piece of shot or shell cut a branch of a tree off close over our reads. Fort Tzee hoisted a flag of truce about 5p.m. We all immediately rushed close up to the Fort. They wished for two hours to bury their dead. The French General said he would give them one hour to surrender - they refused; so double quick back again. French battery opened fire again; Fort ditto. Own battery nearly finished. (French, 3 brass siege 18-pdrs., 4 brass 10-in. mortars).

August 14. - Garrison endeavoured to escape, but most were made prisoners, the Commandant being severely wounded defending the Fort. Killed and escaped 79 (mostly killed), wounded 17, prisoners 49. A report spread that 50 Russians had been found headed up in casks, as they had no means of burying them. Busily employed all day reforming our battery to bear on Fort Nottick and getting the guns up. This was a good deal annoyed by the fire of the forts. A marine shot through the chest by an 18-pounder - of course, killed instantaneously. I was about 5 yards from him at the time; he was lying on his face asleep.

August 15. - Our battery opened at 10 minutes past 8 a.m. Battery consisting of three 32-

pdrs. of 45 cwt., distant about 900 yards from the fort. There were also four 12-pdr. howitzers, though they were of very little use. Forts Nottich and Prasto, as well as the main work, kept up an uninterrupted fire of shot and shell, most of which just cleared the battery and came over and into the camp. All the men ordered to leave the camp and get under cover behind the rocks. About 1 p.m. went in charge of a fatigue party to carry sandbags to the battery, our road lying through the valley, which was ploughed up by the perpetual fire of round shot, was not very agreeable for promenading. Got into the battery all right, after having to go along the brow of the hill only about 100 yards. Fortunately a man in the battery sang out "Down!" pretty loud when he saw a shot fired thereby giving us time to lie down. Just as I got to the battery, poor Wrottsley of the Engineers was carried out (to go to the *Belleisle*, hospital ship), mortally wounded by a cannon ball, which hit him after striking and breaking off one of the trunnions of a gun it hit him at about the left (I think) hip and took off some of the fingers of that hand. Poor fellow, he died just as he reached the ship. He was with us about an hour before he was wounded, under the cover of a large rock, little thinking how soon his death wound would be given. King [1] not wanting any more sandbags I returned to the sandpit with my men to wait for orders.

Was there about half an hour when I received a message that the General wanted to see me, I went to his tent and was much pleased when he offered me the post of Assistant Engineer.

Got into the battery again at half past three. Ord, the Brigade Major R.E., up there in charge of the battery, immediately set me to work to rebuild the embrasures and repair parapet; in the meantime he repaired a platform and replaced the damaged gun.

Mawby up with the Marine Artillery, Poore and Hewett his subs.

Opened fire again on the Fort, which was very soon silenced, though they showed great perseverance; when an embrasure was choked up with rubbish, etc. they would clear it away and go at it again. Mawbey's *broadsides* soon settled them.

By 5 a breach was made practicable by 5.4, so we tried the range of Prasto. The first shot fell about 200 yards short, the second a little short, and the third hit the tower between two of the upper embrasures. That point being settled we again turned our attention to Nottich, and a few minutes before six they hung out a flag of truce. I was despatched to inform the General, and posted back to send Ord down with 100 Marines to take possession. They got down there about dusk, and were so long there that we got alarmed. However, at last they made their appearance with 130 prisoners, the Russians having lost about 25 killed and wounded. This was about midnight.

I remained in the battery till 3 a.m., when returned to camp, the Russians shortly afterward being marched off to the ships. The Russian Commandant when passing the battery the night before, on being shewn the three guns, asked where the *rest* were?

August 16. - The *Leopard* and a couple of the paddle steamers engaged Prasto Fort, and were beaten off, having done very little damage to it-their firing execrable, about five shots out of 100 going near it. They managed to disable one gun, which was under the roof, perfectly unprotected, but did not injure the Fort in the least. A 10-in. gun, which had been landed at the Mud battery, kept up a fire, which only punched a few holes in the roof and knocked a few chimneys down, but not doing any real damage to the Fort.

Fort hung out a flag of truce about 1 p.m. and surrendered unconditionally. All the troops marched down and formed. About 3 the prisoners, about 2,000 in number, were marched out, taking with them what they liked to carry; many of them were drunk.

Went into the fort with King. The place stunk horridly. We found the spirit store open and floating with liquor. Found a few Russians lying about dead drunk, whom the French most unnecessarily prodded up with their bayonets. We found a Russian lying in a dark casemate alongside a gun platform and called in a French sentry. The man had a dark lantern strapped round his waist, and the Frenchman would have bayonetted him (suspecting him of intending to fire the magazine), but we stopped him. The Russian was made prisoner, and said to have been tried by drum-head court-martial and shot.

August 17. - Busy all day surveying. Marines left the camp and returned to Led Sound.

August 18. - Marine Artillery and Marines of Block Ships left.

August 19. - Embarked with Company of Sappers on board the *Julia*, transport. Pretty comfortable there, good grub, etc.

August 20. (Sunday). - At work all day.

August 21. - Sent a line home.

August 22 to 26. - Hard at work, leaving the *Julia* about 8 a.m. and returning at 6 p.m.

Sunday 27 (Sunday). - Went to Prasto. Counted about 40 shot marks, only one entered an embrasure.

August 28 & 29. - Busy with plans of ground.

August 30. - Prasto blown up by the French. Most effectively done.

August 31. - Nottich blown up.

Sept 1. - Small Russian steamer came in under flag of truce.

Sept 2. - Embarked with Sappers on board *Ajax* from *Julia*. French nearly all embarked in the various transports. Dined with Capt. Warden, Sir Charles Napier there, his flag flying in *Ajax*. At 7 p.m. the Main Fort was blown up. *Beautiful*; Fort burnt all night, one blaze of fire. Guns and shells continually going off. Lay awake in my cot nearly all night admiring it.

Sept 3 (Sunday) and 4. - Mined and charged six mines in a casemate of brickwork. Fired them in the afternoon. King nearly *expended*, the two nearest mines exploding when he was only about 15 yards off, owing to defective portfire.

Sept 5. - Nearly completed all mines in brickwork. Fired a mine under Chapel of Main Work.

Sept 6. to 13. - Hard at work destroying all the foundations (principally by mining) and then cut granite by fire.

Sept. 14.. - Went on shore early to make a sketch of the effect of a charge fired under outside wall of Chapel in Main Work. It had a most extraordinary effect, blowing all the stone out in form of an arch and leaving, the brick. Steamed from Bomarsund and arrived at Led Sund about 7 p.m.

Sept. 15. - Went on board *Duke*[2] at 8 ½ a.m. and saw General Jones, who kindly gave me a letter expressing his satisfaction at my services. Rejoined my own ship at 2 p.m. All the old fellows seemed very glad to see me, and in truth I was delighted to see them all again and to get back to the old craft.

Sept. 18. - Blowing hard, so did not sail.

Sept. 19. - Got under weigh at 8 ½ a.m. When a couple of miles out signal made to return as it was getting thick. The French squadron, however, kept on, being homeward bound.

Sept. 20. - Got under weigh at 8 a.m., under steam all day, steering for Nagu.

Sept. 21. - Arrived at Nagu and rejoined the other squadron at 3 p.m. about six miles from Revel.

Sept. 22. - *Locust* and *Wrangler* went in with the Admiral and General to have a look.

Sept. 23. - Admiral went to have a look at Helsingfors - found them throwing up earthworks.

Sept. 24. - Sunday.

Sept. 25. - Received letters from home

Sept. 26 (Tuesday). - Despatched letter home.

Sept. 27 (Wednesday). - Weather Division (the sailing ships) sailed for England. We have remaining 12 sail-of-the-line and three fine screw frigates, besides smaller craft - quite enough to tackle the Russian 26 liners if they dare to show their noses.

Oct. 4, 5, 6. - Blowing a gale of wind.

Oct. 9. - Still blowing fresh.

Oct. 11. - *Bulldog* arrived from Dantzic.

Oct. 12. - Went on shore at Nagu.

Oct. 19 (Thursday). - Got under weigh about 7 ½ a.m.-Rendezvous off Kiel.

Oct. 20. - Wind foul. Blowing very fresh. Boiler burst.

Oct. 21 22. - More moderate.

Oct. 23. - Very strong wind blowing from the west. Ran in under the lee of Bornholm and anchored about three miles off the shore.

NOTES.

1 This Officer's name was not mentioned in Landing State. (Possibly a Naval Officer.)

2 'The Duke of Wellington'

THE BATTALION AT BOMARSUND
LANDING STATE, 8TH AUGUST, 1854

	Col.	Major	Capts.	Lieuts.	Sergts.	Corpls.	Bombrs	Drums	Gnrs	Ptes
Staff	1	1	2	2						
8 Coys			7	15	18	20	1	7	70	541

TOTAL STRENGTH OF BATTALION – 685

OFFICERS LANDED   R.M.L.I.

Colonel Fortescue Graham A.D.C.

Field Officers: Major P.B. Nolloth

Captain W.M. Heriot

Brigade Major: Capt. W.C.P. Elliott

Adjutant: Lieut O.F.C. Fraser

Orderly Officer: Lieut. Jno. M. Lennox

1st Parade Co: Capt. C.O. Hamley
Lieut. H.L. Evans
Lieut. W.R. Jeffreys

2nd Parade Co: Capt. R.K. Clavell
Lieut.W.F.P. Dadson

3rdParade Co: Actg.Capt.Lieut. Geo Naylor
Lieut. I.F. Sanders

4th Parade Co: Captain W.L. Sayer
Lieut. Thos. Bent

5th Parade Co: Capt.H.E. Delacombe
Lieut. Alex. Tait

COMPANY OFFICERS.

R.M.A. – Lieut. H.W. Mawbey
Lieut Wm. Sanders
Lieut. John Poore
Lieut. Henry Hewett
Lieut. Joshua R. Brookes
Lieut. E.C.L. Durnford (Acting Engineer)

6th Parade Co: Capt. R.J. McKillop
7th Parade Co: Capt.Thos.D. Fosbroke
8th Parade Co: Capt. Jno Elliott
                     Lieut.R.W.Bland Hunt
                     Lieut. J.P. Murray

From "*History of the Baltic Campaign.*"

THE BOMBARDMENT OF SWEABORG, 1855.

The following interesting account of the operations of the Mortar Boats from which the bombardment was carried on by the Royal Marine Artillery under the direction of its own officers is from a letter written by Captain Weymss, of that Corps, then serving on board the *Duke of Wellington*, and senior officer in charge of the R.M.A. attached to the Mortar Boats. The letter begins: "My dear Adair",- and is presumably addressed to a member of that family, then also serving in the Royal Marine Artillery.

Captain Weymss encloses copies of the orders issued by the Commander-in-Chief which it is advisable to read before going on to the letter itself. A striking point in his description of the operations is the light it throws on the primitive and defective armament and methods of those days, which judging from the fact that the best mortar seems to have been cast as far back as 1813, seem to have retrograded rather than advanced since the days of Nelson and Wellington.

A contemporary picture of the bombardment by the Mortar Boats is in the Officers' Mess at Eastney, and has been reproduced on a very small scale on the plate facing page 88, Vol. II. of "Britain's Sea Soldiers."

"*Duke of Wellington.*"
June 28th 1855.

STANDING ORDER No. 13.
The undermentioned ships are to have attached to them as tenders the Mortar Vessels severally expressed against their names, and each ship is to bear as supernumeraries the Warrant Officers in charge of stores on board her Mortar Vessel, and such Royal Marine Artillery as may be sent to her from my Flagship, as part of the crew of such vessels, observing that such Mortar Vessel is to be manned in other respects by the ship to which she is attached according to the following scheme.

(Signed) R. S. DUNDAS,
R. Adl. and C.-in-Chief.

To the respective
Flag Officers, etc.
The Complement of Mortar Vessels.
1 Warrant Officer in charge of stores.
3 steady good Seamen;

5 ordinary Seamen.
2 Boys, 1st class;
1 Boy, 2nd class.
1 Sergt.,
1 Corpl. or Bmr. Royal Marine Art'y.
6 Marines.

Then follow the names of 16 Line-of-Battle Ships and their respective Mortar Boats.

H.M.S."*Duke of Wellington.*"
28th June, 1855.

STANDING ORDER No. 14.

With reference to my Standing Order No. 13 of that date, it is my direction that a Subaltern Officer of the Royal Marine Artillery be borne on the supernumerary list of the undermentioned ships under my command for every two Mortar Vessels, and a Captain in each of the ships named in the margin in every six Mortar Vessels, and whenever the Mortar vessels may be engaged, the whole firing is to be directed by the senior Captain of Marine Artillery present, who is to have a boat placed at his disposal by the ship to which he may be attached for the purpose of visiting the different ships and giving orders as to the charge and length of fuse to be used.

Duke of Wellington
Exmouth
Royal George

(Signed) R. S. DUNDAS,
R. Adl. and C.-in-Chief.

The respective
Flag Officers, etc.

Subalterns R.M.A. to go to the following ships : *Nile, Collossus, Edinburg, Majestic, Orion, Cressy, James Watt, Caesar*

Memorandum.
"*Duke of Wellington,*"
Nargan (?)
20th July, 1855.

The Commander-in-Chief has issued the following Regulations with reference to his Standing Order of 28th June last regarding the Mortar Boats :-

(1) The Mortar Boats are divided into two Divisions, commanded by Messrs. (?) Blane and Howarth, the whole being under the command of Lieutenant Hobart, senior lieutenant of the *Duke of Wellington*.

(2) The working of the Mortar Boats in action being under the direction of the Royal Marine Artillery; the officers in command of these vessels are to comply with the requisition of the Artillery Officer or Non-commissioned Officer in charge, and they are to be careful that every necessary arrangement is made to keep the vessels efficient and ready for service. Anchors, cables, fire-hoses and every article of equipment to be in readiness for use, and the vessel to be kept clean and orderly.

(3) The Officers in charge are to assist the Artillery Officer in every way, and to consult them, more particularly the Captains of Divisions and the Captain of Marine Artillery commanding, as to alterations or wants of the different vessels, and in action they are to see all ready for increasing or decreasing their distance as may be required.

(4) Captain Weymss, R.M.A., will command the Marine Artillery attached to the Mortar Boats.

(5) A Captain and 4 Subalterns are allotted to each Division; they will take up their quarters on board the vessels against which their names are placed.

(6) Divisional Captains are to make their reports and receive orders from Captain commanding or senior officer of Royal Marine Artillery present.

1ST DIVISION.		2ND DIVISION.	
Redbreast	Capt. Lawrence	*Prompt*	Capt. Schomberg
Beacon	Lieut. Halliday	*Porpoise*	Lieut. Woolcombe
Grappler	Lieut. Horsay	*Rocket*	Lieut. Searle
Carron			
Havoc	Lieut. Brydges	*Drake*	
Growler	Mr. Blanc (Mate)	*Surly*	Lieut. Ansell
Manly		*Blazer*	Mr. Howarth (Mate)
Mastiff	Lieut. Durnford	*Pickle*	Lieut. Wriford

By Command of Commander-in-Chief,
(Signed) F. P. PELHAM,
Captain of the Fleet.

To respective Flag Officers,
Captains, etc.

THE BOMBARDMENT OF SWEABORG.

"It has been a great week for the Marine Artillery, at least if the same idea strikes people at home as has struck the Admiral and the officers of the Squadron. I wish you to send this letter to the Commanding Officer, who I conclude is Colonel Parke, and also send it to Colonel Dwyer, who will like to hear of our men in the Baltic. Shew it also to all our officers - the subject must be interesting though the writing may be bad. I will omit such details as you will have seen in the dispatches, and confine myself to the part our people played, which, I am happy to say, was very considerable in proportion to the mischief done.

I have told you already that the whole direction of the Mortars was placed in our hands.

We arrived at Sweaborg on Monday the 6th. The weather was at first bad, but on Tuesday we got into an outer line, forming a curve round the front of Sweaborg, whence we could easily haul into action.

I took up my abode on that day on board Wriford's boat, the *Pickle*, intending to fire the first shell from her to try the range. On Wednesday we remained there waiting for the French and at half past 1 on Thursday morning we began to haul into the line we were to take up in action. At 5 o'clock we were all ready, and remained so until half past 7, when an officer in a gunboat came to me on board and communicated the Admiral's order to commence.

No shot had been fired when *Pickle* sent up her first shell with 17 lbs. of powder. It fell into the centre of the store-houses we were directed to burn - between the church and Citadel.

Then Lawrence and Schomberg, with whom I had arranged beforehand, sent up a shell each from *Redbreast* and *Prompt*, both telling well. The French then took it up and the fire was kept up with great vigour. In five hours the town was on fire in many places. Three magazines blew up - the effect of one was like a volcano, lasting minutes.

Our officers and men behaved admirably, the men declining to be relieved, though I had organised relief for them out of the Marine Artillery of the Squadron. I must consult Lawrence and Schomberg before I mention names of N.C. officers and Gunners - in fact it would be difficult to select.

In the evening of the first day *Pickle's* mortar burst into two equal parts through the vent, the chamber being gullied. We had just begun to run zinc into the cavities thus formed-which usually came out after some 15 or 20 rounds had been fired. Our 13-in. mortars are very defective, in shape and materials, the iron being very bad, and the vent, I think, in a wrong direction.

The *Pickle's* stood only 114 rounds, averaging 17 lbs. *Growler* (slung) 360, and burst, her slinging apparatus remaining intact.

Havoc, *Surly* and *Drake* gave in more or less with their swinging gear, owing to the bolts supporting the muzzle band drawing, but they held out till the last, and I should fall back on them were further action required.

The whole number of rounds was 3,140, including 19 carcases - perhaps more - certainly not less.

In the evening of Thursday the conflagration was considerable, and the sight was very picturesque, the shells flaming in their beautiful curves, and many of the French ones falling or bursting short. The two hours' rocket amusement putting one in mind of the Surrey Zoological and the blazing town altogether made a wonderful addition to the starlight night.

On Friday we continued the bombardment; more of the town caught fire - dock, arsenal, building slips - and I never saw such a terrific appearance as was presented at midnight. I was then going round with Schomberg, and heard that two more mortars had burst and several more were dangerous, the zinc having come out of the holes.

I therefore went on board the *Duke* to ask the Admiral for orders and acquaint him that the mortars would not hold out for another day's bombardment. He said he wished the firing to be kept up during the night, as the French had landed guns on an island, and he did not wish to appear to desert them. So I kept up a fire from certain mortars, and at half past 4 on Saturday morning, the enemy's fire having long ceased, a signal was made to cease firing.

The next day - or rather that day - I surveyed the mortars, in company with Captains Ramsay and Schomberg, in order to report to the Admiral. He is greatly pleased with the effect.

Two Indian Officers, who had served lately at Sebastopol, laughed at the idea of our doing anything, but now they confess themselves wrong, and say the result is beyond anything they ever witnessed or could have conceived. Nugent of the Engineers the same.

We remained all Saturday within range of the enemy's guns, and hauled off early on Sunday morning.

The Russian artillery was annoying to us floating magazines, but as the effort of a fortress of the renown of Sweaborg, the effect was puerile.

A handsomely worded order has been issued in which our people are especially mentioned, and on Sunday evening the Admiral called me to his cabin and directed me to express personally to the officers the sense he had of their zeal, and his opinion of the great destruction we had caused.

My opinion had been all along that the effect of our shells would be terrible and the enemy's fire weak, but it was an anxious moment for me while we lay for three hours under those great batteries - failure would have been so fearful a disaster to us all. I soon, however, saw that we had the ascendency - the rapidity and extreme accuracy of our fire preventing them from putting out the conflagration, and increasing the combustion by the numerous fires we lighted.

This contest, in which we have gained so great an advantage on such easy terms, will produce more important results than the mere burning of Sweaborg - it proves that vertical fire is irresistible, and that we can do the same with most other seaports of the enemy.

The *Growler's* mortar, which fired 360 rounds, was almost the only one cast in 1813, the rest, for the most part, being cast in /54, a significant fact. It burst with 18 ½ lbs. of powder, the others with 16 ½ or 16. Our distance from the batteries was 3,250 yards."

EXPERIENCES OF AN OLD ROYAL MARINE IN NEW ZEALAND.
(Reprinted from the Globe & Laurel of 1st Jan, 1893.)

Corporal R. J. Coulter has sent us the following interesting account of his services prior to joining the Corps. He writes: -

I am 50 years of age, and have been connected with H.M. Service for a period of 33 years, and am at present serving as a N.C. Officer in the Chatham Division of Royal Marines. I am an Australian, Sydney, New South Wales, being my place of birth, and the residence of my parents, relatives and friends, and I commenced my military career on the establishment and enrolment of the Sydney Volunteer Corps in 1859, doing garrison and other duties when required, in the absence of the regular forces.

On the breaking out of the war in New Zealand in 1863 we were at once called to perform active service, as the military forces were under orders for New Zealand. Volunteers were at once enrolled to proceed to the seat of war.

A Colonial Military Staff was appointed by the New Zealand Government to select both Officers, N.C. officers and men, fully qualified and found medically fit for military service, a representative being chosen for each colony to raise the required number.

New South Wales was the first to come boldly and openly to the front, and the committee of selection was appointed, viz.: - Colonel Hamilton, Colonel Richardson, Capt. and Adjt. Lavers, H.M. 12th Foot, assisted by Qr. - Mr. General Harrison, representing the New Zealand Government, the whole being under the immediate supervision of the Brigadier-General Commanding viz., Colonel Pitt, H.M. 40th Foot, Commanding the Regular Forces in Australia.

As the enrolment and medical examination of Officers and men proceeded, sailing and other ships were at once chartered by the government to convey those selected for active service from Sydney to Auckland.

The first detachment of Colonial troops for the seat of war, viz., 250 N.C. officers and men, left on the 23rd August, 1863, and your humble servant was selected by the Board of Examiners to take command of this detachment, stores, etc., obtaining a commission as Ensign out of a list of 122 candidates (military and civil) this being the first given to Volunteer Officers of the Colonial Volunteer Forces for the seat of war.

On arriving in Auckland on the 30th August, 1863, many thousands were awaiting our landing on the pier, as no military aid had yet reached their shores from England or India, ships being daily expected with reinforcements. Proceeding to barracks I reported myself to Colonel Kenny, Deputy – Adjutant -General. I returned on board, landed our men and marched to the barracks, or camp, for inspection. Other detachments were arriving, and from the numbers the first four Colonial Regiments were completed up to 1,000 strong, Officers, N.C. officers and men, bearing the distinction of the 1st, 2nd, 3rd and 4th Waikato Militia. We were at once attached to the regular forces, the whole being under the command of Major-General Galloway, H.M. 70th Foot, Auckland District. As we settled down into military and camp life, detachments were sent to the front to relieve the military. I proceeded with our company, 120 strong, under the command of Captain Drury, to St. John's Redoubt, a distance of 40 miles from Auckland, relieving a like number of the 18th Royal Irish.

Shortly afterwards the campaign gradually got warmer, The Maories had come down in large numbers, and behaved in a cruel and barbarous way to many of the old European settlers who had not left their homes, although they had often been warned to do so by the civil and military authorities. This being the case, and daily and hourly massacres taking place through the tomahawk and scalping-knife of the savage, the General Officer Commanding, viz., Major-General Cameron, gave orders for a Flying Column to be at once formed to stop their depredations. The Right Wing was under the command of Major Rutherford, H.M. 70th Foot, who had at his disposal detachments of the 70th, 18th, 65th and 14th Regiments, and half of my own company, assisted by 40 men of the Forest Rangers, under Captain Jackson. I was specially selected by Colonel Haultain, who commanded our Regiment, as the Subaltern to accompany the column and represent our Corps, receiving 5s. a day in addition to my regimental pay, making it 13s. 7d. per diem for this special duty.

Major Ryan, H.M. 70th Foot, had command of the Left Wing, composed of detachments of the 40th, 43rd, 70th and 12th Regiments, and Capt. Drury with the other half of our company, together with a like number of Forest Rangers under Major Von Tempsky, well known to all during the whole of the campaign. This gallant officer was subsequently killed in action, leading his fighting bushmen. Commencing our heavy work with the aid of guides, we drove the Maories back, stormed, burnt and destroyed their villages, killed a great many in the performance of our duty, made forced marches by day and night, penetrated unknown parts to take them by surprise, until we had completely driven them well in advance of the main body, so that the General could commence hostilities. The Maories at once flew back to the Waikato country, and erected formidable pahs or strongholds, we continuing to advance upon them to find out their whereabout, and engage and drive them from their positions. The last engagement took place on the 31st March, 1865, at Orakan, part of my company being attached to a body of 800 officers, N.C. officers and men, told off to drive the enemy out of this important and well-fortified stronghold. The whole of the attacking force was under the command of Brigadier-General Carey, he having, as chief of his staff, Captain and Brevet-Major Baker, 18th Royal Irish (now D.A.Q.M.G. on the Staff of H.R.H. Duke of Cambridge).

On the attacking force arriving at our redoubt, viz., Kihi-Kihi, at 2 a.m., they halted, and our Colonel had to tell off from our number 2 officers and 50 men to go with them and form part of the advance guard and storming party. I was at once ordered to go, and my men were joined in with the 200 selected to storm the position, this small body being under the command of Major Ring, 18th Royal Irish, composed of the 18th, 65th, 12th Regiments and our detachment, with a small number of the Forest Rangers, under Major Von Tempsky. When we found out the enemy's position, Major Ring led us into action, and advancing in extended order, under heavy fire, called upon us to charge; we fixed bayonets and entered their position to drive them out, but our gallant Major was the first to fall, receiving a gunshot wound in the right thigh, dying shortly afterwards. Major Baker at once came amongst us and volunteered to take his place, but the enemy being too strong in numbers for our small storming party, we at once retired under cover, until the main body had surrounded the enemy, when we commenced at a distance of about 100 yards from their position to throw up a flying sap and worked up to their pah. By the use of hand grenades and a 12-pounder at the head of the sap we soon began to make it very hot for them inside, and rather than remain they broke out in rear. On the afternoon of the 3rd day, many, I am sorry to say (as they were called upon to surrender) were killed and wounded by the heavy fire from our rifles when they were making their escape through the swamp.

This being over, brought about the termination of the Waikato Campaign, William Thompson, or in their native tongue, Wiremu Tamahina - their fighting chief and ringleader - came in with many of his well-known chiefs and followers, and surrendered to Sir George Gray, the Governor. The Imperial Troops were shortly afterwards withdrawn from the colony, and the Colonial Regiments settled upon the land in the several districts set apart for their location. Towns were laid out, buildings erected, transport by land and water increased, and I suppose to-day, what with the increase of population and the rapid stride that the colony has made during the past 26 years, many of the small townships formed during my time have considerably enlarged, and now not being built of wood, are of brick and stone.

Leaving New Zealand in the month of Sept., 1866, when peace was fully proclaimed, I finished my colonial military career, and after an absence from military life, found myself in England, having had four years of Civil Service duty in India, through the Bombay Presidency. Inclined again to take a part in H.M. Service I joined our noble and gallant Corps on the 15th January,

1873, and am now entering upon my 21st year of service.

ASHANTEE, 1873.
By Major Moore, R.M.A.

In July 1873 orders were received at Eastney for 1 Captain, 1 Sub and 50 men to embark the following day at 2 p.m. in H.M.S. *Simoom*, for Cape Coast Castle.

On embarking we found 150 Infantry were coming also, some of which we took in at Plymouth - the officers were Capts. Crease, R.M.A., Alnutt, R.M.L.I., Lieuts. Cray, Hearle, Stephens, R.M.L.I., and myself. The ship was full up with stores and provisions for the West Coast, and the men hadn't room to sling their hammocks. The voyage in the hot weather in the Tropics was most trying, the whole of the troop deck being occupied with provisions, and only a narrow passage being left, which at night was almost impassable from the hammocks slung overhead and the men lying on the deck. The officers going the rounds having to creep over the latter and under the former. On arrival at Cape Coast Castle we found that the detachment embarked about two months previously under Col. Festing had been invalided, only 3 officers, viz., Col. Festing, Capt. Despard and Lieut. Allen, and 3 or 4 men left.

The action at Elmina had been fought, and the Ashantees had been driven from the immediate vicinity of Cape Coast Castle. Their exact whereabouts was not known, and owing to this uncertainty, and the preparations for an advance taking some time, no movement was made till information arrived that Sir Garnet Wolsley had been appointed Governor and C. in Chief of the Gold Coast. The contemplated advance was then postponed till his arrival. Immediately on that taking, place, Col. Festing, who had been in command, was ordered to command the advanced post at Dunquah, and an expedition under Col. Wood (afterwards Sir Evelyn Wood) was organised to attack some disaffected villages some 8 or 9 miles from Elmina. The Barracouta was ordered to take the *Simoom's* Marines from Cape Coast Castle to Elmina, and they were landed at daylight with a rocket contingent of bluejackets; there was also a rocket manned by Houssas under Lieut. Allen R.M.A.. The Marine officers on this occasion were Capts. Crease, Allnut, Lieut. Gray and myself - the other two Subalterns having been sent up country to train native levies. 150 Marines, Artillery and Infantry, formed the main body, and there were some natives acting as advance and rear guards. About 9.30 a.m. we arrived at Essaman, when an attack was immediately made on the village. The natives kept firing into the bush on either side of the narrow path, but would not advance so the Marines were ordered to do so. This they did under a fire from all sides, apparently, in my opinion, coming principally from our own native levies. We entered the village and found everyone had cleared out. Several native levies, 2 officers (Col. McNeil and Capt. Fremantle) and 1 marine were wounded. After resting for a time the wounded were put in hammocks and we marched on to another village, which had been previously bombarded from the sea, and we found deserted. We returned to Elmina after a most fatiguing day at about 8 p.m. and were eventually conveyed to *Simoom*. As our destination was kept secret and no orders about provisions to be taken having been received, nobody had anything to eat but a little ship biscuit for 24 hours. As we had been on board for four months in a debilitating climate, such a strain naturally told on the men, and there was a considerable sick list on the following day. A week or so after this we were again landed, and formed the principal part of an expedition destined, I believe, to attack the Ashantee Army, in conjunction with Col. Festing's force at Dunquah. Owing, however, to our advance not being properly timed, or else some misapprehension of the orders on Col. Festing's part, we didn't meet at the place appointed - a small village some 18 miles from the coast - so after waiting an hour or two we marched back to Alrakrampa, whence we had started in the morning. Alrakrampa had been roughly fortified and a clearance made all round the village of about 100 yards. It being situated in the midst of thick bush, made the latter work imperative, and which saved the village when attacked by the Ashantees later on. This work had been done by natives working under some special service officers. The march from Alrakrampa and back was made with the greatest precaution though the path being only a foot wide and the bush impenetrable on either side to any but a native, no precaution except silence seemed of any good. The Ashantees were believed to be all round us on this occasion, but nobody saw one, except a Marine Artilleryman who said he did, and promptly fired his rifle, for which he was severely reprimanded by the General.

We got back to the ship on the fifth day, again much fatigued, as, being the only white troops, all outposts at the halt and picquets by night and day in camp had to be found by the Marines. Capt. Allnutt and I started with this force, but the former falling out after going a few miles out of Cape Coast Castle, the command of the Marines devolved on me, till Capt. Crease, who had been employed at Cape Coast Castle as Colonial Engineer, arrived and relieved me. Two naval officers were also attached, as Capt. Fremantle, R.N. had brought more than were required for the bluejackets with the force. On our leaving Alrakrampa some 20 Marines and Bluejackets remained behind, under Lieut. Wells, R.N. A day or two after we got back, news arrived that Col. Festing had been attacked when attempting to join us, and amongst others Lieut. Eardly Wilmot, R.A. had been killed. Fifty Marines were then ordered up to Assayboo, the first village on the road now being made to the Prah, to keep open the communication. Capt. Allnutt and I were the officers. Assayboo was about four miles from Alrakrampa, and the enemy was supposed to be between the two, which supposition turned out to be true. The Marines had a small 5 ½in. howitzer, which was manned by the R.M.A. The village was placed in a state of defence and every precaution taken to prevent surprise. The day after our arrival firing was heard in the distance, which we afterwards found was the enemy attacking Alrakrampa. Some wounded men were brought down from Dunquah, and appeals for help from an officer of the West Indian Regt., who stated that he was surrounded by the enemy about 3 miles beyond us on the road. Our orders being however to hold Assayboo, I was not allowed to take a few men to his relief, though I wished to do it. The next day Sir Garnet, with a force of sailors and the remainder of the *Simoom's* Marines, which had now dwindled to very few on account of sickness, arrived and we were ordered on to the relief of Alrakrampa, which we effected that night. We arrived in the midst of a great deal of firing, but this was confined to the natives, who had to be driven on in front of the Marines. We entered the village through a filthy marsh, which wet everyone to the knees - not a pleasant preparation for night on outlying picquet, of which I had command. The next day there was a great din from the Ashantees, shouting and tom-tom beating, and an attack was momentarily expected. However, after waiting till the middle of the day and finding the noise growing less, some scouts were sent out, and it was discovered that the whole of the enemy had departed, a few women being captured - a number of cooking utensils left behind, and one of their chiefs lying dead on a sort of bier beside an open grave testifying to a hasty departure. The bush all round was tainted with dead bodies, which could only be detected by the smell, not being visible in the thick undergrowth. A party of natives under some English officers was sent in pursuit of the enemy, but they returned next day having come up with the rear of the Ashantees and losing several men. They, as usual, stampeded after firing their rifles, and if the Ashantees had stopped to pursue them, none of officers would have escaped. Nothing more, however was seen of the Ashantees this side of the Prah, so that the bluejackets and marines can claim to have cleared the country of the enemy before any white regiment had appeared. In a day or two the General and his staff left, leaving Alrakrampa in command of Major Russell (afterwards General Sir Baker Russell) with 50 Marines (Capt. Allnutt and myself) and some native levies. We were there for 4 weeks, when owing to the unhealthiness of climate, which was aggravated by the dreadful smells from the decomposing bodies, our numbers were reduced to 30, the others being sick. Orders having been received to return to the Coast, we started with a long procession of cots bringing up the rear - I was in one of them, but not being able to stand the jolting (it bringing on bleeding from the lungs), I was left behind with my servant. A few days after I was taken to Cape Coast Castle and in hospital there I found Capt. Allnut, who was invalided home a week or two after, Lieut Gray, who died, and the majority of the men. The whole of the *Simoom's* detachment were then sent in the *Amethyst* to Ascension - the white regiments having arrived. Out of the original of 150 men, 40 had either died or been invalided. Of the remaining 110, only 16 appeared at Divisions in the morning, all the others being sick. The officers sent to Ascension were Capt. Crease, Lieut. Stephens and myself, all invalided - the others returned to England in a few weeks, but I was not allowed to come home till May, when I had recovered from an illness that nobody ever thought I should get over. Seven men, I believe, died at Ascension, the remainder got home, but several afterwards either died or were invalided out of the Service.

NOTE - Of the 200 Marines originally sent out in *Simoom*, 50 Infantry were supernumeries for the West Coast Station; the remaining 150 (50 Artillery and 100 Infantry) were what I have called the *Simoom's* Marines.

―――――

THE OCCUPATION OF PORT HAMILTON, 1885-87.

The occupation of Port Hamilton by a detachment of Royal Marines from the end of July, 1885 to the end of February, 1887, is not mentioned in Colonel Field's book "Britain's Sea Soldiers, "though other similar episodes in the history of the Corps are referred to. Forty years have elapsed since this event, but an account of it from the pen of a survivor of the garrison may yet be of interest.

Port Hamilton is an anchorage enclosed by three small islands, which, with several outlying islets is termed the Nan How group. It is situated off the south coast of Korea, about 120 miles to the westward of Nagasaki. The anchorage, which is shown on Admiralty Chart 1280, is capable of sheltering a fleet of deep draught vessels. The reasons for its occupation and for its subsequent evacuation are to be found in Blue Book "China, No. 1 (1887)." Briefly they were as follows:- In the seventies of last century Admirals Ryder and Shadwell, former Naval Commanders-in-Chief on the China station, and Sir Harry Parkes, the British Minister in China, had advocated the acquisition of Port Hamilton as a naval base. Admiral Sir Cooper Key and Lord Carnarvon's Royal Commission on the "Defence of the British Possessions and Sea-borne Trade Abroad" had also recommended in 1882 that it should be acquired. At that time Russia was regarded as a probable foe; her base in far eastern waters was Vladivostock. Hong Kong was then the only British base in China. The steam power and coal carrying capacity of the men-of-war of those days was so inferior, that they could make but little, if any, headway against a strong N.E. monsoon. It was therefore considered that a base in the northern part of the station was required, and Port Hamilton was selected. No steps, however, were taken by the Government of the day until hostilities with Russia were iminent early in 1885. On 14th April of that year the Commander-in-Chief of the China Squadron was ordered to occupy it, but not to hoist the British flag unless a Russian man-of-war came in. The Chinese Government was informed that it was only a temporary measure, in view of its probable occupation by another Power. The entrances to the harbour were protected with booms and mines, and a submarine cable laid to the North Saddle Island, off the mouth of the Yangtze River, where it connected with the Hong Kong-Shanghai cable. Corea, to whom the island belonged, was then China's vassal. Both these countries protested against the occupation of a place that formed part of the Kingdom of Corea; Japan and Russia also protested, and the latter threatened to occupy some other portion of Corean territory if Britain did not evacuate Port Hamilton. Diplomatic correspondence ensued; the Commander-in-Chief, Sir William Dowell, and his successor, Sir Vesey Hamilton, were ordered to report on the place as a naval station. Both reported unfavourably, and considered that unless strongly fortified, its possession would rather hamper than assist naval operations in those waters, as it would be necessary to detach a part of the fleet for its defence. Eventually, the Russian war scare having passed, and China having guaranteed that no other Power should occupy Port Hamilton, it was decided at the end of 1886 to evacuate it.

The garrison that occupied it was detailed from the battalion of Royal Marines serving at Suakin in April, 1885, under the following circumstances. The war scare with Russia caused the Soudan operations to be stopped. The Marine battalion was ordered home, and was already embarked when instructions were cabled from England to detach Captain C.G. Gordon, Lieuts. A.E. Horniblow and H.W.L. Holman, R.M.L.I., with about 70 N.C.O. s and men, for service in China. The senior N.C.O. was Colour-Sergt. Walters, of the Plymouth Division. The detachment was immediately moved to another transport, the officers having only then campaigning kit, and many of the men nothing but the uniform they were wearing at the moment, as there had been no time to muster their bags and valises. After three weeks delay at Suakin the detachment was sent to Suez to meet a transport sailing thence on 18th May. There was a ten days wait there before this vessel, the S.S. "Hankow" arrived. She brought out 25 N.C.O.'s and men of the Royal Marine Artillery, under Lieut. W.F. Trotter, R.M.A. ; also Lieut. Randall Macdonell, to replace Lieut. A.E. Horniblow, invalided from Suakin. After touching at Aden and Singapore, Hong Kong was reached on 1st July, by which time the war scare was over, but a considerable portion of the squadron remained at Port Hamilton. The C.-in-C. cabled home for authority to send the Marines brought by the "Hankow" up to garrison the place. This was granted. Tents and other stores were drawn at Hong Kong, and the men re-equipped there, before sailing in the S.S. "Pembroke Castle" on 18th July, 1885; Port Hamilton was reached in four or five days.

Before narrating the experiences of the Marine garrison at this distant and isolated spot, a description of the islands and their inhabitants at that period may be of interest. The three islands enclosing the anchorage were called Sodo, Sunhodo and Observatory Island, or Ai-to (Japanese Island). The first-named was the easternmost and largest. It was 3 ½ to 4 miles long by about ½ mile in average width, and consisted of a succession of rugged peaks, the highest being 762 feet. The tops were covered with thick bamboo grass, and the lower slopes with dense scrub, interlaced with vines. Patches of ground which had been cleared, levelled and cultivated, existed here and there, principally near the villages. A few small woods, chiefly consisting of fir trees, were scattered about. There were two large villages on the shore of the harbour, one at the northern end and one opposite Observatory Island. Two or three scattered groups of a few huts each existed on the western side, where there were also some paddy fields, which harboured snipe in winter. Sunhodo, the eastern most island, was about 2 ¼ miles long by about 1/3 mile in average width. It was not quite so rugged as Sodo; its highest point was 784 feet. Observatory Island, situated between the southern ends of the two larger islands, was ¾ mile long by ¼ mile broad; the highest point was 335 feet. There was no level ground on it, but several patches of cultivated land existed on the west side. The eastern side was steep and covered with dense scrub. A small natural boat harbour, or camber, at the northern end had been improved by Japanese fishermen, and was used by them to shelter in during bad weather. The fleet constructed a bund round this camber, and erected a wooden shed to store mining gear. Observatory Island was chosen as the site for the telegraph station and camp for the following reasons:-

(1) It was the only place where boats could be kept in all weathers.
(2) Submarine mining work could be more secretly carried on there.
(3) It was the most convenient place for telegraph station.
(4) No natives lived on it.

About 10 acres of land on this island were rented from the native owners, at rentals satisfactory to themselves, for the telegraph station and camp.

On the two larger islands mere foot-tracks connected the villages. A road was made on Observatory Island from the landing place, through the camp, to the officers' mess, which was half way up the hill.

There were a few springs on the two larger islands, and some small streams flowing into the harbour, but the water when analysed was found to be impure, and the streams ran dry after a short spell of hot weather. On Observatory Island there were no springs, so water had to be condensed by one of the ships for the garrison and telegraph operators. A small gunboat was generally moored in the channel between it and Sodo for this purpose. At first water had to be fetched daily, but later large iron tanks were sent up from Hong Kong; they held enough to supply the garrison for a month in winter and a fortnight in summer.

The inhabitants, of whom there were about 2,000, were Coreans, of a very low type. A few years before they had been described as "beyond the pale of civilised nations." They were half starved and inexpressibly filthy. Many of them suffered from various diseases and malformations, such as hare-lip, etc.; cholera and smallpox were endemic. Some of them took advantage of the presence of the Fleet to consult the naval doctors about their ailments. A chief who did so was found to be so verminous on baring his chest for examination, that the doctor explained through the interpreter, that he must first wash, and gave him a piece of soap for the purpose; this the chief promptly ate.

When a headman died, his body was placed on the beach, under the low bushy cliffs bordering it, and covered with a kind of round straw hut about four or five feet high, with a conical thatched roof, and left for several weeks before final burial. The graves were covered with mounds of earth about two or three feet high, round in shape, and were scattered about the hillsides, usually shadowed by clumps of fir trees.

The following incidents show the half starved condition of the natives. About 300 of them were employed after the arrival of the Fleet constructing a breakwater on the bank that runs from Shoal Point on Sunhodo towards Observatory Island. At the request of the headmen they were paid in rice instead of money, owing to the shortage of food.

In the summer of 1886 a party of natives from the opposite village on Sodo landed on Observatory Island in the early hours of the morning, and stole about a hundred-weight of weevilly ship biscuit, that had been condemned, and was stored behind the officers' mess hut for feeding their poultry. Three youths were caught in the act of carrying off the last load. They were placed in charge of the guard, and the headman of their village was requested to return the biscuit and give up the thieves for punishment. He was somewhat truculent at first, but when informed that he would be flogged himself if he did not comply, he stated that the biscuit had been eaten already, and sent over three men, said to be the thieves. They were sentenced to two dozen lashes each with a rope's end, and the youths to one dozen each. Each in turn was laid with bare back over a rock on the shore opposite their village, while a hefty sergeant laid on the lashes with the side-rope from the gangway of a gunboat. One of them after receiving his punishment rolled over in a sitting posture on to the rocks heated by the August sun, which greatly added to his discomforture. When the sentences had been administered the men were allowed to return to their village, the population of which assembled on the beach, and several men were laid out and beaten. It was not definitely known whether they were the same men who had already been flogged, but it was presumed that they were, and that the chief had ordered them another beating for allowing themselves to be caught.

One winter's evening two of the officers, returning from shooting on Sodo, were waiting for their boat on the shore by the village opposite Observatory Island, when they saw two or three natives dropping large stones on something, evidently alive, under a piece of sacking. On investigation it proved to be a dog. As it was already badly hurt, they shot it, and in a very few minutes it was skinned, cut up, washed in the sea and carried off to the village for food.

The inhabitants possessed few cattle, but no sheep and until the arrival of the Fleet, no poultry. Sheep could not live on the islands, on account of the bamboo grass, which killed them if they ate it. Their principal diet was millet and fish. The soil was fertile, and two crops a year were grown. The women did all the hard work in the fields, while men kept watch over them. On the approach of a European they hid. According to report, if a married woman was unfaithful, she was burnt alive, and once during the occupation it was rumoured that such an execution had taken place in the village at the north end of Sodo. It was never definitely ascertained if this rumour was true, but one evening there was certainly considerable commotion there, and a large fire could be seen from Observatory Island.

The young women dived for edible seaweed, with the usual male guard to ward off strangers. At certain seasons the men fished at night, with flares in their boats to attract the fish, which were then speared.

Neither deer, rabbits, or other wild animals existed in the islands. A few rabbits were brought over alive by some naval officers, for the purpose of being turned loose, but the senior naval officer at the time would not allow this to be done, fearing that they might multiply too much and play havoc with the natives crops. They were therefore turned out on a small uninhabited islet a mile or two from the southern entrance of the harbour, which was consequently named "Rabbit Island." It is not known whether they survived; certainly none were seen when some of the officers visited the islet some months afterwards. Vermin of the weasel type were at one time suspected of carrying off young poultry, but none were ever actually seen. No traces of rats were ever discovered on Observatory Island, though they may have existed in the villages on Sodo and Sunhodo.

The only birds definitely known to breed in the islands were black pigeons and crows. The former were about the size of an English wood pigeon, and were very good eating. They are called according to the natural history book, the crow pigeon of Japan. The so-called crows may have really been ravens, as they were very similar in size and appearance to the ravens in the Tower of London. At any rate, they were large, fierce birds, with enormous beaks, and carried off young poultry, eggs, etc. Two of them were once seen to attack a small sucking-pig, pecking at its eyes. On another occasion two flew up and went for a hawk in mid air, as it was carrying off its prey. One was caught on the back of a domestic pigeon, pecking a hole in the back of its skull. Many varieties of migratory birds rested on the islands when on their way south in autumn; among them were blue doves, quail, snipe, woodcock, wild geese, and the greater bustard. The doves arrived towards the end of September or early October, and stayed a few weeks; the quail came in much about the same time. On first arrival they were found in small flights on the cultivated ground; later, as the weather grew colder, they took to the thick grass on the hillsides, where some of them stayed throughout the winter. Only small numbers of the other birds named above dropped on the islands; however, a few of each were shot. Several varieties of wild duck were killed, but none of them were edible. An albatross was once found swimming in the centre of the harbour, and shot by an officer of the garrison. Hawks abounded, and with the crows were a perfect pest to the officers' poultry. Numerous sea eagles hovered over the shores, and several were brought down; the largest killed measured over 7-feet from pinion to pinion. He had been observed to settle, and was stalked by two of the officers, one of whom brought him down with a charge of the largest sized shot just after he had risen. Although he had a hole under his right wing big enough to put two fingers into, he made several attempts to rise again, but was unable to do so. He fought like a fury, until he was seized by the tips of his pinions and held, while one of the men slipped a cord round his neck and strangled him. Another, when cut open after being shot, was found to have a small puppy, apparently a few weeks old, in his crop. One of these birds was caught alive when gorged with eating a dead crow and with his wings sodden by rain. He was kept alive in captivity for nearly a year, but died just before the flag was hauled down. It had been intended to present him to the Zoo at Hong Kong.

After the Fleet anchored at Port Hamilton in April, 1885, the officers started a game club, for the purpose of importing and turning down pheasants and partridges. The birds were brought from Corea, China and Japan, and let loose on Sodo and Sunhodo. The partridges soon died off, and as the climate and nature of the country did not apparently suit them, no more were imported. The pheasants, however, throve, and eventually multiplied to such an extent that the natives, who had no firearms, complained of their depredations on their crops. This was, however, after the evacuation. During the period the islands were occupied by the British the pheasants had not increased sufficiently to justify shooting them, and a fine was imposed on any sportsman who inadvertently shot one. The Japanese and Chinese pheasants inter-bred and some very fine crossbred birds resulted. Officers from ships that visited the islands a few years after their evacuation had good sport with the pheasants, though they were somewhat difficult to get at owing to the nature of the country.

Oysters abounded on the rocks, but were not easy to gather; cut fingers usually resulted from attempts to do so. The Coreans, however, were only too pleased to gather them, and would barter a hundred for a handful or two of ship biscuit. The oysters were small, and if not equal to our natives, were very good to eat. Moreover, they were free from pollution by sewage, and so there was no danger in eating them, as there is in some places. Some of them contained pearls, and one naval officer obtained half-a-dozen fairly good ones.

The climate of Port Hamilton was on the whole healthy and not unpleasant. No serious sickness occurred in the garrison while there, nor were there any deaths, except that of a private who broke out of the island one night in a native boat and in attempting to land on the rocks on Sodo fell into the water, and being unable to swim, was drowned. His body was recovered some weeks later outside the harbour on the western shore of Sunhodo, and was buried on Observatory Island, where there is a small cemetery with six or seven British graves. All those buried were naval ratings or marines from the fleet, and all were killed by or died from the effects of gun or other accidents, except one sick bayman, who was landed from a man-o'-war suffering from small-pox and quarantined in the hospital hut on Observatory Island, where he died. Prior to the arrival of the garrison there had been several weeks of heavy rain, so it was moist as well as hot, but two summers' experience showed that the heat at that period of the year, though necessitating white helmets and uniform, was not excessive. Being about 40 miles from the nearest land, the sea breezes kept the islands comparatively cool. Provided a white helmet or sun hat was worn, there was no time of day when one could not be out of doors. In fact, July and August were the only months when it was really hot, and then it was no worse than a very hot summer in England.

THE OCCUPATION OF PORT HAMILTON, 1885-87. (Part II.)

The winters were not unpleasantly cold, except when the N.E. winds swept across from Corea. These sometimes brought showers of snow or sleet, but the snow never lay. At other times during the winter it was quite possible to play tennis on fine days and even to sit out of doors in sheltered sunny spots. Camellias grew wild not only on shrubs, but on large climbable trees, in fact, the woods on Observatory Island were to some extent composed of these trees. They blossomed profusely in the spring, but a few flowers were out at Christmas time, and were used to decorate the officers' mess table.

On the whole, considering that the infantry portion of the garrison had previously served for a year in the sweltering heat of Suakin, followed by three weeks in Hong Kong during July, it is probable that the eighteen months at Port Hamilton, in good fresh sea air, with no drink, nor the other temptations of a garrison town, was beneficial rather than the reverse.

The S.S. "Pembroke Castle" arrived with the garrison towards the end of July, 1885. A submarine cable station had been already installed on Observatory Island. It consisted of a hut, with two rooms each 12-ft. square, as dwelling and office combined, for the two telegraph operators, Messrs. Macpherson and Weeks, who were loaned by the Eastern Telegraph Company. A smaller hut served as kitchen and dwelling for their cook. The cable broke during the autumn of 1885, and owing to the war scare being over and to the uncertainty regarding the retention of Port Hamilton, it was never repaired, and both telegraphists left.

The only possible site for the men's tents was a neck of land sloping towards the camber, then covered with a half-grown millet crop. On the hillside above, and at right angles to the men's tents, there was just sufficient fairly level space to pitch those of the officers and the marquee used as a mess tent. Before the camp was quite ready for occupation, and while the detachment still lived on board the "Pembroke Castle," a typhoon passed over and blew down all the tents. The guard left on shore took refuge in the telegraph operators' kitchen. For twenty-four hours there was no communication with the island. When the storm had abated the tents were re-pitched and the garrison landed on 29th July, 1885. It was borne on the books of the senior naval officer's ship, from which it was rationed and paid. The garrison was under the Naval Discipline Act, but Sir Vesey Hamilton, after taking over command of the station in the spring of 1886, conferred on the senior Marine officer of the garrison the same powers of punishment as the captain of a man-o'-war. Incidentally it may interest present members of the Corps to learn why this regulation was made. A Marine battalion was sent to Egypt in 1882, at the time of the bombardment of Alexandria; it was when first landed, and before being transferred to Ismalia as part of the army that defeated Arabi Pasha at Tel-el-Kebir, under the Naval Discipline Act. Consequently the Colonel commanding the Marine battalion had no power of punishing his men beyond that which the regulations of those days allowed the Captain of a man-o'-war to confer, at his discretion, on the marine officer of his ship. It was recognised by the authorities that it was an anomalous position for a Lieut.-Colonel with many years service to have no power of maintaining discipline in his battalion, and to have, perhaps, to submit to a Lieutenant in command of a gunboat coming on shore to punish his men. Consequently a regulation was incorporated in the Admiralty Instructions, that when a body of Marines was landed under the Naval Discipline Act, the Commander-in-Chief or senior naval officer could confer on the senior marine officer the same powers of punishment as the captain of a man-o'-war. Captain Gordon knew of this regulation, but at first could not find it in the Instructions. The Commander-in-Chief was desirous of conferring on him complete power of punishment over his men, but the captain of the ship on whose books the garrison was then borne, strongly protested at not having disciplinary powers over them. The Admiral reluctantly informed Captain Gordon that, much as he himself wished it, he was, in view of this protest, and in the absence of any regulation giving him the authority to do so, unable to confer on him the necessary power. At the last moment Captain Gordon and the Admiral's secretary, in searching the Admiralty instructions, again found the new regulation pasted in on a slip. That settled the matter. The only occasion on which there was any serious breach of discipline occurred just before Sir Vesey Hamilton arrived, at the end of May, 1886. Some ten or a dozen men broke out of camp during the night and crossed to Sunhodo in native boats. A sentry gave the alarm, and a roll call was immediately taken, to find out who were absent. Meanwhile a boat was sent in pursuit. One of the culprits, in attempting to land, was drowned, and as mentioned above, was buried on Observatory Island. It was this episode that led to Sir Vesey Hamilton conferring on the senior officer of the garrison the same disciplinary powers as the captain of a man-o'-war.

After the detachment had landed it enjoyed a month of fine but hot weather. The men were employed levelling sufficient ground on the hillside for the huts, which were being built in Hong Kong by an American contractor, under the supervision of the Royal Engineers. Life in the tents was rendered unpleasant by mosquitoes, which swarmed. They, as well as other insects, were attracted by the lights in the officers' mess tent, and after dinner drove them to take shelter under mosquito curtains in their own tents, or to go out sea fishing.

The S.S. "Glenagle," with the huts, the contractor, and about 20 Chinese carpenters, arrived towards the end of August. There were three large huts for the men, each having a sergeant's lobby at the end. On the hillside above there were a hospital, sergeants' mess, canteen and stores. Higher up still was the officers' mess, kitchen and store. Large baulks of timber, which had been used for the booms protecting the harbour entrances, were half buried on the spaces levelled, and the huts bolted on to them.

About the end of August or early in September a second typhoon visited Port Hamilton. It commenced in the middle of the day, about 3p.m.; the officers' mess tent was blown down, and by 4 p.m. the storm was raging. The officers and the American contractor sheltered in the telegraph hut, where eight people, including the two telegraphists, passed an unpleasant night in two small rooms, each 12-feet square. About 4 a.m. it was feared the hut might be blown down, and some of the occupants stood on the verandah waiting to jump. However it survived. The men held up their tents as long as possible by clinging to the poles and guys. Eventually they gave it up and sought what shelter could be obtained under hedges and walls. Some of them sheltered in one of the partially erected huts, but during the night the wind penetrated the window and door spaces, acted on the roof and sides, and blew the hut over. Some of the men were hurt and had to be carried into the telegraphists' kitchen for shelter and medical attendance. The typhoon was at its worst about 4 a.m. A ten-oared cutter and a four-oared teak gig moored in the camber were both wrecked; the latter was whirled clean out of the water and dashed on the rocks. The gunboat "Merlin," which was moored between Observatory Island and Sado was very nearly driven ashore on the former. Her anchors fouled the telegraph cable and that saved her. During the day the typhoon gradually passed over, but no communication with the ships was possible till the day after. Damage done by the storm was immediately made good and work on the huts renewed; they were ready for occupation before the winter. As a precaution against further typhoons, chains with cat screws for tautening them up, were led over the roofs of the huts, and their ends fastened to pigs of ballast buried in concrete. However, during the remaining period the island was occupied no more typhoons passed over it.

The huts had been badly put together, and the heating arrangements were inferior. In the officers' messroom two ordinary cabin stoves, of the pattern then supplied to small ships, were placed one at each end on opposite sides; iron funnels led from their tops straight up through the roof, consequently nearly all the heat went straight up and was wasted. When the N.E. winds blew the room was so cold and draughty that the officers dined in great coats. However, when Sir Vesey Hamilton visited Port Hamilton the following spring he authorised considerable expenditure to make the huts more comfortable. The officers' messroom was provided with two American stoves, and the funnelling from each led round the room and out through the roof over the other stove. The result was that room was warm and comfortable in winter, and it was seldom that both stoves were needed. The mess hut consisted of one large room, with a back and front door, two bedrooms opening into it on one side and three smaller ones on the other.

After the huts had been completed and occupied there was very little for the men to do beyond keeping their accoutrements and huts clean, water fatigue, guard duties, and infantry drill once a week. Each of the men's huts was in charge of an officer, who inspected it every morning. One subaltern was on duty each day as orderly officer, and during his tour of duty did not leave Observatory Island. The men were put through a course of musketry on an improvised range on Sunhodo in the spring of 1886.

A canteen was managed by Lieut. Holman with Sergeant Corbyn as canteen sergeant. It proved both popular and profitable. The men were very glad to supplement their rations with tinned foods, particularly salmon and lobster. Beer, when obtainable, was limited to one pint man per diem, owing to the difficulty of getting supplies. It may be remarked here that communication with the outside world, except by cable, until it broke, was entirely by man-o'-war. When the Fleet lay at Port Hamilton there was fairly regular communication with Nagasaki or Shanghai, usually the former, owing to its proximity. Vessels were then specially sent over to bring mails, bread, beef, or in summer live bullocks, and other stores for the fleet and garrison. At other times the connection with those places was not so regular. However, it was generally possible to get over sufficient beer and other stores to last until a fresh supply was obtainable. Cricket gear was purchased for the men out of the canteen profits, and when the garrison was withdrawn each man received several pounds out of the surplus.

When a ship happened to be going to and returning from Nagasaki, a certain number of men were allowed to go over on general leave; one officer at a time could also get away in like manner. Each one in turn visited Japan, which was then a more primitive and more interesting country than to-day, though it was already beginning to be Westernized. Some of the officers also managed to get to Fusan and other parts in Corea for shooting. The officers' recreations were tennis, sea bathing and fishing in summer, rough shooting and occasional tennis in winter. Prior to the arrival of the garrison the naval officers had begun to make a tennis court by levelling a piece of ground near the camber, covering it with flat stones, piling on granite sand quarried on the island and rolling it in with a stone roller procured from Nagasaki. It proved a great boon to the officers of the garrison and fleet. While under canvas in August, 1885, the former and the two telegraphists usually had an hour's play from 7 to 8 a.m., and then a bathe before breakfast. In the afternoon the naval officers landed for play. It was often possible to get a game in winter on fine days; in fact, on each Christmas Day play took place. The sea bathing was excellent, the water being beautifully clear and quite unpolluted. A convenient bathing place was found on the rocks facing Triangle Peak on Sodo. It was not considered safe to swim too far from the shore, as there were sharks about. Moreover, care had to be exercised in getting out of the water, not to tread on oysters or sea eggs. Not much fishing was done after the first summer, when it was usual to fish at night to avoid the mosquitoes, as the Japanese fishermen who frequented the island were always ready to sell some of their catch. But little else than bream were obtained; however these made a welcome addition to the menu. The shooting was rather poor, on account of the rugged nature of the country and the scarcity of birds, but it afforded a pleasant means of recreation, even though bags were small.

The mess caterer, Lieut. Trotter, imported sheep, goats, fowls, ducks and geese. The sheep were originally brought over to kill off as required, and the goats for milk, but later they were bred. The poultry multiplied rapidly and were very profitable. Many of them took to the bush, and became so wild, that they had to be shot when required for table. Fresh bread and beef were at first only to be had when a ship arrived from Nagasaki with supplies, but during the last six months a Japanese compradore was allowed to set up a bakery on Observatory Island and import bullocks to supply the fleet and garrison with bread and beef. The officers were allowed a Chinese steward, cook and boy. While under canvas a good deal of tinned food had to be used, but when the farmyard was established after moving into the huts, the officers lived very well.

Captain Gordon, on first arrival, asked for pay and allowances on the same scale as the battalion in Japan from 1870 to 1874 drew, i.e., double pay and field allowance. However, the Admiralty could not see their way to give double pay, but field allowance was granted, and later ration money of 1/6 per diem to all ranks was paid in addition to ration.

Surgeon Seymour, R.N., who accompanied the detachment from Hong Kong had already applied to leave the service; his successor, Surgeon A.G. Wildey, R.N., arrived a few months after, and Dr. Seymour then left and settled in Japan. In the summer of 1886 Captain Gordon was allowed to return to England, at his own expense, on urgent private affairs. Captain Trotter, who had just been promoted, succeeded him.

In January 1887 orders were received to evacuate Port Hamilton. The huts were sold as they stood to a Chinese contractor from Nagasaki. The officers' surplus stock was sold partly to the ships and partly at Nagasaki. Owing to the number of sheep and poultry that were bred, there was a good deal to dispose of, and the surplus mess funds yielded each officer nearly £20. H.M. Troopship "Himalaya" took the garrison and stores to Hong Kong, which was reached just in time for the race week, after which she sailed for England, calling at Singapore, Colombo Aden, Suez, Port Said, Malta and Gibraltar, and reached Portsmouth in the middle of April 1887. Lieut. Holman and many of the N.C.O.s and men had left England on the 10th February, 1884 for Egypt and the Sudan, the remainder had joined the battalion there later. As the Himalaya was steaming out of Port Hamilton, a white object was seen on the hillside of Observatory Island. Inspection through field glasses showed it to be a sheep. One had been found missing some time previously, and was believed to be dead, but evidently it had got into the thick scrub and stayed there. The period spent at Port Hamilton was by no means unpleasant and was a novel experience.

SEPOY MARINE BATTALION.

It is not generally known that in the days when the East India Company controlled India a Marine Battalion was formed for duties very similar to our own. It was composed of Sepoys, as there were objections to Hindoos embarking on board ship for Marine duties.

Their uniform was very similar to other Native regiments, but they wore an anchor under the number of the regiment, and the Battalion feather was black.

Their number changed on several occasions, due to the reorganisation of the units in the Indian Army.

In 1777, when the Battalion was raised at Bombay, it was known as The Marine Battalion. In

1818 the Marine Battalion was formed into a Regiment and nominated The 11th Regiment Native Infantry, but only "Breame," the 1st or Marine Battalion, wore the anchor.

In 1824 it became the 21st (Marine Battalion); in 1861 the 21st Regiment of Bombay Infantry (The Marine Battalion); in 1901 The 21st Bombay Infantry (The Marine Battalion); in 1903 The 21st Bombay Pioneers.

On a renumbering scheme the same year it became the 121st Pioneers, and was liable to general service. Up to this date the Regiment's Headquarters had been at Bombay for 127 years; it was now moved to Poona. In 1922 it again became a Bombay regiment, and was called the 10th Battalion 2nd Bombay Pioneers (Marine Battalion).

In 1928 the Corps of Bombay Pioneers was formed by amalgamation of the battalions of Bombay Pioneers, the 1st Battalion being known as the 1st (Marine Battalion). It is not at present known if authority has been sanctioned for the 1st Marine Battalion, Corps of Bombay Pioneers, to wear the Anchor and Laurel Wreath, with the motto in Hindustani corresponding to "Per Mare Per Terram," but the badge was worn by the 10th Battalion 2nd Bombay Pioneers up to the reorganisation in November, 1928.

In 1810 the duties of the Marine Sepoys serving on hoard the Hon. Company's cruisers were laid down as follows:-

The Sepoys are to assist in working the ship below, in hauling up and paying down cables, in hoisting in and out boats, water and provisions, in short, in manning the tackle falls on all occasions.
They are to draw and hand along water for the purpose of washing the ship, and are to personally clean out their own berths.
They are not to wash their clothes but upon days specially appointed by the regulation of the ship. They are not to be compelled to go aloft, to scrub the decks, or perform any menial office.
In case of misconduct, a N.C.O. is to be confined, the next senior to be selected to perform his duties till he can be tried.
In no case is a N.C.O. to be struck or to have corporal punishment. Privates are, for crimes of serious nature, to be confined till they can be brought to trial; but for offences of less importance, when absent from the Presidency and the support of discipline requires immediate punishment, they are to be punished with a "Rattan," according to the degree of the offence, by the Drummer or Fifer, in presence of the detachment, to whom the cause of the punishment is to be clearly explained; or for misconduct not demanding corporal punishment, they may have allotted to them the task of picking oakum or knotting yarns, while their comrades are relieved from duty.

Their chronicles of service are too many to enumerate within this short article, but it appears that their services were utilized for fighting on shore with other regiments, sometimes as a battalion and sometimes in small detachments of one or two companies.

Detachments of vessels not only fought the Hon. Company's cruisers, brigs of war, gallivants, etc., but were often collected and landed as a company or larger force, either on their own, or to assist the troops on shore and afterwards frequently returned on board to chase pirates or prevent the retreat of merchants attempting to make away with their goods.

Further, on more than one occasion, they were employed on board ships of the Royal Navy. Commander Hayes wrote in one of his despatches, when recommending a detachment for special honour: - "The Corps in question is one of the oldest in India, and it has seen more service than any native regiment in the Company's Army."

After nearly every war or small action they appear to have received the greatest praise for their gallantry from their commanders.

On more than one occasion, when the French took some of the Sepoys prisoners, their loyalty was shewn by their refusal to enter the French service, in spite of being offered large bribes.

During one campaign it is recorded that the Marines "gave up their tents, carpets and cumblees for making sandbags, in their zeal for victory."

We read that on the *Falkland* foundering, a Marine, who was sentry on the treasure chest, never left his post until the vessel went down under him, and even then he contrived to save the bag of rupees under his charge. On another occasion a small detachment defended the treasure chest against a Bengal regiment which had broken into open mutiny, and they did so successfully, killing 26 of the mutineers.

The Marines were evidently looked upon as men who were capable of any service anywhere.

In 1817 a detachment was sent to Sydney, New South Wales, as a guard over convicts, and in 1865 volunteers were called for to accompany Dr. Livingstone on his exploring expedition to Central Africa, and twelve out of the forty volunteers went.

In the following year a company proceeded with the pioneer force to Abyssinia, and received great praise from Lord Napier of Magdala.

The strength of the Corps varied from time to time. Originally it was five companies, and as far as can be ascertained, its greatest strength was two battalions.

It was generally commanded by a major or a captain until 1866, when it became a colonel's command. By this time it was more or less a normal regiment of Native Infantry. The actual date of the Battalion ceasing to perform Marine duties is not known, but the process was probably a gradual one.

In 1857 there were many serving in vessels. In 1861 an order came out which read as follows;-

"The Marine Battalion is brought into the line of Native Regiments, and is designated the 21st Regiment of Native Infantry, or Marine Battalion," but as late as 1866 we read of "Small parties on board the gunboats *Hugh Rose* and *Clyde*."

TAMAAI - 13th March, 1884.
Reprinted from Globe & Laurel, March, 1895.

Just eleven years ago occurred the first English expedition to the Eastern Soudan. It will be remembered that the defeat of General Baker's force (4th February, 1884) at El-Teb, following as it did the annihilation of General Hick's army at Kasghil, created a most pitiful impression in England.

The situation was briefly this: -

Two armies led by English commanders, and officered in great measure by Englishmen, had been successively destroyed; of the Egyptian garrisons of Sinkta and Tokar, one was known to have been sacrificed, and the other might share its fate any day; Suakim itself was seriously threatened.

So, on the 6th February, 1884, H.M. Government decided to undertake the defence of Suakim, and in answer to a demand from Admiral Hewett, who was in command of the British Squadron at Suakim, promised him 500 Marines, 140 of whom were then on their way home on the *Orontes* from China and the East Indies, the remainder being sent at once from the ships of the Mediterranean Squadron, under the command of Major Colwell, R.M.L.I., of the flagship *Alexandria*.

On the 12th of February, however, in consequence of a telegram announcing the fall of Sinkat, it was decided to despatch a British force to endeavour to effect the relief of the garrison of Tokar.

The command of the expedition was given to Major-General Sir Gerald Graham. Colonel Tuson, C.B., A.D.C., R.M.A., as Colonel, and Captain Poe, R.M.L.I. as Adjutant of the R.M. Battalion were sent out from England, and on the 28th of February the following force was concentrated at Trinkitat: -

2850 Infantry (including 380 R.M.A. & R.M.L.I.)
750 mounted troops
150 Naval Brigade
100 Royal Artillery
80 Royal Engineers
6 machine guns
8 7-pounders Royal Artillery

On the afternoon of the 28th February, the force marched out and bivouacked at Fort Baker, and on the 29th advanced and defeated with great slaughter the rebels who were entrenched at El-Teb. On the following morning the march was continued to Tokar, which place was reached without any further fighting. On the 4th March, Sir G. Graham and his force returned to Trinkitat, bringing with them the inhabitants of Tokar, and on the following morning embarked for Suakim where the Government had decided to concentrate it, with a view to giving effect to a proclamation issued by Sir G. Graham and Admiral Hewett, denouncing Osman Digna, the leader of the rebels, and calling on the rebel chiefs to submit. No answer having been received to this proclamation, another was issued on the 8th March, warning the Arabs of Sir. G. Graham's intention of marching on their camp at Tamaai, and again urging them to submit. In answer to this a defiant reply was received, signed by a large number of Sheiks.

The British force consisted now of the 10th and 19th Hussars, the 42nd Black Watch, the 3rd Kings Royal Rifles, the 75th Gordon Highlanders, the 65th York and Lancaster, the 89th Royal Irish Fusiliers, a Naval Brigade from the ships in the Harbour, a Battalion of R.M.A. and R.M.L.I., the Mounted Infantry, and two Batteries of Royal Artillery.

So, on the 10th of March there was a move forward nearly south from Suakim to a zeriba made some weeks before by Baker Pasha, about eight miles out; this was re-constructed and water stored there, and the 42nd Regiment was left to protect it.

At 6 p.m. on the 11th, the Artillery and Infantry advanced to Bakers zeriba, reaching it about 10.30 p.m. The general total of the force of Artillery and Infantry amounted to 116 Officers and 3216 Non-Commissioned Officers and men.

The Royal Marine Battalion included R.M.A. and R.M.L.I. from all parts of the China, East Indian and Mediterranean Squadrons, and now totalled 14 Officers, 464 Non-Commissioned Officers and men, in six companies, under the command of Colonel Tuson, R.M.A.; the other Officers being: -

	Major Colwell, R.M.L.I.	Major	*Alexandra*
A Co.	Bt.-Major A. Allen, R.M.A.	}	*Temeraire*
B Co.	Bt.-Major Tucker, R.M.A.	}	*Superb*
B Co.	Lieut. Aston, R.M.A.	}	*Alexandra*
C Co.	Lieut. F. White, R.M.L.I.	} Company	*Temeraire*
D Co.	Lieut. Kysh, R.M.L.I.	} Officers	*Alexandra*
D Co.	Lieut. Rogers, R.M.L.I.	}	*Superb*
E Co.	Lieut. Prendergast, R.M.L.I.	}	*Superb*
F Co.	Bt.-Major Schomberg, R.M.L.I.	}	*Monarch*
	Captain Baldwin, R.M.L.I., Adjutant*		*Euryalus*
	Captain Morgan, R.M.L.I. Staff Officer to Colonel Tuson		
	Staff-Surgeon Martin, R.N.	} Medical	
	Surgeon Cross, R.N.	} Staff	

Lieut. Kysh in addition to his Company duties, was Acting Quartermaster and Transport Officer 34th Co., Clr-Sergt. Hirst was Acting Sergeant-Major.

The troops left in camp and garrison at Suakim, consisted of the Cavalry Brigade, and Mounted Infantry, with orders to join the Infantry early next morning, and the following details left to protect the camp and town, viz., 100 Royal Marines (Artillery and Infantry), in Fort Euryalus guarding the town with five guns in position; Officers - Lieut. Brittan, R.M.A. and Surgeon McCarthy, R.N.; all the sick and weakly men left in charge of the main camp, the tents being left standing, under the command of Lieut.-Colonel Gordon, D.A.A.G.

At daybreak on the 12th, the Cavalry and the Mounted Infantry watered at Suakim, and joined the force at Baker's zeriba (mentioned above), about 7 a.m. Their strength was 41 Officers, 696 Non-Commissioned Officers and men. On arrival, the Mounted Infantry were at once sent to the front.

About 10 a.m. it was reported that the enemy was in force some six miles distant. Accordingly orders were given for the expedition to advance as soon as the men had had their dinners; it began to move off about 1 p.m. The afternoon was hot, and frequent halts were necessary. About 5 p.m. the Cavalry scouts came in, reporting that the enemy was advancing to attack in force. General Graham at once formed up the troops in a defensive position on a favourable piece of ground having a clear space in front, and as there was now barely an hour of daylight left, directed the engineers and pioneers of Battalions to form a zeriba round the camp, by cutting down the prickly mimosa bushes, which grew plentifully about. About half-past 6 p.m. a convoy arrived safely, carrying two days supply of water for men, with rations and reserve ammunition.

Before this the enemy had fired a few shots, but disappeared on a few rounds being fired from the 9-pdr. and Gardner guns.

About a quarter to 1 a.m. there was an alarm, and the enemy opened a distant dropping fire, which continued throughout the night, causing but few casualties, but disturbing the men's rest. The casualties included one man of the 65th killed, one Officer and four men wounded, besides two camel-drivers, and some horses struck: Major Colwell's horse was shot at this time.

About 7 a.m. on the 13th, the Cavalry arrived, and at 7.30 the Mounted Infantry were sent out to feel the enemy. Information was received from a native spy that the bulk of Osman Digna's force would be in a deep khor or watercourse the sides of which would serve as an intrenchment. The advance was made by two Brigades in direct echelon of Brigade squares from the left; the troops carrying 100 rounds of ammunition per man, all transport animals being left behind, together with two companies of the 75th, to defend the zeriba. The 2nd Brigade, under Major - General Davis, led and was in the following formation: on the left flank four companies of the 42nd, in open column of companies; on the front face, three companies of the same Regiment, and at an interval of thirty paces, three companies of the 65th; on the right flank three companies of the 65th, the

Royal Marines forming the rear face of the square. † Inside the square were the guns of the Naval Brigade, and the 9-pdr. Mule Battery.

The following is the account of the attack on the 2nd Brigade, as given in General Graham's despatch.

"The 2nd Brigade began to advance from the place of formation about half-past eight a.m., and owing to some delay, in getting the 1st Brigade forward, were somewhat further in advance than I had intended when they first came in contact with the enemy. This occurred about nine a.m. when a large number suddenly appeared from the edge of a ravine, in the immediate front of the Brigade.

These were soon cleared off; the Royal Highlanders (42nd), distinguished themselves by the gallant manner in which they cheered and charged up to the edge of the ravine; but at this moment a more formidable attack came from another direction, and a large body of natives, coming in one continuous stream, charged with reckless determination, utterly regardless of all loss, on the right hand corner of the square, formed by the 1st York and Lancaster (65th). The Brigade fell back in disorder, and the enemy captured the guns of the Naval Brigade, which, however, were locked by Officers and men who stood by them to the last.

"When first coming into action, the 9-pdr. Battery of four guns, under Major Holley, R.A., had been ordered outside the square on the right flank, and when the disordered retirement took place in the 2nd Brigade, this Battery was for a time unprotected by Infantry, and exposed to the assault of the enemy, now coming on in crowds. Yet Officers and men stood firmly to their guns, raking the advancing enemy with case, which told with deadly effect.

"The 1st Brigade were attacked about the same time, but stood firm, and the Cavalry moved up to protect the flank of the 2nd Brigade, which was soon rallied, and advanced to retake the guns of the Naval Brigade. The zeriba was also threatened, but the little garrison stood to its arms, and drove the enemy back. After this there was no more serious fighting, and the enemy retreated sullenly, making an occasional stand, towards the camp and village of Tamaai, which was occupied by the 1st Brigade about 11.40 a.m., when I despatched a telegram to Admiral Hewett, announcing victory.

"The 2nd Brigade held the heights above the springs, where the Cavalry watered. Ambulances and mule cacolets were sent for to bring away the dead and wounded, all being brought into the zeriba occupied the previous night, where tents and all necessary medical requirements had already been brought up. The Cavalry returned again to Baker's zeriba. The night was undisturbed by any fire from the enemy but voices were heard shouting and wailing from the battle-field.

There was but a temporary check in one portion of the force, during the action of Tamaai, and for that many reasons may be given. At the moment of receiving the attack, the front face of the square of the 2nd Brigade was slightly disordered, owing to the gallant rush of the Royal Highlanders, in charging the enemy at the top of the ravine. For this disorder I am to some extent personally responsible, as the charge took place under my eyes, and with my approval. My own observations of the attack were made from the right front angle, formed by the two half-battalions of the 1st York and Lancaster, where I posted myself as soon as I saw the enemy's attack, and it was here the main rush came. It is the habit of these Arabs to attack the angles of squares, as they know that least fire can be brought to bear on them from these points. As the 9-pdr. Battery was on the right, the sailor's guns were on the left, but I at once sent for them to meet this attack from the right. The Arabs, however, gave no time for further arrangements, but throwing themselves with desperate determination upon the angle of the square, broke it, carrying all before them. There were many attempted rallies among the York and Lancaster and at one time I was almost surrounded by the enemy, one of whom got over my horse's quarter. In the rear of the square were the Royal Marines, than whom there can be no finer troops, and on whom I had counted as a reserve in the last emergency. Such, however, was the sudden nature of the disorder, and the impetuosity of the rush, that the Royal Marines were for a few minutes swept back, and mixed up in the general confusion. Yet, I submit, there was no panic among the men; they had been surprised, attacked suddenly, and driven back by a fanatical and determined enemy, who came on utterly regardless of loss, and who were, as I have since learned, led by their bravest chiefs. As soon as the men had had time to think, they rallied and reformed. This check affected only the 2nd Brigade. The remainder of the force, the Cavalry, the Royal Artillery, and the 1st Brigade were firm and perfectly in hand, repulsing all attacks, and co-operating to assist the 2nd Brigade in driving back the enemy, who suffered tremendously tor his temporary success, and never charged home again that day."

The foregoing despatch perhaps scarcely does justice to the events of the day. To deal with the matter more in detail: On leaving the scene of the bivouac, the two Brigades were separated by about 1,000 yards. The first Brigade, under General Buller, marched on the rear side of the other, at a distance varying from 600 to 900 yards in an oblique line. The rear Battalions and the half-Battalions on either flank of either Brigade marched at wheeling distances, so that on the word to form outwards being given, two complete squares could be formed. The two Brigades were thus placed so as to form two independent oblongs, the front face or line of each Brigade being 200 yards in length, the sides about 100 yards. The main body of the Cavalry were echeloned on the left rear of the 2nd Brigade. The morning was bright and clear, but there was no wind to carry off the smoke.

When the leading 2nd Brigade square got within 200 yards of the ravine, a series of broken and irregular rushes was made by the Soudanese on the front and right, but none of them reached within 20 yards of the British line.

Then, apparently, an order was given to charge and the front rank of the square charged up to within thirty yards from the edge of the ravine; the enemy were now swarming on the ridges on the opposite side of the ravine, and the Naval machine guns, which had been run out a few yards, in front of the right corner of the square, were turned upon them. Many of the enemy were observed running down the slopes, and disappearing among the rocks in the little valley intervening. Under cover of the smoke hundreds of the Soudanese crept up the near side of the ravine, and threw themselves upon the right front and right flank of the square. The 65th, unable to

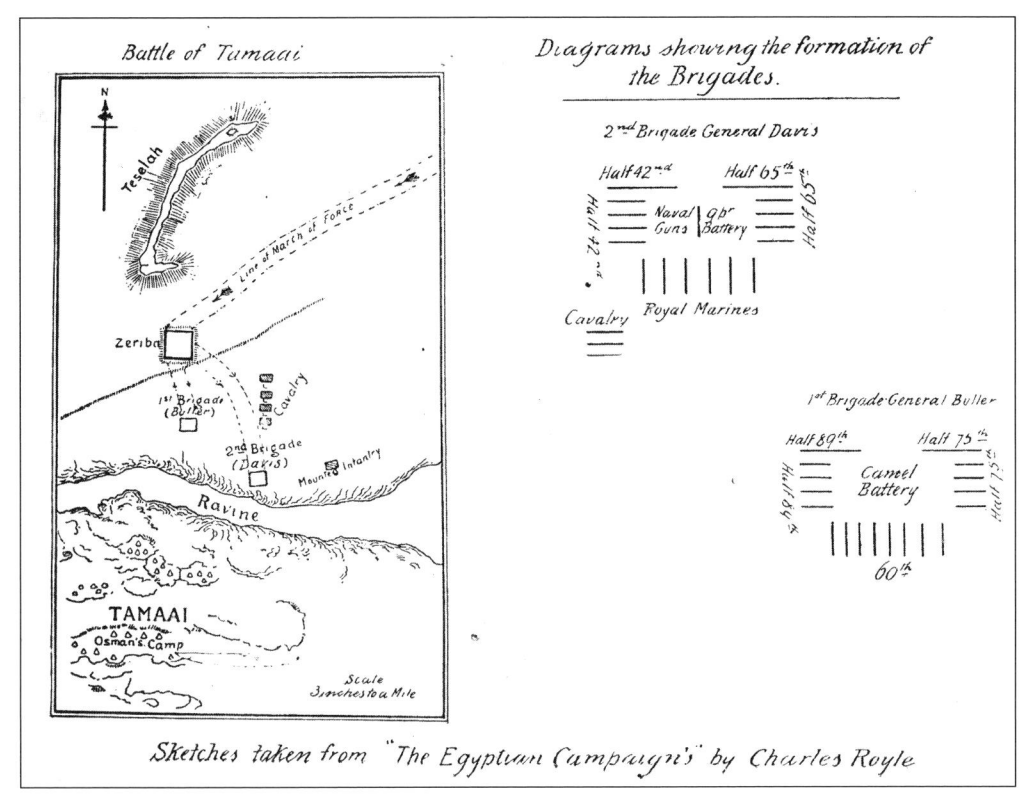

Sketches taken from "The Egyptian Campaigns" by Charles Royle

resist the onslaught, were forced back upon the Marines in rear, and the right of the 42nd became exposed, and the enemy, rushing in were among the Highlanders on their flank and rear cutting and spearing in every direction. The men were so huddled together, that many of them were unable to use their rifles or bayonets. The Marines in rear of the Brigade were wheeled up to support the 65th, and close the gaps in the formation, but it was too late, and they too were thrown back and borne away on the line of retreat. According to "The Egyptian Campaigns," by Charles Royle, as the Marines were being swept away, Major Colwell, R.M.L.I, shouted in stentorian tones, "Men of the Portsmouth Division, rally," which they did, 150 of them closing together in a compact little body, forming a little square. The Highlanders and 65th also formed one or two such groups and materially assisted in bringing about the general rally, which soon followed.

In spite of every effort, however, it appears that the whole force fell back about 800 yards. The Naval Brigade which had been sent to the front with their machine guns, during the rush lost three of their Officers, and many of their men, and the guns had to be abandoned.

It is due to the soldiers of the 2nd Brigade to say that although driven back, there was no such thing as a stampede: they retreated backwards, face to the foe, loading and firing all the time they were not engaged in meeting the attack with thrusts of the bayonet. The rally took place in about twenty minutes. This was greatly assisted by the cross fire of the 1st Brigade, from its position at some 400 or 500 yards from the ravine, and by the fire from the Cavalry, who were dismounted for the purpose, and fired volleys into the enemy's right flank. Covered by this fire, the retreating troops were halted and reformed this time in "line" with the Marines on the right, the 65th in the centre, and the 42nd, with the Naval Brigade in their rear, on the left. After a quarter of an hour's halt, and a fresh supply of ammunition being served out to each man, the 2nd Brigade once more moved forward to the attack. The first Brigade had now moved up 200 yards closer to the ravine, and halted, pouring a raking fire into the enemy, and preventing any attempt to again rush the flank of the 2nd Brigade. In ten minutes, the lost ground had been regained, and the guns recaptured.

It was now the turn of the 1st Brigade, which, still in square formation, was sent to take a second intervening ridge, some 800 yards off. The Soudanese, disheartened, kept up a feeble fire, retreating as the Brigade advanced, and the second ridge was carried without difficulty. From the top of this ridge, Tamaai could be seen in the valley below, with the tents and huts of Osman Digna's camp. By 1140 a.m. these were in possession of the British forces.

The British losses were five Officers and 86 Non-Commissioned Officers and men killed; eight Officers and 100 Non-Commissioned Officers and men wounded; missing, nineteen men.

Of the above, it is said that three Officers and eleven men were killed at the taking of the Naval guns, and that loss of the 2nd Brigade, at the time of the square being broken, was 70 in killed alone.

The number of the enemy was reported by General Graham as being from 10,000 to 12,000, and the loss as over 2,000 in killed alone.

The loss of the Royal Marine Battalion amounted to three killed and fifteen wounded, including Surgeon Cross, R.N., viz: -

Killed	R.M.A.	8th Co.,	Gnr. Thomas Tastin
	R.M.L.I.	24th Co.,	Pte. William Lock
		42nd Co.,	Pte. Arthur Giles
Wounded	R.M.A.	10th Co.,	Gnr. Fred. Eveleigh
		8th Co.,	Gnr. James W. Davis
	R.M.L.I.	2nd Co.,	Sgt. Wm. Trowbridge
		21st Co.,	Pte. Dan. Beautyman
		25th Co.,	Pte. Wm.F. Harris
		31st Co.,	Pte. Geo. Southern
		28th Co.,	Pte. Robt. Boundery
		19th Co.,	Pte. Wm. Chalkley
		6th Co.,	Pte. John Shaw
		39th Co.,	Pte. Wm. Chas. Sugg
		47th Co.,	Pte. Edwd. Horsewell
		38th Co.,	Pte. Rd. M'Donough
		30th Co.,	Pte. Hy. E. Skinner
		14th Co.,	Pte. John Wilkie
	R.N.		Surgeon Cross

Also wounded during previous night, in the zeriba, by the enemy's dropping fire, 3rd Co., Pte. William Smith: 46th Co., Pte. Davis Thomas.

On the following day (14th) Osman Digna's camp was burned, and the force returned to Suakim.

On the 17th March Captain Baldwin, R.M.L.I. and his detachment rejoined H.M.S. *Eurayalus* and the men belonging to H.M.S. *Briton* rejoined their ship also. Lieutenant Aston, R.M.A., was now appointed Acting-Adjutant to the Battalion.

On the 27th of March, Tamanib was occupied after some desultory firing, and the village burned. The British force was then at once broken up, the troops from Egypt returning to Cairo, and the remainder proceeding to England. The 3rd K.R. Rifles and the Battalion of Royal Marines were left as a temporary garrison for Suakim.

The Royal Marine Battalion embarked on board the *Utopia* on the 14th April, 371 strong, and rejoined their ships in the Mediterranean; the men belonging to the paid off ships from the China and East Indian Stations having left when the expeditionary force was broken up (29th March, 1884.)

*Captain Poe had been wounded at El-Teb, and invalided home.
†Major Schomberg's Company (F) was however ordered into the right face of the square just before it was broken.

———

THE VITU EXPEDITION.
25th, 26th, 27th and 28th October, 1890.
(Reprinted from the Globe & Laurel of 15th October. 1893)
(By Act. QM.S. F. L. Hammond, R.M.L.I.)

A short account of the Vitu expedition on the East Coast of Africa, though some time ago, and probably almost passed out of memory of many of those who were engaged in it, may yet serve to recall to mind the many incidents and lively times we had in the preparation and accomplishment of this expedition. We had been having a merry time at Mauritius, whither we had been giving leave, on the East African blockade being raised. On our return to Zanzibar we received information that a few German colonists who had settled in the town of Vitu had been foully massacred. As this place was within the British sphere of influence in the new delimitation of the East African Coast, and as the Sultan of Vitu refused to give up the assassins to justice, this line of action was determined upon. A nice business we had in preparing our straps, etc., everything having to be scrubbed clean of pipeclay and soaked in coffee grounds; also our helmets, so that we should expose our appointments as little as possible to the enemy, and as many of our readers are aware, a ship is but a sorry place to do much soldiering in, more especially when all hands are busy in the excitement of preparing for active service. The expedition was commanded by Vice-Admiral Sir E. R. Freemantle, K.C.B., R.N., with Captain The Hon. Curzon-Howe, R.N., as chief of his staff. The Royal Marines of the squadron formed a Battalion of their own, under the command of Lieut-Colonel Poole, R.M.L.I. of H.M.S. *Boadicea*, Lieut. Lalor, R.M.L.I., doing duty as Adjutant to our Battalion. The whole force was composed as follows: -

Field Battery 4.7 Pounders }	180 men
" " 4 Gardner Guns }	
2 Battalions R.N., Six Companies	450 men
R.M. Battalion, 4 Companies	200 men
Indian Contingent (from Mombassa) Iscaris	150 men

There were also about 250 of the Sultan of Zanzibars Army, used mainly as porters, and these with about 200 Coolies brought out total to about 1,500 men all told, roughly speaking about 1,000 fighting men and the others as coolies, carriers, etc. As water was scarce, and the ground to be covered on the march nothing but jungle and thick grass, and the marches performed during the day with a terribly hot sun, we had one too many coolies, although 500 camp followers appear a large number for an expedition of a thousand fighting men. On Friday (24th Oct.) H.M.S. *Boadicea*, accompanied by the other ships of the Squadron, proceeded up the coast to Lamu. On their attempting to land at some of the villages on the coast, the natives fired on the boats, and the signal was then hoisted to man and arm boats; the ships having done so, a landing was effected under fire of the enemy; after a slight resistance the natives were driven into the bush and the villages destroyed by fire. I cannot give from memory the names of these places, they were merely coast Kails (*i.e.*, small village) and are not shown on a map.

On Saturday (25th Oct.) the East African Fleet assembled off the town of Kipini and anchored about four miles from shore. H.M.S. *Conquest*, which had been sent on in advance, had already landed and occupied the town. We commenced the work of disembarkation immediately the anchorage had been effected. The following was the dress of the Royal Marines in this expedition: Helmets and puggarees, canteen and great-coat (1 flannel, 1 pair socks, towel and soap, and cap inside of great-coat), the whole fastened behind on the belt and braces, eighty rounds of ammunition in the pouches, haversack containing one day's provisions of biscuit and preserved meat, water-bottle full, blue serge suits, and leggings. For a few days previous to our arriving at Kapini we had been well doctored with quinine, as all along the African coast and creeks malaria and ague is very prevalent. I consider our immunity from such greatly due to the very sensible issue of this preventive. On our landing being safely effected through a heavy surf, we sent on at 3p.m. an advance guard of 200 men, R.N. and R.M.L.I. and the Field Battery under the command of Commander Montgomery, R.N. About 3 miles from Kipini they were able to fix up a strong zeriba before night came on, and it was well they did, for the enemy made a most determined attack upon them, greatly outnumbering our small advanced party, and with savage fearlessness advanced to within a few yards of the square several times, but the steady and well-directed fire of the machine-guns and rifles was too much for them, and they had reluctantly to retire to the jungle. The remainder of the force bivouacked for the night on the beach at Kipini, remaining fully accoutred, few slept; it was bitterly cold, and our outposts having heard firing alarmed the camp, consequently we were continually "standing to arms, though nothing transpired. We were glad when "cooks" were sounded at 3 a.m., and the camp resumed an animated and lively appearance, for all were eager to commence active operations. After a hurried breakfast of biscuit and cocoa we formed up for our march, a company of the Royal Marines forming the rear-guard, and by 5 a.m. we were well on our way. By 8 a.m. we had arrived at the zeriba, where the advanced guard had bivouacked the previous night; we then learned that the enemy had made a determined attack, but had after an hour's fighting been repulsed with considerable loss, though it was impossible to form any accurate idea of their casualties, as they had carried away with them most of their wounded and dead. We were very fortunate, only having one severe casualty on our side. After a halt of half-an-hour to refill our water-bottles, etc., we recommenced our march, moving off in square formation, with flanking parties on either side of the square to search the Jungle. By this time the sun was well over our heads and beating down upon us fiercely. The jungle and grass through which we were marching was so thick that our advance was necessarily slow. After an hour's marching a few shots were fired into the square, and the halt was sounded, but it was evident only a few scouts were about, so after a short stay we commenced our march again. Frequent halts were now necessary, as owing to the rough ground we were going over the square was often out of formation. The rear-guard, composed of a company of Royal Marines, had all their work cut out in keeping the water-carriers and coolies up in their places. At 11.30 a.m. we made a halt of two hours for midday meal and another issue of water, the men being cautioned to be most sparing of their water, as it would be the last issue they would receive until we reached the Kall wells that night, and most likely we should meet the enemy there in force. Here we left our heavier baggage with a small party, Admiral Freemantle being determined to reach the wells that night. At 1.30 p.m. we recommenced our weary march, for weary it was, as being cramped up in a ship so long many of the men were not in very good marching order. It was very noticeable that many of the men who were in the habit of wearing boots as little as possible in the ship now began to feel it severely. It is, in my opinion, a great mistake and should be discouraged as much as possible, as without their boots the men are often suffering from sea-cuts or swollen feet. By 4 p.m. we came in sight of the Kall wells, and though a few shots were occasionally dropped into the square from the hills, nothing could be seen of the enemy. By 5 p.m. we were at the wells; you may imagine the disappointment of the troops when these supposed wells turned out to be nothing but a swampy marsh, and the water of which was thick and dirty. At any other time we should probably have turned away from it with disgust, but the men were parched and dry with the heat, and it was no time to be fastidious, in fact they were thankful to get anything to satisfy the burning thirst from which many were suffering. The men were almost done up, as it had been a long march through nothing but jungle and grass, and we were very glad that the position was not occupied by the enemy, and that we were able to get into the place selected for one night's bivouack without resistance. All hands were at once employed (with the exception of the Indian contingent, who were sent out in skirmishing order to search the hills to our right for the enemy) in building zeribas of brushwood cut down with the cutlasses, biscuit boxes, etc., and such stuff as could be procured from the rough and broken ground. We formed our men in three zeribas in echelon, (1),R.M. Battalion. (2) Indian Contingent and native followers, 3) Royal Naval Battalion, having the guns of the Field Battery at the corners of each zeriba. Before we had been long at this work several of the enemy were seen on the hills to our right, who commenced a dropping fire into the zeribas, and our line of skirmishers were seen retiring, keeping up a running fire the meantime. "To Arms" was at once sounded; fortunately no one had straggled far from the encampment, consequently we were soon in position. The Royal Marines were ordered out at once to engage the enemy, advancing in attack formation. As we got well up the hill we reinforced our fighting line, and the Royal Navy (2 companies) coming up as our left support, and the Iscaris (late skirmishing) coming up as our right support, the firing became general. Evidently the enemy were taken almost unawares, they seemingly having intended surprising our zeribas after nightfall; after a sharp engagement they were repulsed with heavy loss. As the forest was pretty thick, and our zeribas not yet formed we did not follow up their retreat, but pouring a few volleys as a parting warning, we hastened back to our encampment to complete our preparations for the night. We were again fortunate in having no severe casualties; this I attribute to the enemy's high firing, most of them firing from the hip, and as we charged up hill the shots were too high. Several of the men's rifles jammed, and even with a cleaning rod it took them some time to get their barrels free again. As soon as we had completed our zeribas for the night we had tea and biscuits, and then, with a sharp look-out, prepared for coming events, feeling sure that now they had come in touch with our position they would harass us throughout the night; yet, although we waited patiently that night, with the exception of a few false alarms, nothing else transpired. It was as bitterly cold at night as it had been hot during the day, so that few slept: it was too cold and damp, and the expected attack kept everyone on the alert. At 4 a.m. (Oct. 27) we sounded "cooks," and after a hasty meal we formed up for march, and by 5 a.m. were well on our road. We were now about three miles from Vitu, advancing in square formation. The first hour passed away quickly, and we plodded silently on; by 6 a.m. we fell in with the enemy's scouts, and from this time until the taking of the place the fire was incessant. We had some difficulty at first in keeping the square formation intact, but as we advanced, and we received a heavy fire on our right and rear force, all was plain sailing as the niggers (coolies) saw there was as much danger one way as the other, consequently kept well in the square. By 7 a.m. the engagement had become general. The Admiral made a feint attack to the right of the stockaded town, and then, changing position, advanced smartly on to the main entrance to the town; a body of the enemy made an attempt to force our right rear, but a few sharp volleys drove them back. As soon as their line of skirmishers had been driven back into the stockade, we brought our Field Battery to bear on the town, also using Hale's war rockets, whilst the Brigade got into position for the coup de main. Under cover of a heavy fire from the side faces of the square, Mr. Jennings (Gunner, H.M.S. *Boadicea*) gallantly advanced and laid a mine of gun cotton under the main entrance of the stockaded town; whilst this was being done we prepared for the final charge. Our formation was as follows: - The R.M. Battalion (with the exception of one company as rear guard) in the centre, facing the entrance, Lieut. J. N. Lalor, R.M.L.I., leading the fighting line, Lieut. J. H. Abrahall, R.M.L.I., the support, Lieut.-Colonel Poole in command and left a Battalion of the Royal Navy, whilst our Field Battery occupied small knolls to our right and left. Keeping up an incessant bombardment of the town, the Indian Contingent remaining in the centre of the now skeleton square, in order that they might be moved to the weakest point in case of a counter attack. The Order was now given to fire the mine, which was successfully done, the bugles sounded the charge and with a ringing British cheer our men advanced to the charge, and Vitu was stormed and taken, the enemy retiring precipitately through the town to the forest and jungle in rear. As we advanced into the town, almost every sort of arm was to be found, the retiring enemy evidently throwing down all encumbrances that were likely to impede their retreat. There were a great many of the enemy killed and wounded; only a few casualties on our side, none fatal. The town of Vitu is well situated, and the palace and houses much better built than one would have expected to see in this part of the African coast. The appearance of the interior of the town would suggest we had been too soon upon them, after their reverse the previous night. The stockade was to a great extent naturally fortified, and was situated in a splendid position for defensive operations; in fact, 200 men of an European army could have successfully resisted a much larger force than ours. After a thorough search of the buildings of the town, and a liberal issue of water, we evacuated the place and encamped outside for the mid-day meal, a small party being detailed to put the town in flames. A few stragglers of the enemy appeared on the hill and commenced a long-range fire, but were soon silenced by a few well-directed volleys from a skirmishing party. At 3 p.m. we commenced our return march, retiring in square formation. It was rather an amusing sight to see some of our fellows, who had burdened themselves up with curios, such as shields, spears, revolvers and old fire-arms, dropping them one by one as the march became weary and irksome. We made a halt at the Kall wells that night, re-occupying the zeribas of the previous night. We breakfasted at 3 a.m. the following morning (28 Oct.), and by 5 a.m. were well on our way to the coast. As the day advanced the heat was intense and several were affected by sun stroke; this was rather hard on the stretcher party, comprised as they were of idlers from the ships, and armed to the teeth. Many will smile as they recollect the strong and rather forcible remarks these long-suffering warriors indulged in as they trudged along with their heavy burdens. I am glad to say none of these cases of sunstroke amongst the men of the expedition proved fatal. As the day wore on our halts became more frequent; the men were weary, and many who had resorted too often to their water-bottles during the heat of the day were now suffered from parched and swollen lips. By 4 p.m. the welcome news was passed along the column that Kipini was in sight; by 5 p.m. we were on the beach and ready for embarkation. The Royal Marine Battalion embarked on their various ships that evening. Thus ended the first armed expedition undertaken entirely by a Naval Brigade on the East Coast of Africa. The Officers of Royal Marines who took part in the expedition were Lieut.–Colonel E. Poole, R.M.L.I., Lieut. J. N. Lalor, R.M.L.I., and Lieut. J. H. Abrahall, R.M.L.I.

As it is now three years ago, and this account is written principally from memory, I trust any imperfections will be favourably treated by any of our readers who may have taken an part in this expedition.

THE WORK OF AN OFFICER OF THE MARINES IN THE OPENING UP OF JAPAN.

Extracts from a letter to the late Col. L. Edye,

From Lt-Col. (afterwards Gen.) Fagan, R.M.L.I.
7th June, 1892.

"About the beginning of the year 1873 the Japanese Government contracted a loan in Europe for the purpose of developing a railway system through the interior of their beautiful country.

At about the same time I had been in communication with some of their officials of the Public Works Department, with a view to taking part in the trigonometrical survey of the country, a class of work which has always had a peculiar attraction for me, and which was at that time about to be undertaken.

In January, 1874, I was sounded as to whether I would be willing to assist in the preliminary surveys in connection with a scheme for pushing the trunk line of railway through the centre of the country. This offer I was, with the kind assistance of our Ambassador (Sir Harry Parkes) and the sanction of the Colonel of our Battalion (Richards), enabled to accept, and in February, 1874, I placed myself at the disposal of the Imperial Government, and went off up country to commence operations, with field instruments borrowed from our own Government and from the friends in the Settlement, who came to wish me Godspeed. This work kept me till the following autumn, when I returned to the coast, knocked over by fever and ague, and my weight which had been 12 st. 10 lbs. had gone down to 9 st. 10 lbs. It took me about a couple of months of rest to get into working trim again, when I went back with our Ambassador and a party who were going on a tour, in the Government dispatch vessel, to Nagoja (pronounced Nangoya), where much of the famous cloisonné ware is made, at the head of Oevari Bay, and about 20 miles only from the scene of my former labours. This province Mino was the theatre of the late disastrous earthquakes. I lived for many months in the town of Kano, which has suffered a great deal, and which is only one mile from Gifu (to which we often went), which has been completely destroyed.

After mapping, and picking a way for the railway through a very rocky gorge about 20 miles from Kano, I returned to spend the winter at office work, etc., in Kioto, in the western capital. Thence I went, in the early spring of 1876 to Isuruga on the west coast, where I remained for some time surveying the coast and providing details for my successors at some future date to work on, when about to locate the line and select the anchorage, etc., for a first-class port on the western coast of the Empire.

In the autumn, as there was no immediate prospect of further operations being undertaken, they having come to the end of their loan, I packed up my traps, and travelling via America, arrived in England in December, 1876.

I may mention that in the 27 days' passage across the Pacific I picked up a stone in weight, or rather more than ½ lb. per diem, which confirmed me in my opinion that a complete change of climate had become necessary to me.

Before leaving I sent over to the Commander-in-Chief at Shanghai, to offer my services with the advance guard of any force going into the interior of China-Pekin, etc. - about which there was a talk at that time; but having received his assurance that there was nothing doing of that sort on the tapis, and that all differences had been amicably arranged, I considered myself free to go on my way to England rejoicing.

In conclusion, I may mention that on the whole I was much pleased with the interior of the country and with the people with whom I was brought in contact; I never had an uncivil word from the civil population, and I have every intention of looking up some of my old friends (if they are still alive) in Oevari plain again, with my wife, when I have more leisure.

At present I have the satisfaction of knowing that my work has borne fruit, and that express trains are now running between the two capitals, as also to my old house at Isuruga.

I have often thought that they might have sent me their Order of the Rising Sun, but my one regret has been that I worked so hard.

Yours sincerely,
G. T. FAGAN."

P.S. - If you come down here you shall have a gargle out of the pewter mug which accompanied me in my travels, and which now an honoured relic, is inscribed with about 50 names of the numerous places of interest &c., in my travels in the above parts. Between February and November in 1874 I shifted my whole party no less than 56 times.

I have my journals still unopened.

THE WAR ON THE GAMBIA.
OPERATIONS OF COLONEL CORBETS COLUMN.
BRILLIANT SUCCESS.
(Reprinted from G. and L. of 16th April, 1894)

The second Flying Column, under Lieut.-Colonel Corbet. R.M.L.I., composed of one company Royal Marines, one company West India Regiment, and a 7-pounder gun (Royal Marine Artillery), left Bathurst at 7 a.m. on Thursday, 22nd February, and marched to Bakotti about twelve miles distant, where the Administrator and Admiral Bedford joined the column, and proceeded to Sukotta, about two miles outside British territory. On arriving at that village, the headman was sent for, and ordered to surrender all guns and powder and to destroy his stockade. But few guns being forthcoming, Colonel Corbet proceeded into the stronghold and threatened to burn it. This produced some more guns, and a thorough search resulted in about a hundred being seized. These were then destroyed, together with a large quantity of powder found in the magazine.

The stockade having been pulled down and burnt, the column returned to Bakotti and bivouacked there. Next morning, at daylight, the march to Busamballa was resumed. Two rivers had to be forded en route. Jundun, an open town, was reached about noon, and searched for arms and powder. After leaving that village the column entered upon the densest imaginable bush, the path of a width of about eighteen inches only permitting of progress in single file, and making the work of dragging the 7-pounder, which was performed by the Marines, very trying indeed.

Shortly before three, on emerging from the thick bush, Busumballa came in sight some 300 yards distant. The moment the head of the column appeared in sight fire was opened from the stockade and also by a large number of men lying hidden in the grass, forming a line reaching from the stockade to the thick bush, and barring any further progress. Without loss of time the 7-pounder was brought to the front, and a couple of shells fired into the village, one of which set it on fire, and soon cleared it of its defenders, who went to join the men in the open. Colonel Corbet having disposed of the village, then advanced on the men outside, disposing his men in skirmishing order, with the 7-pounder in the centre. The enemy retired slowly, firing heavily but without effect, the advancing line pouring volley after volley into them at a distance of about 150 yards. Suspecting that the design of the enemy was to lure him into the thick bush, Colonel Corbet discontinued the pursuit and turned his attention to the destruction of the stockade. Busamballa was a very good specimen of a stockaded village and evidently of recent date. There were two stockades - the outer of bamboo, about 15 feet high, forming a screen of great toughness, being tied with split bamboo and lashed to strong posts at frequent intervals, but at the same time permitting the garrison of the village to see through it; the inner stockade, about 12 feet distance, and the same height as the outer one, composed of trunks of trees, set three deep and embedded in the ground, just allowing a gun to be pushed through between their lower ends. Inside the stockade there was a ditch a couple of feet deep, and the earth from it had been thrown up against the stockade. A very skilfully flanked, gateway was placed in the centre of each side of the stockade.

Two sides of the stockade being attacked by flames from the burning village, Colonel Corbet, with a rope that had been brought for the purpose, had a large portion of the remainder pulled down, using fifty or sixty men at a time, and dragging it down in lengths of a few feet at a time. After, blowing up the principal gate with gun cotton the column resumed the march to Aboka in British territory, which had been appointed as the next resting place. Aboka was reached at 8 p.m.

Thus ended a trying day of over thirteen hours marching and fighting, during which time a distance variously computed to be between 20 and 24 miles had been traversed, dragging a field gun; no mean performance under an African sun.

The following morning at daylight the column marched to Cape St. Mary, some eight miles, to protect British interests in that neighbourhood, and on the next day advanced some six miles further to the front to bar the way to Bathurst, in case Fodi Silah - as was expected – should attempt to invade British territory.

The entrenching tools which were promised not having arrived when the column left Cape St. Mary, and only two hours of daylight remaining when Sabazee, the appointed position, was reached, it was necessary to decide how best to utilise the remaining time. The bush round the bivouac was accordingly cleared away. It was resolved to trust to a steady rifle fire to keep the enemy at a distance should he attack. It was the best policy, and was more in accordance with British tradition than any attempt at providing cover by utilising any of the neighbouring hamlets as a shelter.

By burning and otherwise, Colonel Corbet had cleared the bush to a distance of about 120 yards to each flank. The front was pretty clear for some distance and the rear for some 200 yards. Water had to be procured from a well discovered nearly half a mile away, so all water bottles and kettles were filled before nightfall. All being ready every man was told off to his appointed place, all stores and ammunition in the centre, and a chain of sentries placed at a distance of a hundred yards round the bivouac. When all was quiet the alarm was sounded to test how long it took for each man to reach his post, and about ten seconds was sufficient. The only officers present besides Colonel Corbet in command were Lieutenant Cowie, W.I.R., and Surgeon Bowden, R.N.

At about half-past five in the morning a sentry on the right gave the alarm and came running in. Two large parties of the enemy, each numbering about a hundred, appeared through the darkness, rushing on the force. Quick as lightning the section on the right was in its place, and a volley poured into their ranks checked the enemy's rush while still a couple of hundred yards from the bivouac. In a few minutes fire was opened by the enemy from the front and left also, the men on the right taking advantage of all cover to get to within 100 yards' distance. Until it became light there was nothing to be done but keep the fire of the enemy under by frequent volleys poured into the bush.

As soon as it became light Lieut. Cowie was sent out to clear the bush on the left, and afterwards a party of Marines to do the same on the right. This course was advisable, as the fire was very close and annoying. Several Martini-Henry guns, presumably brought up by the enemy, from Madini Creek, were used. Their bullets could be plainly heard whistling overhead. The woodwork of the rifle of a man of the West India Regiment was smashed by a bullet, but luckily no one was hit, as the firing was too high.

After the action had been progressing for some time a large body of horse and foot, estimated at nine hundred or a thousand, was seen to be passing across the front in a diagonal direction at a distance varying from one thousand to fifteen hundred yards. Colonel Corbet at once directed most of his fire upon them, and effectively shelled them with the 7-pounder. The shells were seen to burst beautifully in their midst before they retreated from view. This was the main body of the enemy returning from a foray into British Kombo. After this experience they never again ventured into our territory.

Feeling now confident of his ability to hold the position, and hoping to draw the enemy into the open, Colonel Corbet ordered a general retreat of the whole force, but the enemy, though somewhat emboldened, still clung to cover. About half-past seven an advance was therefore made, and the enemy rapidly retreated across the border.

The coolness of all concerned is said to have been most marked. The fire, which (with the exception of a few shots fired by individual marksmen) was entirely by section volleys, was delivered with as much precision as if on parade. Private Kenn, R.M.L.I., an excellent shot, distinguished himself by going out to the front, in company with the Sergeant-Major of the West India Regiment, and dislodging a group of men whose fire was very troublesome, one of whom he shot as they were running for better cover.

The rest of the day was spent in making a sheltered trench with improvised tools; and the next day the force moved to another position, where, entrenching tools having arrived, a strong earthwork was soon thrown up. This position was called Fort Britannia. After a week spent there, the force was withdrawn and the Marines marched to Bathurst to embark for the attack on Gunjur.

The casualties were four wounded – Corporal Chaplain, Privates Farmer and Budd, R.M.L.I. and one West India man. It is indeed marvellous that the list was so small, as for half-an-hour at the worst time the bivouac was swept by a hail of slugs and bullets.

The admirable success of this small force in the action of Sobajee against overwhelming numbers was undoubtedly due to the splendid position taken up by Colonel Corbet, and to his skill and resource when making use of the precious hours of daylight. He saved Bathurst from any attack, and too much credit cannot be given him for the manner in which he conducted his operations.

EXPERIENCES OF No. 1 COLUMN.
Commanded By Lieutenant-Colonel A. D. Corbet, C.B., R.M.L.I.,
In The Gambla Expedition, 1894.
(By One who was There.)
(Reprinted from the G. and L. of 15th Feb., 1895)

Our Column, composed of fifty men of the *Raleigh's* Royal Marine detachment, with a 7-pdr. field gun (land service), and a Company of about fifty strong of the 1st Battalion W.I. Regiment, under Captain Westmoreland, Lieuts. Cowie and Carre-Smith, left Bathurst early on the morning of the 22nd February, 1894. Surgeon Bowden, R.N., was in medical charge, and some forty carriers were in attendance - a nondescript lot of all sorts and sizes, but wonderful hands at carrying loads up to eighty pounds, though about sixty pounds is the usual amount.

All being ready, the men carrying a blanket rolled with towel, soap and shirt inside, and sixty rounds of ammunition in their pouches, a start was made for Sukutta, a village situated just outside

British territory, and about twelve miles distant from Bathurst. This village we were to disarm, and if resistance were offered, burn. A couple of miles outside Sukutta we were met by the Headman of the place, who expressed a desire to comply with all our demands, and pushing on, we found the inhabitants engaged in pulling down the stockade. A demand for their arms and powder produced some guns, but no powder, so Colonel Corbet, taking with him an interpreter and his orderly, Corporal Hunt, proceeded into the town to the central square, where the inevitable palavers are held, and informed the Headman that unless more arms were forthcoming and the powder magazine pointed out, he should be under the painful necessity of burning down their town. This produced more arms and the key of the magazine, a mud-built structure, with walls of considerable thickness. About forty or fifty small bags of powder were found in the magazine and destroyed, and a search party discovered some more guns, making a total of about a hundred, which were all broken up. It may be said here that the guns used by the Mandingoes are of the usual "trade gun" description, long-barrelled muskets, sometimes with flint, but usually with percussion locks, and as a rule, in the French district, of French make. The usual charge is a handful of coarse powder, two or three spherical bullets and a dozen or two jagged bits of iron for use at close quarters. The town being disarmed, the Administrator and Admiral Bedford, who had accompanied the column thus far, entered escorted by the whole party, had a palaver with the Headmen and informed them they were now British subjects. Corporal Hunt then produced a Union Jack from the breast of his serge tunic, lashed it on to a bamboo pole, stuck it into the roof of the Headman's hut, the troops saluted, and the British Empire was so much the bigger. After making a bonfire of the remains of the stockade, the troops returned a couple of miles to a friendly village called Bakotti and bivouacked there.

The programme for next day was to march south into hostile territory, take the villages Jundum and Bassambulla, and return for the night to Aboka, a village some miles east of Bakotti, and near Lamir Creek on the Gambia River, where boats were to meet us and convey us back to the ship. But something was to happen which was to overturn these arrangements and keep us on shore fifteen days longer. Soon atter daybreak next morning we started, leaving behind Lieut. Carre-Smith, ill with the fever which so few escape, and which, ultimately, after our return on board, prostrated a large proportion of our party, in spite of the daily dose of quinine swallowed religiously by all hands. Whether it is a true malarial fever or due to exposure to the sun seems doubtful, but it is probably the latter.

Led by two guides, one of them the son of the "King" of Bakotti, a picturesque looking person whom we dubbed the Heir Apparent, our force passed through a thickly - wooded country for some miles, crossing two streams, to ford which it was necessary to make a considerable detour, and meeting here and there patches of open cultivated ground of some extent.

When within about three miles of Jundum we entered upon bush of the densest character, the narrowest bush path compelling us to march in single file, while the advanced guard fired volleys at frequent intervals as a precautionary measure into the bush in front and on either flank. About noon Jundum was reached, an open village, the Headman of which met us with a white flag flying, but, cutting short their insatiable desire for palaver, we reached the village, found a few arms and some powder, which we destroyed, informed the Headman their village was now in British territory, and moved on through, if possible, thicker bush than we had yet encountered. After dragging the 7-pounder with much difficulty and many capsizes through two miles of this, we reached the edge of the bush and came in sight of Bussumballs, and bringing the gun to the front, we entered the clearing in the centre of which stood the village.

Hardly had we appeared before fire was opened from the stockade, and simultaneously from a body of skirmishers lying in the grass, and reaching from the stockade to the thick bush at the edge of the clearing on our left front. In half a minute a common shell rattled through the stockade, followed by a shrapnel which burst over the centre of the village and set it on fire, the thatched roofs being soon in a blaze. The village being now, in the words of the London Fire Brigade reports, "well alight," and the garrison given notice to quit, we turned our attention to the men in the open.

As we advanced in skirmishing order the field gun in the centre, the Heir Apparent, who was armed with a musket of enormous length, apparently inflamed with ardour at the sight of his hereditary foe, bounded forward in front of the field gun (which had just been loaded with shrapnel), squatted on his haunches, and elevated his piece at an angle of forty-five degrees in the direction of the clouds floating overhead. A fearful explosion followed, and H.R.H. nearly measured his length on the ground. Advancing rapidly, we closed somewhat on the enemy, who retired, firing heavily but ineffectually, while we returned their fire with section volleys and an occasional shell, though rarely getting nearer than 150 yards. With the exception of an attempt to turn our left flank, which was soon disposed of, the enemy made no stand, and it became evident their design was to draw us away from the village and into the thick bush, to lure us in fact down to Medina Creek, a few miles distant, where, as we were shortly to learn, our Naval Brigade, a few hours earlier in the day, had been forced to take to their boats, after suffering terrible losses.

Taking steps to prevent being surprised, we desisted from pursuit, and set to work to destroy the portion of the village stockade which the flames of the burning huts had not reached. The easiest way to destroy an old stockade is by fire, but this was a comparatively new one, so, having provided a length of rope before leaving the ship for the purpose, we pulled it down in lengths of ten or twelve feet at a time, employing fifty men on the job. It was now four o' clock, and within two hours of sundown, so, by way of a parting shot, Sergeant Milton placed a charge of gun-cotton under the main gateway of the stockade, and up it went. Bussumballa, unlike the other stockaded towns we saw, which were usually an irregular oval, was a perfect square, and of recent construction. There were two stockades, the outer of split bamboo, forming a screen of great toughness, while allowing the garrison to see what was going on outside, the inner being constructed of the trunks of small trees, about a foot in diameter at the base, standing three deep and some fifteen feet in height, well embedded in the ground. A ditch, about two feet deep was dug inside, and the earth was thrown up in front. A distance of about twelve feet separated the two stockades, while in the centre of the inner side of each was a zig-zag entrance, flanked at each turn, the stockade at that point being of extra strength. A bush or a piece of light matting concealed the entrance from the view of anyone at a distance. It may seem strange that with a stockade of such strength a better stand was not made, but the Mandingo, in common with most savage or semi-savage tribes, has a wholesome dread of being surrounded and caught in a trap, and his first and overmastering thought is how to make sure of his retreat. Threaten his flanks or rear, and he feels it is time to be off.

The march to Aboka took us four hours, the last two in the dark, and glad we were to reach our bivouac, where we found shelters of matting had been run up for us, for the night winds were cold with a heavy dew. These shelters are very useful, and we got quite adepts in a short time at running them up, the supply of matting being practically unlimited, as it is used for hut building, fencing, and a variety of purposes. The "modus operandi" is to take a suitable piece of matting, bend it into a circular form, leaving a doorway, lash it to poles driven into the ground, take a long bamboo for a centre pole, lash some slighter ones with split bamboo to its upper end, and to the poles supporting the walls, so as to form the framework of the roof, thatch it with palm leaves, and the house is complete.

Fires were then lighted, the seven-pounder was divested of sundry bunches of fowls, thoughtfully left behind by our Bussumballa friends, which had made it on the return journey present somewhat the appearance of a poulterer's shop at Christmas time, and stewed chicken was the order of the day.

The carriers, squatting around their own fires, jabbered away far into the night, but we, hunger being satisfied, were soon ready for a good sleep after our twenty mile march.

In the middle of the night Colonel Corbet was aroused by a messenger, bringing a note from the Admiral, acquainting him with the disastrous affair at Medina Creek the day before, in which some sixty officers and men of the Naval Brigade, out of two hundred, had been killed and wounded and requesting him to move with all speed to Fort St. Mary, about eleven miles distant, to protect the district in case the enemy, emboldened by success, should make an incursion into British territory. Next morning, soon after daylight, we were off, none of us feeling very bright after the exertions of the previous day, and with the terrible news of the reverse experienced by the Naval Brigade, fresh in our minds.

A pony, picked up somehow, was utilized to give any men unable to march an occasional lift, and at nine o clock we reached the Fort, which is situated on the sea shore, and must have been in its day of considerable strength.

Hardly had we settled down, when orders arrived for us to leave the next day, on being relieved, and take up a position near Sabagee, five miles further to the front, so as to protect our territory from attack, and the friendly villages in rear from pillage. Next afternoon (25th February) on relief arriving, we marched out, having to send into Bathurst two of our party, unable to proceed further, and arrived at our destination at 4 p.m., with only two hours of daylight left in which to strengthen our position. Intrenching tools, though sent for, had not arrived, so it was resolved to utilize the time in clearing away the bush by burning, and otherwise obtain a good field of fire, and trust to discipline and straight shooting to do the rest. Our position sloped gently to the front, and was fairly clear of bush except on the flanks, where it approached to within about 100 yards. This we burnt and cut down with what tools we could improvise as much as possible. Having filled every available vessel with water, for the nearest well was some distance off in the bush and we knew not when we might be cut off from access to it, we placed the stores and ammunition in the centre, the men were fallen in a circle, according to their sections the Marines taking the right half, the West India Regiment the left half of the circle, the seven-pounder being in front with a shell fused ready to insert. Sections were commanded by Corporals Wetheral, R.M.A., Tilley, Chaplin and Morris, R.M.L.I. but when the field gun was being worked, Corpl. Wetherall and four gunners took charge, and Lce. - Corpl. Healy commanded the remainder of the section. Sergt. Milton, R.M.A., was the only Sergeant present with the detachment. It must be understood that at this time we were the only organised body capable of taking the field. Five miles in rear was Fort St. Mary, held by a small party of bluejackets, and in front was an unknown number of Mandingoes, estimated according to some accounts at as many as two thousand, flushed with their repulse of the Naval Brigade. About 5.30 next morning a sentry on the right gave the alarm, and we could just make out in the dim light two parties of men, each numbering about a hundred, rushing towards our right flank, having plainly been attempting to steal round our rear, for we found their tracks afterwards in the long grass. They appeared to have been marching about six deep.

In a few seconds every man was in his place, and our right section poured in a volley which made them disappear into the bushes, while still some two hundred yards away from us. Almost immediately a heavy fire broke out in front and on our left fank, and the bushes seemed alive with men. Lying down, we fired volleys by sections into the bush wherever the flashes of their guns appeared thickest. For more than half an hour the fire was very heavy, slugs were flying about too thick to be quite pleasant, and the unmistakeable whiz of Martini bullets was to be heard just overhead, telling us that some of the rifles lost by the Naval Brigade were being used against us. Corpl. Chaplin, Privates Farmer and Budd of the R.M.L.I., and a private of the W.I. Regiment were wounded by slugs, but after having their wounds dressed, returned to the fighting line. After a time our volleys began to tell, and the enemy drew further back into the bushes. As soon as it became light enough Lieut. Cowie was sent with a party of the W.I. Regiment to clear the bush on the left, and on their return, a party of Marines to drive the enemy back on our right. An attempt was then made to draw the enemy, if possible, into the open, by sending a section well out to the front, and suddenly recalling it at the double. As the section reached us we fired a volley, and all bolted to the rear as if panic-stricken, hiding behind some mat shelters that had been run up. Somewhat emboldened, the enemy advanced to the edge of the bush, but not a man showed himself in the open. However, our fire, when resumed, seemed somewhat more effective. Soon after the head of a strong column of the enemy, led by mounted men, came in sight, 1100 or 1200 yards off on our left front. We at once opened fire on them with the seven-pounder, and poured in some long range volleys as they moved across our front, and disappeared behind a wood some 1500 yards to our right front, in the direction of their own territory. They numbered apparently about 900 or 1000, and marched in order, five or six deep. While part of our force were engaging them, the remainder kept those of the enemy in our immediate neighbourhood occupied. This force, we learnt afterwards, had burnt one or two small hamlets in British territory before encountering us. Disheartened, apparently, by the failure of the main body to come to their assistance, the fire of the enemy slackened, and at half-past seven we advanced and drove them across the border, nor did they ever again venture into British territory. No bodies were found on the field, for the Mandingoes at all hazards remove their dead, and some blood-stained guns were all they left behind. It was said that at Medina Creek, where the Mandingoes ventured into the open, whenever one of them fell, he was at once seized by his comrades and bumped over the ground to the rear, in a way warranted to extinguish the vital spark in a very short time, if not already extinct. Native reports put the loss of the enemy at two hundred killed and wounded, including three headmen killed by a shell while leading the main body past us. A number of empty Martini cartridge cases were found on the field, showing that several of the rifles lost at Medina Creek were used against us, but the Mandingoes luckily did not know how to use them, and fired too high. The rest of the day we spent in still further clearing the bush around and in constructing a zareba with the aid of a few tools picked up in a neighbouring village. The following day, 27th February, in accordance with orders, we moved back some three miles, as our being so far to the front made the work of sending out supplies rather heavy, and a position was selected at the junction of the four chief "roads" of the district, with good water close at hand, where, entrenching tools having arrived, we threw up a redoubt of sufficient strength, which received the name of Fort Britannia. Though in Bathurst a panic seems to have existed, the days passed quietly enough, and our patrols discovered no sign of the enemy. Fodi Silah, however, the rebel chief, occasionally sent a letter, threatening to burn us out, and breakfast with us as he put it. Possibly he found the early breakfast we provided for him at Sabagee rather indigestible.

On 1st March 1st Battalion West India Regiment arrived, and leaving again with our company of the Regiment on the following day they retook Bassimbulla, which had been re-occupied and partially rebuilt.

On the 6th March we were withdrawn, and picking up some twenty or thirty scouts at Bathurst Barracks, embarked on board the *Alecto*, a paddle gun vessel of a light draught, for river service, where we were reinforced by thirty men from different ships.

Next morning we anchored some 700 yards off Gungur beach, preparatory to an attack on that place, which lies about one and a half miles inland. The town of Gungur is situated about twenty miles south of Bathurst, and was Fodi Silah's last stronghold, as well as one of its oldest towns, and contained a mosque of great sanctity. An obstinate resistance was therefore likely, though, as the W. India Regiment was approaching from the North, it was thought the fear of being taken between two fires would be too much for the Mandingoes, and such proved to be the case. The *Satellite*, *Magpie* and *Widgeon* anchored as close to the shore as their draught of water would permit, and there we remained at anchor three days, the town being bombarded for an hour each morning, the fire being directed by men stationed in the tops, and the bush in the rear of the landing-place, which was full of men, being occasionally shelled and swept by volleys of musketry from a picked party of Marines, all marksmen, stationed on the *Alecto's* hurricane deck. A heavy fire was kept up in return, and boats sent in to reconnoitre the landing place, or, as was sometimes the case, merely to draw the enemy fire, were received with a tremendous fusilade, but though the boats were occasionally struck by slugs, and the ships by Martini bullets, there were no casualties. On the morning of the 9th, information having been received that the W.I. Regiment was nearing Gungur, the beach was shelled for half-an-hour, some beautiful practice being made, and a force of 150 bluejackets and 80 Marines was landed simultaneously, some in large native canoes towed round from Bathurst for the purpose and some in ships boats. There was a considerable surf running, but all got ashore without mishap, though not without a wetting. The beach was rushed with fixed bayonets, but though the crest immediately in rear of the bushes on the top was found to be honeycombed with rifle pits for a considerable distance, the birds had flown. Column of route was then formed with thirty Marines as a rear guard and the remaining fifty in advance. The road led through fairly thick bush, but we were unmolested, and arrived at Gungur only to find the W.I. Regiment in possession and the town in flames, no resistance having been met with. The meeting with our dusky friends was very cordial, as the Marines marched into their lines with Bugler Coles at their head sounding the general salute with might and main to acquaint them with our approach. Our valiant native "scouts," who had hitherto remained in rear, contrary to the usually accepted doctrine as to the duties of scouts, now rushed to the front, and in the twinkling of an eye each man had captured and tied by a cord half–a-dozen stray goats, and appeared hung over like a Christmas tree with a selection of iron cooking pots, looted out of the still burning town. Very picturesque they looked, if not exactly warlike. Poor fellows, they had to return to Bathurst, and were looted in their turn, arriving home after all goatless, if not pot-less. A couple of hours were spent in completing the destruction of the stockade and town, the former being single, and about ten feet high, with various entrances, closed with wooden doors about four inches thick, and only admitting one person at a time. Fragments of shell strewn around showed the fire of the ships to have been well directed. We were all on board our ships before dark, and that night left for Bathurst, rejoining our own ships next morning. The W.I. Regiment marched back to Bathurst, burning a couple of small towns on their way, while Fodi Silah fled into French territory and gave himself up with a couple of hundred of his fighting men to the authorities. Our last sad duty was to collect the remains of those who had been left on the field at Medina Creek, and bury them with all honour in Bathurst cemetery, and there they lie - officer and man, Bluejacket and Marine, and who would wish to lie in better company.

ORIGIN OF DIVISIONAL FUND.

Extract from Plymouth Div. Orders, 18 Nov. 1784:

"The *Charity Fund has been kept for many years back in a close unmilitary manner, so as even to cause a suspicion. The Committee lately appointed to enquire into the state of this Fund have reported that the said Fund appears to them to be deficient £192 4s., which sum has been endeavoured to be recovered, but hitherto without effect.

To prevent the like evils in future the *several* Funds of this Division are to be thrown into one and henceforth to he called the *Divisional Fund*, while it is to be open to the inspection of the Corps, and every quarter a Committee will be appointed to state what has been received and what has been advanced, and then to strike the proper balance.

The Fund is literally meant to supply the little contingencies not authorized by the Board of Admiralty, though absolutely necessary for the utility of the Corps in general, and will now be similar to all Corps, who have what they call a Regimental Fund."

Plymouth Div, Order, 18 Nov., 1791:
The Commanding Officer directs that all men allowed to work are stopped in the Squad Office eighteen pence a week, according to the usage, for the support of the Divisional Fund, and every man permitted to work is to be returned to the Commanding Officer.

Marine Office, 6th Dec., 1821:
………..and you will also cause a stoppage of 3/- a week to be made from each Tailor and Shoemaker, placing them on the same footing with other working men, for the benefit of the Divisional Fund.

R.M.O. Letter of 18th Oct., 1858:
States that payment to Master Tailor and Workmen for making up clothing and necessaries is to be paid without a deduction towards Divisional or other Funds.

R.M.O. Letter of 7 Nov., 1864:
Directs that one-fourth of the profits of the Commissariat Canteen System is to be invested in the funds at the close of each half-year, and added to the Divisional Fund Account.

17th Feb., 1869 - 237 Circular, R.M.O.:
The contribution of one-fourth of the profits of the Commissariat Fund hitherto ordered to be invested for the Divisional Fund is to be discontinued, and a contribution of one-third of the profits realised is to be transferred to the Divisional Fund, not less frequently than half-yearly, for current expenses, the surplus of which, if any, may be invested, the remaining two-thirds of profits to be administered by the Commissariat Committee under the name of the Commissariat Fund. The average profits are not to exceed 8 per cent., and the prices of the articles are to be reduced accordingly. Should the receipts exceed or fall short of the 8 per cent. of stock sold, the Stock Account Book is to be credited or debited accordingly and the price list re-adjusted.

J. W. C. WILLIAMS, A.A.G.

* Nothing more known about this.

ANNUAL INSPECTIONS.

4th May, 1869 - Circular 293, R.M.O.:
(1) By G.O.C. District, with reference to their efficiency in the field (H.R.H. the Field Marshal C.-in-C. to issue the necessary instructions).
(2) By D.A.G. R.M., re the interior economy (in all its details) of the general state of efficiency of the several administrative departments, comprising the Divisional Staff and of the peculiar characteristics of the administration of authority vested in the Commanding Officer for the maintenance of discipline.
(3) By the Director General of Naval Ordnance to test the proficiency of the officers and men of the Infantry and Artillery Divisions, as regards their knowledge of gunnery, and to enquire into the state of the gunnery efficiency generally, and he is to be accompanied by the A.A.G., R.M.

THE DIVISIONAL COLOURS OF THE ROYAL MARINES.
Compiled by General Sir H. E. Blumberg, K.C.B. Royal Marines.

NOTE. - In making this revision of the article I wrote for the Globe and Laurel in 1913, I have tried to bring it up to date, and to embody the considerable amount of information that has since come to light; but there are many gaps, which only time can fill. Official records have been consulted and assistance obtained from the standard work on the subject by the late Mr. Milne - "Standards and Colours of the British Army;" and a book by Mr. S. C. Johnson - "Flags of our Fighting Army." I am very grateful to all those who have helped in the laborious researches through old records, which have resulted in new facts being brought to light.

THE DUKE OF YORK AND ALBANY'S MARITIME REGIMENT.
1664 -1689.

Before 1633 armies and the retainers of feudal nobles, etc., carried banners and insignia, which displayed all manner of Arms, devices, etc., usually those of the King or Baron whom they followed; but in the Civil Wars we get definite records of the first real regimental flags, and Regimental Colours came into general use. These usually consisted of (1) a Colonel's Flag; (2) a Lieutenant-Colonel's Flag; (3) the flags of each Company Commander, to distinguish each company.

(Editor's Note: For pictures of these colours see the dust cover of this book and RMHS Special Publication No 23, The Story of Colours in The Royal Marines by Major A J Donald RM.)

On 13th February, 1661, was published the first Royal Warrant to control the Regimental Colours, and it gives us some idea of the Colours of that time. This Warrant refers principally to the Colours of the Regiments of Foot Guards, but a very interesting point is contained in the last four lines: "Of the usual largeness, with stands, heads and tassels." . . . . "Some of our Royal Badges painted in oil, as our trusty servant Sir Edward Walker, Knight, Garter Principal King of Arms, shall direct."

So we learn that early standards were painted, not embroidered, and the designs were to be regulated by the Garter King-of-Arms, as they still are. By 1684 the King's Colour was embroidered, but the other Colours were frequently painted until the post-Waterloo period; however, by that time a regiment that had its colours painted was rather looked down on.

The first Marine Regiment, the Duke of York and Albany's, following the custom of that time, carried several colours. Thanks to the researches of Major Edye in his "History of the Royal Marine Forces" (of which only the first volume was printed) we know that these colours were - described heraldically:-

The Colonel's - a Field Or (i.e., a plain sheet of yellow).
(Editor's Note. See the dust cover for example in colour.)

The Lieutenant-Colonel's on a Field Or, a cross gules fimbriated argent (i.e., on a plain yellow sheet, a red cross with white edges).
(Editor's Note. See the dust cover for example in colour.)

The Major's - on a Field argent, a sunburst proper, over all a cross gules, fimbriated of the first (i.e., on a white sheet, a red cross with white edges, and a yellow sunburst issuing from the four angles of the cross).
(Editor's Note. See the dust cover for example in colour.)

The Company Colours - as for the Major's, but with either a cypher or number in, the centre; probably the latter, as in the Coldstream Guards.
(Editor's Note. See the dust cover for example in colour.)

The original drawings of these Colours are in the Royal Library at Windsor Castle, and Her Majesty Queen Victoria gave permission for their reproduction by Major Edye; they have also been reproduced in "Britain's Sea Soldiers," Vol. 1, p. 16. The staves had pike heads with gold tassels.

In 1676 Captain Charles Middleton's Company was detached to form part of a composite regiment to quell troubles in Virginia (N. America); this company carried a colour: "The field white, waved with lemon, equally mixt with ye red cross quite through, with J.D.Y. in cypher in gold" (Edye). This colour has a spear head on staff (perhaps the forerunner of the later skeleton spear head used until 1894 (see "B.S.S." Vol. I, p. 16.) The cost of painting on both sides "in oyle" was £18 2s. 0d.

In 1680 a reinforcement was required for Tangier (N. Africa), which was besieged by the Moors, and a composite regiment of 600 men in five companies was drawn from the 1st Guards, Coldstream, The Duke's (i.e., Marines) and the Holland Regiment (i.e., The Buffs). A Colour was sanctioned for each of these companies. The design is not specified, but the "Duke's" company was to have crimson, white and yellow (i.e., the same as the Virginian Company), but "18 large cypres." Edye suggests that these were the ciphers of the Duke of York and those of the Captains of Companies from which the men were drawn. The cost is interesting:-

4 ells Crimson Taffeta at 13 shillings	£2 12 0
4 ells White Taffeta at 11 shillings	£2 4 0
4 ells Yellow Taffeta at 11 shillings	£2 4 0
	£7 0 0
For making one Ensigne	£1 10 0
For painting in oyle with fine gold	
18 large cypres at 7/6 apiece	£6 15 0
For one Ensigne staff	8 0
For one Tassel of yellow, white and red	2 6
(Edye)	£8 15 6

Milne gives the account of an observer, Nathan Brooks, at a great review held on Putney Heath on 1st October, 1684, in which he describes the Colours carried by the various regiments. There were present (to give them their present designations) 1st and 2nd Life Guards, the Blues, 1st Royal Dragoons, the 1st (Grenadier) Guards, Coldstream Guards, Royal Scots, The Queen's, The Duke's (Marines), Buffs and King's Own. Of the Duke's he says: "The Admiral flyes the Red Cross, with rays of the sun issuing from each angle of the Crosse-Or."

There is no record of the disposal of these Colours when the regiment was disbanded on 28th February, 1689, nor whether there was any change when they became the Prince George of Denmark's Regiment in 1685 (i.e., when the Duke of York ascended the throne as James II.), although the uniform was changed from yellow to red.

TORRINGTON AND PEMBROKE'S MARINES. 1690-1699.

In 1690 two Marine Regiments were raised, named after their Colonels - the Earls of Torrington and Pembroke - both of whom were Naval Officers. Luttrell says - "these two regiments were to be clothed in blew (blue), lined with white, and to have grenadier caps" (Edye). There is no record as to the colours carried, but Luttrell says they had no ensignes. It is not clear whether he is referring to colours or to officers of that rank; Edye thinks the latter; anyway, since that date Marines have always had 2nd Lieutenants and not Ensigns.

In 1698, owing to the casualties they had sustained, they were combined into one regiment, known as Brudenell's, whilst three line regiments - Colt's, Mordaunt's and Seymour's - were turned into Marine Regiments and placed on the naval establishment. There is no record of the Colours carried by these regiments, but it is probable that they carried the three Colours - the Colonel's, i.e., one plain colour; the Lieut.-Colonel's, i.e., one with same ground with a red St. George's Cross on a white field, and the Major's, i.e., probably with some device. Milne says "During the reign of William III. standards and colours were reduced gradually from one per troop or company to three for a regiment."

Speaking of the four regiments in 1698, Edye says (p. 555): "There is no record of their carrying Colours, and the inference undoubtedly is that none were borne." However, it is difficult to believe that the three line regiments at least did not have their Colours. Of course, the two Marine regiments were commanded by Naval Officers, and further, they seem to have been almost wholly embarked as detachments in quite the modern way, and to have been regarded as a nursery for seamen, so that Major Edye 's deduction is probably correct as regards them.

THE MARINE REGIMENTS. 1702-1713.

According to the Warrant of Queen Anne (now in the Officers' Mess at Chatham) 6 Regiments of Marines were raised in 1702 and 6 Line Regiments were allocated for Sea Service. Three of the six Marine Regiments were transferred to the Line in 1713 and wear the Battle Honour, "Gibraltar 1704-5," viz.: - 30th (1/E. Lancs), 31st (1/E. Surrey) and 32nd (1/D.C.L.I.), the others were disbanded. The six Line Regiments are now the R. Warwicks (6th), Green Howards (19th), Lancashire Fusiliers (20th), 1/Border (34th), 1/R. Sussex (35th), 2/Worcester (36th). The King's Own (4th) also served as Marines from 1703 to 1711.

It is undoubted that all these regiments carried Colours, because the Prince of Hesse (commanding the Marines at the taking of Gibraltar in 1704), arranged to signal to Admiral Sir Geo. Rooke, by "raising all the Colours of the Regiments." The design of these Colours is unknown and the Librarian of the War Office tells me that no help can be obtained from the regimental histories.

Milne says, "As regards the devices borne upon the Colours of the Army during the reigns of William III and Queen Anne, nothing appears to be known . . . . It may be certain, however, that it was the colours of the Senior Officers that survived, and that the Colonel's and Lieut.-Colonels' flags headed our regiments in Marlborough's campaigns."

In Johnson's book are shown some examples of slightly later date, where the Colonel's crest is embroidered in the Colours: (see also the R. Warrant of 1741 below).

Milne also says, "The Union with Scotland, 1707, had a marked effect upon the appearance of the Colours of the Army; The Red Cross of St. George, used generally with a white edging or border to separate it from the varied ground of the Lieut.-Colonel's, Major's or Captain's flags (and also no doubt to satisfy heraldic requirements the Red Cross on a white field) was simply placed with the white edging intact upon the Scottish ensign.- The White Saltire Andrew of St. Andrew on a blue field; this forming the combination known as the Great Union or Union Flag."

THE REGIMENTS OF MARINES. 1739-1748.

In December, 1739, an order in Council authorised the raising of 6 Marine Regiments, and in 1740 more were added.

Before giving a description of the Colours carried, it is interesting to note that the Adjutant-General's Department of the War Office commenced about 1743 to regularise the many different devices then appearing on Regimental Colours. A Royal Warrant was issued in 1743 which laid down *inter alia:* -

"No Colonel is to put his arms, crest, device or Livery on any part of the appointments of his regiment."

The first Colour of every Marching Regiment of foot is to be the Great Union; the second colour is to be of the facing of the regiment, with the Union in the Upper Canton; except those regiments faced with white or red, whose second colour is to be the Red Cross of St. George in a White field, and a Union in the Upper Canton.

In the centre of each colour is to be painted in Gold Roman figures the number of the rank of the regiment within a wreath of Roses and Thistles.

"All the Royal Regiments, the Fusiliers and the Marine Regiments (and several others) are distinguished by particular devices and therefore are not subject to the preceding articles for Colours."

I have put the order about the Red Cross in italics as it may have a bearing on the Marine Colours from 1755-1802 when the facings of the Corps were white, - we have no exact particulars of these colours except those of the Battalion at Belleisle, described below, when the Regimental Colour appears to have been plain white.

This Warrant was followed by a series of orders from which we learn that the size of the flags was 6 feet 6 inches horizontally, and 6 feet 2 inches vertically; the width of the St. George's Cross 1 foot 1 inch, the width of the white edging, 5 inches, the width of the St. Andrew's Cross, 9 inches. The length of the pikes was 9 feet 10 inches and of the Spear Head 4 inches; the length of the cords and tassels 3 feet, each tassel was 4 inches.

By the courtesy of the Librarian of the Royal Library at Windsor Castle, I am enabled to give a copy of the MS. of the Royal Warrant of 1751 (now in the Royal Library) in which the Colours of the 1st Marine Regiment (44th of the Line), disbanded in 1748, are given in Colour. (*See Illustration*).

This Warrant says: - "All the Marine regiments to wear in the centre of their colours a ship with the sails furled, the rank of the regiment underneath. but their Caps, Drums and Bells of Arms to be according to the general direction of the Marching Regiments." This Warrant also repeats the above quoted provisions of the R. Warrant of 1743 as regards the King's Colour and the Second Colour.

DESCRIPTION.

King's Colour. - The Union Flag; In centre a full rigged ship with sails furled, with the rank of the regiment underneath.

Regimental Colour. - Square flag of the Colour of the facing of the Regiment, with small Union in Upper Canton; in centre a full rigged ship with sails furled, with rank of regiment beneath.

Skeleton spear heads with Gold Cords.

(Editor's Note. See the dust cover for example in colour.)

Colonel Field (B.S.S. Vol. I, Chap. VI) has given us the facings as follows:-

Regiment	Line	Facing
1st Regiment	44th of the line	Yellow
2nd "	45th "	Green
3rd "	46th "	Yellow
4th "	47th "	White
5th "	48th "	Primrose
6th "	49th "	Green
7th "	50th "	White
8th "	51st "	Yellow
9th "	52nd "	Dark Buff
10th "	53rd "	Light Buff

There were also 3 Regiments, raised in North America, afterwards formed into one known as Gooch's Marines and taking precedence as 43rd of the Line.

It would be interesting to know if the 4th and 7th Regiments had a white Regimental Colour, or white with red St. George's Cross.

In 1747 all these regiments were transferred to Admiralty control, and by Admiralty Orders of May 1747 all the facings were ordered to be yellow, and it was further ordered that the Foul Anchor was to be embroidered on the caps, which has therefore become one of the oldest badges of the Corps. As the Warrant of 1751 was published after the ten regiments had been disbanded, the drawings in the Royal Library probably followed the latest Admiralty order as to facings, viz., that of 1747.

1755 TO PRESENT DAY.

As War with France was threatening, an increase of the Forces was decided on. In April 1755 the Ministry therefore authorised the Admiralty to raise a force of 5,000 Marines, in 50 independent companies, so the Corps on its present footing came into existence. The old system of raising regiments had been found inconvenient, and it was a common practice in those days to raise independent companies, each of a specified strength. These were divided into three groups and quartered at Chatham, Portsmouth and Plymouth, which became the Divisional Headquarters as we know them to-day. The allocation of the companies can be seen in the Marine Officers' Lists, and even in the Navy Lists as late as 1888. It is curious to note that from 1755 down to quite modern times the numbers of the Corps were increased or decreased by raising and disbanding companies, the numbers and strength of which were varied annually by Order in Council.*

Probably owing to this method of raising, and possibly, as Colonel Field suggests, because they were clothed as Fusiliers or Grenadiers, Colours do not appear to have been issued at first.

*NOTE. – The Army Annual Act lays down the exact numbers of the Army, but it only says "A Force of Marines." The numbers were fixed by O. in C. Lord Fisher, however, since 1904 varied the numbers inside the Order in Council of that date.

1760. THE BELLEISLE BATTALION.

When a Battalion was put under orders for the expedition to Belleisle a single pair of Colours was ordered to be handed to them. On 24th October, 1760, the Admiralty letter ordered Colonel Burleigh, Commandant at Plymouth, to send a pair of Colours to the Battalion (Plymouth Letter Books). The bill for this pair is as follows: -

Messrs. Wm. Nicholson.
24th October, 1760.

To	Silk, making Union Sheet of Colours	£5	15	6
To	Embroidering the Arms of the Lord High Admiral within a large Ornament of Roses and Thistles	£5	5	0
To	Silk and making a plain sheet with a small union	£4	14	6
To	painting the sheet as above	£3	0	0
To	two Colour Staves and Cases	£2	6	0
To	two pair of Rich Crimson and Gold Tassels and Cord	£2	12	6
		£23	13	6

"B.S.S." Vol. 3., p. 113

Col. C. Field found this Bill in the Admiralty "Out Letters" in the Record Office. It was approved for payment on 9th March, 1761. and signed by "Anson" (Lord Anson) G. Hay and "J. Forbes," and was ordered to be paid by the Paymaster of the Marines.

Description.- From this we may deduce that they were as follows :-
KING'S COLOUR.- The Union (as in 1751) on which were embroidered the Arms of the Lord High Admiral (i.e., the Foul Anchor) with a large wreath of Roses and Thistles.
REGIMENTAL COLOUR.- Silk plain white sheet with small union in upper Canton, the Anchor and Wreath as on King's Colour, but painted on the sheet. The dimensions must have been those laid down in 1751.
(Editor's Note. See the dust cover for example in colour.)

It seems clear that the sheet of Regimental Colour must have been plain white, but there is some uncertainty as to whether there was a Crown above the Anchor or not. The probability is that the Crown was not over the Foul Anchor (which was the same as that now on the Navy List), as the Crown only forms part of the Badge when the King himself is Lord High Admiral, as Charles II. and James II. were.

(Admiralty Librarian)

N.B.- The illustration has been reconstructed from the above Bill and reference to other colours of same date.

Milne, speaking of the Army Colours of the period, beginning with 1751, says: "….. extremely plain at first, only the number within its flowery surroundings, the flowers will be observed to become more ornate; tokens of honour (the remembrance of some gallant action or campaign) added from time to time, and alternately the name of various victories duly and discreetly authorised to be emblazoned; and all surrounding and centreing upon the old regimental number (for Marines the Foul Anchor) ever enhancing its value in the eyes of those who had the honour of serving under it."

THE 1765 COLOURS.

A note in the papers of the late Colonel W. Gage Armstrong, R.M.L.I. (who made such a complete extract of the Plymouth Order and Letter Books) that a pair of Colours had been given to the Chatham Division about this date, led to a search being made in the Records of the Chatham Division, with the following interesting result: -

Admiralty Office,
26 July, 1765.

Sir,
The Storekeeper of His Majesty's Yard at Deptford having been directed to send by the first convenient opportunity to Chatham a Pair of Colours directed to you, I am commanded by My Lords Commissioners of the Admiralty to acquaint you therewith, that you may receive the same

for the use of the Marine Officers and Private men of your Division.
I am, Sir,
Your most obedient servant,
(Sgd.) PHILIP STEPHENS.

The Commanding Marine Officer at Chatham.

The receipt of these Colours was acknowledged on 2 August, 1765. ("From Chatham Letter Books.")

A careful search in the Portsmouth Division Records resulted in the finding of the following letter: -

Admiralty Office,
16 July, 1765.

Sir,
With respect to that part of your said letter wherein you represent that it will be a very great advantage to the discipline of the Corps to give the men better accoutrements than those they have at present, that the want of pouches makes it impossible to put them through all the firings of a Battalion, as the largest Cartouch Boxes hold but eighteen rounds of powder, and many which hold but nine; I am also to acquaint you their Lordships have under consideration the alteration of the accoutrements, and that you will soon receive their determination, and with regard to that paragraph of your before-mentioned letter setting forth, that it would also be advantage that your officers and men should be acquainted with the use to be made of Colours in a Battalion *and desiring those in store at Portsmouth may be delivered to you*. I am likewise to inform you that the storekeeper at Portsmouth is directed to cause those Colours to be delivered, upon application being made by you for that purpose.
Sir,
Your most humble servant,
PHILIP STEPHENS.

Colonel Boisrond, at Portsmouth.

The words printed in italics would seem to show that the Old Marine regiments (1739-1748) must have returned their Colours to the local yard, and that these were re-issued to the Divisions in 1765; because even if Chatham or Portsmouth had received the Belleisle Colours, how are we to account for the other pair. So far no record has been found of Colours having been issued to Plymouth at this time. Unless we may assume that the Belleisle colours having been issued by that Division were returned there. Various interesting problems are raised by these two letters; (1) May we assume that the badge of the Full-rigged Ship was worn as the Colours until they were worn out; (2) At what date were they replaced: (3) Presumably as the Belleisle Colours were new they followed the Admiralty Order of 1747 re The Foul Anchor. (See also under 1810, unfortunately the Badge is missing.) (4) The Laurel Wreath gained at Belleisle first appears on the Colours of 1827.

As the Keeper of the Great Wardrobe supplied Army Colours up to 1789 the designs may yet be found among his accounts in the Public Record Office, and the dates of issue possibly from the Storekeeping Records of the Admiralty.

1766 TO 1810.

The records of this period are very scrappy. The first definite record is a letter from the Admiralty to the Commandant at Plymouth:-

2nd Feb. 1775.
Commanding Officer, Plymouth.
I am commanded by the Lords Commissioners of the Admiralty to signify their directions to you to send the Colours *of your* Division to Boston with the Marines, and to acquaint you that they will be replaced by new ones.
(Sgd.) PHILIP STEPHENS.
Plymouth Letter Books (Col. Armstrong)

These must have been taken out by the reinforcing draft of 41 of and 673 n.c.o. s and men that reached Boston in May, when the two Battalions of Marines were organised under Major Pitcairne (vide Gillespie, p. 191). These were presumably the Colours carried by the 1st Marines at the battle of Bunker's Hill, 17 June, 1775, as only the Grenadier and L.I. Company of 2/Marines were in the battle.

The late Captain Portlock-Dadson told me that when he visited Greenwich in 1864 he saw hanging in the Painted Hall eight or twelve Marine Colours - (these were the 1810 Colours, see later) - and that the Curator, an old man who had lost both his legs, told him that among them was a Colour which had been carried at Bunker's Hill.

In 1913 I was shown at Messrs. Spinks, in Piccadilly, the medals and orders of Major-General Sir James Lyon, which had been bought at Christie's in December 1912; with them was an embroidered letter-case containing a piece of red silk, with some white, as if it was part of a St. George's Cross on a white field, which was said to be a piece of the Marine Colour carried at Bunker's Hill. With it was a letter from Lieut.-Colonel Timmins (S.O.R.M. at Trafalgar in 1805) as follows: -

"Lieut.-Col. Timmins has the honour of enclosing to Sir James Lyon* a portion of the Colour borne by the Marines at the battle of Bunker's Hill.
Wednesday Morning."

*NOTE.- Sir James Lyon was G.O.C. of the Portsmouth Garrison and was in command of the Parade when Colours were presented to Portsmouth Division, by H.R.H. the Duke of Clarence, 27th October,1827. He himself had served in the Fleet in 1794, and was the son of an officer killed at Bunker's Hill.

On back of letter: "Remnant of the Colours borne by the Battalion of Marines engaged at Bunker's Hill.
TOYLORD (?), 18 May, 1818."

This precious relic is now in the Officers' Mess at Plymouth. When the Detachment under Major Ross was being prepared for the expedition to Botany Bay, he appears to have requested that the 4 companies might be supplied with a Sett of Colours. On 2 Jan., 1797, the Admiralty reply to the Commandant at Plymouth is as follows:

"Major Ross having requested that the Detachment of Marines for Botany Bay may be supplied with *one of the Setts of Colours now at Plymouth* Headquarters I am directed to signify their directions to you to supply the same accordingly, - if they can be spared.
(Signed) Philip Stephens"

This letter is in the Plymouth Letter Books (Col. Armstrong's extracts) and show two points: that those companies carried Colours; and secondly, that probably one "Sett" was that ordered for Belleisle (see p. 192) and that Plymouth Division also had a set issued in 1765. Which set went to Australia – probably the Belleisle Colours – and what became of them?

At the defence of Acre, General Berthier, the French G.O.C., says that the Marine sortie parties carried Colours ("B.S.S." Vol. 1 I, p. 217). Colonel Field has verified this from the journal of Mid. Budd, R.N.: "Monday, 7th Jan., 1799 - Moored in the harbour of Constantinople. Fired a salute of 21 guns and manned ship on occasion of Marine Corps being presented with a stand of Colours from H.B.M. Ambassador's lady."

Chatham orders make several mentions of Colours, *e.g.*, "Divisional Colours will be carried by the Guard of Honour ordered to attend H.M. George III. at the Thanksgiving Service at St. Paul's in 1797." (The Guard marched there and back.)†

Some day, probably, the design of these Colours will come to light, but they probably very much resembled the Belleisle Colours.

†Gillespie in his History says that bodies of Marines drawn from Chatham and Portsmouth attended the Thanksgiving Service at St. Paul's on 19th Dec., 1797; and that they were drawn from men who had served in the recent campaigns, and together with the seamen were allotted for the protection of the trophies which their valour had conquered.

In 1800 we come on further records: -

On 13th December, 1800, there is a Plymouth Divisional Order giving direction that in consequence of the O.-in-C. 5th November, 1800, certain alterations were made in the Royal Ensigns, Armorial Flags and Banners following on the Union of Great Britain and Ireland. In 31st December Orders, an extra Corporal was promoted from the 1st January in each Company to commemorate the commencement of the new century and of the happy Union between the Kingdoms of Great Britain and Ireland.

On 22 Dec., 1800, the Commanding Officer at Plymouth wrote to the Lords of the Admiralty:

"You will be pleased to inform my Lords Commissioners of the Admiralty that the Colours of this Division are become totally unfit for further use, being old and worn out, and to request their Lordships will be pleased to order another sett to be forwarded here, and agreeably to the plan proposed relative to the Union.

(Sgd.) J. BOWATER."

There is an answer from the Admiralty, dated 28 Dec., 1800 – "that the Division will be supplied with new Colours agreeable to the Union, and that the Navy Board had been directed to supply the same."

The last sentence seems to refer to the Union with Ireland, which was finally signed in 1801, when the general plan adopted (according to Milne) was to sew red strips along the white limbs of St. Andrew's Cross, to provide for the St. Patrick's Cross, and to add the Shamrock to the wreath of Roses and Thistles.

There is also a letter of May 1801, asking that the Navy Board may supply new Colours in lieu. (Col. W. G. Armstrong).

The next record is a letter from the Commandant at Plymouth to Lieut.-General Johnstone, the Commandant in Town (i.e., A.G.R.M.), under date 1 Nov., 1802: -

"In reply to your letter of 30 Oct., I beg leave to inform you that though the Colours of this Division are in a good state, yet as the Corps has been made Royal since they were issued, it will be necessary that the Divisional Colours should be altered accordingly, nor until this is done can we strictly be called Royal.

(Sgd.) J. BOWATER."

Note the speed of transmission of letters between London and Plymouth.

(I wonder if the Colours had been replaced in 1800 or 1801, or whether behind lies a story! I remember that in 1894, when new colours were under consideration for Portsmouth, the colours at Plymouth were in a very dilapidated condition. For some reason the Commandant (the late Major-General N. F. Way, C.B.) did not wish to have a new set; accordingly the ladies of the Division got to work and repaired them perfectly, so that on the day when they were finally replaced in 1896 they were almost as good as new.)

That new Colours were supplied early in 1801 to all Divisions is corroborated by the Portsmouth Letter Books dated 1st Jan., 1801. The C.O. had represented that there were no Divisional *Silk* Colours in store, conformably to the new regulation, and requesting to be supplied therewith, the Lords Commissioners of the Admiralty replied that they "had given instructions to the Navy Board accordingly."

These letters would seem to make it clear that a general issue of new Colours was supplied in 1801, which is confirmed by the report of their condition by Commandant Plymouth on 1 Nov., 1802, which answers my questions at the bottom of the page above.

But I have since come on a startling piece of evidence in reference to the probable pattern of the Divisional Colours: On 1st Nov., 1802, the Commandant at Portsmouth, replying to Commandant R.M. in Town (i.e. D.A.G.) about the change of colour of the facings, etc., to Blue, on the Corps becoming Royal, says:-

"Our present Colours were received about 18 months since, and are perfectly good, but in consequence of the late alteration in our uniforms and appointments (see the Orders of May, 1802) the Regimental Colour is of no use whatever, for I need not remark it would be preposterous to *take out a Red Colour* with Blue Facings."

"I feel incumbent to remind you that the Egyptian Regiments have been honoured with a Mark of Royal approbation in their Colours, and I trust it will be admitted that our services have upon every occasion been as zealous and exemplary as any other of His Majesty s troops; and as we had a battalion of more than 500 men serving in that country. I hope you will use every endeavour that a distinction as honourable to the discipline and bravery of that army is not withheld from the Corps of Marines."

Signed, T AVARNE, Maj-Gen

Lieut.-Gen. – Souter-Johnstone
(*the A.G.R.M. of that day*)

The second paragraph, of course, refers to the grant of the "Sphynx with Egypt" granted to the Line Regiments for the campaign in 1801, (this of course was prior to the grant of the Globe.) But what are we to make of the *Red Colours?* – there is a lot to be found out yet about the Divisional Colours. (H. E. Blumberg 16.6.32)

In 1806 a Battalion of Royal Marines was landed from the Fleet and took part in the ill-fated attack on Buenos Ayres. They carried a Union Jack and a small Red Ensign, evidently made on board with the letters R.M.B. in white. When the garrison surrendered, these flags, together with the Colours of the other regiments, were given up to the enemy, and they are now hanging in the Convent of San Domingo.

Although the Woolwich Division was formed in 1804, the Brigade Major at Chatham tells me that a careful search of the Woolwich records reveals nothing as to whether Colours were issued on its formation.

THE 1810 COLOURS.

From this time onwards the records are more definite. In 1810 General Barclay (the Commandant in Town) was ordered by the Admiralty to provide Colours of proper pattern for the several Divisions of Marines and these were apparently supplied in 1810 and 1811. Presumably they were in accordance with the latest regulations, e.g., the new Union Flag and the Blue Silk for the Regimental Colour; they appear to have been embroidered.

(Editor's Note. See the dust cover for example in colour.)

"20 Feb., 1811. Major-General Bright (Commandant, Plymouth). I have also to acquaint you a sett of Colours for the Division under your command will be sent from London this day directed to you.

(Sgd.)JOHN BARCLAY."

(C.O.'s Letter Book, Ply.)

Description. - In 1912 I went to Greenwich to look for the 1810 Colours, which according to Nicholas' History of the Royal Marines (published in 1845) were in the Painted Hall, and which he regrets were removed from their proper resting Places, the Divisional Headquarters. But all I could find was one pair in a very bad state, although Colonel Portlock-Dadson told me that in 1864 he saw eight or ten Colours hanging in the Painted Hall; this pair can now be seen in the Royal Naval Museum.

King's Colour.- The Union Flag, but no badges were discernible.

Regimental Colour.- Dark Blue Silk, with remnants of a Union Wreath of Roses, Thistles and Shamrocks. The poles are of ash, with spear heads.

No further information is forthcoming, but presumably, as in 1760, the Foul Anchor must have been in the centre. What we should like to know is what scrolls and mottoes were borne and where the Laurel wreath was placed. (In the illustration the Foul Anchor is copied from a contemporary helmet plate now in Officers' Mess at Plymouth.)

On 17 Dec., 1810, the British Envoy at Lisbon presented a pair of Colours to the 1st Battalion, commanded by Major R. Williams (afterwards Major Commandant of the Artillery Companies, and later Commandant of the Portsmouth Division). This Battalion saw service in Portugal, America and Canada, and in 1814 was broken up and distributed among the gunboats on the Great Lakes.

On 5 August, 1812, approval was given for a pair of Colours to be given to the 2nd Battalion, commanded by Major J. Malcolm, under orders for the Peninsula. On 6 August, 1812, in acknowledging the order the Commandant of the Portsmouth Division says: "He does not know where the different sets lately provided to the Divisions were ordered, as they were sent down by the Naval Board." (Note.- From this and previous letters it would appear that the Navy Board supplied Marine Colours.)

As this Battalion sailed on 14th August for the Peninsular War in Spain, it is believed that they took the Portsmouth Division Colours (a note in the index of the Letter Book lends colour to this idea). After service on the North Coast of Spain, this Battalion went to N. America for the latter part of the war 1812-14, being present at the capture of Oswego on the Canadian Lakes and the capture of Washington, U.S.A., etc., and was eventually broken up and distributed among the gunboats. Nicholas gives a full account of these Battalions, and says that their Colours were sent to Greenwich. It would seem that the piece of a Colour said to be that of the 2nd Battalion at Bunker's Hill, now in the Officers' Mess at Eastney, really belongs to this Battalion, because in the first place only the Grenadier and L.I. Companies of 2/Marines were engaged at Bunker's Hill. Also the donor of this fragment, General Whylock only joined the Corps in 1804, became full Colonel 1851, retired full pay as a Major-General 20th June 1855; served in Spain and Mediterranean 1808-9 and 1812-13; was O.C. Detachments at the storming of Sidon 1840. It would therefore seem as if the Colours of Malcolm's Battalion were torn up, as was often the case at that time.

Disposal.
Correspondence in the Royal Marine office, dated 6th August, 1828, shows that these 1810 Divisional Colours, when replaced in 1827, were ordered to be sent to the Chapel of Greenwich Hospital by the Lord High Admiral, the Duke of Clarence (afterwards H.M. William IV.); Divisions were also ordered to attach to the staves any details of presentation, service, etc.

A letter from Greenwich to the late Major Edye dated 1st Dec., 1892, says: "We have the Colours of the R.M. sent to Greenwich by William IV.; you shall have full information by Saturday.
Yours sincerely,
(Sgd.) G. F. LAMBERT.

This is endorsed in pencil- "In the School."

Enquiries made by me of the Chaplain on 21st Jan., 1930, elicited that the only pair now at Greenwich is the old pair that I saw in 1912. Among Major Edye's papers is a letter from a member of the Royal Household, signature illegible, dated 23rd August, 1892, from which the following is extracted: -

"I cannot imagine what can have become of the old Colours which were sent on board the *Royal Sovereign*, unless they are stored carefully away in Portsmouth Dockyard. I think I may say they are not in any of the Royal Palaces, for I have ransacked them completely. I found some Colours of great historic interest, but not any belonging to the Marines . . . I think that the *Royal Sovereign* yacht was a Portsmouth ship and always had her moorings in that harbour."

This may have been one of the sets of 1810 Colours. Enquiries in Portsmouth yard this year (1930) have elicited that there are no colours there now. These colours belonged to the Plymouth Division, being sent on board the *Royal Sovereign* after the presentation of the 1827 Colours in December 1827. (Col. W.G.Armstrong).

THE 1827 COLOURS.

The design of these Colours materially differs from those hitherto in use. It had become customary to place Battle Honours on the Regimental Colour, and a list of actions, about 106 in number, was submitted to H.M. George IV. in order that he might select those to be placed on the Colours (for full list see a contemporary pamphlet reprinted in *Globe and Laurel*, Vol. 1. p. 210), but "The greatness of their number and the difficulty of selecting amidst so many glorious deeds, such a portion as could be inserted in the space, determined His Majesty, in lieu of the usual badges and mottoes on the Colours of the troops of the Line, to direct that the 'Globe encircled with Laurel' should be the distinguishing badge as the most appropriate emblem of a Corps, whose duties carried them to all parts of the globe, in every quarter of which they had earned laurels by their valour and good conduct"- (from speech of H.R.H. the Duke of Clarence, Lord High Admiral, at Portsmouth); and in his speech at Chatham, H.R.H. referred to this and other badges, and at Woolwich he pointedly said that *"Gibraltar"* was for the capture and *defence* of the Rock in 1704-5. He also said His Majesty had given them the most peculiar and honourably distinctive badge of his own cypher; further that it might be known to posterity that King George IV. had bestowed on them such an honourable mark of his appreciation, H.M. directed that *whatever King or Queen they might serve under hereafter, though the cypher of the reigning sovereign must of course appear on their standard, still on those of the Royal Marines the cypher G.R. IV. was for ever to remain.*

These Colours are rather inaccurately illustrated in Cannon's Historical Record of the Royal Marines (published in 1845), but the design can be seen in the pair now hanging in the Officers Mess at Plymouth.
(Editor's Note. See the dust cover for example in colour.)

King's Colour.- The Union. In centre the Globe, silver, encircled with the Laurel Wreath, gold with red berries; above the globe, the Foul Anchor, gold entwined with the Royal Cypher G.R. IV., ensigned with the Crown; above "Gibraltar" in black letters on yellow scroll; under the Globe a yellow scroll, bearing the motto "Per Mare per Terram," which lies across stems of laurel wreath.

Divisional Colour. —Dark Blue Silk, with Union in upper canton the same badges as on the King's Colour. The poles had the usual spear heads, gold and silver tassels and cords. The cost of the four pairs of Colours was £207 8s. 0d,

Presentation. - The Colours were presented by the Duke of Clarence, the Lord High Admiral, as follows: -

To Chatham on 26 Sept., 1827
To Portsmouth on 27 Oct., 1827
To Plymouth on 21 Dec., 1827
To Woolwich on 10 Oct. 1827
(R.M.O. Records)

It is an interesting note of Corps history to recall that two of the Drummers who witnessed this presentation at Plymouth also saw the new Colours presented in 1858, and finally yet another new set, when pensioners in 1896, viz., Major and Q.M. Uriah King and Q.M.S. Jew.

On 4th Dec., 1829, the R.M. Office directed the Commandant at Woolwich to send his two Colours to Mr. Morton, of 52 Upper Charlotte Street, Fitzroy Square, London, and "to permit them to remain there for such short time as may be required to enable him to introduce them into a painting of H.R.H. the late Lord High Admiral, on which Mr. Morton is now occupied, for the officers' mess rooms of the several Divisions,"- where they can now be seen to-day.

Disposal.
An order was sent from the R.M. Office, dated 6th August, 1858, that on the receipt of the new Colours the 1827 Colours were to be returned to the R. Marine Office.

As regards the Portsmouth set, the late Major and Quartermaster Murphy, R.M.L.I., told me that he remembered that the old Colours were torn up on parade when the new Colours were presented in 1858 (Major Murphy was then a boy of eleven or twelve years old and joined the Corps shortly after as a drummer). No record exists of the disposal of the Chatham or Woolwich sets.

On 6th Nov., 1861, a pair of the 1827 Colours were sent from the R.M. Office to the Commandant at Plymouth, to be handed over to Lieut.Col. Lowder for the use of the Marine Battalion under orders for Mexico. Lieut.-Col. H. S. Bourchier, wrote in 1912 "I carried these Colours myself when we landed at Vera Cruz."

On 5th Dec., 1863, a letter was sent from the D.A.G.R.M., directing that the Colours lately carried by the Mexican Battalion were to be prepared for issue to the Battalion under orders for Japan. The late Lieut.-Col. H. J. Norcock, wrote to me in 1912 "I carried these Colours myself when we marched out of barracks to embark." They must therefore have been at the storming of the batteries at Simonoseki in 1864, and must have been the last R.M. Colours carried in action (see also "B.S.S.", Vol.II., p. 146). This pair of Colours now hangs in the mess room at Plymouth. From Colonel Armstrong's papers we learn that he found these Colours in the Commandant's office, and obtained the permission of the Commandant, Colonel McArthur, to fix them on the picture of the Duke of Clarence, who had originally presented them.

Another Battalion of Royal Marines served as a garrison in Japan from 1870 to 1875, and a photograph in the officers' mess at Chatham shows that they had colours. There is no record of these, but they may possibly have been another pair of the 1827 Colours sent from the R.M. office.

THE 1858 COLOURS.

In 1858 it was decided that the Royal Marine Colours were to be replaced, and the design was entrusted to the Inspector of Colours at the College of Heralds. This officer appears to have departed from the instructions given by King George IV. and to have followed the principles approved for the Army about 1855. The laurel wreath was removed from around the globe and put back into its old place round the Foul Anchor, and the cypher of George IV. was entirely omitted. H.M. Queen Victoria herself approved the design and the Board Letter notifying her approval was dated 17th Feb., 1858 (R.M.O. records).

It is interesting to note that the Bugle was never incorporated in the Colours, though on 30th Jan., 1855, the following minute had been promulgated by the Admiralty:-

"Most humbly submitted your Majesty by the Lords Commissioners of the Admiralty:

"That the Corps of Royal Marines may be designated a Light Corps, and equipped and instructed as such, agreeably to your Majesty's Regulations for Light Infantry Regiments of the Line, this training being considered best adapted to the nature of the service which the Corps is generally required to perform on shore."

Appd. (Signed) VICTORIA R.

Description (see illustration).
Poles with spear head; the size of the Colours was 6ft. 2ins. by 5ft, 6ins.

Queen s Colour .- The Union; in centre a gold Crown on upper limb of St. George's Cross Royal Marines in black on a gold scroll beneath on transverse arms of cross.

Divisional Colour. --Dark Blue Silk, with Union in upper canton; the Royal cypher V.R. in each of other corners in gold. In centre the Globe (silver) encircled with a circular red scroll inscribed "The Royal Marines " in gold, surrounded by a wreath of roses, shamrocks, thistles and oak leaves, with red and white bow. Below (or in base) the Foul Anchor, gold, encircled by a laurel wreath, green with red berries; beneath this a yellow scroll inscribed "Per Mare Per Terram" in black; below this a yellow scroll inscribed "Gibraltar" in black. These Colours were supplied by Messrs. Hamburger and Rogers, who also supplied those in 1894 and 1896.

(Editor's Note. See the dust cover for example in colour.)

Presentation. - It was decided that the Naval Commanders-in-Chief at the several Ports were to make the Presentations, and as far as can be ascertained, there was very little ceremony. Plymouth orders merely state "Division will parade in Review order to-morrow for presentation of Colours."

The dates and the several Commanders-in-Chief were: -
At Chatham, 28th June, 1858, by Vice-Admiral E. Harvey.
At Portsmouth, 8th July, 1858, by Admiral Sir G. F. Seymour.
At Plymouth, 17th June, 1858, by Rear-Admiral Sir Thos. Pasley.
At Woolwich, 15th July, 1858, by Commodore Chas. Shepherd.

Disposal. - On presentation of the new (i.e., the present) Colours in 1894-96, the 1858 Colours were disposed of as follows: -

CHATHAM DIVISION were presented to H.R.H. the Duke of Edinburgh; a silver circlet was put on them to record the fact, and they were taken to Clarence House. These Colours are now hanging in the North-West corner of St. George s Hall, Windsor Castle, having been placed there in September, 1901.

PORTSMOUTH DIVISION. This pair were hung in the Officers' Mess at Forton; on amalgamation of R.M.A. and in 1923 they were laid up in St. Andrew's Church at Eastney.

PLYMOUTH DIVISION are now hanging in the Officers' messroom at Plymouth.

WOOLWICH DIVISION, On the break up of the Division in 1869 they were sent to the Royal Marine Office, where they remained until 1895. On 3rd Oct., 1895, they were sent to Deal and hung in the Officers' Mess. room until. 22nd March, 1909, when the Commandant (Col. E. A. Wylde) obtained permission to lay them up in the Depot Church, where they now are.

*NOTE. - When the Royal Marine Battalion was landed for the Capture of Kinbourn (Crimean War) October, 1855, Lieut. Hugh Rose carried Colour which had been lent by Capt. King, R.N. It was a silk Union Jack properly mounted and was returned to Capt. King on the return of the Battalion to the Ships. (Capt. Portlock-Dadson).

THE 1894-96 COLOURS.

In 1891 it was reported that the Portsmouth Division Colours were in such a bad state that it was necessary to replace them.

In 1892 the Garter King of Arms, or rather the Inspector of Regimental Colours in his office, was asked to prepare designs. In the first place the Army Colours had recently been reduced in size to 3ft. 9ins. by 3ft, with a bullion fringe round them; the Lion and Crown had superseded the spear heads on the poles, which had been reduced in length to 8ft. 7 1/2. ins. Following the 1858 pattern, and embodying these modifications, a design was prepared and submitted, but the historians and senior officers of the Corps, remembering the speeches of the Duke of Clarence represented that the cypher G.R. IV. should appear.

After a good deal of correspondence and preparation of drawings of the 1827 Colours from the pair in the Plymouth Mess, the design of the Garter King of Arms was dropped and one following the 1827 design, but of small size and without the bullion fringe, was submitted to H.M. Queen Victoria, who personally made several alterations, including inserting her cypher. V.R.I. in the three corners of the Divisional Colour, and finally approved the Colours as they now appear in her own handwriting. (The original drawing with the alterations and signature are in the R.M.O. Records.)

Description.

Queen's (now King's) Colour. - The Union: in centre the Foul Anchor with the Royal cypher interlaced, ensigned with the Imperial Crown. "Gibraltar" on a scroll above; in base the Globe surrounded by a laurel wreath, motto "Per Mare Per Terram" on a yellow scroll beneath.

Divisional Colour. - Dark Blue Silk. In the centre the Foul Anchor interlaced with the cypher. G.R. IV., ensigned with the Imperial Crown; "Gibraltar" on a scroll above; in base the Globe surrounded by a laurel wreath; motto "Per Mare Per Terram" on a yellow scroll beneath. In the upper dexter canton the small Union, in the remaining three corners the Royal and Imperial cypher.

It will be noticed that contrary to the Army practice the Queen's Colour bears the distinctive badges of the Corps, as the Marine Colours always have since the beginning.

Presentation. - H.M. Queen Victoria conferred a signal honour on the Portsmouth Division by presenting the Colours personally at Osborne on 28th August, 1894. The presentations to the Chatham and Plymouth Divisions were made by H.R.H. the Duke of Edinburgh, the Honorary Colonel of the Corps, who presented them to Chatham on 22nd June, 1896 and to Plymouth on 3rd July, 1896.

(Editor's Note. See the dust cover for example in colour.)

NOTES.

1. In an old book "Drum and Flute Duty for H.M. Army" that was in the possession of the Drum-Major of the Portsmouth Division, I ascertained that the Royal Marines had a special salute on the drum for receiving the Colour.
2. Following on the loss of life incurred in saving the Colours in the Afghan War, and again in the Zulu War, it was henceforth forbidden to carry Colours into action; so that we may say that the Colours of the Battalion for Japan in 1864 were the last R.M. Colours to be carried in action.

3. In the War 1914-18 no battalion actually carried Colours, but in some cases platoon flags were carried. At the battle of Passchendale (in Flanders) on 26th October, 1917, A Company, 2 R.M.L.I., gallantly led by Lieut. P. Ligertwood, who had connected his men with spunyarn to prevent their leaving the narrow tracks through the mud, crossed the Paddebeeke and made good their position there. He had provided each of his platoons with a small red flag, which had been blessed by the battalion Chaplain, and these were carried forward, and served as rallying points for the platoons; three of these now rest at Chatham, Portsmouth and Plymouth; the bearer of the fourth was killed and the flag lost in the Flanders mud. Lieut Ligertwood, who had gained his commission from the ranks during the war, unfortunately died of his wounds ("B.S.S." Vol. III., p. 335.) The casualties in this battle were: 1/R.M.L.I.- 4 officers killed, 6 wounded; 270 n.c.o.'s and men killed and wounded. 2/R.M.L.1.- 4 officers killed, 4 wounded; 391 n.c.o.'s and men killed and wounded.

4. Owing to the large number of battles in the war of 1914-18, H.M. George V. ordered that those selected which had hitherto been confined to the Regimental Colour, were to be inscribed on the King's Colour, and each regiment was allowed to select 10 from a list prepared by the War Office to be so inscribed.

If it had been customary for the Royal Marines to inscribe such honours, it is interesting to note that they would have had to select from the following, in addition to the Naval actions, such as Jutland, and more particularly Zeebrugge: -

Chatham Bn.	Portsmouth Bn	Plymouth Bn	Deal Bn
R.M.L.I.	R.M.L.I.	R.M.L.I.	R.M.L.I.
Antwerp	Antwerp	Antwerp	Antwerp
France & Flanders	France & Flanders	France & Flanders	France & Flanders
1914	1914	1914	1914
Anzac	Anzac	Landing at Helles	Landing at Helles
Helles	Helles	Helles	Helles
Krithia	Krithia	Krithia	Krithia
Egypt 1915	Egypt 1915	Egypt 1915	Egypt 1915

After 13th July, 1915, the Battalions were so reduced owing to casualties (the Portsmouth Battalion had not one officer left), that they were amalgamated into 1st and 2nd Battalions R.M.L.I. in August 1915.

1st R.M.L.I. formed from Chatham and Deal Bns.	2nd R.M.L.I. formed from Portsmouth and Plymouth Bns
Helles	Helles
Krithia	Krithia
Gallipoli 1915-16	Gallipoli 1915-16
Macedonia 1916	Macedonia 1916
Somme 1916-18	Somme 1916-18
Ancre 1916-18	Ancre 1916-18
Arras 1917-18	Arras 1917-18
Vimy	----
Scarpe 1917	Scarpe 1917
Arleux	Arleux
Ypres 1917	Ypres 1917
Passchendaele	Passchendale
St. Quentin	St. Quentin
Albert 1918	Albert 1918

| Bapaume 1918 | Bapaume 1918 |

Owing to the casualties in the Retreat of March 1918, culminating in the final counter-attack on 6th April in Aveluy Wood, in which both Battalions charged in line, it was found impossible to reinforce both up to strength, and they were amalgamated into one, 1st R.M.L.I.

1st R.M.L.I.

Drocourt-Queant Line	Cambrai
Hindenburg Line	Pursuit to Mons
Canal du Nord	France and Flanders 1916-18

5. After the Armistice, 11th November, 1918, the 1/R.M.L.I. (the sole remnant of the R.M.L.I. Brigade) settled down in the neighbourhood of Mons. The Colours of the Chatham Division were sent to them, which they carried until the cadre returned to England on the final break up of the R.N. (63rd) Division, 6th June, 1919, when they were returned to Chatham ("B.S.S." Vol. III., p. 381).

PART II.

SUMMARY OF THE PRESENTATIONS OF COLOURS TO THE ROYAL MARINES AT VARIOUS DATES.

No accounts prior to 1827 exist.

1827.

The following account of the ceremony at Portsmouth is taken from a contemporary pamphlet (which is printed in full in *Globe and Laurel*, Vol. 1. pp. 197-210).

PORTSMOUTH. The troops in garrison paraded in line on Southsea Common, under command of Major-General Sir James Lyon, K.C.B., on 27th October, 1827, in the following order: Royal Marine Artillery, 58th Foot, Provisional Battalion (Depots 27th, 28th and 95th Regts.), Royal Marines, a Light Infantry Battalion (Depots of 51st and 60th Regts.). In front a Guard of Honour of Royal Artillery. The new Colours, in charge of Colonel Phillott, R.A. and Lt.-Colonel Darley, 58th Regt.

On arrival of H.R.H. the Lord High Admiral (later William IV.) with the Naval C.-in-C., the Commissioner, the D.A.G.R.M. (Major-General Campbell) and Staff, he was received with a general salute, and then passed down the lines and returned to the saluting point. The Royal Marines then advanced in Line, and on the march formed open column of companies right in front. Upon the centre arriving opposite H.R.H. they halted and formed three sides of a square. The R.M.A. formed in close column in rear of the right face, the 58th and Provisional Battalion in rear of the rear face, and the Light Infantry Battalion in rear of the left face.

The Royal Marines saluted the old Colours, which, being dropped, were not again raised.

H.R.H. then directed all Officers and Sergeants of every Corps to be formed in the centre of the square - as well as the young gentlemen of the R.N. College - who were formed into two lines by the Lieut.-Governor and his staff.

H.R.H., with Lady Stopford on his right arm and Lady Lyon on his left, accompanied by a large party of officers and ladies and gentlemen, entered the square, together with the Guard of Honour. He commenced his speech: "Col. Moncrieffe (the Commandant), Lt.-Col. Sir Richard Williams, Officers, N.C.O.'s and Privates of the Royal Marines and Royal Marine Artillery, as Lord High Admiral and General of Marines.... " (The whole speech can be read in the Globe and Laurel.)

H.R.H. then delivered the King's Colour to 2/Lieut. Johnson-How and the Divisional Colour to 2/Lieut. Geo. Griffin. Colonel Moncreiffe replied, after which the Brigade saluted and cheered, and H.R.H. returned to the saluting point. The troops then formed contiguous column and deployed into Line; they then fired a *feu-de-joie*, broke into open column of companies and marched past in review order in slow and quick time and in quarter distance columns wheeled into contiguous columns, deployed into line, and saluted when H.R.H. left the ground.

Divisional Orders, Portsmouth Division. 27th October, 1827, contain a letter from the D.A.G. (Major-General Campbell) to the Commandant, enclosing the following memorandum from H.R.H. and also conveying his own congratulations on their good discipline and fine appearance.

Memorandum, Portsmouth, 27th Oct., 1827.
H.R.H. The Lord High Admiral congratulates Colonel Moncreiffe, the officers and men of the Portsmouth Division of Royal Marines on the distinguished marks of His Majesty's favourable consideration, which they have this morning received, and which H.R.H., both as Lord High Admiral and General of Marines, has felt much gratification in personally obtaining for and presenting to the Corps.

H.R.H. derives additional satisfaction from the confident assurance that these honourable badges will stimulate their future conduct, and that wherever their King and Country may require their services, they will be marked by the same undaunted courage, discipline and loyalty as they have hitherto displayed. H.R.H. cannot conclude this order without calling to the minds of Lieut.-Colonel Sir R. Williams, K.C.B., the Officers, N.C.O.'s and Privates of the Royal Marine Artillery, that as being an integral part of the Corps of Royal Marines, they must participate in the honour and distinction thus conferred by their Most Gracious Sovereign; and as H.R.H., both as Lord High Admiral and General of Marines, trusts and believes that this highly distinguished and drilled Corps will equally continue to merit the approbation of their King and the gratitude of their Country.
By Order,
(Signed) Wm. DAVIS, Adjutant.

WOOLWICH. The presentation at Woolwich was marred by rain. The full account is given in *G. and L.* 1905, p. 71. The following extracts may be of interest: After receiving H.R.H. and marching past in slow and quick time, the rain became so heavy that the Battalion was ordered to quarters: crowds kept pouring into the barrack field, until it seemed to be a forest of umbrellas. As there was no hope of the weather clearing, H.R.H. ordered the parade to be held in the riding school (presumably the R.A. School, a place of evil memories to many R.M. officers!) with as many of the Artillery Brigade as could be accommodated. In the centre was a platform for the Duchess of Clarence, the Princess Augusta and other ladies, with the principal officers. H.R.H. then addressed Colonel McCleverty (the Commandant) and the Royal Marines, pointing out the badges, etc. It is interesting to note that in this speech H.R.H. says "for the Capture and *Defence* of Gibraltar, 1704-5" H.M. had selected "Gibraltar" as one of the badges.

After the general salute and three- cheers the Commandant addressed H.R.H. and then the Duchess, Princess Augusta, with the Generals and effective Field Officers of the Artillery, Engineers and Marines, repaired to the "Green Man" at Blackheath, when H.R.H. entertained the company to a dejuner of great profusion and splendour.

From Blackheath many of the principal officers, and especially the Field Officers and Staff of the Brigade of Engineers and Artillery, returned to Woolwich, being engaged to dine with Colonel McCleverty and the Royal Marines in their barracks; about 90 sat down and well kept up *the joyous feeling of the day*. The N.C.O. s, Royal Marines, invited the Staff Sergeants of the R.A. and RE., with their families, to a dinner and dance in a temporary building, which would have been illuminated, but that the rain defeated all efforts in this respect.

PLYMOUTH. The following account of the presentation at Plymouth is taken from Mr. Whitfield's "Plymouth in Times of Peace and War." - H.R.H. the Duke of Clarence presented the Colours, and made a speech lasting *one and a half hours*. Rain fell all the time with remarkable violence, but the Duke "in a firm and manly voice" persisted to the end.

In the evening the barracks were illuminated, each entrance gate displayed the emblem of the Lord High Admiral, the crossed Double Anchors and Cables, with the letters W and A (later Queen Adelaide) surmounted by a coronet. Another transparency (whatever that may have been) depicted Fame drawing aside a curtain and displaying to Britannia the new flag, surrounded with trophies of war. (The full local newspaper account may be seen framed in the Commandant s Office at Plymouth.)

THE 1858 COLOURS.

It has been impossible to trace any account of these presentations, though doubtless there must be a record in some of the local papers. In any case there seems to have been very little ceremony *e.g.*, the Plymouth orders merely state that "The Division will parade in Review Order to-morrow for presentation of Colours." In some cases the presentation seems to have coincided with the D.A.G.'s inspection.

THE 1894-96 COLOURS.

Her Majesty Queen Victoria conferred on the Portsmouth Division the signal honour of presenting the Colours personally at Osborne on 22nd August, 1894. The presentations to the Chatham and Plymouth Divisions were not made until 1896, when H.R.H. the Duke of Edinburgh, the Honorary Colonel of the Corps, presented them at Chatham on 22nd June, 1896 and at Plymouth on 3rd July, 1896. These ceremonies were the first occasions which I have been able to trace where the old Colours were trooped before the presentation of the new Colours. The religious service appears also to have become standardised, because none was held in 1827.

PORTSMOUTH.

A Battalion of six companies, under Lieut.-Col. F. Baldwin, was conveyed in gunboats from Gosport to Cowes and marched up to Osborne House. They were then formed in line on the lawn facing the N.W. front of the house; a battalion of R.M.A., under Lt Col Pengelley, was formed up on either flank at right angles to the R.M.L.I.

About 5 p.m. Her Majesty drove on to the ground, and was received with a general salute by the troops under Lieut.-General Davis. C.B., Commdg. Southern District. With Her Majesty were the Princess Louise and the Duchess of Connaught, and in a second carriage Princess Beatrice and the ex-Empress Eugene, H.R.H. The Duke of York (now H.M. King George V.). accompanied Her Majesty on foot, with the Naval C.-in-C., Sir E. Commerrell, V.C.

Her Majesty drove down the line and then returned to the saluting point. Col. Commandant J.Philips, C.B., then assumed command. The old Colours were trooped (Major H. C. Money, with Lieuts. F. Phillips and Whitmarsh, being the officers of the escort), and were then marched to the rear of the Battalion to the tune of "Auld Lang Syne" and cased. The line then advanced to 50 yards from Her Majesty's carriage and formed hollow square, with the drums piled, on which the new Colours were laid; the band was also in the centre. After the singing of the hymn "Brightly gleams our Banner" - the first and last verses being sung by the whole Battalion, the second and third verses by the right and left half Battalion respectively; the prayers of consecration were read by the Chaplain, the Rev. C. E. Yorke, R.N.

Majors Quill and Money then handed the new Colours to Her Majesty, who delivered them to Lieuts. J. B. Pym and J. E. Crowther. Queen Victoria then said: "I have much pleasure in presenting you with these Colours. They carry on them the badge of my uncle, George IV., and the motto defining your services by land and sea. I am confident that they will always be safe and honoured in your keeping." Colonel Philips replied, and the Battalion reformed line and saluted the Colours, which were then marched to their places in line whilst the National Anthem was played.

The troops then marched past in column, reformed line advanced in Review Order, and gave a Royal Salute by command of Colonel Philips. Her Majesty expressed her satisfaction at the appearance of the troops and the manner in which the ceremony had been performed.

Her Majesty provided the troops with refreshments in the meadow near the Royal Stables (lately the R.N. College) and the officers were entertained at Barton House Farm.

As an instance of Her Majesty's solicitude for the troops (she was a soldier's daughter, and prided herself on it), having heard that they could not return to Gosport until a late hour, she telegraphed the next day her hopes that they had reached their destination all right. It is sad to recall that these Colours were carried at Gosport at the funeral in January of 1901 of this most gracious sovereign. H.R.H. The Duke of Connaught also telegraphed his congratulations on the honour conferred on them.

The W.Os., Staff Sergeants and Sergeants celebrated the presentation by a dinner and entertainment at Forton, and the Junior N.C.O.'s held a smoking concert.

For fuller details see *Globe and Laurel* 1894, p. 97.

CHATHAM.

The details of presentation were much the same in this case (see *Globe and Laurel*, 1895-96, p. 102). A Battalion of eight companies, under Lieut.-Colonel A. B. Crosbie, A.D.C. paraded on the Great Lines. H.R.H. The Duke of Edinburgh was received by a Guard of Honour of the Royal Scots and escorted to the ground by a troop of the Royal West Kent Yeomanry. Colonel Commandant G. H. T. Colwell, C.B., received H.R.H. with a Royal Salute. Colonel F. H. Poore, R.M.A. attended H.R.H. as equerry.

The Consecration Service was read by Rev. Dr. Dickson, LL.D., R.N., the Chaplain, and the Colours were handed to the Duke by Majors Horniblow and Matson, who delivered them to Lieut. W. E. G. Connolly and Lieut. J. H. Lambert. The Duke then made a speech (which as it has not hitherto been published, is reproduced in full): -

"Col. Colwell, Officers, Non-commissioned Officers, Buglers and Privates of the Chatham Division, Royal Marines. It is peculiarly gratifying to me as your Honorary Colonel, as having been so intimately connected in my capacity as a Naval Officer with your Corps, and serving with its members in all parts of the world, that the duty of presenting you with new Colours should have fallen upon me. It is not necessary for me to speak of the way in which the Royal Marines have at all times done their duty, and will, I doubt not, at all times do it in future, not to mention the various occasions upon which the reigning Sovereign has shown marked appreciation of their faithfulness by bestowing some special distinction on the Corps. These facts are well known to all present here to-day, but in presenting the new colours I would draw attention to the fact that in addition to the monogram of Her Majesty, they hear that of King George IV, who in 1827, when the Duke of Clarence was fulfilling the same duty which it is my privilege to perform to-day, directed that the

Colours of the Royal Marines should for ever after bear his monogram, in addition to that of the reigning Sovereign, and this is a distinction which I know is highly prized in the Corps.

In delivering these Colours into your custody, I feel satisfied that they will be in safe hands, and that it will be the pride of the Corps to show in the future, as in the past, their loyalty and devotion in the service of their Queen and Country."

Colonel Colwell replied, and mentioned the fact that the Colours which were being replaced were presented to the Division in the same year in which H.R.H. had entered the Royal Navy, viz, 1858.

H.R.H. then returned to the barracks, and after being photographed with the officers lunched with them in the Mess. The officers' friends were entertained in the theatre. As the Duke left the barracks all ranks were on the pavement and cheered him as he drove away.

In the evening the Sergeants' Mess gave a dinner and smoking concert, and on 17th July the Officers gave a ball, a special dancing floor being laid in the drill shed. On 30th June Colonel Colwell, with Lieuts. Connolly and Lambert, took the old Colours to Clarence House, where they were handed to H.R.H., a silver plate with an inscription having been placed on them to record the fact.

The Dean of Rochester (Dean Hole) had offered them a resting place in Rochester Cathedral, but as H.R.H. had accepted them, the offer had to be declined.

PLYMOUTH.

On 3rd July, 1896, H.R.H. The Duke of Edinburgh, attended by the D.A.G., General Sir H. Tuson, K.C.B., the D.A.A.G. Colonel C. H. Scale, and his Equerry, Colonel F. H. Poore, R.M.A., arrived at Millbay station at 7 a.m. He was received by a Guard of Honour and Band and escorted to barracks by the Mounted Company of the 2nd Vol. Bn. Devon Regiment. He breakfasted with the Commandant (Colonel E. L. Rose).

In the forenoon the Battalion paraded on the Brickfields, under Colonel R. B. Kirchoffer. H.R.H. who wore the full dress of a Colonel Royal Marines, with the Star and Ribbon of the Garter, was received by the Colonel Commandant with a general salute.

The Service of Consecration was read by the Rev. S. S. Browne, R.N. Majors Cotter and Barrett then handed the Colours to the Duke, who delivered them to Lieuts. R. Prynne and H. M. Howard. He then addressed the Battalion, to which Colonel Commandant E. L. Rose replied. The Duke then returned to barracks and lunched with the officers and afterwards was photographed with the Officers and Colours; he then left Millbay for Windsor, a Guard of Honour being mounted at the station. (See *Globe and Laurel*, 1895-96, p. 110.)

On 31st July the Officers gave a ball, a special floor being laid in the drill shed and the supper in the mess room, the new Colours being marched from the drill shed with ceremony to their permanent home in the Officers' Mess-room, where they hang in company with their fore-runners of 1858 and 1827.

―――――

COLOUR SUPPLEMENT.
(Editor's Note. See the dust cover for examples in colour.)

The breadths in the Union Flags are not quite accurate.

1827 Colours. - It is uncertain whether the Laurel wreath round the Globe was Gold or Green. It is shown Green in the drawing at the R.M.O., but in the old Colours at Plymouth it is now of a brownish tinge which looks much more like faded gold.

1858. - The Anchor on the Regimental Colour is smaller than that on the Colour now hanging in the Eastney Church.

1894-96.- The Fluke of the Anchor is too spread and there should be a Lion over the Crown similar to Cap Badge on the Colour Staves.

―――――

THE DIVISIONAL COLOURS.
A Correction.

On pp. *193 and *194 of my article in the December number, I quoted a letter showing that the Plymouth Colours were sent with the Draft in February 1775 to the Battalion at Boston, North America, and therefore deduced that only the 1st Battalion had Colours. I have just discovered in the Portsmouth Letter Books, Vol. 3, that a precisely similar letter, addressed to the Commanding Marine Officer Portsmouth, was sent from the Admiralty on the same day!

I think we can therefore assume that both 1st and 2nd Battalions carried Colours in North America in 1775-1778. I wonder what became of them when they returned to England; the Battalion (the two battalions were amalgamated in 1777) returned to Portsmouth. Also whether these were the Colours issued to Portsmouth in 1765, and if so, were they the old Colours of 1740-1748? Here is a chance for some of the antiquarians of the Portsmouth Division.

H. E. BLUMBERG

March, 1931.

―――――

THE SWORD IN THE ROYAL MARINES
By General H. E. Blumberg, K.C.B., ret.

On looking through the illustrations in Colonel Field's History of the Corps, one notices that the earliest pictures show that officers carried swords of the rapier type, possibly what are called "small swords." The handling of a sword was then a necessary part of the education of a gentleman, and they were all probably expert in its use; the sword belt was an embroidered shoulder belt with crimson sword knot.

When the present Corps was formed in 1755 the sword appears to be nearly straight, with a brass hilt and leather scabbard, with a gold sword knot; it was worn suspended from a waistbelt; officers also carried a fuzee (short musquet) and bayonet. Sergeants also wore swords and carried halberds; they were allowed to wear swords for walking out, after side-arms had been forbidden to be worn when walking out, owing to rows in the streets, 1760 (Ply. Orders). On 28th July, 1771 (Ply. Orders) officers were ordered to provide themselves with new pattern swords; the new pattern must have been the silver-hilted cut and thrust swords described later, the scabbard was leather (see the illustration of the officer in 1778, Vol. 168).

In April 1772 the men's waistbelts were ordered to be made into crossbelts, and presumably officers adopted the crossbelts at the same time (Ply. Orders) fastened by a clasp.

On 4th November, 1780, Sergeants were ordered to carry halberds (and presumably their swords) on all duties; Grenadier and Light Companies to carry firelocks.

On 27th April, 1784, an oval plate with foul anchor was ordered to be worn on the crossbelt instead of the clasp (Ply. Orders).

On 13th Feb., 1796 (Letter Books) it was reported to the Admiralty that deviations were being made from the official patterns of the officers dress swords, gorgets, etc., and the Board ordered a strict observance of the patterns but evidently by the following year they had yielded to pressure, as by the letters of 3rd June, 1797, orders were given for the silver lace to be replaced by crimson and gold and "the swords to be the old-established silver-hilted cut and thrust blades, with crimson and gold sword-knots as worn by Officers of the line." The breastplate on the crossbelt was in future to be "square, with the Royal crest of the Lion and Crown." The gorgets to be plain and to have the King's arms and anchor as at present (Letter Books).

I have not been able to find that the Marine Officers ever carried the "spontoon" - a sort of half-pike carried by subalterns in the army.

On 23rd Sept., 1797, Orders were given for supply of Pikes to Sergeants. It would be interesting to know the pattern, as they replaced the halberds. It is interesting to note that in November 1786, when the draft for Botany Bay, to escort the convicts, was being got ready, the arms of the detachment were changed, the men being armed with short Army musquets with steel rammers and the sergeants with sergeants carbines, also with steel rammers (Letter Books).

The hilt of the officers' sword must have been changed back to brass somewhere about 1820, when many changes were made in uniform.

On 8th Nov., 1827 (Ply Orders) pikes were abolished for sergeants, who carried them, and in future "Sergeants are to commence duty with arms and accoutrements when men are under arms; at other times to wear their swords."

But matters die hard in the Marines: sergeants continued to wear swords, or rather sword bayonets (long) until the introduction of the Lee-Metford rifle in 1894, when the triangular bayonet was replaced by a sword bayonet for all ranks; there was also an idea that they were armed with a shorter rifle, probably a survival of Botany Bay, but I never could detect any difference. The R.M.A. were also supposed to have a shorter rifle, and they always had the sword bayonet, but not the horrible weapon in use by the R.G.A.

But so far we have heard nothing of the training in the use of the sword. Ply. Orders 14th June, 1830, supply a clue: The Garrison Commander in issuing a very complimentary report on the inspection of the Division he says, "but he finds great fault with, the inefficiency of the officers in sword exercise." It is possible that this was that wonderful collection of flourishes meant to represent cuts and guards, which was known for many years as the "Infantry Sword Exercise." The same remark may be found in many annual reports of the D.A.G., at which this performance provided one of the set pieces.

Somewhere about this year the sword belts were for a time black.

In 1835 Field Officers were ordered to wear gilt scabbards for levees, but black leather with gilt mountings for all other orders of dress.

In 1838 the Officers of the Artillery companies were allowed to wear sling belts, when on artillery service, but the cross belt on all other occasions.

So far we have heard nothing about the handling of this lethal weapon, but on 13th Nov., 1842 (Ply. Orders) a notice appears that "the superintendent of Sword Exercise, H. Angelo, Esq., is making his inspection; Officers to attend at Government House on his arrival." It is curious, in view of what occurred in 1893, that this gentleman appears to have been an Italian.

When the tunic ousted the coatee in Crimean times the waistbelt replaced the crossbelt; the belts were pipeclayed generally, though for a time black belts were worn; the locket clasp bore the words "Per Mare Per Terram," and the tongue of brass had the Lion and Crown crest.

In 1867 the steel scabbard replaced the leather for captains and subalterns, and a gilt one for field officers; whilst in 1868 gold belts and slings (R.M.L.I. crimson and gold) were introduced for levees and full dress. The clasp for the dress belts in the R.M.A. was a gilt hook with an oval gilt piece on either side, on which was mounted the silver Lion and Crown. The R.M.L.I. had a crimson and gold belt with the usual locket, but the outside was the laurel wreath in gilt and the tongue bore the silver Lion and Crown. It must have been about this time that the swords that remained in use for many years were introduced. For the R.M.L.I. the hilt was made of brass bars with the Royal cypher; the blade was a cut and thrust - not very long and rather curved. It was a heavy, ill-balanced weapon, and many officers equipped themselves with "a tailor's sword," that looked all right but could be bent into all sorts of graceful curves if leant on; it was awkward if this happened just before moving off to march past. The R.M.A. were equipped with a long artillery sword, with steel bar hilt, really meant for use mounted.

Reverting to the training in the use of the sword, I must first digress a little. When the proposals were first made in 1877 that the Light Infantry should be granted a penny a day as trained men in Naval Gunnery, the question arose as to the details of the course. At that time the seamen qualifying for T.M. had also to pass in cutlass drill; therefore the Sea Lords of the Admiralty insisted that the Marines should also qualify in this valuable weapon. In vain it was pointed out that the Marines were armed with a bayonet and not a cutlass, but the old Sea Dogs stuck to their guns, or rather cutlasses, and one can only imagine that a way out of the impasse was found by ordering the R.M.L.I. officers to learn the cutlass drill in lieu of the infantry sword exercise. Many weary hours were spent by captains and subalterns in acquiring this art, generally under the parade sergeant-major, particularly just before D.A.G.'s inspection. The value of the exercise is best illustrated by the complaint of the wounded bluejacket, who said "I made the first cut and showed the first guard and he stuck me in the stomach."

I do not remember if the R.M.A. followed the cutlass exercise, or whether they followed the Royal Artillery and learnt the cavalry exercise. About 1894 a change came o'er the spirit of the dream; the Army gymnastic staff, whose word was then law, discovered an Italian fencing master, I believe by name Masiello, who had quite a new method; the position on guard was with a straight arm, with a most extraordinary collection of acrobatic cuts and guards; we were informed that it took six months to learn the grip of the handle alone, which was quite sufficient to determine the majority of us that it was not for us! Hours of drill in empty barrack rooms, or on parade, taught us a semblance of the correct attitudes - of course the handling and use of the sword was a minor matter.

The trouble, from our point of view was it entailed the expense of new swords, which we could ill afford, because the blade was quite straight, with supposed sharp edges near the point; the hilt was the cumbrous basket steel hilt - in fact the present pattern sword. Somehow the R.M.A. managed to retain their old swords - about the only arm of the service that did so - vide the fearsome weapons of the cavalry.

The weight of the new swords made it almost impossible to learn the new system, for we did not then have the modern fencing sabres. Many officers refused to get the new blade, especially those with old family swords, and contented themselves with getting the hilt changed. The scabbards were of steel, as the sensible Sam Browne equipment was not authorised for Marines until about 1897, and then only on rare occasions.

Dismounted officers always wore their swords hooked up, and mounted officers in Review Order and Undress wore a sabretache of patent leather, introduced in 1872. Originally designed as a useful pocket for carrying papers, with a patent leather stiff front, useful as a writing-pad or sketching board; needless to say the tailors soon adorned them with brass badges - the Lion and Crown, with Gibraltar on a scroll above, and Per Mare Per Terram below; the R.M.A. in addition had crossed guns. It was useful for only one purpose, viz., to steady the scabbard when the sword was drawn. In full dress, as distinct from review order, which fortunately was never worn mounted, there was no sabretache for the infantry, but the R.M.A. had a very elaborately embroidered red and gold one. When the uniform was altered in 1907 the old white belts were abolished and the gold belts came into use for review order; the sabretache also was done away with. The King's Birthday and other shows therefore gained an added amusement for the mounted officer, who had now a loose scabbard swinging round his head if he moved out of a walk, for needless to remark, the Marine - being a fine crusted Conservative - did not adopt the sensible army practice of putting the sword in a frog on the saddle.

Gradually our P.T. enthusiasts developed a more sensible method of training in the use of the sword, and before the war training in the use of the sword was transferred to the gymnasiums, and the farce on parade ceased.

And then came the War 1914-18, when the sword, like many other things, was relegated to the limbo of forgotten things; but it is good to see that it is now restored to its ancient prestige. When worn with the sensible S.B. equipment it is no longer a snare and delusion to the unwary subaltern, as it was in the days when it dangled at the end of two long white slings, which not only covered the owner with a fine white dust, but also occasionally assisted to lay him prone in the dust.

Swords were formerly always worn on duty, even at mess by the officer of the day, though later he was allowed to remove the sword and hook up the slings. They were always worn at dances (and inspection dinners) when full dress was worn, as it always was at very small affairs.

Besides Commissioned Officers, swords were only worn by Warrant Officers, Q.M.S. and Q.M.S.I. and the Drum-major. The Sergeant-major was the only man who was allowed to draw his sword, and then on two occasions only (one, I can hear the young officer say, trooping the Colours), but there was another occasion. Formerly when a man was sentenced to discharge with ignominy, it was usual after the sentence was read on parade for the drums to play him out of barracks to the tune, I believe, of the "Rogues' March," and as he went out of the gate the Sergeant-major gave him a final kick and handed him a shilling on the point of his sword; the balancing feat must have taken a bit of doing.

I have ventured to put these few notes from various sources together, but I hope that Colonel Field will one day give us a full account out of the vast store of his knowledge.

HONORARY COLONEL COMMANDANT
By General Sir H. E. Blumberg, K.C.B. ret.

Although the present appointment of Hon. Colonels Commandant were only instituted in

1923, we must go back into history to trace their origin. At the end of 1760 the following order was promulgated by His Majesty the King: -

"His Majesty, anxious to reward such officers as had distinguished themselves in the service of their country on this occasion (*i.e.*, the great victories of 1759) - (see Beatson Naval and Military Memoirs, Vol. II.) appointed: -

Admiral Lord Boscawen to be General of His Marine Forces, with a salary of £2,000 a year (for victory of Lagos).

Vice-Admiral C. Saunders, Lieut. - General of the same, with a salary of £1,200 (Naval C.-in-C. at Quebec).

And the following Captains of the Navy to be Colonels of the above Corps, with a salary of £800 a year each –

Capt. Sir Piercy Brett, Knight, R.N., at Portsmouth.

Capt. Augustus Keppel, R.N., at Plymouth.

Capt. Richard Viscount Howe, R.N., at Chatham."

These were purely sinecure appointments and carried no duties, though from the letters at Chatham Captain Horatio Nelson, who was Colonel from 1 June, 1795 to 19 Feb., 1797. seems to have taken an interest in his Division.

The Captains vacated their appointments on promotion to Flag rank.

Among the Generals was H.R.H. the Duke of Clarence, afterwards King, William IV.

This system remained in force until 1837.

By Order in Council, 20 March, 1863, a General Officer of Marines was appointed as Colonel to each of the five Divisions (as the principle adopted in the Army for Colonelcies of Regiments) and "to raise the pay of these officers from £702 12s. 6d. to £900 a year."

They had nothing to do with the Command of the Division, as the Order said: -

"This measure will, in our opinion, give general satisfaction, as it will not only afford means of conferring a reward upon a very meritorious class of old officers, but will be beneficial in giving it the advantages of a few honorary appointments."

These appointments were abolished by O. in C. 22 Feb.,1870, when a reorganisation and retirement scheme came into force.

In 1883 Admiral H.R.H. the Duke of Edinburgh was appointed Honorary Colonel of the whole Corps, an appointment which held till his death in 1900.

In 1901 H.R.H. the Prince of Wales (His present Majesty) was appointed Colonel-in-Chief, an appointment which he graciously retained on his Accession to the Throne, and still holds, an honour of which the whole Corps is very proud.

In Sept. 1923 His Majesty was graciously pleased to sanction the appointment of a General Officer, Royal Marines, as Colonel Commandant in an Honorary capacity to each of the Royal Marine Divisions. (These appointments were on the precedent established for the Rifle Regiments, and each Hon. Colonel Commandant was appointed definitely to a Division, as they are to be a Battalion.)

The Order directed that they were to be filled by selection from the Active and Retired lists, subject to His Majesty's approval; to be vacated at 70 years of age.

The appointment to carry no extra emoluments, claim for full pay time, or abatement of income tax for upkeep of uniform.

These officers to be allowed to visit the Division to which they are appointed once a year, a government railway warrant being allowed.

The first holders were: -

Chatham:
General Sir Wm. Adair, K.C.B. Although over 70 years of age, the Admiralty in consideration of the long and celebrated services of the Adair family in the Corps, allowed him to retain the appointment until 75 years of age.
Portsmouth: Major-General Sir A. Paris, K.C.B.
Plymouth: General Sir Charles Trotrnan, K.C.B.

In 1932 an Order in Council was promulgated approving of the appointment of Admirals of the Royal Navy being appointed as Honorary Colonels Commandant.

THE COMMANDING OFFICERS, ROYAL MARINES
1755 ONWARDS.
By General Sir H. E. Blumberg, K.C.B. Royal Marines (Retd.)

The section below, up to the new section "Regiments Afloat" has numerous, hand written (ink) amendments. These have been incorporated where legible. Ed

By the kindness of the Admiralty Librarian I have recently had access to some of the old *London Gazettes* and Marine Officers List, and after comparison with the Divisional Letter Books, it is hoped that the following lists are as accurate as possible; they show that some of the lists at the Divisions are not quite correct.

In the *London Gazette* of 26th April, 1755, there are gazetted the full list of Commanding and Field Officers, the Companies allotted to each Division and Officers appointed to each of the fifty companies.

From this we learn that Portsmouth was the Senior Division, beginning with No. 1 Company and having 20 companies. Plymouth was next, beginning with No. 2 Company, and Chatham third, beginning with No, 3 Company.

After the demobilisation in 1763 (after the Seven Years War) and the reorganisation, the companies were renumbered, Chatham became the First Division, beginning with No. 1 Company, Portsmouth second with No. 2, and Plymouth third with No. 3.

Up to 1771, when the rank of Colonel Commandant was instituted, there was only a Lieut - Colonel and Major at each H.Q., although many officers held higher rank by Brevet. In 1771 the Commandants were also appointed Captains of Companies, at Chatham of No. 1 Company, at Portsmouth of No. 2, and at Plymouth of No. 3; and later on, when Colonels Commandant in Second, of whom there were sometimes two, and all holding the rank of Lieut.-General or Major-General, the only way of identifying the Commandant is to see to which Company he was appointed. With these preliminary notes we can return to the lists. The actual dates of promotion are given in the old Marine Officers lists.

Portsmouth.
    Lieut.-Col. JAS. PATERSON, 23 March, 1755.
    Major R. Bendyshe, 5 April, 1755
    On 19 Dec. 1755 Lt.-Col. Paterson was promoted to Colonel (L.G. 3 Mar. 1756), and became Commandant in Town as a sort of A.G.R.M.
    Major BENDYSHE was promoted to Lieut.-Col. 19 Dec., 1755.

On 17 Feb. 1756, Lieut.-Col. Dury. Commanding at Plymouth, was informed by Admiralty that he had been appointed to Command at Portsmouth and appears to have taken over his

Command in April. Colonel Bendyshe was transferred to Plymouth.

Lieut.-Col. T. DURY became Bt. Colonel 14 Apr., 1756, and Major-General 23 Feb.,1761.

On promotion to Major-General he must have been made actually, though not in name, Commandant Resident in Town, because Major Boisrond, who had evidently been told off to "Command the Belleisle Bn. (vide Ply. Letter book 24 Oct. 1760) seems to have been withdrawn at this time; and certainly from 1763 all letters are addressed to Col. Boisrond at Portsmouth, though Dury is borne at Portsmouth till about 1771 in the Marine Officers lists. Strength is lent to this by various letters between those dates, when disputes as to contractors' supplies are referred to him, and he gives decisions against C.O. at Portsmouth.

Lieut. – Col. H, Boisrond, Feb. 1761 to 15 April 1772 (promoted to Colonel Commandant and Captain 16 April 1771). He commanded the Bn. at Quebec, as he is shown in 1760 M.O. list as Lieut.-Col. in America only, dated Jan. 1759.

No. 2 Co., Col. Commandant H. Smith, 16 Ap., 1772 to 24 Dec. 1791, when he was appointed Commandant in Town and A.G.

No. 2 Co., Col. Commandant W. Souter (later Souter – Johnstone) 24 Dec. 1791 to 1 Feb. 1793, exchanged to Plymouth. Commanded No. 2 Grenadier Co. at Bunkers Hill, and later brought the Battalion home.

No. 2 Co., Col. Commandant H. Innes. 1 Feb. 1793 to 5 Nov. 1794. From Plymouth exchanged to Chatham.

No. 2 Co., Col. Commandant Maurice Wemyss, 5 Nov. 1794 to 10 Dec. 1797. Commanded Marines at Battle of Buxar 1764. Tried by G.C.M. and placed on half-pay.

No. 2 Co., Col. Commandant Thos. Avarne, 9 Feb. 1798 to 24 Dec. 1803. Commanded No. 1 Grenadier Co. at Bunkers Hill, and Marine Grenadier Cos. at capture of New York and Philadelphia, 1776-1778. (N.B.- During the interregnum the Division was apparently commanded by the A.G. R.M., Lt.-General Souter-Johnstone). To retired full pay.

No. 2 Co., Geo. Elliot, 24 Dec. 1803 to 28 April 1814.

No. 2 Co., Major-Gen. R. Williams, 28 April 1814 –

Plymouth
Lieut.-Col. T. DURY. 24 Mar. 1755: for his career see Portsmouth.

Major F. Leighton, 5 April 1755. He seems to have left the Corps very soon.

Lieut.-Col. R. Bendyshe, - 14 April 1756. Transferred from Portsmouth 14 April 1756, and exchanged to Chatham 1 July 1758. Lieut.- Col.19 Dec. 1755.

Lieut. - Col. Jas. Burleigh, 1 Jul 1758, exchanged from Chatham. Lieut.- Col. 22 April 1758. Retired full pay 14 April 1771.

No 3 Co., Col. Commandant John Bell, 15 Ap. 1771 to 15 Sept. 1784. To retired full pay.

No. 3 Co., Col. Commandant A. T. Collins, 15 Sept. 1784 to 4 Jan. 1793. Died in London 4 Jan. 1793. From Chatham. Most distinguished service at Louisburg 1758, Belleisle 1761, Havana 1762. Commanded Marine Battalions in America 1776. Father of Col. Collins of Australian fame.

No. 3 Co., Col. Commandant Harrie Innes, 4 Jan. 1793 to 1 Feb. 1793, Exchanged to Portsmouth.

No, 3 Co., Col. Commandant Wm. Souter (Souter - Johnstone), 1 Feb. 1793 to 15 Feb 1795. Appointed Commandant in Town and A.G. For services, see Portsmouth.

No, 3 Co., Col. Commandant John Bowater. 19 Feb. 1795 to 27 Dec. 1803. To retired full pay.

No. 3 Co., Col. Commandant R. Bright. 27 Dec. 1803 to 28 April 1814. To retired full pay. Very distinguished service in West Indies.

No. 3 Co., Col. Commandant R. Winter - never joined.

No. 3 Co., Col. Commandant T. Strickland, 26 May 1814 to 1 Oct. 1819. Promoted to Lieut. - General.*

No. 3 Co., Col. Commandant Watkin-Tench 1 Oct. 1819 to 21 Aug. 1821, Deprived of his Command for forwarding what was considered an improper memorial to Admiralty. Relieved of his command 8 Aug. 1821 He was one of the Founders of Australia and has written a book on it.

*It was ruled in Sept. 1819 that Commandants were to vacate command on promotion to Lieutenant –General.

Chatham
Lieut.-Col. Charles Cordon, 25 March 1755 to 22 April, 1758. Retired half-pay.
Major Jas. Burleigh.
Lieut.-Col. Jas. Burleigh, 22 April. 1758 to 1 July, 1758. Exchanged to Plymouth.
Lieut.-Col. R. Bendyshe, 1 July, 1755. Lieut. - Col. 19 Dec. 1755. Brevet Col. 19 Feb. 1762.

To retired pay.

No. 1 Co., Col. Commandant Jas. Mackenzie. 16 April 1771 to 1 Aug. 1783. Commanded Bn. at Belleisle, severely wounded. To Commandant in Town and Adjutant General.

No. 1. Co. Colonel Commandant Arthur Tooker Collins, 1 Aug. 1783-14 Sept. 1784. Transferred to Plymouth.

No. 1 Co., Col. Commandant Walter Carruthers, 15 Sept. 1784 to 24 Dec. 1791. Died at Chatham.

No. 1 Co., Col. Commandant John Tupper, 24 Dec. 1791 to 29 Dec. 1794. Promoted Commandant. in Town and A.G. Commanded 2/Marines at Bunkers Hill and brought Marines out of action; with Rodney at battle of Saints, 12 April, 1782.

No. 1 CO., Co., Col. Commandant Harrie Innes, 5 Nov. 1794 to 23 Dec. 1803. From Portsmouth. Tried by G.C.M. in 1802, but acquitted.

No. 1 Co., Col. Commandant John Barclay, 24 Dec. 1803 to 24 Sept. 1806, Appointed Commandant in Town and A.G.R.M.

No. 1 Co., Col. Commandant Henry Anderson, 24 Sept. 1806 to 24 July 1809.

No. 1 Co., Col. Henry Bell, 25 July 1809 to 28 April 1814. Appointed Commandant in Town and A.G.

No. 1 Co., Col. Commandant Robert Winter, 29 April 1814 to 30 Sept. 1819. Presumably appointed Lt.-General (see Note).

No. 1 Co., Col. Commandant Lawrence Desborough, 1 Oct. 1819 to 28 July 1821.

No. 1 Co., Col. Commandant James Campbell, 29 July 1821 to 19 June 1825. To D.A.G., R.M. (First D.A.G.).

No. 1 Co., Col. Commandant James Boscawen Savage, 20 June 1825 to 7 March. 1831. Appointed. D.A.G., R.M.

Woolwich.
No. 144 Co., Col. Commandant Fletcher, 29 Aug. 1805 to 7 Nov. 1808. Tried by G.C.M. and dismissed Service, commuted to relegation to half-pay.
No. 144 Co., Col. Commandant A. Burn, 7 Nov. 1808.

COMMANDANTS IN TOWN AND TO ATTEND THE ADMIRALTY IN NATURE OF ADJUTANT GENERAL.

Col. Jas. Paterson, 19 Dec. 1755 to Dec. 1760. Retired when Naval Officers were appointed Generals and Colonels of Marines, sinecure, but paid appointments that lasted till 1832.

Major-General Theo. Dury. Unofficially seems to have done the duty 23 Feb. 1761, onwards, though borne on strength of Portsmouth Division.

Order in Council 22 July, 1783, provided definitely for a "Commandant to reside constantly in London to attend the Admiralty in the nature of Adjutant General": -

Col. Comdt. and Lt. - Gen. John Mackenzie, 1 Aug. 1783 to 23 Dec. 1791.
Col. Comdt. and Lt. - Gen. Henry Smith, 24 Dec. 1791 to 28 Oct. 1794.
Col. Comdt. and Major - Gen. John Tupper, 29 Oct. 1794 to 26 Jan. 1795 Discharged Dead.
Col. Comdt. and Lt. - Gen. Wm. Souter (later Souter - Johnstone), 15 Feb. 1795 to 20 Dec. 1803.
Col. Comdt. and. Lt. - Gen. John Campbell, 21 Dec. 1803 to 23 Sept. 1806. (N.B. - This must have been by selection as he was Colonel Commandant in Second at Plymouth).
Col. Commandant and Lt. - Gen, John Barclay, 24 Dec. 1806 to 28 April 1814.
Col. Comdt. and Major - Gen. Sir H. Bell, 29 April 1814 to 31 July 1825.
Order in Council 19 July 1825 provided for placing Sir H. Bell on Retired full-pay, and this entailed the appointment of a Colonel Comdt. and D.A.G., and an A.A.G., in lieu of the post of Secretary to the Commandant in Town.
Col. Comdt. and Major - Gen. James Campbell, 1 Aug. 1825 to 16 Mar. 1831.
Col. Comdt. and Major - Gen. Sir J. Boscawen Savage, C.B., K.C.H., 17 March 1831 to 31 Dec. 1837.
Lieut. - Col. Sir John Owen, K.C.B., K.H. 1 Jan. 1838 to 12 Dec. 1854.
Lieut. - Col. S. R. Wesley, R.M.L.I., 14 Dec, 1854 to 13 Dec. 1861.
Lieut. - Col. and Colonel G. C. Langley, R.M.A 1 Jan. 1862 to 30 Jan. 1867.
Col. Comdt. S. N. Lowder, C.B., R.M.L.I 1 July 1867 to 9 July 1872.
And so on.

During these years there were two attempts to establish a post of Inspector General, but they both failed; there was no room for that officer and the Adjutant General.

By Order in Council, 31 Jan. 1831: Major - Gen. Sir James Cockburn, Bart., K.C.B., who seems to have been an Army officer, held the appointment from 2 March 1831 to 10 Aug. 1836, when it was abolished by Order in Council 1 Aug. 1836.

Again, by Order in Council 6 Jan. 1862, an Inspector General and Brigade Major were provided in addition to D.A.G., R.M.

Major-Gen. A. B. Stransham, R.M.L.I., a very distinguished R.M. officer, held the appointment from 9 Jan. 1862 to 8 Jun. 1867, and was, succeeded by Major-Gen. J. 0. Travers, C.B. R.M.L.I., (who had commanded the Marine Brigade in China) from 9 Jan. 1867 to 18 Dec. 1868, when the appointment was abolished.

Add Note.
By O. in Council, 20 Aug. 1779, 2 Additional Commandants were added. They were appointed to No. 5 and No. 6 Companies respectively at Portsmouth and Plymouth as 2nd Commandants.

The first holders were: Col. C. Gauntlett, Portsmouth. Died Feb. 1780, Col. A. T. Collins, Plymouth.

––––––––

REGIMENTS AFLOAT.
By Gen, Sir H. E. Blumberg, K.C.B., R.M. (ret.)

In the "Globe & Laurel" editorial for Sept. reference is made to regiments that served afloat and bear distinctions for such service.

Passing over the period of the 17th and early part of the 18th centuries. when the majority of regiments, including the Guards, appear to have served afloat as Marines, and also those regiments originally raised as Marines and transferred to Army later, and coming to the period of the present Corps from 1755 onwards, the regiments still in the Army List and bearing Naval Distinctions are: -

The Queen's (R. West Surrey Regt.), the old 2nd Foot, who were present at Howe's victory of "Glorious 1st June. 1794 " - Naval Crown with date.
1/Worcester Regt. (the old 29th Foot), who also wear the same distinction for the same battle.
2/Welch Regt. (the old 69th Foot), This regiment were often afloat and wear the Naval Crown, 12th April, 1782 (not 1792) for Rodney's celebrated victory in the West Indies, the "Battle of the Saints." They were also present in Nelson's ship, the Captain, at the battle of Cape St. Vincent, 1st Feb., 1797, when the Captain of Marines was killed and many men of the 69th killed and wounded.
The Rifle Brigade also wear the Battle Honour "Copenhagen," but whether this is for the battle in 1801, when there are many soldiers in the casualty lists, or for that in 1807, I am unable to say.

In the series of battles fought between Admiral Sir E. Hughes and Admiral Saffren in the East Indies, 1782-1783, detachments of the 78th and 98th Regiments were serving as Marines, and suffered casualties. Whether these battalions are the same as the 2/Seaforth Highlanders and 2/N. Staffords I am afraid I cannot say; I believe the 78th are.

Many other regiments served afloat, particularly in the period 1793-1802; e.g., the 50th R. West Kent.

In 1795 the men of the 86th, 2/90th, 91st and 118th Regiments, which had principally served afloat, were allowed to transfer to the Marines, but I believe most of these battalions were disbanded and are not the same as the battalions that bear those numbers to-day.

At the end of 1795 large drafts of Marine officers and men were ordered to embark in Home and Mediterranean ships to replace Line regiments.

11/9/32.

H.E.B.

NOTES FROM CORPS HISTORY
Extracted from Divisional Order Books and Letters.
By Gen. Sir H. E. Blumberg, K.C.B., R.M. (ret.).

Nowadays we have become accustomed to watching Tattoos and Tournaments in which representations of our predecessors in beautiful old uniforms parade, turned out in the most immaculate manner; whilst the pictures of Colonel Field and Capt. Hicks have shown us the details of those uniforms. But a perusal of the old Divisional Records show us another side of the picture. For instance: -

23 March, 1785 (Plymouth): "Some waistcoats and breeches appear to be shrunk very much; a temporary loop of thread or string is recommended to be fixed from one button of the waistcoat to one of the trouser buttons, so that the slovenly appearance of so short a waistcoat and the soldier's shirts bellying out may be avoided."

And again in Oct. 1802 there is an amusing correspondence between the Adjutant General, the Navy Board (who supplied the *cloatthing*) and the Commandant at Portsmouth. The latter complains about the "facetious reply" of the Board to his complaint, and he sets out in a letter of 27th Oct., 1802, the grounds of his complaint: -

"Complaint against the uniform breeches supplied to the R. Marines; they are very much too short in the fork and are so tight that the men who are at all muscular in their make find it difficult to get them on, and being sewed close to the edges of the cloth, it is impossible to make them larger; the consequence is that it becomes necessary to use those marked 5ft. 8in. and 9in. for men of 5ft. 6in. and 7in., and it often happens that none can be found sufficiently large for the Grenadiers; the obvious inconveniences are that from being so confined men cannot march with the requisite ease, and the breeches wear out much sooner than the allotted time, from being stretched and exposed to perpetual friction. The men also make a slovenly appearance on parade, as there is generally a space between the waistbands of the breeches and the lower parts of the jackets, exhibiting the shirts, exposing the belly and loins to cold, which occasions a variety of complaints.

* * * *

It can have been no soft job being a Tailor in the early days. An order of 9th July, 1766 (Plymouth) says: - "They are to work in the Black Hole in Frederick Square (now occupied by Raglan Barracks). Hours of work, 4 a.m. to 8 p.m., with one hour for dinner. A Sergeant to be told off to supervise them."

That same Black Hole was also prescribed for Sergeants found drinking with the men; for a second offence to be tried by Court-Martial.

* * * *

On 27 March, 1766 (Portsmouth) it was ordered that Sergeants should wear sashes, the same as other troops.

* * * *

In 1785 the system by which companies bought their own necessaries or slops, in fact the bulk of the Cloathing, except the King's Cloathing (i.e., Uniform Jacket, waistcoat and breeches) was abolished on 1st July, and a contractor in London was appointed to supply all Divisions at the same quality and price, according to sealed patterns. It is amusing to read the difficulties raised by the Divisions to the new arrangements, which evidently were not popular. By Board Order of 1st August, Squad Officers, who had hitherto been charged with these duties, were abolished, and Squad Sergeants, who were only required to keep the accounts, were appointed two at each Division, one at £30, the other at £20 a year, in addition to their pay in lieu of poundage (?) and all other perquisites and emoluments.

From various letters this system was not very satisfactory and the men never seem to have been out of debt. This system remained in force until 30 June, 1807, when the supply of necessaries was undertaken by the Navy Board.

* * * *

In November, 1785, the Commandant at Portsmouth reported that it had been customary to supply men on embarkation with great coats, soap, thread and needles, but that no provision had been made in the contract for these articles. Also he asked who was to pay for altering the clothing and mending the shoes.

* * * *

The Quartermaster's Department may be interested to learn that the Quarterly list of Remains was instituted on 30 June, 1785.

* * * *

It may be of interest to read what the kit was in those days and its price. Contract made with Mr. Prater in London 30 Sept., 1785: -

Shirts	5/-
Shoes	5/2
Hose	2/6
Leather Stock and Turn – over	7d
Knapsack	3/7
Cockade	6d.
Heel Ball	1d.
Knife and Fork	11d.
Sleeve Buttons	1d.
Stock and Buckle	5d.
Leather Cap	2/3 (?)
Shoe and Knee Buckles	11d.
Rose	2 ½ d.
Yarn Gloves	7 ½ d.
Brushes and Black Ball	1/-
Short Linen Gaiters	1/1
Long Black Cloth ditto	4/2
Long Trousers	3/9
Turnscrew, Worm and Hammer	7d.
Brush and Wire	1d.
Combs	7d.

It was not until 22 June, 1792, that the following articles were supplied to the men free with the Ammunition Clothing: -
1 pr. Black Cloth gaiters.
1 pr. Breeches, besides the Ammunition pair.
Altering clothing to fit.
1 Hair Leather (2 ½ d.).
Proportion of expense of Waistcoats 1 /- per year.
Worm Turnscrew Picker and Brush every five years; also emery, brickdust and oil.
N.B. - Barrels of Musquets were always bright.

Among the articles that were still issued on repayment were: -
A Powdering Bag and Puff every 3 years.
Grease and Powder for the hair.
Washing was charged 4d. a week.

* * *

It was not until 28 Sept., 1808, that it was ordered that the hair of all soldiers, liable to foreign service, was to be cropped; the same order was applied to the Marines, so presumably the queues and hair powder ceased at this time.

* * * *

In view of the colour of the present day Khaki Great Coats, it is interesting to learn that this was not their first appearance in the Corps. When a new issue became necessary in 1786, the coats ordered by the Commandant at Portsmouth were made "Light Drab Cloth, such as Artillery use, instead of the blue fearnought." He was apparently jumped on for having ordered them locally and not from the contractor, and apparently had to pay for them himself, the contractor offering to supply a better quality at 13/6 each. "They were to be issued to the Marines on shore by the Q.M. and to those who embark and mount guard." Of course the N.C.O.s and Men paid for them. It is not clear whether they were drab or blue.

* * * *

On 27 March, 1766, it was ordered that new Clothing was to be issued in time to be fitted before the 1st. June, *i.e.*, the birthday of King George III; and this custom was continued throughout Queen Victoria's reign, when new clothing was always taken into wear on 24th May, hence probably the origin of the Clothing date 23 April.

A subject that was very familiar to pre-war Marines, when the band clothing had to be paid for out of local funds, had a very early precedent vide the following correspondence in May 1788:

The Admiralty picked up a charge of £6 16s. 2d. in the Portsmouth Accounts for lace for the Sergeant-Major's and Drum-Major's uniforms; also charges of cutting and making and trimming the said uniforms. They say "No charges are found in the accounts of other Divisions." (I wonder! - Ed.). "The Quartermaster is not to make such charges." But now the cream of the joke - "Expenses ought to be defrayed at Portsmouth in the same manner as other Divisions." The R.M.O. evidently had a sense of humour in those days; the Commandant in town had been Commandant at Chatham for many years!!

* * * *

In these days of railways, motor transport and aeroplanes, it is hard to realise that movements between Divisions, when not made by sea, were carried out by route march, the officers being supplied with routes and billetting orders for the impressment of carriages. In some cases when drafts sent from Portsmouth to Plymouth, and vice versa, there are orders for an exchange of officers to take place at Dorchester or similar places.

But the following brings home the distances traversed by escorts sent to fetch deserters (who were very numerous) from all parts of the Kingdom, who had been committed by the magistrates. April 1774: "it has been represented . . . that the Sergeants, Corporals and. Privates are put to great expense for breeches, shoes and stockings, and that it is not in their power to appear so clean as their characters and station require." The Admiralty therefore ordered the Deputy Paymaster to pay the following allowances to deserter Escorts and charge them in the Contingent Account.

To be equally shared among the party –

				Parties of 2 men	Parties of 3 men
Between	8	&	20 miles	2/-	3/-
"	20	&	50	4/-	6/-
"	50	&	100	8/-	12/-
"	100	&	150	10/-	15/-
"	150	&	200	12/-	18/-
Above 200 miles				15/-	£1 1s

* * * *

Those of us who remember the despair of the Corps at having to surrender their short L.E. rifles in 1914, and to receive all sorts of weird arms in lieu, may perhaps be consoled that this was not the first occasion on which something similar befell the Corps. On 11th Nov., 1803, owing to shortage of arms for the rapidly expanding Army, the Master General of the Ordnance suggested that there might be a lot of Musquets at R.M. Headquarters not in use, and Commandants were ordered to hand them over to the local Ordnance Depots.

* * * *

It is very difficult to obtain any details as to the drill and training of officers and men; but at least things are better than the following: Col. Mackenzie (Chat.), on 30th July, 1775, pointed out the great disadvantage of placing newly-appointed Second Lieutenants, who have never been in the Service, on the Sea roster in the places of those whose vacancies they took; "by which it happens that these young officers are embarked before they are qualified in the requisites personally necessary for their appearance on duty, and consequently sometimes embarked in sloops by themselves, they will be ignorant of the great charge and command of troops in action, or other necessary parts of the Service.

My Lords agreed that "Giving time to the newly-appointed Second Lieuts to perfect themselves in their duty at Quarters before they are sent to sea or on other service is highly necessary and proper." They are therefore to be placed at the bottom of the sea roster according to dates of their respective appointments, and not to be sent to sea until the whole of the Lieutenants before them on the roster shall have been embarked or allowed one tour before they were relieved.

The Sea Roster was kept by Divisions and not for the Corps generally, and numerous were the complaints and difficulties to which this gave rise.

* * * *

It may be of interest to know how the Ball Cartridge was made. 12 July, 1779:
Powder 3 drachms (1/2 oz.)
Balls, 14 in number make one lb.
Fine paper, one sheet makes 16 cartridges.
Thread, 1 oz. will tie 1,000 cartridges.
One whole barrel of powder makes 4,266 cartridges for Musquets.

But we fear our I. of Small Arms would not be content with the following allowances for practice:

Spring Allowance, 25 March -
20 Rounds Ball cartridge   }
40 Rounds Blank   } per Musket.
2 Flints   }

Autumn Allowance, 29 Sept.-
10 Rounds Ball cartridge   }
20 Rounds Blank   } per Musket.
1 Flint   }
Issued on Certificate of average numbers at Headquarters.

It was not until February 1807 that we find any mention of the Bayonet exercise; when on 6th February the Commandant at Portsmouth says that his new Adjutant, Lieut. Faden, is anxious to instruct N.C.O.s and Men of Division in Bayonet exercise, and "in the event of its being deemed of the importance it appears to him (C.O. evidently doesn't think much of it) that Lieut. Faden should be allowed to extend his instruction to the other Divisions. The Board approved of the instruction being given.

* * * *

Major Moncrieffe, evidently the F.O. of the Week, asked the Second Commandant to forward a letter in 1808 proposing the use of our old friends the *Drum, Plummet* and *Pace Stick*; or, as he called it, the step measurer - "Nothing of this kind having ever been used at this Division (Portsmouth) since General Elliott took command, while training officers and men to march, merely at random, without due regard to correct time and proper length of pace." Also that "*facings*" (*i.e.*, Turnings) should be performed precisely according to His Majesty's order. He asked that his letter might be sent to the Board; the 2nd Commandant refused, and he sent it direct himself on 26th July, with the natural result that it was at once sent back to the C.O. for report!! It is interesting to note that on 5th August, Major Moncrieffe was transferred to the Woolwich Division. – Those old Commandants were not to be trifled with.

* * * *

We rather wonder how the following would be received nowadays: - On 14th August, 1778, a 2nd Lieut. Johnson had been reported for absence without leave, and orders issued for his arrest by the Marshal of the Admiralty. On 9th September he turned up at Portsmouth, bringing 12 recruits; on which the Admiralty are graciously pleased to pardon him and order him to return to duty.

* * * *

It is a mistake to think that Commissions were not granted from the ranks before 1913. The first Sergeant-Major at Plymouth, John Christian, was promoted in 1756 and made Adjutant, an appointment he held for 19 years, and when later promoted to Capt.-Lieutenant, he was Adjutant at Portsmouth for many years. Sergeant-Majors Rudd and Olive also were promoted at Portsmouth and Plymouth; whilst at the time of the great Mutinies in 1797, Sergeants Sweet, Gilborne and O'Neale were promoted, whilst there are mention of men who were promoted to ensigncies in some of the Highland regiments. Whilst there are cases of Squad Sergeants and Pay Clerks being promoted to Second Lieutenants. The promotion of Staff Sergeants to Quartermaster did not come until well on in the 19th century.

* * * *

The following is a quaint method of providing for the children of all ranks. - I wonder what the Treasury would say to-day: -

11th June, 1793; "Children of N.C.O.'s and men, over 6 years of age, may be shown on muster rolls as Drummers (i.e., draw the pay); they will be struck off as service requires it and those of mature age and fitness can be raised."

* * * *

Those officers who have been Adjutants will readily recognise this letter - 24 Feb., 1808: The Captain of H.M.S. *President* sent in a Drummer with a complaint about his Drumming, and the Adjutant reports that he has examined him and found him all right. The list of drum-beatings is interesting: "He beat Revalie (sic), Troop, Retreat, Taptoo, To Arms, Grenadiers March, Pioneers March, Duke's March, and all beats practised on the Drum, and find him perfectly correct in his duty." I wonder if in the archives of the Drums any of these calls can be identified.

* * * *

The Corps must have been nearly the first public body to introduce Schooling, vide the following order: - Plymouth, 6th May, 1784 - "School to be opened at Orderly Room tomorrow at 9.0 a.m. for benefit of such children of N.C.O.s and Men as may be of proper age to be instructed in reading and writing. Soldiers who desire to qualify for promotion can also attend, provided it does not interfere with duties. Sergeant Jewell is appointed Master; Hours, 9-12, 2-5 p.m. Children who want flogging to be reported to the Adjutant."

* * * *

School for girls was not started until 1820. 26th Oct., 1820: "School for Education in Reading and Plain Work of a limited number of female children of N.C.O.s and Men is established now under Mrs. Yeomans, wife of Sergt. Yeomans. 2d. per week for each child to be paid by parents and guardians to Lieut. and Q.M. Little.

* * * *

BAND COMMITTEE. - lts origin can be traced in the following order of 2nd Oct., 1784: After detailing the duties of the two Adjutants, the Office and the Field, it says the Field Adjutant is "to take the Band and Drums and Fifes under his entire care as to Dress, Interior Economy and beating of the Drummers. The executive part of the Music of the Band is to be under Lieutenants Gilson and Gordon, who have volunteered and undertaken to make them a *Martial Band and capable of Softer Music.*" What would be the comment of our Directors now?

* * * *

It was apparently the custom to publish the misdeeds of Officers and others in Public Orders, and the following is an amusing incident, though we think "Miss 1932" would not have been thrown into the same flutter as "Miss 1808":

The Commandant is making a report to the Admiralty, 5th March, 1808, regarding 2nd Lieut. N - "His conduct has been so unofficerlike, and so much unlike a gentleman; he was reprimanded in Public Orders, since which period he has rudely assaulted the Mistress and Pupils of a Boarding

School adjoining the Barracks, and particularly on Sunday last, immediately after Divine Service, by mounting a ladder, looking over the wall and driving the mistress with her young pupils into the house, and thus depriving them of their usual air and exercise. He has also boasted of writing letters to the young ladies of the school, and when this was represented to him as improper, said he had done it and should do it again, and this at a public meeting of the officers." Commandant proposed to try him by G.C.M.. Apparently he walked back and wrote an abject letter of apology, which was accepted. This officer had very distinguished service later on.

* * * *

Many of the "Old Soldiers" will remember the "Bunce" of evil memory. It may interest them to know that on 4th January, 1787, the following letters were exchanged between the Admiralty and the Commandant at Portsmouth. The Commandant having proposed that "it would prevent a nuisance in the Barracks if Pewter Chamber Pots were provided and placed on each landing place in the Barracks," the Board order the C.O. to cause a sufficient number to be provided to allow of one for each room, and to place one in each room and not on the landing as proposed by the Barrackmaster.

THE ROYAL MARINES AND H.M. DOCKYARDS.
By Gen. Sir H.E. Blumberg, K.C.B., R.M. (Rtd)

It is not known to the writer how the Dockyards were guarded or policed in the early days. They were apparently administered by the Navy Board, a subservient Board to the Board of Admiralty; the Executive Officer was apparently a Commissioner, who was something like the Admiralty Superintendent of the present day, but I am not clear whether he was a civilian or a naval officer - anyway, they seem to have been very unpleasant old gentlemen.

The first record we have of our connection with them is in 1764, when the Admiralty suddenly seem to have been struck with the idea of policing the Yards with Marines. Hitherto the Yards had been looked after by Watchmen selected from the labourers of the Yard; they are sometimes called "Rounders" as well.

On 13th October, 1764 Their Lordships being of opinion that the guarding of H.M. Dockyards with Marines instead of Watchmen selected from the labourers of the Yards, as is now the practice, may contribute greatly to the security of the Magazines and Stores, as well as to the safety of H.M. Ships. . . ., and the Navy Board having concurred with their Lordships and reported that as there are 22 stands (*i.e.*, at Portsmouth, others were much the same) where watchmen are placed, it, will be necessary to post an equal number of Centinels each night. . . .and half that number to perform the duty in the day time. . . . .; guard should consist of as many men as will admit of three reliefs, viz., 66. Said guard, with proper number of officers, should march into yard every day and remain on duty for 24 hours." The orders to the Commandants were that the guards were to commence on Monday next; that the Captain of the Guard was to obtain from the Commissioner of the Yard orders, instructions, etc., and that all duties were to be performed "in the most punctual garrison duty." To report to the Commissioner of the Yard and show the same attentions to his person as are made to Governors of Garrisons, etc.

If numbers at Headquarters were not sufficient (as they generally were not) the Commandants were to apply to the Naval C.-in-C. or S.N.O. for men to be landed from the guardships to complete the guards as necessary. . . "which guard is not to be neglected on any account whatever".

These orders made a great difference to the Divisions, not so much to Portsmouth, but at Plymouth it led to two Parade Companies being placed in barracks at Dock, *i.e.*, Devonport, and the officers' mess in Marlborough Square; the actual order was - "that Marlborough and Granby Squares within the lines of Plymouth Dock were to be allotted for use of H.M. Marine Forces, of 500 men, with usual proportion of officers, which detachments are to take care of the Barracks and do all necessary (? duties)." On 25th January, 1765, Frederick Square was added.

At Chatham officers and men were billetted in Old Brompton.

An Admiralty letter dated 20th October, 1764, gave full details and orders. Their Lordships considered it necessary that orders and regulations should be established for the government of the Marine Forces which are appointed to mount guard in HM. Dockyards, so that Officers and Workmen. . . .and Officers and Private Marines and others may know what is required of them respectively.

The Navy Board was directed to order the Commissioners of the Yards, in conjunction with the Commanding Officer of the Marines at the respective Ports, to issue such regulations as they consider necessary for the Yard and to send them to their Lordships.

The Commanding Officers to draw up such regulations as are required and in the meantime the following regulations were to be observed.

1

Captain of the Guard is to receive the Parole from the Commissioner and all such orders as he shall communicate from time to time for the King's Service, and he will be responsible for their execution.

The Commissioner is not to interfere in the discipline of the Marines doing duty in the Dockyards, the care of which is to remain in the charge of their officers. In case of any complaint of misbehaviour, he is to address the Field Officer of the Day or the C.O. of the Marines at the Port, or finally to the Board, in order that the delinquents may be dealt with according to the Articles of War.

2

The Captain is to make a report of his guard to the Commissioner, and a copy is to be given to the Adjutant on duty, which he is to deliver to the F.O. of the Day for information of C.O. at the Port.

3

The same honours to be paid to the Commissioner as are shown in the Army to the Commanders of Garrisons and every kind of personal attention tending to preserve the respect due to his office.

4

The Marines, as well as Officers as others, are to be instructed that when they have any cause of complaint against any of the Artificers or others belonging to the Yards, not immediately relating to their duty on their posts, they are to make it known to their Commanding Officer, who will report it to the Commissioner of the Yard, in order that due satisfaction may be obtained, and all subject of personal abuse and enmity between the parties in the Civil and Military Service of the Crown guarded against and prevented as much as possible.

5

It is likewise expected of the Officers and Artificers of the Yards that they do, on like occasions, make their complaint to the Commissioner, who will take the necessary measures thereon; and it Is not doubted that every step will be taken on either part to preserve that mutual harmony and good understanding so becoming to the Particulars themselves, and so necessary in every shape for the advancement of the King's Service.

6

The Guards are to be ordered under Arms during the night at the direction of the F.O. of the Day or Captain of the Guard, and the roll called from time to time to see that none of the men are absent.

7

The F.O. of the Day or Commanding Officer of the Marines of the Port are to be allowed to enter the Dockyard Gates night or day, to go the Rounds or attend the Roll Call, and inspect the conduct of the Guard as often as may be necessary.

8.

All orders for the Military Duty in the Yards which may affect the Commissioned Officers or Persons in the Fleet in their necessary intercourse therewith, are to be particularly communicated to the Admiral or Commander-in-Chief of the Port for their information and government.

9.

The Commissioner is to endeavour to provide by suitable regulations against accidents by fire, either from lighted pipes or candles improperly carried into the Magazines; as also for the posting of the guards in such cases, that no useless persons be admitted within the gates upon any alarm: and for the disposition of the Artificers of the different classes according to their professions when called for on such occasions, and he is to cause the keys of the Fire Engine Stores to be lodged with the Officer of the Main Guard.

BADGE OF ROYAL DOCKYARD BATTALION.

10.

The Gates of the Yards are to remain under the care of the Porters in the daytime as usual, and Warders to be placed thereat, in addition to the Centinels, from the beating of Reveille until the beating of Tattoo, who being acquainted with the workmen, may take care that none but the proper Persons are suffered to come in; but the keys of the said gates are to be lodged with the Captain of the Guard when the working hours of the Yard are over in the evening, and delivered back into the care of the Porters at the beating of Reveille in the morning; and no persons are to be admitted into the Yards in the intermediate time, but such as have occasion to repair thither on the King's Service.

I am to signify their Lordships' directions to you to order the Guards which shall from time to time be appointed to do duty in Chatham Portsmouth, Plymouth, Yards to pay the strictest attention and obedience thereto.

(Signed) PHILIP STEPHENS.

Commanding Officer, Marines,
Chatham, Portsmouth, Plymouth.

Careful though these orders were they did not avert trouble. As usual, the first effect was the request to increase the size of the guards; the next point that cropped up was that there were only two Majors or Field Officers at each Division, and therefore at the end of October permission was given for the senior Captain to be put on the Field Officers' roster. There was also evidently a shortage of N.C.O.'s, because an Order in Council, 5th October, 1764, approved of each company being increased by one sergeant and one corporal and reduced by two privates, making the companies 50 privates.

A letter of 28th June, 1765, shows some of the difficulties: "An accident, which might have proved fatal, to a shipwright at Portsmouth, by the violent and indiscreet behaviour of one of the Centinels posted at the Hulk (presumably where some of the artificers lived), and the many altercations which happen between them and the officers of the Yard will require the attendance of a Person of more knowledge and temper at that post than new-raised Marines are generally indued with." The Commissioner therefore proposed that a Sergeant should take over from the Warder every night, and the C.O. of the Marines is ordered to provide a Sergeant at the Hulk as requested.

The Dockyards must have been pretty beastly places, as we find one of the Commandants on 16th December, 1766, complaining that the great sickness among the Marines at one Division was due to the Dockyard Guard duty taking in so large a circuit, in several parts of which they are subject in rainy weather to be ankle deep in mud, and he proposed that a Guard House to hold 30 men and an officer should be built on the north side of the Yard. The Navy Board were ordered to report on the proposal, and if necessary to submit estimates of the cost; it was apparently built.

When war broke out with the American Colonies in 1774-5, the Marine Guards seem to have been withdrawn from the Dockyards, but I have not been able to find the date.

However, in July 1775 we see that the Dockyard Matey was of the same brand as in 1914-18:

"The Navy Board having represented that a number of shipwrights at Portsmouth have absented themselves, and they have reason to apprehend they may obstruct and assault the orderly well-disposed workmen and thereby deter them from going to their duty in the Yard, Commissioner Gambier is authorised to apply to you (i.e., the Commanding Officer of the Marines) and the C.O. of the Land forces for a sufficient number of men as well for the security of the Dockyard as to assist the Civil Magistrates in preserving the Peace until the refractory workmen shall be brought to order. You are to supply as many Marines as you can."

Anyway, as soon as peace was re-established, as it was by the Treaty of Paris, 2nd and 3rd September, 1783, then the Marines were called on to take over the Guards again.

Admiralty Letters 19th June, 1783: "A Captain's Guard to be mounted in the Dockyard at Portsmouth, etc., to do duty there until further orders, in the same manner and under the same regultions as *were practised in during the last Peace*."

Apparently this arrangement was confirmed by further letters dated 24th December, 1783 "The Admiralty ordered the Marine Guards to do duty in the Dockyards at Portsmouth, Plymouth and Chatham in the like manner and under the same regulations as was practised during the former peace; the same may greatly contribute to safety of H.M. Magazines and Stores, as well as to the safety of the ships in the said Yards. Guard to be of the same strength as in former peace. (At Portsmouth the strength daily was one Captain, two Lieutenants, 129 N.C.0.s and Privates.) The Guard House and Watch Houses now occupied by the officers and watchmen are to be delivered up to the Marines and such alterations and additions to be made as shall be necessary for their accommodation and convenience.

But the arrangement cannot have been very satisfactory, because it was discontinued in the following year. On 28th December, 1784, an Admiralty Letter decided that the Yards are to be guarded in future by warders, rounders and watchmen, being labourers and others belonging to the Yards; with the addition of a Subaltern's Guard of Marines to serve as patrols within the Dock Wall, as directed by the Commissioner of the Yard. This Guard consisted of 36 privates with a proportion of N.C.O.'s. This Guard continued for many years with variations, as we shall see.

This order had a very unpleasant result for the Corps; evidently numbers in excess of the establishment laid down in August 1783 had been retained to furnish the guards; these were now ordered to be discharged, being properly accounted with as regards their pay, etc. "No men to be discharged who are over 5ft. 6in. in height or under 40 years of age." And this was followed on 1st March 1786 with a reduction of 10 companies, leaving only 60 and three Lt.–Colonels and three Majors were also reduced.

War threatening again, on 24th September, 1787, there is an Order that the Dockyard Guards are to be withdrawn and held in readiness for sea service, but they were restarted on 20th March, 1788. But on 27th April, 1789, in order to provide men for embarkation, 12 men were taken from each guard at night after the Warders had taken charge of the Yard, the full guard mounting during the day.

On 31st May, 1790, there was a bitter complaint from the Commandant at Portsmouth "that men have only one night in bed"; and further, that recruiting parties could not be sent out. The Admiralty approved of the Marine Dockyard Guard being withdrawn, but it was reinstated on 3rd April, 1792.

But we are now approaching the period of the Great French Wars, and on 9th January, 1793, an Admiralty letter was issued to all Divisions that the Dock and Hospital Guards would be taken over by the Army, so that the Marines might be embarked.

And this continued all through the Wars, the duty being done either by the Army or the Militia. Though when peace reigned for a short period in 1802, on 19th December, Admiralty ordered that the Divisions were to furnish Dockyard Guards while there were sufficient men at Headquarters to perform the duty without inconvenience to the service. But the Army resumed the duty on 11th March 1803 (date when war broke out).

I cannot say when arrangements were made for the Police to take over the Yards, but it must have been soon after Sir R. Peel introduced the Police Forces in England.

But during the great number of years that the Dockyards, Whale Island, etc., were being constructed by convict labour there was always a Marine Convict Piquet on duty at the Dockyard Gates; these guards certainly continued at Chatham and Portsmouth up till about 1896.

Apparently, some Admiralty official had been reading the old records, for at the conclusion of the Great War 1914 - 19 the proposal was made that the Royal Marines might resume their old duties of guarding the Dockyards in place of the Metropolitan Police. The paucity of numbers, to say nothing of modern training, were sufficient to prevent a recurrence of these duties; the outcome of the proposals, however, was the present efficient body of Royal Marine Police.

In 1803, when a wave of military feeling spread over Great Britain, inspired by their fear of Napoleon's invasion, the formation of Volunteer regiments became fashionable, and the following Admiralty letter shows how the Dockyards reacted.

28th September, 1803: "The Artificers in the Dockyards have volunteered to form Volunteer Battalions to be embodied and trained to arms. The Commissioners became the Colonels, and so the following orders were sent to the Marine Commandants. "A proper number of Sergeants are to be employed in training and exercising the said artificers every *Sunday* till further orders; at such hours as convenient arrange accordingly."

I am unable to say how the Yards were guarded during the early years of the 19th century, but the Metropolitan Police Divisions as now existing were established in 1860, at Portsmouth on 1st October, 1860; at Devonport on 22nd Oct., Chatham and Sheerness on 3rd October, and Pembroke on 17th December, 1860, and now the wheel is coming full circle, Pembroke having been taken over by the Royal Marine Police in 1929, Sheerness in 1930 and Chatham in 1932.

During the 19th century the Dockyards were being greatly extended, largely by convict labour, and the Royal Marines used always to furnish, except at Devonport, a convict picquet or guard during working hours.

In addition to the Volunteer Dockyard Battalion raised in 1883, there appear to have been large numbers of volunteers raised in the Dockyards in 1847, the Marines again finding the instructors. This was a much more ambitious attempt, as they appear to have had guns and pioneers, or as we should say to-day, engineers, whilst they were also exercised in boat drill; they had a band, and were spoken of as a Brigade.

Among the instructions for the formation of the Battalions, Artillery Companies and Engineers, it is said that the *Police* are not to be included in any of the battalions, but to be trained in carbine exercise and to form a Fire Brigade. So there must have been some form of Police in Dockyard in those years. The Brigades were eventually disbanded by Order in Council, 6th April, 1858, except the Brigade at Malta, when the Adjutants and Drill Sergeants were granted small pensions.

ORIGIN OF COLOUR SERGEANTS.
By Gen. Sir H. E. Blumberg, K.C.B., R.M. (Ret.)

With a view to improving the discipline of his Army, Lord Wellington had long advocated that the pay of the Non-Commissioned officers should be increased; but the Government, with the pay of the Army several months in arrears, would not entertain this proposal. They, however, approved the grant of higher pay to one Sergeant in every troop of cavalry to be called a Troop Sergeant-Major, and in July 1813, the W.O. informed Lord Wellington that one Sergt in every company was likewise to receive higher pay than his fellows, wear the regimental colours embroidered as a badge of honour below his chevron and to be called the Colour-Sergeant (Fortescue History of the English Army, vol. ix, p. 100).

On 17th March, 1814, the Commandant of the Portsmouth Division Royal Marines, who had reported to the Admiralty the meritorious conduct of Sergeant Barnes in the recapture of the Transport *Mary* and had suggested his promotion to Colour-Sergeant, according to the late War Office Regulation, was informed that My Lords of the Admiralty do not know that H.R.H. the Prince Regent has made any such regulation for the Royal Marines.

But the Admiralty were unable to retain this attitude for long, because on 22 August, 1814,

Orders were issued that the rank of Colour-Sergeant was introduced into the Royal Marines with 6d. a day extra pay.

Chatham were to promote 18 Sergeants, Portsmouth 14, Plymouth 15, Woolwich 12; all to date 1 July, 1814; apparently, at first no provisions were made for paying them afloat, because on 2 August, 1815, there is a letter from the Admiralty saying, ...additional pay allowed to Colour-Sergeants is to be paid to them for the term of their serving at sea on their joining Headquarters."

As regards the actual badge itself, we see in the Army Order the origin of the Colours; and probably of that peculiar single chevron worn beneath them: -

As regards the Corps peculiarity of the crossed swords, it seems to me that this might have been suggested by the fact that Marine Sergeants from the beginning had always worn swords, in fact they were their mark of rank; as I said in my article on "The Sword in the Royal Marines," the R.M. Sergeants in the days of the old triangular bayonet when swords had been abolished, always wore a sword bayonet, which was a weapon with a long flatish blade, and a handle that could be gripped as a sword handle without the guard.

The 1854 Badge illustrated in B.S.S., vol. ii, p. 78, shows the badge as it originally was; when the elaborate badges illustrated on p.307 was introduced I am unable to say, but it seems to have gone away from the original idea.

RECRUITING IN THE ROYAL MARINES
Compiled By General Sir H. E. Blumberg, K.C.B.

Recruiting for the Royal Marines has always except in modern times, been rather a difficult business, and made more so in former times by the Admiralty policy of discharging men and reducing the Corps to bedrock on the conclusion of a war, and having to increase it to four or five times its peace strength immediately on the outbreak of the next. As wars followed each other at exceedingly brief intervals, recruiting was in a constant state of flux.

When the 50 Companies were raised in 1755, there were no doubt many men of the old Marine Regiments, disbanded in 1748, available, and they flocked to the Colours, as did their officers. We see the first Divisional Orders, May 1755, appointing Company Sergeants, followed by an order, 7th May (Ply.) - "Names of men who have previous service to be reported to the Commanding Officer, so as to make them Corporals." But this was not sufficient to provide N.C.O.s, and there is an Admiralty Letter, 16th May, 1755: "Ten men from each of the Regiments of Foot commanded by Lieut.-General Wolfe, Major-General Rockland and Colonel Honeywood, to be sent to make Sergeants and Corporals for the Marine Companies." There is also a State Paper (Calendar of State Papers 1760-65, No. 937) showing that Sergeants and Corporals were obtained from the Out-pensioners of Chelsea Hospital and from invalids doing duty in garrison, who were entered into the Marines to "instruct the recruits and new raised men in the Manual Exercises."

No doubt the first duty was to send out Recruiting Parties, usually consisting of an officer, a sergeant, a corporal, a drummer and a private, who marched off to different parts of the country. Each party was provided with a "Beating Order, signed by the Admiralty, giving them authority to recruit; a copy of the Recruiting Instructions and a Route or Billeting Order, authorising Magistrates, Constables and Local Authorities to provide them with food and accommodation at rates fixed by Parliament. These arrangements went on till nearly the end of the 19th century. These orders were sent to Divisions from time to time by the Admiralty, and it was necessary to issue fresh ones when the Board of Admiralty was changed.

Men were enlisted for life, but from numerous applications for discharge made after the Seven Years War (1756-63) it is clear that men had been taken during hostilities for "three years or the duration of the war" (c.f. Po. Letter, 2 Feb., 1764, etc.) as was done in the War 1914-18.

Recruits were only obtained by the payment of Bounties or Levy Money; some of which went to the recruit, some to the recruiting party and some to the "bringer." As we shall see, the amounts varied from time to time, but at first it was two guineas, though a Portsmouth Letter says "Foreign Protestants had been enlisted during the war (Seven Years) for as little as £1 7s. 0d.

In those old days boys were apprenticed to their masters for a term of years, and could not be enlisted; the letter books contain many orders directing the return of such men to their masters who had claimed them, but in 1807 the Board decided to prosecute such recruits for fraud and perjury (A.L. 24 July, 1807).

Also from a letter of 3rd Oct., 1766, we learn that Militia Drummers could not be enlisted into another corps and had to be given up.

On 22nd April, 1773, it was ordered that Recruits were to be 5ft. 5n. in height and not under 18 or over 28 years of age, but when war broke out two years afterwards with America, the height quickly dropped to 5ft. 4in. (A.L. 24 Aug., 1775).

Also recruiting was opened in Ireland, as on 23rd June, 1775, the Admiralty issued an order that "Parties are to be sent to Ireland: lists of suitable officers to be sent to the Admiralty. Officers and Parties to proceed by the best route to Dublin and apply to Major Brown, who is superintending." On 15th June Lieut.-Col. Gauntlett was sent over in charge.

But matters came to a head in 1776. 20th Feb., 1776 "Owing to the difficulty of raising recruits other Corps offering greater bounties – the Admiralty gave orders for the Levy Money to be raised to four guineas for every recruit. The order of 24th Feb. says, "Levy Money was only £3 per man, whereas the Army are giving 5 guineas. We are willing to give every encouragement to Recruits who shall voluntarily enter H.M. Marine Service." Recruiting officers were informed that they would be allowed 4 guineas for every man after 1st March, who are approved at Headquarters, which their Lordships considered will have a proper proportion to the Levy money of the Army; the particular advantages of the Marine Service being considered." Here we see the trail of the Accountant General of the Navy so constantly met with in our history.

But a letter of 19th March, 1776, is rather puzzling, unless it means that the amount was what was paid to the man himself: "With reference to the orders of 24th Feb. My Lords think it will tend to encourage proper men to offer themselves if the Levy Money is declared at the Drumhead, and that it will be proper to fix the same at Two guineas and a Crown."

One can imagine the small party marching into the market places of our small towns and villages, the Drummer beating his drum and the Sergeant proclaiming the advantages of the service and pressing the shilling into the hand of a more or less unwilling recruit.

Apparently a row blazed up in Sept. 1776 about the payment of this money, and the Colonel at Chatham reported that the recruit's receipt was always signed on the back of his attestation form. But this report is interesting as one of the Lieut.-Colonels makes the remark that men were "enlisted into the First Division of Marines," i.e., Chatham.

The extraordinary straits to which the recruiting authorities were reduced is shown in a queer bargain made with a Lieut. Bowden and approved by the Admiralty on 15th April, 1777. Lieut. Bowden was to be -

(a) Allowed 2 guineas Levy Money for every recruit, with subsistence from date of attestation.
(b) Allowed 100 guineas for every 100 men sent to and approved at Headquarters over and above the Levy money aforesaid.
(c) Allowed 20 guineas (over and above the 100 guineas) for every 100 men approved, in lieu of all losses he may incur from death, desertion or otherwise.
(d) Should 20 recruits of each 100 be but 5ft. 3in. under the age of 28, they are to be approved, provided they are stout, active, and properly made.

The first lot were to be sent to Chatham, then to Portsmouth and Plymouth. The Commandants to send the certificates to the Admiralty. But the Accountant General's reservation in 1776 was bearing its fruit, for Chatham reported in Jan. 1778 that they were very short of recruits and that there were also shortages at Portsmouth and Plymouth, owing to the large bounties being offered by the Army; so that on 15th Jan. 1778 My Lords raised the amount to 5 guineas for every recruit raised and approved after 1 Feb., 1778.

Apparently also Committees of private citizens had been formed all over the country to raise men for the Services; these Committees offered a Bounty in addition to the Government Allowances, and on 1 Feb., 1778, there is a letter ordering a Captain to attend a meeting of such a Committee in order to receive and enter such men as volunteer for the Marine Service, and reference is also made to Committees at Bath and elsewhere.

In 1778 the height had again been fixed at 5ft. 4in. There is a quaint complaint on 22nd June, 1778, from a Capt. Mcleod of the Marines, that the "Quartermaster at Portsmouth had been granted a Bounty of 4 guineas a man for 20 recruits from Germany, whom he (Mcleod) had entertained (i.e., raised)" and the Commandant is called on to report.

But for sheer impudence two letters of 14th Aug. and 9th Sept., 1778, are hard to beat. A Second Lieutenant J------ had been reported for absence without leave, and the Marshall of the Admiralty ordered to arrest him when he arrived at Portsmouth Headquarters, bringing with him 12 recruits. My Lords were pleased to pardon him and order him to return to duty.

In 1779 Parliament began to take a hand, as an Act was passed "to regulate recruiting of Land Forces and Marines." This necessitated more parties being sent from Headquarters, a difficult matter in those days, and as a result (A.L. 11, April, 1779) the country was divided into 11 districts, and the War Office made certain regulations; the Admiralty ordered the Marine recruiting parties to place themselves under the G.O.C. of the District in which they were, but to continue to report to their own Commandants and the Marine Agent, and to be available for any Marine duty. Copies of the Act and Articles of War were sent to each party, with parcels of Posters of the advantages offered to volunteers. The Act provided that Recruits were to be in common stock, "except in case of Marines, who are to have of the volunteers a number proportional only to the number of their parties in the District." Twenty shillings was to be paid out above the Bounty for necessaries for each volunteer and for each impressed man.

It is interesting to note that when the National Service Acts came into force during 1917 (during the War 1914-18) men were allowed to volunteer for the Royal Marines before being taken for the Army. And yet a letter of 2 Nov., 1779 shows that Recruiting Officers were to attend the meetings of the Magistrates to "receive impressed men for the Marines." In spite of all efforts there are references to soldiers of the Line being embarked in the Fleet in lieu of Marines; whilst in 1781 Prisoners of War, lately taken in the Dutch ships, were allowed to volunteer for the Marines; and on 10th March, 1781, the Admiralty definitely approved of Foreigners, except Frenchmen, being enlisted into the Marines. But we must remember the smallness of the British population of those days and the fact that we were fighting the world, as well as the Americans.

In December, 1781, there is a letter which says "that there were a number of Germans at Forton Prison who wanted to enlist in to the Marines," but the Admiralty consider that they must be regarded as French prisoners and that it cannot be done.

But on 15th Aug., 1782, the Board issued an order that must have added to the difficulties of the recruiting authorities: -

"Whereas we are of opinion that great benefit will arise to H.M. Service by allowing Marines, who may qualify for seamen, to be entered as such, and discharged from the Marine Service without returning the enlisting money paid to them as Marines. On any Marines volunteering, the Captain of the ship is to call the First Lieutenant, Master and Boatswain of the ship and examine them in the presence of the Commanding Marine Officer, and if they pass a list, attested by the Captain of the ship and the Marine Officer, is to be forwarded to the Admiralty, in order that they may be discharged to the sea Service; if their debts exceed the sea pay due to them as Marines, the excess is to be transferred to their growing wages. The Marine Officer is to send the list to the Divisions, and also take charge of their Uniform Clothing (if not long enough in use to entitle them to retain it). The Commandant at Headquarters on receiving the list is to strike them off the books and embark Marines in their place.

(Signed) KEPPEL.
CHAS. BRETT.
J. J. PRATT.
JOHN AUBREY."

A curious letter of 1783 says that Irish recruits were raised "in consequence of the vote of the House of Commons, in Ireland, and that they were enlisted in the usual manner for life."

But peace was now in sight, and instead of recruiting, come the orders for demobilisation and discharge.

In 1786 each Division was allotted the Counties in which they were allowed to recruit and send their parties; a system that remained in force for many years, but letters show that they had often to ask permission to go outside their own boundaries. In 1787 the height was fixed at 5ft. 5in. for young lads of 18 to 20; 5ft. 6in. for men not exceeding 23 years of age.

On 16th November, 1787, the Bounty was reduced to three guineas, of which the recruit was to have one and a half guineas.

In 1790 the standard of height was 5ft. 6in. and five guineas bounty was allowed: but growing lads of 5lt. 4in. could be accepted. But once again war was approaching and standards soon fell. Recruiting was again opened in Ireland 14th October, 1790, with Lieut.-Col. Rotherham in charge, Lieut.-Col. Innes in Dublin and Lieut.-Col. Duval in Cork; five officers from each Division were sent over, making 15 in all. It was stopped soon after, but re-opened in 1793 when war was definitely declared. This, though necessary, had very unfortunate results, because among the recruits were the "United Irishmen," who gave such trouble in the mutinies of 1797 and 1800, and some of whom were shot with some ceremony on the Hoe at Plymouth.

These Irish recruits also gave trouble in another way, for we find a complaint in 14th May, 1806, that they generally bring women over with them, who when the men embark are left destitute, and the Commandant requests that the Admiralty will give orders that they should not be allowed to embark on the Tenders bringing over the recruits.

On 30th March, 1793, the Commandant at Portsmouth is ordered to signify the Admiralty approval to Lieut. Williams, for arriving at Headquarters with 140 Recruits from Manchester in good order; and when one thinks of the conditions under which he had to march them right across England, this must have been no light task.

But when war broke out in 1793 the Corps was so reduced in numbers that large numbers of troops of the Line had to be embarked in lieu, and for the first few years of the war the books are full of orders for the relief of soldiers as Marines became available.

In this regard there is an interesting and pathetic letter from Portsmouth, dated 16 July, 1794, reporting that "the casualties in the Fleet under Lord Howe (the Battle of the Glorious First of June) require more than he has at Headquarters," and asking for drafts from Plymouth; the reply was that there were none available at Plymouth.

On 8th May, 1795, the Bounty was raised to 8 guineas, but on 11th May, 1795, there was a new organisation of the country for recruiting purposes. It was divided into four districts
No. 1 H.Q. at Norwich, in charge of F.O. from Chatham
No. 2 H.Q. at Nottingham, in charge of F.O. from Portsmouth
No. 3 H.Q. at Shrewsbury, in charge of F.O. from Plymouth
No. 4 H.Q. at Ripon, in charge of a F.O. from Plymouth
By 15th Nov., 1795, the bounty for each approved recruit was £15, of which the recruit got 4 guineas and a crown from the recruiting officer.

On 7th Nov., 1795, the C.-in-C., F.M. H.R.H. the Duke of York, gave directions that N.C.O.'s and soldiers of the 86th, 90th (2nd Bn.), 91st and 97th Regiments, who had been doing duty as Marines on board the Fleet, might be enlisted into the Marines, and the Admiralty approved of their receiving a bounty of five guineas; Commandants were directed to communicate with C.O.'s and make the necessary arrangements. Naturally, there was a good deal of trouble with the local G.O.C.'s, and on 23rd Nov. the 118th Regiment was added to the list. We learn from the Plymouth letters that of the 91st Regiment, who were at Liskeard, "almost every man at his H.Q. and on board the ships at Plymouth had volunteered for transfer, when proper persons were sent to receive them."

From the orders and letters of this date, we gather that Marines were now becoming available, and that they were being drafted to the Fleet to relieve soldiers. Also about that time a number of Dutch prisoners of war were allowed to enlist.

France had overrun many of the countries of Europe, and forced their inhabitants to serve in her Army and Navy, so that many prisoners of war were very glad to accept service with the British. For instance, on 9th May, 1796, the Admiralty approved of a party of 70 or 80 Dutch and German prisoners of war from Portchester Castle who wanted to enlist as Marines; and again, on 30th April, 1799, permission was given to enlist Austrian and German prisoners of war, as well as Dutchmen; but this policy had its dangers, as was shown at Curacoa later on and the Island of St. Marcou.

On 25th June, 1801, in dealing with a question of discharge by purchase, it is notified by the Admiralty that the cost of raising two recruits was £52. It is curious that during this war discharge by purchase was allowed, but on condition of paying the cost of raising two recruits in "his stead."

After the temporary cessation of hostilities in 1802, Levy money was fixed at 8 guineas on 23rd June, 1803, and recruiting was opened in Scotland, a Major-General Campbell from Plymouth being sent in charge and three parties from each Division.

As an indication of the numbers of foreigners that must have been serving in the Corps, Portsmouth reported that the number of recruits raised from 1st May to 30th June, 1804, was 167, including 62 foreigners, and a return dated 11th Nov., 1804, of men enlisted for Portsmouth since April 1804 shows what a heterogeneous collection they were

At Headquarters, from Prison Ships	73
In West Indies, by order of Admiral Duckworth	10
In Mediterranean, by order of Lord Nelson	37

The nationalities comprised 2 Brabant, 14 Italians, 10 Spain, 7 Switzerland, 16 Piedmont, 4 Portugal, 1 Porto Rico, 6 Austrian Netherlands, 1 Denmark, 7 Germany, 4 Genoa, 1 Guinea, 1 Holland, 9 Poles, 30 Naples, 1 Rome, 2 Milan, 3 Sicily, 1 Syracuse; whilst in a Plymouth return, dated 1st Jan., 1811, out of 928 ranks serving on shore there were:-

4 Spaniards 126 Germans 158 Prussians 98 Dutch 4 Maltese 7 Swedes
3 Danes 5 Portuguese 1 Russian.
Total 406. The total numbers of the Corps at this time were 31,400.

After Malta had been transferred to the British, Major Weir, on the 14th April, 1805, opened a Recruiting Station there, which was not closed till September 1807.

When the Artillery Companies were formed in August 1804 a letter from the Commandant at Portsmouth is interesting as to the method of obtaining men: "I beg to suggest that the most expeditious way of completing the company here, will be to select such men as appear fit for this service of the Chatham and Plymouth Divisions allowing them the same privileges of selecting men of this Division from ships arriving at their ports; and I have further to observe that should this method meet with Their Lordships approval, the great delay and expense attending their marching would be avoided by an order to transfer the attestations of men chosen for this duty from one Division to another." But it was not always so easy. In Nov. 1811, when each Artillery Company was increased by 3 Corporals, 4 Bombardiers and 58 gunners, there was great difficulty in obtaining men; officers were sent to visit the ships in port, then in December to visit ships and frigates as they arrived in harbour; also on 26th December to visit Channel Fleet, and the age was extended to 30 years, and finally on 28th December officers were sent to the Baltic Squadron, as the ships at Plymouth and in the Downs had failed to supply what were required.

Some time in 1803 or 1804 recruiting was opened for Boys, and a considerable number were entered; they seem to have been definitely embarked as Boys at a special rate of pay. On 11th Nov., 1807, fresh instructions were issued about the enlistment of boys under 16 years of age and 5ft. 2in. in height. Ships appear to have been allowed a definite complement of boys. On 10th March, 1812, an order says that Boys on completing the age of 18 were to be placed on the same rate of pay and allowances as men.

Difficulties were also being caused by the Militia Acts. A Portsmouth return from 1st Jan. to 31st July, 1805, shows: -

Men Recruited	480
Boys	122
Volunteers from Militia:	
Sergeants	14
Corporals	5
Privates	371
Foreigners enlisted in Mediterranean	82
Foreigners enlisted in West Indies	15
	_____
	1070

On 1st July, 1806, men from the Irish Militia were allowed to volunteer for the Marines on the same terms as the English men.

On 15th Dec., 1806, there is a very interesting instruction, showing how the Levy Money was to be distributed: -

	Men			Boys		
Bounty to Recruit -	£	s.	d.	£	s.	d.
On being attested, in Money	2	2	0	1	1	0
On Immediate Approval, Money	2	2	0	1	10	0
Necessaries	0	12	0	0	12	0
On Final Approval, Money	3	12	0	2	2	0
Necessaries	*3	*3	0	*3	*3	0
To the Officer -						
Intermediate Approval:						
For Attestin		1	0		1	0
Surgical Examination		*2	6		*2	6
Postage, Stationery, etc.		*7	0		*7	0
On Final Approval, to cover all incidental expense		*10	6		*10	6
To the Party -						
Reward	1	1	0	1	8	0
For conducting Recruit to final place of approval		*5	0		*5	0
To Bringer of Recruit, whether belonging to Party or otherwise.	3	3	0	3	3	0
	17	1	0	10	15	0

*Not allowed at Headquarters.

N.B - If a recruit deserts after 24 hours, or within four days, the officer refunds 1s. and 20s. smart money.

On 24th March, 1808, an important modification of the period of service was made, for men volunteering for the Marines from the Militia, during hostilities. They were allowed to enlist for Limited or Unlimited service, an extra bounty of £1 being allowed in the latter case: the allowances of officers detailed to get them to volunteer from the Militia regiments were also fixed.

There is an interesting counsel's opinion on 28th February, 1811, that a recruit could not be attested before expiration of 24 hours from time of being enlisted (50 Geo. 3rd C. 14). and on 7th March there was a further opinion that the recruit was allowed 24 hours to return and pay the smart money.

On 9th March, 1812, a new Attestation Form was introduced, extending the Oath of Service to His Majesty to include "His Heirs and Successors."

On 14th March there is an interesting Admiralty letter, which throws light on Limited and Unlimited Service.

Marines enlisted for Limited Service to be allowed to extend for Life and to receive five guineas bounty under following conditions: - Men enlisted for Seven years not to be allowed to extend till the last year of service, and must not be over 30 years of age, healthy, and such as to be retained on a Peace Establishment. Men enlisted for Five years or during the War, to have the same terms if they have entered the seventh year of service. Those enlisted as Boys to commence time from age of 17.

When the R.M. Battalions were in America in the War of 1812-14, numerous runaway negroes took refuge with the British Fleet. A number were enlisted as Marines, and were termed Colonial Marines; there were sufficient of them to form three companies of the 3rd Battalion at Tangier Island in the Potomac River. When the war was over some of them drifted to England, where it was ruled that they could not continue as Marines (A.L. 26 April, 1815), but could be entered as seamen, or else sent back to the West Indies for discharge, which as a matter of fact was done.

With the coming of the long peace all foreigners were discharged and the Corps settled down to the distribution of the country into recruiting districts, and certain towns became recognised as the H.Q. of each district. Officers and N.C.O.'s being sent from H.Q. as part of their regular duty; Volunteers being given the preference; a very pleasant two or three years being enjoyed between embarkations, whilst the recruiting fee added a small addition to the very inadequate pay of those days - a system that lasted until 1895.

The Marine Acts of 1847, modified by that of 1853, made a vast change in the Marine Service. Enlistment was no longer for life, but was limited to 12 years, with an option of re-engaging for at first 12 years, later altered to 9 years - Acts which still govern the Corps and leave us the only long service unit in the Army.

Bounties were abolished in 1870 (O. in C.. 17 Aug.. 1870). but Levy Money of about £1 was paid to cover expenses; this was fixed again on 31 Dec. 1883 (O. in C.), but on 8th Jan. 1906 it was reduced to 10s.

Gradually the Officer in charge of the London Recruiting Office became recognised as the Head of the Marine Recruiting Service, and all recruits passed through London before being sent to the Divisions or Depot. In 1899 his title was changed to Inspector of Marine Recruiting, and by 0. in C. 19th May, 1899, he was given an assistant, one of the new recruiting Staff Officers, Class II, being appointed.

But the greatest change was made in 1895, when the H.Q. recruiting parties were replaced by Retired Officers, who were appointed 22nd June, 1895, to take charge of each district. Ten were appointed: three First Class at a salary of £350 a year and seven Second Class at a salary of £200 a year; on 28th March, 1903, the classification was abolished and all received a salary of £200 a year, and three sums of £200 were awarded as premiums to those whose districts had shown the best results of the year.

On 4th Nov., 1901, the serving Recruiting Sergeants were replaced by Pensioner Recruiters, who received their pensions, 2s. a day, and free uniforms.

In 1903-4 a great reform was made by the introduction of the regulation that recruits had to produce certificates of character from previous employers, etc. This did away with a class of men who were a perfect curse to the Army and Navy; to wit, those men who enlisted, and after having made themselves a nuisance to all who had to deal with them, would then either desert, or else after trial by court-martial, would be discharged with ignominy. They would soon after be found in another regiment, or the Navy, repeating the process.

In 1914 a Quartermaster was added to the staff of the I. of Marine Recruiting, owing to the large increase of work.

During the War of 1914-18 the R.M. Recruiting Service was faced with many problems. The Long Service enlistments for 12 years were continued, but recruits were also entered for three years or the duration of the war; whilst the R.M. Acts of 1916 enabled the provisions of the old Acts, dealing with men being retained for two years beyond the 12, or 21 years in times of emergency, to be extended to include the duration of the War. With the institution of the National Service Acts, the R.M. were allowed their choice of Volunteers, but the long service enlistments were not interfered with in any way. The Recruiting Staff had to secure men for many different purposes: men at R.E. rates of pay and necessary training for the Divisional Engineers and Royal Marine Engineers; at A.S.C. rates of pay and knowledge of horses for the Divisional Train; for the Labour Corps; as R.A.M.C. men for the Medical Unit of the R.N. Division. But perhaps the most extraordinary was the enlistment of about 100 London Bus Drivers, who, in September 1914 were taken to the Recruiting Office, and after being attested, drove their buses down to the barracks at

Portsmouth and Chatham, and after calling in at Quartermaster's Stores and being rigged out with a certain amount of kit, continued their drive to the docks at Dover and Southampton, where they embarked for Dunkirk, and soon after found themselves doing invaluable work at Antwerp, and later with the Army in the first Battle of Ypres and elsewhere.

In 1917 the Headquarters of the Recruiting was reorganised and the Inspector of Marine Recruiting became the Director of Recruiting, with an Assistant Director and a suitable staff.

Post War recruiting has been an easy matter, with the vastly reduced numbers and increased pay, so that it may safely be said that now the Corps can pick and choose from the best in the country.

ANTWERP, 1914.
Copy of a Letter from Colonel F. W. Luard, to His Brother,
Rev. E. P. Luard, about 20th October, 1914.

When I left Lille about October 3rd, the big Anglo-French flanking movement was just south of that place, and both belligerents were piling up troops on either side to outflank the other, so that the extremity of the flanking movement was gradually extending north.

The 7th and 8th Divisions, we supposed, were destined to join the Belgian Field Army and prolong the line northwards, between its northern extremity and Antwerp. Our task was to delay the fall of Antwerp while the gap was being filled, and this we accomplished.

I left Lille on the morning of Saturday, October 3rd, and reached Antwerp at 3 a.m. on Sunday, 4th. At 7 a.m. the same morning we marched to the outer defences about five miles outside the city. I met Churchill on the road and had some conversation with him. Three battalions of my Brigade at once relieved hard-pressed Belgian troops in the trenches, leaving my battalion, which had just had a 13 hour night journey in the train, in reserve at General Paris's headquarters.

During the afternoon half my battalion was also sent into the trenches. All that afternoon and evening my other half battalion and headquarters was very badly shelled, and again in the early morning, when I lost some men.

On Monday the 5th some Germans got across the River Nethe on the right and drove in the Belgian troops there, and my battalion was sent to do a counterattack. We picked up the half-battalion in the trenches and made our counter attack when the Germans retired, and the Belgians reoccupied their trenches. I left two companies in the trenches there that night, and the other two dug themselves in at Headquarters and made a dug-out for the General during the night.

On Tuesday the 6th the Germans gave the trenches a terrific dusting with artillery and we lost a lot of men. Meanwhile the Belgian Field Army (except certain units co-operating with us) were getting out of the town.

The Germans again got over the river with machine-guns, and towards late afternoon the trenches became untenable, and we got orders to move to an intermediate position in rear, which the Belgian engineers had been digging for us. This we occupied about dusk. The German patrols were soon all round us marking down our position. We could hear them in the woods calling to each other with cleverly imitated night-birds calls, invariably answered faintly by another in the distance. (Later on I found on a German prisoner an "ocarina"- a sort of wind instrument with which they make their cries.

About two hours before dawn that night we were suddenly ordered to evacuate this new position and retire to the inner defences of the city. At dawn the German artillery made mincemeat of the trenches we had just vacated.

On Wednesday 7th and Thursday 8th the Germans bombarded the city rather than the defences, with a view (we supposed) of inducing the civil authorities to bring pressure on the military to save useless loss of life and property by surrendering.

The Naval Brigades of the Division had now arrived and were in the trenches of the inner defences, but did not suffer any considerable losses, as the enemy were firing over them into the city. My Brigade was in reserve, and during these two days we were dodging shell behind buildings and in ditches during the bombardment. We could not dig ourselves in as our tools had been sent to other battalions the day before and had not been returned.

Meanwhile the Belgian Field Army continued its evacuation of the city to join the big Belgian concentration to the S.W. of the Scheldt.

At 7 p.m. Thursday 8th my battalion was ordered to reinforce Naval Brigade, as adjoining Belgian troops were hard pressed. At the same moment the orders for the Final Retirement, which had been carefully prepared in advance, should have been received. They did not, however, reach me, and I only got verbal orders to relieve the Naval Brigade in the trenches, carry out some firing to simulate occupation, and immediately follow Naval Brigade in retreat as their rear-guard. When I got to the trenches the commander of one of the Naval battalions had just been killed, and the retirement was very much delayed because he could not be found. It was pitch dark, which added to the difficulties. In the end the Brigade did not get off till two hours after it should have started. It lost its way in the long march through the town, and arrived at a part of the river where there were neither boats nor a bridge. I eventually took charge of it, found a bridge higher up, had it cleared of a dense stream of refugees, and got it over just before dawn. It should have been across about 10 p.m. - shell-fire going on all the time, but we lost no men from it.

Meanwhile the rest of the force had long ago passed over, and the last bridge was blown up as soon as we were over it.

I found no Staff or orders on the far side of the bridge, and so I marched west on the main road, expecting at each village to come up with Headquarters, or to get instructions. After 12 miles march beyond the river (i.e., 24 miles since the start) I halted at St. Nicholas, an important village, to bivouac and requisition food. It was now 5 p.m. and my men had had no rest or food for 24 hours. While arranging requisitions I got news that the Germans were in action in the next village westward, about five miles away, and we could hear the firing. We therefore started off again, northwards, without waiting for food. There was a railway some 8 miles to the north, where there was a service of refugee trains to Ostend.

On we went, while night again came on. When we had done 32 miles we got to a small station. We had sent ahead to telephone for a train. We entrained in the dark in a long line of open trucks, already filled with refugees, women and children and Belgian soldiers. Somehow or other we all got on board, 400 Naval Brigade, 400 of my men on top of the others, all dead beat, and thought that all our troubles were over. After the train had started about 20 minutes it was fired on from both sides of the line. We ran on a mile or so and stopped dead about 9 p.m. The Germans had shifted the points into a blind siding, jammed them so as to be irreversible, and removed a rail so that the leading trucks were derailed. Firing began again from the front of the train on all sides. We got some men together from the nearest trucks and some German troops came up in close order. We let fly at a few yards range killing half a dozen, wounding as many others and taking several prisoners, while the rest bolted. Then firing began again from all sides. By this time we had got enough men out of the train to reply vigorously. After about a quarter of an hour the enemy's fire died down.

The train, however, was unmoveable, and we concluded that they had found us more than they thought and had drawn off for reinforcements. Some of the women and children and a few men had been wounded and a few women killed. We ran down the train and called to the men to come out, collected as many as we could in the total darkness, and decided to resume the march on foot with as many as could undertake it.

Many however, I fear, were too much exhausted to try. About a dozen only Naval Brigade men decided to come on with us, the remainder stayed behind and were taken prisoners. Many of the men at the back of the train were I think, still fast asleep, utterly done up. Some had taken their boots off their swollen and bleeding feet and could not get them on again.

With the rest we started forth once more on foot down the railway track-eight miles more (making 40 in all) brought us to a little town called Selsaate, where we waited till dawn and then got a train to Bruges. A few hours later the Germans were in Selsaate.

At Bruges we got a meal, the first for 48 hours, during which we had marched 40 miles day and night without food, rest or water.

We found the rest of the Brigade at Ostend. They had long given us up for lost. The General was very much relieved to see me.

I was only able to bring away about half my Battalion; the rest are prisoners in Germany.

This is not a very glorious recital, but we did the best we could under very difficult circumstances.

I found afterwards that most careful and precise orders for the retreat should have reached us before we left, but had somehow miscarried.

We were very much exhausted for a few days, but picked up afterwards.

V.C. WON BY MAJOR (TEMPORARY BRIGADIER-GENERAL) F. W. LUMSDEN, D.S.O., R.M.A.

(Reproduced by permission)
ADMIRALTY,
35 SPRING GARDENS,
S.W.1.
11th June, 1917.

Circular.
THE COMMANDANTS, ROYAL MARINES.

The following extract from the supplement to The London Gazette, Dated 8th June, 1917, is notified for information: -

His Majesty the KING has been graciously pleased to approve of the award of the VICTORIA CROSS to the undermentioned Officer: -

Major (now Temp. Brig.- Gen.) Frederick William Lumsden, D.S.O., R.M.A.

For most conspicuous bravery, determination and devotion to duty.

Six enemy field guns having been captured, it was necessary to leave them in dug-in positions, 300 yards in advance of the position held by our troops. The enemy kept the guns under heavy fire.

Major Lumsden undertook the duty of bringing the guns into our lines.

In order to effect this, he personally led four artillery teams and a party of infantry through the hostile barrage. As one of these teams sustained casualties, he left the remaining teams in a covered position, and, through very heavy rifle, machine gun and shrapnel fire, led the infantry to the guns.

By force of example and inspiring energy he succeeded in sending back two teams with guns, going through the barrage with the teams of the third gun. He then returned to the guns to await further teams, and these he succeeded in attaching to two of the three remaining guns, despite rifle fire, which had become intense at shore range, and removed the guns to safety.

By this time the enemy in considerable strength, had driven through the infantry covering points, and blown up the breach of the remaining gun.

Major Lumsden then returned, drove off the enemy, attached the gun to a team and got it away.
DAVID MERCER,
Adjutant General, R.M.

Telegram.

From Commanding 32nd Division, France.
To Headquarters, R.M. Artillery, Portsmouth

All ranks of the 32nd Division desire to congratulate you on the V.C. gained by Brigadier General Lumsden.
They are proud of having in the Division so gallant a representative of the R.M.A.

Telegram.

From Commanding, R.M.A.
To Headquarters, 32nd Division, B.E.F.

All ranks Royal Marine Artillery much pleased with your message about Brigadier-General Lumsden and wish your Division every good fortune and more fine work ahead.

ROYAL MARINES DRUMMERS' LOOPING LACE
By Colonel C. Field, R.M.

Probably the white lace with the blue "Stars" upon it, which was a distinguishing part of the Drummers' uniform, has gone the way of the time-honoured red tunic, when the Corps given a blue full-dress, corresponding to neither Artillery or Infantry traditions. But being blue, it was very likely considered that, since of late years the Artillery had abandoned "looping lace," a good excuse was presented for doing away with it.

At one time, not so very long ago, there was a good deal of discussion among officers interested in the past history of the Corps, as to the origin of the peculiar blue pattern upon our drummers' lace. I have referred to it above as "Stars," but this is merely for want of a better name for upon examination it will be seen that the little blue decorations are of an absolutely nondescript design thus differing from the similar laces worn in the Army, the Guards having a blue "Fleur-de-lis" and the Line a red "Crown."

At the time our own lace was under discussion, there was a suggestion that the blue crab-like objects were intended to represent "Suns," and that these "Suns" had some connection with "The Glorious Sun of York," thereby preserving relation of the present Corps to its earliest predecessor the "Duke of York and Albany's Maritime Regiment."

It is to be feared, however, that the "wish was father to the thought." Setting aside the very far-fetched theory that the pattern represented "Suns "- and "Blue Suns" at that - a very curious colour in which to depict the "orb of day" - there are at least two facts go to upset this theory.

In the first place it is extremely doubtful if either the "Rising Sun" or "The Sun in Splendour" was a badge of James Duke of York. The former was a badge of the Black Prince and the latter of Richard II: and it was the latter which was in 1861 selected as the badge of the 10th Company of the Grenadier Guards. The "Sunrays," so-called, borne on the Major's and Company Colours of the Maritime Regiment - and in a similar way on the Colours of various other Regiments - were -probably not a badge in this respect at all. It is observable that nothing of the kind appears on the Colonel's and Lieut.-Colonel's Colours. Venn in "Military and Maritime Discipline" (1672) says: "As for the dignity of the Ensign in England (not meddling with the Standard Royal), to a regimental dignity; Colonel's Colours, in the first place, is of a pure and clean colour without any mixture; the Lieut.-Colonel's only with St. George's Arms in the upper corner next the staff; the Major's the same, but in the lower and outmost corner, with a little stream blazont, and every Captain with St. George's Arms alone, but with so many spots or devices as pertain to the dignity of their several places."

It will be observed that this writer refers to an earlier pattern of Colour, with the St. George's cross in one corner instead of over the whole flag, and in many regiments the distinction between companies was indicated by the "device" of "little streamers," their number varying according to the company. I cannot help thinking that the "Sun-rays" have some connection with these streamers. Incidentally, it may be remarked that there are twelve on the Major's (and Company's) Colour, corresponding with the number of companies in the regiment, and possibly, at a guess, there may have been one ray less in each company down to the 12th, which may have had only three. The Buffs, by the way, had a distinct and unmistakeable "Sun in Splendour" upon the centre of the St. George's Cross in their Major's and Company's Colours, which seems much more likely to have been a regular Regimental Badge than the "Sun-rays" under discussion.

Another fact which militates against the "Glorious Sun of York theory is that both the 84th and 97th Regiments formerly wore exactly the same pattern lace as ours, but not in the same colours. They have no connection with the Duke of York.

In the 18th and in the last years of the 17th centuries practically each regiment had its own particular lace; all N.C.O. s and men wore it, but the Grenadier company and the Drummers wore more of it. This lace was not, latterly at any rate, of the same thickness and texture of the modern "looping lace." There is a little book in the Library of Windsor Castle in which are pasted specimens of the Army Regimental Laces of 1751. These laces are wider and more like worsted tape, and are, with very few exceptions, all *striped patterns*.

As regards Marine Regimental lace the first we hear of it is the "Gold-coloured" lace with which the hats of the Admiral's Regiment were bound - obviously not suitable for decorating its yellow coats. Then we come to the Marine Regiments of Queen Anne's day. We do not know the lace of all of them, but it is known that "Holt's Marines" wore one of a mixture of "red, black and white," and "Fox's" a plain white lace, although one company of it - perhaps the Grenadier company - was gorgeous in silver lace.

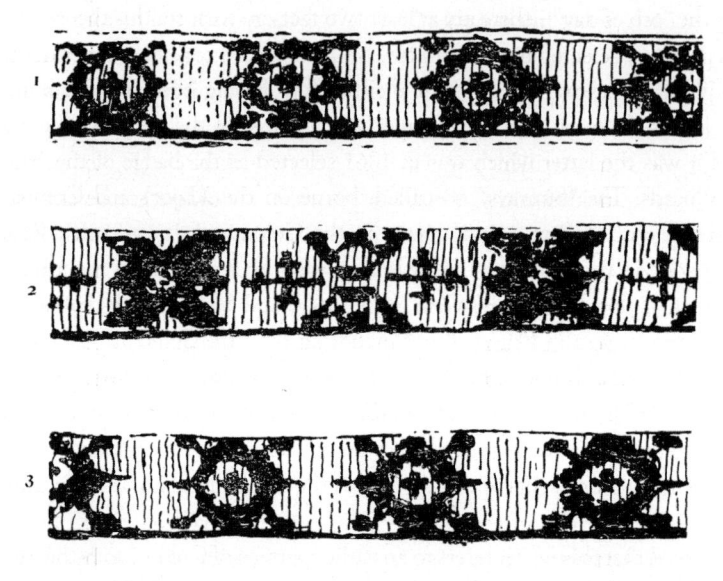

1. OLD R.M.L.1. PATTERN.   2. OLD R.M.A. PATTERN.   3. LATEST PATTERN.

Only three of the ten Marine Regiments of 1739-1748 seem to have had any lace at all. These were the 4th (with an elaborate red, white, blue and yellow lace, and the 5th and 9th with plain white lace. When in 1747, just before their abolition, it was decided to do away with the different facings of these Regiments in favour of a universal facing of a "bright full yellow," the Drummers were ordered to wear a yellow coat, "with a proper lace thereon." This is vague. It may mean a suitable lace, or more probably laced in the way proper for drummers, with the Regimental lace - whatever that may have been.

The next allusion to Marine Lace I found in a little work called "Milian's Succession of Colonels." It was a sort of Army List, published from time to time and one or two years of it used to be in the small collection of books in the Officers' Mess at the Depot, Deal, but they seem now to have disappeared. According to this, after the establishment of the present Corps in 1755, it was "Blue with a Red Worm," i.e., line. How long this lace lasted does not appear, but reference is made to a Tri-coloured lace about the beginning of the 19th century, and in the Windsor Castle Library is a sheet of coloured prints shewing the colours of the coats, facings and lace of all the Regiments of the British Army, including the Royal Marines. It was published in 1806, and the Marine lace is shewn as - A narrow white stripe, a wider blue one, another narrow white one, and a red stripe the same width as the blue. This is evidently the "Tri-coloured lace."

When this lace was abolished cannot be said, but when it went it was probably not replaced so far as the rank and file were concerned, and it was then, most likely, that the present Drummers' Looping Lace was selected, since in a series of coloured lithographs by E. Hull, published 1829-30, the only laced uniforms are those of the Drummers, who are evidently wearing the same lace that is now, or was till recently, uniform.

The pattern chosen is not likely to have any connection with the history or traditions of the Corps, but was probably selected by a committee of taste, which considered it either the prettiest or the most suitable - or possibly the cheapest - of the patterns submitted by the lace-makers.

The very pretty Marine Artillery looping lace was very likely chosen about the same time, a time which may have coincided with the date on which it was ordered to be clothed as the Royal Artillery (26 Oct., 1816). Its Drummers, however, wore red instead of blue. The lace, as shewn in the accompanying sketch, was of a softer and less orange shade of yellow than that of the modern braiding, and the blue rather lighter than that of the Infantry lace. The latter, by the way, underwent a slight and almost unnoticeable change during its existence, the earlier pattern having a thin edge or selvage, making the raised portion a shade narrower than the latter type. The blue, too, is of a rather darker shade.

Although it seems evident that there is nothing of an heraldic or historical interest in these laces, it is to be hoped that one of them, preferably the old R.M.A. one will be retained for the Marine Drummers of the future. The Corps, though wearing blue, is not to be officially recognised as Artillery, and more than half of it is composed of Infantry, so that this decoration for the Drummers tunic would be most appropriate - Artillery lace used in the Infantry style.

HISTORY OF THE GLOBE AND LAUREL.

After due consideration and much correspondence with other Divisions the *Globe and Laurel* was started at the Chatham Division in May, 1892.

The infant paper commenced its life as a humble little journal, "for private circulation only," with an issue of 500 copies, Major G. T. Onslow and Captain C. G. Brittan being the Editors, each putting down £1 for immediate expenses.

The journal was to be not only a temporary chronicle of passing events, but a permanent record of the doings of the Corps, and there can be no doubt that it has attained its object.

In the first number the following paragraph appeared: "It is almost needless to state that no letters or articles of a controversial or complaining nature will find a place in the journal." This rule has been carefully kept throughout.

The first number was an immediate success, and a second edition had to be printed, bringing the number of copies up to 1,200.

There is no indication in the early days of the journal as to who were the Editors, but so far as can be ascertained the heat and burden of the day was borne by the two officers mentioned above, and later by Major T. J. P. Evans and Lieutenant G. E. Matthews.

The first number, consisting of only four pages, increased while in the press to six, was printed by the Divisional printing office. It was soon found it was impossible to continue this arrangement, and after much deliberation, counting the cost, etc., the work was entrusted to Messrs. Ive & Lowe, of Chatham, who performed it in a highly satisfactory manner, until the headquarters of the paper was transferred to Portsmouth. The September, 1892 number was, however, for some reason unknown, printed at the Divisional printing office.

The first number of the journal was published at 1d. per copy, 1½d. post free, but owing to increase in size, and having to go to a firm of printers instead of utilising the Divisional printing office, the price was increased to 2d. and 2½ d. post free for a few months, returning to the original price on the introduction of advertisements in October 1892. The officers at this time paid 6d. for their copies.

In August of that year it appeared with a cover bearing the Corps crest. At this time the general circulation of information was poor, and accordingly the paper filled a want by containing much Service information of interest, as well as news of sports at the various Divisions, but news from the sea was scarce.

Major W. T. Adair was a regular contributor in these early days, with his "Notes by the Way" and some interesting articles dealing with Corps history. During this period also appeared short histories of the Royal Marine Artillery, by Captain R. H. Alexander, the 1st or Chatham Division, by Lt.-Col. J. A. Sweny, and the 3rd or Plymouth Division, by Lt.-Col. W. G. Armstrong.

In 1893 the first Corps Almanac was published, compiled by Lt.-Col. W. G. Armstrong, and revised by him in 1894. It was again revised and brought up to date by General Sir H. E. Blumberg in 1903 and also in 1922.

In August, 1895, at the request of many subscribers abroad the list of "Embarked" and "Disembarked" became a feature of the paper. This list was for some time discontinued during the war, but was reintroduced in November, 1920, and has remained ever since, except for a few months in 1923.

In November 1895, after a sojourn of more than 3½ years at Chatham, the G. & L. was transferred to Portsmouth. The removal was occasioned by the Chatham Editors leaving the Division, and no volunteers being forthcoming to take up the office. Several officers at Portsmouth volunteered their services to watch over and control the second stage of the paper, chief of whom was Lt.-Col. L. Edye. Up to this date the publishers arranged for and took the proceeds of the few advertisements in the paper, but then Messrs. Charpentier became the printers, and the Editors retained in their own hands the whole of the advertisements. It was hoped by this means that the paper would be wholly self-supporting, without the necessity for appeals to the generosity of messes, canteens and individuals for special donations.

In December, 1895, correspondents (then called assistant editors) were obtained at Eastney, Chatham, Plymouth and the Depot, and also one on the China station. Colonel W. J. Gaitskell was Eastney (Assistant) Editor from October 1895 to May 1906, and Captain D. Mercer was the first correspondent for "Per Mare," and sent in useful contributions for some years. In this month's issue of the G. & L. Captain W. P. Drury commenced a series of short stories. These stories were at once a huge success, and in May, 1896, they were published by the G. & L. in book form, under the title of "The Petrified eye and other Stories." The copyright was kindly given to the G. & L. by Capt. W. P. Drury for the benefit of the paper. This publication went through several editions, greatly to the benefit of the G. & L. funds. The Corps paper is much to be congratulated on the fact that they were permitted to be the first to publish a work of fiction by Colonel Drury, and were fortunate enough to receive many contributions from him through the succeeding years.

By December, 1896, the number of assistant editors at sea had greatly increased, there being one in China, Malta, Pacific station and Cape of Good Hope station. In spite of this, news from the sea was very meagre compared to that from the shore. During this period of the paper a great deal of interesting matter concerning the past history of the Corps appeared and was continued for many years. The contributions were mostly from Colonel L. Edye and Capt. W. F. Portlock Scott Dadson, both of whom had the most wonderful knowledge on the subject.

Captain Portlock Dadson was one of the oldest surviving officers of the Corps, being a Crimean veteran, and he had for years been indefatigable in collecting every scrap of information about the Corps that he possibly could.

Colonel L. Edye was the author of "The History of the Royal Marine Forces" (1664-1701) published in 1893. The rough MSS. of Vol. II. (1702-1705), which was never published, is now in the possession of the Admiralty Library - the fair copy being at the bottom of the Atlantic, whither it was sent by a German submarine.

During this time, thanks to donations, etc., the Corps paper was fairly flourishing, but in April 1899 it was decided to endeavour to increase the number of advertisements, and they were put in the hands of a London agent, Mr. C. Vernon, 118 Newgate Street.

By May 1899 the number of pages had increased to 16, of heavier paper. This was made possible partly by the increase in advertisements, but chiefly due to the liberality of private donors and voluntary extra subscriptions; 4,000 copies were being sold. Illustrations were paid for by an annual grant of £5 from each Division and Depot canteen, and any money over went to the Reserve fund. In January a new design of cover made its appearance.

About January 1901 Capt. H. E. Blumberg, Adjutant at Forton, took over the duties of Editor, and continued till June 1904. Under his editorship the circulation increased to 5,000 and the balance credit to nearly £300. On giving up the editorship he stated that he was under a debt of gratitude to Capt. W. F. Portlock Scott Dadson, who seldom let a month go by without supplying copious notes. He was also indebted to Major D. A. Hailes for his serial under the heading "Naval General Service Medal," and to Lt.-Col. Parkins Hearle for some very interesting articles dealing with the Royal Marines in connection with the foundation of our Australian colonies.

During this period, as there was no Treasurer or Assistant Editor, the work of producing and sending out the paper was very onerous for the Editor to manage single-handed, his only assistant being a corporal, who was changed fairly frequently.

The *Globe and Laurel* was now transferred to Lt.-Col. G. T. Onslow, at 7 Whitehall Place, London. During this period the practice of addressing all bundles for ships to the O.C. detachment was started, and has continued ever since. This was found necessary owing to the fact that the individual acting as correspondent had occasionally left the ship when the parcel arrived, and it in consequence went astray.

In May 1905 the journal was transferred to Plymouth, but the work of the Treasurer was carried out in London till May 1910, when it was done by Major D. A. Hailes at the recruiting office in Manchester. In April 1913, however, it was decided that the work of Editor and Treasurer ought to be carried out at the same place, in order to save correspondence and the continual forwarding on of letters, etc. From May 1905 till March 1906 Captain F. J. W. Harvey was Editor, then Major E. M. C. Ommanney and Captain R. D. Ormsby carried on the work of Editors of the journal with good results, till they went to sea in March 1909, when Captain H. La T. Darley took over.

During the first year at Plymouth, though the circulation of the journal was 3,000, it had not been paying its way. The annual subscription of £5 from the Divisions and Depot had been allowed to drop, and the officers had ceased to pay 6d. for their copies, and few donations had been received. By March 1911, when the paper was transferred to Chatham, the circulation remained much the same but owing to substantial assistance from Divisional canteens and donations the paper was again able to pay its way, in spite of the fact that the number of advertisements had considerably decreased. The balance now stood at £155. Photographs were not published at this time unless the cost of the block was paid for by the sender.

In April 1913 the paper was transferred to Eastney. Since November 1895 Messrs Charpentier & Co., Portsmouth, had been the printers, wherever the editorial staff was, but in May 1914, owing to a decreasing circulation and the necessity for economy, the tender of Messrs. Gale & Polden was accepted. It was with regret that the Editors changed their printers, Messrs. Charpentier, as for

18 years they had helped in every way possible to make the paper a success. Later on there was a balance of £234 in the Fund and the size of the journal was increased to 20 pages.

Then came the War, and great difficulties in production. The paper was, of course, full of reports from the various theatres of war. There was no lack of material for insertion in the paper but the difficulty was to decide what to put in as practically all had appeared in the daily papers, and further, the censorship prevented any reference to actual names of ships, battalions or batteries. The editorial staff was continually changing, and from November 1914 they had to arrange for their own advertisements; but in spite of these difficulties the paper carried on and paid its way.

During this period Lt.-Col. Humphery Oldfield was the Editor, and deserves great credit for the way he kept the paper going, in addition to performing the duties of Instructor of Musketry and Barrack Master.

In April 1917, when the journal was transferred to Plymouth, the balance in the fund. was £237. Major W. P. Drury then became the Editor, with Major H. W. Channer as his assistant, and Messrs, Swiss & Co, Fore Street, Devonport, took over the printing. The cover was re-designed shortly afterwards. In June the price was raised to 3d. a Copy, and the number of copies sold was 4,000.

Under this regime the paper flourished. It was full of interesting matter and the Editors' personal contributions were of a very high character. Photographs and cartoons appeared, sketches by Captain J. S. Hicks became a regular feature and the number of correspondents increased. Unfortunately Major Drury had to give up in May 1918, owing to ill-health. The circulation was now over 6,000 copies, advertisements had been charged for at a higher rate and additional pages of these inserted, but it was found that the Journal was only just paying its way.

Then came two severe blows; first, the printers much to their regret were unable to continue their contract, except at greatly increased rates, owing to the extraordinary cost of material, labour, etc.; second, the new postal rates. To meet this emergency the light blue ink cover was abandoned, a lighter weight paper used, and the size of the paper reduced to 16 pages. Under these trying conditions Major J. Macnair Smith assumed the Editorship and Major H. W. Charmer still continued to assist.

During this period the paper gradually returned to its pre-war style, reporting results of sport R.M.R.A. and Royal Tournament, and other matters of that nature, though accounts of Marines finishing up odd jobs in the various corners of the globe still made their appearance.

By January 1920, due to demobilisation and reductions, the number of subscribers was greatly reduced and by October it was found necessary to charge 3½ d. per copy for copies ordered in bulk in order to defray postage.

In March 1921 Lt.-Colonel T. B. Luard took over the Editorship, Lt.-Col. H. W. Channer remaining on as assistant editor. The number of subscribers still continued to fall off, and by February 1922 the number was only 2.000.

About this time we joined an advertising society called "The Combined Regimental Publications." which specialised in getting advertisements for all service Journals, which they supplied already printed, ready to bind up.

Although this was of value, the sums for advertisements were not received till from three to six months after insertion, and in consequence it was not possible to meet bills as they came in.

In October 1922 the paper sustained a great loss in Lt.-Colonel Channer having to give up owing to ill-health, after 5½ years as Assistant Editor. His keenness in all matters concerning the Corps made his services of the greatest value and he was personally responsible for many of the Journals most popular columns.

The following month the paper was transferred to Chatham and Mckays Ltd. became the printers. The Editor in his final notes said he was particularly indebted to General Sir Herbert E. Blumberg for revising the Corps Almanac and contributing articles, and also for his help and advice on many occasions. He also thanked Colonel C. Field for his historical studies of great and permanent interest to the Corps.

On taking over the work of Editor at Chatham Lt.-Colonel C. Mayhew at once began to tackle the financial side, there being a debit of £4. He managed to arrange that each Division and Depot should subscribe annually at the rate of £25 a year. By this means he got a balance of approximately £9 by June the following year. The journal then assumed a new cover, designed by Captain J. S. Hicks. In October 1923 Lt.-Col. C. Mayhew was transferred to Deal, and Colonel R. V. T. Ford took over the duties with a balance of £91, and continued to improve the financial side of the paper.

Seven months later Lt.-Col. H. A. H. Jones became Editor for four months. During his regime the advertisements were printed on separate pages, interspersed with reading matter in the journal.

In September 1924, when Major and Bt. Lt.-Col. G. P. Orde took over the duties, the circulation was just over 2,000 and the balance approximately £150. With the help of the Adjutant-General, who appealed to the various F.R.M.Os. of Fleets, Fleet, Ship and Divisional correspondents volunteered their services. Special headings for "Per Mare," "Per Terram" and "Sports" sections of the paper were introduced, and news from the fleet began to increase. A new dark blue cover was introduced for the journal, the design of which was changed two months later for one by "Col." The number of pages was increased to 24, and at the request of subscribers the names of the first six on the promotion roster of N.C.Os. and candidates were published in the October issue and subsequent numbers of the journal. In February 1925, when Lt.-Col. Arbuthnot became Editor, the number of pages was again reduced to 20, owing to the Treasurer pointing out that the funds would not allow of the larger numbers.

In April 1925 the Royal Marine Officers' Central Fund was started, the annual subscription to which included 5/- for *The Globe and Laurel*. This was of great assistance in retaining a number of willing, but forgetful, subscribers.

In October 1925 the journal was transferred to Eastney; Messrs. W. H. Barrell. became the printers and Major A. L. Forster became Editor until May 1926, when he turned over the duties to Major W. L. Huntingford, with a balance of about £40.

In 1926 special pages of the "Records of the Royal Marines" were introduced. This new departure was suggested by Colonel C. Field, because since the publication of his "Britain's Sea Soldiers" a considerable amount of additional information as to the past operations of the Corps had become available, both from the mass of notes, extracts from official documents, and other material which had been collected by the late Colonel L. Edye, and from other sources. In order, therefore, that such historical information should be kept together, for the benefit of present and future members of the Corps, he put forward the above proposal, and has up to date practically edited and supplied the greater part of the contents of the "Record Pages."

In January 1927 the size of the paper was increased to 24 pages and the dark blue cover replaced by the present design, but varying in colour each month. In January 1928 the size was increased to 28 pages exclusive of advertisements.

In April 1927 the Society "Combined Regimental Publications" was absorbed by the present Association of Service Newspapers, thus safe-guarding the interests of Service journals and further the value of advertising space was raised to more than double. The result of these changes was to make the journal self-supporting.

In May 1928 Lt.-Col. B. C. Gardiner became Editor; the circulation was then 2,600 and the balance approximately £150. At this time the contributions for "Per Mare" section had increased sufficiently to fill nearly half the journal. and the "Per Terram" section had also considerably increased.

In January 1929 the colour of the cover was stabilised and the size of the paper increased to 32 pages of reading matter. Cartoons were introduced, and later complete seniority lists of N.C.Os. and first 200 candidates, giving pension dates of sergeants and above were published. At the same time a new contract was made with the printers, greatly reducing the cost of publication.

On January 1st, 1930, the circulation was 3,300, a pleasing feature being the large increase in the number of past members of the Corps who take in the paper, so that we can now truly say our circulation is world-wide. Our balance is just over £400.

FIELD GUN COMPETITIONS HELD AT PORTSMOUTH.

Year	Sub-Lieutenants' Cup.	Brickwood Trophy.
1900	R.N. College.	
1901	Royal Marine Artillery.	
1902	H.M.S. *Excellent*.	
1903	Royal Marine Artillery.	
1904	Ditto	
1905	Ditto	
1906	Ditto	
1907	Ditto	R.M.L.I. Portsmouth Div.
1908	Ditto	R.N. Barracks
1909	Ditto	H.M.S. *Excellent*
1910	H.M.S. Excellent	
1911	R.M.L.I.	
1912	Royal Marine Artillery	
1913	Ditto	
1923	Ditto	Royal Marine Artillery.
1924	Royal Marines	Royal Marines
	(Record run, 1 min. 24 2-5 secs)	
1925	Sub-Lieutenants, H.M.S. *Excellent*.	Sub-Lieutenants, H.M.S. Excellent
	(Record run 1 min. 24 s.)	
1926	Royal Marines.	Royal Marines.
1927	Royal Marines.	Royal Marines.
1928	Royal Marines.	Royal Marines.
1929	H.M.S. *Excellent*. (Seamen)	H.M.S. *Excellent*. (Seamen)
		(Record, 1 min. 18 1-5 secs)

A RECORD OF ROYAL MARINE SUCCESSES AT THE TOURNAMENT.
1894-1929.

Year	Event	1st	Runners up
1894	Physical Drill Display	R.M.A.	
1895	Physical Drill Display	R.M.A.	
1896	Physical Drill Display	R.M.A.	R.M.L.I. Deal (3rd)
	Bayonet Exercise	R.M.A.	R.M.L.I. Deal
1897	Physical Drill Display	R.M.A.	R.M.L.I. Deal
	Bayonet Exercise	R.M.A.	R.M.L.I. Deal

Year	Event		
1898	Physical Drill Display	R.M.A.	
	Bayonet Exercise	R.M.A.	
	Tug-of-war (Catch Wt.)	R.M.A.	
1899	Physical Drill Display	R.M.A.	R.M.L.I. Deal
	Bayonet Exercise	R.M.A.	
	Tug-of-war (Catch Wt.)	R.M.A.	
1900	Physical Drill Display	R.M.L.I. (Deal)	R.M.A.
	Bayonet Exercise	R.M.L.I. (Deal)	R.M.A.
	Tug-of-war (110 Stone)	R.M.A.	
	Tug-of-war (Catch Wt.)	R.M.A.	
1901	Tug-of-war (110 Stone)	R.M.A.	
	Tug-of-war (Catch Wt.)	R.M.A.	
	Bayonet Combats	R.M.A.	R.M.L.I. Deal
1902	Bayonet Combats	R.M.A.	R.M.L.I. Chat.
	Tug-of-war (110 Stone)	R.M.A.	
	Tug-of-war (Catch Wt.)	R.M.A.	
1903	Bayonet Combats	R.M.A.	R.M.L.I. Chat.
	Tug-of-war (110 Stone)	R.M.A.	
	Tug-of-war (Catch Wt.)	R.M.A.	
1904	Tug-of-war (110 Stone)	R.M.A.	
	Tug-of-war (Catch Wt.)	R.M.A.	
	Bayonet Combat	R.M.L.I. (Chat.)	R.M.L.I. (Deal)
1905	Tug-of-war (110 Stone)	R.M.A.	
	Tug-of-war (Catch Wt.)	R.M.A.	
1906	Tug-of-war (110 Stone)	R.M.A.	
	Bayonet Combat	R.M.L.I. Chat.	
1907	Bayonet Combats	R.M.A.	
1908	Tug-of-war (110 Stone)	R.M.A.	
1909	Bayonet Teams	R.M.A.	
	Tug-of-war (Catch Wt.)	R.M.A.	
1910	Bayonet Teams	R.M.A.	
1911	Tug-of-war (130 Stone)	R.M.A.	
	Bayonet Team (Offs.)	R.M.A.	
1912	Tug-of-war (110 Stone)	R.M.A.	
	Tug-of-war (130 Stone)	R.M.A.	
	Bayonet Teams	R.M.A.	
1913	Bayonet Teams	R.M.A.	
	Tug-of-war (110 Stone)	R.M.A.	

	Tug-of-war (130 Stone)	R.M.L.I. (Ports.)	
1914	Tug-of-war (110 Stone)	R.M.A.	
	Tug-of-war (130 Stone)	R.M.A.	
	Bayonet Teams	R.M.A.	
1919	Bayonet Teams	R.M.A.	
	Bayonet Assault	R.M.L.I. (Ports.)	
	Tug-of-war (130 Stone)	R.M.A.	
1920	Tug-of-war (110 Stone)	R.M.A.	R.M.L.I., Deal
	Tug-of-war (130 Stone)	R.M.L.I (Ports.)	
	Bayonet Assault	R.M.L.I. (Ports.)	
	Bayonet Teams	R.M.A.	R.M.L.I., Deal
	Inter-Port Field Gun Competition	R.M.	

(R.M.A. team best times)

1921	Bayonet Teams	R.M.A.	
	Tug-of-war (130 Stone)	R.M.A.	
	Bayonet Assault		R.M.L.I. Deal (3rd)
	Inter-Port Field Gun C.	R.M.A.	
1922	Bayonet Teams	R.M.A.	
	Tug-of-war (110 Stone)	R.M.A.	
	Tug-of-war (130 Stone)	R.M.A.	
	Inter-Port Field Gun C.	R.M.A.	
1923	Bayonet Team	R.M.A.	
	Tug-of-war (110 Stone)	R.M.A.	
	Tug-of-war (130 Stone)	R.M.A.	
1924	Tug-of-war (130 Stone)	R.M., Portsmouth	
	Bayonet Team	R.M., Portsmouth	
	Tug-of-war (110 Stone)	R.M., Portsmouth	
1925	Tug-of-war (130 Stone)	R.M., Portsmouth	
	Tug-of-war (110 Stone)	R.M., Portsmouth	
	Bayonet Teams	R.M., Portsmouth	
	Inter-Port Field Gun C.	R.M. (Cup for best run)	
1926	Bayonet Teams	R.M. Portsmouth	
	Tug-of-war (110 Stone)	R.M. Portsmouth	
	Tug-of-war (130 Stone)	R.M. Portsmouth	
1927	Bayonet Teams	R.M. Deal	
	Tug-of-war (110 Stone)	R.M. Portsmouth	
	Tug-of-war (130 Stone)	R.M. Portsmouth	
1928	Bayonet Teams	R.M. Portsmouth	
	Tug-of-war (110 Stone)	R.M. Portsmouth	
	Tug-of-war (130 Stone)	R.M. Portsmouth	
1929	Bayonet Teams	R.M. Portsmouth	
	Tug-of-war (110 Stone)	R.M. Plymouth	

| | Tug-of-war (130 Stone) | R.M. *Renown* |
| | Inter-Port Field Gun C. | R.M. |

INDIVIDUAL SUCCESSES.

Year	Event	Result
1898	Bayonet	Sergt. J. Cole, R.M.L.I. (2nd)
1899	Sword v. Bayonet	Sergt. J. Cole, R.M.L.I. (2nd)
	Sword v. Sabre	Sergt. J. Cole, R.M.L.I. (4th)
	Bayonet	Sergt. J. Cole, R.M.L.I. (1st)
1900	Lance v. Bayonet	Sergt. J. Cole. R.M.L.I. (1st)
	Sword v. Bayonet	Cpl. W. Riddell. R.M.A. (1st)
		Sergt. J. Cole, R.M.L.I. (2nd)
	Foil	Q.M.S. Medlon, R.M.L.I. (2nd)
	Sabre	Q.M.S. Medlon, R.M.L.I. (4th)
	Bayonet	Sergt. J. Cole, R.M.L.I. (1st)
1901	Bayonet	Sergt.W. Riddel, R.M.A. (2nd)
1902	Lance v. Bayonet	Sergt. J. Cole, R.M.L.I. (3rd)
	Sword v. Bayonet	Sergt. J. Cole, R.M.L.I. (1st)
	Sabre	Cpl. C. Watts, R.M.L.I. (4th)
	Bayonet	Sergt.W. Riddell, R.M.A. (2nd)
		Sergt. Cole (3rd)
1903	Bayonet	Sergt.W. Riddell, R.M.A. (2nd)
		Clr.-Sgt. Hickman, R.M.L.I. (3rd)
		Cpl. O'Connor. R.M.L.I. (4th)
	Sabre	Sergt. Marshall, R.M.L.1. (4th)
1904	Bayonet	Pte. G. H. Shaul (1st)
		Sergt.W. Riddell. R.M.A. (2nd)
		Sgt. J. Tyler, R.M.L.I. (3rd)
		Sgt. F. Burton, R.M.L.I. (4th)
	Sabre	Sergt. J. Tyler, R.M.L.I. (4th)
1905	Bayonet	Gnr. H. C. Randall (1st)
		Sgt Dallison, R.M.L.I. (3rd)
		L/Sgt. W. Riddell, R.M.A. (4th)
	Sabre	L/Sgt. W. Riddell, R.M.L.I. (1st)
	Bayonet (Officers)	Capt. G. L. Raikes, R.M.A. (2nd)
1906	Bayonet (Open)	Gnr. W. Oboy, R.M.A. (1st)
		Corpl. Lalley, R.M.A. (3rd)
	Bayonet	Bdr. H. C. Randall (1st)
	(Championship) Gnr.	W. Oboy (2nd)
	Bayonet (Cadets)	2/Lt. R. C. A. Glunicke (2nd)
	Foil (Cadets)	2/Lt. Gibbs (3rd)

	Sabre	Clr.-Sergt. Trott, R.M.L.I. (1st)
1907	Bayonet (Officers)	Lt. W. W. Godfrey, R.M.L.I. (2nd)
	Bayonet (Open)	Pte. Morgan (3rd)
		L/Sgt. W. R. Spencer (4th)
	Bayonet (Cham'p)	Gnr. W. Oboy (2nd)
1908	Bayonet (Officers)	Capt. A. E. Syson, R.M.L.I. (3rd)
	Bayonet	Gnr. A. B. Richardson (1st)
1909	Bayonet (Officers)	Capt. A. E. Syson, R.M.L.I. (2nd)
	Foil	Sergt. W. Riddell, R.M.A. (2nd)
	Bayonet (Open)	Gnr. F. Coleman (1st)
		L/Sergt. W. R. Spencer (4th)
	Bayonet (Cham'p)	Gnr. A. B. Richardson (1st)
		Corpl. H. C. Randall, R.M.A. (2nd)
1910	Bayonet (Officers)	Capt. R. E. Kilvert, R.M.A. (1st)
	Bayonet (Open)	Gnr. G. Milne (2nd)
		Pte. Powell (3rd)
		Q.M.S.I. Russell, R.M.A. (6th)
		Corpl. M. Hawes, R.M.L.I. (8th)
	Bayonet (Cham'p)	Gnr. F. Coleman (1st)
		Corpl. H.C. Randall, R.M.A. (2nd)
		Gnr. A. B. Richardson (3rd)
	Sabre (Officers)	Capt. A. E. Syson, R.M.L.I. (2nd)
	Foil	Sergt. Cutcher, R.M.L.I. (5th)
		Pte. Powell (6th)
1911	Sabre (Officers)	Capt. A. E. Syson, R.M.L.I. (2nd)
	Foil	Sergt. Cutcher, R.M.L.I. (3rd)
	Bayonet (Open)	Gnr. F. H. Durham (1st)
		Sergt. Lalley, R.M.L.I. (4th)
	Bayonet (Cham'p)	Gnr. F. Coleman (1st)
		Corpl. H.C. Randall, R.M.A. (2nd)
		Gnr. F. H. Durham (3rd)
1912	Bayonet (Open)	Gnr. G. Milne (1st)
		Gnr. C. A. P. Tosdevine (2nd)
	Bayonet. (Cham'p)	Gnr. G. Milne (2nd)
		Gnr. F. Coleman (3rd)
	Bayonet (Officers)	Lt. J. M. Tuke, R.M.A. (1st)
1913	Bayonet (Officers)	Lt. A. L. Forster, R.M.A. (3rd)
	Bayonet (Open)	Gnr. A. J. Harland (3rd)
		Sergt. J. Clark, R.M.A. (4th)
	Bayonet (Cham'p)	L/Sgt. H. C. Randall, R.M.A. (1st)
		Gnr. F. Coleman (2nd)
		Gnr. F. H. Durham (3rd)

		Gnr. A. B. Richardson (6th)
	Sabre	Sergt. W. Starling, R.M.L.I. (4th)
1914	Foil	Sergt. Bailey, R.M.L.1. (3rd)
	Sabre	Sergt. C. J. Watts, R.M.L.I. (2nd)
	Bayonet (Open)	Musn. Smith, R.M.B. (1st)
		Q.M.S. F. Russell, R.M.A. (2nd)
	Bayonet (Cham'p)	Bdr. F. H. Durham (1st)
		Gnr. A. B. Richardson (2nd)
		Sergt. Sgt. M. Hawes R.M.L.I. (3rd)
1919	Bayonet (Officers)	Bt. Major H. C. Harrison R.M.A. (2nd)
	Foil	Clr.-Sgt. F. W. Dash, R.M.L.I. (2nd)
		Clr.-Sgt. C. J. Watts, R.M.L.I. (5th)
		Sgt. M. Hawes, R.M.L.I. (6th)
	Foil (Cadets)	2/Lt. A. C. Warren (1st)
	Sabre	Sgt. M. Hawes, R.M.L.I. (2nd)
		Clr.-Sgt. F. W. Dash, R.M.L.I. (3rd)
		Sgt. C. R. Potter, RM.L.I. (4th)
		Clr.-Sgt. H.C. Randall, R.M.A. (5th)
	Sabre Officers	Major W. K. Garnier, R.M.L.I.(5th)
	Bayonet Open	Gnr. J. Penfold (1st)
		Clr.-Sgt. M. Hawes, R.M.L.I. (3rd)
		Corpl. C. G. Duncan, R.M.A. (4th)
		Q.M.S.I. D. A. Board, R.M.L.I. (5th)
	Bayonet (Cham'p)	Lt. F. H. Durham, R.M.A. (1st)
		Sergt. H. C. Randall, R.M.A. (3rd)
		Gnr. A. B. Richardson (4th)
		Musn. Smith, R.M.B., (5th)
		Sergt. G. Milne, R.M.A. (6th)
1920	Sabre	Clr.-Sgt. M. Hawes, R.M.L.I. (2nd)
		Sgt. C. R. Potter, R.M.L.I. (3rd)
	Bayonet Open	Cpl. C. A. P. Tosdevine, (2nd)
		Gnr. W. C. Hamilton (3rd)
		Corpl. A. H. Hunting R.M.L.I. (5th)
	Bayonet (Cham'p)	Sergt. G. Milne, R.M.A. (2nd)
		Sgt. A. B. Richardson, R.M.A. (3rd)
1921	Sabre (Cadets)	Prob. 2/Lt. F. St. G. English
	Sabre	Sgt. C. R. Potter, R.M.L.I. (4th)
	Bayonet	Gnr. C. G. Duncan (1st)
1922	Sabre	Sgt. C. R. Potter, R.M.L.I. (2nd)
		Capt. W. A. Pinkerton (6th)
	Bayonet	Gnr. Penfold (2nd)
		Lt. Col. G. L. Raikes, R.M.A. (6th)

	Foil	Sgt. C. R. Potter, R.M.L.I. (4th)
		Capt. Matthews (8th)
	Epee	L/Cpl. L. V. Clarke (4th)
		Lt. V. D. Thomas, R.M.A. (8th)
1923	Sabre	Q.M.S. M. Hawes } R.M.L.I. (4th)
		Sgt. F. A. Peasnell } R.M.L.I. (4th)
	Foil	Sgt. F. A. Peasnell } R.M.L.I. (4th)
	Bayonet	Q.M.S.I. M. Hawes, R.M.L.I. (3rd)
		Sergt. F. A. Peasnell, R.M.L.I. (5th)
1924	Foil	Q.M.S.I. F. A. Peasnell (4th)
		Corpl. P. J. Jerred (6th)
	Epee	Corpl. L. V. Clarke (4th)
	Sabre	Corpl. L. V. Clarke (3rd)
	Bayonet	Q.M.S.I. F. A. Peasnell (3rd)
		Corpl. F. C. Richardson (4th)
1925	Bayonet	Sergt. R. Spanton (1st)
		Mne. C. C. Duncan (3rd)
1926	Bayonet	Mne. C. G. Duncan (2nd)
1927	Bayonet	Clr.-Sgt. A. G. Miller (2nd)
		Mne. C. G. Duncan (3rd)
1928	Sabre	Q.M.S.1. F. A. Peasnell (4th.)
	Bayonet	Clr.-Sgt. A. G. Miller (1st)
		Corpl. A. V. Perry (2nd)
1929	Foil	Corpl. L. V. Clarke (5th)
		Q.M.S.I. F. A. Peasnell (7th)
	Sabre	Corpl. L. V. Clarke (2nd)
	Bayonet (Cadets)	2/Lt. R. St. C. Arkwright
	Bayonet	Corpl. A. V. Perry (1st)
		Cir.-Sgt. A. G. Miller (2nd)
		Mne. A.F.D. Austin (3rd)
		Lt. J. M. Phillips (5th)
		Sergt. F.C. Richardson (6th)

NATIONAL RIFLE ASSOCIATION
Established 1860.

Held at Wimbledon 1860 - 1889 (inclusive)
Held at Bisley, 1890 - to date.
COMPETITIONS OPEN TO ROYAL MARINES.

THE GENERAL EYRE. (1868 – 1897) Teams of 2, Snap Shooting
- 1873   R.M.L.I. Chatham.
- 1874   R.M.L.I. Portsmouth
- 1886   R.M.L.I. Portsmouth
- 1894   R.M.A.

Won outright in 1897 by 2nd Queen's Regiment.

BRINSMEAD CHALLENGE SHIELD. (1882). Teams of 6, fire with movement.
- 1882   R.M.L.I., Portsmouth.
- 1885   R.M.L.I., Chatham.
- 1887   {R.M.A.
         {R.M.L.I., Portsmouth.
         {13th Middlesex R.V.
- 1888   R.M.L.I., Portsmouth.
- 1891   {R.M.L.I., Portsmouth
         {13th Middlesex R.V.
- 1896   R.M.A.
- 1902   R.M.A.
- 1907   R.M.A.
- 1910   R.MA.

From 1914 conditions changed to a team aggregate in 1st Stage of St. George's.
- 1924   Royal Marines, Portsmouth.
- 1925   Royal Marines, Portsmouth.
- 1930   R.M., Portsmouth.

INTER-SERVICES MATCH. (1927).
- 1927   Royal Marines (Corps Team).

UNITED SERVICES CHALLENGE CUP. (1880).
- 1895   Royal Marines (Corps Team).
- 1909   "   "
- 1919   "   "
- 1922   "   "

CANADA CHALLENGE SHIELD. (1913). Open to Royal Marines.
   1923   R.M.A.

WHITEHEAD CHALLENGE CUP. (1894). (Revolver).
   1926   Royal Marines (Corps Team).
   1928   "   "
   1930   "   "

CHEYLESMORE. (1903).
   1907   R.M.L.I., Portsmouth.
   1908   "   "
   1909   "   "

DUKE OF WESTMINSTER'S CHALLENGE CUP. (1892). Open to Royal Marines 1908-1914.
   1910   R.M.L.I., Plymouth.
   1911   R.M.L.I., Portsmouth.
   1912   R.M.L.I., Plymouth.
   After this it became an Individual Competition.

MAPPIN CHALLENGE CUP. (1978). Open to Royal Marines, 1908.
   1922   R.M.A.

RANELAGH CHALLENGE CUP. (1887). Open to Royal Marines, 1919.
   1919   R.M.A.
   1920   R.M.A.

ROBERTS CHALLENGE CUP. (1904). Open to Royal Marines, 1908.
   1911   R.M.L.I., Portsmouth.
   1926   Royal Marines, Portsmouth.

BARGRAVE DEANE CHALLENGE CUP. (1894). Open to Royal Marines, 1919. Revolver teams.
   1922   R.M.L.I., Portsmouth.
   1923   R.M.L.I., Portsmouth.
   1925   Royal Marines, Portsmouth.
   1927   Royal Marines, Depot.

SPECTATOR. (Two rifles).
   1907   R.M.A. (2nd Prize).

IMPORTANT INDIVIDUAL SUCCESSES. ARMY AND NAVY CHALLENGE CUP (1868 to 1893)
- 1873   Sgt. G. Cox R.M.L.I.
- 1874   Staff Sgt. W. Climes, R.M.L.I.
- 1886   S.M. B. Tucker, R.M.L.I.
- 1891   Sgt. W. H. D. Phillips, R.M.L.I. In 1894 this competition was merged into the Imperial Challenge Cup open to all Services. It was discontinued after 1898.

ALL-COMERS AGGREGATE.
- 1908   Capt. R. C. Colquhoun, R.M.L.I.
- 1926   Q.M.S. G. R. King (late R.M A.).

GRAND AGGREGATE.
- 1924   Q.M.S. O. G. Bacon, R.M.
- 1926   Q.M.S. G. R. King (late R.M.A.).

CORONATION CUP. (1902). Open to R.N. and R.M.
    Winner- Capt. J. L. Homer, R.M.A.

DAILY TELEGRAPH CUP.
- 1924   Q.M.S. O. G. Bacon, R.M.

DAILY GRAPHIC CUP. (Now The Times).
- 1920   S.M. J. Bacon, R.M.A.
- 1929   Sgt. A. J. Howard, R.M.

DUKE OF CAMBRIDGE.
- 1925   Q.M.S. O. G. Bacon, R.M.

WIMBLEDON CUP. Service Rifle.
    Q.M.S. G. R. King, (late R.M.A)

GRAPHIC AND DAILY MAIL.
- 1928   Q.M.S. King (late R.M.A.).

PRINCE OF WALES PRIZE.
- 1924   Q.M.S. O. G. Bacon, R.M.

SECRETARY OF STATE FOR WAR,
- 1923   Q.M.S. G. R. King, R.M.A.
- 1928   Sgt. C. V. Borrett, R.M.

VOLUNTEERS' AGGREGATE.
   1890   L/Cpl. A. Fletcher, 3rd V. B. Hants (late Cr'Sgt. R.M.A.).
   1898   "   "   "   "   "   "

BELGIAN CHALLENGE CUP B.S.A.
   1930   Captain H. S. Teek.

————

The History of the Royal Marines Divisions
1755-1923

Compiled by The Late General Sir H E Blumberg KCB and Colonel C Field
Royal Marines

THE PORTSMOUTH DIVISION R.M.
1755 - 1923.

Compiled from:-
Articles and cuttings from old Orders published in the Globe & Laurel from time to time.
Records in the Superintending Civil Engineer's Office, H.M. Dockyard, Portsmouth.
"Britain's Sea Soldiers," Vol. 1., p. 275.
"Britanic Magazine," July 1807.
"Royal Port Garrison and Borough of Portsmouth," by Henry Slight, 1838.
"Metrical History of Portsmouth," by Henry Slight, 1820.
Annual Register for 1778.
"The Life of Edward Lord Hawke," by Capt. Montagu Burrows.
"Gentleman's Magazine," April 1761, p, 185.
"St. Vincent's Magazine," 1929

OLD CLARENCE BARRACKS.

From 1755 to 1765 the officers and private men were billeted in the Town of Portsmouth. In order to relieve them from the inconvenience and hardships to which they were exposed in quarters, buildings which had been erected in 1613 as the King's Cooperage and Brewery, were turned into a Barracks for them, and called Clarence Barracks, and on May 20th, 1765, the Marines took up their quarters there. The Barracks had "accommodation for 500 men and 8 officers" at this time, but further additions were made to it in 1828.

These Barracks were of the old enclosed barrack-square type, surrounded by high buildings and entered by an arch opposite the east end of Barrack Street; the actual site was behind the present Naval Club, between Pembroke Street, Barrack Street, St. Nicholas Street and Penny Street.

> "In Penny Street,
> Henry the Eigth, in warres with Fraunce,
> Bade seven great Brewing stores advaunce,
> With implements, to serve his shippes
> When they might take them warlike trippes;
> But in late times the Bands Marine
> In martial pomp adorn the scene,
> And oft, with heavenly music's aid,
> Invite us to the promenade.
> Near this, with all accommodation
> Befitting Military Station,
> Stand Four-House Barracks - but, for me,
> I never yet found more than three."

There was a Royal Marine Infirmary, with large garden, in Lake Lane.

OLD PORTSMOUTH.

At this date elaborate fortifications encircled "Old" Portsmouth and Portsea a portion being close to the R.M. Barracks, where the new Clarence and Victoria Barracks now stand. The whole of Landport, Fratton and Southsea lay out beyond the glacis. These old lines were demolished about 1874-5, and at the same time the Mill Pond, covering a large area of what now forms the United Service Recreation Ground was filled in. Beyond this area was a land of level fields, corn, market gardens and clumps of trees at long intervals. A circle of outlying forts from Spithead to Portsdown now took the place of the Portsmouth and Portsea ramparts and moats.

THE BARRACKS.

The number of men in barracks must at times have been few, for in July 1801 we read "the whole of the Marines at Headquarters were embarked this morning on board the *Malta*, of 84 guns, for distribution among the ships of the Channel Fleet."

On the other hand, at times the barracks must have been very full, for on Wednesday, 5th May, 1802, when the Officers of the Royal Marines dined together at their mess-room to celebrate the distinguished honour of "Royal" being conferred on them by His Majesty, there were 90 officers assembled (a number of these officers were possibly on half-pay). On this occasion there were 21 healths drunk and several of them with "three times."

About this time a new mess-room was built for the officers, and "in November 1811 the Duke of Clarence, Lord High Admiral, inspected the Portsmouth Division, and partook of a truly sumptuous cold collation in the new mess-room."

On the 2nd July, 1814, an order was received to make a great reduction at this Division. "All foreigners and men over 40 years, and all not 5ft. 3in. in height, were ordered to be discharged." The barracks soon filled up again, as the following year the 2nd Battalion Royal Marines returned from America, and on the 15th May the officers of this Battalion entertained their Colonel, Sir James Malcolm, K.C.B., at the George Inn, High Street, with an elegant dinner."

In 1842 a very handsome clock was erected over the officers' quarters, about which the Marines and the surrounding inhabitants were very pleased.

In 1848 the land on which the present Clarence Barracks stand, and which belonged to the Admiralty, was exchanged for Forton Barracks, which was in possession of the War Department, and the Portsmouth Division transferred to Forton.

FORTON BARRACKS.

The date when Forton was first utilised as a prison for French prisoners is not known, but in 1755 it was decided "that Portchester Castle was a better place for the reception of French prisoners than the premises of a certain Mr. Ward at Fortune (Forton) near Gosport." After this it was used temporarily as a hospital for Marines - this may have been while Haslar Hospital was undergoing alterations, which it did about this date. In 1761 2,000 French prisoners were removed from Portchester Castle to Forton, where they were guarded by the Regiment of Old Buffs.

In 1777, in pursuance of an Act of Parliament empowering His Majesty to secure and detain persons charged with or suspected of the crime of High Treason committed in any of H. M. colonies or plantations in America, or on the high seas, or the crime of piracy, "a certain messuage or building called Forton, in the parish of Alverstoke, in the County of Southampton, was appointed a place of confinement for such prisoners."

> "And Forton's Keep, a dread abode,
> Where 'neath misfortune's heavy load,
> Ambition's slaves, for despot's crime,
> Were captive kept in warlike time."

In 1778, early one morning in September, "it was discovered that 57 prisoners, all Americans, had effected their escape in the night. The black-hole in which the refractory had been confined, was immediately under the room where the other prisoners slept; those in the dungeon had for several days undermined and worked a subterraneous passage, which led beyond the wall that enclosed the prison, so that they had only to open the ground upwards into the country, when they knew there was no guard to discover them. A hole sufficient to admit a man through was made from the ceiling of their bedroom down to the black-hole, by which they had conveyed up the rubbish, brought from working below, some of which they had put into their beds, and some into the chimney, and the hole was easily covered over with a bed when any person came into the room, to prevent any suspicion of their intention."

During the Napoleonic wars Forton was once again used as a depot for confinement of prisoners of war. Amongst the Admiralty records are registers covering the years 1793 to 1814. The prisoners were kept in hulks in Forton creek and in wooden barracks at Forton. At one time as many as 4,000 French prisoners were kept there.

On 22nd July, 1807, a fire broke out in the old buildings of Forton prison. These buildings were undergoing repair for the accommodation of French prisoners, and the fire is supposed to have been occasioned by the boiling over of a quantity of pitch in the workshop; a great part of the buildings were consumed.

ENTRANCE GATE, R.M. BARRACKS. FORTON, 1896

About this time the wooden buildings were pulled down and a large military hospital was built. Originally this was probably intended for the French prisoners. Attached to what was later H Company block was a dark room, used as a mortuary, and a portion of the ground near the present gun battery was the burying place for French prisoners.

The buildings were described by a contemporary as "four very lofty and extensive brick pavilions, connected by arcades of great extent, with a parade ground of some acres. On the opposite square is the entrance gate, with the apartments for officers."

At the close of the Napoleonic wars these buildings appear to have been utilised for the accommodation of Army units, and in 1848 were in possession of the Ordnance Department.

Just outside the barracks stood the "Forton Arms" - afterwards the official residence of the Commanding Officer.

On the 29th March, 1848, the Marines took possession of Forton Barracks. It would appear that at this time the Barracks only consisted of the four large blocks of buildings connected by arcades and the main arch with the buildings on either side, except the East and West houses. The Barracks was encircled all round either by buildings or walls.

THE FIELD. The Barrack Field was purchased in three lots, the middle strip shortly after the Marines took over the Barracks, and the east and west portions in 1856. About 1901 the football field was levelled, and about two years later a pavilion was built. In 1902 a piece of ground to the east of the field was levelled and four tennis courts and three croquet lawns made.

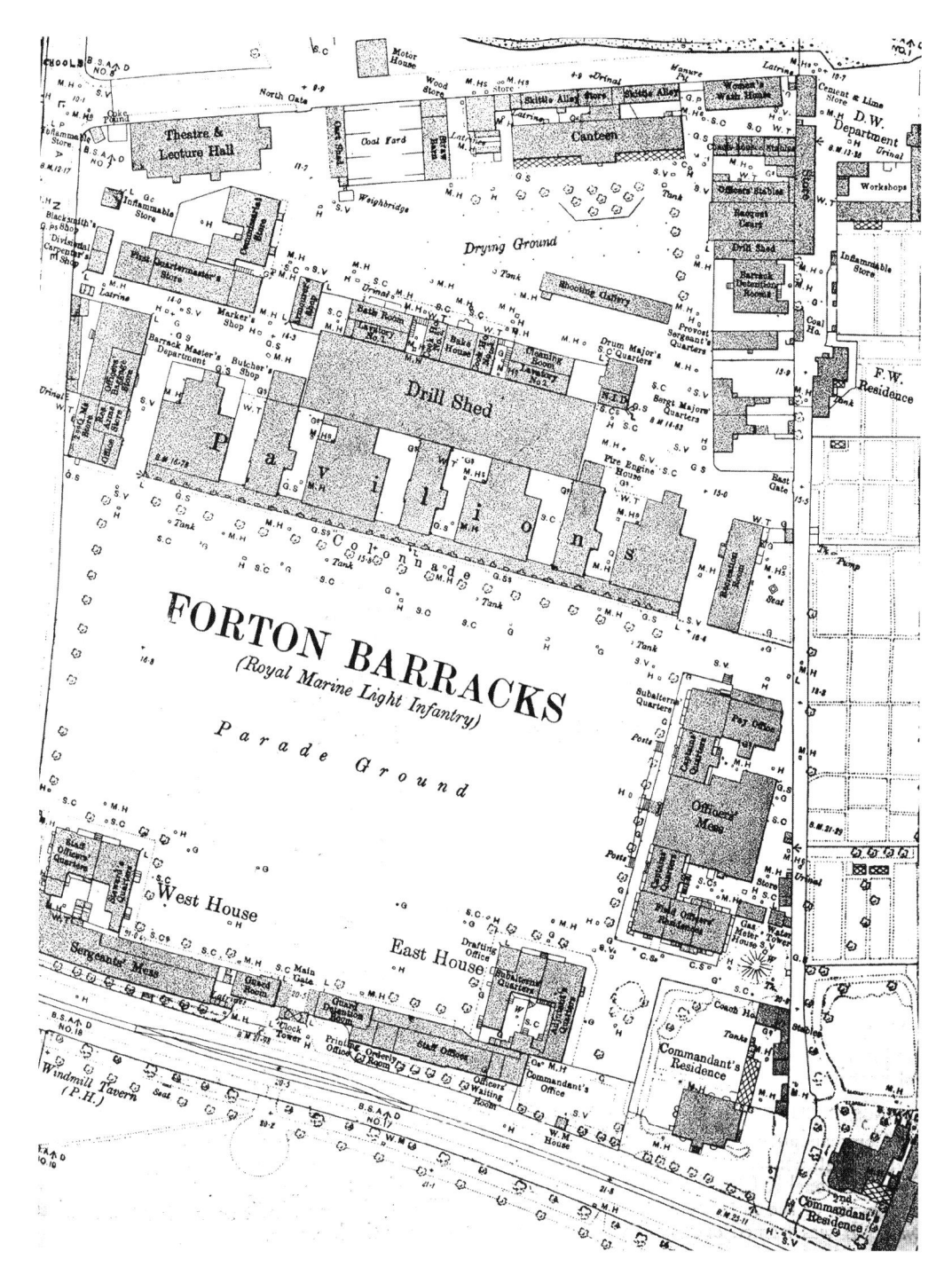

SWIMMING BATH. The site of the Swimming Bath was reclaimed by the Admiralty from the foreshore between 1841-56 and 1867-85. There is no record of the date of construction of the open-air bathing pond.

ALLOTMENT GARDENS. The Millpond was purchased by the Admiralty from the Bishop of Winchester in 1858, and was reclaimed 1866-69, and became the Divisional Allotment Gardens.

SERGEANTS' MESS, DIVISIONAL SCHOOLS AND SHOEMAKERS SHOP. The building on the western side, in line with the blocks, was the Sergeants Mess. The Divisional Schools were located in the block of buildings to the west of the main arch.

In August, 1900, the Sergeants took over the Divisional School Buildings as their Mess, the Schools having been transferred to the buildings on the Mill Lake.

In 1901 the conversion of the old Sergeants Mess into a Shoemakers' shop and store was completed and the building was taken into use.

WEST HOUSE. The West house was built in 1849 as subalterns' quarters, but about 1893 they were turned into the Adjutant's house, which in 1900 became Staff Officer's house. On the alteration of status of the Warrant Officers of the Corps the West house became the Warrant Officers' Mess.

EAST HOUSE. The East house was built in 1849 as single officers' quarters. The one-storied building on the east side of East house became the quarters of the Office Adjutant. In 1893, when he was replaced by a Major Staff Officer, no change was made until an opportunity offered in 1900, when an exchange was effected between the Staff Officer and the Adjutant. Prior to 1894 there had been no Field Adjutant's quarters, presumably because that officer was supposed to be unmarried.

In 1904, when a drafting officer was appointed, he was given the subalterns' quarters on the west side of East house as his office.

BUILDINGS ON EITHER SIDE OF THE MAIN ARCH. The Commandant's Office, which was joined on to the East house, was one of the original buildings. Colonel R. Clavell, when Commandant put a drawing of the forts, etc., at Cronstadt on the wall. It was framed over, and was thought to be a picture, till at the time of amalgamation the frame was taken down, and it was found the picture was painted on the wall. Adjoining the Commandant's Office were the Staff Office and orderly room extending to the main gate, except for the strong room and cells. The Adjutant had a desk in the orderly room till 1908, when he was given a separate office.

The barrack guard room was on the opposite side of the arch, and beyond it the Divisional Schools, afterwards used as the Sergeants' Mess.

OFFICERS' MESS, FIELD OFFICERS' QUARTERS AND PAY OFFICE. These buildings were erected in 1849. The Band Gallery in the Officers' Mess was added later. There was a big alteration made in the Mess about 1900, when an upstairs breakfast room was made, and the two rooms downstairs became ante-room and library. The ante-room was previously the breakfast room. The mess room was a fine room on the upper floor, overlooking the parade. The stables were built soon after the Marines took over the barracks.

QUARTERMASTER'S STORE, RACQUET COURT AND C00KHOUSE. The Quartermaster's Store was built in 1851, and in the following year the Racquet Court and Cookhouse. The racquet court, which was not the correct size, and so seldom used, was turned into a store about 1902.

CEDAR COTTAGE. Cedar Cottage was originally built as a private residence in 1849; it was outside the barracks, on the main road, beyond the Commandant's House. It was purchased by the Admiralty in 1857 and became the 2nd Commandant's House.

CANTEENS. The wet canteen, built in 1872, was a one-storied range of buildings just behind the shooting gallery.

In 1920 the committee of the men's canteen determined to make the tap-room into a more habitable place, and with great taste and judgment the place was re-decorated and furnished with tables and chairs, etc., so that it resembled a comfortable club, its former aspect of sawdust and bare forms became a thing of the past.

Forton canteen was peculiar, in that it always had a room where men could receive their friends, and there was also a bedroom, where relations visiting men who were sick or going abroad, could be accommodated.

The dry canteen was built some time after the wet canteen. It was a small building adjoining the 1st Quartermaster's Store and next to the Theatre.

RECREATION ROOM. The Recreation Room, built in 1877, was a fine two-storied building, with billiard rooms and refreshment bar on the ground floor and library above.

This faced the Pay Office, and stood between the pay office and the houses of the Sergeants Major. The latter were comparatively modern buildings.

In 1909 a waste piece of land at the rear of the recreation room was converted into a recreation garden. It was fenced off from the remainder of the barracks, being approached through the recreation room. Lounge chairs and small tables were placed in the garden for the use of the men.

GUN BATTERY. On the transfer to Forton the Commandant was instructed to "cause the sea service gun drill battery on Southsea Common to be given over, with its equipment, to the charge of the Director of the Laboratory for the use of the Artillery companies of the Corps," but it is believed that the Marines from Forton were detached to the Gunwharf (old victualling store) Barracks to do gunnery at this battery till 1876, when a battery was built at Forton. The officers detached from Forton were full members of the Victualling Store Barracks' Mess by R.M.O. order of 18th April, 1848. Extra gunnery pay was granted to Marines in 1875.

About 1894-6 a light gun and M.G. battery was added at Forton, and a new brick building that was used for shooting appliances was completed about 1902.

THE PARADE GROUND was the largest of all Divisions, and as the acoustic properties were very bad, those unaccustomed to it found it very difficult to conduct drill.

DRILL SHED AND BOWLING ALLEY. The Drill Shed was built in 1879 and Bowling Alley in 1885. The bowling alley was just behind the canteen.

THE BOAT HOUSES were just outside the rear barrack gate, where the pulling boats were kept, the steam pinnace being usually kept at the Clarence Yard.

THEATRE. By December, 1893, a theatre, concert room and gymnasium combined was completed; the building was situated by the rear gate and had seating accommodation for about 600. Three sides were of corrugated-iron, lined with matchwood boarding, and the fourth side was brick, this being the boundary wall between the barracks and the road; the floor was parquet. The stage was heightened and the room much improved in December 1894. For many years the Forton Theatrical Society flourished, and during the winter season gave Fortnightly entertainments.

STAFF SERGEANTS' QUARTERS. During 1894 a fine block of buildings was erected in the field in front of the barracks, giving comfortable quarters for Staff Sergeants and Colour Sergeants of the Division.

COTTAGE HOSPITAL. In 1898 a Cottage Hospital was built at Forton, in the drill field, near the road on the right hand side of the Windmill public house. It was a two-storied building. Of good design, and contained two wards of six beds each, and gave a better look-out than the old sick quarters in the barrack square. The old dispensary was then only used for consulting rooms for women and children.

BROWNDOWN. The exact date Browndown rifle range was opened is not known, but we read that in 1862 the annual competitive contest was held at Browndown. During 1891-2 the ranges were extensively altered to suit the magazine rifle, and were ready for use by 1st May, 1892.

FORTON BARRACKS BY W.L.WYLIE. R.A.

Detachments from the Chatham and Plymouth Divisions then came to Forton to go through their annual musketry, as their own rifle ranges were not available for the Lee-Metford rifle. Gravesend was ready about July 1895 and Plymouth some time later. Detachments were quartered in hutments at Browndown and also in Fort Gomer. The camp was enlarged about 1912, and electric light added about 1922.

DIVINE SERVICE. There never was a church belonging to the Division; the troops always attended St. John's, where a special service was held before the ordinary morning service. There are several memorial tablets in the church to the memory of Marines.

MANOEUVRE GROUNDS. When the Marines first went to Forton, Haslar Common was used for drills and inspections, though the R.M.L.I. used to go over to Southsea Common for the reviews of the Garrison of Portsmouth. Later Grange Field took the place of Haslar Common, and many an Adjutant-General's inspection has taken place on this field with a brigade of Marines from Forton taking part. The Marines continued to use Grange Field until it was taken over by the R.A.F. during the war 1914-18.

WAR MEMORIAL. In 1919 the Marines at Forton decided to combine their own War Memorial with that of the Town, thus enabling the Gosport War Memorial Hospital to be established.

AMALGAMATION. In 1923, when the re-amalgamation of the R.M.A. and R.M.L.I. was finally ordered, the barracks at Forton were in such a decayed condition, and estimates for their repair (approx. £60,000) were so large that they could not be entertained by the Admiralty, and consequently the *Portsmouth Division was once more transferred across the water and accommodated in the Eastney Barracks.* The officers, n.c.o.'s and men who were not required to complete the establishment were transferred to Plymouth and Chatham.

THE DEPARTURE FROM FORTON. The last Church Parade took place on 29th July, when the Adjutant-General, Sir H. E. Blumberg, and Major-General St. G. B. Armstrong (Commandant) attended. After the service the Commandant addressed the officers, n.c.o.'s and men of the Portsmouth Division on parade. There was a very large number of ex-members of the Division present.

On the 1st August, 1923, the transfer of the Colours to Eastney took place. They were taken under escort of four officers and 100 rank and file, under the command of Major M. Filmer-Bennett, the colour-bearers being Lieut. R. H. S. Teek and 2nd Lieut. J. L. R. Pym. It is interesting to note that the father of Lieut. Pym received the Colours from H.M. Queen Victoria in 1894.

HISTORY OF THE DEPOT ROYAL MARINES, DEAL.

Dockyard Gates – Circa 1860

By Major C. H. Congdon, R.M.

EARLY DAYS.
In sight of treacherous Goodwin's faithless sands,
An impious and remorseless town there stands,
Peopled by men whose cruelties of mind
Make them savages of human kind;
Wretches abandoned to the worst crimes of crimes
That e'er were practiced in most guilty times;
Deal is its name, to mariners well known,
Where there is not a vice but what's its own,
But fraud, oppression, theft and rapine reign.

This was written in 1710, many years of course before the Corps had any associations with the place, although there was an Inn situated in the High Street in 1660 called "The Three Marines."

It was probably not until the reign of Henry VIII. that the strategical importance of Deal was fully appreciated. Leland, the Royal librarian described it as "half a myle fro the shore of the se, a fisher village iii myles or more above Sandwic, upon a flat shore, and very open to the se." flanked on one side by the cliffs of Kingsdown and Dover, and on the other side by the sands and marshes of Sandwich Bay, and sheltered by the Goodwin Sands, that has made the coastline of Deal and Walmer the natural landing place for an invasion of England.

There can be no doubt that it was on Deal Beach that Caesar made his first landing. "The combat" wrote Napoleon III, "was certainly fought on that part of the shore which extends from Walmer Castle to Deal." So it would seem highly probable that the South Green, where so many interesting combats of a different kind take place to-day, was the scene of that more bloodthirsty contest "Early Britons v Roman Legions."

From that time until the end of the 18th century little information of interest can be discovered regarding the sites of the present Barracks, the building of which seems to have been begun shortly after the outbreak of the French Revolution. Before 1795, when it appears that some of the present barracks were ready for occupation, troops seem to have been quartered from time to time in Deal. The "Old Barracks" are referred to more than once in the vestry minute book. These Barracks, which were situated in Queen Street, probably on the site now occupied by the Convent, were demolished in 1816. One reads of a vestry meeting on July 29th of that year, in connection with some proposed alterations to the parish church, that Mr G.J.P. Leith informed the vestry "that he would contribute part of the materials comprising the Barrack in Queen St., Deal, consisting of roof, timbers, tiles, flooring, in aid of the building.

DEAL DOCKYARD.

It is also certain that Marines, probably detachments from Chatham or Woolwich Divisions, were quartered in the Royal Naval Yard. This was situated just to the north of Deal Castle, in the area now occupied by the South Eastern Hotel, and extending nearly as far as the shore end of the Pier. Built originally early in the 17th century, it gained considerable importance during the wars with France in the late 18th and early 19th centuries, until it was demolished in 1864.

In the graveyard of St. George's Church may be found several references to this yard: one of these speaks of "George Lawrence, Esq.," who died on "Oct. 31st, 1807, in the 81st year of his age. Twenty-eight years Naval Storekeeper at Deal." Nelson, when lying off Deal in the *Unite* in the summer of 1801, refers to him "As I understand from Mr. Lawrence that 12 or 14 flat-bottomed boats would be ready to put in the water at the latter end of this week; I wish very much that directions may be given to fit 8 of them with brass 8-inch howitzers and the remainder with 12-pounder carronades."

JUBILEE GATE

These boats formed part of the abortive cutting-out expedition on Boulogne when Napoleon was gathering his "great army of invasion".

THE NORTH, SOUTH AND CAVALRY BARRACKS.

The actual date when the foundation stones of the present North and South Barracks were laid is not certain,* but in the accounts of the Barrack Master General for December 1st, 1795, items are given indicating that these Barracks were in course of erection for infantry and cavalry. On the infantry barracks £4,700 had been spent, £3,226 was due, and it was estimated that £7,824 would be necessary to complete the building. The corresponding figures for the cavalry are £4,851, £1,185 and £301 so it seems evident that the Cavalry barracks were the first to be started. These were occupied soon after their completion by the famous 15th Light Dragoons, and the former by various regiments of the line, until in 1869 the whole became Admiralty property.

These accounts, however, contain particulars of other barracks, most of them of a temporary character. Among these are mentioned "Barracks at Deal for 300 Infantry," erected (Works Department please note!) at a cost of £312, and there is a reference that others were to be provided for 58 men and 63 horses.

Thus we see the origin of the "Cavalry Gate" South Barracks, and the reason for the tethering rings for horses on the building now used as the Staff Office, Small Arms Office, etc.; while some of the original stalls are used as pioneers' and barrack store rooms.

*A stone let into the wall on the N.W. corner of the Cavalry Barracks wall bears traces of what appears to be the figure 4. This may possibly be part of the date '94, the year in which the wall was built.

CAVALRY BARRACKS

In the South Barracks the drill shed, canteen, and the rows of buildings facing the South Green (in which the Sergeants' Mess is situated) are of a much later date; the original canteen being situated in the buildings now used by the Works Department. The stables in rear of the Officers' Mess were built in 1893, and in the same year the gymnasium annexe was completed.

In the North Barracks all the buildings to the West of the main row of blocks, including the end blocks, theatre, canteens and cookhouse, were not erected until the latter part of the last century.

Shortly after the second peace of Paris (1815) a considerable proportion of the troops were withdrawn from Lower Walmer; whereupon (from 1816 to 1831) a part of the South Barrack was used as quarters for the Blockade Men employed in putting down the smuggling which was then very prevalent. The present Officers Mess was used as the headquarters of this force, which consisted of seamen borne on the books of H.M.S. *Ramillies* (until 1829) and H.M.S. *Talavera*. In connection with these blockade men, the "windows" in the wall of the South Barracks, flanking the Dover Road, are of interest. There can be seen a set of four windows now blocked up, about 100 yards on each side of the Jubilee Gate, and their origin is obscure. One old resident of Walmer states that his father told him that the blockade men's quarters were along this wall, and that the windows belonged to them, another suggestion is that they were intended as part of the barrack defences against possible invasion, and that, in an emergency, they could form gun embrasures. On the other hand, it is more than probable that they were intended solely for decoration, to break up, as it were, the extended length of blank wall.

There can be no doubt, however, that the Cavalry and North Barracks were unoccupied from 1816 until 1818, since we find an application being made, in 1816, to the War Office "for leave

391

to occupy some part of the barracks for the use of the poor." In the following year the vestry directed that representations be made "to the Commissioners for the Barrack Affairs or other proper Authority" to the effect that "the present Cavalry Barracks" (wherein, incidentally, the Commandant's Office is now situated) "would make a very desirable Poor House, and the parochial authorities would be glad to acquire them for that purpose, if the same can be rented on moderate terms." There is no record of any reply to these overtures, but there is distinct evidence that the South Barracks remained in the occupation of the Blockade Men until the abolition of that service in 1831, when they became a station for Coastguards.

The South Barracks continued to serve as a Coastguard Station until 1840, when, in common with the North Barracks, they were occupied by a detachment of Royal Artillery.

As for the Cavalry Barracks, the War Office seems speedily to have determined that they should serve a worthier purpose than that of a Poor House, for in 1818 we find detachments both of the 9th Lancers and the 11th Hussars quartered there. They appear, however, to have been unoccupied, at least by cavalry, from 1828 to 1853; though as some of the Coastguardmen stationed in the South Barracks during the greater part of that interval were mounted, no doubt the stables were found serviceable.

From 1839 to 1869 the Barracks continued to be occupied by Line Regiments, but in the latter

NORTH BARRACK

year, having then been used for about 10 years as a joint depot for the 2nd Queen's, the 7th Royal Fusiliers and the 23rd Welsh Fusiliers, forming together the VIth Depot Battalion, they were transferred to the Admiralty in exchange for Barracks and other property situated in Woolwich, and have ever since been used as part of the Depot, Royal Marines.

ESTABLISHMENT OF THE DEPOT.

"The new depot barracks for recruits of the Royal Marines is now in full operation at Walmer, and a library and school has just been formed. Each married man of the establishment has a plot of land allotted to him for cultivation. The present number of inmates, principally recruits from the three Divisions of Chatham, Portsmouth and Woolwich, is 400 and as a proof of the advantages, of removing young recruits from temptations incident to garrison towns, it is worthy of remark that during the three months since this depot has been opened, no inmate has been charged before a magistrate."

Illustrated London News, 24th Aug, 1861

THE FIRST DAYS OF THE DEPOT, R.M.

Although it was not until 1869 that the North, South and Cavalry Barracks were taken over, the Depot R.M. had already been in existence for some eight years.

On 4th May, 1861, we find the Royal Marine Office approving the supply of "coals, candles and straw for the use of the ranks about to occupy Deal Barracks," and addressing the authority to "Lt.-Colonel W. R. Maxwell, Commanding detachment Royal Marines, Deal" at 34 Beach Street, Deal, a house long since demolished, and situated just outside the North East gate of the Naval Yard.

But on the 7th of that month, the address is altered to "……. Commanding Depot R.M., Deal," and that title is used in all subsequent correspondence, so that it would seem safe to infer that the official birthday was on that date.

On 20th June the first Officers' Mess committee meeting was assembled, when it was determined:

1st - "That in order to form a fund for the establishment, etc., of a mess, each officer on joining shall pay an entrance of two days' pay"; and later

3rd - "That Mr. Geo. Morton of Deal be engaged as Mess man, etc."; moreover,

7th - "That on Fridays, when any officer gives notice for a friend coming to dinner before 10 a.m., each member pay for a pint of wine in proportion, as at Headquarters."

The manner in which "Mr. Geo. Morton" became "mess man" is not without interest. In subsequent R.M.O. correspondence is found a postscript as follows:-

"P.S. - A beating order is herewith transmitted to enable you to enlist the mess man in question. Should it so happen that any eligible recruits offer themselves from time to time, whom you may consider it desirable to enlist for the Corps, you will be pleased to forward them to Chatham for approval."

This "Beating Order," issued "By the commissioners for executing the Office of Lord High Admiral of the United Kingdom, etc.", is worded thus:-

"These are to authorise you, by beat of drum or otherwise, to raise volunteers at Deal for Her

Majesty's Corps of Royal Marines, for the purpose of completing the said Corps to its establishment and all Her Majesty's Justices of the Peace, Constables, and other Civil Officers whom it may concern, are hereby required to be assisting unto you in providing quarters, impressing carriages, and otherwise as there shall be occasion.

Given under our hands, etc."

And so our good Mr. Morton, after duly being given the rank of sergeant "without emoluments, and having been fitted into his uniform at Chatham, became messman, in which capacity he served for some years, until, unfortunately, he became bankrupt.

On Wednesday, 8th May, 1861, a detachment of 1 Capt., 1 Lieut., 9 Sergts., 7 Corporals and 35 Privates was despatched from Chatham and Woolwich Divisions to form the nucleus of the new Establishment, and, on the following Saturday, 100 recruits from each of these Divisions "not in the first squad under instruction," together with I Capt., 1 Lieut. and "three undisciplined Second Lieutenants" arrived at Deal to commence training.

All these ranks were accommodated in the "R.N. Hospital" (East Barracks), where small detachments of the Royal Marines had been stationed since the end of the Crimean War (1854).

By August the Depot appears to have been in full swing, as the following extract from the *Illustrated London News* of the 24th of the month would indicate: "The new depot barrack for recruits of the Royal Marines is now in full operation at Walmer, and a library and school has just been formed. Each married man of the establishment has a plot of land allotted to him for cultivation. The present number of inmates, chiefly recruits from the three Divisions of Chatham, Portsmouth and Woolwich, is 400; and as a proof of the advantages of removing young recruits from temptations incident to garrison towns, it is worthy of remark that during the three months since the Depot has been opened no, inmate has been charged before a magistrate."

THE EAST BARRACKS.

The present buildings, now called the East Barracks, were erected, with few exceptions, in 1812, but before that date an "Old Hospital" occupied the same site. Pritchard (in his "History of Deal," published in 1864) gives its origin thus: "In the French and American Wars of the early period of the reign of George III. two Naval Surgeons, named Packe and Leith, contracted with the Admiralty to victual and to render Medical assistance to the sick and wounded as might from time to time be required." This and other fortunate (sic) contracts laid the foundations of both these families, and enabled the latter to purchase, of the Knatchbull family, Walmer estate." Elvin, in his "Records of Walmer," commenting on this states: "The story, at all events, accounts for Mr. Leith's possession of the hospital; but what shall be said of a system which allowed the sick and wounded to be put out to farm? It could have little to recommend it, and by the beginning of the present (19th) century, if not sooner, the Admiralty had acquired possession of this building themselves.

"Though, this hospital was clearly intended as a Naval Hospital, its wards were on more than one occasion crowded with sick and wounded soldiers, during the protracted wars of the time of George III. This was the case, for instance, in the year 1793, when the Duke of York was compelled to raise the siege of Dunkirk and, as Pritchard says, 'The dying and the dead' were brought ashore at Deal 'in boat loads'; a circumstance that no doubt explains the mention in the Parish Registers of the 'Camp Hospital', by means of which additional accommodation seems to have been provided at this juncture. In this connection it is further chronicled that 'the number of corpses buried in St. George's Chapel Burial Ground numbered no less than 1,045 in the year.' "

In the year 1809, during a violent thunderstorm, the hospital was struck by lightning and rent

DEAL CASTLE AND THE OLD NAVAL HOSPITAL 1792
From A Drawing Made In That Year. (At The Depot, R.M.,)

from roof to foundation, though most providentially, not one of the numerous patients sustained any injury. This incident which was in many respects remarkable was subsequently communicated to the authorities by the Governor of the Hospital, Commander Peter Dower, in the following terms:- "On Friday, 7th inst. (July), about a quarter to midnight, this hospital received much damage from lightning. It appears to have been attracted by the Mill on the beach side, the sweep of which is shattered, and from thence struck the central chimney of the hospital, levelling it with the roof, and igniting some shavings in the grate below. It seems that the lead on the top conducted the electric fluid to the extremity of the southern end of the body of the hospital, where, meeting with some obstruction, it rent that head and tore off the weather tiling, passed into the tenth (or upper) ward; fused the top part of the foot post belonging to an iron bedstead, in which lay a patient. From thence it passed round, excoriated the lower part of the iron bedstead, and set fire to the floor boards, tearing away the ceiling, and passing into the eight (or middle) ward, fusing the lower window weight, jambs and walls. Continuing downwards, it took again the iron weight of the window in the sixth (or lower) ward, driving out, as before, glass, frame and wall, and passing round the iron bedstead nearest the wall, in which lay another sick person with a fractured skull: it fortunately did him no injury, except a little bleeding subsequent to the concussion. In the eleventh ward it entered by a window jamb on the west side, attracted by a nail, and tore up the flooring of the room above, scattering the splinters of the woodwork in all directions round the ward, but not injuring a pane of glass, nor any of the numerous patients. I have to thank God that none of the latter were injured, though the electric fluid passed round and fused the ironwork, which in this instance acted as a conductor and being covered with the blankets, prevented further annoyance than the singeing of a rug. I also take the opportunity of suggesting to the Board the necessity of conductors, as this building is high and exposed. The damage, I apprehend, is considerable, by the ruin of the chimney pot, etc., which fell upon the slating and broke the circular glass window in the operation room; and I have given immediate directions for the most urgent part of the repairs, requesting the Board's sanction thereto."- (Abstract from the report of Governor Dower to the Transport Office).

Shortly after this the authorities seem to have decided on the demolition of the old building and on 4th June, 1812, the foundation stone of the Royal Naval Hospital (now known as the East Barracks, though still called "R.N. Hospital" on modern charts) was laid by Commander Dower "in the presence of all the Officers." By the end of the year the building was sufficiently far advanced to receive its first batch of patients. When first completed it was capable of accommodating about 300, which is said to have been "nearly the number therein after the Battle of Waterloo," but it was so constructed that it might at any future time, at a very slight additional cost, be sufficiently large for the reception of fully 500.

As early as 1817 some Royal Marines were quartered in Barracks at the Hospital, but they were withdrawn after the following year. Like the Army (South, North and Cavalry) Barracks, the Naval Hospital, or at least some portion of it, was at some time occupied in the Coast Blockade for the repression of smuggling. It was thus used in 1824, when the sailors employed in this service were present here in considerable numbers - many were also billeted in Sandown Castle.

In September of that year the Admiralty appointed a Chaplain "to do duty to the Blockade men," and for many years subsequent to this a portion of the hospital was used as a Coast Guard Station.

THE BURIAL GROUNDS.

Within the limits of the present Barracks are two burial grounds, both of which have now been disused for several years, one within the North and the other within the East Barracks walls.

The former, which is situated at the back of the north cookhouse, is about half an acre in area, and is called in the local registers, the "Military Ground." Some 740 burials are recorded to have taken place in it, though in all probability that is far short of the actual number. Many of the men who died in Walmer during the French wars were buried here in *pits*. Elvin, in his "Records of Walmer" quotes a letter from an old resident: . . . the pits were there - all sunk in - up to about 1852, when the Rifles lay here, and the burial ground was levelled and planted. There was not a shrub in it till that time, and it was a most desolate, neglected place. The pits were all along the wall that separates it from the barrack yard (now the cookhouse wall - traces of these pits can still be seen).

There are no monuments of particular interest in this ground except, perhaps, the following: "Algernon Stephens, late Lieutenant 1st Royals, the colours of which Regiment he carried at Waterloo, died Jan. 8th, 1865." The last interment here, recorded in the parish registers, was on Nov. 19th, 1877, but there are many tombstones bearing dates later than that, the most recent being 1882.

The disused Naval burial ground, which is situated at the back of the East Barracks, behind the tailors' shops and quartermaster's offices, is enclosed in high walls, which completely block it out from the eyes of the public, by whom its very existence is almost forgotten. Its area measures upwards of an acre, and although the parish registers prove that at least 1,685 burials have taken place there from first to last, it contains only 19 memorial stones all told, most of which are set up against the wall of the tailors' shop and are of comparatively recent date. The first interment here took place in 1794, the same year that the War Office probably started building the Cavalry Barracks.

Among the monumental inscriptions in this ground is a plaque on the western wall, "In memory of Perser Dower, Commander R.N., who died the 30th October, 1837, aged 85 years. He laid the foundation stone of these buildings, and was for many years Governor of the Hospital."

KINGSDOWN RIFLE RANGE.

The first payment of rent in respect of the Rifle Range seems to have been made in 1856, and was apparently 1s. per annum. No documentary proof of this, however, can be traced. In the year 1872 the Admiralty wished to erect a small store, latrine and stable, and approached the owners for permission to do so. On 18th November of that year an agreement was entered into with the Admiralty, in which it was stated that for some years past the Admiralty had had the use of "certain beach lands at Kingsdown" at a yearly rent of 1s. for the purpose of a Rifle Range, but in addition the Admiralty now agreed to pay all the rates and taxes.

On 31st December, 1889, a further lease was granted to the Admiralty at a rent of £2 per annum for the first 14 years, and £5 per annum for a further 7 years; but in 1895, when the owner of the land on the top of the cliff fronting the range began building operations inside the "danger zone," all firing had to be suspended. By 1897 the range had been oriented with new butts and firing points, so that no land on the cliff top was in danger, and practices on the range recommenced.

In 1901 negotiations were opened by the Admiralty for the purchase of the freehold, as the owners had decided not to renew the lease except at a much higher rental. The result of these negotiations appears to have been abortive, and the land was sold in bulk to a building syndicate.

This action on the part of the owners had the result of causing the Admiralty to acquire the land from the syndicate by compulsory arbitration in 1903, and it has remained Admiralty property ever since.

Lately the inroads of the sea have been very considerable, necessitating three of the shorter range firing points being built out into the sea, while a strongly cemented sea wall has been provided to protect the outer flank of the butts. This erosion, particularly in the last few years, has also threatened the existence of the road running under the cliff, linking up the points and giving access to the butts. To preserve this road a sea wall is being built in continuation of the wall protecting the butts. The reason of this sudden erosion is doubtful. It may be due to the extension of the works in Dover harbour, or to the groins that have recently been built into the sea at North Deal. But whatever the cause, there is no doubt that the natural configuration of the coastline at Kingsdown is undergoing a very rapid change, and the time seems to be fast approaching, when recruits carrying out "field practices" will have to proceed by boat between successive firing points.

KINGSDOWN RIFLE RANGE.

THE GARRISON CHURCH.

For many years before the present Church was built Divine Service at the Depot was conducted in the building called, and still known as, "The Chapel-School," because of its double use as a place of worship on Sundays and a school for children and men on week-days. This doubtful system of economy was formally adopted by the War Office in garrison towns, and a similar chapel still exists on the Western Heights of Dover. The arrangement was very unsatisfactory, and it is related that the church fixtures, such as the altar, font and pulpit were sometimes utilized on week-days for the storage of "superfluous scholars and materials." Incidentally, this chapel was built in 1858, eleven years before the Admiralty took over the North Barracks.

Eventually it was decided that the Depot ought to have a proper church of its own. Lord Selbourne took a keen interest in the idea, and it was mainly owing to him that the work was put in hand. There appears to be no foundation to the allegation that the funds, originally intended for rebuilding the officers mess were diverted to the Church.

The design of the building was prepared at the Admiralty, and is almost the same as that of the churches at Eastney, Keyham and Chatham. The foundation stone was laid by Lord George Hamilton, Captain of Deal Castle, and a former First Lord of the Admiralty, on 9th June, 1905, and the Church was dedicated by the Archbishop of Canterbury on 26th January, 1907.

Only two marriages, for which special licences were necessary, have taken place in the Church.

During an air raid on Dover on Sunday, 23rd January, 1916, a shell fired from Dover entered the east wall of the Church, doing some damage to the Chancel. This occurred about 1 p.m.; had it come an hour earlier, when the usual service was being held, the consequences might have been more serious.

R.M. INFIRMARY.

An account of the building of the Infirmary is given in the Globe and Laurel of March 24th, 1901:-

"The very handsome new hospital, situated in the Blenheim Road, was completed and opened last autumn. The wards, kitchens and general arrangements are all of the very latest pattern, and a most complete steam laundry, capable of doing washing for the whole of the Barracks as well as the hospital has just been added. The hospital has accommodation for about 105 patients, of whom 21 can be received on the zymotic side and 84 in the general wards. As soon as the new hospital was taken over, the old hospital, re-named the "East Barracks," was handed over to the Works Department for conversion into barrack rooms. These rooms will be ready for occupation about 1st April, and will give accommodation for about 350 extra men. "

Since this was written further accommodation in the hospital has been made for 12 patients on the zymotic side.

Under war conditions the hospital can accommodate 162 patients - 111 in the general wards and 51 in the zymotic wards.

THE DEPOT DURING THE WAR.

At 7 a.m. on 30th July, 1914, the "Assembly" was sounded in the streets of Deal by the Depot buglers, and a few days later notices were to be seen inviting applications for employment of trench digging at Dover. The annual "tattoo" was postponed, after a full-dress rehearsal had taken place.

It is of interest to record that the Royal Naval Division was formed at Walmer. During the latter part of August naval uniform began to be seen in Deal, and by the end of that month many hundreds of seamen, including R.N.R., R.F.R. and R.N.V.R. had arrived. Two Naval Brigades were formed (Commodores W. Henderson and Oliver Backhouse). At the beginning of September one of these Brigades was moved to Betteshanger, between Deal and Sandwich, while the other was augmented, and on 4th October was embarked at Dover for Antwerp, accompanied by the R.M. Brigade, which had been in camp at East Valley (near Martin Mill). Of these the remnants returned on 12th October, when, it is recorded, "dense crowds lined the streets to witness the march of the weary men from the station to the barracks. There were touching scenes as wives recognised their husbands and children their fathers, returned safely from a terrible, if brief, experience of actual war."

On 27th October the remnants of the Naval Brigade which had accompanied the Marines to Antwerp and returned to Deal, left finally for the Crystal Palace, to be sent later to Blandford for further training.

But the connection of the locality with the R.N. Division had by no means ceased. The R.N. Divisional Engineers, which included Depot Field, Signal and Transport companies, had been in training near Oxney (near Dover), and these were now brought to Walmer and billeted in unoccupied houses. The R.N.D.E. remained in Walmer for several months, and eventually left for Blandford in April 1915. The R.M. Labour Corps, the "home base ledger" of which was kept at the Depot, was established early in 1917. The personnel were all over military age, and after a short stay for elementary training and inoculation, were sent to France at frequent intervals. At the end of the war they returned to Deal for demobilization.

Many incidents of interest - too many to recount in this brief record - occurred in the Downs and the district. Four air raids took place, and whether the objective was the Barracks, or whether the enemy wished to unload the unexpended portion of his day's ration of bombs, will probably never be known. Only one of these, which occurred on 20th February, 1916, did any material damage to the Barracks, if the chips out of the South Barrack wall flanking the Dover Road, can be called "damage." These still remain, and it is only a few months since the remark was heard "it's about time the Marines got that wall repaired." But surely this record of the war situated as it is in such a conspicuous position, deserves a better fate.

As might be expected, there were many rumours of intended enemy landings in the neighbourhood of Deal. A R.M. Emergency Force was formed from the ranks serving at the Depot, and Operation Order No. 1 to this Force, which was dated 6 p.m. 24th February, 1916, reads as follows:-
1. It is expected that a hostile landing may be attempted tonight, or in the course of the next few days.
2. The emergency force under the command of Lieut.-Col. Godfrey will man the beach trenches at night from 6.30 p.m. to one hour after reveille.
3. No. I Company will man the trenches from Kingsdown Coastguard Station to Walmer Castle (not inclusive); Old Soldiers platoon to remain in barracks.

4. No. 2 Company will man the trenches thence to Deal Castle (not inclusive); Old Soldiers platoon to remain in barracks.
5. No. 3 Company will man the trenches thence to Sandown Castle (inclusive); Old Soldiers platoon to remain in barracks.
6. One machine-gun and one crew will go with each Company - the remaining 3 guns will remain in barracks.
7. Men will take one blanket each and great coats, and will not be in marching order, but will take filled water-bottles and haversacks.
8. Lieut.-Colonel Godfrey's Headquarters will be OFFICERS' MESS, SOUTH BARRACKS, etc.

Immediately after the issue of this order the "Cinque Port Fencibles" were mobilised to augment this battalion. This force of volunteers, which was first created in 1793, at the instigation of William Pitt, consisted of residents in the district over military age. It was formed shortly after the outbreak of war, and other local contingents were drilled in the Marine Barracks.

On mobilisation they armed with long rifles, taken from the squads at the Depot who had not undergone their musketry course. Detachments from Northbourne and Sandwich also came in, and altogether about 195 turned up. They were issued with haversacks and 150 rounds of ammunition per man, and after remaining in the South Barracks drill shed till midnight, they were sent to the trenches, which had been dug in the beaches between Kingsdown and Deal. Early next morning after a "snowy night with three-quarters of a gale blowing" they returned to the Depot and were not called upon again to man their trenches. Some incidents in connection with this defence force are both interesting and amusing, as for example, the commandeering of local fish handcarts, which were collected in the North Barracks, for use as stretchers for wounded. The association of the "Fencibles" with the Royal Marines is maintained by an annual dinner, at which the Commandant of the Depot is usually the principal guest.

It will be recalled that it was at the Depot that the famous Fourth Battalion R.M. was trained, before the historic raid on Zeebrugge. Captain (now Rear-Admiral) A. F. B. Carpenter. V.C., R.N., in his book "The Blocking of Zeebrugge" writes: "The Marine Infantrymen were put through intensive training at one of the southern depots (Deal, of course, is meant). This training was arranged and personally supervised by Lt.-Col. Elliot, whose powers of imagination were of a high order, and whose optimism was very encouraging . . . I remember a lady telling me that she and her friends had been much interested on recent nights in watching a large party of Marines indulging in peculiar antics on a hill opposite her house; also that the hill was partly covered with strips of canvas, in a seemingly aimless fashion. I expressed my astonishment at the strange proceeding. Incidentally the canvas strips were laid out to represent different portions of Zeebrugge Mole, though at that period the men believed they represented some enemy position elsewhere."

H.M. The King visited the Depot on 7th March 1918, and inspected the Fourth Battalion and the various departments in the Barracks, including the Infirmary, where he presented the D.S.C. to a wounded trawler skipper, and three D.S.C.'s and a bar to the D.S.C. to Naval Officers. The use of the term "King's Squad" for the senior Squad of recruits at the Depot dates from this visit.

In addition to this honour the following letter was received the next day. The signal is now framed and hung in the Commandant's office.

BUCKINGHAM PALACE.

General White,

I am glad to have had an opportunity of inspecting the Depot of the Royal Marines, and I desire to express my entire satisfaction both with the system of training and with the serious and earnest spirit shown by officers and men to attain a high standard of War efficiency.

It was a pleasure to see the orderly state of the various branches of your Depot, and I welcome the opportunities given to all ranks for recreation and sport.

For some 250 years the Royal Marines have rendered splendid service to the Country, and during this great war they have had the unique record of taking part in all naval actions and of being employed in every theatre of war. Everywhere your Corps has added fresh glory to its record, and never has your name stood higher than to-day.

When you serve afloat or on land, remember the achievements of those who have passed through the Depot before you, and so continue to foster that *esprit de corps* and fellowship with the Navy which have always been famous in the traditions of the Royal Marines.

I am prouder than ever to be your Colonel-in-Chief.

(Signed) GEORGE R.I.
7th March, 1918.

In March 1919 Vice-Admiral Sir Roger Keyes, C.M.G., D.S.O., presented to the Depot a 12-in. cartridge case, which came from the Kaiser William II. Battery, Knocke, Belgium, and was in action on the 23rd April, 1918. The beam from which the cartridge case is suspended is part of the deck of H.M.S. *Vindictive*. The hours are struck on this gong as on board ship, to accustom recruits to ships' bells when they eventually go afloat.

After the attack on Zeebrugge the remnant of the Fourth Battalion returned to Deal, and the two V.C.'s awarded to the Battalion were allotted by vote to Capt. Bamford, D.S.O., R.M.L.I. and Sergt. N. A. Finch, R.M.A. All that was left of the Battalion entrained for their respective headquarters on Saturday, 27th April and were given an enthusiastic send-off by the civil population.

On 19th July, 1919, Peace Day was celebrated at Deal. Laker, in his "History of Deal," says: "The co-operation of the Royal Marine authorities provided a telling, feature of the celebrations at mid-day. A battalion in blue uniform, headed by the drum and fife band, marched from the barracks to the sea front by way of the Strand, Victoria Road and King Street, and lined the Parade (sea front) from Deal Castle to the top of King Street. The W.R.N.S. formed up on the green in front of the Castle, and the trim little lads of the Depot R.M. Cadet Corps marched to the Pier, headed by their own drum and fife band. Behind the long line of Marines was a dense crowd of civilians. Precisely at noon a signal was given from the bandstand, and this repeated from the Pier, was the indication for the firing of a feu-de-joie, which was given with splendid precision. At a further signal from the Pier there was a flash of steel in the bright sunlight as the Marines fixed bayonets and presented arms for the Royal Salute. Led by the Lord Mayor the civilians sang the National Anthem, and His Worship then read a letter from the Lord Lieutenant of the County conveying a message from the king."

12-IN. CARTRIDGE CASE FROM KAISER WILLIAM II BATTERY, KNOCKE, BELGIUM

On the 10th May. 1928, H.R.H. the Duke of York paid an unofficial visit to the Depot. The compliment paid to the Corps by this visit was undoubtedly due to the good impression made by the R.M. detachment of H.M.S. *Renown* during the tour of T.R.H. the Duke and Duchess of York.

The Duke visited the gymnasium and garrison church, and thence through the North Barracks to the swimming bath. He was shewn recruits at various stages of instruction, from the simplest elementary movement onward. On his return to the officers' mess, the officers and warrant officers had the honour of being presented.

H.R.H. then lunched with the officers in their mess and afterwards inspected the British Legion on the South Barracks green.

THE DUKE OF YORK IN NORTH BARRACKS.

The following is an extract from the letter afterwards written to the Commandant from the Comptroller: -

H.R.H. the Duke of York wishes me to lose no time in writing to say what great satisfaction it gave him to visit the Depot of the Royal Marines at Deal yesterday. The Duke was much struck by the very thorough training, on the most modern lines, given to the young recruits, and the marked progress made by the various squads in the few weeks that they have been under training . . . . "

Thus we will bring to a fitting close this chapter in the story of the Depot- a story not perhaps entirely devoid of interest, but in which there are doubtless many omissions and possibly some errors. For such the chronicler apologises, with the hope that any reader of this journal, who may be in possession of other incidents of historical interest, will communicate with the Editor.

RECORD OF THE BANDS OF THE PORTSMOUTH DIVISION, R.M.L.I.
AND OF THE
DEPOT, ROYAL MARINES, DEAL.
Compiled by Capt. H. T. Tollemache, R.M.

From extracts from the "Globe and Laurel" and the "Musical Times," and from information supplied by Captain J. S. Nicholson. Lieutenant F. J Ricketts, Band Sergeant G. Handford and Mr. W. H. Legallez, ex Band Sergt. Thanks are also due to Captain G. Miller, Grenadier Guards, to Colonel B. C. Gardiner, C.B., and particularly to General Sir H. E. Blumberg, K.CB., who has kindly read over the proofs and added much valuable information.

DEPOT BAND.

When Colonel N. F. Sampson Way, C.B., was commanding the Depot (1889-1892) and the 2nd in Command was Lieut.-Colonel E. W. G. Byam (afterwards Commandant at Gosport), efforts were made to raise a band at the Depot. The issue of the *Mercury* of February 1st, 1890, contains the following notice: "The long cherished idea of a Military Band at Walmer is, we understand, shortly to be realised, the Lords of the Admiralty having received the concurrence of the Treasury in sanctioning the proposal."

An Order in Council of 21st March, 1890, gave authority for 17 musicians in lieu of 17 privates R.M.L.I., stating that the establishment of band would "tend to discipline and good health among recruits." (All recruits, both R.M.A. and R.M.L.I., passed through the Depot at that time.)

No doubt the band also had its N.C.O.'s, with 6 buglers and 4 privates attached, the same as a Headquarter band. In 1900 the musicians were increased to 25, thus being placed on the same footing as Headquarter bands.

A grant of £100 per annum was also made by the Government, and it is understood that the Depot band also received a share of the officers' band subscriptions.

A sergeant, R.M.L.I., was allowed as Bandmaster (it was not until 1897 that a warrant officer was allowed), and Band Sergeant Batson was selected. Batson had already served for 26 years with the Band of the Portsmouth Division, R.M.L.I., and had formerly acted as Band Sergeant under Major Miller.

DEPOT BAND, 1922

The first public appearance of the Band in the Depot seems to have been at a smoking concert in connection with the R.M. Cycle Corps, which owed its origin to the keenness of Major Edye, R.M.L.I., then serving at the Depot. The concert took place on 22nd May, 1890. It is recorded that "at every instrument the execution was admirable. At the close of the performance the members of the new band were loudly cheered, and all, colonel, officers, n.c. officers and men alike, appeared to be highly delighted with the prospect of the new and promising departure in the way of producing a first-class instrumental band for the Walmer Depot."

Considerable difficulty was experienced in obtaining suitable musicians, and there are many quaint legends as to their recruitment. One relates that a cornet player was obtained from a painless dentistry caravan, where his job was to play his high notes at the critical moment.

At the Depot Sports the new band played alternately with the band of the Chatham Division, R.M.L.I., and the first public appearance in Deal seems to have been at the Regatta in September, 1890, when the band played on the Parade. It also gave performances in the Marine Terrace Gardens, as the Rink in South Street was then termed, in connection with "assaults-at-arm" by the gymnastic instructors of the Depot, and on a portable bandstand on Deal sea-front. These open-air performances were a feature of Deal's season, and attracted huge crowds. It took part in its first torchlight tattoo in 1900.

Bandmaster Batson was succeeded in 1897 by Mr. J. S. Nicholson, who came to the R.M.L.I. from the 15th King's Hussars, in which regiment he had served for 17 years. The String Band was formed during his directorship. He became one of the two senior bandmasters in 1916, and was promoted to Musical Director (Lieutenant) as provided by Order in Council of 19th May, 1914.

He became Director of Music when the title was changed in 1921, and retired as Captain on the disbandment of the band. Under his regime, which had lasted 26 years, the band grew in efficiency and became well known, especially in Kent.

Mr. Nicholson had the unique honour of being presented twice in one month to H.M. The King, once when playing at a military lunch, when His Majesty specially sent for him and congratulated him on the splendid efficiency of the band, and once when conducting the string band at a fashionable London festival.

The band proceeded to France in, January 1917 and served there for three months, during which period it gave approximately one hundred concerts and played the 1st Battalion R.M.L.I. back to billets at Engelbelmer on 22nd March, 1917, after the battle of Miraumont, having met them at Martinsart.

In 1918 the band played in the Albert Hall at a special boxing match, which H.R.H. The Prince of Wales attended. Two days later it proceeded to Belgium to entertain various Divisions, and by permission of Lieut.-Colonel N. S. Clutterbuck commanding 1st Battalion R.M.L.I., gave concerts in aid of the War Widows and Orphans, at which it was accorded very enthusiastic receptions.

The following is an extract from a speech made by the Burgomaster of La Bouverie at one of these concerts:-

"The committee who organised this fete beg me to thank you very deeply for the generous audience you kindly brought to this patriotic fete. In our country, where musical art is extensively patronised, your performance of to-day was highly appreciated. We love your land, your King, and your Army that brought us deliverance, and here, where military and civil men are together, we are always very glad to tie again the friendly and grateful chains that bind us to your compatriots.

I congratulate your talented bandmaster and his very good musicians. I beg him to accept this recollection of our fete: It is the usual lamp that guides the brave miner into the depths of the gloomy coal mine. Moreover it is the characteristic emblem of our country, where coal-mining is the most important industry. Bravo to the famous band of the Royal Marines. Bravo to its talented Master. Hurrah to England, its King, its Navy and Army, and thank you again!"

Lord Charles Beresford engaged the band to play at a Rose Show in Trafalgar Square in 1920, and it was subsequently engaged to play at a dinner at Greenwich, which was attended by Their Royal Highnesses the Prince of Wales and the Duke of York.

In 1922, with the Band of the Portsmouth Division, R.M.L.I., it attended the funeral of Prince Louis of Battenberg, and played from St. James' Palace to Westminster.

The Band was disbanded in 1923 on the amalgamation of the R.M.A. and R.M.L.I., its place being taken by the band of the Portsmouth R M.L.I. In actual fact, this new Depot Band was composed of nearly equal numbers of musicians from both bands.

BAND OF THE PORTSMOUTH DIVISION
Marines, 1755-1802; Royal Marines, 1802-1855; Royal Marines Light Infantry, 1855-1923; Depot Royal Marines, 1923 - 30.

The origin of the Band is obscure. It is believed to have been the oldest of the Divisional Bands, and must therefore have been raised prior to 1767, because on the 10th March, 1767, the Plymouth Division made "an agreement with Mr. Antonio Rocca to be enrolled as a Private Marine on 2nd April, 1767, and to receive his discharge when obligation ceases. He was to be allowed to play at halls and concerts for his own advantage with his band, but the service to come first." (Plymouth Order Books.) The probability is that the band at Portsmouth was much the same. Plymouth Orders of 18th June, 1768, also say "Band of Music to wear white stockings and breeches and black buckle gaiters at Guard Mounting."

Bandmasters were usually foreigners, and when they held rank at all, it was only as Staff Sergeants. An Order of Plymouth Division dated 2nd October, 1784, directs the Field Adjutant take "Band, Drums and Fifes under his entire care as to dress and interior economy, and the "beating" of the drummers (*i.e.*, the drums, not their persons, though that also came under his care. - Ed.). The executive part of the music of the band to be under Lieutenants Gibson and Gordan, who have volunteered and undertaken to make them a Martial Band and capable of softer music. The Master of the Band is as heretofore to instruct the Fifes in Martial Tunes only." This appears to be the origin of the Band Committee, and no doubt all Divisions were much the same.

MASTER OF THE BAND 1829

Little is known of the early history of the band, but in 1800 we find a notice of the Portsmouth Division Marines Band taking part in a concert at the Portsmouth Assembly Rooms, then the resort of the fashionable world. Early in the century, too, we find it in gorgeous attire, playing every morning on the old Governor's Green in Portsmouth, during the changing of the town guard. It then consisted of:

2 Flutes
2 Oboes
8 Clarinets
2 Bassoons
4 Horns
2 Trumpets
2 Serpents
1 Bass Horn
4 Trombones
3 Time beaters
Total 30

The "Time-beaters" were black men. The regimental drummers assisted when necessary.

On 11th December, 1797, orders were issued that "A Captain's Guard of Marines, with the Band of the Division under your command, is to march from Portsmouth to attend in Town on 18th inst. which, if possible, is to be commanded by officers who were in the action of 1st June. 1794 (Glorious 1st of June. - Ed.), 14th February (?) - (probably 14th August - Battle of Cape St. Vincent - Ed.) and 11th October last (Camperdown), in order to attend His Majesty to St. Paul's Cathedral on the 19th inst., to offer thanksgiving for the many signal and important victories obtained by his Navy in the course of the present war."

Colours were at first ordered to be taken, but on 14th December this was corrected, as the guard was "not as a guard to His Majesty in procession," but to form part of the procession to St. Paul's with the colours taken from the enemy.

In 1812 it accepted a private engagement, and played at Shadwell House, Wickham, on the coming of age of a young Guards officer.

In February 1821 Lieut.-Colonel Sir Richard Williams R.M. Barracks, Portsmouth, reported to the Admiralty that the period of service of the Master of the Band having expired, he had been discharged in consequence of His Majesty (King George IV) having been graciously pleased to order him to be received into his private band. The letter continues: "I have now an opportunity of enlisting an efficient person, without bounty, to fill that vacancy, named John Smally, aged 29 years, 5 feet 7 inches in height, and reported fit by the surgeon." This appointment was approved by their Lordships.

In the same year Colonel Commandant Robert Moncreiffe, R.M. Barracks, Portsmouth, reported that by His Majesty's Command the Band of the Portsmouth Division had been embarked in the *Active*, to accompany the Royal Squadron to Ireland. Local papers describe how the band went to His Majesty's Palace in the Park at Dublin, and how they played several pieces for His Majesty after dinner on the deck of H.M. Royal Yacht *George*, and were "applauded by the King most heartily."

In 1822 there is a record of a private engagement at a concert given at the Green Row Rooms at Portsmouth. In the same year it attended His Majesty during an autumn cruise; and it seems again in the autumn of 1823 in the Royal Yacht.

It grew in importance during the life of the Prince Consort, being frequently ordered to Osborne, and staying there sometimes for a week at a time. These honours remained until the death of Queen Victoria, when Osborne ceased to be a royal residence.

In 1855 Mr. Earle, then Bandmaster to the Corps, formed a "String Band," since when the band continued to be "double-handed."

In 1858 it had the honour of accompanying Her Majesty Queen Victoria and the Prince Consort in the Royal Yacht when they went to Cherbourg, to be present at the opening of the Grand Napoleon Dock.

It has the distinction of being selected to accompany His Majesty King Edward VII., then Prince of Wales, in H.M.S. *Serapis*, when he visited India in 1875-76 and held the big Durbar there. In commemoration of this occasion the band were authorised to wear the Prince of Wales plume upon the regimental badge in their helmet plates and caps, which they continued to do until their final disbandment in 1930.

By Order in Council of 29th November, 1881, Warrant Rank was introduced into the Corps, and the Bandmasters became Warrant Officers.

In 1884 the band came under the directorship of Mr. George Miller, in succession to Mr Kreyer. Mr. Miller had been bandmaster of the 16th Foot, and afterwards received the appointment of Bandmaster at Sandhurst Military College - when he by chance became acquainted with Sir Arthur Sullivan. There were 115 applicants for the vacant post at Portsmouth, and at this time it was the fashion in all well regulated regiments to have a German bandmaster (and a French cook). The choice was finally reduced to six, of whom Miller was the only Englishman. His acquirements and experience were so unique, however, and his backing by Sir Arthur Sullivan, the Duke of Edinburgh (Colonel-in-Chief of the Corps) and Mr. Dan Godfrey, so influential, that he was selected, and was appointed Bandmaster (W.O.) on 18th November, 1884.

In 1885 the band played at the wedding of Prince Henry of Battenberg.

In Order in Council dated 20th June, 1886. we find the first mention of Musicians allowed by establishment.

Mr. Miller was given the Jubilee Medal in 1887 and the additional Bar in 1897.

In 1892, when His Majesty King Edward VII., as Prince of Wales went on a cruise of convalescence, the band had the honour of accompanying him, and to use His Majesty's own words - characteristic of the band was its depth of tone, "helped him to get well." In the same year 2nd Lieut. Miller gained the Bachelor of Music degree at Cambridge.

Records show that between the years 1890 and 1897 the band played before Her Majesty Queen Victoria, by command, no less than 66 times. It always went to the Royal Yacht when the Queen was at Cowes, but was replaced in King Edward VII.'s reign by the Royal Marine Artillery Band, who were allowed extra personnel for this duty.

When the Adjutant, Captain F. Luard, initiated Torchlight Tattoos, which are now such a great attraction, about the year 1897, the band was the mainstay, and with Mr. Miller's marching songs formed the principal attraction.

MAJOR GEORGE MILLER M.V.O., MUS. BAC., L.R.A.M.

1904, when Captain H. E. Blumberg was Adjutant, the old uniform and drill were introduced for the first time in England on the 200th anniversary of the capture of Gibraltar, and the band under 2nd Lieut. Miller added greatly to the completeness of the spectacle by providing the old airs of the period.

The band accompanied the training battalions to Aldershot on several occasions, and in the big manoeuvres on Salisbury Plain in 1898 it accompanied the 2nd Battalion R M L.I. all through. Mr. Miller, in spite of his age, insisted on accompanying it and leading on foot, and by his encouragement and writing of marching songs was of great assistance.

He was a great upholder of the Military Band, and during his regime the band was noted for its playing on the march, which he never allowed it to shirk. This tradition was well maintained until their final disbandment. A great characteristic of the band was its depth of tone, due to the excellent euphoniums and the old circular basses, to the use of which it clung., Mr. Miller was made Honorary 2nd Lieut, on 28th December, 1898, and 2nd Lieut., on 15th November, 1899. He was the first Bandmaster in the Royal Marines (and almost the first in the Army) to receive this rank.

At Queen Victoria's funeral in 1901 the band played the procession from Osborne House to the East Cowes Pier, and during the embarkation in the Royal Yacht. For this they played a German march, which had been obtained for the funeral of Prince Henry of Battenberg in 1896 and rearranged by Mr. Miller, with a most wonderful and poignant drum accompaniment, with which Her Majesty had been very pleased. The drummers of the R.M.A. and the R.M.L.I. were massed for this occasion, and those who were present say that it was one of the outstanding features of that sad day and there were very few dry eyes at East Cowes.

The Chatham Band R.M.L.I. accompanied Their Royal Highnesses the Duke and Duchess of York (now Their Majesties King George V. and Queen Mary) on their cruise in H.M.S. *Ophir* in 1901, but prior to sailing 2nd Lieut. Miller was sent for by His Majesty and decorated with the Victorian Order 5th Class. In making the presentation His Majesty spoke of the pleasure, which the playing of the band had given to Her Majesty the late Queen.

Subsequently in attendance, first upon King Edward during a cruise of convalescence in 1902 and then upon Queen Alexandra, it went with the Royal Yacht to Portugal, Malta, Italy and Denmark. At Lisbon the late King Carlos made 2nd Lieut. Miller a Chevalier of the Portuguese Order "Notre Dame de La Conception."

At the Coronation Review at Aldershot in 1902 the Massed Bands of the four Divisions accompanied the Royal Marine Brigade. 2nd Lieut. Miller, the senior bandmaster, knowing the great importance of drums in playing the march past on such a big scale, had ordered all the bands to bring as many drummers as they could manage. This they had omitted to do, bringing the one or two musician side drummers only. Fortunately the Portsmouth Band R.M.L.I. had brought about 30 or 40 drummers, and 2nd Lieut. Miller decided to give the others a lesson. At the church parade before the review he massed all the drummers he could collect. The playing of the hymns by massed bands and drums under his direction, particularly "Onward, Christian Soldiers," equalled any cathedral organ.

In 1903 the Glasgow Trades Exhibition presented a sum of money and a diploma of merit to the band, after permission had been given for it to remain an extra week after the termination of their engagement. This allowed of buying two valuable instruments, a "cor anglais" and a violin, which could not possibly have been afforded otherwise. At this time the band went to Glasgow continually. The composition of the band in 1911 was:-

MILITARY

1 Flute	4 Trumpets
2 Oboes	2 Cornets
*14 Clarinets	3 Trombones
2 Bassoons	1 Tenor Horn
4 Horns	1 Euphonium
3 Basses	2 Drums

Total 39

* Including Saxophones and Alto Clarinets.

ORCHESTRAL.

2 Flutes	2 Drums
2 Oboes	3 Trombones

2 Clarinets	1 Harp
2 Bassoons	8 1st Violins
2 Horns	5 2nd Violins
2 Trumpets	3 Violas
3 Double Basses	2 Violoncellos

Total 39

In 1910 a great boon was granted, by which Musicians of Divisional and Depot Bands were allowed to be classed for pension as Corporals, after five years in the recognised establishment of musicians. In 1914 this was extended to the four privates and six buglers who had been attached to the Bands as part of the recognised establishment, and both classes were made eligible for Long Service and Good Conduct gratuity as Corporal. It was not until 1922 or 1923 that all became musicians.

In 1912 a remarkable incident occurred at the Market Hall at Aberdare. During a concert which was being given by the band, several thousands of people were present, when the light failed. 2nd Lieut. Miller took in the situation admirably, and the band continued playing. The programme was abandoned, but the band gave a fine selection of music in the dark for over two hours.

The band always played "Christchurch Bells" as a troop at Church Parade, ever since it can be remembered. It is believed that this is an old Army custom, and is still continued in many regiments. It has no connection with the "Easter Hymn" which was ordered to be played at Church Parade at Plymouth on 8th March, 1791.

For many years the band always played at Henley, going under canvas during the regatta, a holiday which they much enjoyed; and they were also great favourites at Oxford, playing, at the College dances, until the war and consequent expense put a stop to it.

By Order in Council of 19th May, 1914, the Corps was allowed two Musical Directors. with the rank of Honorary Lieutenant, eligible for promotion to Captain after ten years and to Honorary Major after 15 years, and to be compulsorily retired at the age of 65 years. 2nd Lieut. Miller accordingly became Major.

The Portsmouth Band was the first of the Divisional Bands to be sent over to France. They proceeded in November 1916, and rendered excellent service, playing not only for the R.M.L.I. Battalions of the 63rd R.N. Division, but also for the R.M.A. Howitzers in that sector. They met the 2nd Battalion at Abbeville and played them to rest billets at Rue, after the battle of Ancre. They remained in France until January 1917, but Major Miller, whilst doing most invaluable work was taken ill and had to be invalided to England a few weeks before the band returned. He was invalided from the service in March 1917 as the result, having directed the band for 32 years. During this time he and his band had become famous all over the country, so much so, that in the North Country and Midlands the band was known as "Miller's Band." He composed many works,

BAND PORTSMOUTH DIVISION R.M.L.I., 1921

and was the originator of Marching Songs. During his regime the band secured more commissions from Royalty than any other band, and his death in 1927 closed the career of a great and famous Bandmaster. It is authoritively stated that no Bandmaster in any service has received so many Royal acknowledgments for duty done, for pleasure given, or for the band's stirling worth.

He was succeeded by Lieut. B. W. O'Donnell, F.R.A.M., who came from the 7th Hussars in India.

Order in Council of 10th June, 1921, allowed five Directors of Music to the Corps, so that all Bandmasters became Commissioned Officers. They were made Lieutenants on appointment, and Captain after eight years, and the senior Director of Music became Major, provided that he had 15 years' service. It is interesting to note that the Bands of the Royal Marine Artillery and of the Portsmouth and Plymouth Divisions Royal Marine Light Infantry gave a massed concert at Glasgow in 1922, the Musical Directors being three brothers, Lieutenants P. S., B. W. and R. P. O'Donnell respectively.

In 1923, on the amalgamation of the R.M.A. and R.M.L.I., the band, as has already been stated, became the band of the Depot Royal Marines, still remaining under the Directorship of Lieut. B. W. O'Donnell. In 1925 it was chosen to accompany H.R.H. the Prince of Wales to South Africa and South America in H.M.S. *Repulse*. Lieut. O'Donnell was decorated with the Victorian Order after this cruise. In 1927 Lieut. O'Donnell, on retiring to take up appointment as Conductor of the British Broadcasting Company's Military Band, was succeeded by Lieut. F. J. Ricketts, Bandmaster of the Argyll and Sutherland Highlanders. In the same year the band combined with the band of the Royal Corps of Signals in concerts, and in 1928 with the band of the Chatham Division under Captain P. S. O'Donnell, in concerts given at the Kelvin Hall. Glasgow, in which town it gained great popularity. The last concert given by the Band prior to its disbandment was at the Kelvin Hall.

On the disbandment of the band on 1st October, 1930, Lieut. Ricketts became Director of Music at the Plymouth Division, and the musicians were approximately equally divided between the three Divisional Bands.

There were many families in the Band in which son had succeeded father (the names of Miller, Legallez, Newbold and Williams will be recalled), and with its disbandment there passed a unit which had attained fame and had been in existence for at least 160 years.

RECORDS CORRECTION.

We are asked by Captain H. T. Tollemache to correct a statement which appeared on p. 236 of the Record section of the Journal for September. It is stated therein -There were many families in the Band in which son had succeeded father (the names of Miller, Legallez, Newbold and Williams will be recalled): This is incorrect as regards the Legallez family, as the two Band Sergeants of that name were brothers, Frank Legallez being seven years junior to W. H. Legallez.

HISTORY OF THE R.M.A. DIVISION.

Prior to the Royal Marine Artillery being formed into a separate Division they led a nomad existence between Chatham, Portsmouth, Landguard Fort and Plymouth. In 1804 an Artillery Company was raised at each of the Marine Divisions - Chatham, Portsmouth and Plymouth. The Officers were on the general list of the Corps, and the men were picked as for Grenadier Companies in the line regiments.

The officers selected to command the companies were Captain R. Williams†, Portsmouth (senior officer), Captain T. Abernethie*, Plymouth, and Captain W. Minto, Chatham.

†Bt. Lt.-Colonel Sir Richard Williams, K.C.B., was the first Commanding Officer officially appointed as such. He was appointed Major Commandant of the R.M.A. on 1st January, 1816. They were not entirely independent however, as they came under the nearest Royal Marine Division for all administration, pay, etc. †Sir Richard Williams remained in command of the R.M.A. till 1827, when he was appointed to command the Portsmouth Division. He was succeeded by Captain T. A. Parke as senior officer R.M.A. Companies.

*Captain Abernethie became Senior Officer R.M.A. Companies on the promotion of Capt. Williams to Major in 1809 and on his own promotion in 1815 Captain Minto assumed the duties until Sir Richard Williams was again appointed.

The newly formed branch of the Corps was at once utilised, for in September 1804, in consequence of the differences existing between the commanders of bomb-vessels and the officers Royal Regiment of Artillery, it was deemed expedient to remove the Royal Artillery from the bomb vessels and supply their places by the Royal Marine Artillery. These were almost immediately required to prevent the collection of the enemy's flotilla at Boulogne, and although the men were only half trained, they appear to have acquitted themselves well. The detachments were, however, relieved by fully qualified Marine Artillerymen as they became available.

In 1805 a company was added at Woolwich, and the following year a portion were sent to Landguard Fort to carry out experiments for rangetakers for 13-in. and 10-in. sea service mortars.

On the 21st March, 1813, the R.M.A. Company at Chatham went to Fort Pitt Barracks, Chatham, and by order of the Commandant Chatham Division their new parade was called Melville Parade, in honour of Lord Viscount Melville, who first established the R.M.A.; the walk was called Clarence Walk, in honour of the Duke of Clarence, Lord High Admiral and General of Marines, afterwards King William IV., and the terrace was called Minto Terrace, in honour of Captain Minto, then Commanding Officer of the Chatham R.M.A. Company.

In 1816 all four R.M.A. Companies were transferred to Chatham. At this time the ordnance for their practice consisted of two iron and service mortars, one 18-pdr. iron gun, mounted on a sea service carriage, with breechings and carriage as used in H.M. ships; a brigade of light 6-pdr. and two light 5-in. howitzers .

In 1817 the R.M.A. were increased to eight companies, when, "in order that they might be fully instructed in field practice and the services with projectiles, etc., Fort Monckton, situated at the entrance of Portsmouth Harbour, at the Kicker Point, with the barracks at Haslar, were given up to them. Quarters were built for the officers, a mess room and an academy were formed, and the business of education immediately commenced under the able Mathematical Master Mr. Joseph Edwards.

This was a great improvement to the circumscribed means for practice in gunnery at Chatham. "Practising (sic) batteries were formed in Stokes Bay and field equipage and everything necessary were provided. They successfully combined theory with practice, and were enabled from actual ranges to form from their own immediate observation the tables of practice from charges of 2 pounds to 20 pounds of powder."

On leaving Chatham these quarters were not immediately available. In consequence, about 7th June, 1817, four companies, under the command of Sir Richard Williams marched into Fort Cumberland, the remaining four being stationed at the four several headquarters of the Corps. Their stay at Fort Cumberland appears to have been of very short duration, for in December the same year we find an order by the Commanding Officer R.M.A. stationed at Fort Monckton, Stokes Bay, warning the men of the R.M.A. against the habit of cutting the hair from the cows tails in the fields for the purpose of making brushes for their musket locks.

In 1822, in consequence of fever and ague having broken out among them, they were sent to the Upper Barracks, Chatham, where they remained for nearly two years, after which the R.M.A. (800 strong) left Chatham for Portsmouth. "The premises of the late W. Turner, Esq., in the High Street, and in St. Thomas' Street, were purchased by the Government for the permanent accommodation and lodging and mess rooms for the Officers." These premises. 110 High Street, are now occupied by the Phoenix Lodge No. 257 in the Grand Lodge of England and one of the oldest Marine Lodges, nearly all the R.M.A. officers who were Freemasons belonged to this Lodge.

"The men were accommodated in the Victualling Store in the 'new' Gunwharf, which was converted for their use," and a small detachment was stationed at Fort Cumberland. Permission was given for them to use various Artillery buildings on Southsea Common, the place of arms at Eastney, the Ravelin and Magazines at Fort Cumberland and also to erect butts and batteries on the ordnance waste at Fort Cumberland. They were also allowed by the Duke of Norfolk to carry out their exercises on the south side of Hayling Island.

In 1827 "the Duke of Clarence inspected Mortar practice at Fort Cumberland, also a new mode of disembarking heavy pieces of ordnance when the surf was so great on a beach that no boat could ground the beach to do it. A line was thrown ashore from the boat by which the gun was lashed to a small mortar. The guns were then disengaged from the boat, and the party to whom the line had been conveyed drew it to the shore. Afterwards the gun carriage was sent ashore in a similar way, the gun refixed to the carriage and fired. The whole service was effected in 14 ½ minutes."

In 1828 the Four-house barracks adjoining the old Clarence Barracks was appropriated to the use of the R.M.A. companies. They were thus quartered quite close to the Portsmouth Division.

In 1830 the Naval School of Gunnery was started in the "*Excellent*." In the establishment of officers and crew of the "*Excellent*" a Lieutenant, R.M.A. three n.c.o.'s and two privates R.M.A. were included in the complement.- "They were appointed for the theoretical instruction of Naval Officers and seamen gunners, and also to instruct them in the laboratory works required for the Naval service, such as making rockets for signals, filling tubes, new priming them, and filling cartridges, etc., etc."

Towards the end of 1831, as a result of the growth of the "*Excellent*," the R.M.A. were reduced to four companies and the next year were abolished, though an extra Field Officer as Director of Laboratory, a Sergt.-Major and two companies were allowed to the Portsmouth Division, to act as Artillery Companies. They thus again came under the immediate command, of Sir Richard Williams. This nucleus occupied a few rooms, with two or three at Fort Cumberland, where all training was carried on.

In 1835 their strength began to gradually increase, till in 1841 it was three companies.

In 1837 "Major-General Sir James Cockburn inspected the Field Battery of the R.M.A. and then the laboratory and repository exercises and drills at the 'Fire Barn' which was situated on Southsea Common opposite to Clarence Parade West. After this various gun and mortar practices were carried out, as well as practice with Congreve rockets, at Fort Cumberland. He afterwards witnessed the firing of live shell. etc., at a floating target at a distance of 1,100 yards; the shell burst with beautiful effect and precision just as it reached the destined spot.

On the increase of the R.M.A. their Headquarters were moved back to the Gunwharf Barracks (old Victualling Store), and as there became insufficient room for the men there and at Fort Cumberland, companies were distributed between the Marine Divisions, one company being for a time at the old Mill Bay Barracks. Plymouth. By 1847 they had increased to ten companies.

The R.M.A. Officers' Mess at this time must have been in the Gunwharf Barracks, for on the 11th November, 1842, we read of the Officers giving a ball there, with the Marine Band in attendance.

In 1848, when the Portsmouth Division was transferred from Portsmouth to Forton Barracks, the Commandant Portsmouth Division was instructed to cause the sea service gun drill battery on Southsea Common to be given over with its equipment to the charge of the Director of the Laboratory for the use of the Artillery companies. and it continued to be so used by them till 1859, when they moved to Fort Cumberland. This was the old R.N. Reserve Battery at the back of Southsea Castle.

In 1858 the Admiralty exchanged the Gunwharf Barracks for Fort Cumberland, and the R.M.A. Headquarters took possession the following year. On 22nd October, 1859, the R.M.A., now 16 companies, were formed into a separate Division, and ceased to be attached to Forton Barracks for administration, pay, etc. By Order in Council of 21st March, 1862, the officers were placed on a separate list, and the Corps became Royal Marine Light Infantry and Royal Marine Artillery. Up to this date the names were Royal Marines Light Infantry and Royal Marines Artillery.

FORT CUMBERLAND.

Fort Cumberland, built by English convict labour, was completed in 1803. The convicts appear to have lived in the Fort after its completion, as one reads that in 1805 the convicts became very troublesome, and the men of the 8th Veteran Battalion had to be called out.

1n 1806 they again gave trouble.

In 1810 the convicts living in the Fort (between 200 and 300 strong) made a desperate effort to escape, but failed to overpower the guard of the Veteran Battalion.

The Fort, which was part of the Duke of Richmond's plan for fortifying the coast, was looked upon as extravagant and unnecessary. It was built round Cumberland Farm House, used by the Duke of Cumberland, of Culloden fame, as a shooting lodge, which building, occupying a slight rise, is known as "Monkey Island." This, when the R.M.A. first occupied Fort Cumberland, was used as the Commandant s, Adjutant s and Paymaster s offices, Orderly Room and Junior N.C.O.s' library, later as Repository lecture rooms, and more recently, when all the inside beams and flooring

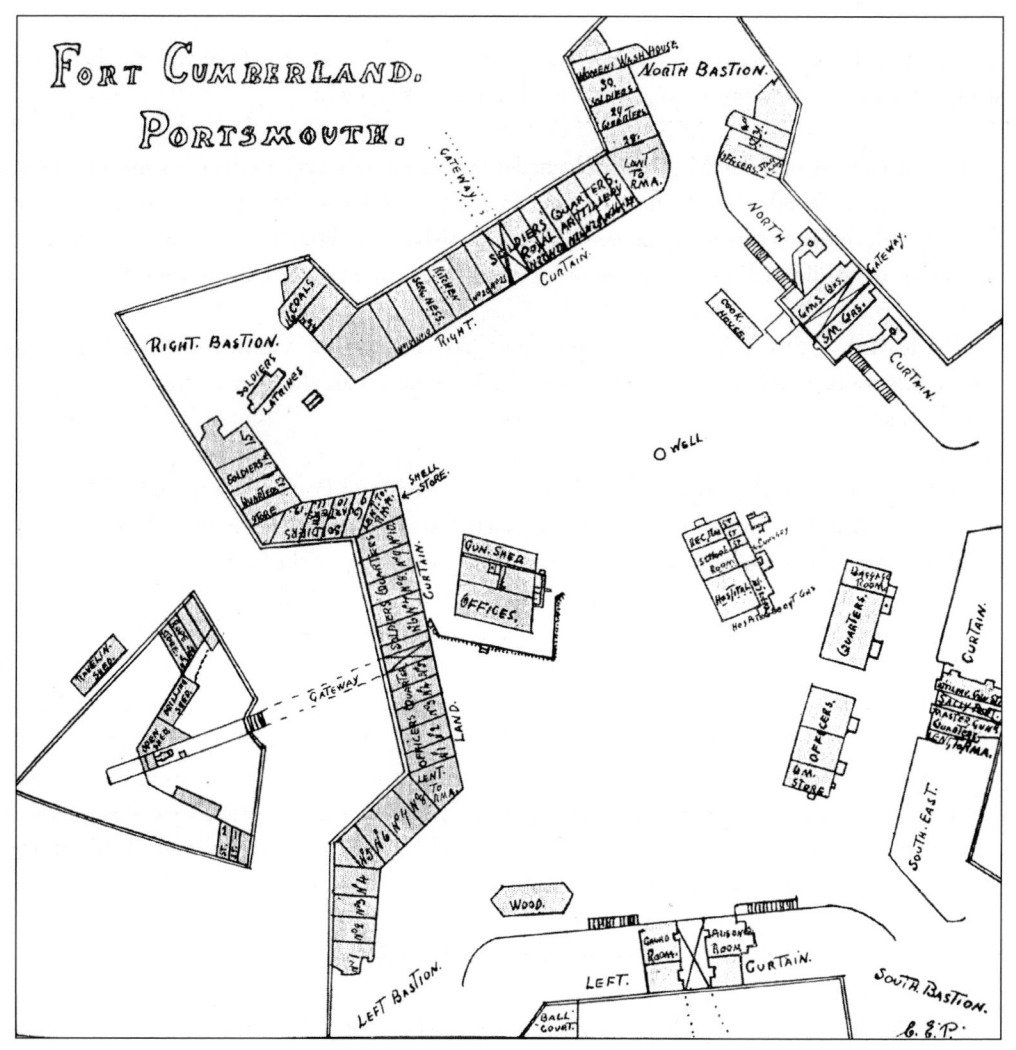

Fort Cumberland

rotted away, was gutted, re-roofed and made into a rope shed. The other old building, said to have been a keeper's lodge, with some farm buildings or barns attached, was utilised as a School, the Infirmary and Infirmary Sergeants quarters being added.

In course of time the school room was embodied in the infirmary and was used as such until an infirmary was built in Eastney Fort East, when it became the Land Service lecture room.

The Cook House was built in 1860, and the Officers' quarters, 1-4, with a billiard room at the north end, and quartermaster's store at the south end about the same time. It is said that the officers' quarters were converted from quarters used by officers or warders of the convicts, and they do appear to be over 100 years old. The bricks were made from clay from the Glory Hole; traces of brick-kilns still exist in the musketry drill field and one or two of the allotment gardens between the field and the road.

From about 1882 to 1890 the room built as a Q.M. store at the south end was used as a classroom for the Prob. 2nd Lieuts. R.M.LI. who underwent their military course there. The Military Instructor lived in the house next door.

The Fort was drained and water laid on in 1859-60, prior to which the water supply consisted of a well in the centre of the parade, the water of which was rather brackish (but considered "by no means unwholesome"). This was closed in and lost sight of until a tractor one day sat down on it. Rats infested the Fort to such an "annoying degree" as to warrant application being made for a rat-catcher.

Two batteries were constructed in Fort Cumberland, by the Dockyard, one a broadside battery in the N.E. bastion, the other a pivot battery near the south gate.

Near Langstone Ferry was the Point battery of two guns, Armstrong Pattern, mounted in 1860, the convicts' mortuary being used as the Officer Instructor's office.

The Officers occupied the casemates in the land curtain Nos. 1-5; No. 1 was used as the anteroom and library, and the remaining casemates by the men (R.A. and R.M.A.), except that used by the master gunners R.A., viz., the one in rear of No. 3 house. The R.A. manned the guns, 18 and 32-pdrs. M.L., occupying No. 16-32.

The only means of recreation for the men were one skittle alley (lighted by tallow candles), parallel bars, and quoits in the ditch, while the junior N.C.O.s had a bagatelle table in the canteen parlour. Later a theatre was started in the battery near the N.E. bastion.

At one period boxing was a popular source of amusement, and a very formidable team of bruisers came into existence.

The Officers had the fives courts (ball court) outside the south gate, and indulged in a great deal of boating.

In No. 1 passage can still be seen two iron hooks secured into the staircase and used for gymnastic purposes.

The cells or strong room (situated to the east of the south gate) contained an iron cage for the reception of refractory prisoners. The old Guard Room is situated to the west of the south gate. It is interesting to note that all entrances to the Fort had very strong double doors (inner and outer), and it may reasonably be supposed that these were kept either barred and locked, or so locked at sunset, the only exit and entry after that time being by a small wicket gate in the south of the doors, the keys these gates being always retained by the Commander of the Guard.

The R.A. had charge of armaments at Fort Cumberland and both forts at Eastney.

Under an old Army Occupation return the Fort held 23 officers and 701 men, but shortly after the R.M.A. took over the official return showed only half this number.

EASTNEY AND SOUTHSEA.

At this time from Eastney to the South Parade Pier (original pier, opened 1879) and northwards of this line, the country consisted of open fields, except round about the present Canoe Lake which was a rough wilderness of furze bushes with a natural lake in wet weather. There was a stump of a windmill and a cottage surrounded by a high wall, where the corner house of Granada Road, "Beach Tower," now stands. The only buildings in this space were Craneswater, Cumberland House, Norman Court, Cheduba and Willurah.

Further to the west was the East Hants cricket ground, which was situated where Taswell and Worthing Roads now are, the pavilion being at the north end in Duncan Road.

Southsea Common was more or less a snipe marsh, and officers proceeding from the Gunwharf Barracks to Fort Cumberland often took a shot gun with them in winter, in the hope of picking up a snipe on the way.

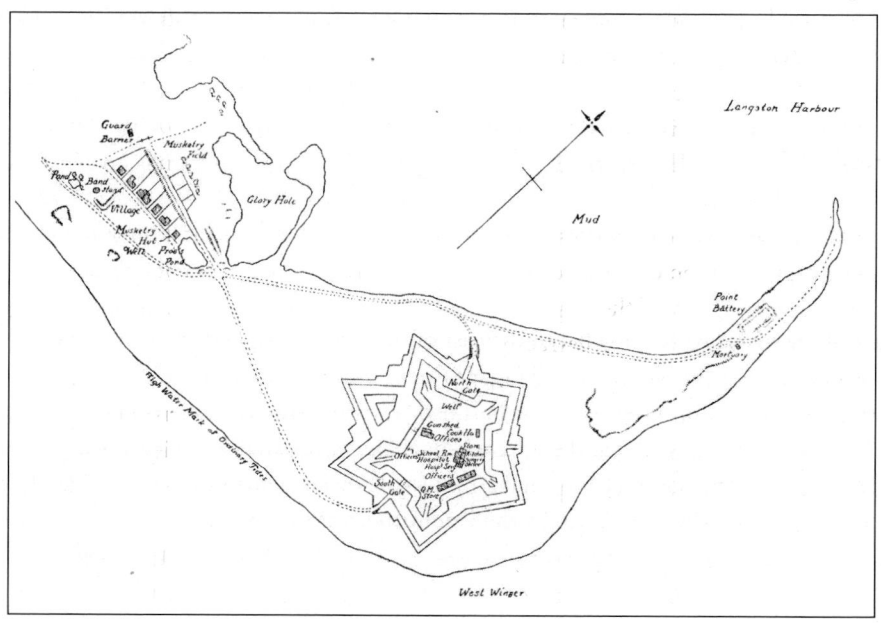

Eastney village, consisting of a few small cottages and a farm, used to stand just west of Proe's Pond, round which, there was an orchard. The whole estate east of the present sports field was sold to the crown in 1845. James Osmond, trustee of the Order of the Baptists, a sect at that time much persecuted, occupied the farm in 1716. Meetings were held at the farm and converts baptized by immersion in the small pond, well stocked with carp, frogs and sticklebacks.

Proe's house, close to the pond of that name, was demolished in 1877, its end being hastened from all accounts by the firing of guns and mortars in its vicinity. The pond was not filled in till 1925-6. Proe (formerly spelt Proux) was a French refugee employed by the English Government during the wars at the beginning of the last century. Having rendered some personal service to the Duke of Kent, he was allowed to live there rent free. His widow continued to reside there until 1862, although the property had been purchased by the Crown, a concession in consideration of the fact that she had occupied this and the adjacent property for nearly fifty years. Mrs. Proe's cart, driven by the excellent Miss Proe, may be seen in the picture of Proe's farm. It was a sort of appendage of Fort H.Q. Mess, and trundled in and out to High Street (then the centre of life) several times a day carrying officers. It was eventually superceded by an omnibus, which every morning brought out the Commandant, and later on (two hours later, say) restored him to his friends in Southsea. It is believed Proe's cart had at times also fulfilled the same honourable office.

On Mrs. Proe's death the cottage became the quarters of Staff Sergeant Rowlatt, Musketry Instructor, and with another small brick hut was taken over by the Musketry Department.

Coastguard cottages extended along the front beyond the barrier to the westward, the small cottage at the cross roads being used as a guardroom for a corporal's guard. Later this was the musketry rangeman's quarters, and then a store. This was demolished in 1896.

EASTNEY BARRACKS.

In 1862 the new barracks at Eastney were commenced. They were thus described by a writer of that date:, "The Barracks will stand on an extensive piece of ground, and its front will have a strong defensive work consisting of a long curtain with a heavy work at either end (Eastney Fort East and Fort West) in line with the sea beach, each containing two guns in cavalier bastions and seven guns in embrasures. The whole is fronted and flanked by a deep ditch, having a low wall next the escarp of the work for rifle fire. The escarp of the work itself is reveted with flints and concrete."

A critic of the same date writes thus about them: "The new Barracks for the R.M.A. at Portsmouth have just been commenced in the rear of a heavy Coast Fort commenced at the same time, and mounting guns of the largest calibre, so that in case of attack, all shots missing the batteries will plump right into the barracks.

In December 1863 the contractor complained of great inconvenience caused by the numberless soldiers, in some cases accompanied by their wives and families, wishing to view the men's quarters; these were the earliest buildings completed.

On the 7th November, 1864, the first detachment (Depot from Fort Elson) marched in, but it was not until the 1st April, 1865, that a part of the new barracks was turned over to the Barrackmaster,

PROE'S FARM. THE ORIGINAL BUILDINGS.

and a volunteer detachment from the Chatham and Woolwich Divisions occupied rooms 7-8, 13-16, the Band 17-18, and the Canteen rooms 19-20. There were quarters for four staff sergeants behind the guardroom, there being two, back to back, on either side of the armourer's shop, and in addition quarters for the paymaster's chief clerk over the old pay office. The two quarters at the eastern end were occupied by the sergeants-major until 1899, when new houses were built for them in front of the provost sergeant's quarters; the old sergeants-major quarters became offices for the 1st and 3rd Q.M. The officers occupied G block for their mess and ante-rooms until the block comprising officers' mess and single officers' quarters was completed at the end of 1865. In 1894 the officers' mess was improved by the addition of a conservatory. Before this was built the mess room was so cold that in the winter officers often had to wear their great coats at mess.

The field officers' quarters (Teapot Row) were built in 1866, also the block of buildings containing the Commandant's office. Originally, besides the two married quarters on the south side there were two flats above the Commandant's office, the lower one being the Adjutant's quarters, and the top floor being usually allocated to a junior officer on the headquarter staff. This block went by the name of "Scandal Alley."

THE PARADE LOOKING EAST, CIRCA 1870

By 1867 the R.M.A. were in complete occupation of the Barracks, including the married quarters and schools north of the main block of buildings. The drill shed, detention quarters and officers' stables were also built.

The drainage was at first defective, and several deaths occurred from typhoid. The ventilating shaft near the boathouse was erected in consequence.

S.S. BATTERIES.

As previously stated, the R.M.A. had a gun drill battery on Southsea Common till 1859, when a battery was built at Eastney. It was situated near the cross roads on the opposite side to Ivy Cottage, and contained 64-pdrs. Mounted on trucks. Practice was carried out from them at targets moored in the Langstone channel. This battery was known as the garden battery, and the small pond to the south of it as the garden pond.

Near this battery, out in the open, were two 10-in. mortar batteries and one 13-in. mortar on a turn-table, of the same pattern as those used in bomb boats during the Crimean war. They were fired at a mark (disc on a pole) on the glacis near the south gate of Fort Cumberland, about 700 yards range. The mortar shells were not filled, only fired with a time fuze. They were collected for future use from where they happened to fall about the glacis. The actual mortars can now be seen round the parade and on top of two of the arches in the Barracks.

There was also in use about this time an old S.S. Battery, situated at the Point near Langstone Ferry, which was used when all the R.M.A. were at Fort Cumberland till about 1876-7. It is believed the armament was 32-pdr. S.B. guns. Near this battery was a 6-pdr. S.B., mounted on a platform, which by turning a winch wheel was made to represent a ship rolling. Recruits fired from this solid shot (recovered afterwards from the sand butt) at a target 600 yards distant and quite close to Fort Cumberland. The platform was afterwards moved to where the M.G. battery now stands, and a 9-pdr. M.L. was fired from it out to sea.

The drill shed was used for standing gun drill in 1865, but in 1868 a lecture hut was fitted up for the instruction of sea service squads: formerly this hut was a store room for the Point Battery.

After this the main battery was built; there were one 10-in., one 9-in., one 8-in. R.M.L., 64-pdr. and some 7-in. on the broadside, and two 40-pdr. R.B.L. and one or two 20-pdr. Armstrong, also Nordenfelts in the Bow battery. In the Battery were kept one or two 9-pdr. field guns on naval carriages.

In 1885 a 6-in. B.L. 80-pdr. Armstrong had been added on the broadside, and a Hotchkiss 6-pdr. and Nordenfelt 6-pdr. in the Bow battery. 64-pdr. firing from the main battery took place at moored targets out to sea, and in later years 4.7 - and 12-pdr. guns were used for practice.

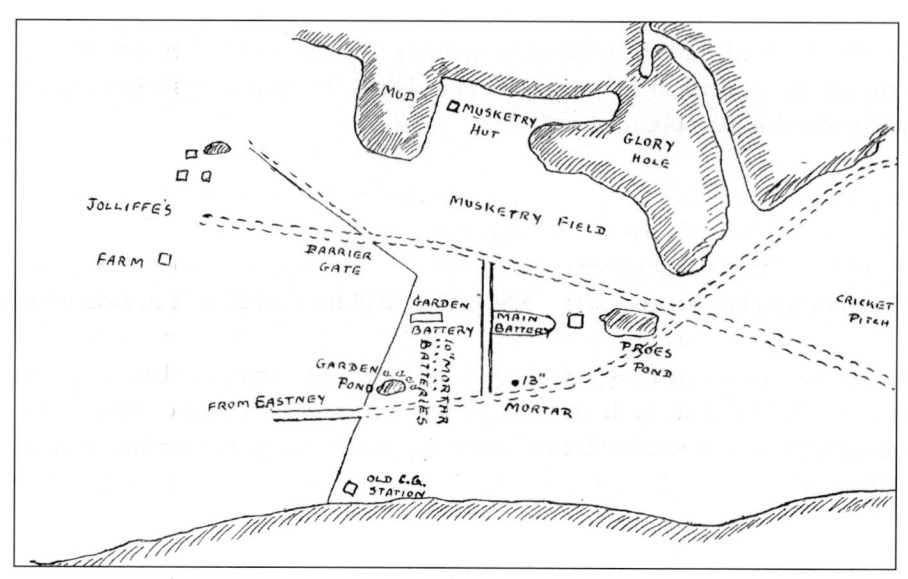

PLAN SHOWING GARDEN BATTERY AND MORTAR BATTERIES

In 1886 the wooden structure inside the barracks N.E. of the gymnasium was built and mounted 6-in. B.L. guns (V.B. Mountings). It was at first used for recruit classes, and later for spotting and deflection teacher.

Throughout the war this building was used as the Brigade Depot Q.M.'s store and office and since January 1921 as a shoemakers' shop.

In 1893 a 9.2-in. gun was mounted in a firing position (en barbette) due east of the main battery near Proe's Pond. This gun was of obsolescent type when mounted. It was used by the R.M.A. for drill and was also included in the defence scheme of the Port, but was never actually fired.

In 1896 an ammunition room, with offices for the I. of G. and Q.M.S. I. of G. was built between the main and garden batteries, and the M.G. Battery between the main battery and the 9.2-in. In it was a 3-pdr. Hotchkiss mounted on a revolving platform. Firing was carried out to sea, and the noise from the corrugated-iron roof and sides was terrific.

The garden battery was demolished when these new buildings were taken over, and as soon as the demolition was complete the old mortar parapet was levelled and the garden pond filled in.

By 1898 all M.L. guns had disappeared and the armament of the main battery, consisted of two 6-in. Q.F. guns in casemates, one 4.7-in. Q.F. and 6-in. Q.F.C. on the broadside, and 12-pdr. Q.F.'s in the Bow battery.

The 10-in. M.L. gun (which had been retained to enable R.M.A. detachments competing at Shoeburyness to have 10-in. gun drill) was eventually turned over to the I. of G. repository.

In 1913 the 12-in. turret was taken into use, and in 1918 the Director Tower was fitted in place of the rangefinder, which had been in use since 1902. The bell used as a ship's bell in the battery was originally the bell of the old Crinoline Church.

RIFLE RANGES.

In 1885 a 600 yard Range was in use, with four iron plate targets, and about 1887 Blands Butts No. 4 (Musketry Hut) was completed. With the issue of the .303-in. rifle in 1895 it was found that the existing range was no longer safe, and in 1896-7 the dockyard constructed an 8-target range (canvas targets), with a huge stop butt behind, and at the same time built a "floating" road on faggots across the mud, to divert the Hayling Island traffic during such times as firing was taking place. This range was lengthened to 800 yards, the last 200 yards being reclaimed from the "Glory Hole."

Prior to this, the old Mortar Butt on the glacis near the south gate of Fort Cumberland was used when firing at 800 yards from a firing point a short distance in front of present musketry hut.

In 1902 a 1,000 yards firing point was built to give practice to skilled shots, and a small four-target range (two mantlets, fitted with four Spencer targets) was constructed to the eastward of the main range and running back to 500 yards. This range enabled recruits and trained soldiers to carry out practices at the same time, and also offered greater facilities for naval and military units to carry out musketry courses on the Eastney range.

About 1912-3 the main range was extended by the addition of eight more targets on the east end of the existing butt.

GROUNDS.

The lawns and shrubberies were laid out under the direction of General Barnard, C.B., when Commandant. In 1865 R.M.A. fatigue parties constructed the new road from the Barrier Gate to Eastney Barracks, the hedge being planted and gardens laid out at the same time. The Parade Ground was completed four years later. The officers' tennis courts were going in 1878, and La Crosse was introduced by Major F.H. Poore in 1879 and played on the Parade.

The men's (gunners) lawn, which had at various periods during many years been used as a drill ground, also for football and hockey by officers, was re-conditioned in 1921 and laid out as tennis courts.

GOLF.

In 1890 a nine-hole golf course was made on the glacis of Fort Cumberland. The greens were never very good, but it continued to be played on till about 1902-3.

DRILL FIELD.

All the grounds which are now used for football, cricket, W.O.s. and Sergeants tennis courts, allotments, etc., originally belonged to Farmer Joliffe, whose farm extended to the north beyond the present Henderson Road.

At this time the drill field was an arable field of 33 acres. In 1889 the Portsmouth Corporation wanted ground east of Fort Cumberland for an outfall and tanks for their drainage system. After negotiations the field was bought from the owner by the Corporation and exchanged with the Government for the ground beyond the fort.

The present bank-bounded cricket ground was commenced the following year, the rest of the field being gradually laid down to grass, to be used when ready for drill purposes. About 40 tons of chalk was obtained from Paulsgrove chalk pit to be laid under the centre of the cricket ground. Capt. A. L. S. Burrowes was the chief architect and leveller of this, and it is believed it was opened for cricket matches in 1892. In 1893 it was in going order and the pavilion up. Before this the pitch on Fort Cumberland glacis had been used for purely R.M.A. cricket, both among officers and men, all regimental and garrison matches being played at Hilsea (present Grammar School ground), then the garrison ground. The present U.S. Recreation Ground was opened in 1881, when all regimental and garrison matches were played there till 1914. Since the war the U.S. Ground has seldom been used by R.M. officers or men.

In 1898 the redoubt at the back of the Officers' mess in the drill field was levelled and the ditch filled in. This had been originally built partly for instruction and partly defensive work upon which to practice "the attack," but it proved of little use. This gave an additional two acres of ground to the drill field. In 1901 a further improvement was made, the piece of the drill field east of the officers' mess was levelled, drained and fenced for a football ground, and after being sown, was ready for the season 1902-3; the cost was £100 and the labour was principally provided in barracks.

MAKING THE FOOTBALL GROUND, 1901-2.

In 1907 the Sergeants' tennis courts were made. The School of Music ground was levelled and first used in 1909, and the adjacent ground has been gradually levelled since. The sports pavilion near No. 1 football ground was erected out of the R.M.A. War Memorial Fund. The W.O.s' tennis courts were made in 1922.

THE SCHOOLS.

The Schools were used for boys and men of the Division, and also for the sons and daughters of the Marines. In 1894 they were placed under inspection by the Education Department, to enable them to become eligible for a grant, and in 1921 the Education Authorities forced the Admiralty to close the school for boys and girls, and the Marine staff returned to duty. After this date only serving Marines and Musicians received instruction there. About 1904-5 part of school buildings were converted into married quarters.

RECRUITS.

In 1869, on the establishment of the Depot, Royal Marines, Deal, on its present basis, the Depot Company was transferred there, and remained till November 1893, when owing to overcrowding, they were, with their instructors, gymnastic staff, etc., in all about 200, brought back to Eastney, temporarily returning to the R.M. Depot at the end of 1896. In September 1897, on the increase of the Corps, the recruits were again brought to Eastney, and occupied portions of E. F and G blocks.

In 1901 the old married quarters were converted to single men's quarters, the recruits, then 450 in number, were transferred to these buildings, the recruits occupying the major portion and H.Q. companies occupying the remainder.

R.N. SCHOOL OF MUSIC.

On July 22nd, 1903, the R.N. School of Music was formed at Eastney and took over part of the eastern half of the old married quarters (K block). The first party consisted of 34 ratings from H.M.S. *Impregnable* and *Lion,* under Ch. Bandmaster Lidiard.

In 1908 the R.N. Band were all concentrated at Eastney and took over H block in addition, and in course of time the whole of the buildings.

SICK QUARTERS.

Prior to 1866 part of an old building in Fort Cumberland was used as a Hospital, but after that year an Infirmary was built in Eastney Fort East. The present Infirmary was built in 1881.

In 1900 a disinfector was installed, and in 1918, after the influenza epidemic, a spraying chamber was built.

In 1904 the Dispensary and women's waiting rooms were completed. Formerly a portion of the building between the schools and the old married quarters was used for this purpose, with an entrance from between the main gate and the coal shed, opposite the guard room.

Highland House was the "sick house" for married families between 1892 and 1904, after which date a house in Highland Road was used.

HIGHLAND HOUSE.

Highland House was bought by the Crown and converted into a Quartermaster's residence in 1888, and remained so until 1892. After this it became the "sick house" for married families until the end of 1904. From this date the house was more or less derelict, till taken over by the foreman of works in 1907. In 1926 it became the Chaplain's house.

The SIGNAL SCHOOL.

(Ivy Cottage) was originally built as a mess for the *"Excellent's"* seamen when going through field gun training on the Eastney ranges.

CHURCH.

In 1905 the Church of St. Andrew's was completed and took the place of the old Crinoline structure, which stood on the ground between the Field Officers' quarters and the Officers' gardens. The "Crinoline" Church was built as a hospital for the Crimea; (Editor's Note: this was actually a myth, it was never in the Crimea - see RMHS SP44 The Crinoline Church by Dennis Bill) on its return it did duty for St. Simon's and St. Bartholomew's until the permanent churches were built, and was then bought by the Admiralty for duty at Eastney. It held 800.

The foundation stone of the new church was laid by H.R.H. the Princess of Wales on the 16th March, 1904, and was dedicated by the Lord Bishop of Winchester on the 17th November, 1905. It was constructed of Rowlands Castle red bricks, with Portland and Bath stone dressing. It has accommodation for 1,000 people, and is of the early English style of architecture. The reredos was erected out of the R.M.A. War Memorial Fund.

The MEMORIAL TO GENERAL LUMSDEN, V.C., D.S.O., was erected by his comrades of all ranks in R.M.A. and Divisions of the Army in which he served in France and Belgium.

OTHER BUILDINGS ERECTED SINCE 1867.

1870-1 The Clock and Water Tower. This was originally built to provide the necessary force of water for the fire mains. The clock was made in 1784 by Wm. Dutton, London, and was formerly the Woolwich Dockyard clock.

1884 Racquet Court - thoroughly re-conditioned in 1901.

CRINOLINE CHURCH

MARRIED OFFICERS' QUARTERS AND TOWER

1886 Carpenters' Shop and Shooting Gallery.

1887 Blacksmiths' Shop.

1890 Wooden floor of drill shed replaced by asphalt. Soon afterwards a roller skating club was formed at Eastney.

1892 Band Practice Room and Tailors' Shop.

1893 Clothing Shed between the Store and Armourers' Shop.

1895 Bowling Alley converted into a billiard room for the men.

1898 Gymnasium.

1899 The New Theatre. The original theatre was built out of canteen funds.

1900 New Boiler House,

1901 Old Married Quarters converted to single men's quarters.

1904 The Canteen was rebuilt and enlarged.

1905 A Telephone Exchange was installed in the barracks and situated in the guardroom. The Swimming Baths and Technical Training Instruction Room (now used as a garage) were built. The technical training classes were formed at Eastney two years previously, and were the origin of what is now termed Vocational Training.

The new Pay Office building was completed.

1911 Sergeants' cubicles.

1913 Three new Coastguard houses were built in place of the old cottages, and in 1923 the remaining Coastguard buildings were completed. These are now Staff quarters.

In 1921 the new Cookhouse was built; the old cookhouse then became the butchers' shop and provision store. The Barber's shop was removed to the old butcher's shop and the old barber's shop pulled down. At the same time the junior N.C.O.s' Club was removed from the bar parlour in the wet canteen to its present position near the barber's shop.

In 1921-2 the promenade in front of the barracks was made and Eastney Barracks grounds ceased to extend to the sea.

In 1923 the R.M.A. and R.M.L.I. were re-amalgamated into the Corps of Royal Marines, and Eastney Barracks became the Home of the Portsmouth Division.

THE WOOLWICH DIVISION.

Until 1805, there had been no Regiment associated with the garrison of Woolwich other than the Royal Artillery but in that year, consequent on the vast and increasing importance of the Royal Navy, a 4th Division of Royal Marines was ordered to be formed by Lord Barham.

It was humorously termed the "Court Division," owing to its proximity to London. It was at first small and was located in the Dockyard and in the *Dover* - 44 guns - which had been prepared as a floating barracks for the new Division. The *Dover* was placed alongside the upper end of Woolwich,

R.M. BARRACKS NEARING COMPLETION. THE LONDON ILLUSTRATED NEWS, JAN. 22, 1848

near the mast houses, close to the quay. From the quay to the ship was a platform, which made the vessel quite easy of access and in every sense as commodious as land barracks. On board this vessel were generally from three to four hundred of the Woolwich Division with a proportionate number of Officers. A certain number of N.C.O.s and men had their wives and families on board.

On the 20th August, 1806, there was a fire on board the *Dover*, there were about 50 women and 25 children on board at the time. All were safely got out of the ship though one man who returned for some reason, was lost. The ship was burned to the water's edge.

In 1808 the Woolwich Division was increased to the same strength as the other Divisions and the Government purchased Whitby's Brewery, a series of buildings covering some 8 acres of rising ground next Frances Street, and with some slight alterations adapted them for the Marine Barracks.

Frances Street was for the most part the product of the R.M. Barracks. A residence was found for the Commandant in the Manor House on "Mount Pleasant" (Bowater House) and the second Commandant resided in the house which is now a shop at the corner of Ogilby Street. All the other houses in the same road were occupied by married Officers, others residing in Bowling Green Road and George Street.

The buildings were not suitable for a Barracks and so later the Division was moved to the Western part of the Royal Artillery Barracks, but in 1846 these were required for the new 10th Battalion, Royal Artillery, and so the Admiralty pulled down the old buildings used as a Barracks by the Marines and erected the Cambridge Barracks in their place. During the alterations the Division was temporarily quartered on board the *Benbow*, 74-gun ship, at this time lying alongside the quay at the west end of the Dockyard.

The Barracks faced the Common and was described as follows in the Illustrated News of January 22nd, 1848.

"This extensive pile of buildings has been designed by Mr. J. T. Crew, in conjunction with Sir W. Denison, now Governor of Van Diemen's Land. These new barracks have cost £100,000; they will accommodate 1150 men (officers included), with every convenience for cleanliness and comfort. A novel feature in the plan is that a kitchen or mess is appropriated for every 40 men, apart from their sleeping room an advantage which is not possessed by any other barracks in the kingdom.

The rear buildings, forming the boundary to the plan, contained extensive lavatories, bake-house, wash-house, laundry, bath-room, music-room, butchers and sutler's shops, and cleaning sheds. Beneath the barracks and running the entire length of the building, is a tunnel 25 feet in sectional area, into which warm air is forced, after passing between metal chambers heated by hot water: and from this tunnel a flue is carried into each room, with an exit flue for the foul air near the ceiling line. There are roomy corridors to the barracks, and covered ways, which gives every advantage for drilling men in wet weather. Contiguous to the main building are schools for 100

R.M. BARRACKS COMPLETED. *(Reproduced By Kind Permission Of "Illustrated London News")*

boys and 100 girls: baggage stores for Officers and Men: stabling for Officers; cells, guardroom and magazine.

The Officer's quarters and the mess department form the two sides of the front quadrangle. The entrance gate, with the Officer's library, guardroom and drill sheds, are not yet completed.

The contractors for this work are the Messrs. Rigby of Westminster; and the whole has been executed under the superintendence of Mr. Crew."

It was thus described by Major Poyntz, R.M.L.I. in his work *Per Mare Per Terram*, "Our Woolwich Barracks were modern and therefore possessed all possible requirements even to a Turkish Bath, a delightful resort on one of the good old English dull muggy afternoons, combining Eastern luxury with a good cigar and a well made cup of coffee, calculated to put one in a good temper for the rest of the day."

There was a bathing pond on the South side of the Common nearly opposite the Royal Military Academy on the North side of the Common. The heavy gun drill battery was at the East end of the Barrack Square. In 1862 we read. Major General Stransham 'witnessed the representation of a Naval bombardment of gunners at present undergoing a course of drill. The heavy armstrongs and 68-pounders were loaded, run out and fired.'

The Officers' Mess contained a fine mess room. On one occasion as many as 90 Officers dined there together.

The Woolwich Common was used for Drill at Manoeuvre.

In 1858 there was a big review on the occasion of the Queen's Birthday and we read that after marching past, the Brigade, composed of R.H.A. R.F.A., and two Battalions of Marines formed up on the top of the Common facing the Barracks and there carried out manoeuvres, opening fire and finally 'preparing for cavalry' after which there was a General salute. There were, no doubt many such reviews.

At inspections, several hours were spent in testing the efficiency of the Officers and men. After a Brigade and Battalions had been exercised "several companies marched past in quick and slow times under their Officers and a series of evolutions were carried out including the sword exercise."

There was a rifle range on the Plumstead Marshes which was used by the Marines in common with the Army Regiments. There was also a long rifle range belonging to the Volunteers at Woolwich which appears to have been used by the Marines. Their rifle meetings were social affairs and in 1860 the C.C. Royal Artillery and Colonel Stransham, Commandant R.M. and a large number of Officers and men assembled in the Plumstead Marshes to witness a "scientific shooting match," between officers and men of the R.M. Division arranged by Captain Suther, musketry instructor of the Corps. There were 200 competitors. A number of tents were erected and "provisions copiously supplied and carefully served." The Band was in attendance.

In 1858 the Church in the Dockyard was completed and the Lords of the Admiralty came down to inspect the building which was in Gothic style, from designs by Mr. Gilbert Scott.

The Woolwich Division provided a guard for the Deptford Dockyard. This guard was commanded by a Captain R.M., and was relieved every three months. The exact strength is not known, but in 1852 we hear of a Detachment leaving Woolwich for guard duty at Deptford Dockyard, composed of seven N.C.O.s and 156 Privates under the Command of a Lieut. R.M.

In 1861 the Barrack quarters occupied by this guard were condemned and new buildings erected.

They also provided an Arsenal Guard which was an Officers day and night guard. The Officer was privileged to wander through any of the workshops during working hours.

THE RED BARRACKS (ORIGINALLY THE INFIRMARY)

The hospital originally built in 1815 stood in rear of the Barracks but in 1859 it was converted into men's quarters and offices required for the Barrack establishment and a new infirmary was built at the Western end of the Barrack limits on the ground once occupied by the Manor House of the Bowaters, previously mentioned.

In October the new R.M. infirmary having been thoroughly surveyed by the Sanitary Committee and pronounced fit for the reception of invalids the transfer of the patients from the Hospital commenced when 83 Marines and 34 Seamen took possession of the new establishment.

In this year also, the Barrack quarters underwent considerable improvement, these were large rooms in several of which the Corporal superintendent of the room and his wife occupied a cubicle in the centre and the men were all round the room.

In 1869 the strength of the Corps was reduced and the 4th Division abolished. Most of the Officers were placed on half pay and the N.C.O.s and men not required to complete Deal and other Divisions were given a day's pay and marched out of Barracks and dismissed and the gates locked. The men required for Deal with their families were sent round by sailing ketch and dumped on the beach at Deal.

The '*Urgent*' brought round the officers, N.C.O.s and privates with their wives and families and baggage to Portsmouth and another vessel those for Plymouth. Major General Sir A. B. Stransham, G.C.B. R.M., in one of his letters stated that the N.C.O.s and men of the dissolved Woolwich Division wore at the third button of the tunic a small piece of crepe or black stuff.

The Marine Barracks was then sold to the War Office and turned over to an Infantry Regiment being re-named the Cambridge Barracks. At the same time the Infirmary was transformed into the Red Barracks and transferred to the Ordnance Store Corps (now the R.A.O.C.), The Red Barracks is the most conspicuous and striking feature of the Town of Woolwich.

OFFICERS AND COLOURS 1869

The whole of the Red Barracks are now used by the Military College of Science (old Ordnance College) and the personnel are housed in the Cambridge Barracks.

REMINISCENCES.

On October 10th, 1827, Colours were given by King George IV. and presented by the Duke of Clarence.It was intended that they should be presented in the Barrack field but the day was so wet that the Riding school was used. After the ceremony H.R.H. entertained the effective Generals and Field Officers of the Artillery, Engineers and Marines and their ladies to a 'dejenner,' at the 'Green Man,' Blackheath.

In 1858 new colours were presented by the Commodore of the Port without any ceremony.

There was evidently a Band belonging to the Division at an early date, as in 1835 we read "the Drum-major of the Woolwich Division is in future to have but one Dress Coat in two years, instead of annually, as the cost (30 guineas) is defrayed out of the Divisional Fund." In 1861 the R.M. Band performed regularly on the Common on Wednesdays and in the grounds of the Royal Military Repository on Fridays, and in 1867 in the Rotunda gardens a short distance off to the South on the left of the Charlton Road.

The short paragraph quoted above also gives us the information that a Divisional Fund had been started at Woolwich on the same lines as our other Divisional Funds, which date back to somewhere about 1784 (Plymouth).

The greater portion of the money for the Divisional Fund was from fees paid by shop people, builders, etc., for the services of Marines who were apparently allowed to work for them on the understanding that a portion of the fees paid (1/6 per week.) was paid into the Divisional Fund. Tailors and shoemakers were stopped 3/- a week for the Divisional Fund between 1821 and 1858. Other sources of income were:-
(a) A portion of the fines for drunkenness.
(b) Part bounties for recruits.
(c) Payments by outliers to be allowed to sell provisions in the Barracks before the establishment of Canteens.
(d) After 1864 a quarter of the profits of the Commissariat Canteen system. This was increased to half in February, 1869, the other two thirds being paid into the Commissariat Fund.

In December, 1862, it was announced at Woolwich that the Admiralty had decided that as soon as the present contract for the supply of ready made men's shirts and underclothing expired they would, in order to improve the condition of and to give employment to the wives of Seamen and Marines during the times their husbands were absent on service and the women as well as widows and others in distress, issue the materials for them to make up.

By EUSTACE G. BIRD, Capt., R.M.L.I. (retd.)

I joined at the end of 1867, and was posted to No. 1 Parade Company with Captain Drury, who had recently re-joined Hd. Qrs. from San Juan island, where a detachment of Royal Marines had held one end of the island, and United States Marines held the other, till arbitration settled who was entitled to possession. The old German Emperor William I. decided that the Americans were to have it, and they, I suppose, to show there was no ill feeling in the matter, erected memorials on the sites of the camps with elaborate ceremonials.

No. 1 Company at that time was partly made up of men enlisted for the R.M. Artillery. Colonel Suther was the Commandant, and I well remember his remark to me when I went in to report myself on joining. He shook hands with me and said, "Well, my boy, I hope you may have as good a time in the Corps as I have had!"

When I arrived the afternoon before, in a cab loaded up with my barrack-room effects, the first person I spoke to was Captain Mitchell - afterwards a Colonial Governor. He evidently took in the situation and came forward to render first aid - "You're a new commission, are you not?" and finding that his supposition was correct, he shouted to an orderly, and very soon after baggage and furniture were unloaded into my new quarter.

Jack Straghan was the Adjutant, and a better one never existed, being always fair and just, but at the same time strict in all his duties.

The Division was numerically a strong one at that time, and on field days on the Common we used to muster three battalions and form a brigade of our own, with Colonel Suther as Brigadier or sometimes Colonel Rodney. The Common made an excellent drill ground on account of its size, and it was always a magnificent sight to see the Royal Horse Artillery gallop past the saluting base.

The Arsenal Guard was the only officers guard that we had to provide - a day and night guard - but as the officer was priviliged to wander through any of the workshops during working hours, one had opportunities of seeing many operations of great interest. The Woolwich "infant" guns were being manufactured at that time, and Boxer cartridges in various stages were to be seen. Moreover, Colonel Boxer's pretty daughters were to be seen on their lawn opposite the guard-room, Lieut. Sidney Alston and Capt. Allnutt being so specially favoured as to become the husbands of two of the sisters.

All the barrack buildings were imposing and solidly built, in an area of many acres, entirely walled in, the Church being the only edifice outside its limits. The hospital, now used as a separate barracks, was also a very fine building standing at the western end of our limits.

The first floating dock that went to Bermuda, was launched from the North Woolwich side of the river just about this time. North Woolwich gardens used then to be rather a "shady" spot, but I believe it has improved greatly since. The train service to London, only about eight miles off, used to be very convenient.

Blackheath for football used to be, and still is, a great meeting ground, as I then played for the Marlborough Nomads.

Mr. Childers' reign as First Lord of the Admiralty was not a happy one for the Royal Marines. Not only was the Woolwich Division swept out of existence, but some 200 men in the ranks of the above Division were summarily dismissed from the Service, many of them with G.C.Bs. I do not remember the wording of the order that came from the Admiralty, but I believe it was in effect that certain entries in a man's defaulter sheet, no matter how many years previously that entry had been made, were to suffice to condemn any man in the entire force of the R.Ms. to immediate dismissal. The result was that several hundreds of men in uniform, with sandwich boards stating that they had been discharged from the Corps, paraded for some days in front of the Admiralty. The scandal resulted in many being reinstated.

* * * *

By T. W. HOLDSTOCK (Sergt.-Major, late Chatham Division)

The punishments up to 1868 were flogging, drumming-out, and discharge with ignominy.

Flogging took place in rear of the barracks, early in the day, but none since 1866. Drummers used to do the flogging, for which they received three-farthings a day. This was discontinued when flogging was abolished. Each drummer gave twelve strokes; if more were to be inflicted, the next drummer came in. The flogging was under the control of the drum-major, who gave the time each stroke should be given - generally every thirty seconds - in order that the drummer could disentangle his "nine-tails". A doctor had charge of the man physically, and could stop the punishment at his discretion, as many did. Drummers used to practice flogging in their barrack-room; the three-farthings a day they got was called "flogging money."

Drumming-out was a sad affair, in which the whole division took part. After the victim had been stripped of his facings, ornaments, buttons, etc., by the drum-major in the centre of the parade, he was marched round the large square, formed by the men on parade, under charge of the "Provost Sergeant". The drums and fifes followed, playing the "Rogue's March," to the front gate when he would he handed to the drum-major, who would take him into a small room to the side of the gate and there tattoo a B.C. on his left breast. The prisoner was then kicked out of the gate by the smallest drummer-boy, into the arms of a civil policeman, who took him away to gaol to do any imprisonment in addition awarded to him.

Discharge with ignominy was similar to drumming-out, but without the drumming. The man was simply stripped of ornaments, buttons, etc., tattooed, marched to the gate and kicked out.

All these punishments were discontinued in 1868.

The pay was given out on parade, if fine, and under the colonade if wet, three times a week. There were no fires in the barrack-rooms, but hot pipes, and no meals were taken in the barrack rooms, which were simply bedrooms.

The barracks being of nearly white brick, was played on by the boat's crew every Saturday. There were two fine colonades, upper and lower. All meals were taken down below in the basement, where the only fires were.

Passes, called the "11 o'clock passes," were the only ones given; no night passes, unless special. Belts, when going out after sunset, were not allowed to be worn, as they used to come into use in street fights, which did occur at times, if an unpopular regiment happened to be stationed at Woolwich, or a quarrelsome draft paid off from sea.

It was quite a common thing to see Marines pay off after being away on a four or five years' commission, march into barracks looking half sailor and half marine, because in those days their clothing was not sent out to them as it is now, when a marine looks as smart coming home as he does going away.

The barracks were always full of men, as no large ships ever fitted out there. The last big ship commissioned at Woolwich Dockyard was the *Bristol* frigate, 42 guns, and the old line-of-battle ship *Meemee*, three-decker, for China, in 1868. She took a large draft, and the last Woolwich detachment to return to barracks from a large ship was that from the old *Victoria*, 104 guns and now a coal hulk in Portsmouth Harbour.

THE DRUM AND FIFE BAND

The detachment at Deptford was relieved every three months and was quite numerous.

The annual sports were held on Woolwich Common.

The last wife of a marine who embarked with her husband paid off early in 1865. Her name was Perry, whose son eventually became a drummer boy and her husband a nurse in the naval hospital. Her duties on board being more that of a laundress for officers' washing.

Many of the old marine pensioners, who could not get into Greenwich Hospital, joined the battalion of "enrolled pensioners," who used to drill on Woolwich Common. They had their own drums and fifes, and it was a noted fact that one side drummer had a wooden leg, and could march past with any of them.

The band of the Division wore white cloth tunic and shako until 1867, when it was changed for the present scarlet and gold one now in use.

The splendid drum and fife band was second to none, Guards not excepted, under that splendid drum-major Charles Duncan, a handsome fellow, 6 feet 2 inches in height.

In the picture of the drum and fife band, T. W. Holdstock, afterwards Sergt.- Major at Chatham, is looking over the left shoulder of another drummer, who is holding a son of the Sergt.-Major with his right arm. (Feb. 1867).

The drummer with three Crimean medals flogged the last man who had to be flogged at Woolwich. He used to say before flogging a man "Lord strengthen my arm and harden my heart." The drummer immediately below him, and next to the bugle-major, was the son of the last woman who embarked on a man-o'-war with her husband, an officer's servant.

Until the division was broken up the drum was used as much as the bugle for calls. The fall in for parade was drummed, also first post, reveille retreat, officers' dinner call, defaulters, and the "roast beef of Old England" by one drummer and one fifer at dinner time.

Sir Michael Costta came down from London to hear the splendid band play their last programme, under Mr. Winterbottom. At the end he said, with tears in his eyes, "What a sin to break up such a band."

This brings us up to March 1869, when the men, at a full parade, were informed that the Division would be dissolved by March 31st, 1869. The Adjutant, Capt. Straghan, a splendid man read the Admiralty order, and informed each company which division it was to be transferred to. The Chatham party left first, Portsmouth March 9th and Plymouth later to finish up. Before dismissing the parade the Commandant Colonel Suther, addressed the parade, his last words being "act on the square."

PICTURES, TROPHIES, &C., OF INTEREST WHICH BELONGED AT ONE TIME TO THE WOOLWICH DIVISION.

Picture - King William IV.

H.R.H. the Duke of Clarence, K.G., Lord High Admiral and General of Marines (afterwards King William IV.) presented new colours to the various Divisions in 1827.

It was arranged to have a full length portrait of H.R.H. painted by Sir Thomas Lawrence, and three days pay was to be collected from all officers to pay for it, the Duke regretting that he could not afford to make the presentation. Two days pay had been collected when George IV died, and one of the first acts of the Duke on becoming King was to write to Colonel Savage, the Commandant of Chatham, saying he was then in a position to present a portrait to each of the Divisions.

Five portraits were accordingly painted by Mr. A. Morton, the Woolwich colours being sent up to London for the purpose of the painting by order of the Royal Marine Office. The details of the pictures were identical at all Divisions, except that in the picture for the R.M.A. there is a representation of a mortar in place of the King's Colour. The frames were made of oak from H.M.S. *Victory*, and were designed by 2nd Lieut. Gascoigne (afterwards General Gascoigne) and cost £100 each.

The *Hampshire Telegraph* of April, 1831, says: "The five portraits of the King, painted by Mr. A. Morton, munificent presents by His Majesty to the several Divisions of Royal Marines, have been arranged in the Palace of St. James for His Majesty's inspection, when he was pleased to express his approbation of their performance. In compliance with orders for an officer from each Division to repair to London to make a selection by lot, Lieut. and Adjutant Davis was sent from this Division (Portsmouth) for that purpose, and on Monday the selection was made at St. James' Palace. The first choice devolved on Adjutant Davis, and that which is considered the best painting consequently is consigned to this Division - they are all, however, masterly productions."

The whereabouts of the Woolwich picture is not known, though several attempts have been made to trace it.

Picture - Lord Barham.

In red robes with ermine cap. In left hand a parchment book inscribed "Establishment of the Fourth Division of Royal Marines, 1805."

Lord Barham was a good friend of the Corps, it was by his order, when First Lord of the Admiralty, that the Woolwich Division was established.

The picture hung in the officers' mess until the abolition of the Woolwich Division in 1869, when it was sent to Forton. It is now in the Eastney Mess.

It was stated by General Sir A. B. Stransham K.C.B. R.M., who was at one time Commandant of the Woolwich Division, that periodically up to a certain date (1836-7 of his own knowledge) on the anniversary of the establishment of the Woolwich Division the picture was taken down from the wall by the mess waiter and taken to the Mess President of the day, who said a few appropriate words, and then the waiter carried it round to everyone seated at the table, and the President toasted the picture."

Picture - Col. Thomas A. Parke, C.B., A.D.C.

Painted for the officers of the Woolwich Division and presented by them to the R.M.A. in 1869. It is now in the officers' mess Eastney.

Colonel Parke served in the R.M.A. companies during nearly all his early service. He was in the *Triumph* at Camperdown, 1797, commanded the Marine Artillery serving in North America, 1813- 15, acting against the enemy in Georgia, in the operations on the *Chesapeake*, and assisted in the capture of American camp at Hampton. 1838-9 he succeeded Lt.-Colonel Owen in command of the R.M. Battalion in Spain. He was 2nd Commandant at Portsmouth 1840-2 at Commandant at Woolwich 1842.-51.

Engraving - The Battle at Bunkers Hill, near Boston, 17 June, 1775.

Presented by Captain Portlock-Dudson to the Woolwich Division. On the break-up of this Division the picture was returned to the donor who presented it to the Portsmouth Division.

General Stransham's Clock.

On top: Globe and Crown.

Supporters: Dexter, a Sergeant, R.M.L.I., with rifle.

Sinister, a Private, R.M.L.I., round side cap with ornaments, Globe and Laurel surmount by bugle and holding a gunnery sponge.

On front of the clock-

Woolwich Division Royal Marines, Feb. 1866

Woolwich Division April 1869

Portsmouth Division June 1886

On the abolition of the Woolwich Division the clock went back to General Sir A. B. Stransham, K.C.B., R.M., who parted with it. It was bought by the Forton Mess from a dealer in 1886. It is now in the officers mess at Eastney.

Burmese Bell.

Inscription: "This Bell was taken from a Pagoda in the stockade of Bassain in Burmah, in May 1852, by the Royal Marines, mainly of the Portsmouth Division, who served in Burmah under Col. T. Elliott, C.B.. C.M.G., R.M.L.I., who was in command during the assault on the stockade.

Col. J. Elliott wrote: "The Bell was presented to me as the senior officer of Royal Marines serving in Burmah in 1851 and 1852 by the G.O.C. General Godwin. It was taken from a stockade at Bassein, which stockade was stormed by a detachment of Marines under my command, in which service I was wounded . . . On my return to Woolwich in 1853 I presented it to the Woolwich Division."

Col. Elliott again became possessor of the Bell on the breaking up of the Woolwich Division in 1869. He presented it to the Portsmouth Division in 1876.

Candelabra ("The Woolwich Folly").

Trunk and branches adorned at foot by devices Globe and crown (two), topmasts with topsails lowered.

Sir Charles Mitchell (late R.M.L.I.) wrote in 1898, "Made when Colonel Swaine was President of the Mess (Woolwich) in 1853 or 1854, and cost £450."

Sir A. B. Stransham wrote: "The late Lady Stransham on festive occasions used to send natural climbing plants, such as convolvulus, etc., to twine up the trunk and branches, and it looked well." He also wrote that the silver sconces were fixed against the trunk afterwards, to make the affair more massive; these formerly hung by the sides of the mess room chimney-piece. The battles recorded on the pieces were selected by him when Commandant.

The story that the three pieces were once one huge piece may be true, though it was in three Pieces some time before it left the Woolwich mess. The reason for cutting it up is said to have been that the mess room table would not stand the enormous weight and broke - hence the name the "Woolwich Folly." It is possible, however, that the name only refers to the expense, and that the large centre piece was humorously termed the "trunk," and the smaller side pieces the "branches." There are silver ribbons, with battles recorded on them, on the trunks of the smaller side pieces, as well as on the trunk of the large centre piece.

The largest of the three pieces (the trunk or centre piece) was given to the Plymouth Mess, and the two smaller (the branches or side pieces) to the Portsmouth and Chatham messes respectively.

* * * *

R.M.O. LETTER RESPECTING THE BREAKING UP OF THE OFFICERS' MESS OF THE WOOLWICH DIVISION AND THE DISPOSAL OF THE MESS FUND, PLATE AND OTHER PROPERTY.

As the reduction of the Woolwich Division of Royal Marines now ordered necessitates the breaking up of the officers' mess and library establishments, the Lords Commissioners of the Admiralty are pleased to direct-

That all money, plate, linen and other property belonging to the Woolwich mess be taken account of by a committee of officers, in order that on the breaking up of that mess the whole may be divided and apportioned to the messes of the other three divisions, according to the number of Woolwich officers respectively transferred to those divisions.

That the share of money or property, or both, thus apportioned, be received by those messes in lieu of the entrance money that would under ordinary circumstances be due from officers thus joining.

It is to be clearly understood that at the breaking up of the Woolwich mess no apportionment of money or property to individual officers will be allowed, and that the distribution of the Fund and property of the present Woolwich mess is to be strictly in aid of the funds of the other three messes into which the officers now composing the Woolwich mess will be absorbed.

All articles of furniture and all fittings (not positively fixtures) the property of the Government to be handed over to the charge of the Barrack Master, who will give a receipt for the same.

The large picture of the late King William IV. is to remain in its present position until the pleasure of their Lordships respecting its future disposal shall have been notified.

The Committee appointed to carry out the distribution are to keep a correct account of all their proceedings, the minutes of which are to be submitted to and to receive the approval of the Colonel Commandant of the Division.

The pictures (with one exception, William IV. Rex), trophies, candelabra, and other articles of a decorative character, which at any time may have been presented to the Woolwich mess, my Lords consider should be disposed of as far as possible in accordance with the wishes of the officers generally, and not to be deemed liable to distribution.

By Command,
S. NETHERVILLE LOWDER, D.A.G.
Royal Marine Office, 19th Feb., 1869.

In this connection the following letters are of interest
Admiralty, 7 New Street, Spring Gardens, S.W.
No. 309 Circular.

25 May, 1869.

MEMO. FROM THE D.A.G., R.M.

The Lords Commissioners of the Admiralty have been pleased to direct in pursuance of their orders of the 2nd ult., laying down that the property held by each of the Headquarter Messes, R.M. Light Infantry, belongs to the *Officers of the Corps* collectively, and in consideration of the embarrassed condition of the Fund of the Officers' Mess at the Depot, that each of the Headquarter Messes at Chatham, Portsmouth and Plymouth be called upon to contribute a small portion of plate, linen and table equipment, and a sum of Thirty pounds (£30) for the benefit of the Depot Mess.

J. W. C. WILLIAMS, A.A.G.
[ED. We have not been able to obtain a copy of the order of 2nd April, 1869, laying down that "the property held by each of the Headquarter Messes R.M.L.I. belongs to the Officers of the Corps collectively."]

LETTER RE MESS PROPERTY ON THE OCCASION OF THE FORMATION OF THE ROYAL MARINE ARTILLERY DIVISION.

The Colonels Commandant and Officers Commanding, Royal Marines Light Infantry. R.M. Barracks, Forton.

13 Jan., 1860.
Sir,

We have the honour to submit for your consideration the following propositions, unanimously agreed to by the joint committee of the Artillery and Lt. Infantry Division of Royal Marines, with reference to the distribution of Mess articles, etc. consequent on the formation of the Artillery Division.

To have the whole of the property of both Messes valued by an appraiser, to add thereto the mess funds in hand on 31st Oct., 1859. Then to take the number of officers of both Divisions on the 31st Oct., 1859 (the date of the formation of the Artillery Division, which on investigation they find to have as follows, viz., Artillery Division 64, Lt. Infantry Division 109), and to divide the total amount in proportion to these numbers.

The furniture supplied by order of the Lords of the Admiralty to both Messes, and heirlooms, (viz., pictures, busts, snuff boxes, etc., etc.) not to be included in the valuation, but to be retained by the present holders.

The joint committee have to observe that in reckoning the foregoing numbers they have thought it equitable not to include the officers attached to the Portsmouth Division studying at the College - 13 in number.

Appd.   ALEX. ANDERSON, Col. Cmdt., Ports. Div.
JOHN FRASER, Col. Cmdt., Arty. Div.
Major-Gen. WESLEY, D.A.G.

* * * *

Respecting the Amalgamation of R.M.A. and R.M.L.I. and Abolition of Forton Barracks.

..... Colonel Commandant R.M.A. and R.M.L.I. will assemble Committees of the several Messes, Canteens, etc., to decide as to the disposal of property, funds, etc.

As the Portsmouth Division is the oldest, from which the R.M.A. funds were originally derived, those of the R.M.L.I. Division are to be considered the Parent Funds, and used for the new Division. It is for consideration whether the several R.M.A. funds should be placed in Trust and the interest used for the new Portsmouth Division, or divided between the new Division, Depot, etc., or alternatively, that the funds of Eastney and Forton should be combined.

The Trustees must be consulted as to any action necessary. (*Ed.* - The Trustees are the members of the Mess for the time being.)

It is desirable that arrangements should be made to suitably accommodate in the various Messes, Institutes, etc., at Eastney the pictures, furniture. etc., of the corresponding messes, etc., at Forton. Lists of articles belonging to both Divisions which it is not possible to accommodate, or which may be considered surplus, and their proposed disposal should be submitted.

17 April, 1923,   H. E. BLUMBERG, A.G., R.M.

ED. - Forton brought over the whole of their various Mess Funds, etc., and Eastney put in a similar sum. A portion of the remainder of the Eastney monies was devoted to the publication of the History of the R.M.A., and the remainder was invested and put in Trust.

The Eastney pictures, trophies, silver, glass and stocks of wine are in the same Trust, but are lent to the Portsmouth Mess on the condition that they are kept up. The purchase of R.M.A. medals for the Eastney collection is the first charge on the interest of the invested capital, the remainder is divided up between the three Divisions in the proportion of 4/6ths to Portsmouth and 1/6th each to Chatham and Plymouth.

The surplus R.M.A. and R.M.L.I. pictures, trophies, silver, etc., are on permanent loan to other R.M. messes, with the exception of certain articles which had been purchased by one or other of the messes, and not considered of any corps interest, which were otherwise disposed of.

THE PLYMOUTH DIVISION, ROYAL MARINES.
By Colonel R.D. Ormsby, C.B.E., R.M.

NOTE. A short history of the Plymouth Division by the late Lieut.-Col. W. G. Armstrong, R.M.L.I., appeared in Vols. I. and II. of the "Globe and Laurel." The following notes are based to a great extent on this previous record. The compiler of these notes is greatly indebted to Generals Sir H.E. Blumberg, K.C.B., and St. G.B. Armstrong, C.B., C.M.G., for much valuable revision and information.

From 1664 until 1755 troops who served as Marines and portions of Marine regiments were frequently quartered in the town of Plymouth or at Dock, now known as Devonport. When the Admiralty raised 50 Companies of Marines in 1755, a group of these Companies formed the Third or Plymouth Division. The first order of the Division is dated 7th May, 1755.

It requires a knowledge of the ground and some imagination to picture the Plymouth of that day. There is a good collection of old prints of Plymouth in the Plymouth Museum which is of value in this respect. The Hoe extended over all the ground occupied by Lockyer Street, Windsor Terrace and buildings that exist in rear. There were of course no Great Western Docks. Stonehouse was a village, probably straggling along to join Plymouth on the line of the present Union Street. Dock, now Devonport, was a small town which had grown up in the vicinity of the South Yard of the modern Dockyard. The road from Plymouth to Dock was over Millbridge: there was also a ferry at the site of the present "Halfpenny Bridge" which was not built until about 1815.

In 1755, as far as can be ascertained, there were no houses on the narrow neck of land separating Millbay from Stonehouse Pool. What is now known as Millbay Quarry (in the vicinity of Andrews' repair depot) was a hill called Battery Hill, with the ground sloping in a westerly direction over the sites of Emma Place and Caroline Place. Durnford Street was undulating ground rising to the height of Eastern Kings. It is probable that the stone used for the construction of the Marine Barracks was quarried from this cliff, the remainder of which can still be seen at the end of Durnford Street, in the vicinity of the house known as Mount Stone.

At first the Marines were billeted near the Barbican, with the Orderly Room in Southside Street, which until recently could be identified as a printing establishment in the latter street. The small open space used as a parade ground is still known as "Parade," but the Hoe was used for drill and ceremonial parades. The first parade was ordered on the Hoe on 12th May, 1755. On 20th May, 1759. the Marines were ordered to use the "New Quay" as an alarm parade. There were no barracks in Plymouth other than the Citadel. Military Barracks had been built in Dock by 1765, stretching from George Barracks, Mount Wise to Marlborough Barracks, on the site occupied by the present Raglan Barracks.

The first mention of an Officers' Mess Room is 30th April, 1769 this room was situated in Marlborough Street at Dock. Important occasions were celebrated by the officers meeting at hotels, e.g. the Coronation dinner on 19th September, 1760, was at the "Red Lion."

In 1756 four companies of Marines were sent to Dock, with outlying detachments at Plympton and Tavistock. The whole Division moved to Dock in 1764, but returned to Plymouth in 1772, Companies and detachments appear to have gone between the two places a good deal, with the men at Dock sometimes in barracks and sometimes in billets, but always in billets at Plymouth. The Infirmary was at Millbay Prison (Millbay Barracks) in December 1783.

On Sept. 11th. 1779, 1 lieutenant and 29 n.c. officers and men were sent to garrison St. Nicholas Island (Drake's Island) and to be exercised frequently at the great guns.

In 1781 the work of building new Barracks for the Marines had begun. This date (i.e. G.R. 1781) can still be seen on top of the two water pipes near the Officers' Mess. On Monday, 6th October, 1783, the first Guard was mounted at the new barracks, consisting of 1 sergeant, 1 corporal and 12 privates, and it is interesting to remember that this daily guard-mounting has taken place on the same spot for nearly 150 years.

On Monday, 8th December, 1783, the Plymouth Division occupied the new Barracks for the first time. They consisted of quarters for the men running north and south with seven passages, the end ones having four rooms each including basements, the remainder eight rooms. At right angles with this building at each end were the north and south wings for officers. The south wing had the Commandant's and 2nd Commandant's house at either end with 24 single or 12 double quarters for officers in between. The north wing was similar to the south wing, with a Field Officer's house at each end.

ROYAL MARINES BARRACKS, STONEHOUSE.

In rear of this north wing the ground rose steeply to the level of Caroline Place. In the northeast corner of this hill, known locally as "Bunker's Hill" the Infirmary and Surgeon's quarters were built. The quartermaster's stores and provost cells were adjacent to the Infirmary. There were also on Bunker's Hill the divisional stables and a two-storied building known as the Drill Room. The ground floor of this building was the drill room at one end of which was a wooden "broadside" gun for handspike drill. On the first floor were the Divisional Schools and a Tailor's Shop. It was not until 1857 that clothing was made at headquarters; previous to that date clothing was "altered to fit" in the Tailor's Shop at so much per suit. When the Artillery Companies were attached to the Division a very small gun drill battery was built on Bunker's Hill. There was a double door from Bunker's Hill on to the main road. The approach to Bunker's Hill from the Barrack Square was by a winding road leading up from between the north and east blocks. There were also two wide flight of steps leading up from the rear of the north block.

The Officers' Mess House was a detached building separated by a passage from the men's quarters. In the basement of this building was the canteen, The Sergeants' Mess was in the present "O" passage. The parade was 115 yards long and 40 yards broad, bounded on the western side by railings, with two gateways and a guard-room. In rear of the main block was a sea wall separating the Barracks from the water of Mill Bay.

The creek, which is now covered by a portion of the G.W.R. Docks, was known as Firestone Bay. The anchorage was much used by yachts and the old yacht club stands in Millbay Road near the Laundry and is now occupied by the S.W. Counties Agricultural Association.

At this date (1783) there were no other buildings in the present Durnford Street area, with the exception of the Longroom, which appears to have been a fashionable assembly room, but after the Barracks were built the village of Stonehouse began to expand at a rapid rate. This Longroom building eventually became the Infirmary and Boys' School, and is now used as a School and Shoemakers' shop.

Of the original barrack buildings described above much remains to the present day. The original main block is that at present comprised between "I" passage and "O" passage, now occupied by "E" and "G" Companies. The Commandant's House is the present Barrack-master's House, the original front door of which is indicated by stone steps leading to what is now a window.

The 2nd Commandant's House has become part of the Officers Mess. The first Officers' Mess is now the ante-room, and the canteen has become a part of the Officers' Mess Sergeant's quarters.

The present hall of the Officers' Mess was at first a paved courtyard, the entrance to the mess being a doorway leading to the present inner hall. This courtyard was eventually roofed over and two ground-glass plates were inserted in the floor to give light to the wine cellars beneath. The inner and outer porches were added at subsequent dates. The hall received a wooden floor, a fireplace was built, and the entrance to the inner hall was enlarged in 1905.

The original north wing has disappeared, the present north wing having been built at a later date, when much of Bunker's Hill was quarried away. The site of the original Infirmary and Surgeon's quarters is now occupied by the Barrackmaster's and 1st Quartermaster's stores. The entrance of the Surgeon's house may still be recognised in the somewhat dilapidated glass roofed room, with its vine, in rear of the Barrackmaster's office.

The sea wall ran approximately on the line of the present ablution rooms and cookhouse, and men could embark from a landing place by the wall. The barrack railings ran from the present Barrackmaster's house to the corresponding corner of the north wing, now represented approximately by "C" passage in the new north wing.

The first additions to the original buildings were made in 1818, when permission was given to build over the passage separating the Officers' Mess from the main block, in order to provide accommodation for Officers, as some rooms in the south wing had been appropriated as offices. The rooms now used as a library and breakfast room were probably used as the Mess room until the present mess room was built. The attics over these rooms were originally used as Subalterns' quarters. The quarters underneath the attics were made into the Billiard room in 1862. At the same time a colonnade was built between the two gateways in the barrack railings. This colonnade had a guard-room, an officers' guard-room, and guard-room cells on the ground floor, with the Orderly Room, Paymaster's Office and Divisional Library upstairs. Few alterations were made until after the Crimean War, when much new building took place. The late Major J. J. Hoare has supplied some very interesting details concerning the Barracks previous to 1860. A large scale ordnance map, dated 1857, has also furnished much valuable information.

At the period of the Crimean War the offices of the Commandant and Adjutant were in the passage next to the Commandant's (now Barrackmaster's) house. Two of the basements were used as "Grand Divisional Pay Offices," two Captains of Companies in each of four rooms. At this time, according to Major Hoare, Captains used to pay their Companies three times a week, on Tuesdays, Thursdays and Saturdays.

In the main block was the Sergeants Mess, in a room in the present "O" passage. The Band and Drums were in two rooms in the present "L" passage, one of which was subsequently used as the Pay Captain's office, and is now used by the Company Ledger Clerks. The archway under this room was not made until after 1857. Five of the basements in the main block were used as quarters by the two Sergeant-Majors, the Barrack Sergeant, the Quartermaster Sergeant and the Boat Sergeant, the remainder being used for stores, etc.

In rear of the main block, running from north to south, were a barber's shop, next the Surgeon's quarters, a Ball Court on the site of the present Theatre, and at that time used as a barrack store. Then the straw barn, lavatory, ash pit, armourer's shop with armoury over it, blacksmith's shop, with carpenter's shop over it, wash-house, cleaning room (for equipment), with ablution and bathroom underneath, lavatory, Works Department office, and store with shop underneath. The present Officers' Mess Room was built in 1858. Under the ante-room was the wet canteen, as has already been stated. Opposite the mess kitchen was a small house for the canteen butler; this house no longer exists; then the barrack wood store, now used as Barrackmaster's paint store.

In the space now occupied by the present Company Sergeant-Major and Staff Quarters, were two coal yards, as shewn on the map of 1857, the inner one of which soon became the Commandant's garden, and close to which were a stable and coach-house for the Commandant.

The ground occupied by the Mill Bay Barracks was acquired by the Admiralty in three parcels in 1758, 1795 and 1796, and as already noted, the Infirmary of the Marines was here in 1783. The Mill Bay prison was either built or adapted for the accommodation of French prisoners of war, the cemetery for whom was on the site occupied by the Crescent. The possession of these Barracks was transferred from the Admiralty to the War Office, and vice versa, on several occasions. These Barracks were used by the Marines for many years. R.M.A. companies were quartered there, and recruits from time to time. The R.M.A. details left for Portsmouth in 1859. When the large alterations were completed at the Stonehouse Barracks, at some time between 1862 and 1871, Mill Bay Barracks were handed over to the War Office in exchange for barrack rooms at Fort Stamford. These Barracks reverted to the Admiralty after the South African War, but were not again occupied. They were again transferred to the War Department in 1908, and were finally pulled down and the site converted into a recreation ground, facing the Duke of Cornwall's Hotel.

To be quartered in Mill Bay Barracks was a distinct inconvenience to Officers, as they had to come to the Stonehouse Barracks for dinner. At a much later date the subaltern of the day had to visit the guard there. On Saturdays this officer had in addition to visit the Marines on main guard at Devonport, in the guard-room opposite Mount Wise cricket ground, so that Saturday in particular was a day of compulsory exercise.

In 1857 considerable alterations and additions were begun at the Barracks in Stonehouse. Bunker's Hill was excavated sufficiently to give room, and the main block was extended and three passages added. The cliff in rear of the north block gives an idea of the excavation required. A new Gun Drill Battery was built at the Longroom (the present lower Battery). A new Infirmary was established at the Longroom House; this work was completed in 1859. A new house was built for the Surgeon in 1861.

Before the new north wing and the western side could be commenced it was necessary for the Admiralty to acquire the land which was then occupied by the eastern side of Durnford Street and Barrack Street. This Barrack Street ran parallel to the then barrack railings, guard-room, etc., and contained nine public houses and one brewery, which all faced the barracks. Back to back with these houses were the houses on the eastern side of Durnford Street. This area had become an unsavoury rookery, and on the site being acquired by the Admiralty the houses were pulled down and the extensions of the barracks were begun. The first work taken in hand was the new north wing, the construction of which made the parade ground 136 yards long and 55 yards broad, instead

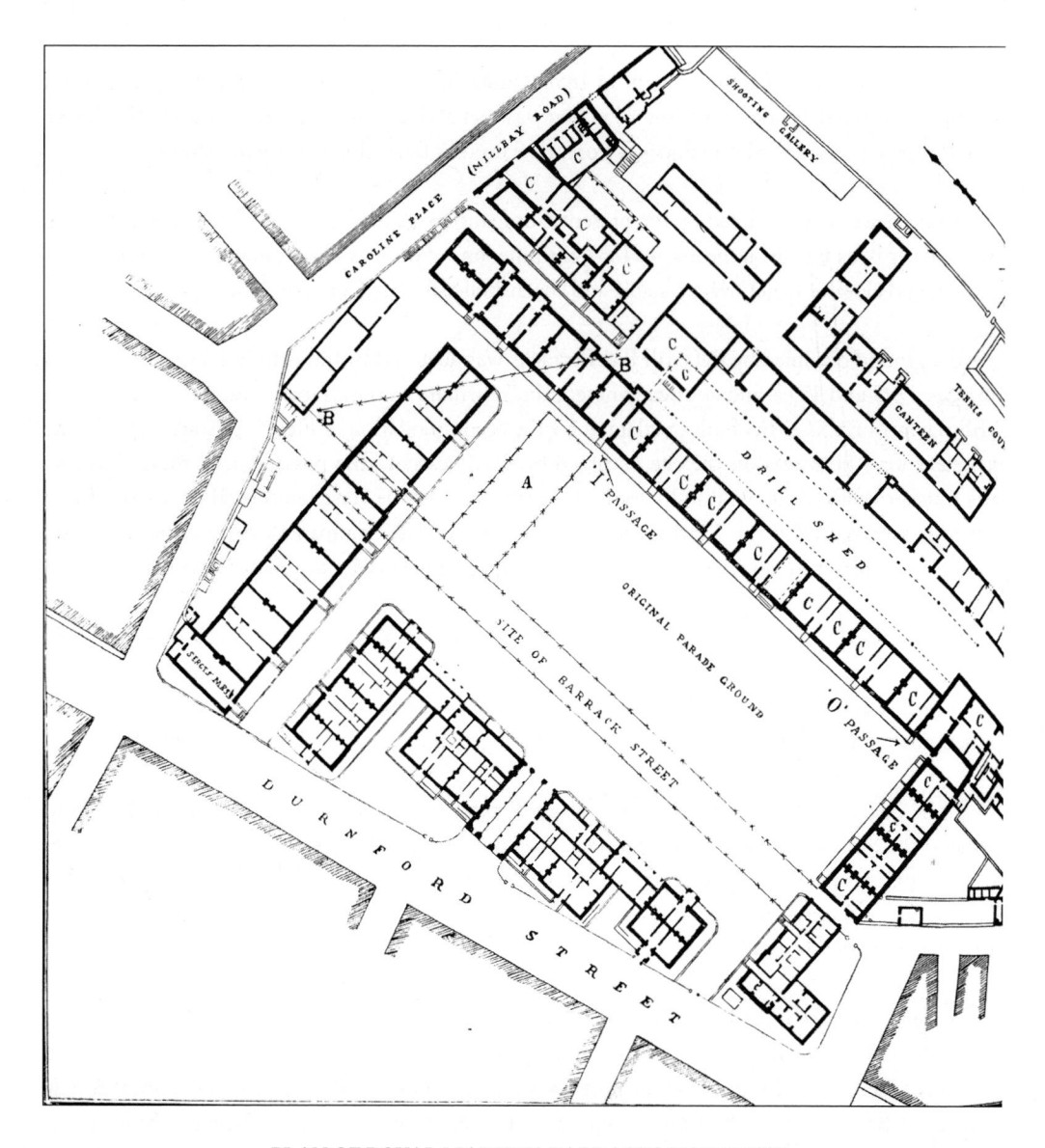

PLAN OF ROYAL MARINES BARRACKS PLYMOUTH
PRIOR TO ALTERATIONS IN 1900

of 115 by 40. This wing was finished in 1864. The present western front was finished in 1867. Few alterations have been made in this part of the barracks since that date, and these chiefly consist of rearrangement of the accommodation. A set of Captain's quarters were eventually incorporated into the Commandant's, 2nd Commandant's, Brigade Major's and Adjutant's houses. The present Orderly Room was originally the Court-Martial Room, and the Adjutant's and Paymaster's Office were a set of Captain's quarters. In consequence of the widening of the parade a vacant space was left in continuation of the south wing. On this site were built quarters for married officers, which were finished in 1869. As originally planned, the accommodation was intended for 13 officers, but it

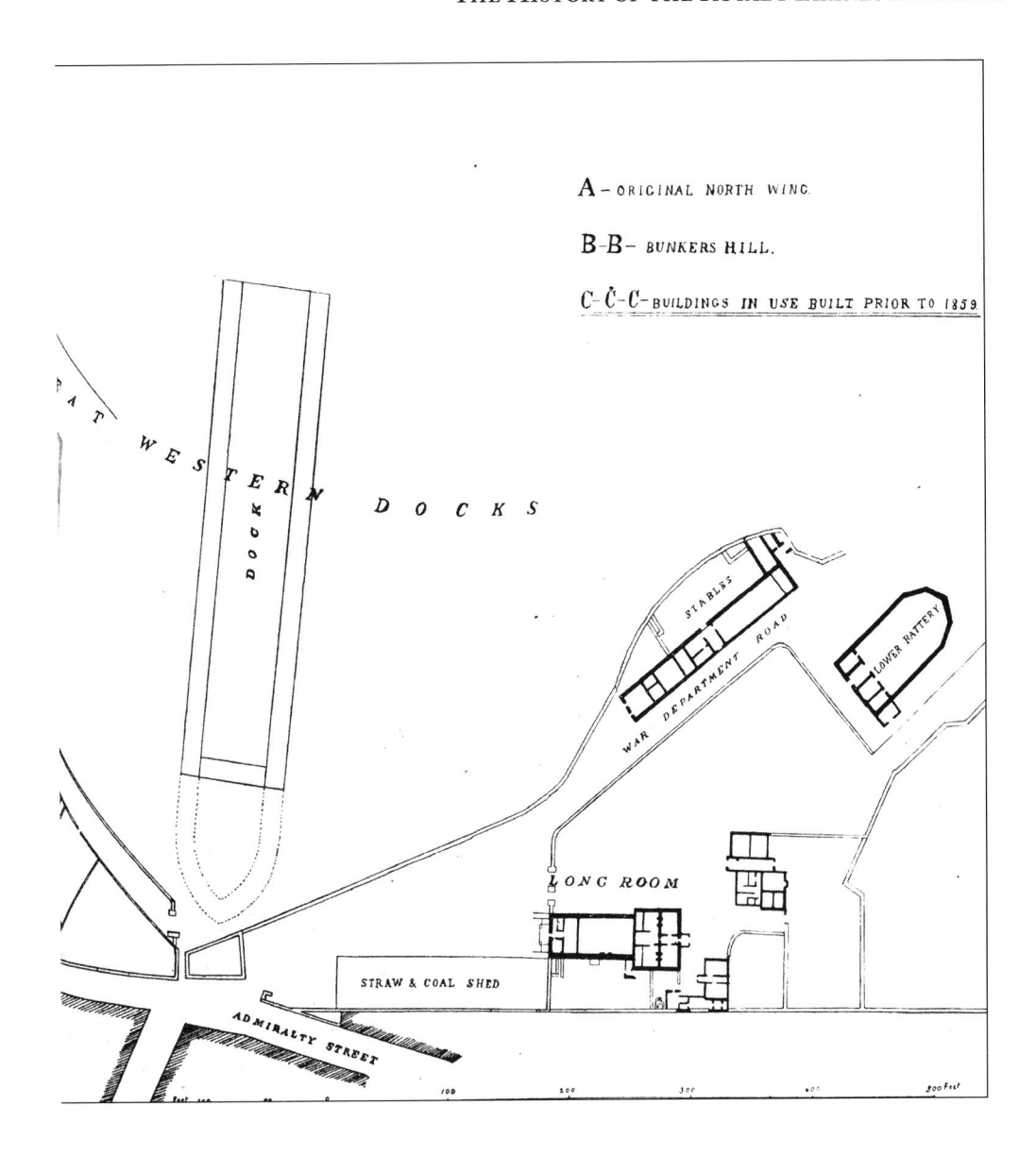

A – ORIGINAL NORTH WING
B-B – BUNKERS HILL.
C-C-C – BUILDINGS IN USE BUILT PRIOR TO 1859.

was so cramped that it was found only possible to make 10 quarters. For many years this portion of the Barracks was familiarly known to the Officers as "The Warren." In 1895 serious cases of typhoid caused much needed alterations to be made to the drainage. The reconstruction into seven flats was not carried out until 1905.

The present condition of the Mill Bay area makes it difficult to realise what was the extent of the water area in ancient times. The "History of Plymouth," by R. Worth, states that anchors have been found where the Octagon now is. The first attempt of importance to provide special accommodation was the formation of the Union Dock in what is now the southern angle between Martin and Phoenix Streets. In 1840 an Act was passed authorizing the construction of the Millbay Pier with a dock adjacent. This dock has since been filled up and the site built upon, consequent on the adoption of a larger undertaking. Mr. I. Brunel, the engineer of the South Devon and Cornwall Railways, was the engineer of the new docks. After experiencing serious difficulties the floating basin was opened in February 1857.

The construction of a floating basin and dry dock by the Railway Company resulted in the reclamation from the sea of a considerable portion of ground, outside of what was the sea wall of the barracks. Part of this ground was bought by the Admiralty and the existing wall was built. At one time the "Sea Gate" of the Barracks opened on to the G.W. Docks area; this gave rise to the privilege still enjoyed by officers and men quartered in barracks of entering the G.W. Docks free of charge. The old sea wall was pulled down and a few feet east of it were built the present ablution rooms, cookhouse, officers baggage store, etc. The space between the barracks and these buildings was roofed in, forming the drill shed, completed in 1873. Prior to the opening of the cookhouse in 1873 all meals were cooked in the barrack rooms, and for many years dinners were occasionally cooked there in winter, as long as the old pattern cooking ranges existed. Up to the year 1881 the following were built: the School on the Millbay Road, known as the Admiralty School, used as a school for girls until it was lent to the local Educational Authority in 1921; the Bowling Alley and Wash-house, the Workshops and Band Practice room, the Canteen block, Racket Court and quarters for the Sergeants-Major. When the new Wet Canteen was taken into use in 1851 the original canteen accommodation under the officers' mess was altered into quarters for the senior sergeant-major, and when the houses were built for warrant officers,

MARINE BARRACKS AT STONEHOUSE, DEVONSHIRE.

these quarters were allotted to the officers' mess sergeant. The racket court, built in 1882, was a fine building, but larger than the regulation size; after a "condemned" existence of some years it has now been converted into three standard squash racket courts. A house was built for the Assistant Surgeon near the Infirmary at the Longroom, and the Divisional stables in 1861. In 1880 the "new" Camber was constructed by the G.W. Dock Company and taken into use for the boats of the Division and of the King's Harbour-master.

The present coal and straw shed and garage for Divisional transport was a drill shed, and had been used as such and for housing the officers' boats for some years prior to the construction of the present drill shed. On the wall opposite to this shed was a cemented strip of the G.W. docks wall, on which bulls' eyes were painted as aiming marks. Most of this strip is now hidden by the officers' garages, but traces of the aiming marks can still be distinguished. The Shooting Gallery was built in 1886 and the upper gun drill battery on Longroom Hill was competed in 1889. In 1900 the Staff Sergeants quarters on the site of the old coal yard were completed, and the adjacent bath-house in 1922. The present Infirmary near St. Paul's Church was completed in 1902, and the old infirmary taken into use as the shoemakers' shop. The Commandant's garden was established opposite the new Infirmary at this time.

CHURCH.

In the early days of the Division men used to attend services at St. Andrew's Church, one of the two churches in the town. An order of 1783 states that the men are to be marched to Plymouth Old Church (St. Andrew's). When the Barracks were built at Stonehouse in 1784 the old chapel of East Stonehouse had fallen into disrepair. An Act of Parliament was made authorizing the taking down of the old chapel and the building of a new one. The Commandant of the Marines was designated as one of the Trustees for the carrying out of this work. This new chapel was called the Chapel of East Stonehouse, and is now known as St. George's Parish Church. For many years the Division attended the parish church, until in 1877 the Division was ordered to attend service in the Lecture Room. In 1878 the lecture room was authorized by the Admiralty to be used for Divine Service until further orders.

Since that date a service has usually been held in the lecture room. Generally speaking the overflow lecture room service went to St. George's Church, played by the drums; at other times the whole parade went to St. George's. For a period before the war the service was held at St. Paul's Church. It was not, however, until about 1922 that the lecture room ceased to be used for other purposes than church services. At one time penny readings, dances and matinees musicales, and at a later date work parties, were held in there. Of recent years laudable efforts have been made to improve the appearance of this room and to render its equipment more consonant with its use. It now contains the handsome roll of honour of those who fell in the Great War and two memorial brasses.

GUN DRILL BATTERY.

As already indicated, a very small gun drill battery existed on Bunker's Hill for the use of the R.M.A. details attached to the Division, with a wooden broadside gun in the drill room for handspike drill. The present lower battery was built in 1857. The date when the drill battery at the Devil's point was taken over is uncertain, but it was enlarged and covered in in 1881. The garden at the Point was in use by officers prior to this date. The present upper battery on the Longroom was finished in 1889, but was not armed until 1893-1896. The drill battery at the Point continued to be used for many years for the preliminary training of recruits and for instruction in the mysteries of the hammock. In 1906 the R.N.R. Battery and buildings at the Point were taken over, but the guns were removed and the battery used as a signals school and the covered drill shed as a gymnasium.

MUSKETRY.

It is not known where ball practice with muskets took place in the early days of the Division. It is very probable that it took place in the ditch of the Citadel, but on the introduction of the Enfield rifle about the time of the Crimean War a range was obtained on the sea shore at Mount Batten. The men used to go to and fro in boats from headquarters. This inconvenient arrangement came to an end when barrack rooms were obtained at Fort Stamford in exchange for Millbay Barracks. When parties were sent to Batten, and a steamboat was not available for towing, a curious type of paddle-boat, worked by hand, was occasionally used. A range was subsequently built on Staddon Heights for the use of the garrison, and was also used by the Marines. When the Lee-Metford rifle was introduced, a great number of ranges in the country were condemned as unsafe, amongst which was Staddon range. The wall for retaining the butts on Staddon Heights still remains as a very prominent landmark, and a fruitful source of varied explanations as to the reason of its existence to newcomers to the West Country Division.

For some years subsequent to the closing of the Staddon ranges musketry instruction at Plymouth was carried out under great difficulties. The range accommodation at Fort Tregantle was very limited, and so the Assistant Instructor of Musketry and the bulk of the instructors were sent to Forton, where the Plymouth details carried out range practices until range accommodation again became available at Tregantle and subsequently at the old range at Mt. Batten. This was a very poor range in every way, and eventually accommodation was again made available at the Tregantle ranges, details being accommodated first at Fort Tregantle and subsequently at Fort Scraesdon. Military Training, subsequently called Field Training, was also carried out at Fort Stamford, tents being pitched on the glacis to accommodate the detachments. Tactical training is now carried out from Fort Scraesdon. Mention should also be made of the 30 yards range which was built at the Devil's Point in 1913, and the shooting gallery built in 1886.

RECREATION GROUNDS.

For very many years the Division suffered from the lack of any recreation ground of its own. Previous to the Great War the officers had three tennis courts on the reclaimed ground by the racket court. The Longroom ground was a rough uneven ground, quite unsuited for any games. This area had been levelled during the war, and in 1920 it was covered with turf and converted into a good football ground. There is sufficient space for a cricket net and one tennis court for warrant officers. The Drummers Pit has been fenced off and four grass tennis courts established for the use of n.c. officers and marines. An excellent swimming pool was built outside the boat camber in 1910. No Division has such facilities for boat-sailing as Plymouth Division. Weekly races for service boats are a feature of the summer season, one day being reserved for officer coxswains and one for n.c. officers or marines.

As has already been mentioned, three standard squash racket courts, built in the old racket court, were opened for play in 1930. Mention should also be made of the Bowling Alley, which was built in 1880, and for which the Division was famous for many years.

THEATRE.

Shortly after the Barracks were built in 1783 a small racket court or ball court was built about 1788. This court was really too small to be of much use, and it was adapted for use as a theatre in 1848. The present theatre is the result of a skilfully designed enlargement and rearrangement of the old theatre and the straw yard which existed at its back. The Theatre has the advantage of being arranged as such with all the requisite equipment of a regular theatre. New seating of modern pattern was installed in 1928, and the equipment for cinema performances is being extended so as to provide for two projectors, etc., for the winter of 1930.

THE PARADE.

Before the year 1910 the parade ground in the Barracks was level, with the result that in wet weather water lay for some time. The corner near the Officers' Mess was particularly noted for its sticky white mud. Between the years 1910 and 1912 four gutterways were laid across the parade and the intervening surface was cambered. This feature has undoubtedly given a drier parade ground but it has entirely upset the symmetry of a ceremonial parade when the troops are in line. Further, the present surface is quite unsuited for horses, in which it resembles the majority of the roads in the vicinity. Previously to the Great War the "Brickfields" at Devonport was frequently used by the Division for drills, and also for ceremonial parades of the garrison. Many noteworthy equestrian feats have been performed on this peculiarly shaped area. A large part of the "Brickfields" is now fenced off, and several football grounds have been made for the use of the garrison, and large ceremonial parades of the garrison are no longer possible.

WATER SUPPLY IN PLYMOUTH BARRACKS.
Compiled by Brigadier R. D. Ormsby, C.B.E.

Most residents in the Royal Marine Barracks of the present day are aware that there were many hardships to be undergone in the earlier days of the Barracks, that is if conditions then are compared with modern ideas of necessary amenities and comfort. When the Barracks at Plymouth were first occupied in 1783, the want of a good supply of water was much felt. The copies of two letters given below are of interest, not only for the subject itself, but as examples of Official correspondence of a hundred and fifty years ago.

The initials A.C. refer to Major General Arthur Tooker Collins, who was Commandant of the Plymouth Division from 1784 to 1793. Major General Collins was the father of Captain David Collins who went out as Judge Advocate with Governor Phillip, the first Governor of New South Wales, and who himself became the first Governor of Tasmania.

P. Barracks, 4th July, 1785.

Sir, - This being a remarkable dry season, our Barracks are so unfortunately situated as not to admit of any water but what is brackish. Our men are obliged to go almost a mile for water which destroys their necessaries and subjects them to be disorderly, therefore If My Lords Commissioners of the Admiralty will be pleased to order a long boat with a proper number of casks from the Dockyard our own boatmen might be employed in bringing water from the Kings Brew House, which would be a sufficient supply.

I am etc., (Sgd.) A.C.

P. Stephens. Esq.
The Honourable,
The Commissioners of H.M. Navy.

The Shortness of your visit to the Barracks prevented me acquainting you with the most distressing circumstance the want of water on the least continuance of sunshine.

Here is a pump which is supposed to supply the Barracks this pump has lately been made intirely new, but it seems to do its office very badly as it has been sometime out of order and the maker has been sent to often yet no one appears to rectify it. I apprehend a pump which is to give a supply to Six Hundred Men daily should be made upon the first principles and not like one which may serve a girl to pump a pail of water now and then.

If you would be so kind as to pay five minutes attention to this pump I am certain you will agree with me that its necessary to give every assistance that acts can procure to supply the Barracks, with water.

I am, Gentlemen, &c., (Sgd.) AC.

Dated 18th June, 1786.

HISTORY OF THE CHATHAM DIVISION ROYAL MARINES.
By Captain V. D. Thomas, R.M.

This short history of the Barracks has been compiled from old Divisional Orders and other files available at Headquarters. Few papers are to be found prior to 1703, but those of interest are quoted.

There is an Admiralty Letter Book of 1763, but the first Commandant's Letter book is dated 1777, and therefore it is only possible to obtain a complete record of correspondence between both departments from that date.

(Editor's Note: The writing, punctuation, layout and grammar of this article is exactly as written by the author - the reader will note that staff duties would appear not to have been considered important.)

History prior to the construction of the Barracks.

The actual date of the Marines being first quartered in the town is uncertain, but there is a record of their being at Rochester in 1708, as the following letter shows:-

Admiralty Office,

24th January, 1708-9.

Gentn.

WHEREAS I am informed by Sr. Wm. Jumper, Super-intendent at Chatham and Sheernefs, that many seamen who came from Deale, Dover and Foulkston, from Merchants Ships, and severall Deserters from ships of Her Majys. doe travel the Country wide of the roade that leads to London, and thereby escape being taken up and sent into Her Majys. Service. And WHEREAS I have therefore given orders to Lieutenant Colonell Webb of the Marines, who is at or near Rochester, to place a guard at or near Ailsford, and at such other place or places as he shall judge convient, for the re-intercepting such Straggling Seamen, and to carry them to the Clerk of ye Cheque at Chatham, to be disposed of as Sr. Wm. Jumper shall direct. I doe hereby desire and direct you to give orders to the said Clerk of the Cheque, that for every such Straggling Seamen fitt for Majys. Service as shall be brought unto him by orders of Lieut. Coll. Webb, or the Commander in Chiefe of the Marines, at or about Rochester for the time being, he does pay the sum of twenty shillings, according to Her Majys. Royall Proclamation, and take a receipt for the same, and you are further to direct the sd. Clerk of the Cheque to inform me himselfe, and to give an account to you, if any of the said seamen doe belong to her Majys. Ships, and if so, you are to cause the money paid for them to be Stoped out of the pay due to them or out of their growing pay, and in order therewith, you are to direct the Clerk of the Cheque to give an Accot. of what Ships they shall be put aboard.

I am,

Your affectte ffriend,

PEMBROKE.

Another record of the early occupation of the Marines in the town of Rochester is an account of a force of 600 Foot Guards and Officers proportionable, and a detachment of one hundred gentlemen of the four troops of Horse Guards, and three score men of the Horse Grenadiers, and Officers proportionable, being dispatched by his Grace the Duke of Ormonde. This force was ordered to proceed to Rochester in 1713, in order to suppress the men of Will's Regiment of Marines, quartered at or near Rochester, who, on orders having been received to disband the Regiment, were assembled in a tumultous manner, in contempt of Her Majesty's authority, and to the disturbance of the peace of her Subjects.

In 1763 there were 16 Companies stationed at Chatham. The first indication of Barracks being built for the Marines is to be found in a letter from the Admiralty Office, dated 21st November, 1764.

Sir,
His Majesty having been pleased to direct that provision be made in the Barracks at Chatham for quartering a body of his Marine Forces, consisting of at least 500 Private men with the usual proportion of officers, and the Secretary at War having in consequence thereof directed the Commanding Officer of His Majesty's Forces at Chatham Barracks to consult with you and report what part of the said Barracks can be spared for the use of the above number of Marines, having in particular regard to the situation of the same, so as to keep the Quarters of the Land and Marine Forces seperate and distinct, I am commanded by my Lords Commissioners of the Admiralty to acquaint you therewith, in order that you may consult with and assist the said Commanding Officer in making such report accordingly.

I am, etc.,

The C.M.Os., Chatham. PHILIP STEVENS.

At this period the Marines were billeted in the towns, and a letter was received by the Commandant from the Lords Commissioners of the Admiralty directing him to state the reason for half the Division being quartered in Rochester, "to the great distress of the inhabitants upon whom they are billeted." No reply to this letter is available.

However, the number of billets do not appear to have been sufficient, and further billets were obtained, as is indicated in the following letter.

By the Commissioners for executing the Office of Lord High Admiral of Great Britain and Ireland, etc.

Whereas you have represented to us by letter of the 5th instant, that you have applied to the justices for enlarging the Marine Quarters (which are at present rather crowded), and to that end desired that 11 Public Houses belonging to the Gillingham Parish, and which constitutes part of Brompton, are within the Lines, and where you have not had a man quartered upon, might be allotted to you, for better enabling, from its continuity to the Dockyard, to have your men quartered near to where their duty requires them: And whereas you have also represented that the Justices seem well disposed, as you informed, to grant your request, but that they have no authority to confine the Constables to a particular spot of any Parish, when a route is general, as yours is. And you having desired a route, particularly specifying the Marine Forces to be quartered in that part of Gillingham Parish called Brompton, may be sent you. You are therefore hereby required and directed, whenever the number of Marines under your Command is more than can be provided for in a proper manner in Chatham to appoint as many as you shall find requisite to be quartered at

Rochester, St. Margaret's, Strood, and particularly that part of Gillingham called Brompton, or at such as those places as may be convient for His Majesty's Service. And all Justices of the Peace, and Constables and other civil officers, whom this may concern, are hereby required to be aiding and assisting to you in the due execution hereof. Given under our hands the eleventh day of July, 1765.

Signed,
EGMONT. CARYSFORT. DIGBY.

The C.M.O., Chatham.

On the 30th July of the same year the Officers of the Division sent a petition to the Lords Commissioners of the Admiralty; Praying to be put into Barracks in order to relieve them from any inconvenience they now labour under.

In 1763 the Lords Commissioners of the Admiralty being of the opinion that the guarding of His Majesty's Dockyards with Marines instead of Watchmen selected from the Labourers of the Yards, as then practised, might contribute greatly to the security of the Magazines and Stores, as well as to the safety of the Ships, signified their directions that the Marines were to "Post a Guard."

This guard was continued until 1868, and the following letter in connection with the Guard is of interest:-

Chatham Dock.
13th April, 1769.

Sir,

As the Marine Guard have from the first doing duty in the Dockyard been accustomed to load, I was surprised at the information of its being lately discontinued, and at the message I received from Lieut. Hill, of your having ordered three rounds of cartridges to be lodged at the Guard Rooms, to be issued to the Guard whenever you might think it proper, as I cannot even consider the Centinels secure from being attacked, if it should be known that their Pieces are not loaded, and much less the vast object they are ordered to defend, or that it will be in their power in dark and windy nights to alarm the different Posts and Guards, I find myself under the necessity to acquaint you herewith and that I must address the Lords Commissioners of the Admiralty on the subject, as I consider myself exposed to censure while the Centinels are allowed to mount without ammunition. I have particular pleasure, sir, in declaring on this occasion that you have ever laboured with me that the Guard shall fully answer the purpose intended.

I am, Sir,
THOS. HANWAY.

In 1776 the Public Houses in Chatham were divided into classes, with the number of Soldiers each house could contain:

- 1st Class :   "Sun; Mitre; Hill Coffee House - 3 Houses at 8 men each - 24 men.
- 2nd Class: "Royal Oak; Union Flag; King's Head; Crown and Anchor; Old Globe; Red Lion; George; Crown and Thistle; Brewer's Arms; Old Barn; King's Head; Golden Lion; Queen's Head; King's Arms - 14 Houses of 6 men each - 84 men.
- 3rd Class: "Prince of Orange; Cross Keys; Trumpet Horn; King's Arms; George; Tobacco Roll; Coach and Horses; Dartmouth Arms; Fountain; Red Lion;

	Tanner's; Swan; Hen and Chickens; Blue-bell; Three Cups; King's Head; Swan; White Heart; Red Lion; Shipwright's Arms; Black Horse; Plough; King's Head; Palmer's Swan, Brompton" - 24 Houses at 4 men each - 96 men.
4th Class:	"Britannia; Cricketers; Ship and Launch; Hit or Miss; Granby; Dover Castle; Three Horse Shoes; Black Boy; Shipp Coffee House; Crown; Sun; White Horse; Hook and Hatchet; George"-14 Houses at 2 men each - 28 men.

It will be noticed how many of the Public Houses mentioned are still in existence, or at all events their names are preserved.

This list also contains the public houses in Brompton, Strood and Rochester, and billeted in all 354 men.

Site for the Barracks.

The site for the Barracks was purchased in 1777. From a plan of Chatham Dockyard dated 1688, it will be seen that there were only four houses in the neighbourhood, in addition to St. Mary's Church. (See plan "A.")

It should be noted that the present steps leading down to the river are shown, but there is no lane running up from the stairs to Dock Road, neither is there a lane running along the Gun Wharf Wall on the site of the present Drill Shed. The building nearest the river appears to be on the site of the present canteen, but what this building actually was is not known.

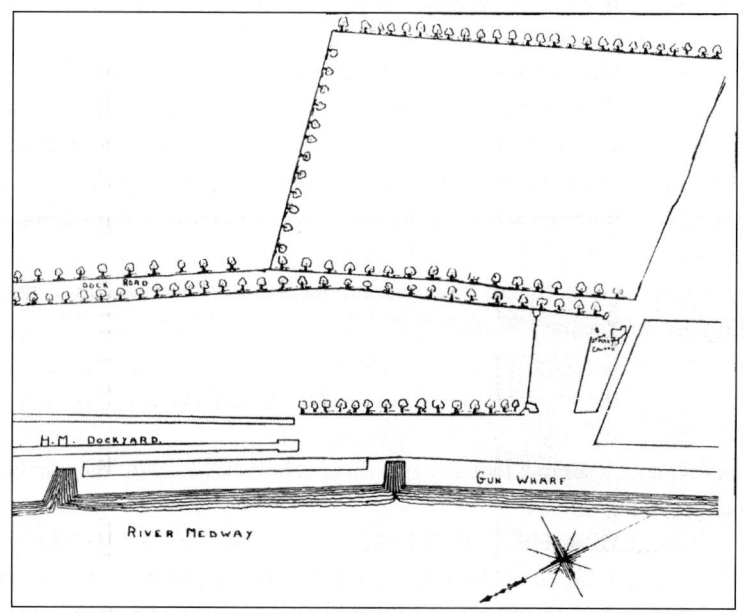

PLANS OF HM DOCKYARD CHATHAM IN THE YEARS 1688, 1698 AND 1774 (PLAN 'A')

Occupation of the Barracks.

A Divisional Order dated 2nd September, 1779, reads as follows:-

The Marine Barracks being so far forward as to be fit to receive some of the Division, to inhabit those rooms proper for that purpose, it is therefore the Commanding Officer's directions that as many of those of the Division now at Quarters as the said Barracks may contain, shall march in on Friday afternoon, thereto remain to lodge and inhabit until further orders.

Description of the Barracks and General History.

The History will be set out in Four Periods and each period will be sub-divided into two parts. Part "A" will consist of the construction of the barracks, and Part "B" any items of interest other than construction.

The periods are as follows:-
1st Period: 1779-1862, when the Barracks remained as they were first constructed.
2nd Period: 1862-1906, on the enlargement of Main Barracks.
3rd Period: 1906-1914, the addition of Melville Barracks.
4th Period: 1914-1930.

1st Period, 1779-1862, Part "A."

The plan of the barracks (see Plan "B") as it appeared when constructed, is taken from facts obtained from the Civil Engineers, Department of the Dockyard, and also from a plan of the buildings between the barracks and St. Mary's Church, but the latter plan is dated 1856, just prior to this land being bought for the enlargement of the barracks. (See Plan "B.")

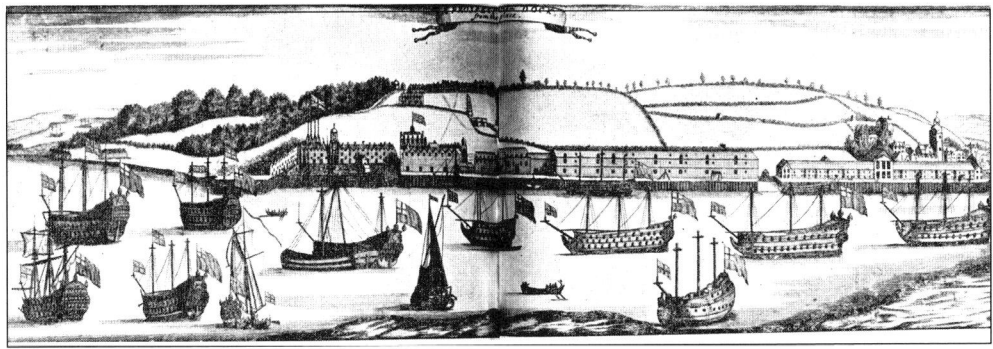

A PROSPECT OF CHATHAM DOCK

Starting on the East side of the barracks along Dock Road, at the South end are the Field Officers and Barrackmaster's houses. On the left of the main gate on entering is the Guard Room, underneath which was the "Black Hole," which according to orders of April 1791 was used as follows:-

"A soldier is not to be confined by a Commissioned Officer to the Black Hole, but on the urgent necessity with which the Commanding Officer on the spot is immediately to be acquainted."

On the North side of the barracks were the Commandant's House and Office, Adjutant's and Staff Officer's houses, and the annex to the Mess, with the main Mess buildings and Mess Room. The North Gate was part of the original construction.

Along the West side of the barracks the boundary ran alongside the Gun Wharf wall as far as the canteen, which did not then exist. At this period there were no buildings on this side, except the men's quarters, as the outer wing had not been built. The Sergeants' Mess was next to the Officers' Mess.

The South wall ran from a point about the position of the canteen to the Field Officers' houses, but as will be seen from the plan the present Guard Room gate did not exist. There was a gate in the South wall and also a wicket gate, the latter being mentioned in Order of 1863 as only to be used by the Field Officers and Barrack master. Outside the South wall was Red Cat Lane, which had on the further side a number of dwelling houses. Mention of this lane is made in Orders of 1849, as two soldiers' wives residing in that lane died of malignant cholera, and the Commandant directed that all living in that locality be removed into barracks and the place put out of bounds.

This definitely settles the position of Red Cat Lane, and the theory of this lane running in rear of the barracks is incorrect. How this lane came to be called by this name is not clear, but it assumed that at some earlier date there was Public House of this name in the area. The Red Lion stands on the present site of the canteen. The Navy and Army Hotel is also mentioned Orders of 1863, when the south wicket gate was left open for the convenience of the Quartermaster' Department to remove stores from that place.

There is now only one building which cannot definitely be fixed and that is the Single Officers' quarters. This was, it is presumed, somewhere on the south side of the barracks, and stood according to Lieut.-Colonel Swiney on the site of the present dry canteen. On looking at the plan this would appear to be possible, but it has not been inserted as it cannot be verified. Mention is made, as will be found later, of officers being quartered in the South Wing.

The Armourer's Shop and Recreation Room were built in 1848, and formed part of the Outer West Wing. The old Stables and Harness-room (Gun Battery) were erected at the same time.

The picture- "A Prospect of Chatham" - in the Officers Mess at Chatham, shows the Barracks as they were at this period.

In 1828 Melville Barracks, as we now know it, was constructed for use as a Naval Hospital, on a portion of the ground used as gardens for the Royal Marines.

1st Period, 1779-1862, Part "B."

BILLETS. - The strength of the Corps about this time was continually changing, and in 1782 there were 37 companies at Chatham, each of 140 privates, giving a strength of 5,200 men, of which only a small number would be accommodated in barracks. In connection with men quartered in the town, various places of parade are mentioned.

In 1790 the Battalion paraded in the Vines, Rochester, including those at headquarters, and those in odd places, at any spot the senior Officers or Sergeant might direct. Later in the same year more troops appear to have been brought into barracks.

"The Troop to beat at seven o'clock this evening, when the whole of the Battalion is to parade at the Commanding Officer's quarters with their arms and necessaries complete. A baggage waggon to be in the yard of the Crown Inn at seven o'clock to he loaded. The General to beat to-morrow morning at three o'clock and the troop at half an hour thereafter, at which time the whole of the Officers and the Battalion, except those in the district of Seal, are to parade opposite the Commanding Officer's quarters to proceed on their route to the Barracks at Chatham; it is expected that the Non - commissioned Officers at the different billets see that the men's quarters are all paid, and that they may leave the town with credit and not have any disagreements with their landlords.

14th June, 1790"

This did not bring all the men of the Division into Barracks, as orders of 1811 direct that "Men quartered in Chatham beyond the Chest Arms be paraded with the Rochester party, and that the Subaltern of that party to visit them in their quarters."

Again, in 1814, "The men who are quartered out in Chatham, Strood and Rochester are at all times in readiness when required to proceed to Rochester Bridge, where a Field Officer will take command of them."

The actual date of men of the Division ceasing to be billeted in the town is uncertain, but it is unlikely that this continued after 1862.

GARDENS. - In 1785 a Garden Fund was started for putting the ground in order that was allotted to the N.C.Os. and private men as a garden, and every man subscribed one day's pay to the same. This subscription was reduced when part of the ground was taken over for a Naval Hospital.

These extracts from Orders show to a certain extent the life of the Division during the period.

GUARDS. - In 1785 the Dock Guard, which has already been referred to, consisted of 1 subaltern 3 sergeants, 3 corporals, 1 drummer, 32 privates; and in June 1814 the strength of the

Guard had been increased to 1 captain, 2 subalterns, 4 sergeants, 6 corporals, 2 drummers and 135 privates. Later, in 1817, the Guards which were provided daily were:-

Barrack Guard -
1 Capt.; 1 2nd Lt.; 3 Sgts.; 2 Cpls.; I Drmr.; 45 Ptes.
Garden Picquet -
1 Cpl.; 3 Ptes.
Anchor Wharf –
1 Sgt.; 1 Cpl.; 12 Ptes.
Dock Guard -
1 2nd Lt.; 2 Sgts.; 2 Cpls.; 1 Drmr.; 39 Ptes.
Again in 1820 further Guards were provided, as shown in the following table:-
Barrack Guard –
1 2nd Lt.; 1 Sgt.; 2 Cpls.; 1 Drmr.; 39 Ptes.
Main Dock -
1 Capt.; 1 2nd Lt.; 2 Sgts.; 3 Cpls.; 1 Drmr.; 63 Ptes.
Lower Dock –
1 2nd Lt.; I Sgt.; 2 Cpls.; 1 Drmr.; 30 Ptes.
Anchor Wharf –
1 Sgt.; 1 Cpl.; 12 Ptes.
Convict Guard –
1 Sgt.; 6 Ptes.
Melville Parade –
1 Cpl.; 3 Gunners.
Brompton Barrier –
1 Sgt.; 24 Ptes.
Lines –
1 Sgt.; 1 Cpl,; 18 Ptes.
Gun Wharf –
1 Sgt.; 1 Cpl.; 15 Ptes.
St. Mary's –
1 Sgt.; 1 Cpl.; 12 Ptes,

The Guard House used by the Dock Guard is three-storey building in the dockyard, which is at present used as a Joiners' Store. There were officers' cabins on each floor. These cabins have now been pulled down (during 1930), as this building is at the present time being altered.

MARCH ROUTE. - 1783: "The Marines. of the Portsmouth and Plymouth Divisions to parade to-morrow morning at 5 o'clock in order to march to their respective Divisions."

PUNISHMENTS. - 1814: "Whereas Lt. and Adjt. Peebles, as Acting judge Advocate, has transmitted to us the proceedings of a General Court-Martial held at Chatham for the trial of

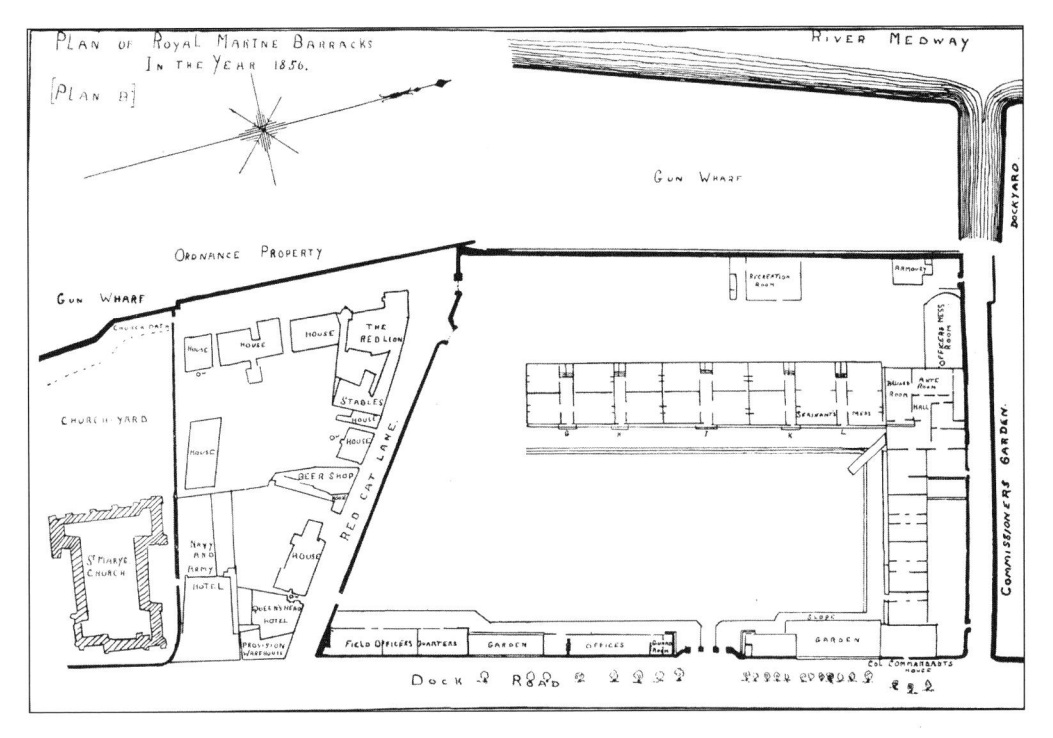

Chas. Collins Pte. Marine, for stabbing Sergt. Abbott in the side with a bayonet, and whereas it appears by the sentence that the Court have maturely and deliberately weighed the evidence were the opinion that the prisoner was guilty of the crime laid against him, but in consideration of the very provoking and irritating behaviour of Sergt Abbott to him, did only sentence him to receive 600 lashes on his bare back with cat o'nine tails by the drummers of the Division, and afterward to be drummed out of the Royal Marine Corps with a halter round his neck.

And whereas we have taken the said sentence into our consideration, we do hereby signify our approval thereof.

My Lords Commissioners of the Admiralty."

The First Division.

The reason for the Chatham Division being styled the "First Division" is not absolutely clear, and there are two opinions on the matter: One is because the Chatham Division were the first Division to occupy Marine barracks, the other is for the service of the Division during the Mutinies in 1797.

With regard to the latter, when in 1797 handbills were distribute among the Marines of Chatham inciting them to mutiny, the N.C.O.'s signed a petition showing their loyalty.

The following are extracts which show the correspondence received by the Commandant from the War Office and Admiralty at that time:

Horse Guards.
25th May, 1797.

Sir,

I have Field Marshals the Duke of York's command to acknowledge the receipt of your letter of the 23rd instant, with its enclosures, for which communication His Royal Highness desires that you will be pleased to accept his best thanks. His Royal Highness has felt great satisfaction at the highly praiseworthy conduct of the Division of Marines under your Command in having in such proper terms evinced their detestation and abhorrence of the vile acts that are now practicing by wicked incendiaries with a view to shake the allegiance of the soldiery. But His Royal Highness trusts that the honourable example set by the Chatham Division of Marines will be followed by every individual of their brother soldiers, and that the British Army will to the latest period preserve its love and attachment to their King and Country, and that they will be as desirous to distinguish themselves for their loyalty as they have ever been emulous to excel all other nations in courage when opposed to the enemy.

I have the honour to be. etc.,
ROBERT BROWNRIGG.

Major-General Innes,
    Commdg. Chatham Division of Marines.
        Admiralty Office.

23rd May, 1797.

Sir,

I have received and communicated to My Lords Commissioners of the Admiralty your letter to me of yesterday's date, enclosing a printed hand-bill which appeared to have been distributed amongst the Marines at Chatham under your command, and an answer thereto which has been transmitted to you signed by the Non-commissioned Officers of the Division now in barracks at that place; and I have it in command from their Lordships to acquaint you, that they view with great satisfaction the spirit, and loyalty and zeal so strongly manifested by the Non-commissioned Officers and Privates of that Division, and , which it is their direction you should communicate to them in a proper manner. I have at the same time the pleasure to add that their Lordships fully approve of all your proceedings on the occasions,

And have the honour to be, Sir, etc.,
EVAN NEPEAN.

Major-General Innes,
    Chatham.

Subsequently in December 1797, when a detachment from Chatham was proceeding to London to take part in a thanksgiving service in St. Paul's for the signal victories in the late war, the Commandant included these words in a Divisional Order:-

"You will not fail to recollect that the Division to which you belong has well earned the Honour of being styled the "First Division" from the eminent loyalty they displayed in its answer to the infamous handbill which was, immediately followed by every other Corps."

Barrack Women.

The first reference appears in 1780. - When any woman employed in Divisional Service in the Marine Barracks or any other building thereunto belonging, comes with child, she is not on any account or pretence whatsoever to be permitted to lodge or inhabit in any of the aforementioned places, after the fourth month of her pregnancy. The Quartermaster and Barrackmaster are in their weekly visitations to be as attentive as possible to the execution of this order, to prevent the very great inconvenience that the neglect thereof may occasion.

Again in 1783 the Pay Sergeants were instructed to see that the Men's rooms never contained less in each, than the smallest number for a Mess which is eight, beside the Barrack Women. When Bibles were issued in 1806, one to every inhabited room, they were turned over to the Women in charge of the room. Later women occupying different barrack rooms (Artillery Rooms excepted) attended for the purpose of drawing for their turn to have Boys messed in their rooms.

The last reference with regard to the Women is found in orders of 1827, when women were allowed to remain in barracks for six weeks after their husbands had embarked.

The date of the removal of the Women from barracks cannot be definitely stated.

Supervision of Barrackrooms.

It will be noted that in an order mentioned above, the Quartermaster visited the rooms, and during this period it was one of the duties of the Quartermaster to supervise all the barrackrooms.

Beer.

June 1794. His Majesty's most gracious bounty of five pints of small beer per day to each N.C.O Drummer and Private man will commence to-morrow and will continue to be served of Saturday's and Wednesday's at eleven o'clock, at which hour the superintendents of each room and the out-layers are to attend to receive their proportions.

In the following month the N.C.O.'s and private men petitioned the Commanding Officer that the supply be reduced to three pints, and he thought proper to comply with their request.

Divisional Library.

The Divisional Library was started in September 1841, and corporals, drummers and privates were stopped 1d. per month for the upkeep of the same.

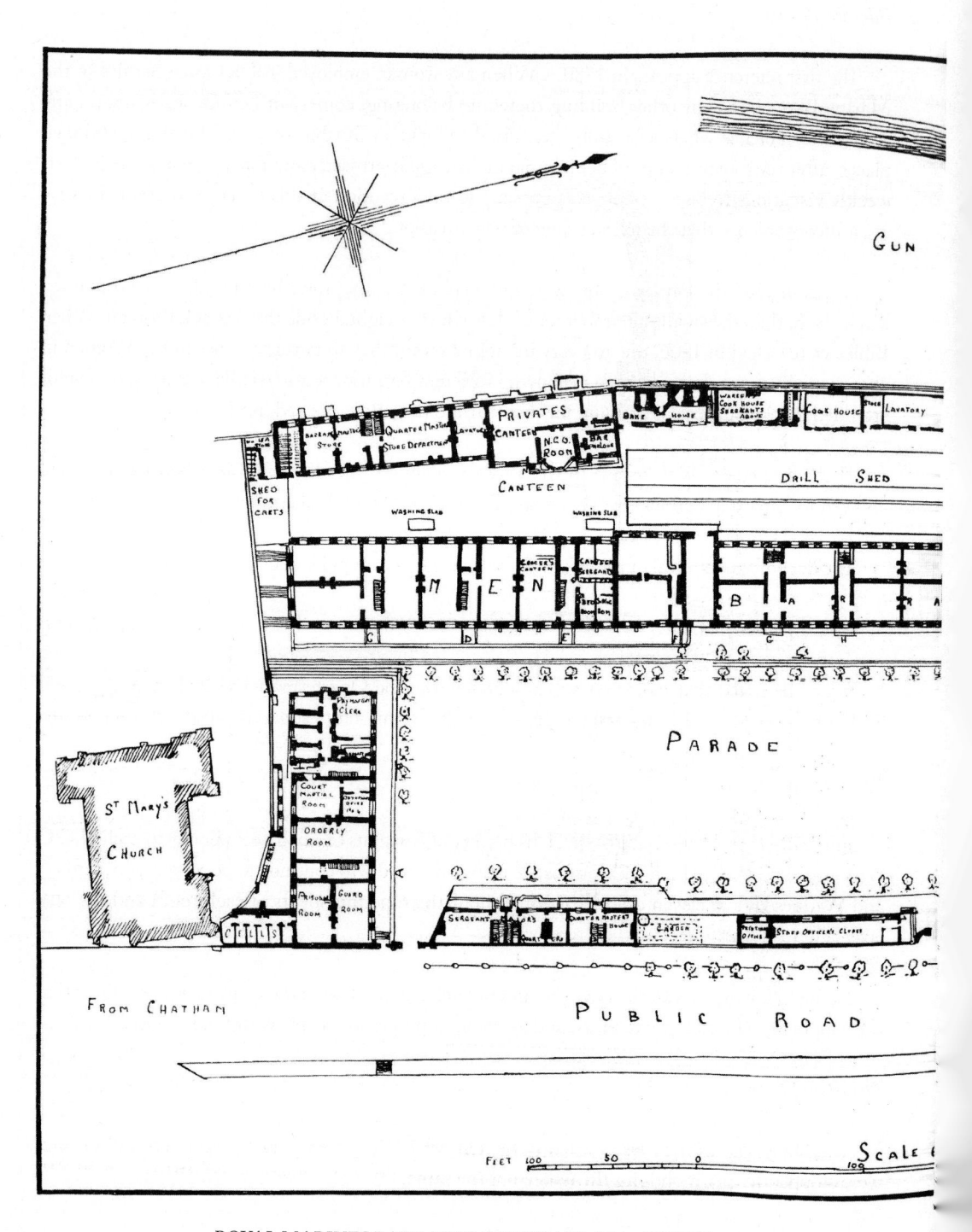

ROYAL MARINES BARRACKS CHATHAM, 1880 – PLAN C

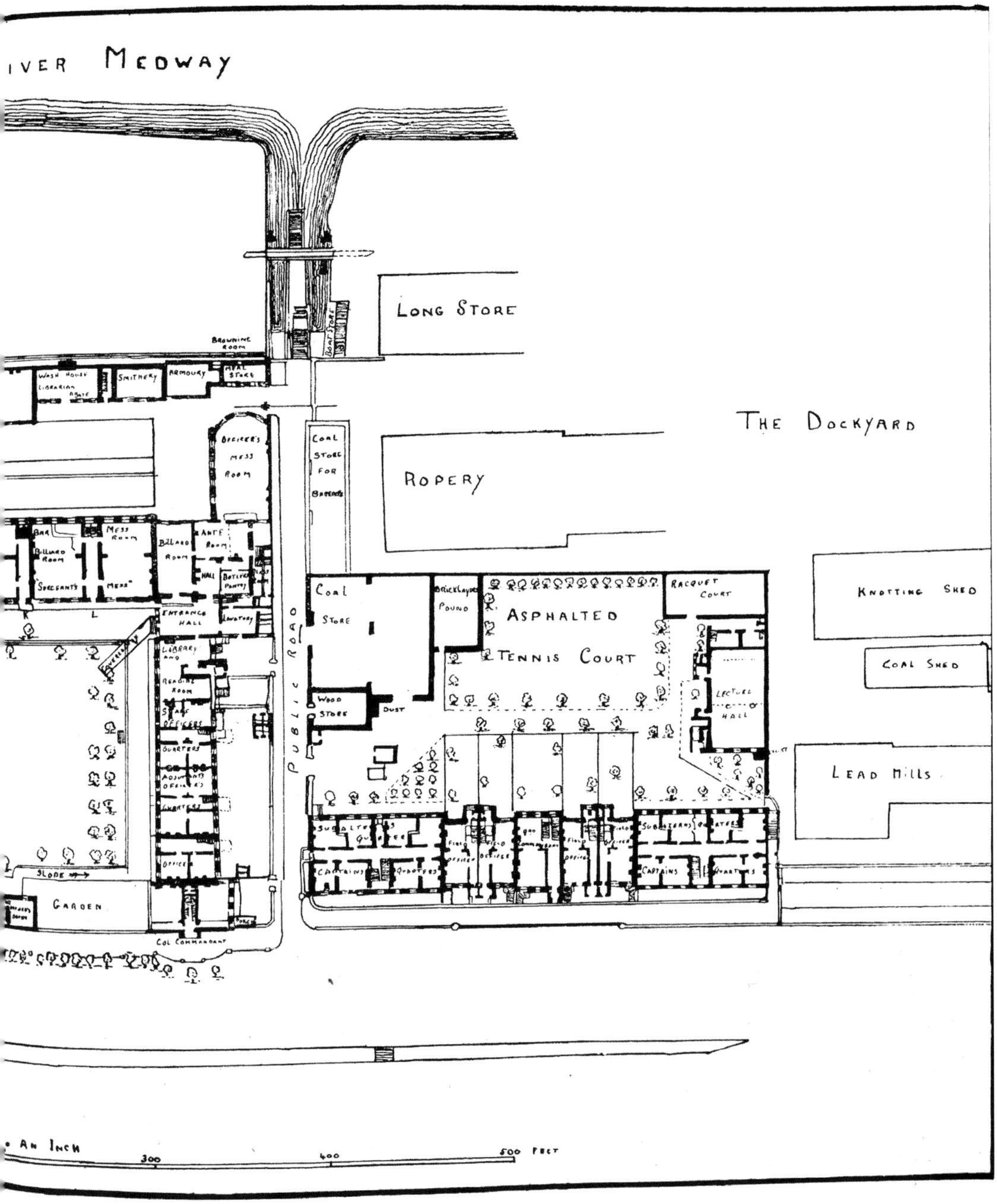
IVER MEDWAY
LONG STORE
THE DOCKYARD
ROPERY
KNOTTING SHED
COAL SHED
LEAD MILLS
ASPHALTED TENNIS COURT
RACQUET COURT
LECTURE HALL
COAL STORE
WOOD STORE
PUBLIC ROAD
SMITHERY
ARMOURY
OFFICER'S MESS ROOM
ENTRANCE HALL
GARDEN
AN INCH
300
400
500 FEET

Sedan Chair.

March 1847. Whenever the Sedan Chair is used the hire of the same is to be paid into the hands of Sergt. Martin, who will render an account to the Commandant of the money so received, and for which he will be entitled to Id. in the shilling, and distribute the rest agreeably to former regulations.

Pay.

February 1798. The Commanding Officer having acquainted the Secretary of the Admiralty for their Lordships information that the Officers, Non-commissioned Officers and Privates have voluntary come forward in contributing a week's pay towards the exigencies of the State, has it in command the proper sense entertained of the handsome manner in which their loyalty to their Sovereign and their regard for the Constitution has evinced upon the occasion.

Employed for Divine Service.

November 1829. The C.O. having observed that none of the Employed N.C.O.'s attended Divine Service, he desires that should duty prevent their doing so in the morning, they will go to Church in the Afternoon.

2ND PERIOD, 1862-1906. PART A.

About 1862 the barracks were enlarged and the present boundaries fixed. All the buildings between the old South Wall and St. Mary's Church (see Plan "C") were demolished and the South and Officers' Gates erected.

Before proceeding with the construction of the barracks during this period, an order of 21st May, 1864, throws some light on the position of the Officers' Quarters:

"Attention of Officers in the South Wing. - The blowing of horns, or other discordant noises in the Officers' Quarters, to the annoyance of those residing in the same or adjoining buildings is strictly prohibited."

There is a legend with reference to the Officers' Quarters and the ringing of bells at St. Mary's Church, but this is not founded on facts, as the tower of that church was not erected until a much later date.

The additions to barracks in 1864 were the erection of "C," "D," "E" and "F" Blocks, the re-construction of the Recreation Room, and the building of the Cook and Bake Houses, which were in the outer West Wing (Plan "C").

In 1865 "A" Block, with Detention Cells, "B" Block and the Paymaster's Offices, the Quartermaster's Stores, Canteen and Quarters, Lavorities, Coal and Wood Stores were constructed.

The next large addition came in 1867, when the Single Officers' Quarters and the Field Officers Houses were built. At that time the site on which they were built was part of the Commissioner's garden, and a part of the garden still remains in the form of a walk between Dock Road and the Dockyard Gate.

In addition to the Terrace, the Drill Shed, Meat and Bread Store (now Cook's Preparing Room and Cupboard), Coal Store, Gas Meter House and the Straw Store and Commandant's Stable (Gun Battery) were erected.

This really finished the construction of Main Barracks, with the exception of the following places:-
1874   Divisional Stables.
1879   Lecture Hall (Globe Theatre).
1876   Guard House and Detention Room ("A" Block).
1884   Miniature Rifle Range in areas of C and D Blocks.
1891   Married Quarters (Gun Battery). The original Practice Battery first started in 1872, and the following additions were made:-
1894   N.C.O.'s Instruction Room.
1895   Ammunition Room.
1900   Heavy Gun Battery, Q.F. Battery and M.G. Shed.
1901   Armourer's Shops and Field Carriage Sheds.
1907   Loading Teacher Shed.

2ND PERIOD, 1862-1906. - PART B.
Garrison Duties.

On the 26th October, 1862, the Garrison Guards were as follows:-
Garrison Main, Brompton Gate, Chatham Barracks, Garrison Hospital, Fort Amhurst, Gun Wharf, Fort Pitt, Dockyard, St. Mary's Barracks, Magazine, Convict and Abattoir.

At this time there were in the garrison two regiments in Chatham and one in St. Mary's Barracks, and the Royal Marines took their turn with these regiments for garrison duty, with the additional help of the Royal Engineers.

Main Guard and Convict Guard were Subaltern's guards.

The Royal Marines provided a detachment at New Tavern, Fort Gravesend until 1871, when it was taken over by the Royal Artillery. The embarkation officer at Gravesend was also found by the Division, and this officer was quartered in the Fort.

There was a detachment at Upnor Castle, but this has been dealt with under a separate heading.

In connection with duties in 1867, orders of 27th March are interesting: -

"Trooping of Colours will take place on Wednesdays and Saturdays, in lieu of Tuesdays and Thursdays,"

In 1868, in consequence of the night duties being discontinued, Convict and Dock Guards were considered as fatigues. Convict Guard was resumed in 1869, and turned into a Picquet again in 1871.

The Royal Marines also furnished a Guard in Fort Amhurst, as part of their Garrison Duties, until 1881, when this guard was discontinued.

During 1877, and again in 1882, the Division found a detachment for Chattenden, but on both occasions this duty only lasted for a short time.

The Main Guard was discontinued as a Garrison Duty in 1878, when the 86th Regiment was detailed to take over this Guard, and this ended Garrison Guards. Garrison duties were, however, continued for Officers, and at this period the following daily duties had to be found:-

Garrison Field Officer and Captain.
Main Guard and Convict Prison.

In addition to the above, Divisional duties took a Duty Captain and Subaltern, and three Officers for Fire duties.

In 1880 the use of Paroles by Field Officers and Garrison Guards was discontinued. The Parole was always given at the beginning of Orders.

It was not until 1891 that the Convict Picquet was discontinued.

COMPANIES.- At the commencement of this period, owing to the smallness of numbers and the fluctuation of the non-Commissioned Officers, and Privates at Quarters, the Battalion was formed into four Grand Divisions, instead of eight Parade Companies. This Order came into force in 1790.

In the year 1873, the following companies were allotted to Chatham:-1, 4, 5, 13, 16, 17, 21, 25, 28, 29, 33, 37, 40, 41 and 45, and these were re-distributed into 8 Parade Companies. These 8 parade Companies were numbered until 1885 when the Division consisted of a series of Companies designated by letters from "A" to "H."

In October 1889 approval was given for each Head Quarters to consist of seven Companies and the Eighth Company was broken up. This continued until 1901 when "H" Company was re-formed.

LIBRARY AND RECREATION Rooms. - The re-constructed Library and Recreation Rooms were opened in July 1865 and the subscription was 3d. per month, but this was reduced to the present rate of 1d. per month in 1891.

OFFICERS — PLAIN CLOTHES. - A Garrison Order of 1852 states:-

"Officers are permitted to wear Plain Clothes for walks into the country and Field Amusements, and when they wish to go in plain clothes to the other side of Rochester, they are to proceed by the Military Road, the New Road, Gravel Walk, Troy Town, through the Vines and by the river side of the Castle, to Rochester Bridge. When they ride or drive through any of the neighbouring towns in plain clothes, they are not to stop, loiter, or get off their horses or out of their carriages in the streets, but to go at once into the country or to Barracks."

Further permission is given in 1867 - "The Major General will not object to Officers wearing Plain Clothes when attending Divine Service at Rochester Cathedral, or when going into society in Rochester."

LIGHTS. - In 1st May, 1868, Divisional Orders contain an order for "Lights" to be put out at 10.30 p.m. No reason for this is given, and this custom is continued to this day. The legends which have grown up round the custom of putting Lights Out at 10.30 p.m. would appear to be incorrect.

BARRACK ROOMS. - During the period, Barrack Rooms were re-allocated on a number of occasions and it is impossible to give all these changes. The rooms were re-allocated on the transfer of the Woolwich Division in March, 1869.

WARD ROOM OFFICERS' SERVANTS. - In November, 1869, the first mention of Servants appears when volunteers for this duty were carefully interviewed by the Commandant.

HARVESTING. - The numbers taking part in this work are not stated, but in 1871 the Colonel Commanding having received most satisfactory accounts of the manner in which the men recently employed harvesting in the neighbourhood had performed their work and had conducted themselves; he had much pleasure in making the same known to the Division.

FIELD WORK. - The Royal Marines in conjunction with the remainder of the Garrison in 1869 helped to construct a Field Redoubt, i.e., the Glacis between Brompton Barrier Gate and the Ball Court. The Division supplied 263 men who worked in three reliefs until the work was completed.

ELECTIONS. - In the early days, as the following order indicates, during the election time, the troops were confined to their Barracks. This routine continued until 1918.

"The whole of the troops of the Garrison will be confined to barracks on those days. The usual patrols will not be sent out, and the Military Police on duty outside the barracks will parade without side arms. Officers going out of Barracks will wear plain Clothes, and married soldiers living out of barracks will proceed to and from their quarters without belts and side arms. Any soldiers having votes will apply to their Commanding Officers for short passes to enable them to go and vote."

SENTRIES. - About 1873 the practice of mounting sentries with sticks was discontinued, and the sentries were posted with their rifles. They were ordered to unfix their bayonets during thunder storms. Until 1906 sentries carried ball ammunition.

CANTERBURY CATHERDAL. - On 3rd September 1872 there was a fire at Canterbury as shown in Orders –

"A party of one Officer and twenty men with a fire hose and reel proceeded to Canterbury to help to extinguish a fire at the Cathedral at that place."

DERBY WEEK. - A memo from the R.M.O. was received in May, 1878 authorizing leave to Officers during Derby Week and the suspension of Field Drill.

SKATING RINK. - Authority was given in 1878 for the Drill Shed to be used as a Skating Rink after 4 p.m. The Skates could be hired from the Recreation room for 1d. per hour paid in advance.

DIVISIONAL RIFLE MEETING. - This was first started in 1880.

NON-COMMISSIONED OFFICERS. - The N.C.O.'s coming under the Adjutant started in 1883, when all matters relating to discipline, clothing, etc., were in the exclusive charge of the Field Adjutant.

INFIRMARY. - The Lords Commissioners of the Admiralty decided in 1885 to separate the R.M. Infirmary at Chatham from the Marine Division, and to place it under the orders of the Commander-in-Chief, Sheerness, as a Naval Hospital.

The combined medical duties relating to the R.M. Division and the Naval Hospital devolved on the Medical Staff of the Hospital. The Deputy Inspector General, Staff Surgeon and 2 Surgeons borne on the strength of the Division being transferred to the Hospital; the Chaplain was appointed to the Hospital exclusively and not available for the Division. The appointment of Purveyor to the Infirmary held by the Paymaster of the Chatham Division was abolished, and the whole of the marine staff were returned to their Headquarters.

FOOTBALL. - The first mention of football on the R.M. Ground on the Lines is found in 1886, and of Rugby Football in 1888.

DIVISIONAL ORDERS. - The earliest available Orders were in a book in manuscript with an index at the end of the book. Later they were written on separate pages, and stuck in a book as at present. It was not until November, 1889 that the orders were printed.

MARRIED QUARTERS. - In the allocation of rooms in 1889 no mention is made of "H" Block, and it would appear that this block was used as married quarters and they were taken over as such by the Works Department in 1890. There were at that time still married quarters on the top of "H" and "L" blocks and they were used until the next year.

GLOBE AND LAUREL - The Globe and Laurel was first edited at Chatham in 1892.

SERGEANTS' DORMITORIES. - In orders of November 1893, the following reference is to be found but what was the object of this order is not clear –

"The Sergeants dormitory is to be taken over as a Barracks room and the N.C.O.s occupying it are to sleep in the rooms of which they are Superintendents."

3RD PERIOD, 1906-1914. - PART A.

In July 1905 H.M. the King opened the present Naval Hospital, and in the next year Melville Barracks was taken over and reconstructed for the use of the Royal Marines.

In Main Barracks during 1905-1906 certain alterations took place, including the billiard room, part of the ante-room, the library and mess bedrooms in the Officers' Mess; the ceiling of the library was raised by taking in the floor above. The Sergeants' Mess was dealt with in a similar manner, and during the alterations the sergeants were accommodated in "I" passage.

The boat shed and public foot bridge leading to the stairs and Hard were constructed in 1908.

3RD PERIOD, 1906-1914. - PART B.

MELVILLE BARRACKS. - In 1907 "H" Company occupied No. 1 Block, and early in the next year the Drummers and R.M. Band No. 2 Block. The recreation room was opened at the same time. In 1911 there was a fire in Melville Barracks.

PLAIN CLOTHES MEN. - Plain clothes were permitted in 1908 for recreation purposes only and in 1909 when proceeding on furlough or pass.

GUARD OF HONOUR. - A Guard of Honour was mounted for H.I.M. the Emperor of Germany at Port Victoria in 1910.

FIELD TRAINING. - During the period field training was carried out at Lodge Hill, Fort Horsted and Chattenden.

4TH PERIOD. 1914-1930. - PART A.

The only new building to be erected during the period was the miniature rifle range in Melville Barracks in 1925. Alterations were carried out in the bathrooms, and in 1929 the N.A.A.F.I. carried out work in the canteen, in order to make the restaurant.

4TH PERIOD, 1914-1930. - PART B. (WAR PERIOD)

From a historical point of view the war period is shorn of interesting incidents, as far as Headquarters is concerned, as it was at that time a sorting place, in order to fill up detachments for the fleet and drafts for the 63rd (R.N.) Division. A number of anti-aircraft guns mounted on the Lines were manned by the Division.

During the war a number of units other than the Royal Marines were quartered in the barracks. During 1915 the R.N. Auxiliary Sick Berth ratings and the Metropolitan Police were quartered in Melville Barracks.

The Headquarters of the R.M. Submarine Miners were transferred from Newcastle to Chatham in 1917 and were accommodated in barracks. They were under the Commandant's orders for discipline and leave, but the technical and interior arrangements were in the hands of the O.C.R.M. Submarine Miners; the pay and clothing was dealt with by the staff of the R.M.S.M., as hitherto.

In 1918 the R.M. Engineers were authorised and Divisional Headquarters were established at Chatham, with offices in No. 4 Field Officers' Quarters and storerooms in the Workmen's Club and concert room, and also in Curtiss's storerooms in the High Street. The Divisional H. Qrs. consisted of H.Q. staff and a Depot Company, and were responsible for the administration and working of the unit on the lines of a division of Royal Marines. The Mobile H.Q.'s of the unit was stationed at Shoreham, Sussex. The unit ceased to exist in April 1919, when all records were turned over to the Division.

During 1918 W.R.N.S. were employed in barracks, and were quartered in hostels in Chatham and Rochester. Their office was situated first in the present Warrant Officers' billiard room, and subsequently in the present Adjutant's office. They were disbanded in October 1919.

The strength of the Division rose considerably, from 3,253 in August 1914 to 6,604 in November 1918.

A parade which took place in 1916 is of interest. On Easter Sunday the Division attended Divine Service on the parade, and the Colours were brought out for this service, as it is as nearly as possible the anniversary of the landing of the Royal Marines on Gallipoli.

4TH PERIOD, 1914-1930. - PART B. (POST WAR)

After the war Chatham ceased to be a garrison town, and after the 4th April, 1919, no mention is made in divisional orders of garrison duty.

11TH R.M. BATTALION. - The Battalion was concentrated at Chatham in 1921. Battalion H.Q. and "D" (Composite) Company were in Main Barracks, "A" (Ch.) Company and "B" (Po.) Company at Fort Borstal, and "C" (Ply) Company in Melville Barracks. In September the companies at Fort Borstal occupied Chatham Lower Barracks until the battalion sailed for Turkey.

CENOTAPH. - The Division provided sentries for the Cenotaph and the Tomb of the Unknown Warrior when they were unveiled in 1920. On subsequent Armistice days, a Guard with the Divisional Band and Buglers from all Divisions, has been on duty at the Cenotaph, and also a party in Westminster Abbey, at the Tomb of the Unknown Warrior.

H.M.S. VANGUARD. - A window was unveiled in Rochester Cathedral in 1920 in memory of the men who lost their lives in H.M.S. Vanguard.

WAR SAVINGS CERTIFICATES. - During the War and up to 1921 the Division subscribed £20,981 1s. 6d. by the purchase of War Saving Certificates.

COMPANIES. - Between 1901 and 1921 there were in Headquarters 8 parade companies, but in December 1921, on account of the reduction in the Corps, the number of the companies was reduced to 4, as at present.

WAR MEMORIAL, GREAT WAR, 1914-1918. - The erection of a Divisional War Memorial was first considered in 1919, when it was suggested that it might take the form of a suitable archway leading into Headquarters, and in order to start a fund one day's pay was on the 11th March 1919 stopped from all ranks. In 1921, as sufficient funds had not been subscribed for the proposed Memorial Archway, the Division was asked to decide on the following alternatives–
1. The endowment of a bed or beds at St. Bartholomew's Hospital, Rochester;
2. Financial grant to some local Service Institution;
3. Memorial metal gates at the Main Entrance into Barracks, instead of the proposed Archway.

At this period the fund stood at £1,289 15s. 4d., made up as follows: Subscriptions £837, Canteen Fund £400, Recreation Room Fund £50, with the hope of an additional sum of £50 from the Divisional Fund.

It was finally decided to endow a bed in the St. Bartholomew's Hospital, Rochester, at the cost of £1,000, and a cheque for this amount was handed over to the Governor of the Hospital on the 18th May, 1921.

This left a balance of £266, and the Division was again asked as to the method of expending the balance. One suggestion was to purchase furniture for a club room for the R.M. Cadet Corps. At a meeting in January 1922 it was decided that the balance remaining was to be used to erect a memorial tablet, and the remainder turned over to Cadet Corps funds.

On 19th October 1922 the Bronze Memorial Tablet was unveiled by the Adjutant General, Royal Marines, Major-General H. E. Blumberg, C.B., At this time, in addition to the bronze tablet, large wooden boards with the names of the men of the Division who lost their lives in the Great War, were hung under the colonnade. In 1929 this Roll of Honour was checked, and it was found in some cases that the names were incorrect, and that the Roll of Honour was incomplete. It was thus decided to take the boards down and to compile a correct Roll of Honour in book form.

After the Armistice Day Service on 11th November, 1930, the Commandant, Brigadier R. F. C. Foster, C.B., C.M.G., D.S.O., placed the Roll of Honour in a case under the bronze Memorial Tablet.

OFFICERS' MESS. - It was not until 2nd July, 1789, that the Officers' Mess House was nearly finished, and it was completed on 17th November, 1789, when the following order was issued:
"As the Mess House is now properly furnished by the Person who is the Mess Holder, and who is ready to mess those Officers who are desirous to diet there. It is therefore necessary that those Officers who intend to eat there will give in their names on Monday at 11 o'clock, in order for forming an Original Mess Body, as after that Formation none will be admitted into the Mess but those who are regularly ballotted for by the Original Mess Body."

There do not appear to have been any large alterations to the mess between its construction and 1906, when the billiard room was altered and the entrance from the hall to the billiard room blocked up. This entrance was on the site of the present fireplace in the hall. The outside staircase, up to the mess bedrooms was built, and this enabled the old staircase, which was in the present library, to be demolished and the library heightened.

Owing to the fact that there are no available records of the Mess prior to 1896, it is difficult to trace any old customs or items of interest about the Mess.

MESS PATRONS. - There are in the Mess room three pictures of Mess Patrons. The first is the Earl of Sandwich, with whom the following Divisional Order, dated November 1788, is connected:

"The Officers who intend to dine in the mess on the 14th instant, to celebrate the anniversary of the birth of the Earl of Sandwich, are desired to send their name immediately to the Adjutant's Office."

To the Earl of Sandwich, who in 1771 was placed at the head of the Admiralty, the Marines owe a debt of gratitude. From him originated the Colonels Commandant of Divisions and many interior regulations. He also enlarged the number of Field Officers, which reform held out hope for the Veteran, who until now had had little hope of being head of the Division. During the year 1771 his portrait was painted by Gainsboro' after Dupoint.

On the death of the Earl of Sandwich in 1792 the Commanding Officer gave instructions that the Officers of the Division should put themselves into military mourning, as a memento of gratitude towards their late patron whenever accounts were received of his being interred.

The second, the Earl of Chatham, whose picture was painted in 1788 by Hoppner.

The third is the Earl of St. Vincent, through whose intercession the Marines obtained the distinction of being styled Royal Marines. He also brought in a new code of regulations for use when on shore. His portrait was painted by Jackson in 1801.

WARRANT OFFICERS' MESS. - The Halsey Committee, which sat in 1919 to consider the rank and status of the Warrant Officers, approved of them having a Mess of their own, and the present site was selected. In order to make the building suitable certain alterations had to be carried out, and a new home found for the Orderly Room and the Adjutant's Office, which were situated in the selected building. The then Chaplain's room and W.R.N.'s office were allocated to the Orderly Room and Adjutant's Office.

It was proposed to obtain a grant from the various funds of the Division to start the Mess, but this was not approved by the Adjutant General.

The building was taken over as a Mess on 23rd March, 1920, and was occupied soon after. There were 18 members when the Mess was opened, but owing to reduction in the number of Warrant Officers this number has fallen at the present time to seven. Alterations were under-taken in 1922, when provision was made in the basement for a kitchen and washing facilities.

SERGEANTS' MESS. - The Sergeants' Mess is part of the original construction, and was altered in 1906, when the height of the rooms was increased. During the alterations the Mess was situated in "I" passage; the Mess was re-opened in February 1907.

The Colours of the Division have been lodged in the Mess on two occasions. The first time was on 12th May 1911, for a Sergeants' Reunion Dinner, and again on a similar occasion in 1913.

A number of changes have taken place with regard to the allocation of rooms for the dormitories; the present cubicles were completed in 1930.

JUNIOR N.C.O.s' CLUB. - The Junior N.C.O.s were originally provided with a room in the mens beer canteen (now the restaurant) and liquor was supplied through a trap door from the men's bar. They also had one room in "H" Block (H. 3) which was termed the Junior N.C.O.s' Room.

In the Welfare proposals, 1919-1920, a request for forming a separate mess was put forward, and the Admiralty decision was that it was approved in principle.

Approval was given in 1920 for the formation of a Junior N.C.O.s' Club, which all junior N.C.O.'s had to join, and in the early part of 1921 approval was given for a bar in the club. When the club first started it consisted of "H" 3 and 4 barrack rooms, and in January 1921 "H" 5 and 6 were added, with the addition of a lobby on the first floor of "H" block and a cellar in the basement. Alterations were carried out in 1929, when the wall between "H" 3 and 4 barrack rooms was removed, and the billiard table which was at that time on the ground floor removed to the floor above. The bar, which had been run by the club, was in 1929 turned over to the N.A.A.F.I.

DIVISIONAL SCHOOLS. - The position of Divisional School prior to 1880 is uncertain, in that year the schools, at the bottom of Dock Road, next to the Town Hall, were constructed. The schools continued until December 1921, when in accordance with Admiralty Instructions they were closed and the buildings turned to the Territorial Army and the Naval Recruiting service.

CADET CORPS. - It was proposed in 1903 start the Chatham Company of the R. M. Cadet Corps, and on 18th September of that year 66 boys were enrolled, and two barrack rooms were allocated for their use. All recruits at that time were either sons of serving or ex-members of the Corps, or those connected with the Royal Marines.; At that time the Divisional Schools were in existence, and thus recruiting from this source was much facilitated, and there was no difficulty in keeping the Company up to full strength.

When the Cadet Corps was first started they were dressed as follows: Khaki tunic, trousers and putties, with Corps buttons and badges, and a khaki felt hat turned up on the left side. Their equipment included a leather bandolier and belt, and they were armed with a short pattern rifle with a leather sling.

The Cadet Corps was affiliated to the Territorial Association and was attached to the Royal West Kent Regiment T.A., and thus was allowed to compete in the King's Shield and similar competitions. Although affiliated to the Territorial Army it was inspected annually by the Adjutant General R.M.

During the early days of the Great War all subscriptions ceased, but they were re-started again in November 1915.

In 1920 the uniform of the Cadet Corps was altered, and then was: Blue tunic and blue breeches, with a red welt, blue putties; blue forage cap with red piping, corps buttons and badges and a leather belt. The company was not armed.

Owing to the closing of the Divisional Schools in 1921, the flow of recruits from sons of members and ex-members of the Corps diminished, and in order to keep the company up to strength it was necessary to take any boys, provided they were suitable, whether their parents were connected with the Royal Marines or not.

During 1930 the War Office gave orders that all Cadet Corps were to be disbanded, and thus on 31st October the Chatham Company R.M Cadet Corps was disbanded. All serviceable equipment and clothing, miniature rifles, and the balance of the Cadet Corps Fund have been put on one side for subsequent use, should it be found possible to restart a similar unit at some future date.

RECREATION GROUNDS. - From 1779-1928 the Chatham Division did not possess a recreation ground of its own. This sounds very remarkable, but it must be remembered that it was not until 1861 that recreation on Saturday afternoons, for well drilled and conducted men, was introduced. During this period athletic sports were held on the Chatham football ground on the Maidstone Road. Cricket and football and later hockey were played on the Great Lines and many were the games that had to be temporarily suspended whilst the Dockyard maties streamed across the pitches on their way to and from work. Football was played on the present No. I ground which was enclosed about 1907 or 1908, but rugby and hockey were still played on the open Lines. At that time this ground belonged to the R.N. and R.M. Recreation Club, who charged a certain sum for every game played on it.

It was not until 1928 that through the concurrence of the Nore Sports Committee and the R.N. and R.M. Recreation Club committee, that the Commander-in-Chief, Admiral Sir Alexander Sinclair, approved of the present No. 1 ground being turned over by the R.N. and R.M. Recreation Club to the Division. In connection with this ground certain improvements were carried out in 1930, namely, the erection of a new fence along the east side, the construction of a covered stand on the south bank, and the repair of the stand on the west side.

In 1929 permission was sought from the G.O.C. Major-General Walker, for the use of a piece of ground on the Lines, directly opposite the No. 1 ground, and this was approved. Subsequently in 1930 permission was given by the G.O.C. to extend this ground to the north, to give enough space for an additional football ground, with a wicket between the two football grounds. During the year this extension was enclosed by a spike fence and a water supply laid on.

DIVISIONAL BAND - The earliest record of the Band is in 1693, when a Warrant authorising its inception was made –
"To Presse or cause to be impressed from time to time such number of Drums, Fifes and Hautboys as shall be necessary for His Majesty's Service, either by land or sea . . . Whereby Captain William Prince, of their Majesty's First Mareen Regiment . . . to impress two Drums and two Hautboys for the service of his company in the aforesaid Regiment."

Mention is made of the band in Divisional Orders in 1772, when Thomas Howard was appointed to act "with the authority of a Sergeant over the Band of Musick."

The Band was in 1773 sent on board the Orpheus at Sheerness, in order to be carried to Spithead, "there being occasion for it when the King reviews His Fleet assembled there." The band at that time was under the care of Acting Sergt.-Major Clements.

The Band was not allowed to play anywhere out of the barracks, but where the Divisional Business calls them, or where Government may take concern, in order that they might not be looked on in the light of common fiddlers. This was in 1781.

About this period the committee of the Divisional Fund recommended that the 12 oldest (or most deserving) privates in the band should be allowed 2d. from the fund whilst its state will allow it.

The complement was in 1815 laid down to be: Band Sergeant 1, Corporal 1, Drummers 20. The Master of the Band to be borne and payed as a Sergeant, a second clarionet as a corporal, and the remainder as drummers, and the whole of those employed in the band are to be included in the 22.

This complement was revised in 1830, and in 1842 the Lords Commissioner of the Admiralty directed that the Officers were to annually contribute one day's pay towards the upkeep of their band.

In 1901 the band was selected to accompany H.R.H. the Duke and Duchess of York (the present King and Queen) on their tour in the Ophir. After their tour they were given the distinction of wearing the York Rose on their head dress.

Towards the end of 1916 the band was attached to the Royal Naval Division in France for a period of six weeks.

PLACES OF WORSHIP OF THE DIVISION.

St. Mary's, the Parish Church of Chatham. – The history of this Church is given, as it stands adjacent to the barracks, and was the place of worship of the Division until 1808, and after that date until 14th March, 1868, a certain number of men regularly attended on Sundays.

On the site of the present Church there have been in the course of time five churches-
1. The Saxon Church mentioned in the list of lands belonging to Odo, Bishop of Bayeux.
2. The Norman Church, probably built about 1120 A.D. Three arches of this Church arc still to be seen in the present church.
3. The Church of the fourteenth century. This church, according to Hasted's Kent, was built in 1516 for "Bifop Thomas de Woldham, by his will, dates that year, bequeathed the fum of 10s. towards this work; but it feems the inhabitants were not able to finish it, for the Pope's letter of indulgence was publifed in 1352, for the remiffion of a year and 40 days' penance to all fuch as fhould contribute to fo pious a work."
   In 1635 the Commissioners of the Navy repaired this Church, rebuilt and enlarged the West end, and erected a steeple. Again in 1707 Commissioner St. Loe built a gallery over the South aisle for the use of the "Navy and Ordinary." This church was burned down in 1786.
4. The eighteenth century Church was built after the fire, and was a large Georgian structure, with galleries round the sides. It was when this church was in being that the following entry was recorded:

"The sum of Two Hundred Pounds having been contributed by the Royal Marine Corps towards rebuilding the Church at Chatham, I am to request that the seats in the said church which were appropriated for the use of the Royal Marine Officers, etc., and which have been taken away from them, may be given up, or the sum of Two Hundred Pounds refunded to the Corps." Dated 1809.

5. The present Church. The work was begun 1884, when H.R.H. the Duke of Cambridge laid the foundation stone of the chancel. In 1897 the foundation stone of the Victoria Tower was laid as a memorial to the second Jubilee of Queen Victoria, and both the tower and the tenor bell were by the late Queen's permission called by her name. The work was completed in 1903 and consecrated by the Lord Bishop of Rochester, in the presence of the Commander-in-Chief, Field Marshal Lord Roberts.

When the Division was first quartered in Chatham the Dockyard Chapel was not built and the Division attended St. Mary's Church. When the Dockyard Chapel was built a number of Marines continued to attend divine service at this Church until the date mentioned above. At the present time an annual Parade Service is always held in the church.

DOCKYARD CHAPEL. - The Church of the Chatham Dockyard is a modern building, having been completed in the year 1808. There is a Royal coat of arms on the front of the west gallery, bearing the date 1811.

The Yard itself originally occupied the site of the present Ordnance Wharf, and was moved to the position it now occupies in the reign of James I. about 1622.

Although there was no Dockyard Chapel until 1808, the list of Dockyard Chaplains goes back to 1626. Church ships were used in the 18th century the *Revenge* and *Bristol* being two of them.

The Dockyard Church was used by the Royal Marines as soon as it was built, and an order of 1809 states: "The Commissioners having reported to the Commanding. Officer that in the gallery of the Dock Chapel allotted to the Marines the division of the pews and walls in several places have been disfigured by letters and other marks, done apparently with the points of bayonets. Any person being discovered to have been guilty of such disgraceful conduct will be severely punished.

UPNOR CASTLE. - The Marines during a large portion of the time of being quartered in Chatham have had a connection with Upnor Castle. The present Castle was built in 1561, but for some time prior to 1778 it was not used as a fort, or were any guns mounted there. About the latter date the Governor General of the Castle was in command of all the forts on the Medway.

In the vicinity of the Castle there was good accommodation for troops.

It is not dear when the Castle was first used as a magazine, but according to Hasted's Kent it was in use as such in 1778.

In 1862 a detachment of one officer and fifty-seven men was quartered in the castle, and later, in 1876 and 1877, detachments were at Upnor and Chattenden. During 1880 the detachment was withdrawn from Upnor, and a year later the Division provided a Guard of a sergeant and eight privates.

The detachment was withdrawn from Chattenden in 1882, and in 1890 the Upnor Guard was a daily garrison duty. The Metropolitan Police took over the duty of guarding Upnor in September 1891, and a year later it was known as H.M. Naval Magazine.

In 1923 the R.M. Police took over the police duties at Lodge Hill, Chattenden and Upnor from the Metropolitan Police, and at H.M. Dockyard, Sheerness, in April 1929.

Chattenden Depot was built for the Army, and was taken into use in 1887 being transferred to the Admiralty in 1906. Chattenden Barracks was the School of Military Railways, and was taken over in the same year.

Lodge Hill Depot was taken into use in 1902. As originally designed, it had a broad gauge connection via Sharnal Street to Teapot Hard on the Medway, where it was proposed to build extensive piers, so that the fleet could embark stores maintained at Upnor. These arrangements were, however, subsequently cancelled after the line had been laid as far as Sharnal Street. The Depot was largely augmented in 1906 and again in 1910.

The present complement of R.M. Police at Lodge Hill and Upnor is 1 Chief Inspector, 6 Sergeants and 46 Constables; and at Sheerness, 1 Chief Inspector, 9 Sergeants and 30 Constables.

RIFLE RANGES. - in the early days of the Marines being quartered at Chatham no record can be found of Musketry exercises, and the first mention appeared in Divisional Orders of 1835:-
"Should the weather be favourable, the Right Wing will march from barracks at half past 8 o'clock to Upnor for Ball Practice, each man being provided with 12 rounds of ball cartridge, and the Commanding Officer is pleased to direct that one shilling shall be given to each soldier who hits the Bull's eye, provided that the largest part of the ball passes through it, but not for merely grazing the bullseye."

From 1876 the ranges at Milton were used, except for short periods, when the range was not available, as in 1877 and 1899, when musketry parties were detached to Walmer and Lydd.

In 1905 the Musketry Staff (as it was then called) was accommodated in a self-contained block in Milton Barracks, Gravesend, and musketry parties were accommodated in Melville Barracks, doing their preliminary instruction in barracks and on the Great Lines. The parties went by train from Rochester or Strood to a halt close by the Range Huts, daily. At some later date parties proceeded to and from the range in winter, and were accommodated under canvas at Milton Barracks in the summer; R.M. detachments from ships in the dockyard were accommodated in Shornmead Fort, close to the range.

It is interesting to note that in August 1914, the Chatham Battalion was quartered at Gravesend, and marched in from there in the dark to embark for Ostend landing there the following morning.

In September 1914 the R.Ms. left Milton Barracks, as the accommodation was required for Reservists called up for the Great War, and the R.Ms. were quartered in two large private houses near the village of Shorne - The Little Hermitage and Gad's Hill House. Excess of numbers were billeted in the village in the winter and under canvas in the summer.

Shorne camp was closed on the 5th June, 1919, and the Weapon Training parties were accommodated in Milton Barracks for two weeks, but owing to Army requirements they were moved to the Drill Hall, Denton, near Gravesend.

Fort Bridgewoods was occupied in October 1919, which is situated close to the Borstal Range, where firing was carried out.

During May 1920 Fort Bridgewoods was given up and Fort Borstal taken over. This Fort was built by convict prison labour and was completed in 1899. Prior to the war the Fort was occupied by Army Weapon Training parties, and during the war was used as the Thames and Medway Machine Gun School, when the wooden huts were erected inside the fort, giving accommodation for 150 other ranks.

The Borstal Range was closed as being unsafe in 1927. Parties were still quartered at Fort Borstal, but firings were again carried out at Milton Ranges for small parties; large parties carried out firings at the Sheerness Range, and were borne V.O. H.M.S. *Pembroke*.

UNITED STATES MARINE CORPS. - The connection between the Division and the U.S. Marine Corps started in 1872, when Lieut.-Colonel Forney, of the U.S. Marine Corps, was granted facilities for collecting information as to the organisation and discipline of the Corps. Later, in 1923, a party of U.S. Marines from the U.S.S. *Pittsburg* visited the Division. When the American Naval Mission was in London in 1929 for the London Naval Conference a number of N.C.O.'s of the U.S. Marine Corps visited the Division as guests of the Division, and stayed for the week-end, being accommodated in the sergeants' mess. A return visit was paid by a party of our N.C.O.'s, who stayed the night at St. Ermine's Hotel, the headquarters of the American Naval Mission.

"The same facilities were again afforded in 1903."

"The close connection of the U.S. Marines with the Corps was established in 1900, when the U.S. Marines under Capt. Myers, and the British Marines under Capt. B. M. Strouts, R.M.L.I., and when he was killed under Capt. L. S. T. Halliday, R.M.L.I., served together, working under each other's officers as necessary; the senior Sergeant of the R.M., was Sgt. Murphy, of the Chatham Division."

"Also in same campaign when the R.M. Bn. under Major Luke. R.M.L.I„ was preparing to form part of the Relief Column, advancing from Tientsien, it was the U.S. Marines, who by lending our Men (who had only their white ducks) Khaki uniforms, enabled our Bn., to form part of the Column."

EAST SURREY REGIMENT. - The present connection between the Royal Marines and the East Surrey Regiment goes far back into history. In 1702 Queen Anne ordered the formation of six additional Regiments of Marines, and Villier's Regiment, in accordance with the seniority of its Colonel, ranked second among the six, and to-day is the First Battalion of the East Surrey Regiment.

Villier's Regiment of Marines fought at Gibraltar, and thus "Gibraltar 1704-5" now heads the long roll of distinctions borne on the Colours of the East Surrey Regiment. After the peace of Utrecht, Goring's Marine Regiment, as Villier's Regiment was then known, was disbanded, but in 1714, in the reign of King George I., the three senior Marine Regiments, those of Wills, Goring and Borr, were restored to life, and Goring s Regiment became the 31st Foot.

The close connection between the Chatham Division and the East Surrey Regiment was the result of the burning of the *Kent*.

On January 12th, 1825, the 31st Regiment marched from Gosport to Chatham, arriving there on January 20th, and on February 7th the Regiment embarked for Calcutta at Gravesend, the right wing and headquarters, under Lieut.-Colonel Fearon, C.B., in the Honourable East Indian Company's ship *Kent*. On March 1st the *Kent*, whilst in the Bay of Biscay, caught fire and finally blew up. The survivors were taken back to Falmouth in the *Cambria*, which came up to the *Kent* when on fire. At Falmouth they were re-embarked and landed at Chatham. On arrival in the garrison the officers were taken into the mess and the men into the barracks and looked after during their stay in Chatham, which did not last long, as on the 19th April they sailed again for India.

In the Mess Room is a picture of the burning of the *Kent*, presented by the Colonel and Officers of the 31st Regiment, and underneath it is a letter of thanks for our hospitality. A silver-gilt snuff box was also presented to the Mess and bears the following inscription –

"Presented to the Chatham Division Royal Marines by the Officers of the 31st Regiment as a trifling testimonial of gratitude for the liberal hospitality and attention extended towards that portion of the Corps shipwrecked by the conflagration of the *Kent* Indiaman in the Bay of Biscay on the 1st March, 1825."

In this way the present custom of the Officers of the Royal Marines and the East Surrey Regiment being honorary members of each other's messes came about.

> **EXTRACT FROM THE HISTORY OF THE EAST SURREY REGIMENT.**
>
> **RAISING OF THE REGIMENT.** Among the regiments raised in 1702 was one of Marines commanded by Colonel Villiers and hence called 'Villiers' Marines'. This regiment was later styled the '31st Regiment of Foot, now 1st Bn The East Surrey Regiment. In the War of the Spanish Succession, Villiers' Marines acted in conjunction with the Navy. It was present with Rooke's Expedition to Cadiz and at the destruction of shipping at Vigo.
>
> **The Capture of Gibraltar.** On July 1st 1704, the Regiment took part in the land attack on Gibraltar, which has been described as one of the boldest and most difficult attacks ever performed. It afterwards took part in the defence of Gibraltar and received its first battle honour of Gibraltar 1704.
>
> **Loss of the Troopship Kent.** In February 1825, the Headquarters and Right Wing of the 31st embarked for India on the Kent; a Ship employed on the route to India - known in those days as an East Indiaman. During a heavy storm in the Bay of Biscay the vessel caught fire and was totally destroyed. The discipline of the men under these terrible circumstances was beyond all praise, and it was chiefly owing to this, that 550 out of 637 people on board were saved. The brig Cambria of only 200 tons, took the survivors to Falmouth, whence they proceeded to Chatham and received a brotherly welcome from Royal Marines. As a consequence of this incident there has always been a special link of friendship between the Royal Marines and the East Surrey Regiment.

Although the original custom of being honorary members of each other's messes was at first confined to the Chatham Division and the 31st Regiment of Foot, it was held by the Regiment that it applied to all the Infantry Divisions and Depot of the Royal Marines. When the 31st Regiment was linked with the 70th Regiment as its 2nd Battalion in 1881, the privilege was not actually extended to the 2nd Battalion until 1924, when the 2nd East Surreys were quartered at Plymouth, the Colonel of the Regiment, Major-General Sir J. R. Longley, interviewed the Adjutant-General, R.M. Lt.-General, Sir H. E. Blumberg, K.C.B., and pointed out how closely interlocked the Battalions now were, and it was agreed that all Regular Battalions and Depot of the East Surrey Regiment and all Divisions and Depot of Royal Marines should be considered honorary members of each other's messes.

This entente has been celebrated and cemented on many occasions when the Regiment and members of the Corps have met, notably at Aldershot and Forton in 1905, also in China in 1926-7, and again recently at Gibraltar. It is now maintained by an annual two days cricket match between the officers past and present of the Corps and the East Surreys.

The extract from the history of the East Surrey Regiment, designed and executed by Corpl. Morris, was sent to the Depot at Deal, and is now hung in the North Colonnade.

The History of the Royal Marines Divisions

Letter from General Sir H. E. Blumberg, K.C.B.

May I add some details to the interesting account of the Chatham Division in your last issues:-

THE FIRST DIVISION.

I think this must have been due to its being the first formed. I believe its first Commanding Officer was Lieut.-Colonel Patterson, whose appointment was dated 23 March, 1755. Lieut.-Colonel Drury, at Portsmouth, was dated 24th March, 1755, and a Lieut.-Colonel Gordon was dated 25th March, 1755, presumably for Plymouth though he does not appear to have served there.

Further, in some correspondence between the Admiralty and the Commandants at Chatham and Portsmouth regarding the method of raising and approving recruits, dated 29th Sept., 1776, the Chatham Commandant (Col. Mackenzie) forwards the orders issued by Lieut.-Col. Marriott in charge of the Chatham recruiting parties, in which he says "He promulgated the Admiralty order of the 19th March, 1776, and told them to follow it, and as is commonly understood to beat up accordingly, by offering and paying two guineas and a crown for every fit and proper man that will enlist in the *First Division of Marines*, as men are much wanted, etc.

BARRACKS.

The date of occupation of the Barracks would appear to have been 1780, because on the 20th June, 1780, Capt. Allan was appointed barrackmaster from quartermaster.

COMPANIES.

The account says that Chatham Division had 16 companies in 1763, but this was after the reduction to 70 companies following the peace. In 1757 the Corps consisted of 129 companies (Chatham 41, Portsmouth and Plymouth 44 each). At the outbreak of the American War, Chatham had 16 companies, Portsmouth and Plymouth 27 each, but by July 1782 these had risen to 157 (Chatham 37, Portsmouth and Plymouth 60 each). The Corps then totalled approximately 25,300 officers and men.

After the demobilisation in 1783 the total companies were again 70, with a total of 4,519 officers and men. In the Napoleonic Wars the numbers rose again, till they were 145 companies (Chatham 43, Portsmouth and Plymouth 51 each) of a total of 24,167 officers and men. There was a slight fall at the temporary peace in 1802, but in 1803 they were back again at 143 (Chatham 47, Portsmouth and Plymouth 48).

In 1814, by O.-in-C. 28th July, 1814, the numbers fell to 25 Field Officers, 14 Staff Officers and 120 Companies; these, of course, now included Woolwich Division and the four Artillery Companies.

All through the 19th century the companies fluctuated, until they finally disappeared from the Navy List about 1890; the men's register numbers having replaced the company designation.

PARADE COMPANIES.

Your correspondent speaks of Parade Companies and Grand Divisions being introduced about 1860. As a matter of fact the same causes had produced the same effects much earlier. A Plymouth Order, date 10th Nov 1756, orders the companies to be formed into squads; in this case 4 Divisional Companies were allotted to each squad. But this varied from time to time, and this organisation evidently went right through the Corps, because both in Plymouth and Portsmouth documents there make frequent references to the squad officers. The duties of those officers we learn from a letter to Portsmouth dated Nov., 1763; they were evidently connected with the clothing and subsistence of the men-" from the various accounts of receipts and disbursements which squad officers are obliged to keep, not only a thorough knowledge of accounts, but a regular and minute exactness therein, as well as some experience of business is requisite . . . ." "The frequent removal of officers from the squad duty to take their tour of sea duty, as directed by the 13 Article of the Regulations of July 1763, must be attended with many inconveniences." The Admiralty consequently decided that for the future "officers upon half pay shall be appointed squad officers to the several Divisions of Marines, with an allowance of Forty pounds a year each for their care and trouble," 1st Dec., 1763.

There is no information as to how many squads there were at each Division, but in 1785 a new system of supplying necessaries to N.C.Os. and men from a contractor in London at a fixed rate for the Corps, instead of by local purchase, was introduced, and in Sept., 1785 the squad officers were replaced by two or three sergeants, who seem to have been a sort of mixture of quarter-master sergeants and sergeants.

DOCKYARD GUARDS.

The details about Dockyard Guards are not quite correct.

The Admiralty Order directing the Marines to provide guards for the dockyards at Chatham, Portsmouth and Plymouth, to relieve the civilian roundsmen, watchmen, etc., is dated 3rd Oct., 1764. The Guard appears to have been a Captain's Guard, and the sentries in three reliefs, and as the Admiralty evidently realised there would not be sufficient officers and men on shore for the duty, the Commanding Officer was authorised to call on the detachments of the guardships (i.e., harbour ships and nucleus crews) for officers and men as required.

The original orders for the Guards are very complete, and at the same time display a good knowledge of human nature, as they evidently expected rows.

The Guards seem to have been discontinued during the American War 1775 to 1783, but on 24th Dec., 1783, the Board ordered the Marines to take over the Dockyards at Chatham, Portsmouth and Plymouth, "as was practised during the late peace (!!)"

But it cannot have been very satisfactory, because on 28th Dec., 1784, the Board ordered the civilian watchmen, warders and rounders to take over again, with the addition of a subaltern's guard of about 36 n.c.o.'s and men to patrol within the dockyard walls. This had the usual result; evidently the Corps had retained men supernumary to the establishment of 1783 for the duty, who were now ordered to be discharged. (N.B. - It is curious that at the end of the war 1914-1919, about 1922, the Admiralty were considering similar proposals, which eventually resulted in the Royal Marine Police as we know them to-day.)

PARLIAMENTARY ELECTION.

This is not quite correct for the early days. The procedure in the earliest times was to march all troops and detachments out of the town where the election was being held, to a distance of at least three miles, three days before the election, until three days after it was over; and Plymouth and Portsmouth orders make many references to the Division having marched to and been billetted at Tavistock, Plympton, Havant, Fareham, etc.

DERBY WEEK.

Certainly up to about 1900 no leave was supposed to be granted during the spring and summer drill seasons, *i.e.*, from April up to September, except for the one exception of Derby Week, and for this reason the Corps Dinner used always to be held on Derby Day.

THIRD PERIOD, 1906-1914.

Not only were the alterations made to the Mess, but perhaps the following alterations are worthy of note:-

In 1907 the Colonel Commandant moved his residence from the old house in the Barracks to the big house in Melville Barracks. His old house was converted into the Infirmary.

The barrack rooms vacated by H Company were turned into barrack storerooms, shoemakers shop, etc.

At that time the Staff Officer's office was in the small house at end of Commandant's garden, and the Superintending Clerk in the room on either side of the gate, so that they could look at each other through the windows. The Staff Office was where the present Barrack Master's Office is. The Orderly Room, Adjutant's Office and Drafting Office were in the lower rooms of the old Field Officers' quarters, the two Sergeant-Majors occupying the top floors.

It must have been about 1912 or 1913 that the old Commandant's House was converted into offices and the Infirmary removed to the end block in Melville.

I see no mention is made of the great alteration in the Divisional Library and Recreation Rooms about 1912. Lieut.-Colonel Drake-Brockman, the Barrack Master, obtained permission to use the range of old buildings comprising an Adjutant's lecture room, a laundry for washing clothes, and carpenter's store, and converted them into the present pleasant library, reading rooms, etc., adjoining the recreation room.

The Dining Halls were introduced Dec., 1922.

H. E. BLUMBERG.

Random Records of the Royal Marines

INDEX.

Action Afloat	124	Gibraltar, Marine Detachments at its Capture		25
A.D.C. to the King, The First R.M.	189	Gibraltar, Progress of the Siege by the Spaniards		22
Admiralty Letter establishing Naval Gunnery School	189	Gibraltar, Cession of		23
Affair of Honour. An	51	Globe and Laurel, History of the		357
Affray between Marines and Shipwrights (1768)	55	"Good Old Days, The", Reminiscences of a Veteran		187
America, Marine Battalions in (1775-6)	65	Grill, A Mixed		37
Anholt, Defence of	165	Hamilton, Port, Marines at (Colonel Holman)		249
Anson and the Marines	36	Heart of the Prince of Hesse		19
Antiquity, Marines of	4	Hernani, Battle of (1837)		197
Antwerp, 1914 (Col Luard)	350	Impressment Duty, Marines on in Plymouth (1803)		158
Artillerymen, Service Afloat prior to 1804	49	Inspections, Annual		286
Australia, First British Settlement in	81	Interregnum, The (1713-1740) (Col. C. Field)		26
Band, The Chatham Divisional (1781)	76	Ireland, Royal Marine Battalion in (1848)		220
Band, The Depot	404	Ireland and the Baltic, Services of Lieyt. A. O. Lewis		
Band, The Portsmouth Division,	404	(Colonel Hailes)		219
Belleisle, Capt. D. Hepburn	53	Japan, Work of an R.M. Officer in (Genl Fagan)		274
Bellisle, Gallant conduct of a party of Marines at	54	Johnson, The Smuggler, Notes on		114
Belleisle, The Marines at (1761)	53	Justice, Captain James, Account of		79
Bomarsund, 1854 (Lieut. E. C. L. Durnford, R.M.A.)	234	King William IV's Approbation of the Royal Marines		189
Boston, 1775, Seditious Rebel Handbill at	64	Landings, Orders for (1708)		22
Cabins, A Question concerning	18	Lexington and Concord, Major Pitcairn at (Col. C. Field)		55
Chatham Division, History of the,	457	Looping Lace, Drummers' (Col. C. Field)		354
Colours, Divisional, History of the		Lord St Vincent and his Portrait		109
(Gen Sir H. E. Blumberg, K.C.B.)	286	Loyalty and Disloyalty (1797) (Col. C. Field)		135
Colours, Presentation of at Constantinople, 1799	90	Lumsden, Brigdr.-General, Bestowal of his V.C.		353
Commanding Officers, Royal Marines	285	Marines in 1758 (An Affair of Honour)		51
Cool Request, A	55	Marine Sepoy Battalion		259
Corps History, Notes on the	291	Marines and the Royal Dockyards		333
Coulter, Corpl. R. J. – Reminiscences of Service,		Marine Regiments, Clothing and Equipment of (1702)		
New South Wales and New Zealand	244	(Col. L. Edye)		5
Court Martial, Brigdr. Seymour empowered to convene (1703)	21	Memorial of Corporal J. Coulter		244
Court Martial, Competence of a Naval	89	Murray, John, The Publisher		78
Coxswain of the Marine Boat, Chatham (1781)	76	Mutiny on board H.M.S. Temeraire (Col. C. Field)		94
Cutting-out Expedition at Corigeou (1815)	170	National Rifle Association, Royal Marine Successes		371
Deduction of 6d. in the pound 1	9	Naval Forces of Great Britain (1833)		196
Depot, Establishment of the (1861)	392	Navarino, H.M.S. Albion at (Lt.-Col. Hurdle)		179
Deserters	20	Navarino, Lieut. Thomas Browne-Gray's account		182
Detachment, A very poor (1707)	27	Night Attack, The 1810		125
Detachments, R.M., Lord St Vincent's Orders for (1798-1800)	139	New Zealand, An Old Marine in		244
Diaries, Clark, Lieut. William, R.M.	113	Nootka Sound, Evacuation of by the Spaniards		80
Diaries, Browne-Gray, Lieut. Thomas (1827)	182	Odessa, Bombardment of (Major-General Fraser)		223
Diaries, Noble, Major Christopher (1792-1822)	143	Order, an unpopular (1782)		77
Diaries, Pridham, Major (1799-1816)	151	Orders, Lord St. Vincent's for Marine Detachments (1798-1800)		139
Diaries, My Uncle's (1796-1820)	149	"Palmerston' Own" (Poem)		205
Divisional Fund, Origin of the	284	Parana River, Operations on the, in 1845 (Col. C. Domville)		217
Documents in connection with the beginning of the present Corps	38	Pay, Lord Howe and his Marine		138
Documents, Miscellaneous	19	Pay, Royal Marine in 1808		164
Douglas, Major-General Sir John:		Pay, Want of in 1708		17
Incidents in the Life of	103	Philips, Lt.Col. Molesworth, 1855 Account of		194
Miscellaneous documents in connection with	105	Plymouth Division, History of		445
Services of	101	Port Hamilton, Occupation of (1885-7) (Colonel Holman)		249
Evening Walk, The, Account of Capt. James Justice	79	Portsmouth Division, History of		379
Excellent, H.M.S., Her Establishment as a School of Gunnery	189	Portugal, Marines for (1832)		187
Extravagance, Marine	220	Precedence of the Corps of Royal Marines		111
Fathers of the present Royal Marine Corps (Colonel Field)	43	Presentment of Death		175
Field Gun Competitions	364	Rations and Victualling in the Royal Marines		128
Foreigners in the Marines	142	(General Sir H. Blumberg)		
"Forty-five, The", Experiences of a Marine		Recruiting Instructions for Marines (1745)		35
(Capt. Richmond Webb)	28	Recruiting in the Marines		340
Gambia Expedition,	The 275	Regent's Allowance, The		168

492

Regiments Afloat (Gen. Sir H. Blumberg, K.C.B.)	289
Reminiscences of General Simon Fraser:	190
Ascension, Life in the island of	207
Balaklava Heights, The Royal Marines on the	225
Dutch Blockade of 1832, The	190
H.M.S. Vernon in the West Indies	192
In the Fleet in the Crimea	221
Landing of the Royal Marines in the Crimea	224
Light Brigade at Balaklava,The	227
Odessa, Bombardment of	223
Syrian Campaign of 1846 (Acre, Lebanon, Sidon, Beyrout)	199
Repentance and Forgiveness (1782)	77
Robinson, Colonel Wm., Memorial and Services of	90
Roman Marines and their Badges	3
Royal Marine Corps a Hundred Years ago –	
(Capt. Glascock, R.N.)	177
Royal Marine Artillery Division, History of the	414
Sepoy Marine Battalion	259
Slow Promotion	194
Supply of Arms 1710	22
Sweaborg, Bombardment of in 1855 (Capt. Wemyss, R.M.A.)	239
Sword, The, in the Royal Marines	
(General Sir H. Blumberg, K.C.B.)	279
Tait, Captain Walter, Note on	194
Tamaai, Battle of	262
Tournament, Royal Marine Successes at the	364
Uniform, Clothing and Equipment 1702 (Colonel L. Edye)	5
Uniform Coat, Lieut. Sampson, R.M. 1803	12
Uniform, Recollections of former	13
(General S. Fraser and Colonel C. Field)	
Van Dieman's Land and Melville Island, Marine at, in 1824	176
Vitu Expedition	269
Wager, The Four Marines of H.M.S.	207
War, The Ashantee	247
War, The Crimean	219, 221, 223, 225, 227, 231, 234, 239
War, The "Forty Five"	28
War, The Great	350, 353
War, The Rebellion in America	55-76
War, The Syrian	199
Water Supply, Plymouth Barracks	456
Woolwich Division, History of the	430